SAXON
ALGEBRA 1

Student Edition

An Imprint of HMH
Supplemental Publishers Inc.

www.SaxonPublishers.com
1-800-531-5015

ISBN 13:   978-1-6027-7301-1

ISBN 10:   1-6027-7301-7

Printed in the United States of America

2 3 4 5 6 7 8 073 15 14 13 12 11 10 09 08

Table of Contents

DISTRIBUTED STRANDS

Algebra Foundations	Inequalities
Functions and Relations	Systems of Equations and Inequalities
Equations	Radical Expressions and Functions
Linear Equations and Functions	Quadratic Equations and Functions
Polynomials	Absolute-Value Equations and Inequalities
Rational Expressions and Functions	Probability and Data Analysis

Section 2: Lessons 11-20, Investigation 2

Section 3: Lessons 21-30, Investigation 3

DISTRIBUTED STRANDS

☐ Algebra Foundations	■ Inequalities
☐ Functions and Relations	☐ Systems of Equations and Inequalities
☐ Equations	☐ Radical Expressions and Functions
■ Linear Equations and Functions	☐ Quadratic Equations and Functions
■ Polynomials	☐ Absolute-Value Equations and Inequalities
☐ Rational Expressions	☐ Probability and Data Analysis

Section 4: Lessons 31-40, Investigation 4

Section 5: Lessons 41-50, Investigation 5

DISTRIBUTED STRANDS

- Algebra Foundations
- Functions and Relations
- Equations
- Linear Equations and Functions
- Polynomials
- Rational Expressions

- Inequalities
- Systems of Equations and Inequalities
- Radical Expressions and Functions
- Quadratic Equations and Functions
- Absolute-Value Equations and Inequalities
- Probability and Data Analysis

Section 6: Lessons 51-60, Investigation 6

Section 7: Lessons 61-70, Investigation 7

DISTRIBUTED STRANDS

Algebra Foundations

Functions and Relations

Equations

Linear Equations and Functions

Polynomials

Rational Expressions

Inequalities

Systems of Equations and Inequalities

Radical Expressions and Functions

Quadratic Equations and Functions

Absolute-Value Equations and Inequalities

Probability and Data Analysis

Section 8: Lessons 71-80, Investigation 8

Section 9: Lessons 81-90, Investigation 9

DISTRIBUTED STRANDS

- Algebra Foundations
- Functions and Relations
- Equations
- Linear Equations and Functions
- Polynomials
- Rational Expressions

- Inequalities
- Systems of Equations and Inequalities
- Radical Expressions and Functions
- Quadratic Equations and Functions
- Absolute-Value Equations and Inequalities
- Probability and Data Analysis

Section 10: Lessons 91-100, Investigation 10

Section 11: Lessons 101-110, Investigation 11

DISTRIBUTED STRANDS

Algebra Foundations	Inequalities
Functions and Relations	Systems of Equations and Inequalities
Equations	Radical Expressions and Functions
Linear Equations and Functions	Quadratic Equations and Functions
Polynomials	Absolute-Value Equations and Inequalities
Rational Expressions	Probability and Data Analysis

Section 12: Lessons 111-120, Investigation 12

Classifying Real Numbers

Warm Up

1. Vocabulary A _____ (*Venn diagram, line plot*) shows the relationship between sets.
(SB 30)

Write each fraction as a decimal.

2. $\dfrac{2}{9}$
(SB 5)

3. $4\dfrac{3}{8}$
(SB 5)

Write each decimal as a fraction in simplest form.

4. 0.6
(SB 6)

5. 5.75
(SB 6)

New Concepts

A **set** is a collection of objects. Each object in the set is called an element. A set is written by enclosing the elements within braces. There are three types of sets. A set with no elements is called the null or **empty set.** A set with a finite number of elements is a **finite set.** An **infinite set** has an infinite number of elements.

$$\{12, 24, 36\} \qquad \{1, 3, 5,...\} \qquad \{ \} \text{ or } \varnothing$$
$$\text{finite set} \qquad \text{infinite set} \qquad \text{null or empty set}$$

The subsets of real numbers are infinite sets.

Reading Math

The three dots inside the braces are called an ellipsis. An ellipsis shows that the numbers in the set continue on without end.

Subsets of Real Numbers	
Natural Numbers	The numbers used to count objects or things. $\{1, 2, 3, 4,...\}$
Whole Numbers	The set of natural numbers and zero. $\{0, 1, 2, 3, 4,...\}$
Integers	The set of whole numbers and the opposites of the natural numbers. $\{..., -4, -3, -2, -1, 0, 1, 2, 3, 4,...\}$
Rational Numbers	Numbers that can be written in the form $\dfrac{a}{b}$, where a and b are integers and $b \neq 0$. In decimal form, rational numbers either terminate or repeat. Examples: $\dfrac{1}{2}, 0.\overline{3}, -\dfrac{2}{3}, 0.125$
Irrational Numbers	Numbers that cannot be written as the quotient of two integers. In decimal form, irrational numbers neither terminate nor repeat. Examples: $\sqrt[3]{5}, \sqrt{2}, -\sqrt{2}, 3\sqrt{3}, \pi, 3\pi$
Real Numbers	The set including all rational and irrational numbers.

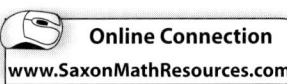

Online Connection
www.SaxonMathResources.com

The Venn diagram below shows how the sets of numbers are related.

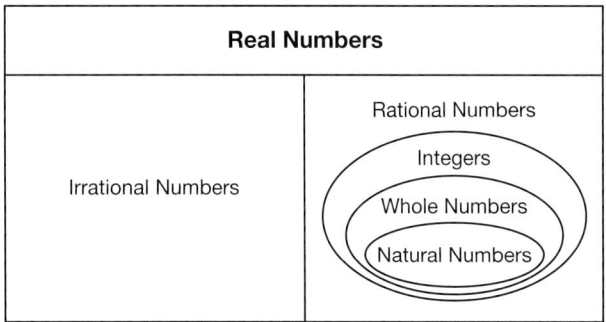

Example 1 **Identifying Sets**

For each number, identify the subsets of real numbers to which it belongs.

a. $\frac{1}{2}$

SOLUTION

{rational numbers, real numbers}

b. 5

SOLUTION

{natural numbers, whole numbers, integers, rational numbers, real numbers}

c. $3\sqrt{2}$

SOLUTION

{irrational numbers, real numbers}

Example 2 **Identifying Sets for Real-World Situations**

Identify the set of numbers that best describes each situation. Explain your choice.

a. the value of the bills in a person's wallet

SOLUTION The set of whole numbers best describes the situation. The wallet may contain no bills or any number of bills.

b. the balance of a checking account

SOLUTION The set of rational numbers best describes the situation. The balance could be positive or negative and may contain decimal amounts.

c. the circumference of a circular table when the diameter is a rational number

SOLUTION The set of irrational numbers describes the situation. Since circumference is equal to the diameter multiplied by pi, it will be an irrational number.

The **intersection of sets** A and B, $A \cap B$, is the set of elements that are in A and B. The **union** of A and B, $A \cup B$, is the set of all elements that are in A or B.

Example 3 Finding Intersections and Unions of Sets

Find $A \cap B$ and $A \cup B$.

a. $A = \{2, 4, 6, 8, 10, 12\}$; $B = \{3, 6, 9, 12\}$

SOLUTION

$A \cap B = \{6, 12\}$; $A \cup B = \{2, 3, 4, 6, 8, 9, 10, 12\}$

b. $A = \{11, 13, 15, 17\}$; $B = \{12, 14, 16, 18\}$

SOLUTION

$A \cap B = \{\ \}$ or $\varnothing$; $A \cup B = \{11, 12, 13, 14, 15, 16, 17, 18\}$

In some lessons, **Explorations** allow you to go into more depth with the mathematics by investigating math concepts with manipulatives, through patterns, and in a variety of other ways.

A set of numbers has **closure,** or is closed, under a given operation if the outcome of the operation on any two members of the set is also a member of the set. For example, the sum of any two natural numbers is also a natural number. Therefore, the set of natural numbers is closed under addition.

One example is all that is needed to prove that a statement is false. An example that proves a statement false is called a **counterexample.**

Example 4 Identifying a Closed Set Under a Given Operation

Determine whether each statement is true or false. Give a counterexample for false statements.

a. The set of whole numbers is closed under addition.

SOLUTION

Verify the statement by adding two whole numbers.

$$2 + 3 = 5$$
$$9 + 11 = 20$$
$$100 + 1000 = 1100$$

The sum is always a whole number.

The statement is true.

b. The set of whole number is closed under subtraction.

SOLUTION

Verify the statement by subtracting two whole numbers.

$$6 - 4 = 2$$
$$100 - 90 = 10$$
$$4 - 6 = -2$$

$4 - 6$ is a counterexample. The difference is not a whole number.

The statement is false.

For each number, identify the subsets of real numbers to which it belongs.
(Ex 1)

  a. -73 **b.** $\dfrac{5}{9}$ **c.** 18π

Identify the set of numbers that best describes each situation. Explain your choice.
(Ex 2)

  d. the number of people on a bus

  e. the area of a circular platform

  f. the value of coins in a purse

Find $C \cap D$ and $C \cup D$.
(Ex 3)

  g. $C = \{4, 8, 12, 16, 20\}$; $D = \{5, 10, 15, 20\}$

  h. $C = \{6, 12, 18, 24\}$; $D = \{7, 14, 21, 28\}$

Verify **Determine whether each statement is true or false. Provide a counterexample for false statements.**
(Ex 4)

  i. The set of whole numbers is closed under multiplication.

  j. The set of natural numbers is closed under division.

Practice   Distributed and Integrated

1. Multiply 26.1×6.15.
(SB 2)

2. Add $\dfrac{4}{7} + \dfrac{1}{8} + \dfrac{1}{2}$.
(SB 3)

3. Divide $954 \div 0.9$.
(SB 2)

4. Add $\dfrac{3}{5} + \dfrac{1}{8} + \dfrac{1}{8}$.
(SB 3)

5. Write $\dfrac{3}{8}$ as a decimal.
(SB 5)

6. Write $0.\overline{666}$ as a fraction.
(SB 6)

7. Add $2\dfrac{1}{2} + 3\dfrac{1}{5}$.
(SB 3)

8. Name a fraction equivalent to $\dfrac{2}{5}$.
(SB 7)

9. Error Analysis Two students determine the prime factorization of 72. Which student is correct? Explain the error.
(SB 12)

Student A	Student B
72	72
$= 9 \cdot 8$	$= 9 \cdot 8$
$= 9 \cdot 4 \cdot 2$	$= 9 \cdot 4 \cdot 2$
$= 9 \cdot 2 \cdot 2 \cdot 2$	$= 3 \cdot 3 \cdot 2 \cdot 2 \cdot 2$

10. Find the prime factorization of 144.
(SB 12)

11. Write 0.15 as a percent. If necessary, round to the nearest tenth.
(SB 5)

12. Write 7.2 as a percent. If necessary, round to the nearest tenth.
(SB 5)

*13. Use braces and digits to designate the set of natural numbers.
(1)

*14. The set {0, 1, 2, 3,…} represents what set of numbers?
(1)

*15. Represent the following numbers as being members of set *K:* 2, 4, 2, 0, 6, 0, 10, 8.
(1)

*16. Multiple Choice Which of the following numbers is an irrational number?
(1)

   A 15 **B** $\sqrt{15}$ **C** 15.15151515… **D** $-\dfrac{15}{3}$

*17. Measurement The surface area of a cube is defined as $6s^2$, where *s* is the length of
(1) the side of the cube. If *s* is an integer, then would the surface area of a cube be a
rational or irrational number?

18. Verify True or False: A right triangle can have an obtuse angle. Explain your
(SB 1) answer.

19. ⎡**Anatomy**⎤ A baby's head is approximately one fourth of its total body length. If the
(SB 3) baby's body measures 19 inches, what does the baby's head measure?

20. True or False: An acute triangle has 3 acute angles. Explain your answer.
(SB 13)

21. True or False: A trapezoid has two pairs of parallel sides. Explain your answer.
(SB 14)

*22. ⎡**Track Practice**⎤ Tyrone ran 7 laps on the quarter-mile track during practice. Which
(1) subset of real numbers would include the distance Tyrone ran at practice?

23. True or False: A parallelogram has two pairs of parallel sides. Explain your
(SB 14) answer.

24. Write Use the divisibility test to determine if 1248 is divisible by 2. Explain
(SB 4) your answer.

*25. Geometry The diagram shows a right triangle. The length of the hypotenuse is
(1) a member of which subset(s) of real numbers?

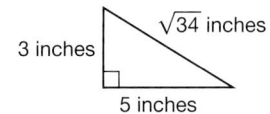

*26. Multi-Step The diagram shows a rectangle.
(1)   **a.** Find the area of the rectangle.

   b. The number of square feet is a member of which subset(s) of real
   numbers?

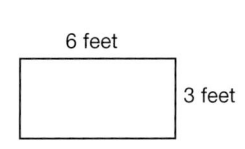

27. ⎡**Lunar Rover**⎤ The surface-speed record set by the lunar rover on the moon is
(SB 2) 10.56 miles per hour. At that speed, how far would the rover travel in 3.5 hours?

28. Write Use the divisibility test to determine if 207 is divisible by 3. Explain
(SB 4) your answer.

29. ⎡**Swimming**⎤ Vidiana and Jaime went swimming before school. Vidiana swam $\frac{3}{5}$ mile
(SB 1) and Jaime swam $\frac{4}{7}$ mile. Write a comparison to show who swam farther. Use <, >,
or =.

*30. ⎡**Banking**⎤ Shayla is balancing her checkbook. Which subset of real numbers best
(1) describes her balance?

Understanding Variables and Expressions

1. **Vocabulary** When two numbers are multiplied, the result is called
(SB 2) the _____. (*quotient, product*)

Add.

2. $\frac{2}{5} + \frac{1}{3}$
(SB 3)

3. $654.1 + 78.39$
(SB 2)

Multiply.

4. $4.5(0.23)$
(SB 2)

5. $\frac{3}{8}\left(\frac{2}{9}\right)$
(SB 3)

New Concepts

A symbol, usually a letter, used to represent an unknown number is called
a **variable.** In the algebraic expression $4 + x$, x is a variable. The number 4
in this expression does not change value. A quantity whose value does not
change is called a **constant.**

> **Example 1** **Identifying Variables and Constants**
>
> Identify the constants and the variables in each expression.
>
> **a.** $6 - 3x$
>
> **SOLUTION**
>
> The numbers 6 and 3 are constants because they never change. The letter x
> is a variable because it represents an unknown number.
>
> **b.** $71wz + 28y$
>
> **SOLUTION**
>
> The numbers 71 and 28 are constants because they never change. The letters
> w, y, and z are variables because they represent unknown numbers.

Math Reasoning

Connect What other term can be used to describe the coefficient in the expression $5mn$?

The expression $4xy$ can also be written as $4 \cdot x \cdot y$. When two or more
quantities are multiplied, each is a **factor** of the product. The numeric
factor of a product including a variable is called the numeric coefficient,
or simply the **coefficient.**

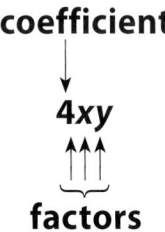

coefficient

4xy

factors

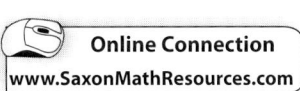

Example 2 | Identifying Factors and Coefficients in Expressions

Identify the factors and coefficients in each expression.

a. $7vw$

SOLUTION

The factors are 7, v, and w. The coefficient is 7.

b. $-5rst$

SOLUTION

The factors are -5, r, s, and t. The coefficient is -5.

c. $\dfrac{y}{3}$

SOLUTION

The factors are $\dfrac{1}{3}$ and y. The coefficient is $\dfrac{1}{3}$.

d. cd

SOLUTION

The factors are c and d. The expression cd has an implied coefficient of 1.

Hint

$\dfrac{y}{3} = \dfrac{1}{3}y$

$cd = 1cd$

Parts of an expression separated by $+$ or $-$ signs are called **terms of an expression.** A term that is in parentheses such as $(y + 2)$ can include a plus or minus sign.

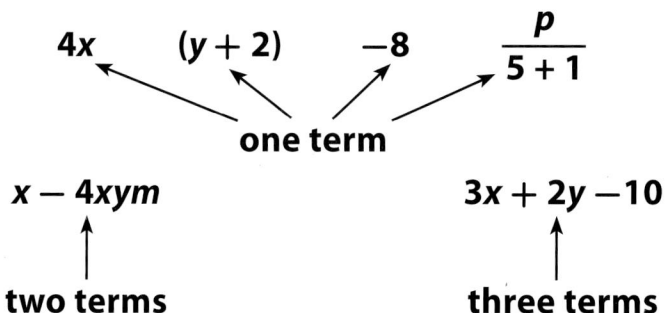

You can refer to a particular term of an expression by its placement within the expression. The terms of an expression are numbered from left to right, beginning with the first term.

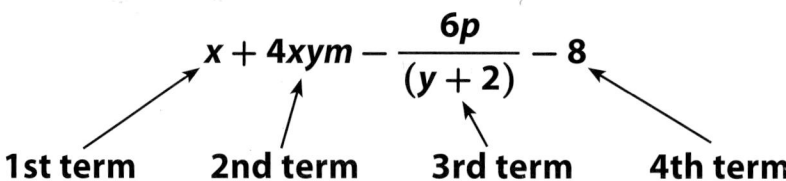

Example 3 Identifying Terms

Identify the terms in each expression.

a. $6xy + 57w - \dfrac{24x}{5y}$ **b.** $m + 3mn - \dfrac{5t}{(d+8)} - 9$

SOLUTION

The first term is $6xy$.

The second term is $57w$.

The third term is $\dfrac{24x}{5y}$.

SOLUTION

The first term is m.

The second term is $3mn$.

The third term is $\dfrac{5t}{(d+8)}$.

The fourth term is 9.

Example 4 Application: Telecommunications

The local telephone company uses the expression below to determine the monthly charges for individual customers.

$$0.1m + 4.95$$

a. How many terms are in the expression?

SOLUTION There are two terms.

b. Identify the constant(s).

SOLUTION The constants are 0.1 and 4.95.

c. Identify the variable(s).

SOLUTION The variable is m.

Lesson Practice

Identify the constants and variables in each expression.
(Ex 1)

   a. $65qrs + 12x$ **b.** $4gh - 71yz$

Identify the factors and coefficients in each expression.
(Ex 2)

   c. $17def$ **d.** $\dfrac{uv}{4}$

   e. $-3st$ **f.** abc

Identify the terms in each expression.
(Ex 3)

   g. $8v - 17yz + \dfrac{63b}{4gh}$

   h. $\dfrac{(4 + 2x)}{38q} + 18s - 47jkl$

Bill's Bikes uses the expression below to calculate rental fees.
(Ex 4)

$$6.50 + 3.25h - 0.75b$$

   i. How many terms are in the expression?

   j. Identify the constants.

   k. Identify the variables.

Find the GCF of each pair of numbers.

1. 24, 32
(SB 9)

2. 28, 42
(SB 9)

Find the LCM of each group of numbers.

3. 9, 12
(SB 10)

4. 3, 5, 6
(SB 10)

Multiply or divide.

5. $\dfrac{3}{4} \cdot \dfrac{8}{15}$
(SB 3)

6. $\dfrac{7}{15} \div \dfrac{21}{25}$
(SB 3)

Identify the coefficients and variables in each expression.

*7. $rst - 12v$
(2)

*8. $2xy + 7w - 8$
(2)

*9. $47s + \dfrac{2}{5}t$
(2)

Identify the following statements as true or false. Explain your choice.

*10. **Verify** All whole numbers are natural numbers.
(1)

11. **Verify** All integers are real numbers.
(1)

12. **Verify** A number can be a member of the set of rational numbers and the set of irrational numbers.
(1)

13. **Multi-Step** Use the following set of data.
(SB 29)

$$3, 6, 4, 3, 6, 5, 6, 7, 4, 3, 2, 4, 6$$

    a. What is the frequency of each number?

    b. Display the set of data in a line plot.

14. All natural numbers are members of which other subsets of real numbers?
(1)

15. **Measurement** Add $7\dfrac{3}{8}$ meters $+ 6\dfrac{1}{3}$ meters. Does the sum belong to the set of rational numbers, integers, or whole numbers?
(1, SB 3)

16. Find the prime factorization of 153.
(SB 12)

17. **Verify** True or False: An obtuse triangle can have more than one obtuse angle. Explain your choice.
(SB 13)

18. **Geometry** A line can be classified as a _____ angle.
(SB 13)

19. **Write** Use the divisibility test to determine if 2345 is divisible by 4. Explain your answer.
(SB 4)

20. Write 0.003 as a percent. If necessary, round to the nearest tenth.
(SB 5)

21. Use braces and digits to designate the set of whole numbers.
(1)

22. The set {1, 2, 3,...} represents what set of numbers?
(1)

*23. Multiple Choice What is the second term in the expression
(2)
$$\sqrt{8} + \frac{gh}{5} + (3x + y) + 15gh?$$

A $(3x + y)$ **B** $15gh$ **C** $\sqrt{8}$ **D** $\frac{gh}{5}$

*24. (Astronomy) To calculate the amount of time it takes for a planet to travel around
(2) the sun, you use the following expression: $\frac{2\pi r}{v}$. Which values are constants, which
are variables, and which are coefficients?

*25. (Entertainment) Admission price for a matinee movie is $5.75 for children and $6.25
(2) for adults. Brad uses the expression $5.75c + $6.25a to calculate the cost for his
family. What are the variables in the expression?

*26. Error Analysis The surface area of a rectangular prism is $2lw + 2lh + 2wh$. Two
(2) students determined the variables in the formula. Which student is correct? What
was the error of the other student?

Student A	Student B
variables: $2lw$, $2lh$	variables: l, w, h

*27. (Cost Analysis) A large medical organization wants to put two cylindrical aquariums
(2) in the pharmacy area. It will cost the pharmacy 53 cents per cubic inch of
aquarium. This is the formula for figuring out the cost: $P = (\pi r^2 h)(\$0.53)$.
a. Find the coefficients of the expression.

b. Find the variables of the expression.

28. Multiple Choice Which shape is not a parallelogram?
(SB 14)
A square **B** rectangle **C** trapezoid **D** rhombus

*29. (Cycling) A bicycle shop uses the expression $5 + $2.25h to determine the charges
(2) for bike rentals. How many terms are in the expression?

30. (Attendance) The attendance clerk keeps records of students' attendance. Which
(1) subset of real numbers would include the number of students in attendance each
school day?

Simplifying Expressions Using the Product Property of Exponents

Warm Up

1. Vocabulary In the term $4x$, x is the _____. (*variable, coefficient*)
(2)

Simplify.

2. $(1.2)(0.7)$
(SB 2)

3. $(0.5)(11)(0.9)$
(SB 2)

4. $\left(\frac{2}{3}\right)\left(\frac{6}{7}\right)$
(SB 3)

5. $\left(\frac{1}{2}\right)\left(\frac{4}{5}\right)\left(\frac{15}{16}\right)$
(SB 3)

New Concepts

An exponent can be used to show repeated multiplication.

$$\text{base} \longrightarrow 5^3 \longleftarrow \text{exponent}$$

The **base of a power** is the number used as a factor. If the **exponent** is a natural number, it indicates how many times the base is used as a factor.

Words	Power	Multiplication	Value
five to the first power	5^1	5	5
five to the second power or five squared	5^2	$5 \cdot 5$	25
five to the third power or five cubed	5^3	$5 \cdot 5 \cdot 5$	125
five to the fourth power	5^4	$5 \cdot 5 \cdot 5 \cdot 5$	625

Caution

Be careful not to multiply the base and the exponent when simplifying powers.

Online Connection
www.SaxonMathResources.com

Example 1 **Simplifying Expressions with Exponents**

Simplify each expression.

a. 7^3

SOLUTION

The exponent 3 indicates that the base is a factor three times.

7^3

$= 7 \cdot 7 \cdot 7$

$= 343$

b. $(0.3)^4$

SOLUTION

The exponent 4 indicates that the base is a factor four times.

$(0.3)^4$

$= (0.3)(0.3)(0.3)(0.3)$

$= 0.0081$

Math Reasoning

Generalize Examine the powers of 10. What pattern do you see?

c. $\left(\dfrac{1}{2}\right)^5$

SOLUTION

The exponent 5 indicates that the base is a factor five times.

$$\left(\dfrac{1}{2}\right)^5$$

$$= \dfrac{1}{2} \cdot \dfrac{1}{2} \cdot \dfrac{1}{2} \cdot \dfrac{1}{2} \cdot \dfrac{1}{2}$$

$$= \dfrac{1}{32}$$

d. 10^3

SOLUTION

The exponent 3 indicates that the base is a factor three times.

$$10^3$$

$$= 10 \cdot 10 \cdot 10$$

$$= 1000$$

The product of powers whose bases are the same can be found by writing each power as repeated multiplication.

$$5^4 \cdot 5^5 = (5 \cdot 5 \cdot 5 \cdot 5) \cdot (5 \cdot 5 \cdot 5 \cdot 5 \cdot 5) = 5^9$$

The sum of the exponents in the factors is equal to the exponent in the product.

Product Property of Exponents
If m and n are real numbers and $x \neq 0$, then
$x^m \cdot x^n = x^{m+n}.$

Example 2 Applying the Product Property of Exponents

Simplify each expression.

a. $x^5 \cdot x^7 \cdot x^2$

SOLUTION

Since each of the factors has the same base, the exponents can be added to find the power of the product.

$$x^{5+7+2} = x^{14}$$

b. $m^3 \cdot m^2 \cdot m^4 \cdot n^6 \cdot n^7$

SOLUTION

The first three factors have m as the base. The exponents can be added to find the product of those three factors. The last two factors have n as the base. The exponents can be added to find the product of the last two factors.

$$m^{3+2+4} \cdot n^{6+7} = m^9 n^{13}$$

Math Reasoning

Estimate Use the order of magnitude to estimate 1,127,000 times 108.

The order of magnitude is defined as the nearest power of ten to a given quantity. The order of magnitude can be used to estimate when performing calculations mentally.

Example 3 Application: Speed of a Supercomputer

In 2006, the fastest supercomputer's performance topped out at about one PFLOPS. One PFLOPS is equal to 10^3 TFLOPS. Each TFLOPS is equal to 10^{12} FLOPS. What was the computer's speed in FLOPS?

SOLUTION

Understand

1 PFLOPS $= 10^3$ TFLOPS

1 TFLOPS $= 10^{12}$ FLOPS

Find the number of FLOPS in one PFLOPS.

Plan

Write an expression to find the number of FLOPS in one PFLOPS.

Solve

To find the speed in FLOPS, find the product of the number of TFLOPS, 10^3, and the number of FLOPS in a TFLOPS, 10^{12}.

$10^3 \cdot 10^{12}$

$= 10^{3+12}$

$= 10^{15}$

The computer performed at a speed of 10^{15} FLOPS.

Check

$$10^3 \cdot 10^{12} \overset{?}{=} 10^{15}$$

$$(10 \cdot 10 \cdot 10)(10 \cdot 10 \cdot 10 \cdot 10 \cdot 10 \cdot 10 \cdot 10 \cdot 10 \cdot 10 \cdot 10 \cdot 10 \cdot 10) \overset{?}{=} 10^{15}$$

$$10^{15} = 10^{15} \quad \checkmark$$

Lesson Practice

Simplify each expression.

a. 6^4
(Ex 1)

b. $(1.4)^2$
(Ex 1)

c. $\left(\dfrac{2}{5}\right)^3$
(Ex 1)

d. 10^6
(Ex 1)

e. $w^3 \cdot w^5 \cdot w^4$
(Ex 2)

f. $y^6 \cdot y^5 \cdot z^3 \cdot z^{11} \cdot z^2$
(Ex 2)

g. If a supercomputer has a top speed of one EFLOPS which is equal to 10^9 GFLOPS, and if one GFLOPS is 10^9 FLOPS, what is the computer's speed in FLOPS?
(Ex 3)

Practice Distributed and Integrated

Find the GCF for each pair of numbers.

1. 15, 35
(SB 9)

2. 32, 48
(SB 9)

Find the LCM for each group of numbers.

3. 8, 12
(SB 10)

4. 2, 4, 7
(SB 10)

Multiply or divide.

5. $\dfrac{9}{16} \cdot \dfrac{12}{15}$
(SB 3)

6. $\dfrac{6}{15} \div \dfrac{24}{30}$
(SB 3)

Identify the coefficients and variables in each expression.

7. $6mn + 4b$
(2)

8. $5j - 9cd + 2$
(2)

9. $23t + \dfrac{4}{7}w$
(2)

Identify the following statements as true or false. Explain your choice.

*10. Verify All real numbers are integers.
(1)

11. Verify All natural numbers are whole numbers.
(2)

12. Verify All irrational numbers are real numbers.
(2)

Complete the comparisons. Use <, >, or =.

13. 42.53 $\bigcirc$ 42.35
(SB 1)

14. $\dfrac{5}{9} \bigcirc \dfrac{7}{12}$
(SB 1)

15. Add $1\dfrac{1}{8} + 7\dfrac{2}{5}$.
(SB 3)

16. Measurement Use braces and digits to designate the set of integers. Which
(1) measurement can be described by the set of integers: temperature or volume?

17. Find the prime factorization of 98.
(SB 12)

*18. Error Analysis Two students are trying to simplify the expression $x^2 \cdot x^5$. Which
(3) student is correct? Explain the error.

Student A	Student B
$x^2 \cdot x^5$	$x^2 \cdot x^5$
$x^{2 \cdot 5} = x^{10}$	$x^{2+5} = x^7$

19. Verify True or False: A rhombus is always a square. Explain your choice.
(SB 14)

20. Write Use the divisibility test to determine if 306 is divisible by 6. Explain your
(SB 4) answer.

*21. The expression 3^6 indicates the number of times 3 is used as a factor.
(3)   **a.** Which number in the expression is the base?

  b. Which number is the exponent?

  c. What is the simplified value of this expression?

*22. Multiple Choice MFLOPS, TFLOPS, and PFLOPS are used to measure the speed
(3) of a computer. One PFLOP is equal to 10^3 TFLOPS. Each TFLOP is equal to 10^6
MFLOPS. How many MFLOPS are in a PFLOP?

A 10^{18} **B** 10^9 **C** 10^6 **D** 10^3

*23. (Cooking) A cooking magazine advertises 4^4 recipes in every issue. How many
(3) recipes are in 4^2 issues?

*24. Multi-Step A business is worth 10^6 dollars this year. The business expects to be 10^3
(3) more valuable in five years.

a. Simplify 10^3 to determine how many times more valuable the business
will be.

b. What will the business be worth in five years? Express your answer in
exponential form, then simplify your answer.

*25. (Population) The population of Bridgetown triples every decade. If the population
(3) in the year 2000 was 25,000, how many people will be living in Bridgetown
in 2030?

26. Multiple Choice Which triangle is a right triangle?
(SB 13)

A a triangle with angle measures of 45°, 45°, and 90°

B a triangle with angle measures of 40°, 110°, and 30°

C a triangle with angle measures of 55°, 45°, and 80°

D a triangle with angle measures of 60°, 60°, and 60°

*27. (Bacteria) The population of a certain bacteria doubles in size every 3 hours. If
(3) a population begins with one bacterium, how many will there be after one day?
Simplify the expression $1 \cdot (2)^8$ to determine the population after one day.

28. Geometry You can calculate the area of a trapezoid using the following equation:
(2) $A = h \times \dfrac{b_1 + b_2}{2}$. Identify the constant(s) in the equation.

*29. (Aquarium) A fish tank is in the shape of a cube. Each side measures 3 feet. What is
(SB 26) the volume of the fish tank?

*30. (Remodeling) Vanessa is remodeling her bathroom. She uses the expression $2l + 2w$
(2) to determine the amount of wallpaper border she needs.

a. How many terms are in the expression?

b. What are the variables?

Using Order of Operations

1. **Vocabulary** A(n) _____ can be used to show repeated multiplication.
(3)

Simplify.

2. $28.75 + 13.5$
(SB 2)

3. $89.6 - 7.4$
(SB 2)

4. $\dfrac{2}{3} \cdot \dfrac{9}{16}$
(SB 3)

5. $4\dfrac{1}{5} \div 3\dfrac{1}{2}$
(SB 3)

New Concepts

To **simplify** an expression means to perform all indicated operations. Simplifying an expression could produce multiple answers without rules concerning the order in which operations are performed. Consider the example below.

Method 1: $\dfrac{2 \cdot (3)^2}{6} = \dfrac{2 \cdot 9}{6} = \dfrac{18}{6} = 3$

Method 2: $\dfrac{2 \cdot (3)^2}{6} = \dfrac{(2 \cdot 3)^2}{6} = \dfrac{6^2}{6} = \dfrac{36}{6} = 6$

To avoid confusion, mathematicians have agreed to use the order of operations. The **order of operations** is a set of rules for simplifying expressions. Method 1 followed the order of operations.

Order of Operations
1. Work inside grouping symbols.
2. Simplify powers and roots.
3. Multiply and divide from left to right.
4. Add and subtract from left to right.

Example 1 **Simplifying Expressions with Parentheses**

Simplify. Justify each step.

$(10 \cdot 3) + 7 \cdot (5 + 4)$

SOLUTION

Write the expression. Then use the order of operations to simplify.

$(10 \cdot 3) + 7 \cdot (5 + 4)$

$= 30 + 7 \cdot 9$ Simplify inside the parentheses.

$= 30 + 63$ Multiply.

$= 93$ Add.

Example 2 Simplifying Expressions with Exponents

Simplify each expression. Justify each step.

a. $4^3 + 9 \div 3 - 2 \cdot (3)^2$

SOLUTION Write the expression. Then use the order of operations to simplify.

$4^3 + 9 \div 3 - 2 \cdot (3)^2$

$= 64 + 9 \div 3 - 2 \cdot 9$ Simplify exponents.

$= 64 + 3 - 18$ Multiply and divide from left to right.

$= 49$ Add and subtract from left to right.

b. $\dfrac{(2 \cdot 3 - 2)^2}{2}$

Hint

Remember to use the order of operations inside parentheses as well.

SOLUTION Write the expression. Then use the order of operations to simplify.

$\dfrac{(2 \cdot 3 - 2)^2}{2}$

$= \dfrac{(6 - 2)^2}{2}$ Multiply inside the parentheses.

$= \dfrac{(4)^2}{2}$ Subtract inside the parentheses.

$= \dfrac{16}{2}$ Simplify the exponent.

$= 8$ Divide.

Example 3 Comparing Expressions

Compare the expressions. Use $<$, $>$, or $=$.

$(1.5 + 3) \div 9 + 3^3 \ \bigcirc \ \dfrac{(18 + 8)}{2} - 8 \div 4$

SOLUTION

Use the order of operations to simplify the two expressions.

$(1.5 + 3) \div 9 + 3^3$ $\dfrac{(18 + 8)}{2} - 8 \div 4$

$= (4.5) \div 9 + 3^3$ $= \dfrac{26}{2} - 8 \div 4$

$= 4.5 \div 9 + 27$ $= 13 - 8 \div 4$

$= 0.5 + 27$ $= 13 - 2$

$= 27.5$ $= 11$

Hint

Remember to compare the original expressions in the inequality.

Since $27.5 > 11$, $(1.5 + 3) \div 9 + 3^3 \ \ominus \ \dfrac{(18 + 8)}{2} - 8 \div 4$.

Example 4 Application: Comparing a Crop Circle to a Soccer Field

Hint

Remember that the formula for the area of a circle is πr^2.

A crop circle in a wheat field has a diameter of 100 yards. Its area is $3.14 \cdot \left(\frac{100}{2}\right)^2$ square yards. A World Cup soccer field is 70 yards by 110 yards. Its area is $(70 \cdot 110)$ square yards. How much larger is the crop circle than the soccer field?

SOLUTION

Find each area and subtract to find the difference.

Area of crop circle: $3.14 \cdot \left(\frac{100}{2}\right)^2$

Area of soccer field: $(70 \cdot 110)$

Difference in area: $3.14 \cdot \left(\frac{100}{2}\right)^2 - (70 \cdot 110)$

Simplify the expression.

$3.14 \cdot \left(\frac{100}{2}\right)^2 - (70 \cdot 110)$

$= 3.14 \cdot (50)^2 - (7700)$ Evaluate inside the parentheses.

$= 3.14 \cdot 2500 - 7700$ Simplify the exponent.

$= 7850 - 7700$ Multiply.

$= 150$ Subtract.

The crop circle is 150 yd^2 larger than the soccer field.

Lesson Practice

a. Simplify $45 - (2 + 4) \cdot 5 - 3$. Justify each step.
(Ex 1)

Simplify each expression. Justify each step.
(Ex 2)

b. $9 \cdot 2^3 - 9 \div 3$

c. $\dfrac{15 - 3^2 + 4 \cdot 2}{7}$

d. Compare the expressions. Use $<$, $>$, or $=$.
(Ex 3)

$\dfrac{1}{4} + 3^2 + 6 \bigcirc 5 - 2 + 2 \cdot 4 + 3 \div 9$

e. Jonah is making a model of the moon using plastic foam. He uses
(Ex 4) the formula $\frac{4}{3}\pi r^3$ to find the volume. The model moon's radius is $\frac{3}{2}$ inches. What is the volume of the model moon? Give the answer in terms of π.

Caution

Do not forget to cube $\frac{3}{2}$ in the expression for the model moon's volume.

Add, subtract, multiply, or divide.

1. $2\frac{1}{4} + 4\frac{1}{2}$
(SB 3)

2. $5\frac{2}{5} - 3\frac{1}{4}$
(SB 3)

3. $1\frac{3}{4} + 4\frac{1}{8} - 2\frac{1}{2}$
(SB 3)

4. $4\frac{1}{3} \div 2\frac{1}{6}$
(SB 3)

5. $3.519 \div 0.3$
(SB 2)

6. $4.16 \cdot 2.3$
(SB 2)

7. How many terms are in the algebraic expression $14x^2 + 7x + \frac{x}{4}$?
(2)

8. Find the prime factorization of 225.
(SB 12)

9. Write Use the divisibility test to determine if 124,302 is divisible by 3. Explain
(SB 4) your answer.

10. Represent the following numbers as being members of set L: $-15, 1, 7, 3, -8, 7, 0,$
(1) $12, 6, 12$

*11. Verify True or False: All whole numbers are integers. Explain your answer.
(1)

*12. To which set(s) of numbers does $\sqrt{5}$ belong?
(1)

13. Write $\frac{1}{6}$ as a percent. If necessary, round to the nearest tenth.
(SB 5)

14. Write $\frac{5}{9}$ as a percent. If necessary, round to the nearest tenth.
(SB 5)

*15. Compare $3 \cdot 4^2 + 4^2 \bigcirc 3 \cdot (16 + 16)$ using $<$, $>$, or $=$. Explain.
(4)

16. Multiple Choice Which triangle is an obtuse triangle?
(SB 13)
  A a triangle with angle measures of 45°, 45°, and 90°

  B a triangle with angle measures of 40°, 120°, and 20°

  C a triangle with angle measures of 55°, 45°, and 80°

  D a triangle with angle measures of 60°, 60°, and 60°

17. Display the following set of data in a line plot:
(SB 29)

$$6, 7, 8, 4, 5, 4, 3, 4, 5, 3, 2, 6, 2, 7$$

18. Verify True or False: A square is a rectangle. Explain your choice.
(SB 14)

19. Measurement Subtract $15\frac{1}{3}$ yards $- 7\frac{4}{5}$ yards.
(SB 3)

20. Error Analysis Two students determine the prime factorization of 108. Which
(SB 12) student is correct? Explain the error.

Student A	Student B
$108 = 2 \cdot 2 \cdot 3 \cdot 3 \cdot 3$	$108 = 2^2 \cdot 3^3$

21. Write Use the divisibility test to determine if 1116 is divisible by 9. Explain
(SB 4) your answer.

22. $\dfrac{n}{6} + 3xy - 19$

(2)

    a. Find the variables of the expression.

    b. Find the terms of the expression.

*23. (**Biology**) A survey found that there were 1100 gray wolves in Minnesota in 1976.

(4) By 2003, the number of gray wolves had increased to 2300. What was the average growth of the wolf population in one year? (Round to the nearest whole number.)

*24. Multiple Choice A bouquet is made from nine red roses that cost $1.75 each and

(4) five white roses that cost $1.50 each. Use the expression $9 \cdot (\$1.75) + 5 \cdot (\$1.50)$ to find the cost of the bouquet.

    A $31.00   **B** $23.25

    C $25.25   **D** $21.75

*25. A can of soup in the shape of a cylinder has a radius of

(4) 3.8 cm and a height of 11 cm. What is the surface area of the can to the nearest tenth? Use 3.14 for π.

$r = 3.8$ cm

$h = 11$ cm

*26. Multi-Step Two friends compare the amount of change they

(4) have in their pockets. Ashley has 12 nickels, 2 dimes, and 4 quarters. Beto has 10 nickels, 4 dimes, and 3 quarters. Who has more money?

    a. Write an expression to represent the value of Ashley's money. (Hint: Use 10¢ to represent the value of each dime, 5¢ for each nickel, and so on). Simplify the expression.

    b. Write an expression to represent the value of Beto's money. Simplify the expression.

    c. Compare the value of money that each friend has. Who has more?

*27. (**School Supplies**) Anthony had 10 packages of markers. Each package contained

(4) 8 markers. He gave 2 packages to each of the other 3 people in his group. Use the expression $8(10 - 3 \cdot 2)$ to determine how many markers Anthony kept for himself.

28. Geometry Use the cube shown to write a formula for the volume

(3) of any cube.

*29. (**Temperature**) The hottest day in Florida's history was 109°F,

(4) which occurred on June 29, 1931 in Monticello. Use the expression $\frac{5}{9}(F - 32)$ to convert this temperature to degrees Celsius. Round your answer to the nearest tenth of a degree.

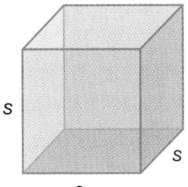

s

*30. (**Billing**) Each month Mrs. Li pays her phone company $28 for phone service and

(4) $0.07 per minute for long-distance calls. Use the expression $28 + 0.07m$ to find the amount she was billed if her long-distance calls totaled 223 minutes.

Finding Absolute Value and Adding Real Numbers

Warm Up

1. Vocabulary The set of _____ (*integers, real numbers*) includes all
(1) rational or irrational numbers.

Simplify.

2. $54.2 - 27.38$
(SB 2)

3. $\dfrac{1}{2} + \dfrac{3}{8}$
(SB 3)

4. $1.09 + 76.9$
(SB 2)

5. $\dfrac{3}{4} - \dfrac{3}{8}$
(SB 3)

New Concepts

The **absolute value** of a number is the distance from the number to zero on a number line. The absolute value of 4 is written $|4|$.

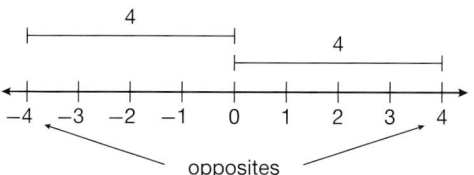

$$|-4| = 4 \qquad\qquad |4| = 4$$

Absolute Value
The absolute value of a number n is the distance from n to 0 on a number line.

Example 1 Finding the Absolute Value

Simplify.

a. $|0|$

SOLUTION

The absolute value of 0 is 0.

b. $|7.12|$

SOLUTION

The distance from 7.12 to 0 is 7.12. So the absolute value is 7.12.

c. $\left|1 - \dfrac{3}{4}\right|$

SOLUTION

First simplify within the absolute-value bars. Then find the absolute value.

$$\left|1 - \frac{3}{4}\right| = \left|\frac{1}{4}\right| = \frac{1}{4}$$

d. $-|11 - 2|$

SOLUTION

First simplify within the absolute-value bars. Then find the absolute value.

$$-|11 - 2| = -|9| = -9$$

Reading Math

Read $-|9|$ as the opposite of the absolute value of 9.

Exploration Modeling Real Number Addition

Find the sum $-5 + 3$.

Model -5 and 3 using algebra tiles.

Group positive and negative tiles to make zero pairs.

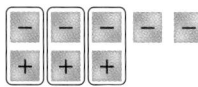

Count the remaining tiles.

$$-5 + 3 = -2$$

Model $-5 + 3$ on a number line.

$$-5 + 3 = -2$$

Use algebra tiles to find the sum. Then model each problem on a number line.

a. $4 + (-3)$ **b.** $-2 + -6$ **c.** $(-7) + 7$

Generalize Determine whether each statement is true or false. Provide a counterexample for false statements.

d. The sum of two positive numbers is always positive.

e. The sum of two negative numbers is always negative.

f. The sum of a positive and a negative number is always negative.

The sum of two numbers can also be found using the rules for adding real numbers. These rules apply to all real-number addends.

Rules for Adding Real Numbers
Adding Numbers With the Same Sign
To add numbers with the same sign, add their absolute values. The sum will have the same sign as the addends.
Examples $3 + 2 = 5$ $-3 + (-2) = -5$
Adding Numbers With Different Signs
To add numbers with different signs, find the difference of their absolute values. The sum will have the sign of the addend with the greater absolute value.
Examples $3 + (-2) = 1$ $(-3) + 2 = -1$

Example 2 Adding Real Numbers

Find the sum.

a. $(-12) + 21$

SOLUTION Since the numbers have different signs, find the difference of their absolute values. The sum is positive because $|-12| < |21|$.

$(-12) + 21 = 9$

b. $(-19) + (-8)$

SOLUTION Since the numbers have the same sign, find the sum of their absolute values. The sum is negative because both addends are negative.

$(-19) + (-8) = -27$

c. $(3.2) + (-5.1)$

SOLUTION Since the numbers have different signs, find the difference of their absolute values. The sum is negative because $|3.2| < |-5.1|$.

$(3.2) + (-5.1) = -1.9$

d. $\left(-\dfrac{3}{5}\right) + \left(-\dfrac{1}{5}\right)$

SOLUTION Since the numbers have the same sign, find the sum of their absolute values. The sum is negative because both addends are negative.

$\left(-\dfrac{3}{5}\right) + \left(-\dfrac{1}{5}\right) = \left(-\dfrac{4}{5}\right)$

Example 3 Identifying Sets of Real Numbers Closed Under Addition

Determine whether each statement is true or false. Give a counterexample for false statements.

Math Language

A set of numbers is **closed** under a given operation if the outcome of the operation on any two members of the set is also a member of the set.

a. The set of integers is closed under addition.

SOLUTION The statement is true because the sum of any two integers will be an integer.

b. The set of real numbers is closed under addition.

SOLUTION The statement is true because the sum of any two real numbers will be a real number.

Example 4 Application: Football

On the first down, the Cougars lost 4 yards. They gained 7 yards on the second down. Use addition to find the total number of yards lost or gained on the first two downs.

SOLUTION A loss of 4 yards can be expressed as -4.

$(-4) + 7 = 3$

The Cougars gained a total of 3 yards on the first two downs.

Simplify.
(Ex 1)

a. $|-3.4|$

b. $\left|\dfrac{6}{7}\right|$

c. $|14 + (-22)|$

d. $-|7 + 16|$

Find the sum.
(Ex 2)

e. $(-23.4) + 18.72$

f. $\left(-\dfrac{2}{3}\right) + \left(-\dfrac{1}{6}\right)$

Determine whether each statement is true or false. Give a counterexample for false statements.
(Ex 3)

g. The set of rational numbers is closed under addition.

h. The set of positive integers is closed under addition.

i. The temperature at 7:00 p.m. was 34°F. The temperature fell 12°F by
(Ex 4) midnight. Use addition to find the temperature at midnight.

Practice   Distributed and Integrated

Add, subtract, multiply, or divide.

1. $1\dfrac{1}{6} + 3\dfrac{1}{3}$
(SB 3)

2. $2\dfrac{3}{8} - 1\dfrac{1}{4}$
(SB 3)

3. $3\dfrac{2}{3} + 1\dfrac{5}{8} - 1\dfrac{3}{4}$
(SB 3)

4. $3\dfrac{1}{3} \div 1\dfrac{3}{5}$
(SB 3)

5. $1.506 \div 0.2$
(SB 2)

6. $2.89 \cdot 1.2$
(SB 2)

7. How many terms are in the algebraic expression $2x^2 + 3x + 7$?
(2)

8. Find the prime factorization of 150.
(SB 12)

9. Write Use the divisibility test to determine if 125,000 is divisible by 10.
(SB 4) Explain your answer.

10. Model Represent the following numbers as being members of set L: $-12, 0, -8, 4,$
(1) $-4, 4, 0, 8, 8, 12$.

11. Verify True or False: All integers are rational numbers. Explain your answer.
(1)

12. Error Analysis Student A said that $\dfrac{\sqrt{2}}{1}$ is a rational number. Student B said that it is
(1) an irrational number. Which student is correct? Explain your answer.

13. Write $\dfrac{5}{8}$ as a decimal and a percent.
(SB 5)

14. Measurement Order the lengths 1.25 yards, 3 feet, $1\dfrac{1}{3}$ yards from least to greatest.
(SB 1)

15. Write 7% as a fraction in simplest form and as a decimal.
(SB 5)

16. Formulate Write an equation using absolute values to represent the sentence.
(5) "The distance from -11 to 0 is 11."

17. Multiple Choice Which angle measures form an acute triangle?
(SB 13)

A 45°, 45°, and 90°   **B** 40°, 110°, and 20°

C 55°, 45°, and 80°   **D** 30°, 30°, and 120°

18. Estimate: $1.48 + $0.12 - $0.27.
(SB 8)

19. Write Use the definition of absolute value to write $|-5| = 5$ in words.
(5)

20. Verify True or False: A rectangle is a parallelogram. Explain your choice
(SB 14)

*21. Geometry The hypotenuse squared (c^2) can be determined by solving for $a^2 + b^2$ in
(4) the Pythagorean Theorem. Using the order of operations, decide if the expression $(a + b)$ should be determined before a^2?

*22. (Weather) One winter day the temperature rose 29°F from a low of −3°F in the
(5) morning. What was the day's high temperature?

*23. (Football) On the first down, the Tigers gained 8 yards. Then they were pushed back
(5) for a loss of $13\frac{1}{2}$ yards on the second down. Write and solve an addition problem to find the total number of yards lost or gained on the first two downs.

*24. Multiple Choice Which of these sets of numbers is closed under addition?
(5)

A integers   **B** rational numbers

C real numbers   **D** all of these

*25. Multi-Step Airplane A took off from an airport that is 43 feet below sea level, and
(5) then climbed 20,512 feet to its cruising altitude. Airplane B took off at the same time from an airport that was 1924 feet above sea level, and then climbed 18,527 feet to its cruising altitude. Which airplane is currently cruising at a higher altitude?

*26. (Banking) Martha had $500 in her checking account. She made a withdrawal of $34.65.
(5) Write and solve an addition problem to find Martha's balance after the withdrawal.

*27. Multi-Step A china cup-and-saucer set sells for $15.25 and a plate sells for $25.
(4) A woman buys 3 cup-and-saucer sets and 4 plates. If she pays a 5% sales tax, how much does she pay for her purchase?

a. Determine how much the woman spends before sales tax. Use the expression $3 \cdot (\$15.25) + 4 \cdot (\$25)$ to solve.

b. How much does she pay with sales tax included? Round your answer to the nearest hundredth. Use the expression $\$145.75 + (0.05) \cdot (\$145.75)$ to solve.

*28. (Stocks) Stock in the ABC Company fell 12.67 points on Monday and 31.51 points
(5) on Tuesday. Determine the total change in the stock for the two days.

*29. Multiple Choice Which expression correctly represents 1.6^5?
(3)

A $1.6 \times 1.6 \times 1.6 \times 1.6 \times 1.6$ **B** $1.6 + 1.6 + 1.6 + 1.6 + 1.6$

C $0.6 \times 0.6 \times 0.6 \times 0.6 \times 0.6 + 1$ **D** $1 \times 1 \times 1 \times 1 \times 1 + 0.6$

*30. (Temperature) At midnight the temperature was −7°F. By noon the temperature had
(5) risen 23°F. What was the temperature at noon?

Subtracting Real Numbers

Warm Up

1. Vocabulary The _____ of a number is the distance from the
(1) number to 0 on a number line.

Simplify.

2. $86.9 - 18.94$
(SB 2)

3. $\frac{1}{3} + \frac{4}{9}$
(SB 3)

4. $41.06 + 83.7$
(SB 2)

5. $\frac{5}{6} - \frac{5}{12}$
(SB 3)

New Concepts

Two numbers with the same absolute value but different signs are called **opposites**. Another name for the opposite of a number is **additive inverse**. The sum of a number and its opposite is 0.

Inverse Property of Addition
For every real number a, $a + (-a) = (-a) + a = 0$.
Example $5 + (-5) = 0$

Addition and subtraction are inverse operations. Subtracting a number is the same as adding the inverse of the number.

Rules for Subtracting Real Numbers
To subtract a number, add its inverse. Then follow the rules for adding real numbers.
Example $3 - 5 = 3 + (-5) = -2$

Example 1 Subtracting Real Numbers

Find each difference.

Math Reasoning

Analyze What is the meaning of $-(-8)$?

a. $(-12) - 21$

SOLUTION

$(-12) - 21$

$(-12) + (-21) = -33$

b. $(-19) - (-8)$

SOLUTION

$(-19) - (-8)$

$(-19) + (+8) = -11$

c. $3.2 - (-5.1)$

SOLUTION

$3.2 - (-5.1)$

$3.2 + (+5.1) = 8.3$

d. $\left(-\frac{3}{5}\right) - \left(-\frac{1}{5}\right)$

SOLUTION

$\left(-\frac{3}{5}\right) - \left(-\frac{1}{5}\right)$

$\left(-\frac{3}{5}\right) + \left(+\frac{1}{5}\right) = -\frac{2}{5}$

Online Connection
www.SaxonMathResources.com

Example 2 Determining Closure Over Subtraction

Determine whether each statement is true or false. Give a counterexample for false statements.

a. The set of integers is closed under subtraction.

SOLUTION

The statement is true because the difference of any two integers will be an integer.

b. The set of real numbers is closed under subtraction.

SOLUTION

The statement is true because the difference of any two real numbers will be a real number.

Example 3 Application: Dive Depth

Nayip collected a water sample at a depth of 23 meters from the surface. He descended another 12 meters to collect a plant sample. Where was Nayip in relation to the surface when he retrieved the plant sample?

SOLUTION

A depth of 23 meters can be written as (-23).

$(-23) - 12$

$= (-23) + (-12)$

$= -35$

Nayip was at 35 meters below the surface when he collected the plant sample.

Lesson Practice

Find each difference.
(Ex 1)

a. $14 - (-22)$

b. $(-7) - 16$

c. $(-23.4) - 18.72$

d. $\left(-\frac{2}{3}\right) - \left(-\frac{1}{6}\right)$

Determine whether each statement is true or false. Give a counterexample for false statements.
(Ex 2)

e. The set of whole numbers is closed under subtraction.

f. The set of rational numbers is closed under subtraction.

g. On January 23, 1960, the Trieste dove to a record depth of 37,800 feet below sea level. The record set previously, on January 7th of the same year, was 13,800 feet less than the dive on January 23rd. What was the record set on January 7th in relation to sea level?
(Ex 3)

Add, subtract, multiply, or divide.

1. $5\dfrac{1}{3} \div 2\dfrac{1}{3}$
(SB 3)

2. $40\dfrac{1}{8} - 21\dfrac{1}{4}$
(SB 3)

3. $5\dfrac{2}{3} + 2\dfrac{5}{6} + \left(-2\dfrac{1}{6}\right)$
(5)

4. $1\dfrac{2}{3} \div 1\dfrac{1}{4} \cdot 1\dfrac{1}{2}$
(SB 3)

5. $0.74 \div 0.2 \cdot 0.3$
(SB 2)

6. $5.4 \cdot 0.3 \div 0.4$
(SB 2)

7. $1.24 \cdot 0.2 \div 0.1$
(SB 2)

8. $112.4 \div 3.2$
(SB 2)

9. Find the prime factorization of 592.
(SB 12)

10. Find the prime factorization of 168.
(SB 12)

11. **Model** Display the following set of data in a line plot.
(SB 29)

$$8, 6, 9, 7, 5, 4, 6, 7, 9, 8, 5, 6, 6, 8$$

12. **Write** Use the divisibility test to determine if 2326 is divisible by 3. Explain your
(SB 4) answer.

13. Write 6% as a fraction in simplest form and as a decimal.
(SB 5)

14. **Measurement** Write 1.25 feet as a fraction in simplest form and compare it to $\dfrac{5}{3}$ feet.
(SB 5) Which is greater?

15. Write $\dfrac{3}{5}$ as a decimal and as a percent.
(SB 5)

16. **Multiple Choice** What is the value of the expression below?
(4)

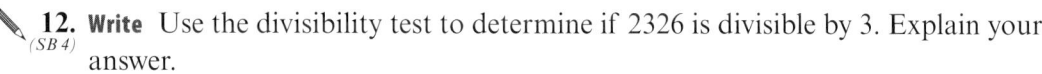

$$\frac{(3 \cdot 20 + 2 \cdot 20) \cdot 6 - 20}{10^2}$$

A 2.8   **B** 58   **C** −14   **D** 5.8

17. Simplify $\dfrac{(45 + 39 + 47 + 40 + 33 + 39 + 41)}{(2 \cdot 2)^2 - 12}$.
(4)

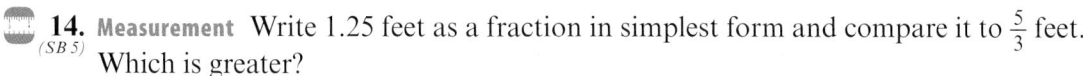

*18. **Multiple Choice** Which of these differences will be negative?
(6)

A $-4.8 - (-5.2)$ **B** $4.8 - 5.2$

C $4.8 - 3.2$ **D** $6.7 - (-7.8)$

*19. (**Football**) Ryan's varsity football team is on its own 25-yard line. The quarterback
(6) stumbles for a loss of 15 yards. What line is Ryan's varsity football team on now?

*20. **Geometry** If one angle in a triangle measures 105.5° and another measures 38.2°,
(6) what is the measurement of the third angle? Use the expression $180 - 105.5 - 38.2$
to solve.

*21. (**Temperature**) On a winter day, a wind gust makes the temperature in Antarctica
(6) feel sixteen degrees colder than the actual temperature. If the temperature is -5°C,
how cold did it feel?

*22. (**Consumer Math**) Leila issued a check for \$149.99 and deposited \$84.50 in her
(6) account. What is the net change in her account?

23. **Multiple Choice** Which triangle is an equiangular triangle?
(SB 13)   **A** a triangle with angle measures of 45°, 45°, and 90°

   B a triangle with angle measures of 60°, 60°, and 60°

   C a triangle with angle measures of 55°, 35°, and 90°

   D a triangle with angle measures of 30°, 30°, and 120°

24. (**Boating**) The tour boat can leave the dock only if the level of the lake is no more
(5) than 2 feet below normal. Before the recent rainfall, the level of the lake was
$5\frac{1}{3}$ feet below normal. After the recent rainfall, the level of the lake rose $3\frac{1}{4}$ feet.
Can the tour boat leave the dock? Explain.

*25. **Geometry** The triangle inequality is a theorem from geometry stating that for any
(5) two real numbers a and b, $|a + b| \le |a| + |b|$. Verify the triangle inequality by
simplifying $|-18.5 + 4.75| \le |-18.5| + |4.75|$.

*26. **Error Analysis** Two students solved this problem. Which student is correct? Explain
(5) the error.

The elevator started on the second floor and went up 8 floors, then down 11 floors
to the garage level, and then up 6 floors. Which floor is the elevator on now?

Student A	**Student B**
$2 + 8 + (-11) + 6 = 5$ The 5th floor	$2 + 8 - (-11) + 6 = 27$ The 27th floor

27. **Multi-Step** A bit is a binary digit and can have a value of either 0 or 1. A byte is a
(3) string of 8 bits.
   a. Write the number of bits in one byte as a power of 2.

   b. Write 32 as a power of 2.

   c. Write the number of bits in 32 bytes as a power of 2.

*28. $16c + (-4d) + \frac{8\pi}{15} + 21efg$
(2)
   a. Find the coefficients of the expression.

   b. Find the number of terms in the expression.

   c. **Justify** Rewrite the expression so that there are no parentheses. Justify your change.

*29. **Multiple Choice** What subset of numbers does the number $-9.0909090909\overline{09}$ belong to?
(1)   **A** integers   **B** irrational numbers

   C natural numbers   **D** rational numbers

*30. (**Oceanography**) The Pacific Ocean has an average depth of 12,925 feet, while the
(6) Atlantic Ocean has as average depth of 11,730 feet. Find the difference in average
depths.

Simplifying and Comparing Expressions with Symbols of Inclusion

Warm Up

1. Vocabulary A _____ is used to represent an unknown number.
(2)

Simplify.

2. $-1.5 + 3^2 - (3 - 5)$
(4)

3. $12 - 4 \cdot 0.5 + (3.4 - 1.7)$
(4)

4. $\left(\dfrac{2}{3}\right)^2 - \left(\dfrac{1}{3}\right)^2 + \dfrac{5}{6}$
(4)

New Concepts

A mathematical expression can include numbers, variables, operations, and symbols of inclusion. Symbols of inclusion, such as fraction bars, absolute-value symbols, parentheses, braces, and brackets indicate which numbers, variables, and operations are parts of the same term. An example is shown below.

$$\left(\dfrac{2x}{3} + 3\dfrac{1}{5}\right) - 2y$$

The expression inside the parentheses is considered a single term. To simplify an expression with multiple symbols of inclusion, begin inside the innermost symbol of inclusion and work outward.

Math Language

( )	parentheses
[ ]	brackets
{ }	braces
$\dfrac{a}{b}$	fraction bar
$\lvert x \rvert$	absolute-value symbols

Example 1 **Expressions with Absolute-Value Symbols and Parentheses**

Simplify each expression.

a. $9 - \lvert 4 - 6 \rvert$

SOLUTION

$9 - \lvert 4 - 6 \rvert$

$= 9 - \lvert -2 \rvert$ \qquad Subtract inside absolute-value symbols.

$= 9 - 2$ \qquad Simplify the absolute value.

$= 7$ \qquad Subtract.

b. $5 \cdot 2 + [3 + (6 - 8)]$

SOLUTION Begin simplifying inside the innermost symbol of inclusion.

$5 \cdot 2 + [3 + (6 - 8)]$

$= 5 \cdot 2 + [3 + (-2)]$ \qquad Subtract inside parentheses.

$= 5 \cdot 2 + 1$ \qquad Add inside brackets.

$= 10 + 1$ \qquad Multiply.

$= 11$ \qquad Add.

It is important to follow the order of operations at all times, even when working inside symbols of inclusion.

Example 2 **Simplifying Expressions with Brackets**

Simplify.

$$3 + 5 \cdot [(9 - 3)^2 - 6]$$

SOLUTION

Begin inside the innermost symbol of inclusion and work outward.

$$3 + 5 \cdot [(9 - 3)^2 - 6]$$
$$= 3 + 5 \cdot [6^2 - 6] \qquad \text{Simplify inside the parentheses.}$$
$$= 3 + 5 \cdot [36 - 6] \qquad \text{Evaluate the exponent.}$$
$$= 3 + 5 \cdot 30 \qquad \text{Subtract inside the brackets.}$$
$$= 3 + 150 \qquad \text{Multiply.}$$
$$= 153 \qquad \text{Add.}$$

To simplify a rational expression such as $\frac{6 \cdot 3}{4 - 2}$, the numerator and denominator must be simplified first.

Example 3 **Simplifying Expressions with Rational Numbers**

Simplify. Justify each step.

$$\left[5 \cdot (4 + 2)^2\right] + \frac{4 \cdot 5}{2}$$

SOLUTION

Justify each step using the order of operations or mathematical properties.

$$\left[5 \cdot (4 + 2)^2\right] + \frac{4 \cdot 5}{2}$$

$$= \left[5 \cdot (6)^2\right] + \frac{4 \cdot 5}{2} \qquad \text{Add inside the parentheses.}$$

$$= \left[5 \cdot 36\right] + \frac{4 \cdot 5}{2} \qquad \text{Simplify the exponent.}$$

$$= 180 + \frac{4 \cdot 5}{2} \qquad \text{Multiply inside the brackets.}$$

$$= 180 + \frac{20}{2} \qquad \text{Simplify the numerator.}$$

$$= 180 + 10 \qquad \text{Simplify the fraction.}$$

$$= 190 \qquad \text{Add.}$$

Example 4 **Compare Expressions with Symbols of Inclusion**

Compare the expressions. Use $<$, $>$, or $=$.

$$12 + [5(7 - 5)^3 - 14] \bigcirc [(9 - 5)^2 + 7] - 3^3$$

SOLUTION Simplify each expression. Then compare.

$$12 + [5(7-5)^3 - 14] \qquad [(9-5)^2 + 7] - 3^3$$
$$= 12 + [5(2)^3 - 14] \qquad = [(4)^2 + 7] - 3^3$$
$$= 12 + [5 \cdot 8 - 14] \qquad = [16 + 7] - 3^3$$
$$= 12 + [40 - 14] \qquad = 23 - 3^3$$
$$= 12 + 26 \qquad\qquad = 23 - 27$$
$$= 38 \qquad\qquad\qquad = -4$$

Since $38 > -4$, $12 + [5(7-5)^3 - 14] \; \bigcirc \; [(9-5)^2 + 7] - 3^3$.

Graphing Calculator

Enter the expression $10 + 8 \div 2^2$ into your calculator. If the calculator follows the order of operations, the answer will be 12.

Example 5 **Application: Half Price Sale**

Beatrice wants to buy 3 DVDs marked $7 each and 4 CDs marked $12 each. Everything in the store is on sale for half off the marked price. Beatrice has $31.50 to spend and a coupon good for $1 off each CD. Use the expression below to determine if Beatrice has enough money to buy all the items she wants.

$$\$31.50 - \left[\frac{3 \cdot \$7}{2} + \frac{4 \cdot \$12}{2} - (4 \cdot \$1) \right]$$

SOLUTION Begin inside the innermost symbols of inclusion to simplify the expression.

$$\$31.50 - \left[\frac{3 \cdot \$7}{2} + \frac{4 \cdot \$12}{2} - (4 \cdot \$1) \right]$$

$$= \$31.50 - \left[\frac{3 \cdot \$7}{2} + \frac{4 \cdot \$12}{2} - \$4 \right] \qquad \text{Multiply inside the parentheses.}$$

$$= \$31.50 - \left[\frac{\$21}{2} + \frac{\$48}{2} - \$4 \right] \qquad \text{Simplify the numerators.}$$

$$= \$31.50 - [\$10.50 + \$24 - \$4] \qquad \text{Simplify the fractions.}$$

$$= \$31.50 - \$30.50 \qquad\qquad \text{Simplify inside the brackets.}$$

$$= \$1.00 \qquad\qquad\qquad\qquad \text{Subtract.}$$

Beatrice has enough money.

Lesson Practice

Simplify each expression.
(Ex 1)

a. $12 + |5 - 11|$

b. $5(8 + 4) \div (15 - 5 - 4)$

c. $5 + [6 \cdot (2^3 + 4)]$

d. **Justify** Simplify the expression. Justify each step.
(Ex 3)

$$4(1 + 2)^2 \div 6 + \frac{8 \cdot 3}{2}$$

e. Compare the expressions. Use $<$, $>$, or $=$.
(Ex 4)
$$(13 + 5) - [5 \cdot 2^2] \;\bigcirc\; [(7 + 11) - 5] - 2^3.$$

f. (Health) Body Mass Index (BMI) is the relation of weight to height. The
(Ex. 5) expression $\left(\dfrac{W}{H^2}\right) \cdot 703$, where W is weight in pounds and H is height in inches, is used to calculate BMI. Explain the steps that are necessary to simplify this expression.

Practice   Distributed and Integrated

Add, subtract, multiply, or divide.

1. $(5 + 2)^2 - 50$
(4)

2. $(3 - 5) + 7^2$
(4)

3. $3\dfrac{1}{3} - 1\dfrac{1}{6} - 5\dfrac{1}{4}$
(6)

4. $2\dfrac{1}{3} \cdot 3\dfrac{1}{4} \cdot 1\dfrac{1}{2}$
(SB 3)

5. $(0.56 + 0.3) \cdot 0.2$
(4)

6. $3.25 \cdot 0.4 + 0.1$
(4)

7. $1.2 \div 0.1 \div 0.1$
(SB 2)

8. $20.2 \cdot 0.1 \cdot 0.1$
(SB 2)

9. **Verify** True or False: All whole numbers are counting numbers. If true, explain
(1) your answer. If false, give a counterexample.

10. The set $\{..., -3, -2, -1, 0, 1, 2, 3,...\}$ represents which set of numbers?
(1)

11. **Justify** True or False: An obtuse triangle has two obtuse angles. Explain your choice.
(SB 13)

12. Find the prime factorization of 207.
(SB 12)

13. Find the prime factorization of 37.
(SB 12)

14. **Write** Use the divisibility test to determine if 10,048 is divisible by 8. Explain.
(SB 4)

15. Write 0.345 as a fraction in simplest form and as a percent.
(SB 5)

16. Write 0.07% as a fraction in simplest form and as a decimal.
(SB 5)

*17. Evaluate $(|-3| \cdot 4) + \left[\left(\dfrac{1}{2} + \dfrac{1}{4}\right) \div \dfrac{1}{3}\right]$.
(7)

*18. Compare: $\dfrac{1}{3} + \dfrac{1}{5} \cdot \dfrac{2}{15} \;\bigcirc\; \left(\dfrac{1}{3} + \dfrac{1}{5}\right) \cdot \dfrac{2}{15}$.
(7)

*19. (Temperature) The following two formulas are used to convert degrees Celsius (°C) to
(7) degrees Fahrenheit (°F) and vise versa: $C = \dfrac{5}{9}(F - 32)$ and $F = \dfrac{9}{5}C + 32$. Explain how the equations are different.

*20. (Fencing) The diagram represents the fencing around a backyard. The fence
(7) is formed with parallel lines and a half-circle. Write and solve an equation to determine how many feet of fencing are needed. Round the answer to the nearest tenth.

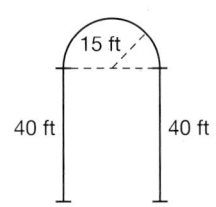

*21. Multiple Choice Simplify $[(10 - 8)^2 - (-1)] + (5 - 3)$.
(7)

    A -38 **B** 7 **C** -80 **D** 37

*22. (Manufacturing) A company produces two different types of 6-sided boxes. Box A is
(7) 12 inches long, 12 inches wide, and 12 inches tall. Box B is 16 inches long,
16 inches wide, and 6.75 inches tall. Both boxes have the same volume, but the
company wants to know which box uses less material to produce.

    a. Write and solve an expression to find the surface area of Box A.

    b. Write and solve an expression to find the surface area of Box B.

    c. Compare the box sizes. Which box uses less material?

*23. Multi-Step A ball is dropped from a height of 25.6 feet. After it hits the ground, it
(6) bounces to 12.8 feet and falls back to the ground. Next it bounces to 6.4 feet and
falls back to the ground. Then it bounces to 3.2 feet and falls back to the ground.

    a. Find the difference in heights between each consecutive bounce.

    b. If the pattern continues, will the ball ever stop bouncing? Explain.

24. Geometry What is the perimeter of the rectangle?
(6)

8.42 units

22.312 units

25. Measurement A valley is 250 below sea level and a small hill is 78 feet above sea
(5) level. Solve $|-250| + 78$ to determine the distance from the bottom of the valley
to the top of the hill.

*26. (Transportation) In the last hour, 7 planes have landed at the airport and 11 planes
(5) have taken off. Use addition to find the change in the total number of planes at
the airport in the last hour.

27. Error Analysis The temperature in the morning was $-18°$F. It increased by $5°$ by noon
(4) and dropped $10°$ in the evening. Two students determined the temperature in the
evening. Which student is correct? Explain the error.

Student A	Student B
$-18 + 5 + 10 = -3$	$-18 + 5 + (-10) = -23$

*28. (Meteorology) The water level of the reservoir in Purcellville, Virginia was 2 feet
(6) below normal. After a heavy rainstorm, the water level increased to 5 feet above
normal. Write and solve a subtraction problem to find the change in the water
level caused by the rainstorm.

29. Multiple Choice Which term in the expression $\frac{\sqrt{9}ny}{nx} + a^2 - \frac{n}{4} + \frac{3\pi}{8}$ contains an
(1) irrational constant?

    A $\dfrac{\sqrt{9}ny}{nx}$ **B** $\dfrac{3\pi}{8}$ **C** $\dfrac{n}{4}$ **D** a^2

*30. Geometry The measure of each interior angle of a hexagon is given by the
(7) expression $\frac{180(6 - 2)°}{6}$. What is the measure of an interior angle of a
hexagon?

Using Unit Analysis to Convert Measures

Warm Up

1. **Vocabulary** The amount of space a solid figure occupies is called the _____ (*area*, *volume*).
(SB 26)

Simplify.

2. $\dfrac{7}{12} \cdot \dfrac{36}{49}$
(SB 3)

3. $\dfrac{8}{9} \cdot \dfrac{15}{36}$
(SB 3)

4. $\dfrac{2}{5} \cdot \dfrac{15}{16} \cdot \dfrac{6}{7}$
(SB 3)

5. $\dfrac{12}{13} \cdot \dfrac{1}{4} \cdot \dfrac{39}{48}$
(SB 3)

New Concepts

Unit analysis is a process for converting measures into different units. A unit ratio, or conversion factor, compares 2 measures that name the same amount.

$$\frac{12 \text{ in.}}{1 \text{ ft}} \qquad \frac{1 \text{ m}}{100 \text{ cm}} \qquad \frac{3 \text{ ft}}{1 \text{ yd}}$$

Since the amounts used in a unit ratio are equal to each other, a unit ratio is always equal to 1. Since the product of 1 and a number is that number, a unit ratio multiplied by a measure will always name the same amount.

Example 1 Converting Units of Length

A cheetah ran at a rate of 105,600 yards per hour. How fast did the cheetah run in miles per hour?

SOLUTION Find a unit ratio and multiply.

Hint

A mile is equal to 1760 yards.

$\dfrac{105{,}600 \text{ yd}}{1 \text{ hour}} = \dfrac{? \text{ mi}}{1 \text{ hour}}$ Identify known and missing information.

$105{,}600 \text{ yd} \rightarrow ? \text{ mi}$ Write the conversion.

$1 \text{ mi} = 1{,}760 \text{ yd}$ Equate units.

$\dfrac{1 \text{ mi}}{1760 \text{ yd}}$ Write a unit ratio.

$\dfrac{105{,}600 \text{ yd}}{1 \text{ hr}} \cdot \dfrac{1 \text{ mi}}{1760 \text{ yd}}$ Write the multiplication sentence.

$= \dfrac{\overset{60}{\cancel{105{,}600}} \text{ yd}}{1 \text{ hr}} \cdot \dfrac{1 \text{ mi}}{\underset{1}{\cancel{1760}} \text{ yd}}$ Cancel out common factors.

$= \dfrac{60 \text{ mi}}{1 \text{ hr}}$ Multiply.

$\dfrac{105{,}600 \text{ yd}}{1 \text{ hr}} = \dfrac{60 \text{ mi}}{1 \text{ hr}}$ Write the ratio of miles per hour.

Online Connection
www.SaxonMathResources.com

The cheetah ran at a rate of 60 miles per hour.

Exploration Using Unit Analysis

If a measure of length changes, then the unit analysis occurs in one dimension. If a measure of area changes, the units for the dimensions of both length and width must change.

Draw two congruent squares with side lengths of 3 inches on a sheet of paper. Label the sides of the first square 1 yard. Divide both the length and width of the second square into 3 equal sections. This will divide the square into 9 congruent smaller squares. Label the sides of the second square 3 feet.

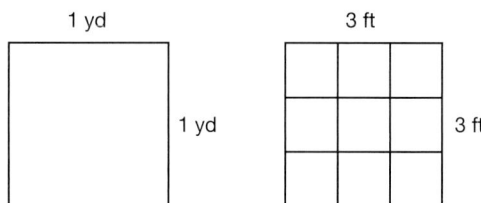

a. What is the area of the first square? Show your calculation.

b. What is the area of the second square? Show your calculation.

c. Write two unit ratios for converting between feet and yards.

d. Which unit ratio should be used for converting yards to feet? Explain your choice.

e. **Justify** Use a unit ratio to convert the area of the first square into square feet. Show your calculation.

f. **Write** Why is it necessary to multiply by the unit ratio twice to convert square yards to square feet?

Extend the example of the area of squares to the volume of cubes. Draw two cubes, one with dimensions of 1 yard and one with dimensions of 3 feet.

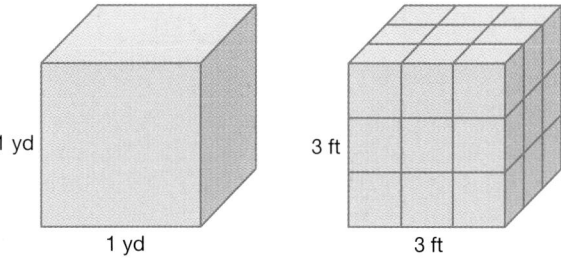

g. What is the volume of the first cube? Show your calculation.

h. What is the volume of the second cube? Show your calculation.

i. **Justify** Use a unit ratio to convert the volume of the first cube into cubic feet. Show your calculation.

j. **Write** Why is it necessary to multiply by the unit ratio three times to convert cubic yards to cubic feet?

Example 2 Converting Units of Area

A gym measures 8.5 meters by 14 meters. The owner bought mats to cover the floor. Each mat is 110 centimeters square. If 95 mats were purchased, are there enough mats to cover the floor?

SOLUTION Find the area and convert the unit of measure.

$8.5 \text{ m} \cdot 14 \text{ m} = 119 \text{ m}^2$	Find the area of the room.
$119 \text{ m}^2 \rightarrow ? \text{ cm}^2$	Write the conversion.
$1 \text{ m} = 100 \text{ cm}$	Equate units.
$\dfrac{100 \text{ cm}}{1 \text{ m}}$	Write a unit ratio.
$119 \text{ m} \cdot \text{m} \cdot \dfrac{100 \text{ cm}}{1 \text{ m}} \cdot \dfrac{100 \text{ cm}}{1 \text{ m}}$	Write the multiplication sentence.
$= 119 \, \cancel{\text{m}} \cdot \cancel{\text{m}} \cdot \dfrac{100 \text{ cm}}{1 \, \cancel{\text{m}}} \cdot \dfrac{100 \text{ cm}}{1 \, \cancel{\text{m}}}$	Cancel out common factors.
$= \dfrac{119 \cdot 100 \text{ cm} \cdot 100 \text{ cm}}{1} = 1{,}190{,}000 \text{ cm}^2$	Multiply.
$95(110 \text{ cm} \cdot 110 \text{ cm}) = 1{,}149{,}500 \text{ cm}^2$	Find the area of 95 mats.
$1{,}149{,}500 \text{ cm}^2 < 1{,}190{,}000 \text{ cm}^2$	Compare the areas.

The area covered by 95 mats is less than the area of the floor, so there are not enough mats to cover the floor.

Math Reasoning

Each mat is 110 **centimeters square.** This means that the length and width are 110 centimeters each.

Example 3 Application: Converting Units of Volume

A hose with a flow rate of 41,472 cubic inches per hour is filling up a pool. The volume of the pool is 1,104 cubic feet. How many hours will it take to fill the pool?

SOLUTION Find the volume and convert the unit of measure.

$\dfrac{41{,}472 \text{ in}^3}{1 \text{ hour}} \rightarrow \dfrac{? \text{ ft}^3}{1 \text{ hour}}$	Identify known and missing information.
$1 \text{ ft} = 12 \text{ in.}$	Equate units.
$\dfrac{1 \text{ ft}}{12 \text{ in.}}$	Write a unit ratio.
$\dfrac{41{,}472 \text{ in.} \cdot \text{in.} \cdot \text{in.}}{1 \text{ hr}} \cdot \dfrac{1 \text{ ft}}{12 \text{ in.}} \cdot \dfrac{1 \text{ ft}}{12 \text{ in.}} \cdot \dfrac{1 \text{ ft}}{12 \text{ in.}}$	Write the multiplication sentence.
$= \dfrac{\overset{24}{\cancel{41{,}472}} \, \cancel{\text{in.}} \cdot \cancel{\text{in.}} \cdot \cancel{\text{in.}}}{1 \text{ hr}} \cdot \dfrac{1 \text{ ft}}{\underset{1}{\cancel{12 \text{ in.}}}} \cdot \dfrac{1 \text{ ft}}{\underset{1}{\cancel{12 \text{ in.}}}} \cdot \dfrac{1 \text{ ft}}{\underset{1}{\cancel{12 \text{ in.}}}}$	Cancel out common factors.
$= \dfrac{24 \text{ ft} \cdot \text{ft} \cdot \text{ft}}{1 \text{ hr}} = \dfrac{24 \text{ ft}^3}{1 \text{ hr}}$	Multiply.
$1{,}104 \div 24 = 46 \text{ hours}$	

It will take 46 hours to fill the pool.

Math Reasoning

Analyze Compare the process of converting feet to inches with the process of converting feet per minute to inches per minute.

Unit analysis can be used for more than just converting units of length. It can also be used to convert units of mass, density, temperature, capacity, or even money. In economics, the value of money is defined by what people are willing to exchange for it. This means that the value of a currency can change relative to the value of other currencies. An exchange-rate listing shows what a currency is worth compared to other currencies at that moment.

Example 4 Foreign Travel: Converting Units of Currency

Jared and his family are going on a vacation to Europe. He takes $225 with him. He needs to exchange this amount for its equivalent value in euros. If the current exchange rate is 1 euro = $1.36, what is the value of Jared's $225 in euros?

SOLUTION

Convert the unit of measure.

225 dollars → ? euros	Write the conversion.
1 euro = 1.36 dollars	Equate units.
$\dfrac{1 \text{ euro}}{1.36 \text{ dollars}}$	Write a unit ratio.
225 dollars $\cdot \dfrac{1 \text{ euro}}{1.36 \text{ dollars}}$	Write the multiplication sentence.
= 165.44 euros	Multiply and cancel.

Check Since a euro is worth more than a dollar, Jared should have fewer euros than dollars after the exchange.

225 > 165.44   The answer is reasonable.

Hint

Choose a unit conversion factor that cancels the units you want to change and replaces them with the units you want.

Lesson Practice

a. A Mourning Dove can reach speeds up to 35 miles per hour. How fast is this in feet per hour?
(Ex 1)

b. An interior wall measures 4.5 yards by 3.25 yards. What is the size of the wall in square feet?
(Ex 2)

c. Della has a small bag containing 50 cubic centimeters of potting soil. Her planter has a volume of 46,300 cubic millimeters. Does Della have enough soil to fill the planter? Explain.
(Ex 3)

d. Arthur just returned from London. He has 16 British pounds to convert to American dollars. If the exchange rate is 1 pound = $2.016, what is the value of Arthur's 16 pounds in dollars?
(Ex 4)

Add, subtract, multiply, or divide.

1. $4\frac{1}{3} \div 1\frac{1}{3} + 3\frac{1}{3}$
(4)

2. $2\frac{3}{8} - 1\frac{3}{4} \div 1\frac{1}{2}$
(4)

3. $2\frac{2}{3} + 1\frac{5}{6} - 6\frac{3}{4}$
(6)

4. $3\frac{1}{3} \div 1\frac{1}{4} \cdot \frac{1}{2}$
(4)

5. $0.37 \div 0.2 \cdot 0.1$
(6)

6. $1.74 \cdot 0.3 \div 0.2$
$(SB\,2)$

7. Given the sets $A = \{1, 3, 5\}$, $B = \{0, 2, 4, 6\}$, and $C = \{1, 2, 3, 4\}$, are the
(1) following statements true or false?

   a. $A \cup B = \{0, 1, 2, 3, 4, 5, 6\}$

   b. $A \cap B = \{0, 1, 2, 3, 4, 5, 6\}$

   c. $B \cup C = \{2, 4\}$

   d. $A \cap C = \{1, 3\}$

8. Compare the expressions using $<$, $>$, or $=$. Explain.
(4)

$$8^2 \div 4 - 6^2 \, \bigcirc \, (6 \cdot 7 \cdot 5) \div 6 - 15$$

9. Draw a line plot for the frequency table.
$(SB\,29)$

Number	2	3	4	5	6	7
Frequency	4	3	2	1	4	3

10. Subtract $78\frac{2}{5} - 14\frac{7}{10}$.
$(SB\,2)$

11. Find the prime factorization of 484.
$(SB\,12)$

12. Write Use the divisibility test to determine if 22,993 is divisible by 5. Explain your
$(SB\,4)$ answer.

13. Write 125% as a fraction in simplest form and as a decimal.
$(SB\,5)$

14. Convert 105 kilometers per hour to kilometers per minute.
(8)

*15. Convert 74 square meters to square centimeters.
(8)

*16. (Camping) Norman's camping tent has a volume of 72,576 cubic inches. What is the
(8) volume of the tent in cubic feet?

17. Multiple Choice Which of these differences will be positive?
(6)

   A $-\frac{1}{2} - \frac{1}{8}$
      B $\frac{9}{12} - 1$

   C $\frac{5}{7} - \frac{3}{10}$
      D $-\frac{14}{15} - \left(\frac{4}{15}\right)$

18. Error Analysis Two students used unit analysis to convert a measurement of length.
(8) Which student is correct? Explain the error.

Student A	Student B
1 cm = 10 mm	1 cm = 10 mm
5540 mm = 5540 mm × $\dfrac{1 \text{ cm}}{10 \text{ mm}}$	5540 mm = 5540 mm × $\dfrac{10 \text{ mm}}{1 \text{ cm}}$
5540 mm = 554 cm	5540 mm = 55400 cm

*19. Multiple Choice Which one of the following ratios can be used to convert 120 cm
(8) into an equivalent measure in inches? (Hint: There are 2.54 cm in one inch.)

A $\dfrac{2.54 \text{ cm}}{1 \text{ in.}}$

B $\dfrac{1 \text{ in.}}{2.54 \text{ cm}}$

C $\dfrac{2.54 \text{ cm}}{1 \text{ in.}} \cdot \dfrac{2.54 \text{ cm}}{1 \text{ in.}}$

D $\dfrac{1 \text{ in.}}{2.54 \text{ cm}} \cdot \dfrac{1 \text{ in.}}{2.54 \text{ in.}}$

*20. (**Weather Forecasting**) One knot is exactly 1.852 kilometers per hour. The highest
(8) wind gust for the day was measured at 38 knots.

a. How many km/hr was the recorded wind gust? (Hint: 1 knot = 1.852 km/hr)

b. How many mph was the recorded wind gust? (Hint: 1 mi = 1.609 km)

*21. Multi-Step How can you find the area of the triangle in square inches?
(8)

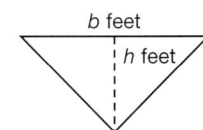

a. Write a formula for computing the area of the triangle in units of
square feet.

b. Write a new formula that computes the area of the triangle in units of
square inches.

c. What is the area of the triangle in square inches if $b = 3$ ft and $h = 2.2$ ft?

*22. (**Chemistry**) Water has a density of 1 gram per cubic centimeter. What is the density
(8) of water in grams per cubic inch?

*23. Justify True or False: A right triangle has one right angle, one obtuse angle, and
(SB 13) one acute angle. If false, explain why.

24. **Error Analysis** Student A and Student B simplified the expression $\frac{24}{8} + (2 + 4)^2$.
(7) Which student is correct? Explain the error.

Student A	Student B
$\frac{24}{8} + (2 + 4)^2$	$\frac{24}{8} + (2 + 4)^2$
$3 + 6^2$	$3 + (2 + 16)$
$3 + 36 = 39$	$3 + 18 = 21$

25. **Geometry** A square pyramid has a base with edges of 8 inches and a height of
(7) 12 inches.

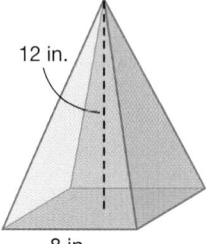

12 in.

8 in.

a. Use the following formula to find the volume: $V = \frac{1}{3}s^2h$.

b. **Analyze** Which term did you simplify first? Why?

*26. **Economics** Use the table of the Profit and Loss Report of ABC Company. What
(6) was the total profit or loss for the year? [( ) indicates a loss.]

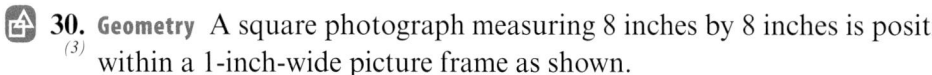

	1st Quarter	2nd Quarter	3rd Quarter	4th Quarter
Profit or Loss	$6 million	($3.5 million)	($2 million)	$5 million

*27. **Multi-Step** Two groups of students measured the length of a tabletop. Group A's
(5) measurement was $56\frac{3}{4}$ inches. Group B's measurement was $57\frac{3}{4}$ inches. If the
actual length of the tabletop was $57\frac{1}{2}$ inches, which group's measurement had the
smaller error?

28. **Error Analysis** Two students simplified an expression containing an exponent.
(3) Which student is correct? Explain the error.

Student A	Student B
$b^2 \cdot c^2 \cdot c \cdot b^2 \cdot b =$	$b^2 \cdot c^2 \cdot c \cdot b^2 \cdot b =$
$b^2 \cdot b^2 \cdot b \cdot c^2 \cdot c = b^5c^3$	$b^2 \cdot b^2 \cdot b \cdot c^2 \cdot c = b^4c^2$

29. **Speed** A giraffe can run 32 miles per hour. What is the speed in feet per hour?
(8)

30. **Geometry** A square photograph measuring 8 inches by 8 inches is positioned
(3) within a 1-inch-wide picture frame as shown.

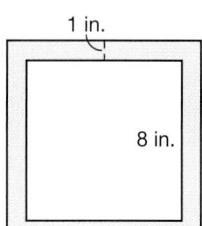

1 in.

8 in.

a. What is the area of the photograph?

b. What is the combined area of the photograph and frame?

c. What is the area of the frame alone?

d. If the 1-inch-wide frame is replaced with a 2-inch-wide frame, how much more
wall space will be needed to hang the framed photograph?

LESSON 9

Evaluating and Comparing Algebraic Expressions

Warm Up

1. Vocabulary When two numbers are divided, the result is called the _____. (*quotient, product*).

(2)

Simplify.

2. $x^5 b^2 \cdot 3b^3 x$
(3)

3. $\dfrac{4^3}{2^3} + 7^2$
(4)

4. $\dfrac{5^3}{3^2 + 4^2}$
(4)

5. $32 \div \left[2 \cdot (8 - 7)\right]$
(7)

New Concepts

Any expression containing only numbers and operations is a **numeric expression**. An **algebraic expression** is an expression with variables and/or numbers that uses operations (e.g., $+$, $-$, $\times$, or $\div$). An algebraic expression is also called a variable expression.

Example 1 Evaluating Algebraic Expressions

Evaluate the expression when $x = 3$ and $a = 1$.

$3x - 4x + ax$

> **Math Language**
>
> **Evaluate** means to substitute values for the variables and to simplify using the order of operations.

SOLUTION Substitute 3 for x and 1 for a in the expression. Then simplify.

$3x - 4x + ax$

$= 3 \cdot 3 - 4 \cdot 3 + 1 \cdot 3$

$= 9 - 12 + 3$

$= 0$

When the variables in algebraic expressions have exponents, it is helpful to write the value in parentheses.

Example 2 Evaluating Algebraic Expressions with Exponents

Evaluate the expression for $y = 2$ and $z = 4$.

$3(z - y)^2 - 4y^3$

SOLUTION Substitute 2 for y and 4 for z in the expression. Then simplify.

$3(z - y)^2 + 4y^3$

$= 3(4 - 2)^2 - 4(2)^3$

$= 3(2)^2 - 4(2)^3$

$= 3 \cdot 4 - 4(8)$

$= 12 - (32)$

$= -20$

> **Online Connection**
> www.SaxonMathResources.com

Two algebraic expressions are equivalent if they can be simplified to the same value. For example, $2 \cdot 2 - 1$ is equivalent to $15 \div 5$. Both expressions have a simplified value of 3.

Example 3 Comparing Algebraic Expressions

Compare the expressions when $a = 4$ and $b = 3$. Use $<$, $>$, or $=$.

$$3a^2 + 2b - 4b^3 \bigcirc 2a^2b^2$$

SOLUTION Simplify the expression on the left and then compare.

$3a^2 + 2b - 4b^3$	$2a^2b^2$
$3(4)^2 + 2(3) - 4(3)^3$	$2(4)^2(3)^2$
$= 3(16) + 2(3) - 4(27)$	$= 2(16)(9)$
$= 48 + 6 - 108$	$= 288$
$= 54 - 108$	
$= -54$	

Since $-54 < 288$, $3a^2 + 2b - 4b^3 < 2a^2b^2$ when $a = 4$ and $b = 3$.

Many real-world situations can be described using math. Algebraic expressions can be used to represent relationships between quantities.

Example 4 Application: Phone Charges

Math Reasoning

Analyze In the expression $20 + 0.45m$, what does the variable m represent?

A cell phone company charges a \$20 monthly fee and then 45 cents per minute. The company uses the expression $20 + 0.45m$ to find the total amount to charge for each month. How much would the company charge for 200 minutes?

SOLUTION Substitute 200 for m in the expression and simplify.

$$20 + 0.45m$$
$$= 20 + 0.45(200)$$
$$= 20 + 90$$
$$= 110$$

The cell phone company would charge \$110.

Lesson Practice

Evaluate each expression for the given values.

a. $3x - 4b + 2bx$; $x = 10$, $b = 2$
(Ex 1)

b. $2ab - 4a^2 + 10$; $a = -1$, $b = 8$
(Ex 2)

c. Compare the expressions when $x = 2$ and $y = 5$. Use $<$, $>$, or $=$.
(Ex 3)
$$(6x^2 + y^3) - 3x^6 \bigcirc 8x^4 - y^3$$

d. (**Climate**) The lowest recorded temperature is $-89.4°C$ in Antarctica.
(Ex 4) The expression $\frac{9}{5}C + 32$ can be used to convert Celsius measurements to Fahrenheit. What is the lowest recorded temperature in degrees Fahrenheit?

Add, subtract, multiply, or divide.

1. $4\frac{1}{3} \div 2\frac{1}{3}$
(SB 3)

2. $42\frac{3}{8} - 21\frac{3}{4}$
(SB 3)

3. $1\frac{2}{3} + 2\frac{5}{6}$
(SB 3)

4. $2\frac{2}{3} \div 1\frac{3}{4}$
(SB 3)

5. $0.75 \div 0.2$
(SB 2)

6. $1.74 \div 0.3$
(SB 2)

7. $1.25 \cdot 0.2$
(SB 2)

8. 12.2×3.2
(SB 2)

9. Verify True or False: A square is a rhombus. Explain your choice.
(SB 14)

10. Simplify $4[(6 - 4)^3 - 5]$.
(7)

11. Convert 1.86 km^2 to m^2.
(8)

*12. Evaluate the expression $14c + 28 - 12cd$ for the given values $c = 4$ and $d = 5$.
(9)

13. A straight angle measures _____.
(SB 13)

14. Find the prime factorization of 125.
(SB 12)

*15. Find the value of the expression $\frac{t-36}{36} + l$ if $t = 72$ and $l = 1$.
(9)

16. Multiple Choice Evaluate the expression $14 + \frac{36}{9} \cdot (2 + 5)$.
(7)

    A 126   **B** 21   **C** 42   **D** 140

17. Simplify $(3 + 12) + (|-4| - 2)^3 + 1$.
(7)

*18. (**Flight**) A rocket is fired upward at an initial speed of 112 feet per second (ft/sec). It
(9) travels at a speed of $112 - 32t$ ft/sec, where t is the flight time in seconds.

    a. What is the rocket's speed after 1 second?

    b. What is the rocket's speed after 2 seconds?

*19. (**Canoeing**) Rachel wants to rent a canoe for 3 hours. Use the expression
(9) $\$6.50 + \$1.75h,$ where h represents the number of hours, to calculate the cost
of renting the canoe.

*20. Error Analysis Two students were asked to evaluate $\frac{y^2}{-x}$ when x is 5 and y is -5.
(9) Which student is correct? Explain the error.

Student A	Student B
$\dfrac{y^2}{-x} = \dfrac{-5^2}{-(5)} = \dfrac{-25}{-5} = 5$	$\dfrac{y^2}{-x} = \dfrac{(-5)^2}{-(5)} = \dfrac{25}{-5} = -5$

*21. Data Analysis The variance of a set of data can be found with the expression $\frac{s}{n}$,
(9) where s is the sum of the squared deviation and n is the total number of data items
in the set. What is the variance for a set of data with 12 items and a sum of the
squared deviations equal to 30?

*22. **Sports** In volleyball, the statistic for total blocks at the net is calculated with the
(9) expression $s + 0.5a$, where s is the number of solo blocks and a is the number
of assisted blocks. What is the total-blocks statistic for a player who has 80 solo
blocks and 53 assisted blocks?

23. **Write** Use the divisibility test to determine if 224 is divisible by 6. Explain
(SB 4) your answer.

24. Write 35.2% as a fraction in simplest form and as a decimal.
(SB 5)

*25. **Multi-Step** The rectangle has dimensions measured in centimeters. What
(8) is the ratio of the area of the rectangle in centimeters to the area of the
rectangle in millimeters?

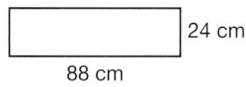

a. Calculate the area of the rectangle.

b. Find the area of the rectangle in square millimeters.

c. Find the ratio of square centimeters to square millimeters for the rectangle.

*26. **Geometry** A right circular cylinder has a base radius of 56 mm and a height of
(8) 128 mm. What is its volume in cubic centimeters? Round the answer to the
nearest hundredth. Use 3.14 for π.

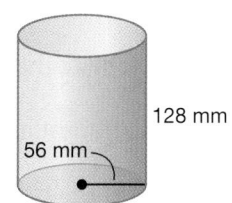

27. **Loans** The formula for long-term loans is $F = P(1 + i)^{n \div 12}$, where F is the future
(7) value of money, P is the present value, i is the interest rate, and n is the length of
time the money is borrowed in months. When solving this equation for F, what
step would you perform after adding 1 and i?

28. **Golf** Below is Rickie's golf score for two golf tournaments. What is the difference
(6) in his final score for the 1st and 2nd tournament?

1st Tournament	1	−2	−3	2
2nd Tournament	−2	−1	1	−1

29. **Error Analysis** Two students were asked to evaluate $(30 - 10)^2$. Student A answered
(4) 400, and Student B answered −70. Which student is correct? Explain the error.

Student A	Student B
$(30 - 10)^2$	$(30 - 10)^2$
$= 20^2$	$= (30 - 10 \cdot 10)$
$= 400$	$= (30 - 100)$
	$= -70$

*30. **Typing** Jared can type 35 words per minute. Use the expression $35m$ to find the
(9) number of words he can type in 15 minutes.

Adding and Subtracting Real Numbers

Warm Up

1. Vocabulary Any real number that cannot be written as a quotient of
integers is called a(n) _____ number.
(1)

Simplify.

2. $(25 \div 5) - (30 \div 10)$
(4)

3. $-4 + (-9) + (-6)$
(5)

4. $(2.45 + 5.75) - (4.85 - 3.75)$
(4)

5. $(j^4 k^5)(4kj^2)(3k^3)$
(3)

New Concepts

When solving a problem containing addition and subtraction of signed numbers, begin by writing the problem as addition only. Next, group and add the terms with like signs. Then add the terms with unlike signs.

Example 1 Adding and Subtracting Fractions and Decimals

Simplify.

a. $-\dfrac{1}{5} + \dfrac{3}{5} - \dfrac{2}{5} - \left(-\dfrac{4}{5}\right)$

SOLUTION

$-\dfrac{1}{5} + \dfrac{3}{5} - \dfrac{2}{5} - \left(-\dfrac{4}{5}\right)$

$= -\dfrac{1}{5} + \dfrac{3}{5} + \left(-\dfrac{2}{5}\right) + \dfrac{4}{5}$ Write the problem as addition.

$= -\dfrac{1}{5} + \left(-\dfrac{2}{5}\right) + \dfrac{3}{5} + \dfrac{4}{5}$ Group the terms with like signs.

$= -\dfrac{3}{5} + \dfrac{7}{5}$ Add numbers with like signs.

$= -\dfrac{4}{5}$ Add.

b. $3.16 + (-1.22) - 4.73 + 5.6$

SOLUTION

$3.16 + (-1.22) - 4.73 + 5.6$

$= 3.16 + (-1.22) + (-4.73) + 5.6$ Write the problem as addition.

$= 3.16 + 5.6 + (-1.22) + (-4.73)$ Group the terms with the same signs.

$= 8.76 + (-5.95)$ Add numbers with like signs.

$= 2.81$ Add.

Hint

Use the rules below for adding integers.

1. Like signs: Add and keep the sign.

2. Unlike signs: Subtract and keep the sign of the greater absolute value.

Online Connection
www.SaxonMathResources.com

Example 2 Ordering Rational Numbers

Order the numbers from least to greatest.

$$\frac{7}{8}, -2, 0.125, \frac{1}{2}$$

SOLUTION

Use a number line to order the numbers. Place each number on the number line.

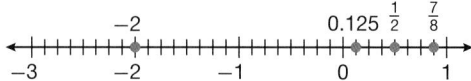

To order these numbers from least to greatest, read the numbers on the number line from left to right.

$$-2, 0.125, \frac{1}{2}, \frac{7}{8}$$

Example 3 Comparing Rational Expressions

Complete the comparison. Use $<$, $>$, or $=$.

$$\frac{3}{8} + \left(-\frac{5}{8}\right) - \frac{1}{8} \bigcirc -2.75 + 6.25 - 3.75$$

SOLUTION

Simplify each expression. Then compare.

$$\frac{3}{8} + \left(-\frac{5}{8}\right) - \frac{1}{8}$$

$$= \frac{3}{8} + \left(-\frac{5}{8}\right) + \left(-\frac{1}{8}\right)$$

$$= \frac{3}{8} + \left(-\frac{6}{8}\right)$$

$$= -\frac{3}{8}$$

$$-2.75 + 6.25 - 3.75$$

$$= -2.75 + 6.25 + (-3.75)$$

$$= -2.75 + (-3.75) + 6.25$$

$$= -6.50 + 6.25$$

$$= -0.25$$

Hint

Convert $-\frac{3}{8}$ to a decimal or -0.25 to a fraction to make comparing the values easier.

Since $-\frac{3}{8} < -0.25$, $\frac{3}{8} + \left(-\frac{5}{8}\right) - \frac{1}{8} \; \textcircled{<} \; -2.75 + 6.25 - 3.75$.

Example 4 Application: Investing

Carly invested $250 in two accounts. The table below shows the ending balance per quarter.

	1ˢᵗ Quarter	2ⁿᵈ Quarter	3ʳᵈ Quarter	4ᵗʰ Quarter
Investment A	$255.75	$258.81	$260.25	$262.99
Investment B	$260.66	$274.22	$268.92	$290.07

a. Which investment grew more?

SOLUTION

Find the differences and compare.

Investment A	Investment B
$262.99 − $250 = $12.99	$290.07 − $250 = $40.07

Investment B grew more.

b. In which quarter did Investment B grow the most?

SOLUTION

$260.66 − $250.00 = $10.66

$274.22 − $260.66 = $13.56

$268.92 − $274.22 = −$5.30

$290.07 − $268.92 = $21.15

The greatest difference is $21.15, which occurred in the 4th quarter.

Lesson Practice

Simplify.

(Ex 1)

a. $\dfrac{4}{9} + \dfrac{2}{9} - \dfrac{5}{9}$

b. $16.21 - 21.54 + 12.72$

c. Order the numbers from least to greatest.

(Ex 2)

$$\dfrac{3}{4}, -1, 0.85, \dfrac{5}{8}$$

d. Complete the comparison. Use $<$, $>$, or $=$.

(Ex 3)

$$3.2 + (-2.8) - 5.2 \;\bigcirc\; \dfrac{7}{12} - \dfrac{5}{12} + \left(-\dfrac{11}{12}\right)$$

e. Jonah ran a race in 32.68 seconds. Jarrod finished 1.92 seconds before Jonah. Gayle finished 3.01 seconds after Jonah. How many seconds did it take Gayle to run the race?

(Ex 4)

Practice   Distributed and Integrated

Add, subtract, multiply, or divide.

1. $\dfrac{1}{2} + \dfrac{3}{5}$
(SB 3)

2. $15\dfrac{1}{3} - 7\dfrac{4}{5}$
(SB 3)

3. $3\dfrac{2}{3} \cdot 2\dfrac{1}{4}$
(SB 3)

4. $3\dfrac{2}{5} \div 1\dfrac{2}{3}$
(SB 3)

5. $78\dfrac{2}{5} - 14\dfrac{7}{10}$
(SB 3)

6. $2\dfrac{1}{3} \cdot 1\dfrac{1}{4}$
(SB 3)

7. $10.2 \cdot 3.15$
(SB 2)

8. $20.46 \div 2.2$
(SB 2)

9. $12.3 \cdot 2.02$
(SB 2)

10. $0.8 \div 0.25$
(SB 2)

*11. Order from greatest to least: $\frac{6}{7}, \frac{3}{5}, \frac{1}{7}, -\frac{4}{3}$.
(10)

12. A(n) _____ angle measures less than 90°.
(SB 1)

13. Convert 8673 g to kg.
(8)

14. Convert 26 mi to km. Round your answer to the nearest tenth.
(8)

15. True or False: $(2 + 5) - (3 \cdot 4) = 2 + 5 - 3 \cdot 4$. Explain.
(4)

*16. Multiple Choice Simplify $1.29 + 3.9 - 4.2 - 9.99 + 6.1$.
(10)

    A -2.9 **B** -1 **C** 1 **D** 2.9

*17. Error Analysis Which student is correct? Explain the error.
(10)

Student A	Student B
$1 - \left(\frac{1}{5} - \frac{2}{10} - \frac{1}{10}\right)$	$1 - \left(\frac{1}{5} - \frac{2}{10} - \frac{1}{10}\right)$
$= 1 - \left(-\frac{1}{10}\right)$	$= 1 - \frac{1}{5} - \frac{2}{10} - \frac{1}{10}$
$= 1\frac{1}{10}$	$= \frac{1}{2}$

*18. (Time) A ship sailed northeast for $2\frac{1}{4}$ hours. It then sailed east for $1\frac{1}{3}$ hours. How much longer did it sail northeast than east?
(10)

19. Model Draw a line plot for the frequency table.
(SB 29)

Number	9	10	11	12	13	14
Frequency	4	3	2	1	0	4

*20. Multi-Step A map shows streets $\frac{1}{1000}$ of their size.
(9)

    a. Write an expression that represents the real length of a block if the length of the block on the map is b.

    b. Find the actual length of a block that is 0.4 feet on the map.

*21. Geometry A parallelogram has a base of z and a height of $2z$. Write an expression to find the area of the parallelogram. If z is equal to 12 cm, what is the area of the parallelogram?
(9)

22. Error Analysis Two students used unit analysis to convert a measurement of area to a different unit. Which student is correct? Explain the error.
(8)

Student A	Student B
1 ft = 12 in.	1 ft = 12 in.
$9 \text{ ft}^2 = 9 \text{ ft}^2 \times \frac{12 \text{ in.}}{1 \text{ ft}}$	$9 \text{ ft}^2 = 9 \text{ ft}^2 \times \frac{12 \text{ in.}}{1 \text{ ft}} \times \frac{12 \text{ in.}}{1 \text{ ft}}$
$9 \text{ ft}^2 = 108 \text{ in}^2$	$9 \text{ ft}^2 = 1{,}296 \text{ in}^2$

23. (**Meteorology**) When a weather system passes through, a barometer can be used to measure the change in atmospheric pressure in millimeters of mercury. What is the pressure difference in inches of mercury for a measured change of +4.5 mm of mercury? Round the answer to the nearest thousandth.
(8)

*24. Multi-Step A plot of land contains a rectangular building that is 9 yards long and 6 yards wide and a circular building with a diameter of 4 yards.
(7)

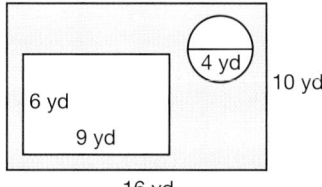

a. Write an expression for the area of the two buildings.

b. Write an expression and solve for how much area on the plot of land is not being taken up by the buildings. Round the answer to the nearest hundredth yard.

*25. Error Analysis Student A and Student B each added the numbers –4.8 and 3.6 as shown below. Which student is correct? Explain the error.
(5)

Student A	Student B
$-4.8 + 3.6$	$-4.8 + 3.6$
$\lvert -4.8 \rvert = 4.8$	$\lvert -4.8 \rvert = 4.8$
$\lvert +3.6 \rvert = 3.6$	$\lvert +3.6 \rvert = 3.6$
4.8	4.8
$+3.6$	-3.6
$\overline{8.4}$	$\overline{1.2}$
8.4	-1.2

26. (**Banking**) Raul had $500 in his checking account. He wrote checks for $157.62 and $43.96. Then he deposited $225. Find Raul's balance after these three transactions.
(5)

27. Write Mutually exclusive means that two sets of numbers have no numbers in common. Name two subsets of real numbers that are mutually exclusive. Explain.
(1)

*28. (**Stocks**) Stock in the 123 Company fell 8.2 points on Monday and 5.3 points on Tuesday. On Wednesday the stock rose 9.1 points. Determine the total change in the stock for the three days.
(5)

*29. (**Football**) The Rams gained 4 yards on the first down, lost 6 yards on the second down, and gained 14 yards on the third down. How many total yards did the Rams gain on the three downs?
(5)

30. Measurement A kite flies 74 feet above the ground. The person flying the kite is 5 feet 6 inches tall. How far above the person is the kite?
(10)

Generating Random Numbers

Graphing Calculator Lab (*Use with Investigation 1*)

A set of random integers has no pattern. Some common methods for generating random integers include rolling a number cube or drawing numbers out of a hat. A graphing calculator can also be used to generate random integers.

Generate three random integers between 1 and 12.

1. Press **MATH** and then press the ▶ key three times to highlight PRB.

2. Select **5:randInt(** by pressing **5.**

3. Identify the range of values. The lowest possible value is 1 and the highest is 12. So, press **1** [,] **12** [)].

4. Press **ENTER** to generate one integer between 1 and 12. An integer between 1 and 12 is 6.

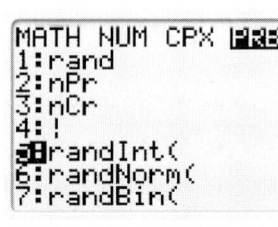

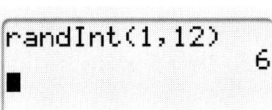

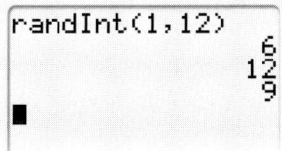

Online Connection
www.SaxonMathResources.com

5. Press **ENTER** two more times to generate two more integers between 1 and 12. Three integers between 1 and 12 are 6, 12, and 9.

Lab Practice

Jared lost the number cubes to his favorite board game, but he does have his graphing calculator. According to the rules, the player should throw two number cubes and move the total number of spaces shown on the top faces of the cubes.

a. What range of numbers does a single number cube generate? What would Jared enter into the calculator to simulate a number cube?

b. How would Jared simulate rolling two number cubes? How would Jared know how many spaces to move?

c. Simulate Jared taking three turns. What number of spaces will he move in each turn? What is the total number of spaces moved?

Determining the Probability of an Event

Math Language

An **outcome** is a possible result of a probability experiment.

An **event** is an outcome or set of outcomes in a probability experiment.

Probability is the measure of how likely a given event, or outcome, will occur. The probability of an event can be written as a fraction or decimal ranging from 0 to 1, or as a percent from 0% to 100%.

Range of Probability

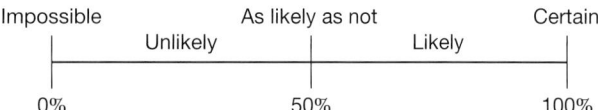

Describe each of the events below as impossible, unlikely, as likely as not, likely, or certain.

1. Jake rolls a number less than 7 on a number cube.

2. February will have 30 days.

3. A tossed coin will land on tails.

4. Shayla correctly guesses a number between 1 and 100.

Experimental probability is the measure of how likely a given event will occur based on repeated trials.

$$\text{experimental probability} = \frac{\text{number of times an event occurs}}{\text{number of trials}}$$

Online Connection
www.SaxonMathResources.com

Materials
• small paper sacks
• small red, blue, green, and yellow paper squares

Exploration Conducting Experiments to Find Probabilities

Place a small handful of colored squares into a paper sack. Draw out a square of paper without looking. Record the color in a frequency table like the one below.

Color	Tally	Frequency
Red		
Blue		
Green		
Yellow		

Repeat the experiment 50 times, replacing the square after each draw.

5. What is the experimental probability of drawing a red square? a blue square? a green square? a yellow square? Express each probability as a fraction and as a percent.

6. **Predict** Which color are you most likely to draw? Explain your reasoning.

Experimental probability is widely used in sports. In baseball, a player's batting average is the probability of a player getting a hit based on his previous at bats. It is typically expressed as a decimal to the thousandths place. For instance, if a player has made 3 hits after coming to bat 10 times, his batting average is .300.

7. (Sports) If a player gets 8 hits in 25 at bats, what is the probability that he will get a hit on his next at bat? Express the answer as a decimal number to the thousandths place.

In addition to sports, experimental probability is often used in banking, insurance, weather forecasting, and business.

8. (Quality Assurance) A piston manufacturer is concerned with the likelihood of defects, as this affects costs and profits. The manufacturer inspects 250 pistons and finds that 8 have defects.

   a. What is the probability a piston will have a defect? Express the probability as a percent.
   b. If the same manufacturer produces 3000 pistons, about how many will likely have defects?
   c. **Evaluate** Pistons sell for $35 and it costs $25 in materials to make each piston. How much profit would the manufacturer likely make on 3000 pistons if defective ones cannot be sold?

Hint

Manufacturing costs must be paid for all pistons made, but only the ones that pass inspection can be sold.

A **random event** is an event whose outcome cannot be predicted. For example, drawing a card labeled 8 from a bin of cards, each labeled with a number from 1 to 100, represents a random event. An experiment could be conducted to determine the experimental probability of drawing a card labeled 8, however, it is not always practical to conduct an experiment to determine an experimental probability. In some instances it makes sense to perform a **simulation** of a random event using models such as number cubes, spinners, coins, or random number generators.

Graphing Calculator

For help with generating random numbers, see Graphing Calculator Lab 1 on page 52.

(Exploration) **Using a Simulation to Find Probabilities**

Saxon O's cereal is having a contest. Each box of cereal contains a prize piece and claims that 1 in 8 pieces is a winner. Conduct a simulation to determine the experimental probability of winning a prize piece within 50 boxes of cereal.

To simulate this problem, use the digits 1 through 8, with 1 representing a winning prize piece. Use your calculator to generate 50 random numbers.

9. According to your simulation, what is the probability of winning a prize in the Saxon O's contest? Express your answer as a fraction and as a percent.

10. **Verify** How does your answer in problem **9** compare to the likelihood stated on the cereal box?

Describe each of the following events as impossible, unlikely, as likely as not, likely, or certain.

a. Gavin rolls an even number on a number cube.

b. In the northern hemisphere, the temperature will get above 90°F in the month of July.

c. The first person that Sonya meets is a left-handed person.

d. A player with a batting average of .875 gets a hit on his next at bat.

Jamie spun a game spinner and recorded the results in the table.

Outcome	Frequency
A	9
B	6
C	10

e. What is the probability of landing on A? on B? on C? Express each probability as a fraction and as a percent.

f. **Predict** Which letter will Jamie most likely spin? Explain your reasoning.

g. (Sports) If a baseball player has 18 hits in 50 at bats, what is the probability that he will get a hit in his next at bat? Express your answer as a decimal number in the thousandths place.

h. According to a survey at Johnson High School, 1 in 4 students has a part-time job. Conduct a simulation to determine the experimental probability of a student having a part-time job in a random group of 25 students.

Multiplying and Dividing Real Numbers

Warm Up

1. Vocabulary Two numbers with the same absolute value but different signs are called _____ (*integers, opposites*).
(6)

Simplify each expression.

2. $(-4) + (-4) + (-4)$
(5)

3. $-8 - 8 - 8 - 8 - 8 - 8$
(6)

4. 5^4
(3)

5. 2^5
(3)

New Concepts

The sum of three 2's is 6 and the sum of two 3's is 6.

$$2 + 2 + 2 = 6 \qquad 3 + 3 = 6$$

Multiplication is a way to show repeated addition of the same number. The repeated addition above can be shown as multiplication of the same number.

$$3 \cdot 2 = 6 \qquad \text{or} \qquad 2 \cdot 3 = 6$$

The properties of real numbers apply to all real numbers, rational and irrational. Use these properties when evaluating and simplifying numeric and algebraic expressions.

The table shows some properties of multiplication when a and b are real numbers.

Math Reasoning

Analyze How are the Identity Property of Multiplication and the Identity Property of Addition alike?

Properties of Real Numbers
Multiplication Property of -1
For every real number a,
$$a \cdot -1 = -1 \cdot a = -a$$
Example $\quad 9 \cdot -1 = -1 \cdot 9 = -9$
Multiplication Property of Zero
For every real number a,
$$a \cdot 0 = 0$$
Example $\quad 9 \cdot 0 = 0$
Inverse Property of Multiplication
For every real number a, where $a \neq 0$,
$$a \cdot \frac{1}{a} = \frac{1}{a} \cdot a = 1$$
Example $\quad 3 \cdot \frac{1}{3} = \frac{1}{3} \cdot 3 = 1$

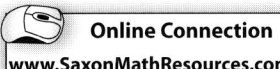
Online Connection
www.SaxonMathResources.com

To multiply signed numbers, use the rules in the table below.

Multiplying Signed Numbers
The product of two numbers with the same sign is a positive number.
Examples $(3)(4) = 12$ $(-5)(-3) = 15$
The product of two numbers with opposite signs is a negative number.
Examples $(-2)(4) = -8$ $6(-2) = -12$

Example 1 Multiplying Rational Numbers

Simplify each expression. Justify your answer.

a. $4(-8)$

SOLUTION

$4(-8) = -32$ The product of two numbers with opposite signs is negative.

b. $(-6)(-0.7)$

SOLUTION

$(-6)(-0.7) = 4.2$ The product of two numbers with the same sign is positive.

To raise a number to a power, use repeated multiplication to simplify.

Example 2 Raising a Number to a Power

Simplify each expression.

a. $(-3)^4$

SOLUTION

$(-3)^4$

$= (-3)(-3)(-3)(-3)$ Use repeated multiplication.

$= 81$

b. $(-3)^3$

SOLUTION

$(-3)^3$

$= (-3)(-3)(-3)$ Use repeated multiplication.

$= -27$

c. -3^4

SOLUTION

-3^4

$= -1 \cdot 3^4$

$= -1[(3)(3)(3)(3)]$ Use repeated multiplication.

$= -1(81)$ Find the product inside the brackets.

$= -81$ Multiplication Property of -1

Math Reasoning

Generalize How does an even or odd exponent affect the product of the power of a negative number?

To divide signed numbers, use the rules in the table below.

Dividing Signed Numbers
The quotient of two numbers with the same sign is a positive number.
Examples $\qquad 6 \div 3 = 2 \qquad\qquad -8 \div (-2) = 4$ $\qquad\qquad\qquad \dfrac{6}{3} = 2 \qquad\qquad\qquad \dfrac{-8}{-2} = 4$
The quotient of two numbers with opposite signs is a negative number.
Examples $\qquad 10 \div (-5) = -2 \qquad\qquad -12 \div 3 = -4$ $\qquad\qquad\qquad \dfrac{10}{-5} = -2 \qquad\qquad\qquad -\dfrac{12}{3} = -4$

Example 3 **Dividing Real Numbers**

Simplify each expression. Justify your answer.

(a.) $-16 \div (-2)$

SOLUTION

$-16 \div (-2) = 8$ $\qquad$ The quotient of two numbers with the same sign is positive.

(b.) $2.8 \div (-7)$

SOLUTION

$2.8 \div (-7) = -0.4$ $\qquad$ The quotient of two numbers with opposite signs is negative.

Dividing by a number a is the same as multiplying by the **reciprocal** $\frac{1}{a}$, or **multiplicative inverse,** of the divisor.

$$12 \div 2 = 12 \cdot \frac{1}{2} = 6$$

The reciprocal of 2 is $\frac{1}{2}$. Multiplying 12 by $\frac{1}{2}$ is the same as dividing 12 by 2.

Example 4 **Dividing Positive and Negative Fractions**

Evaluate each expression.

(a.) $-\dfrac{2}{3} \div \left(-\dfrac{3}{4}\right)$

SOLUTION

$-\dfrac{2}{3} \div \left(-\dfrac{3}{4}\right)$

$-\dfrac{2}{3} \cdot \left(-\dfrac{4}{3}\right)$ $\qquad$ Multiply by the reciprocal of $-\frac{3}{4}$.

$-\dfrac{2}{3} \cdot \left(-\dfrac{4}{3}\right) = \dfrac{8}{9}$ $\qquad$ The product of two fractions with the same sign is positive.

Reading Math

You can write $-\frac{3}{5}$ as $\frac{-3}{5}$ or $\frac{3}{-5}$.

b. $\frac{2}{9} \div \left(-\frac{3}{5}\right)$

SOLUTION

$\frac{2}{9} \div \left(-\frac{3}{5}\right)$

$\frac{2}{9} \cdot \left(-\frac{5}{3}\right)$ Multiply by the reciprocal of $-\frac{3}{5}$.

$\frac{2}{9} \cdot \left(-\frac{5}{3}\right) = -\frac{10}{27}$ The product of two fractions with different signs is negative.

Example 5   Application: Cave Exploration

The Voronya Cave in Abkhazia, Georgia is the deepest known cave in the world. At an elevation of -2140 meters, Voronya is a challenge for experienced cavers. If it takes 8 days to travel to the bottom of the cave, what is the average number of meters the cavers would travel each day?

SOLUTION

Write an expression.

elevation of cave		number of days to travel
-2140 m	$\div$	8 days

$-2140 \div 8 = -267.5$

The cavers would travel an average of -267.5 meters per day.

Lesson Practice

Simplify each expression. Justify your answer.
(Ex 1)

  a. $9(-0.8)$

  b. $-12(-2.5)$

Simplify each expression.
(Ex 2)

  c. $(-4)^3$

  d. $(-8)^4$

  e. -5^4

Simplify each expression. Justify your answer.
(Ex 3)

  f. $-105 \div (-7)$

  g. $63.9 \div (-3)$

Evaluate each expression.
(Ex 4)

  h. $-\frac{4}{5} \div \left(-\frac{9}{10}\right)$ **i.** $\frac{3}{8} \div \left(-\frac{3}{4}\right)$

  j. (Science) During a cold spell in January 1989, Homer, Alaska, recorded
(Ex 5) a low temperature of $-24°F$. The city of Bethel, Alaska, recorded a low temperature twice as cold as the low in Homer. What was the temperature in Bethel, Alaska?

*1. **Verify** True or False: The product of a number and its reciprocal is equal to one.
(11) Verify your answer.

*2. Simplify $-(-4)^2$.
(11)

3. **Error Analysis** Which student is correct? Explain the error.
(10)

Student A	Student B
$\left(\dfrac{11}{12} - \dfrac{2}{4} - \dfrac{1}{3}\right) + \dfrac{11}{12}$	$\left(\dfrac{11}{12} - \dfrac{2}{4} - \dfrac{1}{3}\right) + \dfrac{11}{12}$
$= \dfrac{1}{12} + \dfrac{11}{12}$	$= \dfrac{8}{12} + \dfrac{11}{12}$
$= 1$	$= \dfrac{19}{12}$

4. Simplify $\dfrac{2 \cdot 14 + 3 \cdot 7}{71 - 15}$.
(4)

5. Draw a line plot for the frequency table.
(SB 29)

Number	5	6	7	8	9	10
Frequency	4	2	0	1	0	3

6. A(n) _____ angle measures more than 90° and less than 180°.
(SB 13)

7. Evaluate $3(x + 4) + y$ when $x = 8$ and $y = 7$.
(9)

8. Evaluate the expression $3x^2 + 2(x - 1)^3$ for the given value $x = 6$.
(9)

9. **Multiple Choice** Which rate is the fastest?
(8) **A** 660 ft/15 s

B 645 ft/11 s

C 616 ft/12 s

D 1100 ft/30 s

10. **Justify** Simplify $5 + \frac{9}{3}[4(\frac{1}{2} + 4)]$. Justify each step.
(7)

*11. **Multiple Choice** The temperature at noon was 20°C. The temperature fell 2 degrees
(11) every hour until 3 a.m. the next day. What was the temperature at 11 p.m. that
evening?
A 22°C

B −2°C

C −30°C

D −22°C

*12. (Physics) The magnitude of the instant acceleration of an object in uniform circular
(9) motion is found using the formula $a = \frac{v^2}{r}$, where r is the radius of the circle and v is
the constant speed. Evaluate $a = \frac{v^2}{r}$ if $v = 35$ cm/s and $r = 200$ cm.

*13. (Retailing) A grocery store is having a sale on strawberries. Suppose 560 pints of
(11) strawberries are sold at a loss of $0.16 for each pint. How much money does the
store lose on the sale of the strawberries?

*14. (Ocean Travel) The deepest point of the Kermandec trench in the Pacific Ocean
(11) is 10,047 meters below sea level. A submarine made two dives from above
the deepest point of the trench at a rate of 400 meters per minute. The first
of the two dives was 10 minutes long and the second was 4 minutes. How far
did the submarine travel in each dive?

15. Add $-1.06 + 2.01 + 4.13$.
(10)

16. Multi-Step A purple string is 0.99 m long. A green string is 0.23 m long. What is
(10) the difference in length of the two pieces?

    a. Estimate Estimate the difference using fractions.

    b. Find the exact value of the difference using fractions.

17. Error Analysis Two students solved a homework problem as shown below. Which
(9) student is correct? Explain the error.

Student A	Student B
Evaluate $3g - 4(g + 2b)$;	Evaluate $3g - 4(g + 2b)$;
$g = 9$ and $b = 4$.	$g = 9$ and $b = 4$.
$3(9) - 4(9 + 2(4))$	$3(9) - 4(9 + 2(4))$
$27 - 4(17)$	$27 - 4(17)$
$23(17)$	$27 - 68$
391	-41

18. (Science) Scientists can use the expression $2.6f + 65$ to estimate the height of a
(9) person if they know the length of the femur bone, f. What is the approximate
height of a person if the femur bone is 40 centimeters long?

19. Error Analysis The highest point in North America, Mount McKinley, in the
(6) Alaska Range, is 20,320 feet above sea level. The lowest point in North America
is 282 feet below sea level and is in Death Valley in California. Which student
correctly calculated the difference in elevations? Explain the error.

Student A	Student B
$20,320 - 282$	$20,320 - (-282)$
$20,320 + (-282)$	$20,320 + (+282)$
$20,038$ feet	$20,602$ feet

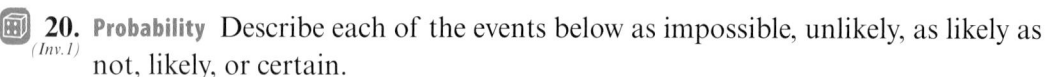 **20.** **Probability** Describe each of the events below as impossible, unlikely, as likely as
(Inv.1) not, likely, or certain.

    a. Joshua rolls an odd number on a standard number cube.

    b. Maria's birthday is September 31st.

    c. The basketball team has won 11 of their last 12 games. The team will win the
next game.

Simplify each expression.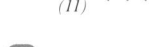

*21. $5(-2)$
_(11)_

*22. $(-3)(\ 5)$
_(11)_

23. $-|-15 + 5|$
_(5)_

*24. $(-3)(-6)(-2)(5)$
_(11)_

*25. $(3)(5)$
_(11)_

26. **Geometry** Can the perimeter of a rectangle be any integer value?
_(1)_

27. **Model** Mary is playing a board game using a number cube to decide the number
_(10)_ of spaces she moves. She moves forward on an even number and backward on
an odd number. Her first 5 rolls were 4, 2, 3, 6, 1.

    a. Model her moves on a number line with zero being the starting point.

    b. Using addition and subtraction, write an expression showing her moves.

    c. At a the end of 5 rolls, how many spaces is she away from the starting point?

*28. **Analyze** Jan bought 2 yards of ribbon. She needs 64 inches of ribbon to make a bow.
_(8)_ Does she have enough ribbon? Explain your answer.

29. **Meteorology** A meteorologist reported the day's low temperature of $-5°F$ at 7 a.m.
_(6)_ and the day's high temperature of $20°F$ at 5 p.m. How much did the temperature
rise from 7 a.m. to 5 p.m.?

30. **Phone Charges** Fast Talk Phone Company charges an initial fee of \$20 plus
_(9)_ 10¢ per minute used. The total bill is expressed as $20 + 0.10m$, where m is the
minutes used. If 200 minutes are used, what is the amount of the bill?

Using the Properties of Real Numbers to Simplify Expressions

1. Vocabulary A(n) _____ expression is an expression with constants
(9) and/or variables that uses the operations $+$, $-$, $\times$, or $\div$.

2. Simplify $6 - |-6| + (-4)$.
(5)

3. Divide $-\dfrac{4}{5} \div \left(-\dfrac{8}{9}\right)$.
(11)

4. Evaluate $2|y| - 2|x| + m$ for $x = -1.5$, $y = -3$, and $m = -1.3$.
(9)

New Concepts

The properties of real numbers are used to simplify expressions and write equivalent expressions. The table shows properties of addition and multiplication when a, b, and c are real numbers.

Math Language

0 is the **additive identity**.

1 is the **multiplicative identity**.

Properties of Addition and Multiplication
Identity Property of Addition
For every real number a,
$a + 0 = a$ Example: $5 + 0 = 5$
Identity Property of Multiplication
For every real number a,
$a \cdot 1 = a$ Example: $5 \cdot 1 = 5$
Commutative Property of Addition
For every real number a and b,
$a + b = b + a$ Example: $5 + 2 = 2 + 5$
$7 = 7$
Commutative Property of Multiplication
For every real number a and b,
$a \cdot b = b \cdot a$ Example: $5 \cdot 2 = 2 \cdot 5$
$ab = ba$ $10 = 10$
Associative Property of Addition
For every real number a, b, and c,
$(a + b) + c = a + (b + c)$ Example: $(1 + 2) + 3 = 1 + (2 + 3)$
$a + b + c = a + b + c$ $3 + 3 = 1 + 5$
$6 = 6$
Associative Property of Multiplication
For every real number a, b, and c,
$(a \cdot b) \cdot c = a \cdot (b \cdot c)$ Example: $(1 \cdot 2) \cdot 3 = 1 \cdot (2 \cdot 3)$
$abc = abc$ $2 \cdot 3 = 1 \cdot 6$
$6 = 6$

Online Connection
www.SaxonMathResources.com

Example 1 Identifying Properties

Identify the property illustrated in each equation.

a. $1 \cdot 8 = 8$

SOLUTION Since 8 is multiplied by 1, its value does not change. This is the Identity Property of Multiplication.

b. $13 + 5 = 5 + 13$

SOLUTION The order of the terms is changed. This is the Commutative Property of Addition.

c. $(3 \cdot 4) \cdot 7 = 3 \cdot (4 \cdot 7)$

SOLUTION The terms and the order are not changed; only the grouping of the factors is changed. This is the Associative Property of Multiplication.

d. $(12 + 9) + 5 = (9 + 12) + 5$

SOLUTION The terms are the same and the same two terms are grouped. However, the order of the grouped terms has changed. This is the Commutative Property of Addition.

Example 2 Using Properties to Justify Statements

Tell whether each statement is true or false. Justify your answer using the properties. Assume all variables represent real numbers.

a. $gh = hg$

SOLUTION The statement is true. It illustrates the Commutative Property of Multiplication.

Check Substitute a value for each variable to determine whether the statement is true.

Let $g = 6$ and $h = 7$.

$6 \cdot 7 \stackrel{?}{=} 7 \cdot 6$

$42 = 42$ ✓

b. $b + 1 = b$

SOLUTION The statement is false. To illustrate the Identity Property of Addition, the equation should be $b + 0 = b$.

Check Substitute a value for the variable to determine whether the statement is true.

Let $b = 13$.

$13 + 1 \neq 13$ ✗

Hint

Compare the left side of the equation to the right side. Determine what changes have been made.

Math Reasoning

Analyze Why does the Commutative Property not apply to subtraction?

Write

Explain why it is necessary to substitute only one value for the variable to show that the statement is false.

c. $d + (e + f) = (d + e) + f$

SOLUTION Substitute a value for the variables to determine whether the statement is true.

Let $d = 5$, $e = 7$, and $f = 9$.

$$5 + (7 + 9) \stackrel{?}{=} (5 + 7) + 9$$
$$5 + 16 \stackrel{?}{=} 12 + 9$$
$$21 = 21 \quad \checkmark$$

The statement is true by the Associative Property of Addition.

Example 3 **Justifying Steps to Simplify an Expression**

Simplify each expression. Justify each step.

a. $16 + 3x + 4$

SOLUTION

$16 + 3x + 4$	
$= 3x + 16 + 4$	Commutative Property of Addition
$= 3x + (16 + 4)$	Associative Property of Addition
$= 3x + 20$	Add.

b. $(25) \cdot y \cdot \left(\dfrac{1}{25}\right)$

SOLUTION

$(25) \cdot y \cdot \left(\dfrac{1}{25}\right)$	
$= (25) \cdot \left(\dfrac{1}{25}\right) \cdot y$	Commutative Property of Multiplication
$= 1 \cdot y$	Multiply
$= y$	Identity Property of Multiplication

Caution

Don't skip or combine steps. For each property necessary to simplify the expression, a step must be shown.

Example 4 **Application: Consumer Math**

Envelopes, pens, and correction tape can be purchased at an office supply store for the following prices respectively: \$2.85, \$5.35, and \$2.15. Find the total cost of the supplies. Justify each step.

SOLUTION

$\$2.85 + \$5.35 + \$2.15$	
$= \$2.85 + \$2.15 + \$5.35$	Commutative Property of Addition
$= (\$2.85 + \$2.15) + \$5.35$	Associative Property of Addition
$= \$5.00 + \$5.35$	Add within the parentheses.
$= \$10.35$	Add.

The supplies will cost \$10.35.

Identify each property illustrated.
(Ex 1)

    a. $5 + (9 + 8) = (5 + 9) + 8$

    b. $0 + 10 = 10$

    c. $15 \cdot 3 = 3 \cdot 15$

    d. $17 \cdot 1 = 17$

Tell whether each statement is true or false. Justify your answer using the properties. Assume all variables represent real numbers.
(Ex 2)

    e. $(ab)c = a(bc)$

    f. $m - z = z - m$

    g. $w + 0 = w$

Simplify each expression. Justify each step.
(Ex 3)

    h. $18 + 7x + 4$

    i. $\dfrac{1}{3}d \cdot 3$

    j. Erasers, markers, and paper can be purchased at the school store for
(Ex 4) the following prices, respectively: $1.45, $3.35, and $2.65. Find the total
cost of the supplies. Justify each step.

Practice   **Distributed and Integrated**

  *1. Identify the property illustrated in the equation $100 \cdot 1 = 100$.
(12)

Simplify each expression.

  2. $-18 \div 3$ **3.** $|12 - 30|$
(11)   *(5)*

  4. $(-3)(-2)(-1)(-8)$
(11)

  *5. True or False: $p(q + r) = (p + q)r$. Justify your answer using the properties.
(12)

  6. Write a fraction equivalent to $\dfrac{2}{3}$.
(SB 7)

  7. True or False: The sum of the measures of complementary angles is $90°$.
(SB 15)

  *8. **Multiple Choice** Which equation demonstrates the Identity Property of
(12)   Addition?

    A $a \cdot 0 = 0$

    B $a + 0 = a$

    C $a \cdot \dfrac{1}{a} = 1$

    D $a + 1 = 1 + a$

  9. Add $\dfrac{11}{15} + \dfrac{1}{30} + \dfrac{3}{60}$.
(10)

10. Error Analysis Students were asked to simplify $\frac{5}{6} \div \left(-\frac{3}{2}\right)$. Which student is correct?
(11) Explain the error.

Student A	Student B
$\frac{5}{6} \div \left(-\frac{3}{2}\right)$	$\frac{5}{6} \div \left(-\frac{3}{2}\right)$
$= \frac{5}{6} \cdot \left(-\frac{2}{3}\right)$	$= \frac{5}{6} \cdot \left(-\frac{2}{3}\right)$
$= -\frac{5}{9}$	$= \frac{5}{9}$

*11. Jon has 5 marbles. His best friend gives him some more. Then he buys 15 more
(12) marbles. The expression $5 + x + 15$ shows the total number of marbles Jon now
has. Show two ways to simplify this expression and justify each step.

12. Multiple Choice What is the value of $\frac{(5x + x)^2(6 - x)}{x}$ when $x = 2$?
(9)

   A 288   **B** 200   **C** 400   **D** 28

*13. Find the value of $(4x^3y^2)^2$ when $x = 2$ and $y = 1$.
(9)

14. Convert 588 ounces to pounds. (Hint: 1 lb = 16 oz)
(8)

*15. Geometry A wall in a rectangular room is 12 feet by 8 feet. Jose calculated the area
(12) using the equations $A = 12 \cdot 8$ and $A = 8 \cdot 12$. Explain why each expression will
give him the same answer.

*16. (Interior Decorating) Tim is building a picture frame that is 10 inches long and
(12) 6 inches wide. He calculated the perimeter using $P = 2(10 + 6)$. His brother
calculated the perimeter for the same frame using $P = 2(6 + 10)$. Will the
measurements be the same? Explain.

*17. (Temperature) To convert a temperature from Celsius to Fahrenheit, Marc uses the
(12) formula $F = \frac{9}{5}C + 32$. He also uses the formula $F = 32 + \frac{9}{5}C$. Which calculation is
correct? Explain.

18. Geometry A rectangle is twice as long as it is wide. If the width of the
(11) rectangle measures 2.3 inches, what is the area of the rectangle?

2.3 in.   2.3 in.

19. Multi-Step In each of the first five rounds of a game; Tyra scored 28 points. In
(11) each of the next three rounds, she scored -41 points. Then she scored two rounds
of -16 points. What is the total number of points that Tyra scored? Explain.

*20. Multiple Choice Order from greatest to least: $\frac{1}{4}, 0.23, -0.24, \frac{1}{3}$.
(10)

  A $-0.24, 0.23, \frac{1}{4}, \frac{1}{3}$ **B** $\frac{1}{4}, \frac{1}{3}, 0.23, -0.24$

  C $-0.24, 0.23, \frac{1}{3}, \frac{1}{4}$ **D** $\frac{1}{3}, \frac{1}{4}, 0.23, -0.24$

21. (Sewing) Maria is sewing curtains that require 124 inches of ribbon trim. She can
(8) only buy the ribbon in whole yard lengths. How many yards does she need to buy?

22. Error Analysis Student A and Student B simplified the expression $9 - 4 \cdot 2$. Which
(7) student is correct? Explain the error.

Student A	Student B
$9 - 4 \cdot 2$	$9 - 4 \cdot 2$
$= 5 \cdot 2$	$= 9 - 8$
$= 10$	$= 1$

23. Write Explain how to use the order of operations to simplify $4(8 - 9 \div 3)^2$.
(4)

24. Simplify $x^2kxk^2x^2ykx^2$.
(3)

25. Error Analysis Two students evaluate the expression $4t + 5x - \frac{1}{x}$ when $x = 3$.
(2) Which student is correct? Explain the error.

Student A	Student B
$4t + 5x - \frac{1}{x}; x = 3$	$4t + 5x - \frac{1}{x}; x = 3$
$= 4t + 5(3) - \frac{1}{3}$	$= 4t + 53 - \frac{1}{3}$
$= 4t + 15 - \frac{1}{3}$	$= 4t + 52\frac{2}{3}$
$= 4t + 14\frac{2}{3}$	

26. (Savings Accounts) The table below shows the transactions Jennifer made to her
(10) savings account during one month. Find the balance of her account.

Jennifer's Bank Account

Beginning Balance	$396.25
Withdrawal	$150.50
Deposit	$220.00
Interest (deposit)	$8.00

*27. (Tug of War) In a game of Tug of War, Team A pulls the center of the rope three and
(10) a half feet in their direction. Then Team B pulls back five feet before Team A pulls
for another eight feet. How far from the starting point is the center of the rope?

28. (Travel) Bill rides a bus for 2.5 hours to visit a friend. If the bus travels at
(11) about 60 to 63 miles per hour, how far away does Bill's friend live? (Hint: To find
distance, multiply rate by time.)

29. Justify Simplify $2^2 + 24 - (3 - 12)$. Explain your steps.
(4)

30. Verify Give an example that illustrates that the sum of a number and its opposite
(6) is zero.

Calculating and Comparing Square Roots

Warm Up

1. **Vocabulary** The number that tells how many times the base of a power is
(3) used as a factor is called the _____ (*variable, exponent*).

Simplify each expression.

2. $-3 + (-4) - (-8)$
(10)

3. $[-(-4)^3]$
(11)

4. $a^3 \cdot x^4 \cdot x^8 \cdot a^4 \cdot z^4$
(3)

5. $\left(-\dfrac{2}{6}\right) \div \left(-\dfrac{3}{8}\right)$
(11)

New Concepts

A perfect square is a number that is the square of an integer. The product of an integer and itself is a perfect square.

$$2^2 = \boxed{} \qquad 3^2 = \boxed{}$$

A square root is indicated by a radical symbol $\sqrt{}$. A radicand is the number or expression under a radical symbol.

$$\sqrt{50} \qquad\qquad 2\sqrt{7}$$

50 is the radicand.   7 is the radicand.

The square root of x, written $\sqrt{x}$, is the number whose square is x.

$$4^2 = 16$$
$$\sqrt{16} = 4$$

A square number can only end with the digits: zero, one, four, five, six, and nine. However, not all numbers ending in these digits will be perfect squares.

Math Reasoning

Formulate What is the inverse of x^2?

Example 1 Finding Square Roots of Perfect Squares

a. Is the radicand in $\sqrt{50}$ a perfect square? Explain.

SOLUTION

50 is not a perfect square. There is no integer multiplied by itself that equals 50.

b. Is the radicand in $\sqrt{64}$ a perfect square? Explain.

SOLUTION

64 is a perfect square; $8 \cdot 8 = 8^2 = 64$. The product of an integer and itself is a perfect square.

Not all numbers are perfect squares, but their square roots can be estimated.

Example 2 **Estimating Square Roots**

Estimate the value $\sqrt{50}$ to the nearest integer. Explain your reasoning.

SOLUTION

$\sqrt{50}$ is not a perfect square.

Determine which two perfect squares 50 falls between on the number line.

50 is between the perfect squares 49 and 64.

Then determine which perfect square $\sqrt{50}$ is closest to.

$\sqrt{50}$ is between the numbers 7 and 8 because $\sqrt{49} = 7$ and $\sqrt{64} = 8$.

$\sqrt{50}$ is closer to the number 7 because 50 is closer to 49 than 64.

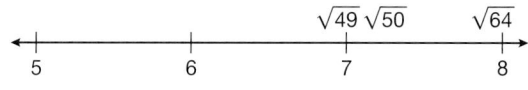

$\sqrt{50} \approx 7$

> **Math Reasoning**
>
> **Analyze** Is 1.44 a perfect square?

When comparing expressions that contain radicals, simplify the expressions with radicals first. Next, perform any operations necessary. Then compare the expressions.

Example 3 **Comparing Expressions Involving Square Roots**

Compare the expressions. Use $<$, $>$, or $=$.
$$\sqrt{4} + \sqrt{36} \bigcirc \sqrt{9} + \sqrt{25}$$

SOLUTION

$$\sqrt{4} + \sqrt{36} \bigcirc \sqrt{9} + \sqrt{25}$$
$$2 + 6 \bigcirc 3 + 5 \qquad \text{Simplify the expressions.}$$
$$8 \text{ⓔ} 8 \qquad \text{Add.}$$

> **Caution**
>
> Square roots must be simplified before performing any other operations. For example, $\sqrt{4} + \sqrt{36} \neq \sqrt{40}$.

Example 4 **Application: Ballroom Dancing**

The area of a dance floor that is in the shape of a square is 289 square feet. What is the side length of the dance floor? Explain.

SOLUTION

The side length can be found by finding the square root of the area.

Area of a square = side length × side length

$$A = s^2 \qquad \text{Write the formula.}$$
$$289 = s^2 \qquad \text{Substitute 289 for } A.$$
$$\sqrt{289} = s \qquad \text{Find the square root of 289.}$$
$$17 = s$$

Each side length of the dance floor is 17 feet.

a. Is the radicand in $\sqrt{225}$ a perfect square? Explain.
(Ex 1)

b. Is the radicand in $\sqrt{350}$ a perfect square? Explain.
(Ex 1)

c. Estimate the value of $\sqrt{37}$ to the nearest integer. Explain your
(Ex 2) reasoning.

d. Compare the expressions. Use $<$, $>$, or $=$.
(Ex 3)

$$\sqrt{16} + \sqrt{441} \bigcirc \sqrt{81} + \sqrt{361}$$

e. The city park has a new sandbox in the shape of a square. The area of
(Ex 4) the sandbox is 169 square feet. What is the side length of the sandbox?
Explain.

Practice Distributed and Integrated

Simplify each expression.

1. $-16 \div -2$
(11)

2. $\dfrac{4 + 7 - 6}{2 + 7 - 3}$
(11)

3. $-2 + 11 - 4 + 3 - 8$
(6)

4. $(-2)(-3) + 11(2) - 3 - 6$
(6)

Evaluate each expression for the given values.

*5. $3p - 4g - 2x$ for $p = 2$, $g = -3$, and $x = 4$
(9)

6. $3xy - 2yz$ for $x = 3$, $y = 4$, and $z = 3$
(9)

*7. $\sqrt{40}$ is between which two whole numbers?
(13)

*8. Multiple Choice Which of the following numbers is a perfect square?
(13)

A 200 **B** 289

C 410 **D** 150

*9. Solve $b = \sqrt{4}$.
(13)

10. Model Draw a model to compare $\frac{5}{12}$ and $\frac{1}{3}$.
(10)

11. Convert 25 feet per hour to yards per hour.
(8)

12. True or False: The square root of any odd number is an irrational number. If false,
(1) provide a counterexample.

*13. Multiple Choice The area of a square is 392 square meters. The area of a second
(13) square is half the area of the first square. What is the side length of the second
square?

   A 14 meters

   B $\approx$ 20 meters

   C 196 meters

   D 96 meters

*14. True or False: $xyz = yxz$. Justify your answer using the properties.
(12)

15. Verify Determine whether each statement below is true or false. If false,
(4) explain why.

   a. $4^2 + 15 \cdot 20$ is equal to 316.

   b. $(4 + 5)^2$ is the same as $4 + 5^2$.

16. Multi-Step Kristin has several ropes measuring $8\frac{1}{4}$ in., $8\frac{3}{16}$ in., $8\frac{5}{8}$ in., and $8\frac{1}{16}$ in.
(10) How should she order them from least to greatest?

   a. Find a common denominator for each measure.

   b. Order the measures from least to greatest.

17. Arrange in order from least to greatest:
(10)

$$1.11, \ 1.5, \ 1.09, \ 1.05$$

*18. Are the expressions $(20k^3 \cdot 5v^5)9k^2$ and $900k^3v^5$ equivalent? Explain.
(9)

*19. (Science) The Barringer Meteor Crater in Winslow, Arizona, is very close to a
(13) square in shape. The crater covers an area of about 1,690,000 square meters. What
is the approximate side length of the crater?

20. (Science) The time, t, in seconds it takes for an object dropped to travel a distance,
(13) d, in feet can be found using the formula $t = \frac{\sqrt{d}}{4}$. Determine the time it takes for
an object to drop 169 feet.

*21. Multi-Step The flow rate for a particular fire hose can be found using $f = 120\sqrt{p}$,
(13) where f is the flow rate in gallons per minute and p is the nozzle pressure in
pounds per square inch. When the nozzle pressure is 169 pounds per square inch,
what is the flow rate?

22. (World Records) The world's largest cherry pie was baked in Michigan. It had a
(1) diameter of 210 inches. If the diameter was converted to feet, would it be a
rational number? Explain.

23. Find the area of the shaded portion of the circle. The radius of the circle is
(4) 4 inches. (Use 3.14 for π.)

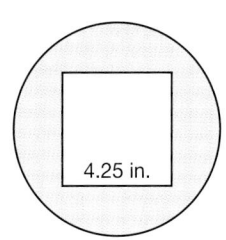

4.25 in.

24. (Banking) Frank deposited \$104.67 into his bank account. Later that day, he spent
(5) \$113.82 from the same account. Estimate the change in Frank's account balance
for that day.

25. Justify Simplify $52 + (1 + 3)^2 \cdot (16 - 14)^3 - 20$. Justify each step.
(7)

26. Error Analysis Two students simplify the expression $2 + 3x + 1$. Which student
(12) is correct? Explain the error.

Student A	Student B
$2 + 3x + 1$	$2 + 3x + 1$
$= 2 + 1 + 3x$	$= (2 + 3)x + 1$
$= (2 + 1) + 3x$	$= 5x + 1$
$= 3 + 3x$	

*27. Justify Arlene has 30 buttons and buys x packages of buttons. There are
(12) 7 buttons in each package. She uses 12 buttons. The number of buttons she now
has is represented by the expression $30 + 7x - 12$. Simplify the expression and
justify each step using the properties.

28. Multiple Choice Which of the following expressions will result in a negative
(11) number?

A $(-6)^2$

B $(-6) \div (-6)$

C $-\frac{3}{4}(6) \div (-4)$

D $-1 \cdot (-6)^2$

29. (International Banking) A Greek company needs to purchase some products from a
(8) U.S. corporation. First, the company must open an account in U.S. dollars. If the
account is to hold \$1,295,800, how many drachma, the Greek currency, should the
company deposit? Use the exchange rate of one Greek drachma for every \$0.004
in U.S. currency.

30. Probability Describe each of the following events as impossible, unlikely, as likely as
$(Inv\ 1)$ not, likely, or certain.

a. Jim rolls a 10 on a standard number cube.

b. Sarah guesses a number correctly between 1 and 900.

c. Mayra dropped a coin and it landed heads up.

Determining the Theoretical Probability of an Event

Warm Up

1. **Vocabulary** _____ (*Closure, Probability*) is the measure of how likely
   (Inv 1) it is that an event will occur.

Simplify each expression.

2. $5 \times 7 - 27 \div 9 + 6$
   (4)
3. $6.3 + (-2.4) + (-8.9)$
   (10)
4. $6 + |-72| + |-5|$
   (5)
5. Write a number to represent the opposite of "twelve floors up."
   (6)

New Concepts

A **sample space** is the set of all possible outcomes of an event. For example, a toss of a fair coin has two equally likely outcomes. The two possible outcomes, heads and tails, is the sample space.

A **simple event** is an event having only one outcome. For example, rolling a 5 on a number cube is a simple event.

The **theoretical probability** of an outcome is found by analyzing a situation in which all outcomes are equally likely, and then finding the ratio of favorable outcomes to all possible outcomes. For example, the probability of tossing a coin and it landing on heads is $\frac{1}{2}$ or 0.5 or 50%.

> **Math Language**
>
> A fair coin has an equally likely chance of landing on heads or tails. The coin is not weighted so that one outcome is more likely than another.

Exploration Finding Theoretical Probability

Place 4 different-colored marbles in a sack. Without looking, draw one marble out of the sack. Record the color in a frequency table.

Color	Tally	Frequency
Red		
Green		
Yellow		
Blue		

> **Materials**
>
> • small paper sacks
> • colored marbles

a. Repeat the experiment 10 times, 20 times, 50 times and 100 times, replacing the marble after each draw.

b. Divide the number of times a red marble is picked by the total number of times you pick a marble. Write this as a probability.

c. **Generalize** What do you notice about the probabilities as the number of times you pick a marble is increased?

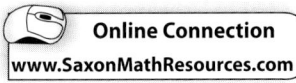

Online Connection
www.SaxonMathResources.com

Example 1 Identifying Sample Spaces

A number cube labeled 1–6 is rolled. List the outcomes for each event.

a. a number less than or equal to 3

SOLUTION

$\{3, 2, 1\}$

b. an odd number

SOLUTION

$\{1, 3, 5\}$

c. a number greater than 4

SOLUTION

$\{5, 6\}$

Theoretical probability can be determined using the following formula:

$$P(\text{event}) = \frac{\text{number of favorable outcomes}}{\text{total number of outcomes}}$$

A **complement of an event** is a set of all outcomes of an experiment that are not in a given event. For example, if heads is the desired event when tossing a coin, tails is the complement of the event. The sum of an event and its complement equals 1.

$$P(\text{event}) + P(\text{not event}) = 1$$
$$P(\text{not event}) = 1 - P(\text{event})$$

Example 2 Calculating Theoretical Probability

There are 4 green, 3 blue, and 3 red marbles in a bag.

Give each answer as a decimal and as a percent.

a. What is the probability of randomly choosing a red marble?

SOLUTION

$$P(\text{red}) = \frac{3 \text{ red marbles}}{10 \text{ marbles in all}}$$

$$P(\text{red}) = \frac{3}{10}$$

The probability of choosing a red marble is 0.3 or 30%.

b. What is the probability of randomly choosing a marble that is not green?

SOLUTION

$$P(\text{green marble}) + P(\text{not green marble}) = 1$$
$$P(\text{not green marble}) = 1 - P(\text{green marble})$$
$$P(\text{not green marble}) = 1 - \frac{4}{10}$$
$$P(\text{not green marble}) = \frac{6}{10} = \frac{3}{5}$$

The probability of not choosing a green marble is 0.6 or 60%.

Math Language

A spinner is divided into four equal parts: blue, yellow, green, and red. If the spinner lands on yellow, then the **outcome** is yellow.

Reading Math

The probability of an event can be written **P(event).** The probability of picking a red marble can be written $P(\text{red})$.

Hint

Probability can be expressed as a fraction, decimal, or percent.

Chance, like probability, is the likelihood of an event occurring.

Example 3 **Calculating Chance**

In a bucket there are 10 balls numbered as follows: 1, 1, 2, 3, 4, 4, 4, 5, 6, and 6. A single ball is randomly chosen from the bucket. What is the probability of drawing a ball with a number greater than 4? Is there a greater chance of drawing a number greater than 4 or a 1?

SOLUTION

$$P(\text{greater than } 4) = \frac{3}{10} \qquad \text{3 out of the 10 balls have a number greater than 4.}$$

The probability of drawing a ball with a number greater than 4 is 0.3, or 30%.

$$P(1) = \frac{2}{10} = \frac{1}{5} \qquad \text{2 out of the 10 balls are numbered 1.}$$

$$\frac{3}{10} > \frac{1}{5} \qquad \text{Compare } \frac{3}{10} \text{ and } \frac{1}{5}.$$

There is a greater chance of drawing a number greater than 4 than drawing a 1.

Example 4 **Application: State Fair**

At a carnival game, you drop a ball into the top of the device shown below. As the ball falls, it goes either left or right as it hits each peg. In total, the ball can follow 16 different paths. The ball eventually lands in one of the bins at the bottom and you win that amount of money. (One path to $0 is shown.) What is the probability of winning $2?

SOLUTION

total number of paths = 16

number of paths to $2 bins = 2

$$P(\$2) = \frac{\text{number of paths to \$2 bins}}{\text{total number of paths to win}} = \frac{2}{16}$$

$$P(\$2) = \frac{1}{8}$$

The probability of winning $2 is $\frac{1}{8}$.

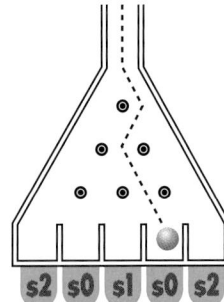

$2 $0 $1 $0 $2

Math Reasoning

Analyze If you drop the ball once, is there less than or greater than a 20% probability of not winning $2?

Lesson Practice

A number cube labeled 1–6 is rolled. List the outcome for each event.
(Ex 1)

   a. a number less than or equal to 4

   b. an even number

   c. a number greater than 2

There are 4 green, 3 blue, and 3 red marbles in a bag.
(Ex 2)

   d. What is the probability of randomly choosing a blue marble?

   e. What is the probability of randomly not choosing a red marble?

f. Suppose there are 8 balls in a bucket numbered as follows; 1, 2, 3, 5, 5, 6, 7, and 7. A single ball is randomly chosen from the bucket. What is the probability of drawing a ball with a number less than 6? Do you have a greater chance of drawing a 7 or a 6?
(Ex 3)

g. A 52-card deck has 4 kings in the deck. What is the probability of randomly drawing a king out of the deck?
(Ex 4)

Practice   Distributed and Integrated

*1. A number cube labeled 1–6 is rolled three times. What is the probability that the next roll will produce a number greater than 4?
(14)

*2. An jar contains 5 green marbles and 9 purple marbles. A marble is drawn and dropped back into the jar. Then a second marble is drawn and dropped back into the jar. Both marbles are green. If another marble is drawn, what is the probability that it will be green?
(14)

3. Convert 20 inches to centimeters (2.54 cm = 1 in.).
(8)

4. Convert 25 feet to centimeters. (Hint: Convert from feet to inches to centimeters.)
(8)

Simplify.

5. $3 - 2 \cdot 4 + 3 \cdot 2$
(4)

6. $-3(-2)(-3) - 2$
(11)

7. $5(9 + 2) - 4(5 + 1)$
(4)

8. $3(6 + 2) + 3(5 - 2)$
(4)

9. Evaluate $\sqrt{31 + z}$ when $z = 5$.
(13)

10. Use $<, >$ or $=$ to compare $\frac{4}{5}$ and $\frac{5}{6}$.
(10)

*11. **Geometry** What is the length of the side of a square that has an area of 49 square centimeters?
(13)

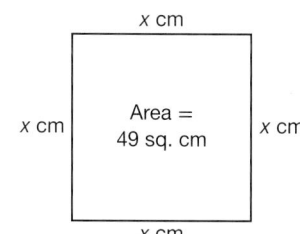

12. **Multiple Choice** Which equation demonstrates the Associative Property of Addition?
(12)

A $(a + b) + c = a + (b + c)$

B $ab + c = ba + c$

C $a(b + c) = ab + ac$

D $a + (b + c) = a + (c + b)$

*13. Justify What must be true of each of the values of x and y if $-xy$ is positive? zero? negative?
(11)

14. Identify the property illustrated in the expression $5 \cdot 6 = 6 \cdot 5$.
(12)

*15. Multiple Choice A number cube labeled 1–6 is tossed. What is the theoretical probability of rolling an odd number?
(14)

    A $\dfrac{1}{2}$

    B $\dfrac{1}{3}$

    C $\dfrac{1}{4}$

    D $\dfrac{2}{3}$

*16. A letter is chosen at random from the word probability. What is the probability of randomly choosing the letter b?
(14)

*17. Multiple Choice A bag contains 4 blue, 6 red, 5 yellow, and 1 orange marble. What is the probability of randomly choosing a blue marble?
(14)

    A $\dfrac{1}{16}$

    B $\dfrac{4}{15}$

    C $\dfrac{1}{4}$

    D $\dfrac{4}{32}$

18. Error Analysis Students were asked to find the square root of 16. Which student is correct? Explain the error.
(13)

Student A	Student B
$\sqrt{16} = 4$	$\sqrt{16} = 8$
$4 \times 4 = 16$	$8 \times 2 = 16$

*19. (Braking Distance) The speed a vehicle was traveling when the brakes were first applied can be estimated using the formula $s = \sqrt{\dfrac{d}{0.04}}$, where d is the length of the vehicle's skid marks in feet and s is the speed of the vehicle in miles per hour. Determine the speed of a car whose skid marks were 4^2 feet long.
(13)

*20. (Physics) The centripetal force of an object in circular motion can be expressed as $\dfrac{mv^2}{r}$, where m is mass, v is tangential velocity, and r is the radius of the circular path. What is the centripetal force of a 2-kg object traveling at 50 cm/s in a circular path with a radius of 25 centimeters?
(9)

21. Verify Convert 2.35 pounds to ounces (1 lb = 16 oz). Check to see if your answer
(8) is reasonable.

22. Write If a computer program is designed to run until it reaches the end of the
(1) number pi (π), will the program ever end? Explain.

23. (Geography) The lowest point in elevation in the United States is Death Valley,
(1) California. Death Valley is 86 meters below sea level. Which set of numbers best
describes elevations in Death Valley?

24. (Temperature) To convert degrees Celsius to degrees Fahrenheit, use the
(2) equation $C = \frac{5}{9}(F - 32)$.
  a. How many terms are in the expression $\frac{5}{9}(F - 32)$?

  b. Identify the constants in the expression.

25. Simplify $-7 + 3 - 2 - 5 + (-6)$.
(6)

26. Error Analysis Ms. Mahoney, the algebra teacher, has two cakes that weigh 3 pounds
(4) and 5 pounds. She cuts the cakes into 16 equal pieces. She asks the students to
write an expression that represents the weight of each piece. Which student is
correct? Explain the error.

Student A	Student B
uses the expression $3 + 5 \div 16$	uses the expression $(3 + 5) \div 16$

27. Model While the Petersen family was waiting for their table, 9 people left the
(5) restaurant and 15 people entered. Find the sum of -9 and 15 to determine the
change in the number of people in the restaurant. Use algebra tiles to model the
situation.

28. Justify Simplify $22 - (-11) - 11 - (-22)$. Justify your answer.
(6)

29. Write Why is the order of operations important when simplifying an expression
(7) like $(5 + 7)^2 \div (14 - 2)$?

*30. (Landscaping) Tanisha is building a fence around a square flower bed that has an
(13) area of 144 square feet. How many feet of fencing does she need?

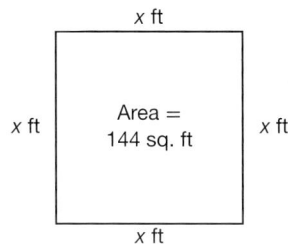

Using the Distributive Property to Simplify Expressions

Warm Up

1. **Vocabulary** In the expression $3x + 5$, $3x$ is a _____ (*variable, term*)
   (2) of the expression.

Simplify each expression.

2. $5 - 7 + 5(3)$
   (4)
3. $(-5) + (-2) + |(-5) + (-2)|$
   (4)
4. Evaluate $7x + 4y$ for $x = 2.1$ and $y = -0.7$.
   (9)
5. Find the product of $\frac{3}{8}$, $\frac{4}{5}$, and $\frac{2}{3}$.
   (11)

New Concepts The Distributive Property can be used to simplify expressions. Since subtraction is the same as adding the opposite, the Distributive Property will also work with subtraction.

The Distributive Property
For all real numbers a, b, c, $\qquad a(b + c) = ab + ac$ and $a(b - c) = ab - ac$ **Examples** $5(2 + 1) = 5 \cdot 2 + 5 \cdot 1 = 15$ $\qquad\qquad 5(2 - 1) = 5 \cdot 2 - 5 \cdot 1 = 5$

Example 1 **Distributing a Positive Integer**

Simplify each expression.

a. $6(4 + 8)$

SOLUTION

$6(4 + 8)$

$= 6(4) + 6(8)$ Distribute the 6.

$= 24 + 48$ Multiply.

$= 72$ Add.

b. $4(5 - 3)$

SOLUTION

$4(5 - 3)$

$= 4(5) + 4(-3)$ Distribute the 4.

$= 20 - 12$ Multiply.

$= 8$ Subtract.

Math Reasoning

Verify Use the order of operations to show that $4(5 - 3) = 8$.

Online Connection
www.SaxonMathResources.com

Use the Multiplication Property of -1 to simplify an expression like $-(5 + 2)$. Rewrite the expression as $-1(5 + 2)$ and then distribute.

Example 2 Distributing a Negative Integer

Simplify each expression.

a. $-(9 + 4)$

SOLUTION

$-(9 + 4)$

$= (-1)(9) + (-1)(4)$ Distribute.

$= -9 - 4$ Multiply.

$= -13$ Simplify.

b. $-9(-6 - 3)$

SOLUTION

$-9(-6 - 3)$

$= (-9)(-6) + (-9)(-3)$

$= 54 + 27$

$= 81$

> **Hint**
>
> The product of a real number and 1 is the real number.

The Distributive Property of Equality applies not only to numeric expressions but also to algebraic expressions.

Example 3 Simplifying Algebraic Expressions

Simplify each expression.

a. $-4(x + 7)$

SOLUTION

$-4(x + 7)$

$= (-4)(x) + (-4)(7)$ Distribute.

$= -4x - 28$ Multiply.

b. $(5 - x)6$

SOLUTION

$(5 - x)6$

$= 6(5) + 6(-x)$

$= 30 - 6x$

> **Reading Math**
>
> There are different ways to write the same expression:
>
> $6 \cdot (5 - x)$
> $(5 - x) \cdot 6$
> $6(5 - x)$
> $(5 - x)6$

Example 4 Simplifying Algebraic Expressions with Exponents

Simplify each expression.

a. $mn(mx + ny + 2p)$

SOLUTION

$mn(mx + ny + 2p)$

$= m^2nx + mn^2y + 2mnp$ Multiply.

b. $-xy(y^2 - x^2z)$

SOLUTION

$-xy(y^2 - x^2z)$ Distribute.

$= (-xy)(y^2) + (-xy)(-x^2z)$ Combine like terms.

$= -xy^3 + x^3yz$

> **Hint**
>
> When multiplying, add the exponents of powers with the same base.
>
> $y(y^2) = y^{1+2} = y^3$

Example 5 Application: Landscaping

Hint

To find the area of a rectangle, multiply length times width.

The turf on a football field is being replaced. The field is 300 feet long and 160 feet wide, not including the two end zones. Each end zone adds an additional 30 feet to the field's length. Write an expression using the Distributive Property to show the entire area of the field. Simplify the expression.

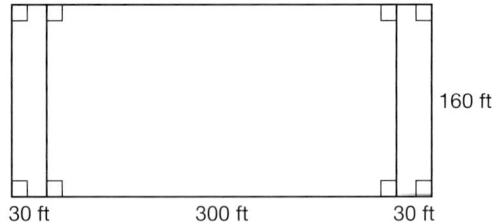

SOLUTION

width	$\times$	length
= 160	$\times$	$(30 + 300 + 30)$

$= 160(30 + 300 + 30)$

$= 160(30) + 160(300) + 160(30)$ Use the Distributive Property.

$= 4800 + 48{,}000 + 4800$ Multiply.

$= 57{,}600$ Add.

Check Use the order of operations.

$160(30 + 300 + 30)$ Perform the operation inside the parentheses.

$= 160(360)$ Multiply.

$= 57{,}600$ ✓

The area of the football field is $57{,}600 \text{ ft}^2$.

Lesson Practice

Simplify each expression.

a. $8(2 + 7)$
(Ex 1)

b. $4(6 - 2)$
(Ex 1)

c. $-(9 + 3)$
(Ex 2)

d. $-14(4 - 2)$
(Ex 2)

e. $-10(m + 4)$
(Ex 3)

f. $(7 - y)8$
(Ex 3)

g. $4xy^3(x^4y - 5x)$
(Ex 4)

h. $-2x^2m^2(m^2 - 4m)$
(Ex 4)

i. A group of 4 adults and 8 children are buying tickets to an amusement park. Tickets are $15 each. Write an expression using the Distributive Property to show the total cost of the tickets. Simplify the expression.
(Ex 5)

Evaluate.

1. $-7(-8 + 3)$
_(15)_

2. $5(-3 - 6)$
_(15)_

3. Evaluate $\sqrt{10,000}$.
_(13)_

4. Solve $c = \sqrt{25}$.
_(13)_

*5. Multi-Step In a shipment of 800 eggs, the probability of an egg breaking is $\frac{2}{25}$.
_(14)_ How many are likely to be broken in the shipment? Justify the answer.

6. The digits 0, 1, 2, 3, 4, 5, 6, 7, 8 and 9 are written on cards that are shuffled
_(14)_ and placed face down in a stack. One card is selected at random. What is the
probability that the digit is odd and greater than 5?

*7. In a bucket there are 10 balls in a bucket numbered 1, 1, 2, 3, 4, 4, 4, 5, 6, and 6.
_(14)_ A single ball is randomly chosen from the bucket. What is the probability of
drawing a ball with a number less than 7? Explain.

*8. Multiple Choice Simplify the expression $-5(x + 6)$. Which is the correct
_(15)_ simplification?

    A $-5 + x - 11$ **B** $-5x + 1$ **C** $-5x + 30$ **D** $-5x - 30$

*9. Find the value of y in the equation $18 - x = y$ if $x = -4$.
_(6)_

10. The water level of the reservoir in Austin, Texas, was 3 feet below normal. After a
_(5)_ heavy rain storm, the water level increased to 5 feet above normal. How much did
the rain storm change the water level?

11. Error Analysis Two students evaluated a numeric expression. Which student is
_(15)_ correct? Explain the error.

Student A	Student B
$-8(-5 + 14)$	$-8(-5 + 14)$
$= 40 - 112$	$= -13 + 6$
$= -72$	$= -7$

12. Write Evaluate the expression $-8(9 - 15)$ using the Distributive Property. Explain.
_(15)_

*13. (**Surveying**) The county surveyed a piece of property and divided it into
_(15)_ equal-sized lots. Use the diagram to write an expression that requires the
Distributive Property to evaluate it. Evaluate the expression to find the total number
of lots on the property.

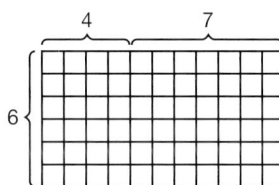

*14. True or False: $m + 0 = m$. Justify your answer using the properties.
_(12)_

15. Convert 3.4 yd^3 to ft^3.
(8)

16. Multi-Step Travis plans to divide his collection of baseball cards among
(15) 8 grandchildren. He will give each child the same number of cards. Each card
is worth \$14. Write an expression to represent the value of each child's cards.
Let c equal the total number of cards in Travis's collection.

17. (**Budgeting**) Kennedy's teacher asked her to plan the budget for the class party.
(15) Kennedy began by writing the expression $g = b + 7$ to represent that the number
of girls equals the number of boys plus seven. Each girl will need \$6. Write and
simplify an algebraic expression that uses the Distributive Property to show the
total cost for girls at the class party.

*18. If a number cube is rolled, what is the probability of it landing on the number
(14) 5 or 6?

*19. Error Analysis Two students are evaluating the expression $\sqrt{36 + z}$ for $z = 13$.
(13) Which student is correct? Explain the error.

Student A	Student B
$\sqrt{36 + z}$	$\sqrt{36 + z}$
$= \sqrt{36 + 13}$	$= \sqrt{36} + z$
$= \sqrt{49}$	$= 6 + 13$
$= 7$	$= 19$

20. Justify The expression $6 \cdot 2 \cdot 4$ would be simplified from left to right using the order
(12) of operations. What property would allow this expression to be simplified from
right to left?

*21. (**Investments**) Susan invests the same amount of money in each of 7 stocks. In one
(12) year, her money increased 8 times. The value of her investment is represented by
the expression $7x \cdot 8$. Show two methods to simplify the expression and justify each
step using the properties.

22. (**Age**) Rickie is $3\frac{3}{4}$ years older than Raymond. Raymond is $2\frac{1}{2}$ years younger
(10) than Ryan. If Ryan is $14\frac{1}{4}$ years old, how old is Rickie?

23. Write Write the procedure for evaluating the expression $16f^2 g^3 - 4f^8 + 12$ for
(9) $f = 3$ and $g = 5$.

24. Model Use the number line to model $x - 8$ when $x = -6$.
(6)

25. (**Astronomy**) In astronomy, brightness is given in a value called magnitude. A
(3) -2-magnitude star is 2.512 times brighter than a -1-magnitude star, a
-3-magnitude star is 2.512 times brighter than a -2-magnitude star, and so on.
If Sirius is magnitude -1.5 and the full moon is magnitude -12.5, how much
brighter is the full moon?

26. Error Analysis Student A and Student B each solved the absolute-value problem as
(5) shown below. Which student is correct? Explain the error.

Student A	Student B
$-\|12 - 15\|$	$-\|12 - 15\|$
$= -\|-3\|$	$= -\|-3\|$
$= -(3)$	$= \|+3\|$
$= -3$	$= 3$

*27. Find the value of y for the given values of x in the equation $x - \|x - 2\| = y$
(6) if $x = -3$.

28. Verify When simplified, will the expression $3 + \frac{2}{3} + \|-5\|$ be positive or negative?
(7) Explain.

29. Probability Thomas spun a game spinner and recorded the results in the table below.
(Inv 1)

Outcome	Frequency
Red	3
Blue	5
Yellow	9
Green	8

Use the table to find the experimental probability of each event. Express each
probability as a fraction and as a percent.

a. landing on red

b. landing on green

c. not landing on green

30. Geometry What is the perimeter of a square with an area of 121 sq. in.?
(13)

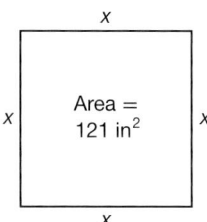

Simplifying and Evaluating Variable Expressions

Warm Up

1. **Vocabulary** The set of whole numbers and their opposites $\{..., -4, -3, -2, -1, 0, 1, 2, 3, 4,...\}$ is the set of _____.
   (6)

Simplify.

2. $-ax^2(dx^3 - a^5x)$
   (15)

3. $\sqrt{36} + \sqrt{81} - 4^2$
   (13)

4. $[-(-5)] - |-7|$
   (7)

5. Which value is equivalent to $\frac{9}{10}\left(-\frac{1}{12}\right)$?
   (11)

   A $-\frac{49}{60}$ **B** $-\frac{3}{40}$ **C** $\frac{3}{60}$ **D** $\frac{3}{40}$

New Concepts

To evaluate an expression that contains variables, substitute each variable in the expression with a given numeric value, and then find the value of the expression.

Example 1   **Evaluating Expressions with Two Variables**

Evaluate each expression for the given values of the variables.

a. $-a[-a(p - a)]$ for $a = 3$ and $p = 4$

SOLUTION

$-a[-a(p - a)]$

$= -3[-3(4 - 3)]$ Substitute each variable with the given value.

$= -3[-3(1)]$ Subtract.

$= -3[-3]$ Multiply inside the brackets.

$= 9$ Multiply.

b. $(-x + a) - (x - a)$ for $a = -2$ and $x = 7$

SOLUTION

$(-x + a) - (x - a)$

$= [-7 + (-2)] - [7 - (-2)]$ Substitute each variable with the given value.

$= [-7 + (-2)] - [7 + 2]$ Take the opposite of -2.

$= (-9) - (9)$ Evaluate inside the brackets.

$= -18$ Subtract.

Hint

Use parentheses when substituting a number for a variable, so that the negative signs and the subtraction signs are not confused.

Example 2 Evaluating Expressions with Three Variables

Evaluate each expression for the given values of the variables.

a. $(yx)(zyx)$ for $x = 2$, $y = -1$, and $z = 4$

SOLUTION

$(yx)(zyx)$

$= [(-1)(2)][(4)(-1)(2)]$ Substitute each variable with the given value.

$= (-2)(-8)$ Multiply inside the brackets.

$= 16$ Multiply.

b. $\dfrac{x(4ap)}{xp}$ for $a = 1$, $p = 5$, and $x = -3$

SOLUTION

$\dfrac{x(4ap)}{xp}$

$= \dfrac{(-3)(4)(1)(5)}{(-3)(5)}$ Substitute each variable with the given value.

$= \dfrac{-60}{-15} = 4$ Multiply and simplify.

An expression can be simplified before it is evaluated.

Example 3 Simplifying Before Evaluating Expressions

Math Reasoning

Verify Evaluate Example 3a without simplifying first to show that the answer is the same.

Simplify each expression. Then evaluate it. Justify each step.

a. $-x(y - 3) + y$ for $x = 0.5$ and $y = -1.75$

SOLUTION

$-x(y - 3) + y$

$= -xy + 3x + y$ Distributive Property

$= -(0.5)(-1.75) + 3(0.5) + (-1.75)$ Substitute.

$= 0.875 + 1.5 - 1.75$ Multiply and add.

$= 0.625$

b. $x(x + 2y) - x$ for $x = \dfrac{1}{2}$ and $y = \dfrac{1}{4}$

SOLUTION

$x(x + 2y) - x$

$= x^2 + 2xy - x$ Distributive Property

$= \left(\dfrac{1}{2}\right)^2 + 2\left(\dfrac{1}{2}\right)\left(\dfrac{1}{4}\right) - \left(\dfrac{1}{2}\right)$ Substitute.

$= \dfrac{1}{4} + \dfrac{1}{4} - \dfrac{1}{2} = 0$ Use order of operations to simplify.

Online Connection
www.SaxonMathResources.com

Example 4 **Evaluating Expressions with Exponents**

Evaluate each expression for the given values of the variables.

a. If $m = -2$ and $y = 2.5$, what is the value of ym^3?

SOLUTION

ym^3

$= (2.5)(-2)^3$ Substitute each variable with the given value.

$= (2.5)(-8)$ Evaluate the exponent.

$= -20$ Multiply.

b. If $a = 3$ and $b = -1$, what is the value of $2\left(\frac{a}{5-b}\right)^2$?

SOLUTION

$2\left(\frac{a}{5-b}\right)^2$

$= 2\left(\frac{3}{5-(-1)}\right)^2$ Substitute each variable with the given value.

$= 2\left(\frac{3}{5+1}\right)^2$ Take the opposite of -1.

$= 2\left(\frac{3}{6}\right)^2$ Perform operations inside the parentheses.

$= 2\left(\frac{1}{2}\right)^2$ Write the fraction in simplest form.

$= 2\left(\frac{1}{4}\right)$ Evaluate the exponent.

$= \frac{1}{2}$ Multiply.

c. If $a = 3$, what is the value of $\left|(-a)^3\right|$?

SOLUTION

$\left|(-a)^3\right|$

$= \left|(-3)^3\right|$ Substitute the variable with the given value.

$= \left|(-3)(-3)(-3)\right|$ Evaluate the exponent.

$= \left|-27\right|$ Multiply.

$= 27$ Take the absolute value.

Example 5 **Application: Investments**

A savings account increases as interest accumulates according to the formula $P_y = 1.04(P_{y-1})$, where P_y is the principal balance at the end of y years and P_{y-1} is the principal balance after $y-1$ years. After 6 years, there is a principal balance of \$1450.00. How much is the principal balance after 8 years?

SOLUTION

P_{7-1} or P_6 represents the principal balance after 6 years

P_{7-1} or $P_6 = \$1450$

$P_7 = 1.04(P_{7-1})$ Write the formula for the principal balance after 7 years.

$P_7 = 1.04(1450)$ Substitute 1450 for P_{7-1}.

$P_7 = \$1508$

$P_8 = 1.04(P_{8-1})$ Write the formula for the principal balance after 8 years.

P_{8-1} or P_7 represents the principal balance after 7 years

$P_8 = 1.04(1508)$ Substitute 1508 for P_{8-1}.

$P_8 = \$1568.32$

Her principal balance is $\$1568.32$ after 8 years.

Lesson Practice

Evaluate each expression for the given values of the variables.

  a. $ax[-a(a - x)]$ for $a = 2$ and $x = -1$
(Ex 1)

  b. $-b[-b(b - c) - (c - b)]$ for $b = -2$ and $c = 0$
(Ex 1)

  c. $(5y)(2z)4xy$ for $x = 3$, $y = -1$, and $z = \dfrac{1}{2}$
(Ex 2)

  d. $\dfrac{4rs}{6st}$ for $r = -1$, $s = -3$, and $t = -2$
(Ex 2)

Simplify each expression. Then evaluate for $a = 2$ and $b = -1$. Justify each step.
(Ex 3)

  e. $-b(a - 3) + a$

  f. $-a(-b - a) - b$

Evaluate each expression for the given values of the variable.
(Ex 4)

  g. If $a = -2$ and $b = 25$, what is the value of $\dfrac{-b(a - 4) + b}{b}$?

  h. If $x = -4$ and $y = -2$, what is the value of $\dfrac{x^2 - x|y|}{x^3}$?

  i. A savings account grows according to the formula $P_y = 1.04(P_{y-1})$, where P_y is the principal balance at the end of y years and P_{y-1} is the principal balance after $y - 1$ years. After 6 years, there is a principal balance of $\$1600.00$. How much is the principal balance after 8 years?
(Ex 5)

Simplify.

1. $2 + 5 - 3 + 7 - (-3) + 5$
(10)

2. $3(7) + 5 - 3 + 7 - 9 \div 2$
(4)

3. Represent the following numbers as being members of set K: $-2, -1, -4, -1, -3,$
(1) $-1, -5, -3$.

Determine if each statement is true or false. If true, explain why. If false, give a counterexample.

4. The set of whole numbers is closed under multiplication.
(1)

5. All integers are whole numbers.
(1)

Simplify by using the Distributive Property.

6. $-4y(d + cx)$
(15)

7. $(a + bc)2x$
(15)

Evaluate the expression for the given values.

*8. $pa[-a(-a)]$ when $p = 2$ and $a = -1$
(16)

*9. $x(x - y)$ when $x = \dfrac{1}{5}$ and $y = \dfrac{6}{5}$
(16)

*10. $\left(\dfrac{x - 3}{y}\right)^2$ when $x = -5$ and $y = 2$
(16)

11. $4(b + 1)^2 - 6(c - b)^4$ when $b = 2$ and $c = 7$
(9)

 12. Geometry The measure of one side of a square is $5x + 1$ meters. What expression
(15) would be used for the perimeter of the square? Explain.

13. Identify the property illustrated in the equation $2 + (1 + 7) = (2 + 1) + 7$.
(12)

*14. Multiple Choice A fish tank empties at a rate of $v = 195 - 0.5t$, where v is the
(16) number of liters remaining after t seconds have passed. If the fish tank empties for 20 seconds, how many liters remain?

   A 205   **B** 185

   C 175   **D** 174.5

*15. Multi-Step A solid, plastic machine part is shaped like a cone that is 8 centimeters
(16) high and has a radius of 2 centimeters. A machinist has removed some of the plastic by drilling a cylindrical hole into the part's base. The hole is 4 centimeters deep and has a diameter of 1 centimeter.

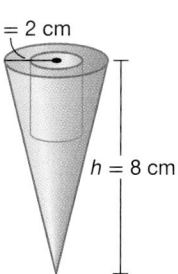

   a. Determine the volume of the cone. Use the formula $V = \frac{1}{3}\pi r^2 h$.

   b. Determine the volume of the cylindrical hole. Use the formula $V = \pi r^2 h$.

   c. Determine the volume of the plastic machine part by subtracting the volume of the cylindrical hole from the volume of the cone.

*16. (**Chemistry**) Boyle's law relates the pressure and volume of a gas held at a constant
$\ (16)$ temperature. This relationship is represented by the equation $P_f = \frac{P_i V_i}{V_f}$. In this
equation, P_i and V_i represent the gas's initial pressure and volume. P_f and V_f
represent the gas's final pressure and volume. What is the final pressure of the
gas if a 3-liter volume of gas at a pressure of 1 atmosphere is expanded to a final
volume of 6 liters?

*17. (**Investing**) Jamie wants to determine how much she should invest in a stock. She uses
$\ (16)$ the equation for present value, $V_p = \frac{V_f}{(1+i)^t}$, in which V_f is the future value, i is the
interest rate, and t is the number of years. How much should her present value be
if she wants the future value of the stock to be $2000 in 10 years at an interest rate
of 0.02? Round the answer to the nearest dollar.

*18. **Multiple Choice** Given the information in the table, which
$\ (16)$ equation best relates x and y?

A $y = x^3 + 5$

B $y = \frac{x^2 + 5}{x}$

C $y = |x^3 + 5|$

D $y = \frac{x^3 + 5}{x}$

x	y
2	13
1	6
−1	4
−2	3

*19. **Measurement** A party planner use the equation $A = Nx^2$ to estimate how much cake
$\ (16)$ is needed for a party with N guests, where x is the width of a square piece of cake.
If each piece of cake will be about 3 inches wide, approximate the area of the base
of a cake pan for the given number of guests.

  a. 50 guests

  b. 150 guests

  c. 350 guests

*20. **Multi-Step** Two teams of students were riding bikes for charity. There were a total
$\ (15)$ of b students on the blue team and they each rode 15 miles. There were a total of
r students on the red team and they each rode 3 miles. The students collected $2
for each mile.

  a. Write an expression for the total number of miles ridden by both teams.

  b. Write and simplify an expression that uses the Distributive Property to show the
  total amount of money collected.

21. **Error Analysis** A bucket contains 10 balls numbered 1, 1, 2, 3, 4, 4, 4, 5, 6, and 6. A
$\ (14)$ single ball is randomly chosen from the bucket. What is the probability of drawing
a ball with a number greater than or equal to 5? Which student is correct? Explain
the error.

Student A	Student B
$P(5 \text{ or } 6) = \frac{3}{10}$	$P(5 \text{ or } 6) = \frac{2}{10} \text{ or } \frac{1}{5}$

22. **Estimate** $\sqrt{36} + \sqrt{40} \;\bigcirc\; \sqrt{25} + \sqrt{80}$. Verify the answer.
$\ (13)$

23. Multi-Step John is using square ceramic floor tiles that are each 18 inches
(13) long. How many of these tiles will John need to cover a floor with an area
of 81 square feet?

24. (Oceanography) *Alvin* (DSV-2), a 16-ton manned research submersible, is used to
(11) observe life forms at depths of up to 8000 feet below sea level. After the hull was
replaced, *Alvin* was able to dive about 2.6 times the distance as before the hull
replacement. About how far was it able to travel after the hull was replaced?

25. Analyze What is the sign of the sum of -8 + 7? Explain how the sign is
(10) determined.

26. Write Why would you want to convert measures from one unit to another when
(8) working with a recipe found in a French cookbook?

27. Justify Evaluate $10(8-6)^3 + 4(|-5 + (-2)| + 2)$. Justify each step.
(7)

28. Error Analysis Two students wanted to find out the change in temperature in
(6) Calgary, Canada. It was -1°C in the morning and was -20°C by nighttime.
Which student is correct? Explain the error.

Student A	Student B
-20 - 1	-20 - (-1)
-20 + (-1)	-20 + 1
-21	-19

29. (Construction) A father builds a playhouse in the shape of a rectangular prism
(4) with a triangular prism on top, as shown in the figure. The volume of the
rectangular prism is $(10 \cdot 5.8 \cdot 8)$ ft³, and the volume of the triangular prism is
$[\frac{1}{2} \cdot (10 \cdot 5.8)] \cdot 4$ ft³. What is the volume of the whole structure?

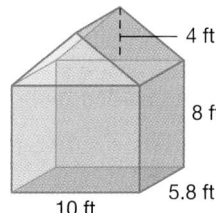

30. (Manufacturing) A manufacturing company produced 500 bowling balls in one day.
(Inv 1) Of those, 10 were found to be defective. The manufacturer sent a shipment of
250 balls to Zippy Lanes.

a. What is the experimental probability that a bowling ball with have a defect?

b. Predict the number of balls in the shipment to Zippy Lanes that will have a
defect.

LESSON 17

Translating Between Words and Algebraic Expressions

Warm Up

1. *(9)* **Vocabulary** An expression that has only numbers and operations is a _____ (**numeric, variable**) expression.

Simplify each expression.

2. *(6)* $5 - 7 + 5 - (-3)$ **3.** *(15)* $(5 + 7)4 + 7(5 - 3)$

4. *(15)* $(x^3 + m^5)x^2 m^2$

5. *(11)* Which value is equivalent to $-(-6)^3$?

  A -216 **B** 216 **C** 18 **D** -18

New Concepts

Algebraic expressions, or variable expressions, are expressions that contain at least one variable. A numeric expression contains only numbers and operations.

Translating Word and Phrases into Algebraic Expressions		
Words	**Phrases**	**Expressions**
Addition sum, total, more than, added, increased, plus	4 added to a number 7 increased by a number	$x + 4$ $7 + x$
Subtraction less, minus, decreased by, difference, less than	the difference of 5 and a number 8 less than a number	$5 - x$ $x - 8$
Multiplication product, times, multiplied	the product of a number and 12 a number times 3	$12(x)$ $3x$
Division quotient, divided by, divided into	the quotient of a number and 6 10 divided by a number	$x \div 6$ $\frac{10}{x}$

Hint

Remember that in multiplication, the coefficient is usually written before the variable.

Hint

"Years younger than" means less than.

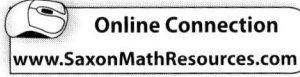
Online Connection
www.SaxonMathResources.com

Example 1 Translating Words into Algebraic Expressions

Write an algebraic expression for each phrase.

a. y increased by 12

SOLUTION $y + 12$

b. the product of x and 4

SOLUTION $4x$

c. 8 less than the quotient of m and 15

SOLUTION $\frac{m}{15} - 8$

d. James is 6 years younger than Lydia, who is x years old. Write the expression that shows James's age.

SOLUTION If x represents Lydia's age, then $x - 6$ represents James's age.

Example 2 — Translating Algebraic Expressions into Words

Use words to write each algebraic expression in two different ways.

a. $m + 7$

SOLUTION

7 more than m;

the sum of 7 and m

b. $y - 9$

SOLUTION

9 less than y;

the difference of y and 9

c. $5 \cdot n$

SOLUTION

the product of 5 and n;

5 times n

d. $x \div 3$

SOLUTION

x divided by 3;

the quotient of x and 3

e. $27 - \frac{1}{2}(18)$

SOLUTION

the difference of 27 and one-half of 18;

27 minus 18 divided by 2

Caution

"Less than" phrases are written in the reverse order of the given form.

two less than x: $x - 2$

Math Reasoning

Generalize Using the operations multiplication and division, explain the relationship between a number and its reciprocal.

Example 3 — Application: Savings

Jayne is saving money to buy a car. She has x dollars saved and is saving y dollars per week. Write an algebraic expression to represent the total amount of money she will have saved after 52 weeks.

SOLUTION

dollars saved	dollars saved each week	amount saved after 52 weeks
x	y	$x + 52y$

Jayne will have $x + 52y$ dollars saved after 52 weeks.

Lesson Practice

Write each phrase as an algebraic expression.
(Ex 1)

    a. the product of x and 8

    b. 18 minus y

    c. 7 more than 5 times x

    d. Raquel is 2 years older than Monica, who is x years old. Write the expression that shows Raquel's age.

Use words to write each algebraic expression in two different ways.
(Ex 2)

    e. $\dfrac{10}{s}$

    f. $5 - r$

    g. $3m + 7$

h. $\dfrac{3}{4}x + 9$

i. $\dfrac{x - 3}{2}$

j. (Savings) Jon has d dollars in a savings account. He withdraws x dollars
(Ex 3) each week for 15 weeks. Write an algebraic expression to represent the amount of money that will be left in the savings account at the end of the 15 weeks.

Practice Distributed and Integrated

Expand each algebraic expression by using the Distributive Property.

1. $(4 + 2y)x$
(15)

2. $-2(x - 4y)$
(15)

3. Write What is a term of an algebraic expression?
(2)

4. Given the sets $A = \{-3, -2, -1\}$, $B = \{1, 2, 3\}$, and $C = \{-1, 1, -2, 2, -3, 3\}$,
(1) are the following statements true or false?

   a. $A \cap C = \{-3, -2, -1\}$

   b. $A \cap B = \{-3, -2, -1, 1, 2, 3\}$

   c. $B \cup C = \{-3, -2, -1, 1, 2, 3\}$

   d. $A \cup B = \{-3, -2, -1\}$

Write the algebraic expressions for each statement.

*5. three times the sum of the opposite of a number and -7
(17)

*6. 0.18 of what number is 4.68?
(17)

7. Add $4.7 + (-9.2) - 1.9$.
(10)

8. Compare $\sqrt{36} + \sqrt{121}$ $\bigcirc$ $\sqrt{100} + \sqrt{49}$ using $<$, $>$, or $=$.
(13)

9. Between which two whole numbers is $\sqrt{15}$?
(13)

10. Justify True or False: $k = 0 \cdot k$, where k is any real number except for zero. Justify your
(12) answer using the properties.

11. Evaluate $(a + 4)^3 + 5x^2$ when $a = -3$ and $x = -1$.
(16)

*12. Justify True or False: $yx^2m^3 = -4$ when $x = -1$, $y = 2$, and $m = -2$. Justify your
(16) answer.

*13. Translate $3(x + 6)$ into word form.
(17)

*14. Multiple Choice Which expression is the algebraic translation of "4 times the sum of
(17) 9 and g"?

   A $4 + 9g$ **B** $4(9 + g)$ **C** $4 \cdot 9g$ **D** $(4 + 9)g$

*15. (Age) Mary is one year younger than twice Paul's age. Write an expression for
(17) Mary's age.

*16. (Finance) Miles spent $7 and then received a paycheck that doubled the money he
(17) had left. Write an expression to represent how much money he has now.

*17. Multi-Step A produce stand sells apples and bananas. Apples cost $0.20 each and
(17) bananas cost $0.10 each.

   a. Choose variables to represent apples and bananas.

   b. Write an expression to represent the total pieces of fruit.

   c. Write an expression to represent how much the fruit costs in dollars.

18. Error Analysis Students are asked to evaluate $\frac{x^2 - 4x}{xy}$ when $x = -2$ and $y = 3$. Which
(16) student is correct? Explain the error.

Student A	Student B
$\dfrac{x^2 - 4x}{xy}$	$\dfrac{x^2 - 4x}{xy}$
$\dfrac{(-2)^2 - 4(-2)}{(-2)(3)}$	$\dfrac{(-2)^2 - 4(-2)}{(-2)(3)}$
$= \dfrac{4 + 8}{-6}$	$= \dfrac{-4 - (-8)}{-6}$
$= \dfrac{12}{-6} = -2$	$= \dfrac{4}{-6}$
	$= \dfrac{-2}{3}$

*19. Geometry The figure below has corners that are square and a curved section that
(16) is a half circle. The dimensions given are in meters. What is the area of the figure?
Use 3.14 for π.

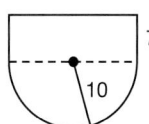

*20. Multi-Step A painter estimates that one gallon of a certain kind of paint will
(4) cover 305 square feet of wall. How many gallons of the paint will cover the wall
described by the diagram below? (Dimensions given are in feet.)

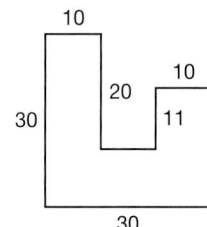

*21. Error Analysis Two students simplified an algebraic expression. Which student is
₍₁₅₎ correct? Explain the error.

Student A	Student B
$2r^3t\,(r^5t^2 + 4r^3t^3)$ $= 2r^{15}t^2 + 8r^9t^3$	$2r^3t\,(r^5t^2 + 4r^3t^3)$ $= 2r^8t^3 + 8r^6t^4$

22. Probability There are 400 students in the cafeteria. Of these students, 120 are
₍₁₄₎ tenth-graders. What is the probability of randomly selecting a tenth-grader?
Express the answer as a percent.

23. Error Analysis Two students simplify the expression $-7 - x + 7$. Which student is
₍₁₂₎ correct? Explain the error.

Student A	Student B
$-7-x+7$ $= x + (-7) + 7$ $= x + (-7 + 7)$ $= x + 0$ $= x$	$-7-x+7$ $= -7 + 7 - x$ $= (-7 + 7) - x$ $= 0 - x$ $= -x$

24. Justify Simplify $-\frac{2}{3} \div \left(-\frac{8}{9}\right)$. Show your steps.
₍₁₁₎

25. Write Must the algebraic expression $x + 7y$ have only one value? Explain.
₍₉₎

26. Measurement Madison used a scale and measured her weight at 85 pounds. How
₍₈₎ many kilograms does Madison weigh? (Hint: 1 kilogram = 2.2 pounds.)

27. (Energy Conservation) Wind turbines take the energy from the wind and convert it
₍₄₎ to electrical energy. Use the formula $P = ad^2v^3\,\frac{\pi}{4}\,e$ to find the amount of available
energy in the air. Describe the steps you would take to simplify the formula.

28. (Finance) Tonia deposited a total of \$174.52 into her checking account. She also
₍₅₎ withdrew a total of \$186.15. Use addition to find the net change in Tonia's
checking account.

29. Justify What is the first step in simplifying the expression $2 \cdot 4 + 5^2 + (23 - 2)^2$?
₍₄₎

30. (Payroll Accounting) Employees at Wilkinson Glass Company earn x number of
₍₁₅₎ dollars per hour. Executives make y number of dollars per hour. Each employee
and executive works 40 hours per week. Write and simplify an algebraic expression
that uses the Distributive Property to show a weekly payroll for one employee and
one executive.

Combining Like Terms

Warm Up

1. Vocabulary A _____ (*constant, variable*) is a symbol, usually a letter
used to represent an unknown number.
₍₂₎

Simplify each expression.

2. $(0.2)^5$
₍₃₎

3. $y^3 \cdot x^4 \cdot y^2 \cdot x^5 \cdot y$
₍₃₎

4. Write the phrase "six more than twice a number" as an algebraic expression.
₍₁₇₎

New Concepts

Two or more terms that have the same variable or variables raised to the same power are **like terms**. Terms with different variables or terms with the same variable or variables raised to a different power are **unlike terms**.

$$\boxed{3x^4} + 5y^4 + \boxed{5x^4}$$

Because the variable x has the same power, $3x^4$ and $5x^4$ are like terms. Because the variables are not the same, $5y^4$ and $5x^4$ are unlike terms. The coefficient is not used to establish whether the terms are like or unlike.

> **Hint**
>
> It may be helpful to circle, box, or underline the terms that are alike before combining like terms.

Example 1 Combining Like Terms Without Exponents

Simplify each expression.

a. $5x + 7x$

SOLUTION

$5x + 7x$

$= (5 + 7)x$ Use the Distributive Property.

$= 12x$ Simplify.

b. $-4y - (-3y) + 5y$

SOLUTION

$-4y - (-3y) + 5y$

$= (-4 + 3 + 5)y$ Take the opposite of -3, and then use the Distributive Property.

$= 4y$ Simplify.

> **Math Reasoning**
>
> **Justify** Why can the order of the factors in a term be rearranged?

c. $6xy - 3a + 4yx$

SOLUTION

$6xy - 3a + 4yx$

$= 6xy + 4yx - 3a$ Rearrange the terms.

$= 6xy + 4xy - 3a$ Rearrange the factors.

$= 10xy - 3a$ Add the like terms.

Example 2 Combining Like Terms With Exponents

Simplify each expression.

a. $x^5 + y^3 + x^5 + y^3$

SOLUTION

$$x^5 + y^3 + x^5 + y^3$$
$$= x^5 + x^5 + y^3 + y^3 \qquad \text{Rearrange the terms.}$$
$$= (1 + 1)x^5 + (1 + 1)y^3 \qquad \text{Use the Distributive Property.}$$
$$= 2x^5 + 2y^3 \qquad \text{Simplify.}$$

b. $3k^2 - 2k^2 + 4k^2 + 2kx^4 + kx^4$

SOLUTION

$$3k^2 - 2k^2 + 4k^2 + 2kx^4 + kx^4$$
$$= (3 - 2 + 4)k^2 + (2 + 1)\, kx^4 \qquad \text{Use the Distributive Property.}$$
$$= 5k^2 + 3\, kx^4 \qquad \text{Simplify.}$$

c. $2x^2y^3 + xy - 8y^3x^2 - 5yx$

SOLUTION

$$2x^2y^3 + xy - 8y^3x^2 - 5yx$$
$$= 2x^2y^3 - 8\, y^3x^2 + xy - 5xy \qquad \text{Rearrange the terms.}$$
$$= 2x^2y^3 - 8\, x^2y^3 + xy - 5xy \qquad \text{Rearrange the factors.}$$
$$= (2 - 8)x^2y^3 + (1 - 5)xy \qquad \text{Use the Distributive Property.}$$
$$= -6x^2y^3 - 4xy \qquad \text{Simplify.}$$

Hint

The coefficient of x is 1.

The coefficient of $-x$ is -1.

Reading Math

It is customary to write the factors of a term in alphabetical order. So, x^2zy^3 is written x^2y^3z.

Example 3 Application: Measurement

Olympic competition offers three equestrian disciplines: dressage, show jumping, and endurance. The diagram represents the measurements for a regulation dressage arena.

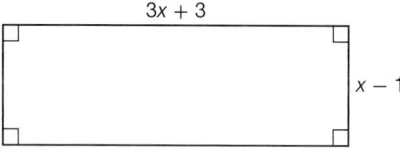

Find the perimeter of the arena as a simplified variable expression. Then evaluate the expression for $x = 19.5$ meters.

SOLUTION

$$P = 2l + 2w \qquad \text{Write the formula for the perimeter of a rectangle.}$$
$$P = 2(3x + 3) + 2(x - 1) \qquad \text{Substitute for } l \text{ and } w.$$
$$P = 6x + 6 + 2x - 2 \qquad \text{Use the Distributive Property.}$$
$$P = 8x + 4 \qquad \text{Combine like terms.}$$
$$P = 8(19.5) + 4 \qquad \text{Substitute 19.5 for } x.$$
$$P = 156 + 4 = 160 \qquad \text{Multiply. Then add.}$$

The perimeter of the dressage arena is $8x + 4$ or 160 meters.

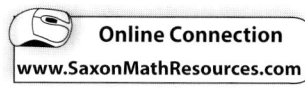
Online Connection
www.SaxonMathResources.com

Simplify each expression.

a. $-2xy - 3x + 4 - 4xy - 2x$
(Ex 1)

b. $7m - (-8m) + 9m$
(Ex 1)

c. $3yac - 2ac + 6acy$
(Ex 1)

d. $x^4y + 3x^4y + 2x^4y$
(Ex 2)

e. $x^2y - 3yx + 2yx^2 - 2xy + yx$
(Ex 2)

f. $m^3n + m^3n - x^2y^7 + x^2y^7$
(Ex 2)

g. A triangular-shaped display case has the
(Ex 3) dimensions shown on the diagram. Find the perimeter of the display case as a simplified variable expression. Then evaluate the expression for $x = 2$ feet.

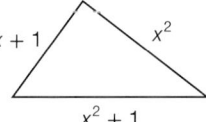

$x + 1$ x^2 $x^2 + 1$

Practice **Distributed and Integrated**

1. Write an algebraic expression for this statement: The sum of 5 times a number and -8.
(17)

Simplify each expression by adding like terms.

*2. $m + 4 + 3m - 6 - 2m + mc - 4mc$
(18)

*3. $xy - 3xy^2 + 5y^2x - 4xy$
(18)

*4. Multiple Choice Simplify $2x^2 + 3x$.
(18)

A $5x^2$ **B** $5x^3$

C $6x^3$ **D** cannot be simplified

*5. (**Reading**) Two classes are keeping track of how many pages they can read. In one
(18) class, the boys read 15 pages per night and the girls read 12 pages per night. In another class, the boys read 7 pages per night and the girls read 9 pages per night. Each class has x girls and y boys.

a. Write expressions representing the number of pages each class read per night.

b. Write an expression for the number they read altogether.

6. Justify After doing three addition problems that included negative numbers, John
(5) found that all three answers were negative. John concluded that any addition problem involving a negative number must have a negative answer. Is John correct? Explain. Give a counterexample if necessary.

7. (**Geography**) The retention pond at Martha's summer home in Florida changed
(6) -3 inches every day for 5 days. After 5 days, the water level was -40 inches. What was the original water level 5 days ago?

8. (**Bowling**) A ten-pin bowling ball has a volume of about 5274 cm³. A candlepin
(8)   bowling ball has a volume of about 48 in³. About how much greater is the volume
      of a ten-pin bowling ball than the volume of a candlepin bowling ball?

Simplify.

9. $\dfrac{-16 + 4}{2\left(\sqrt{13 - 4}\right)}$
(4, 13)

10. $-7 - \left(2^4 \div 8\right)$
(4, 13)

*11. $6bac - 7ac + 8acb$
(18)

*12. $2x^3y + 4x^3y + 9x^3y$
(18)

13. $\left|-15 + \sqrt{81}\right|^2$
(13)

14. $\dfrac{\sqrt{6 - 2}}{2 \cdot \left|-7 + 3\right|}$
(13)

*15. (**Sewing**) Susan started with 11 bows. She can tie 4 bows per minute. Analise ties
(18)   twice as many per minute.

    a. Write expressions representing the number of bows each girl will have after
       x minutes.

    b. Write an expression for the number they will have altogether after x minutes.

16. Multi-Step Marshall, Hank, and Jean are all cousins. Marshall is 3 years older than
(17)   Hank. Hank is twice the age of Jean.

    a. Write expressions to represent the ages of the cousins. Assign the variable j to
       represent Jean.

    b. If Jean is 12 years old, how old are the other cousins?

    c. If Hank was 14, how old would Jean be?

*17. Justify Simplify $8x + x(2x + 5)$ and explain each step.
(18)

18. Evaluate $\dfrac{8ak}{4k(2a - 2c + 8)}$ when $a = \dfrac{1}{2}$, $c = 3$, and $k = -2$.
(16)

*19. True or False: $pm^2 - z^3 = 27$ when $p = -5$, $m = 0$, and $z = -3$. Justify your answer.
(16)

20. Error Analysis Two students are asked to evaluate $x^2y - |4x|^2z$ when $x = -2$, $y = \dfrac{1}{2}$,
(16)   and $z = -1$. Which student is correct? Explain the error.

Student A	Student B
$x^2y - |4x|^2\,z$	$x^2y - |4x|^2\,z$
$(-2)^2\left(\dfrac{1}{2}\right) - |4(-2)|^2\,(-1)$	$(-2)^2\,(-1) - |4(-2)|^2\left(\dfrac{1}{2}\right)$
$= 4\left(\dfrac{1}{2}\right) - |-8|^2\,(-1)$	$= 4(-1) - |-8|^2\left(\dfrac{1}{2}\right)$
$= 2 - (8)^2\,(-1) = 66$	$= -4 - (8)^2\left(\dfrac{1}{2}\right) = -36$

21. Predict How can finding a common denominator tell you that $\dfrac{1}{9} - \dfrac{2}{20}$ will result in
(10)   a positive number?

*22. Multi-Step Tamatha picks 10 peaches a minute for x minutes. Her grandmother
(18) picks 12 peaches a minute for 3 fewer minutes.

    a. Write an expression to represent the number of minutes the grandmother picks peaches.

    b. Write an expression for the number of peaches they pick together and then simplify.

23. Geometry Translate the Pythagorean Theorem into symbols. In a right triangle,
(17) the sum of the squares of the legs of the triangle is equal to the square of the
hypotenuse. Let a and b be the legs of the triangle and c be the hypotenuse.

24. Measurement A railing is being built around a rectangular deck.
(17)

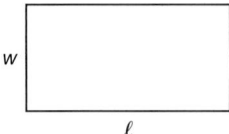

    a. Write an expression to represent the number of feet of railing needed.

    b. The width is doubled. The length is tripled. Write an expression to represent the number of feet of railing needed.

25. Multiple Choice Simplify the expression $7(10 - y)$. Which expression is correct?
(15)

    A $70 - y$ **B** $70 - 7y$

    C $70 - 7 + y$ **D** $70y - 7y$

26. Justify Simplify the expression $-m(mn^2 - m^2n)$ and explain your method for
(15) simplifying.

27. Probability A number is chosen at random from the numbers 1 through 5. What is
(14) the probability that an odd number will be chosen?

28. ⸨Carpentry⸩ A new company buys 140 square feet of carpet to cover the floor in one
(13) of its square offices. The carpet is 4 square feet too small. What is the length of
the office floor?

29. Verify The Commutative Property states that $6 \cdot 4 = 4 \cdot 6$. Show that the
(12) Commutative Property does not apply to division.

30. Error Analysis Two students translate the phrase "the sum of the squares of 8 and p"
(17) into an algebraic expression. Which student is correct? Explain the error.

Student A	Student B
$(p + 8)^2$	$p^2 + 8^2$

Solving One-Step Equations by Adding or Subtracting

Warm Up

1. **Vocabulary** -4 and 4 are _____ because they have the same absolute value but different signs.
   (6)

2. Add $7.5 + (-1.25)$.
   (5)

3. Subtract $12.75 - (-1.05)$.
   (6)

4. Use $<$, $>$, or $=$ to compare $6x + 3$ and $-2x + 4$ when $x = -3$.
   (16)

5. Evaluate $w - (wy - y)$ for $w = -4$ and $y = -1$.
   (9)
      A 1 **B** -1 **C** -9 **D** 9

New Concepts

An **equation** is a statement that uses an equal sign to show that two quantities are equal. A **solution of an equation in one variable** is a value of the variable that makes the equation true.

Example 1   Identifying Solutions

State whether the value of the variable is a solution of the equation.

a. $x + 6 = 9$ for $x = 3$

SOLUTION

$$x + 6 = 9$$
$$(3) + 6 \overset{?}{=} 9 \qquad \text{Substitute 3 for } x.$$
$$9 = 9 \quad \checkmark$$

Solution, $3 + 6 = 9$

b. $x - 6 = 9$ for $x = 3$

SOLUTION

$$x - 6 = 9$$
$$(3) - 6 \overset{?}{=} 9 \qquad \text{Substitute 3 for } x.$$
$$-3 \neq 9 \quad ✗$$

Not a solution, $3 - 6 \neq 9$

> **Math Reasoning**
>
> **Verify** If the same quantity is added to both sides of $x - 7 = 15$, show that the resulting equation is equivalent to $x - 7 = 15$.

An equation is like a balance scale.

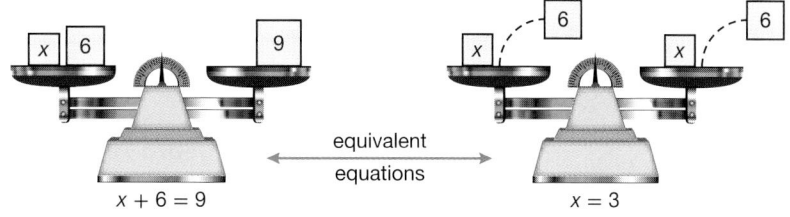

The scale remains balanced when the same quantity is added to both sides, or when the same quantity is subtracted from both sides.

Equivalent equations have the same solution set. By adding or subtracting the same quantity from both sides of an equation, each equation remains equivalent to the original equation. Furthermore, each side of the equation remains balanced as the equation is solved.

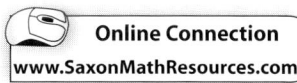

Online Connection
www.SaxonMathResources.com

The Addition and Subtraction Properties of Equality hold for every real number a, b, and c.

Addition and Subtraction Properties of Equality
Addition Property of Equality
You can add the same number to both sides of an equation and the statement will still be true.
Examples $\quad$ $2 = 2$ $\qquad\qquad\qquad\qquad$ $a = b$ $\qquad\qquad 3 + 2 = 2 + 3$ $\qquad\qquad$ $a + c = b + c$ $\qquad\qquad\qquad 5 = 5$
Subtraction Property of Equality
You can subtract the same number from both sides of an equation and the statement will still be true.
Examples $\quad$ $10 = 10$ $\qquad\qquad\qquad\qquad$ $a = b$ $\qquad\qquad 10 - 4 = 10 - 4$ $\qquad\qquad$ $a - c = b - c$ $\qquad\qquad\qquad 6 = 6$

On the first page of the lesson the Subtraction Property of Equality is illustrated with balance scales. Below, the Addition Property of Equality is illustrated.

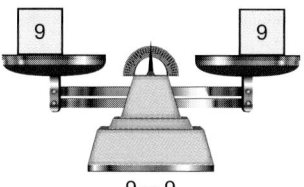 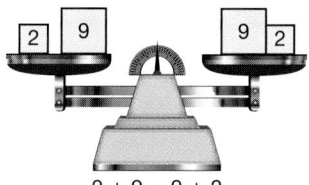

$$9 = 9 \qquad\qquad\qquad 2 + 9 = 9 + 2$$

Inverse operations are operations that undo each other. To solve an equation, isolate the variable on one side of the equal sign by using inverse operations. Use the same inverse operation on each side of the equation.

Inverse Operations

$$\text{Addition} \longleftrightarrow \text{Subtraction}$$

$$\text{Multiplication} \longleftrightarrow \text{Division}$$

Materials

algebra tiles

Hint

The + and − algebra tiles that are the same shape are opposites and undo each other.

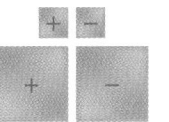

Exploration **Using Algebra Tiles to Model One-Step Equations**

Use algebra tiles to model $x + 6 = 9$.

a. Model each side of the equation.

b. Isolate the x-tile. Add six negative 1-tiles to both sides. Remove pairs that equal zero.

c. What is the solution?

d. Use algebra tiles to model $x - 2 = 4$. What is the solution?

Example 2 Solving Equations by Adding

Solve. Then check the solution.

a. $x - 3 = 12$

SOLUTION

$$x - 3 = 12$$
$$\underline{+3 = +3} \qquad \text{Add 3 to both sides to undo the subtraction.}$$
$$x = 15$$

Check Substitute 15 for x.

$$x - 3 \overset{?}{=} 12$$
$$(15) - 3 \overset{?}{=} 12$$
$$12 = 12 \quad \checkmark$$

b. $-15 = n - 8$

SOLUTION

$$-15 = n - 8$$
$$\underline{+8 = +8} \qquad \text{Add 8 to both sides.}$$
$$-7 = n$$

Check Substitute -7 for n.

$$-15 \overset{?}{=} (-7) - 8$$
$$-15 = -15 \quad \checkmark$$

Caution

Sometimes the variable is on the right side of the equal sign. Use inverse operations to isolate the variable.

Math Reasoning

Justify Does it matter if you add (-7) to each side or subtract 7 from each side? Explain.

Example 3 Solve Equations by Subtracting

Solve.

a. $k + 7 = 13$

SOLUTION

$$k + 7 = 13$$
$$\underline{-7 = -7} \qquad \text{Subtract 7 from both sides.}$$
$$k = 6$$

b. $-21 = p + 9$

SOLUTION

$$-21 = p + 9$$
$$\underline{-9 = -9} \qquad \text{Subtract 9 from both sides.}$$
$$-30 = p$$

Example 4 Solve Fraction Equations by Adding or Subtracting

Solve.

$$x + \frac{1}{4} = -\frac{3}{8}$$

SOLUTION

$$x + \frac{1}{4} = -\frac{3}{8}$$

$$\underline{-\frac{1}{4} = -\frac{1}{4}} \qquad \text{Subtract } \tfrac{1}{4} \text{ from both sides.}$$

$$x = -\frac{5}{8}$$

Example 5 Application: Weather

On January 10, 1911, the temperature in Rapid City, South Dakota, fell 47°F in 15 minutes. What was the temperature at 7:00 a.m.?

Temperature in Rapid City, SD	
7:00 a.m.	
7:15 a.m.	8°F

SOLUTION

Let x = the temperature at 7:00 a.m.

Write an equation.

$$x - 47 = 8$$

$$\underline{+47 = +47} \qquad \text{To isolate the variable, add 47 to each side.}$$

$$x = 55$$

At 7:00 a.m. the temperature was 55°F.

Lesson Practice

State whether the value of each variable is a solution of the equation.
(Ex 1)

  a. $h - 14 = 2$ for $h = 12$

  b. $-11 = j - 4$ for $j = -7$

Solve. Then check the solution.
(Ex 2)

  c. $x - 5 = 17$

  d. $-30 = m - 12$

Solve.

  e. $p + 3 = 37$
(Ex 3)

  f. $-14 = y + 8$
(Ex 3)

  g. $d + 4\frac{1}{2} = 3\frac{1}{6}.$
(Ex 4)

  h. Jagdeesh took the same test twice. On the second test he scored 87, which was 13 points higher than on the first test. What was his first test score?
(Ex 5)

1. Simplify $-3x^2ym + 7x - 5ymx^2 + 16x$.
(18)

Solve each equation.

*2. $x + 5 = 7$
(19)

*3. $x + 5 = -8$
(19)

*4. $x - 6 = 4$
(19)

5. Write the algebraic expression for the phrase "seven times the sum of a number
(17) and -5."

6. Expand the expression $-3(-x - 4)$ by using the Distributive Property.
(15)

7. Simplify $xm^2xm^3x^3m$.
(3)

8. Identify the property illustrated by $3 + 8 = 8 + 3$.
(12)

9. **Write** True or False: $-5^4 = (-5)^4$. Explain.
(11)

10. Sandra lost 8 points for incorrect answers on her quiz, but gained 5 points for a
(10) bonus question. What is the sum of points Sandra lost and gained?

*11. **Error Analysis** A teacher asked two students to solve the following equation
(19) for x: $x + \frac{1}{3} = \frac{4}{9}$. Which student is correct? Explain the error.

Student A	Student B
$x + \frac{1}{3} + \frac{1}{3} = \frac{4}{9} + \frac{1}{3}$	$x + \frac{1}{3} - \frac{1}{3} = \frac{4}{9} - \frac{1}{3}$
$x = \frac{4}{9} + \frac{3}{9}$	$x = \frac{4}{9} - \frac{3}{9}$
$x = \frac{7}{9}$	$x = \frac{1}{9}$

*12. **Multiple Choice** A swimming pool is $\frac{4}{5}$ full. A maintenance man removes some of
(19) the water so that the pool is $\frac{1}{3}$ full. As a fraction of the pool's total capacity, how
much water did the maintenance man remove?

A $\frac{1}{5}$ **B** $\frac{3}{2}$ **C** $\frac{7}{15}$ **D** $\frac{17}{15}$

*13. **Chemistry** Many chemists use kelvins to describe temperatures. To convert from
(19) a temperature in degrees Celsius to kelvins, a chemist will use the equation
$T_{\text{Celsius}} + 273.15 = T_{\text{kelvin}}$. If a gas cools to a temperature of 325.20K, what is its
temperature in degrees Celsius?

*14. **Business** A movie theater needs to sell 3500 tickets over a single weekend to cover
(19) its operating expenses before it starts making a profit. If it sells 1278 tickets on
Friday, what is the minimum number of tickets it needs to sell over the rest of the
weekend in order to make a profit? Write an equation and then solve it.

*15. Write Jeremy is solving the equation $x - 2.5 = 7.0$. What must he do to both side
(19) of the equation in order to isolate x?

*16. Multiple Choice Given the information in the table, which equation best relates
(19) a and b?

a	b
−5	0
0	−5
5	−10
−10	5

A $a - b = 5$ **B** $a - b = -5$ **C** $-5 - b = a$ **D** $a - 5 = b$

17. Error Analysis Two students simplify the expression $6x + 8 - 4x - 2$. Which student
(18) is correct? Explain the error.

Student A	Student B
$2x + 6$ $= 8x$	$2x + 6$

18. Geometry Write an expression to represent the sum of the degrees in
(18) the triangle.

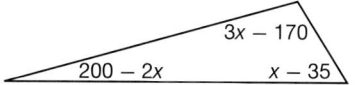

$3x - 170$
$200 - 2x$ $x - 35$

19. Multi-Step At a family camp, the big race is on the final day. Each
(18) family member runs for t hours and the family that runs the farthest
wins. The rate each person ran is shown in the chart. To find how far
they ran, multiply their rate by the amount of time they ran.
a. Write an expression to represent how far each person ran.

b. Write an expression to represent how far the family ran.

c. How far did they run if each person ran $\frac{1}{6}$ hour?

Family Member	Rate (mph)
Julio	4
Jorge	5
Sam	3

20. Error Analysis Two students translate the phrase "five more than the product of a
(17) number and three" into an algebraic expression. Which student is correct?
Explain the error.

Student A	Student B
$\frac{x}{3} + 5$	$3x + 5$

*21. When $x = 1.5$ and $y = -2$, what is the value of $\left| x^2 + y^3 \right|$?
(16)

22. Multiple Choice A store owner makes a pyramid-shaped display using a stack of
(16) soup cans. She arranges the cans so that the highest level of the stack has one
can. The second-highest level has four cans arranged in a square supporting the
top can. The third-highest level has nine cans arranged in a square that supports
the second-highest level. Which of the following expressions best represents the
number of cans in the lowest level of a display that is l levels high?

    A $3l$ **B** $4l$ **C** l^2 **D** l^3

23. Write a. What is the sign of the result when a negative value is cubed?
(5, 16)

    b. What is the sign of the result when the absolute value of an expression is
taken?

24. ⟮**Sites**⟯ Use the table to answer the questions.
(14)
    a. If a building is randomly chosen, what is
the probability that it is exactly 1250 feet
tall?

    b. What is the probability that a building
exactly 1046 feet tall is chosen?

    c. What is the probability that a building
that was built between 1960 and 1980 is
chosen?

Building	Height (ft)	Year Built
Sears Tower	1451	1974
Empire State Building	1250	1931
Aon Center	1136	1973
John Hancock Center	1127	1969
Chrysler Building	1046	1930
New York Times Building	1046	2007
Bank of America Plaza	1023	1992

25. Write What is a perfect square?
(13)

26. ⟮**Personal Finance**⟯ The expression $P(1 + i)^2$ can be used to find the value of
(9) an investment P after 2 years at an interest rate of i. What is the value of an
investment of \$500 deposited in an account with a 3% interest rate after 2 years?
(Hint: Remember to convert the percent to a decimal before calculating.)

27. ⟮**Racing**⟯ The formula for the cylindrical volume of an engine on a dragster is
(4) $\left(\frac{\pi}{4}\right)b^2 s$, where b is the inside diameter (the bore) and s is the distance that
the piston moves from its highest position to its lowest position (the stroke).
Following the order of operations, describe the steps you would take to simplify
the formula.

28. Justify What is the additive inverse of 12? Justify your answer.
(6)

29. Multi-Step Theater tickets cost \$14 dollars for adults, a, and \$8 for children,
(15) c. Additionally, each person who went to the theater on Thursday made a \$5
contribution to charity. Write an expression using the Distributive Property to
show the amount of money that the theater received on Thursday. Simplify the
expression.

30. Probability What is the probability that an ace will be chosen from a full deck of
(14) 52 playing cards? What is the probability of another ace being drawn if the first
ace drawn is not returned to the deck?

Graphing on a Coordinate Plane

Warm Up

1. Vocabulary The distance from a number to 0 on the number line is
(5) the _____.

Simplify.

2. $\left| 3 + (-5) - (-7) \right|$
(7)

3. $\left| 3 + (-5) + (-7) \right|$
(7)

4. $4(8 + c) + 5$
(15)

5. $5y^2 + 3x^4 - 5y^2 - 5x^4$
(18)

New Concepts

A **coordinate plane** is made of two perpendicular number lines, one horizontal and one vertical. The horizontal line is called the **x-axis,** and the vertical line is called the **y-axis.** The number lines divide the plane into four **quadrants,** numbered and named as shown. The intersection of the x- and y-axis is called the **origin.**

Math Language

Perpendicular lines intersect at right angles. The sides of a book are perpendicular. They intersect and form a right angle at the corner of the book.

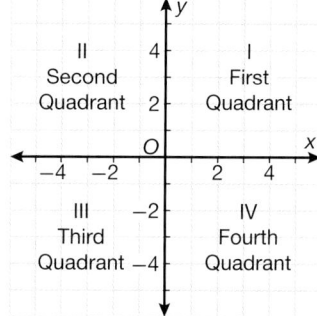

Each point on the coordinate plane is identified by an **ordered pair,** or two numbers in parentheses, separated by a comma. An ordered pair is written as follows: (x, y). The ordered pair that represents the origin is $(0, 0)$.

The first number in an ordered pair is called the **x-coordinate** and indicates the distance to the right or left of the origin. The second number, the **y-coordinate,** is the distance above or below the horizontal axis. A **coordinate** is a number that helps locate a point on a graph.

To find or graph a point, always start at the origin. Then use the sign of the coordinate to determine the location of the point.

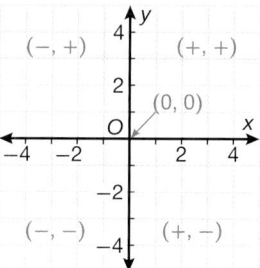

Online Connection
www.SaxonMathResources.com

Example 1   Graphing Ordered Pairs on a Coordinate Plane

Graph each ordered pair on a coordinate plane. Label each point.

a. $(4, 2)$

SOLUTION

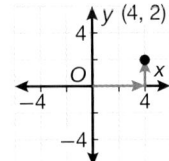

Point $(4, 2)$ is located in the first quadrant, 4 units to the right of the origin and 2 units above the horizontal axis.

b. $(-3, 0)$

SOLUTION

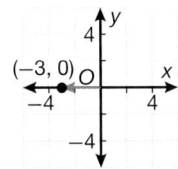

Point $(-3, 0)$ is on the x-axis. It is located 3 units to the left of the origin.

When there is a relationship between two variable quantities, one variable is the independent variable and the other is the dependent variable.

Variables
Independent variable: The variable whose value can be chosen. Also called the input variable.
Dependent variable: The variable whose value is determined by the input value of another variable. Also called the output value.

The dependent variable always depends on what value is chosen for the independent variable.

Example 2   Identifying Independent and Dependent Variables

For each pair of variables, identify the independent variable and the dependent variables.

a. number of traffic violations, cost of auto insurance

SOLUTION

independent variable: number of traffic violations; dependent variable: cost of auto insurance

The cost of auto insurance depends upon the number of traffic violations.

b. electric bill total, kilowatts of electricity used

SOLUTION

independent variable: kilowatts of electricity used; dependent variable: electric bill total

Electric bills are based, or dependent, on the electricity usage. The kilowatts of electricity determine the electric bill total.

A solution to an equation with two variables is an ordered pair that makes the equation true. There are infinite solutions to the equation $y = 4x + 2$. Solutions can be found by substituting values for the independent variable, x, to find the corresponding value of the dependent variable, y.

Example 3 Determining the Dependent Variable

Complete the table for the equation $y = 4x + 2$.

x	y
-2	
0	
2	
$\frac{3}{4}$	

Caution

Be sure to use the order of operations when simplifying either side of an equation.

SOLUTION

Substitute the x-values into the equation to determine the y-values.

First substitute -2 for x in the equation.

$y = 4x + 2$ Write the equation.

$y = 4(-2) + 2$ Substitute -2 for x.

$y = -8 + 2$ Evaluate.

$y = -6$

One solution to the equation is the ordered pair $(-2, -6)$.

Math Reasoning

Generalize How are the independent and dependent variables graphed on the coordinate plane?

Then substitute the other values to complete the table.

$x = 0$

$y = 4x + 2$

$y = 4(0) + 2$

$y = 0 + 2$

$y = 2$

$x = 2$

$y = 4x + 2$

$y = 4(2) + 2$

$y = 8 + 2$

$y = 10$

$x = \frac{3}{4}$

$y = 4x + 2$

$y = 4\left(\frac{3}{4}\right) + 2$

$y = 5$

The completed table shows the ordered pairs for the given values of x.

x	y
-2	-6
0	2
2	10
$\frac{3}{4}$	5

Values are assigned to the variable x. The value of the variable y is dependent on the value chosen for the variable x.

Example 4 Application: Wages

The federal minimum wage is about $5 per hour. The total on a minimum-wage worker's paycheck is dependent on the number of hours worked. The paycheck total can be calculated using the equation $y = 5x$.

Find the pay for 1, 3, 5, and 8 hours of. Make a graph to represent the equation $y = 5x$.

SOLUTION

Understand Since a worker makes $5 per hour, a worker's pay is calculated by multiplying the number of hours worked by 5.

Plan Find the amount of pay, y, when x is equal to 1, 3, 5, and 8 hours. Then graph the ordered pairs.

Solve Substitute 1, 3, 5, and 8 for x.

$y = 5x$	$y = 5x$	$y = 5x$	$y = 5x$
$y = 5(1)$	$y = 5(3)$	$y = 5(5)$	$y = 5(8)$
$y = 5$	$y = 15$	$y = 25$	$y = 40$

The pay for 1, 3, 5, and 8 hours is $5, $15, $25, and $40 respectively.

The ordered pairs are $(1, 5)$, $(3, 15)$, $(5, 25)$, and $(8, 40)$.

Graph the ordered pairs. Connect the points with a smooth line.

Check As the number of hours increases; so does the pay. The pay should increase steadily, which is shown by the straight line on the graph.

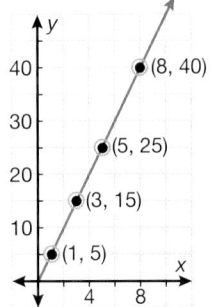

Math Reasoning

Predict How many hours would someone have worked if they are paid $122.50?

Lesson Practice

Graph each ordered pair on a coordinate plane. Label each point.
(Ex 1)

  a. $(0, 5)$ **b.** $(-1, -6)$

  c. $(-2, 0)$ **d.** $(-3, 4)$

  e. $(5, -1)$ **f.** $(2, -4)$

For each pair of variables, identify the independent variable and the dependent variable.
(Ex 2)

  g. the amount paid, the number of toys purchased

  h. the number of hours worked, the number of yards mowed

  i. Complete the table for the equation $y = 2x - 1$.
(Ex 3)

x	-3	-2	-1
y			

j. (**Fundraising**) The prom committee raises money for the prom by selling
(Ex 4) flowers. The money earned for the prom is dependent on the number of
flowers sold. Money earned is represented by the equation $y = 3x - 75$.

Find the amount of money raised when 25, 50, 75, and 100 flowers
are sold. Make a graph to represent the equation $y = 3x - 75$.

Practice   Distributed and Integrated

Simplify.

1. $(+3) + (-14)$
(5)

2. $4xyz - 3yz + zxy$
(18)

3. $3xyz - 3xyz + zxy$
(18)

Solve.

4. $x - 4 = 10$
(19)

5. $x + \dfrac{1}{5} = -\dfrac{1}{10}$
(19)

*6. Graph the ordered pair $(3, -4)$ on a coordinate plane.
(20)

*7. Graph the ordered pair $(0, 5)$ on a coordinate plane.
(20)

*8. **Multiple Choice** Which ordered pair is associated
(20) with point Z?

    A $(3, 0)$ **B** $(0, 3)$

    C $(-3, 0)$ **D** $(0, -3)$

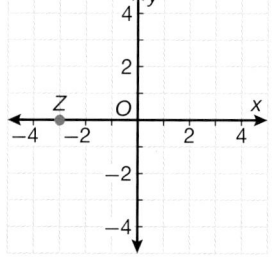

*9. (**Babysitting**) Ellen charges \$3 plus \$1 per child for an hour of
(20) babysitting. To determine her hourly rate, she uses the formula
$r = 3 + c$, where r is the rate and c is the number of children
Complete the table and graph the solutions.

c	r
1	
2	
3	
4	

*10. (**Reading**) Thomas read 10 pages in a book before starting his
(20) speed-reading lessons. After his lessons, he could read 3 pages
per minute. The equation $y = 3x + 10$ calculates the total
number of pages read after x minutes. Complete the table.

x	y
15	
20	
30	
50	

*11. Error Analysis Two students completed an x/y chart for the equation $y = 3 + 2x$ to
(20) find a solution to the equation. Which student is correct? Explain the error.

Student A	**Student B**

Student A

x	y
2	10

$y = 3 + 2(2)$
$y = 5(2)$
$y = 10$
$(2, 10)$ is a solution.

Student B

x	y
2	7

$y - 3 + 2(2)$
$y = 3 + 4$
$y = 7$
$(2, 7)$ is a solution.

*12. Multi-Step For a lemonade stand, profit depends on
(20) the number of cups sold. Profit is represented by
the equation $y = x - 5$, where x is the number of
cups sold and y is the profit in dollars.

x	5	10	20	50
y				

a. Complete the table and graph the solutions.

b. How would you find the profit if 30 cups were sold?

13. Geometry The triangle has a perimeter of 24 centimeters. Find the value for x.
(19)

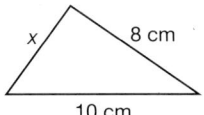

8 cm
10 cm

*14. Multi-Step To climb to the highest observation deck in the Empire State Building,
(19) you have to walk up 1860 steps. Starting at the lowest step, a security guard walks
up $\frac{1}{4}$ the total number of steps during his morning rounds. At the end of his
afternoon rounds, he stands on the 310th step. How many steps did he walk down
during the afternoon rounds?

*15. Error Analysis Two students simplify the expression $5x^2 + 7x^2$. Which student is
(18) correct? Explain the error.

Student A	**Student B**
$12x^2$	$12x^4$

16. Write Why do mathematicians use symbols rather than words?
(17)

17. Multiple Choice Which equation demonstrates the Associative Property of
(12) Addition?

A $6 - 3c = 3c - 6$ **B** $c^3 - 6 = c^3 + 6$

C $(6 - c)^3 = (c - 6)^3$ **D** $(6 + c^3) - 4 = 6 + (c^3 - 4)$

18. Evaluate each of the following expressions when $a = 2$.
(16) **a.** a^2 **b.** $-a^2$ **c.** $-a^3$ **d.** $(-a)^3$ **e.** $|(-a)^2|$

19. Analyze A school is holding a blood drive. If 3 students out of the 50 who give
(14) blood are Type A, what is the probability that a randomly selected student is
Type A? Write the probability as a decimal.

20. Evaluate $\sqrt{441} + \sqrt{1089}$.
(13)

21. Analyze Use an example to show that the Associative Property holds true for multiplication.
(12)

22. Statistics Use the data in the table to find the average yearly change in the deer population during a five-year period.
(11)

Deer Population

Year	Decrease in Number of Deer
2000	10
2001	7
2002	9
2003	10
2004	12

23. (Stocks) A Stock Market Report shows the value of stocks in points. The value of the stock is determined by the number of points. If a stock is at $79\frac{5}{7}$ points and it drops 3 points, what is the value of stock?
(10)

24. (Nutrition) One hundred grams of honey contains about 0.3 grams of protein. How many milligrams is 0.3 grams of protein?
(8)

25. (Tiling) A contractor lays patterned tile floors. He often begins with a polygon and makes diagonal lines that pass from corner to corner of the polygon. He uses the following expression $\frac{n^2 - 3n}{2}$, where n equals the number of sides of the polygon to find the number of diagonal lines for any given polygon.
(7)

  a. Find the number of diagonals for a hexagon.

  b. Model Check your work by drawing the diagonals in a hexagon.

26. Write and simplify a mathematical expression that shows "fourteen minus the quotient of three squared and the sum of three plus six."
(4)

27. Verify Indicate whether each statement is true or false. If the statement is false, explain why.
(2)

  a. The coefficient of x in the expression $x + 3$ is 3.

  b. The factors of the expression $\frac{2mn}{5}$ are $\frac{2}{5}$, m, and n.

28. Name the coefficient(s), variables, and number of terms in the expression $b^2 - 4ac$.
(2)

29. Multi-Step Pencils cost ten cents and erasers cost five cents.
(17)

  a. Write an expression to represent the total number of school supplies purchased.

  b. Write an expression to represent how much the supplies cost in cents.

*30. Analyze A person runs 5 miles per hour. The equation $d = 5t$ tells how far the person has run in t hours. Make a table when $t = 0, 1, 2,$ and 4 hours. Graph the ordered pairs in a graph and connect all the points. What do you notice?
(20)

Graphing a Relationship

A graph is a visual representation of how data change and relate to each other. A graph can convey the numeric relationship between data like time and distance.

Beach Trip Maria takes a trip to the beach. She stays at the beach all day before driving back home. As Maria drives to the beach, her distance from home increases. While she is at the beach, there is no change in her distance from home. As she returns home, her distance from home decreases.

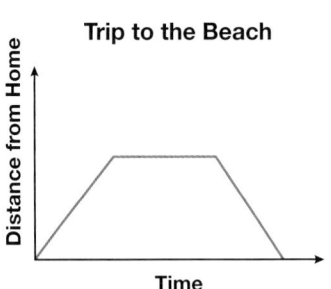

Trip to the Beach

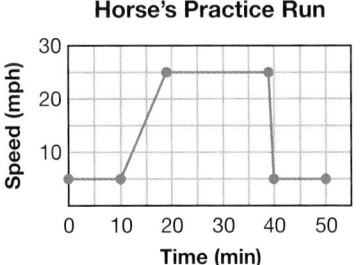

Horse's Speed The graph shows the various speeds at which a horse travels.

Horse's Practice Run

Online Connection
www.SaxonMathResources.com

1. **Analyze** Use the graph to complete the table. Describe the horse's speed in each of the time intervals as increasing, no change, or decreasing.

Interval	Description
0 to 10 minutes	
10 to 18 minutes	
18 to 38 minutes	
38 to 40 minutes	
40 to 50 minutes	

Math Reasoning

Analyze How does the increase in the horse's speed compare to the decrease in its speed? Explain.

You can use a graph to show how data change. When drawing a graph to represent a real-world situation,

- choose appropriate intervals for the units on the axes;
- be sure to space the intervals equally;
- only use values that make sense, such as positive numbers of books or whole numbers of people.

(Cost of Pecans) Customers at a local grocery store pay $3.00 per pound for pecans. They can purchase the pecans in fractions of a pound.

   2. Justify Should the graph representing this situation display negative values for pounds of pecans? Explain.

   3. Estimate What is a reasonable maximum number of pounds to graph?

   4. What is the cost of purchasing 1 pound of pecans? 4.5 pounds?

   5. Draw a graph to represent the situation.

The cost-per-pound data modeled in the graph are continuous. Continuous data are data where numbers between any two data values have meaning. A graph of this data is drawn with a solid line. A **continuous graph** is a graph that has no gaps, jumps, or asymptotes.

Data that involve a count of items, such as a number of people, are called **discrete data.** A **discrete graph** is made up of separate, disconnected points determined by a set of discrete data.

Math Reasoning

Analyze Identify the dependent and independent variables. Explain

(Photography) A sheet of photos at an automatic photo booth costs $5. Patrons may purchase only full sheets of photos. The photo booth can print up to 10 sheets per patron.

   6. Predict What will the graph look like?

   7. What is the least number of photo sheets for purchase? The greatest number of sheets?

   8. Draw a graph that represents the situation.

   9. Write Use the graph to describe Maura's hike on Windy Hill. In the description, use the phrases increasing, no change, and decreasing.

Caution

The phrases increasing, no change, and decreasing describe the elevation of the hiker, not the speed.

Windy Hill Hike

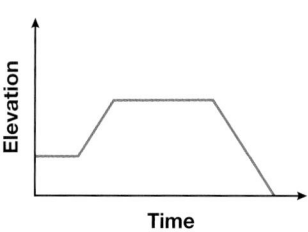

A graph represents the relationship between two quantities. The "Windy Hill Hike" graph shows the relationship between a hiker's time and altitude.

   10. Analyze Describe another set of data that could be related to the hiker's time.

Many quantities can be measured and compared, such as a plane's traveling speed and its altitude.

(Air Travel) A commercial airplane travels at 600 miles per hour and typically flies at a height of about 6 miles. The graph shows the flight time and the altitude of an airplane.

   11. What is the plane's altitude at the beginning and end of its 6-hour trip? Explain.

Plane's Altitude

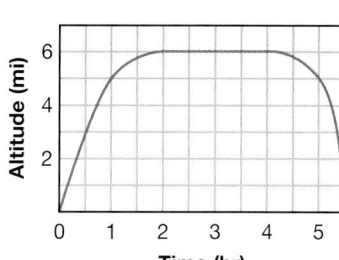

12. **Write** Describe the plane's flight in the first and last hour of the trip.

13. **Write** Explain why the graph of the plane's flight is relatively flat between 2 and 4 hours of the flight.

Investigation Practice

Graph each situation. Indicate whether the graph is continuous or discrete. Then describe the graph as increasing, no change, and/or decreasing.

a. Boxes of greeting cards sell for $5 a box. Income is calculated based on the number of boxes sold.

b. A scuba diver dives to a depth of 100 feet below sea level, then spends some time exploring the aquatic life at that level. The diver then descends to 250 feet below sea level for the remainder of the dive. (Hint: Assume the diver descends about 100 ft per 5 minutes.)

c. A driver brakes as she approaches an intersection. She stops to watch for traffic and pedestrians. The driver continues when the way is clear.

d. **Multiple Choice** The temperature of an ice cube increases until it starts to melt. While it melts, its temperature stays constant. Which graph best represents the situation?

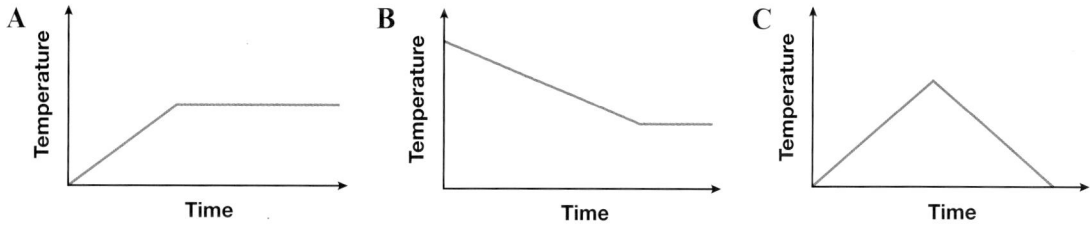

Describe the shape of the graph representing each situation.

e. **Write** A rocket is launched into orbit and, in time, returns to Earth. The graph relates time to the rocket's distance from Earth.

f. **Write** The ink in a printer is used until the ink cartridge is empty. The graph relates time used to the amount of ink in the cartridge.

g. **Write** An employee of a delivery service earns $3 for every package she delivers. The graph shows the employee's total earnings based on the number of packages delivered.

Solving One-Step Equations by Multiplying or Dividing

Warm Up

1. **Vocabulary** In the equation $5x = 10$, x is the _____. (*variable*, *coefficient*)
(2)

2. Multiply $\frac{4}{5}$ and $\frac{1}{2}$. Give the answer in simplest form.
(11)

3. Divide $\frac{3}{4}$ by $\frac{1}{2}$. Give the answer in simplest form.
(11)

4. Evaluate $8n + 2$ for $n = 0.5$.
(9)

5. **Multiple Choice** Which is the solution?
(19)

$5 + x = 7$

A 12   **B** 7

C 5   **D** 2

New Concepts

To find the solution of an equation, isolate the variable by using inverse operations. You must use the same inverse operation on each side of the equation.

Math Language

An **inverse operation** undoes another operation.

Inverse Operations
Add ⟷ Subtract
Multiply ⟷ Divide

Multiplication and Division Properties of Equality
Multiplication Property of Equality
Both sides of an equation can be multiplied by the same number, and the statement will still be true.
Examples $\quad 2 = 2 \qquad\qquad\qquad\qquad\qquad a = b$ $\qquad\qquad\quad 3 \cdot 2 = 3 \cdot 2 \qquad\qquad\quad a \cdot c = b \cdot c$ $\qquad\qquad\qquad 6 = 6 \qquad\qquad\qquad\qquad ac = bc$
Division Property of Equality
Both sides of an equation can be divided by the same number, and the statement will still be true.
Examples $\quad 10 = 10 \qquad\qquad\qquad\qquad\qquad a = b$ $\qquad\qquad\quad \dfrac{10}{2} = \dfrac{10}{2} \qquad\qquad\qquad \dfrac{a}{c} = \dfrac{b}{c}(c \neq 0)$ $\qquad\qquad\qquad 5 = 5$

Online Connection
www.SaxonMathResources.com

Using Inverse Operations

Copy and complete each table. Find the value of x by using the given values for the expression. Then explain how you found the values in the first column.

a.

x	$\dfrac{60}{x}$
	1
	2
	3
	4
	5
	6

b.

x	$4x$
	8
	20
	32
	36
	48
	60

c. **Justify** Is 20 a solution of the equation $\dfrac{60}{x} = 3$? Explain.

d. **Justify** Is 7 a solution of the equation $4x = 54$? Explain.

Example 1 **Solving Equations by Multiplying**

Solve each equation. Then check the solution.

a. $\dfrac{x}{6} = 8$

b. $-11 = \dfrac{1}{4}w$

Hint

Inverse operations "undo" each other. Multiplying by 6 "undoes" dividing by 6.

Math Reasoning

Verify Show that dividing both sides of the equation by 5 or multiplying both sides of the equation by $\frac{1}{5}$, will result in the same solution.

SOLUTION

$$\dfrac{x}{6} = 8$$

$$6 \cdot \dfrac{x}{6} = 8 \cdot 6 \quad \text{Multiplication Property of Equality}$$

$$x = 48$$

Check Substitute 6 for x.

$$\dfrac{48}{6} \overset{?}{=} 8$$

$$8 = 8 \checkmark$$

SOLUTION

$$\dfrac{4}{1} \cdot -11 = \dfrac{4}{1} \cdot \dfrac{1}{4}w \quad \text{Multiplication Property of Equality}$$

$$-44 = w \quad \text{Simplify.}$$

Check Substitute -44 for w.

$$-11 = \dfrac{1}{4}w$$

$$-11 \overset{?}{=} \dfrac{1}{4}(-44)$$

$$-11 = -11 \checkmark$$

Example 2 Solving Equations by Dividing

Solve each equation. Then check the solution.

a. $5x = 20$

SOLUTION

$$5x = 20$$

$$\frac{5x}{5} = \frac{20}{5} \qquad \text{Division Property of Equality}$$

$$x = 4 \qquad \text{Simplify.}$$

Check Substitute 4 for x.

$$5x = 20$$

$$5(4) \overset{?}{=} 20$$

$$20 = 20 \quad \checkmark$$

b. $-12 = 3n$

SOLUTION

$$-12 = 3n$$

$$-\frac{12}{3} = \frac{3n}{3} \qquad \text{Division Property of Equality}$$

$$-4 = n \qquad \text{Simplify.}$$

Check Substitute -4 for n.

$$-12 = 3n$$

$$-12 \overset{?}{=} 3(-4)$$

$$-12 = -12 \quad \checkmark$$

c. $\dfrac{2}{5}p = 7$

SOLUTION

$$\frac{2}{5}p = 7$$

$$\left(\frac{2}{5} \div \frac{2}{5}\right)p = \left(7 \div \frac{2}{5}\right) \qquad \text{Divide both sides by } \frac{2}{5}.$$

$$\left(\frac{\overset{1}{\cancel{2}}}{\cancel{5}} \cdot \frac{\overset{1}{\cancel{5}}}{\cancel{2}}\right)p = \left(7 \cdot \frac{5}{2}\right) \qquad \text{Divide by multiplying by the reciprocal of } \frac{2}{5}, \text{ which is } \frac{5}{2}.$$

$$p = \frac{35}{2}$$

Check Substitute $\frac{35}{2}$ for p.

$$\left(\frac{\overset{1}{\cancel{2}}}{\cancel{5}}\right)\left(\frac{\overset{7}{\cancel{35}}}{\cancel{2}}\right) \overset{?}{=} 7$$

$$7 = 7 \quad \checkmark$$

Write equations to solve real-world problems.

Example 3 **Application: Architecture**

Anita is an architect. She is designing a rectangular room that has an area of 126 square feet. If the length of the room is 12 feet, what is its width?

Understand

The answer will be the width of the room in feet.

List the important information:

- The room is a rectangle.
- The area is 126 square feet.
- The length is 12 feet.

Plan

To find the area of a rectangle, multiply the length by the width.

Solve

$$A = lw \qquad \text{Write the formula.}$$

$$126 = 12w \qquad \text{Substitute 126 for } A \text{ and 12 for } l.$$

$$\frac{126}{12} = \frac{12w}{12} \qquad \text{Division Property of Equality}$$

$$10\frac{6}{12} = w \qquad \text{Simplify.}$$

The width will be $10\frac{1}{2}$ feet.

Check

Area of a rectangle = length × width

$$126 \stackrel{?}{=} 12 \times 10\frac{1}{2}$$

$$126 = 126 \quad \checkmark$$

Lesson Practice

Solve each equation. Then check the solution.

a. $\frac{k}{9} = 3$
(Ex 1)

b. $-20 = \frac{1}{5}m$
(Ex 1)

c. $8y = 24$
(Ex 2)

d. $-15 = 3x$
(Ex 2)

e. $\frac{3}{4}y = 11$
(Ex 2)

f. $8 = -\frac{5}{12}n$
(Ex 2)

g. A rectangular pond has an area of 140 square feet. If the length of the pool is 16 feet, what is its width?
(Ex 3)

*1. **(Safety)** For every 4 feet a ladder rises, the base of the ladder should be placed
(21) 1 foot away from the bottom of a building. If the base of the ladder is 7 feet from
the bottom of a building, find the height the ladder rises up the building?

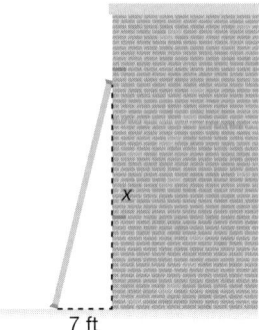

7 ft

2. What is a term of an algebraic expression?
(2)

*3. **Write** Explain how to use inverse operations to solve $\frac{2}{3}x = 8$.
(21)

*4. **(Physics)** In physics equations, a change in a quantity is represented by the delta
(19) symbol, Δ. A change in velocity, Δv, is calculated using the equation $\Delta v = v_f - v_i$,
where v_i is the initial velocity and v_f is the final velocity. If a cart has an initial
velocity of 5 miles per second and experiences a change in velocity of 2 miles
per second, what is the final velocity of the cart?

5. Graph the ordered pair $(-2, 6)$ on a coordinate plane.
(20)

6. **Geometry** The length of a rectangular picture frame is 3 times the width.
(3) **a.** Draw a picture of the picture frame and label the dimensions.

b. Write an expression for the area of the frame.

7. Complete the table for $y = 2x + 7$.
(20)

x	-5	1	4
y			

*8. Solve $\frac{x}{3} = 5$.
(21)

*9. **Multiple-Choice** Which step can you use first to solve $-\frac{x}{9} = -52$?
(21) **A** Multiply both sides by $\frac{1}{9}$.

B Multiply both sides by -9.

C Divide both sides by -52.

D Divide both sides by 52.

*10. **Estimate** Alan makes \$1 for each snow cone he sells. Alan calculates his profit
(19) by subtracting the daily cost of \$195 to run the stand from the total amount he
makes on the snow cones that he sells each day. How many snow cones does Alan
need to sell to make a profit of \$200 a day?

11. Write Explain which terms in $3z^2y + 2yz - 4y^2z - z^2y + 8yz$ can be combined.
(18)

12. (Astronomy) The relative weight of an object on the surface of Jupiter can be found
(9) using $2.364w$, where w is the weight of the object on Earth. The space shuttle weighs about 4,500,000 pounds on earth. What would be the weight of the space shuttle on Jupiter?

13. Geometry The length of a frame is 8 inches. Let w be the width of the frame.
(20) The formula $A = 8w$ calculates the area of backing needed for a framed picture. Complete the table and graph the solutions.

w	A
2	
4	
6	
8	

14. Simplify $-4 - 3 + 2 - 4 - 3 - 8$.
(6)

15. Multiple Choice Simplify $5p + 7 - 8p + 2$.
(18)   **A** $9 - 3p$ **B** $3p - 9$ **C** $13p + 5$ **D** $13p - 9$

16. Verify Evaluate $\frac{2}{3}\left(4 + \frac{3}{4}\right)$ using two different methods. Verify the solution of each
(15) method.

17. Probability A letter of the alphabet is randomly chosen. What is the probability
(14) that the letter is a vowel?

18. Justify The area of a square is 100 square feet, what is the length of each side?
(13) Explain.

19. Measurement A picture framer calculates the amount of materials needed
(12) using $2l + 2w$. If the framer used $2w + 2l$, would the results be the same? Explain.

*20. Multi-Step Alda's school is 1200 yards from her house. She walks 150 yards
(20) per minute. The equation $y = 1200 - 150x$ represents how far she will be from the school after x minutes.
   a. Complete the table and graph the solutions.

x	y
1	
4	
6	
8	

   b. What does it mean to say that after 8 minutes, she is 0 yards from the school?

*21. Analyze A student says that to solve $-\frac{3}{4}x = 12$ you should divide each side
(21) by $-\frac{3}{4}$. Another student says that to solve the equation you should multiply each side by $-\frac{4}{3}$. Will both methods result in the correct solution? Explain.

22. Multi-Step Determine whether $4^3 \cdot \left(\frac{1}{4}\right)^3 = 1$.
$_{(3)}$

    a. Simplify the expressions 4^3 and $\left(\frac{1}{4}\right)^3$.

    b. Write an expression for the multiplication of 4^3 and $\left(\frac{1}{4}\right)^3$ without using exponents. Then check to see if the product of the expressions is 1.

23. Write Will dividing two integers ever produce an irrational number? Explain.
$_{(1)}$

24. Analyze If a student is converting from 225 square units to 22,500 square units, what units of measure is he or she most likely converting?
$_{(8)}$

25. (Golf) A round of golf takes 4.5 hours and each hole takes 0.25 hours. In the equation $y = 4.5 - 0.25x$, x is the number of holes played and y is the remaining time to finish the round. Make a table for 4, 8, 12, and 16 holes and then graph the ordered pairs in your table.
$_{(20)}$

26. Simplify $-|15 - 5|$.
$_{(5)}$

*27. (Pricing) One fruit stand has s strawberries and k kiwis to sell. Another stand has twice as many strawberries and four times as many kiwis to sell.
$_{(18)}$

    a. Write expressions representing the number of strawberries and kiwis each stand has to sell.

    b. Write an expression for the total number of pieces of fruit.

*28. Sketch a graph to represent the following situation: A tomato plant grows at a slow rate, and then grows rapidly with more sun and water.
$_{(Inv\ 2)}$

29. Write an algebraic expression for "0.21 of what number is 7.98?"
$_{(17)}$

30. Error Analysis Two students solve $x - 5 = 11$. Which student is correct? Explain the error.
$_{(19)}$

Student A	Student B
$x - 5 = 11$	$x - 5 = 11$
$\underline{+5 = +5}$	$\underline{-5 = -5}$
$x \quad = 16$	$x \quad = 6$

Analyzing and Comparing Statistical Graphs

Warm Up

1. **Vocabulary** The set of real numbers includes all _____ numbers and
(1) all _____ numbers.

Name the point on the number line that corresponds to each given value.
(SB 1)

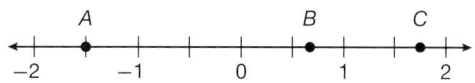

2. −1.5   3. 1.75   4. $\frac{2}{3}$

5. Find the difference between 12.3 million and 20,000.
(7)

New Concepts

Numerical data can be displayed in different ways. **Bar graphs** use vertical and horizontal bars to represent data.

Exploration Analyzing Bar Graphs

A sample survey asked students to name their favorite type of pet. The results are shown in the bar graph.

Math Reasoning

Predict If 1000 students are surveyed, how many are likely to pick dogs as their favorite pets?

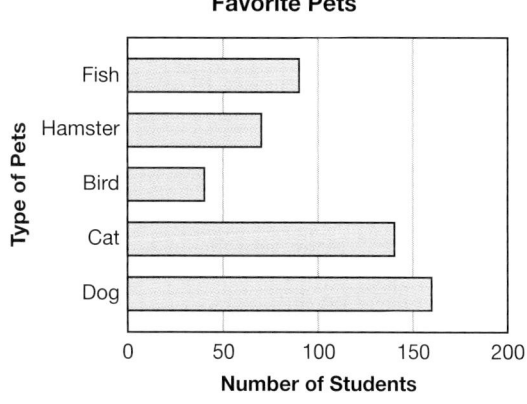

a. What information is shown on the vertical axis? the horizontal axis?

b. Use the graph to complete the table.

Pet	Dog	Cat	Bird	Hamster	Fish
Number of Students					

c. How many students were surveyed?

Online Connection
www.SaxonMathResources.com

d. **Analyze** Which pet did students choose twice as often as the hamster? Explain.

A **double-bar graph** shows groups of two bars side by side. This allows easier comparison of two related sets of data.

Example 1 Interpreting Double-Bar Graphs

Sal and Harry both own sandwich shops. The double-bar graph shows the number of shops they owned at the end of each year. What conclusions can be made from the graph?

Sandwich Shops

SOLUTION

- Harry always had more shops open than Sal, except in 2004, when they both had the same number of shops open.

- The number of shops Harry owned increased from the years 2001 to 2006.

- The number of shops Sal owned increased from the years 2001 to 2004, but decreased from the years 2004 to 2006.

A **stem-and-leaf plot** is a data display that uses some digits as "stems" and others as "leaves." The "stems" have a greater place value than the "leaves." Stem-and-leaf plots are useful for organizing and ordering data.

Example 2 Interpreting Stem-and-Leaf Plots

The stem-and-leaf plot shows the ages of members of a hiking club.

Find the age of members at the hiking club that occurs most often.

SOLUTION Look at the key. The stems represent tens and the leaves represent ones. So 3|2 represents 3 tens 2 ones, which is 32.

The data set:

10, 10, 17, 24, 26, 32, 33, 34, 41, 41, 41, 43, 53, 56, 56, 59

41 is the data value that occurs most often.

The age that occurs most often is 41 years.

Age of Hiking Club Members

Stem	Leaf
1	0 0 7
2	4 6
3	2 3 4
4	1 1 1 3
5	3 6 6 9

Key: 1|0 means 10

In a **line graph,** a line is drawn through points on a grid to show trends and changes in data over time. As with bar graphs, two related data sets can be compared in a **double-line graph.**

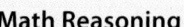

Example 3 Interpreting Line and Double-line Graphs

The double-line graph shows the same data as the double-bar graph in Example 1.

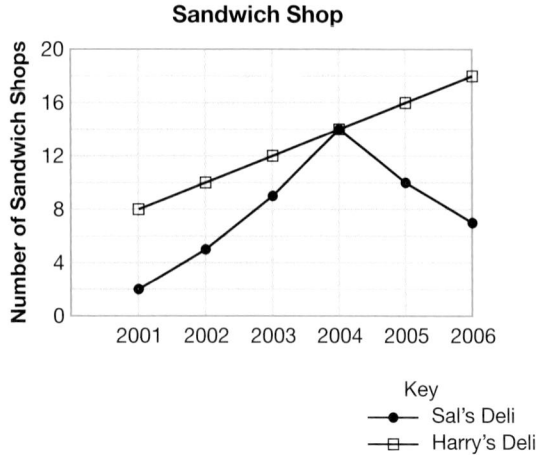

Sandwich Shop

What conclusions can you make from each graph?

SOLUTION

- Sal had fewer sandwich shops than Harry in 2001, but in 2004 they both had the same number of sandwich shops.

- The graph of Harry's shops is a straight line that shows a steady increase in the number of shops each year.

- Harry had 6 more shops than Sal in 2001, they both had 14 shops in 2004, and Harry had 11 more shops than Sal in 2006.

Math Reasoning

Predict If the number of shops Harry owns increases at the same yearly rate, how many shops will he own in 2010?

Example 4 Comparing Data using Double-Bar Graphs

The table shows Andre's bank account transactions.

Month	January	February	March	April	May	June
Deposits	$475	$200	$350	$425	$500	$150
Withdrawals	$100	$275	$350	$400	$200	$225

Make a graph to compare the deposits and withdrawals.

SOLUTION Use a double-bar graph to compare the deposits and withdrawals.

- The graph shows that the deposits were greater than the withdrawals in January, April, and May.

- The withdrawals were greater than the deposits in February and June.

- Andre deposited and withdrew the same amount of money in March.

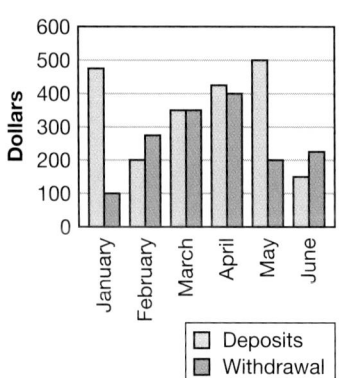

A **circle graph** uses sections of a circle to compare parts of the circle to the whole circle. The whole circle represents the entire set of data.

Example 5 Application: Yearly Sales

The circle graph shows Art Online's total yearly sales by quarter. The total amount of sales for the year was $20 million. Find the sales for each quarter.

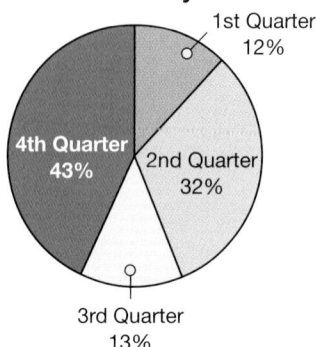

Art Online Yearly Sales

1st Quarter 12%
2nd Quarter 32%
3rd Quarter 13%
4th Quarter 43%

Caution

Circle graphs are sometimes labeled with actual data values instead of percents. Always check the labels and keys of a graph.

SOLUTION

Multiply the percent of sales for each quarter by the total amount for the year.

1st Quarter: $12\% \times 20$ million $= 0.12 \times 20$ million $= 2.4$ million
2nd Quarter: $32\% \times 20$ million $= 0.32 \times 20$ million $= 6.4$ million
3rd Quarter: $13\% \times 20$ million $= 0.13 \times 20$ million $= 2.6$ million
4th Quarter: $43\% \times 20$ million $= 0.43 \times 20$ million $= 8.6$ million

Check Find the sum of the amounts calculated for each quarter.

$2,400,000 + 6,400,000 + 2,600,000 + 8,600,000 = 20,000,000$

Lesson Practice

a. Use the double-bar graph in Example 1. What year shows the greatest difference between the number of shops Sal and Harry owned?
(Ex 1)

b. Use the double-line graph in Example 3. What was the greatest number of shops Sal opened in one year?
(Ex 3)

c. Make a stem-and-leaf plot of the data showing the height in inches of grandchildren in the Jackson family: 56, 52, 68, 49, 49, 40, 72, 71, 43, 54. What height occurs most often?
(Ex 2)

d. Use the data in Example 4. Which month shows the greatest difference between deposits and withdrawals?
(Ex 4)

e. **Predict** Use the circle graph from Example 5. If first quarter sales the next year are $3,000,000, predict the total sales for the year.
(Ex 5)

*1. True or False: A stem-and-leaf plot can help analyze change over time. If false,
(22) explain why.

2. Complete the table for $y = -3x - 9$.
(20)

x	-1	0	1
y			

3. Simplify $2p(xy - 3k)$.
(15)

4. Solve $y - 3 = 2$.
(19)

*5. Solve $x - \dfrac{1}{4} = \dfrac{7}{8}$.
(19)

6. Solve $4x = 2\dfrac{2}{3}$.
(21)

7. Solve $7x = 49$.
(21)

*8. Choose an appropriate graph to display the change in profit of a company over
(22) several years. Explain your choice.

9. Verify Determine whether each statement below is true or false. If false, provide a
(1) counterexample.

 a. The set of integers is closed under division.

 b. The set of irrational numbers is closed under division.

 c. The set of integers is closed under addition.

*10. (Racing) The table shows the Indianapolis 500 fastest lap times to the nearest
(22) second, every 5 years since 1960. Make an appropriate graph to display the
data. Then make a conclusion about the data.

Fastest Lap Times in the Indianapolis 500

Year	1960	1965	1970	1975	1980	1985	1990	1995	2000	2005
Time (seconds)	62	57	54	48	47	44	40	40	41	39

11. Graph the ordered pair $(-4, -1)$ on a coordinate plane.
(20)

12. Error Analysis Two students plotted the point $(-4, 3)$. Which student is correct?
(20) Explain the error.

Student A

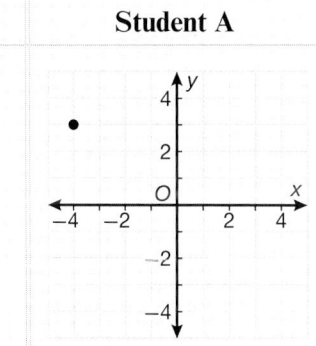

Student B

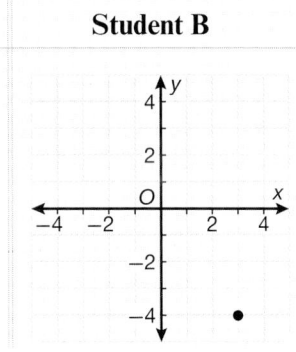

13. Multiple Choice A baker needs 25 eggs for all the cakes she plans to bake. She only
₍₁₉₎ has 12 eggs. If x is the number of eggs she will buy to complete her ingredients list,
which of the following equations best represents how she can find x?

A $12 - x = 25$ **B** $12 + x = 25$ **C** $25 + x = 12$ **D** $x - 12 = 25$

*14. Analyze For the equation $x = 14 - y$, what must be true of each value of x if y is
₍₁₉₎ **a.** greater than 14?

b. equal to 14?

c. less than 14?

*15. Multiple Choice Which graph would best compare the ages of people living in
₍₂₂₎ two different cities?

A circle graph **B** stem-and-leaf plot

C double-line graph **D** double-bar graph

16. (Travel) A man travels 25 miles to work. On his way home, he stops to fill up
₍₁₇₎ with gas after going d miles. Write an expression to represent his distance
from home.

17. Verify Show that each equation is true for the given values of x and y.
₍₁₆₎
a. $x\left(\dfrac{y}{y-x}\right)^2 = -\dfrac{4}{9}$; $x = -4$ and $y = 2$ **b.** $|(x-y)^3| = 27$; $x = -1$ and $y = 2$

18. Write What is a sample space?
₍₁₄₎

*19. (Endangered Animals) The table shows the number of threatened or endangered
₍₂₂₎ animal species as of July 22, 2007. Make an appropriate graph to display the data.
Then make a conclusion about the data.

Number of Threatened or Endangered Species in the U.S. and Foreign Countries

	Mammals	Birds	Reptiles	Amphibians	Fish	Clams	Snails	Insects	Arachnids	Crustaceans
U.S.	81	89	37	23	139	70	76	57	12	22
Foreign	276	182	81	9	12	2	1	4	0	0

20. Generalize Use the pairs of equations. What can be concluded about the Commutative
₍₁₂₎ Property?

$9 - 5 = 4$ and $5 - 9 = -4$

$12 - 6 = 6$ and $6 - 12 = -6$

$7 - 3 = 4$ and $3 - 7 = -4$

21. (Landscape Design) Wanchen is planting a garden the shape of a trapezoid in
₍₄₎ her yard. Use the diagram to find the area of her garden.

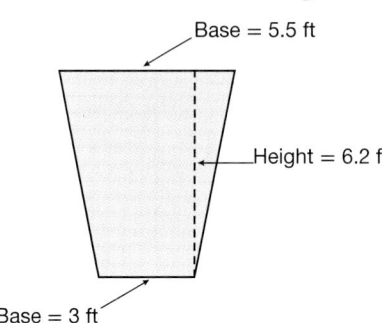

Base = 5.5 ft

Height = 6.2 ft

Base = 3 ft

22. Simplify $-7 + (-3) + 4 - 3 + (-2)$.
(6)

 *23. **Geometry** An arc of a circle is a segment of the circumference of a circle. If
(21) an arc measures 16 inches and is $\frac{4}{9}$ the circumference of a circle, what is the
circumference of the circle?

24. **Multi-Step** A house has an area of 1200 square feet. The owners add on a new
(4) room that is 15 feet long and 20 feet wide. What is the area of the house now?
  a. Write an expression to represent the area of the new room.

  b. Write an expression to represent the total area of the house now.

  c. Find the area of the house now.

25. **Write** Describe a situation that could be represented by the expression $2d - w$.
(9)

26. Simplify $3ab^2 - 2ab + 5b^2a - ba$.
(18)

 *27. The circle graph shows the result of a poll on the sleeping habits of children ages
(22) 9–12. What portion of the children said they slept the recommended $9\frac{1}{2}$ to $10\frac{1}{2}$
hours for their age group? Express the answer as a decimal rounded to the nearest
hundredth.

Sleeping Habits

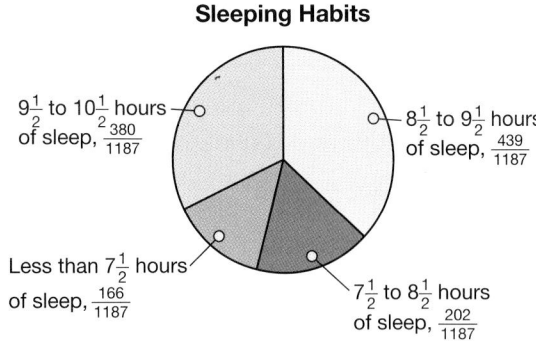

28. Simplify x^2yyyx^3yx.
(3)

*29. **Multi-Step** Enrique pays $31.92 (not including tax) for 6 books that are on sale. Each
(21) book costs the same amount. Enrique pays $\frac{4}{5}$ of the original cost of the books.
  a. What is the sale price of each book?

  b. What was the original cost of each book?

 30. **Probability** In a standard deck of cards, there are 13 cards in each
(Inv 1) of four suits: hearts, diamonds, clubs, and spades. Jose randomly
draws a card from a deck and replaces it after each draw. His
results are recorded in the table. Find the experimental probability
of each event.
  a. drawing a heart

  b. not drawing a club

Outcome	Frequency
Hearts	8
Diamonds	8
Clubs	6
Spades	4

Solving Two-Step Equations

Warm Up

1. Vocabulary In the equation $-5x = 20$, -5 is the _____
(2)
(*variable*, *coefficient*).

Simplify.

2. $3(x - 4)$
(15)

3. $-2(x - 3) + 4(x + 1)$
(18)

4. Evaluate $\frac{3}{4}n + \frac{5}{6}$ for $n = \frac{2}{9}$.
(9)

5. Multiple Choice What is the solution of $-7 + x = 14$?
(19)
A -2

B 2

C 7

D 21

New Concepts

If an equation has two operations, use inverse operations and work backward to undo each operation one at a time.

To reverse the order of operations:

• First add or subtract.

• Then multiply or divide.

Example 1 **Evaluating Expressions and Solving Equations**

(a.) Evaluate $3x - 2$ for $x = 4$.

SOLUTION Substitute 4 for x and use the order of operations.

$3(4) - 2$ Multiply first.

$12 - 2 = 10$ Then subtract.

(b.) Solve $3x - 2 = 10$.

SOLUTION Reverse the order of operations.

$$3x - 2 = 10$$
$$\underline{+\ 2 = +\ 2} \quad \text{Undo the subtraction by adding.}$$
$$3x = 12$$
$$\frac{3x}{3} = \frac{12}{3} \quad \text{Undo the multiplication by dividing.}$$
$$x = 4$$

Online Connection
www.SaxonMathResources.com

Example 2 — Solving Two-Step Equations with Positive Coefficients

Solve the equation. Then check the solution.

$$4x + 5 = 17$$

SOLUTION To isolate x, first eliminate 5 and then eliminate the 4.

$$4x + 5 = 17$$

$\underline{-5 = -5}$	Subtraction Property of Equality
$4x = 12$	Simplify.
$\dfrac{4x}{4} = \dfrac{12}{4}$	Division Property of Equality
$x = 3$	

Check Substitute 3 for x in the original equation.

$$4(3) + 5 \stackrel{?}{=} 17$$
$$12 + 5 \stackrel{?}{=} 17$$
$$17 = 17 \quad ✓$$

Math Reasoning

Write Explain why the first step in checking the solution is to multiply by 4 and the last step in solving the equation is to divide by 4.

Example 3 — Solving Two-Step Equations with Negative Coefficients

Solve the equation. Then check the solution.

$$8 = -5m + 6$$

SOLUTION To isolate m, first eliminate the 6 and then eliminate the -5.

$$8 = -5m + 6$$

$\underline{-6 = \qquad -6}$	Subtraction Property of Equality
$2 = -5m$	Simplify.
$\dfrac{2}{-5} = \dfrac{-5}{-5}m$	Division Property of Equality
$-\dfrac{2}{5} = m$	Simplify.

Check Substitute $-\frac{2}{5}$ for m.

$$8 \stackrel{?}{=} -5\left(-\frac{2}{5}\right) + 6$$
$$8 \stackrel{?}{=} 2 + 6$$
$$8 = 8 \quad ✓$$

Example 4   Solving Two-Step Equations with Fractions

Math Language

When you multiply a number by its **reciprocal,** the product is 1.

$\frac{2}{1} \cdot \frac{1}{2} = 1$

Solve the equation. Then check the solution to see if it is reasonable.

$$\frac{1}{2}n - \frac{1}{3} = \frac{3}{4}$$

SOLUTION

To isolate n, first eliminate the $\frac{1}{3}$ and then eliminate the $\frac{1}{2}$.

$$\frac{1}{2}n - \frac{1}{3} = \frac{3}{4}$$

$$\underline{+\frac{1}{3} = +\frac{1}{3}} \qquad \text{Addition Property of Equality}$$

$$\frac{1}{2}n = \frac{13}{12} \qquad \text{Simplify.}$$

$$\frac{2}{1} \cdot \frac{1}{2}n = \frac{13}{12} \cdot \frac{2}{1} \qquad \text{Multiplication Property of Equality}$$

$$n = \frac{13}{6} \qquad \text{Simplify.}$$

Estimate to verify that the solution is reasonable.

$\frac{13}{6}$ is about 2. Substitute 2 for n. $\frac{1}{2}$ of 2 is 1.

$\frac{1}{3}$ subtracted from 1 is $\frac{2}{3}$, which is close to $\frac{3}{4}$.

So, the solution $\frac{13}{6}$ is reasonable.

Example 5   Application: Fitness

Caution

Read the problem carefully. The number of months is unknown, but the question asks for the number of years.

A gym charges a $90 fee plus $30 per month. Another gym charges a fee of $1500. How many years will it take for the charges at the first gym to reach $1500?

SOLUTION Write an expression to represent the total cost at the first gym.

monthly cost	times	the number of months	plus	the membership fee
30	$\cdot$	x	$+$	90

Use the expression to write an equation equal to the total cost of $1500.

$$30x + 90 = 1500$$

$$\underline{-90 = -90} \qquad \text{Subtraction Property of Equality}$$

$$30x = 1410 \qquad \text{Simplify.}$$

$$\frac{30}{30}x = \frac{1410}{30} \qquad \text{Division Property of Equality}$$

$$x = 47 \qquad \text{Simplify.}$$

47 months is about 4 years. It will take about 4 years for the total charges at the first gym to reach $1500.

a. Justify Which step would you use first to evaluate $9y + 6$ for $y = 2$? Explain.
(Ex 1)

b. Justify Which step would you use first to solve $9y + 6 = 24$? Explain.
(Ex 1)

Solve each equation. Then check the solution.

c. $8w - 4 = 28$
(Ex 2)

d. $-10 = -2x + 12$
(Ex 3)

e. Solve $\frac{1}{8}m + \frac{3}{4} = \frac{7}{12}$. Then check the solution to see if it is reasonable.
(Ex 4)

f. (**Energy Conservation**) The Green family conserves energy by using energy-efficient bulbs. They pay \$125 for energy-efficient bulbs. If the family saves \$7 per month on their electricity bill, and the power company gives them a rebate of \$25, in about how many months will they have paid for the bulbs?
(Ex 5)

Practice Distributed and Integrated

1. Evaluate $(x - y) - (x - y)$ for $x = 3.5$ and $y = 2.5$.
(9)

2. Write Explain how to graph the point $(-2, 4)$.
(20)

*3. Multiple Choice What is the value of x in the equation $3x + 5 = 32$?
(23)

   A 24 **B** 9 **C** 81 **D** $12\frac{1}{3}$

4. Error Analysis Two students solve $-12x = -72$. Which student is correct? Explain the error.
(21)

Student A	Student B
$-12x = -72$	$-12x = -72$
$-\dfrac{12x}{12} = -\dfrac{72}{12}$	$\dfrac{-12x}{-12} = \dfrac{-72}{-12}$
$x = -6$	$x = 6$

*5. (**Altitude**) A plane increases altitude by 350 meters every minute. If the plane started at an altitude of 750 meters above sea level, what is the plane's altitude after 6 minutes?
(17)

6. Verify Is $x = 9$ the solution for $3x - 8 = 22$? Explain. If false, provide a correct solution and check.
(23)

7. Justify Find a counterexample to the following statement: A rational number that is not an integer, such as $\frac{3}{5}$, multiplied by any integer will produce a rational number that is not an integer.
(1)

*8. Multi-Step Three hundred people were surveyed as they left a movie theater.
(22) They were asked which type of movie they like best. The circle graph shows the survey results.

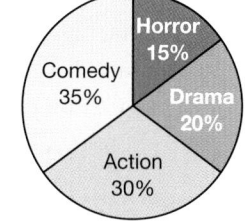

a. Which type of movie was most popular?

b. How many people liked horror movies the best?

c. How many more people liked action movies than dramas?

*9. Choose an appropriate graph to display the number of different types of DVDs
(22) sold at two video stores. Explain your answer.

*10. A class of 20 students answered a survey about their favorite places to go on
(22) vacation. Use the data in the table to make a bar graph.

Beach	Amusement Park	Mountains	Museums
5	8	3	4

*11. Geometry A circle has a circumference of $\frac{8}{9}\pi$ meters. What is the radius of
(21) the circle?

12. Multiple Choice Which equation has solutions that are represented by the
(21) graphed points?

A $y = 2x + 1$

B $y = 2x + 3$

C $y = -2x$

D $y = -2x - 1$

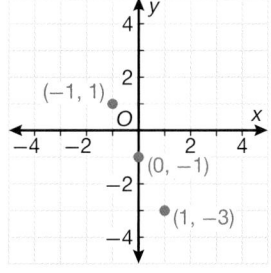

13. ⬭Coins Jenny and Sam took the coins out of their pockets. Jenny has x quarters
(7) and y dimes. Sam has h half dollars and z nickels.

a. Write expressions representing the value of the coins, in cents, in each person's pocket.

b. Write an expression for the total number of cents they have.

14. Verify "12 more than the product of x and 3" can be written as $3x + 12$ or
(17) $12 + 3x$. Substitute 2 for x and show that the expressions are equivalent.

15. Use $>$, $<$, or $=$ to compare the expressions.
(7)
$$24 + \frac{16}{4} - (4 + 3^2) \cdot 2 \ \bigcirc \ 24 + \left(\frac{16}{4} - 4\right) + 3^2 \cdot 2$$

Solve.

16. $y - \frac{1}{2} = -2\frac{1}{2}$ ***17.** $2x + 3 = 11$
(19) (23)

*18. $3x - 4 = 10$ ***19.** Solve $2.2x + 2 = 8.6$
(23) (23)

*20. Statistics A basketball player attempted 1789 free throws. He made 801 of them.
$(Inv\ 1)$ What is the probability that the player will make the next shot he attempts? Write the probability as a decimal rounded to the nearest hundredth.

21. (**Presidential Facts**) Many of our first 43 U.S. Presidents had the same
(14) first name. Use the table.

    a. If a U.S President is chosen at random, what is the theoretical
       probability of choosing one whose name is George?

    b. What is the probability of choosing one whose name is William
       or John?

    c. What is the probability of choosing a president whose name is not
       shown in the table?

Names	Number of Presidents
James	6
John	4
William	4
George	3

22. (**Carpentry**) Alice wants to add a square porch to the back of her house. The area of
(13) the porch is 361 square feet. What is the length of each side of the porch?

23. (**Meteorology**) The highest temperature ever recorded at the South Pole is −13.6°C.
(11) The lowest temperature is about 6 times lower than the highest temperature
recorded. Approximately what is the lowest temperature recorded?

24. Model On Monday the low temperature was −4°F. The temperature rose 21°F to
(5) the high temperature for that day. What was the high temperature on Monday?
Use a number line or thermometer to model the addition.

25. Multi-Step Paula's bank statement showed the following transactions for last month.
(5) The beginning balance was $138.24. There was a withdrawal of $46.59, then a
deposit of $29.83, plus $1.87 in interest added. What was the balance after these
transactions?

26. Simplify $4 \div 2 + 6^2 - 22$.
(4)

27. Write Explain how to simplify $a^3b^2ac^5a^4b$.
(3)

28. Convert 332 meters per second to centimeters per second.
(8)

29. Multiple Choice In 2000, the U.S. economy gained $111,349 million from the sale of
(10) goods exported to Mexico. However, the U.S. economy lost $135,926 million from
the sale of goods imported from Mexico. What was the U.S. balance of trade with
Mexico in the year 2000?

    A $247,275 million

    B $24,926 million

    C $1.2 million

    D −$24,577 million

30. Probability Describe each of the following events as impossible, unlikely, as likely
(Inv 1) as not, likely, or certain.

    a. Tanisha buys a new pair of shoes and the first shoe she pulls out of the box is
       for the left foot.

    b. Ralph rolls a number less than 7 on a standard number cube.

    c. November will have 31 days.

Solving Decimal Equations

Warm Up

1. **Vocabulary** If $10^3 = 1,000$, then $1,000$ is the third _____ of 10.
(3)
   A exponent   **B** base   **C** power   **D** factor

2. Write the numbers below in order from least to greatest.
(SB 1)

$$-2.85, \frac{5}{8}, 0.58, -0.8$$

3. Simplify $4x - 3x^2 + 7x$.
(16)

New Concepts

To write decimals as integers, multiply by a power of 10.

Example **1**   **Solving by Multiplying by a Power of 10**

Solve.

a. $8 + 0.5x = 10.5$

SOLUTION

$8 + 0.5x = 10.5$	
$10(8) + 10(0.5)x = 10(10.5)$	Multiply each term by 10.
$80 + 5x = 105$	Multiply.
$\underline{-80 \qquad -80}$	Subtraction Property of Equality
$5x = 25$	Simplify.
$\dfrac{5x}{5} = \dfrac{25}{5}$	Division Property of Equality
$x = 5$	Simplify.

b. $0.006a + 0.02 = 0.2$

SOLUTION

$0.006a + 0.02 = 0.2$	
$1000(0.006a) + 1000(0.02) = 1000(0.2)$	Multiply each term by 1,000.
$6a + 20 = 200$	Multiply.
$\underline{-20 \quad -20}$	Subtraction Property of Equality
$6a = 180$	Simplify.
$\dfrac{6a}{6} = \dfrac{180}{6}$	Division Property of Equality
$x = 30$	Simplify.

Hint

If the decimals are in the thousandths, hundredths, and tenths places, multiply by a power of 10 that will make the decimal with the least value an integer.
$0.006 \times 1000 = 6$

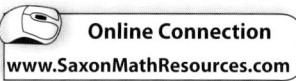
Online Connection
www.SaxonMathResources.com

A decimal equation can also be solved by using inverse operations without multiplying by a power of 10 first.

Example 2 Solving Two-Step Decimal Equations

Solve.

a. $0.2m + 0.8 = 1.8$

SOLUTION

$$0.2m + 0.8 = 1.8$$
$$\underline{-0.8 = -0.8} \qquad \text{Subtraction Property of Equality}$$
$$0.2m = 1 \qquad \text{Simplify.}$$
$$\frac{0.2m}{0.2} = \frac{1}{0.2} \qquad \text{Division Property of Equality}$$
$$m = 5 \qquad \text{Simplify.}$$

b. $-0.03n - 1.2 = -1.44$

SOLUTION

$$-0.03n - 1.2 = -1.44$$
$$\underline{+1.2 = +1.2} \qquad \text{Addition Property of Equality}$$
$$-0.03n = -0.24 \qquad \text{Simplify.}$$
$$\frac{-0.03n}{-0.03} = \frac{-0.24}{-0.03} \qquad \text{Division Property of Equality}$$
$$n = 8 \qquad \text{Simplify.}$$

Math Reasoning

Verify Are $0.2m + 0.8 = 1.8$ and $2m + 8 = 18$ equivalent equations? Explain.

Math Language

$\frac{1}{2}$ **of** $100 = \frac{1}{2} \times 100 = 50$

0.5 **of** $100 = 0.5 \times 100 = 50$

50% **of** $100 = 0.5 \times 100 = 50$

"Of" means to multiply.

Finding a decimal part of a number is the same as finding a fraction or percent of a number.

Example 3 Finding Decimal Parts of Numbers

0.48 of 86 is what number?

SOLUTION

decimal number	of	given number	is	what number
0.48	$\cdot$	86	$=$	n

$$0.48 \cdot 86 = n \qquad \text{Multiply.}$$
$$41.28 = n$$

Estimate the answer to see if it is reasonable.

0.48 is less than 0.50 or $\frac{1}{2}$.

$\frac{1}{2}$ of 86 is 43.

41.28 is close to 43, so the answer is reasonable.

Example 4 Application: Zoology

The height of an average mandrill (a large species of baboon) is 2.54 cm more than 12 times the length of its tail. If the height of a mandrill is 78.74 centimeters, then what is the length of its tail?

SOLUTION

height of mandrill = (12 times the tail length) plus 2.54 cm

Write and solve an equation to find the length of the mandrill's tail.

$$12t + 2.54 = 78.74$$

$$\underline{-2.54 = -2.54} \qquad \text{Subtraction Property of Equality}$$

$$12t = 76.20 \qquad \text{Simplify.}$$

$$\frac{12t}{12} = \frac{76.20}{12} \qquad \text{Division Property of Equality}$$

$$t = 6.35 \text{ cm} \qquad \text{Simplify.}$$

Check

$$12t + 2.54 = 78.74$$

$$12(6.35) + 2.54 \overset{?}{=} 78.74 \qquad \text{Substitute 6.35 for } t.$$

$$76.20 + 2.54 \overset{?}{=} 78.74 \qquad \text{Multiply.}$$

$$78.74 = 78.74 \ \checkmark \qquad \text{Add.}$$

The mandrill's tail is 6.35 cm long.

Hint

Draw a diagram to help visualize the problem.

Lesson Practice

Solve each equation.

a. $0.25 + 0.18y = 0.97$
(Ex 1)

b. $0.05 = 0.5 - 0.15q$
(Ex 1)

c. $-0.5n + 1.4 = 8.9$
(Ex 2)

d. 0.6 of 24 is what number?
(Ex 3)

e. (Highway Mileages) Use the diagram. The distance from Town A to Town C is 52.8 kilometers. What is the distance from Town B to Town C?
(Ex 4)

Practice Distributed and Integrated

1. Multiple Choice What is the solution of $\frac{4}{5}x = -24$ for x?
(21)

A -30 **B** $-\frac{96}{5}$ **C** $\frac{96}{5}$ **D** 30

2. Simplify $3(2x + 5x)$ using the two different methods shown below.
(18)
    a. Combine like terms, and then multiply.

    b. Distribute, and then combine like terms.

*3. Solve $0.45x - 0.002 = 8.098$.
(24)

*4. Justify If you multiply both sides of an equation by a constant c, what happens
(21) to the solution? Explain your answer.

*5. (Stock Market) An investor buys some stock at $6.57 a share. She spends $846.25
(24) which includes a transaction fee of $25. How many shares of stock did she buy?

*6. Multiple Choice 0.8 is 0.32 of what number?
(24)
    A 2.5   **B** 0.25   **C** 0.4   **D** 4

*7. Verify Solve $0.45x + 0.9 = 1.008$. Will both methods shown below result in the
(24) same solution? Verify by using both methods to solve.

    Method I: Multiply both sides of the equation by 1000 first.

    Method II: Subtract 0.9 from both sides first.

8. Identify the coefficient, the variable(s), and the number of terms in the
(2) expression $\frac{9}{5}C + 32$.

*9. Verify Solve $0.25x + \frac{1}{2} = 0.075$. Will both methods shown below result in the same
(24) solution? Explain.

    Method I: First write the fraction as a decimal.

    Method II: First write the decimals as fractions.

*10. Error Analysis Two students use the circle graph to find the total percent
(22) of students who have fewer than two siblings. Which student is correct?
Explain the error.

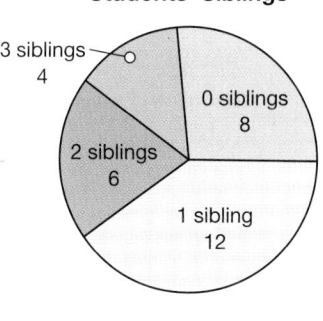

Students' Siblings

Student A	Student B
0 siblings or 1 sibling = 20 20% of the students	Total students: $8 + 12 + 6 + 4 = 30$ 0 siblings or 1 sibling = 20 $\frac{20}{30} \approx 67\%$ of the students

*11. Measurement The graph shows an estimation of the changes
(22) in the diameter of a tree, in inches, every 20 years. What
was the approximate circumference of the tree when the
tree was 100 years old? Use 3.14 for π. Round the answer
to the nearest tenth.

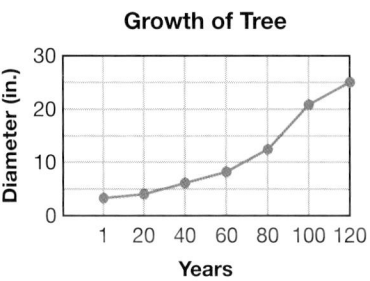

Growth of Tree

*12. The circle graph shows the amount of money Will spent on different snacks at
(22) a store. If Will spent \$12, how much money did he spend on each item?

Will's Spendings

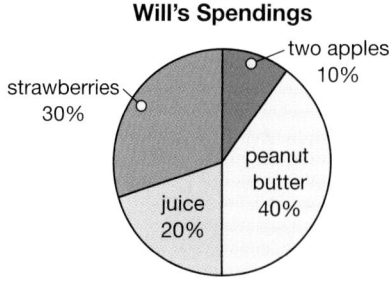

13. Graph the ordered pair on a coordinate plane (2, 1).
(20)

14. Probability A spinner is divided in equal sections and labeled as shown in
(16) the diagram.

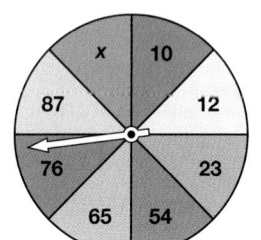

   a. If x is an even number, what is the probability the spinner will land on an even number?

   b. If x is an odd number, what is the probability the spinner will land on an odd number?

   c. If $x = 20$, what is the probability the spinner will land on a number less than 20?

15. Multi-Step Each camp counselor at Camp Wallaby walked 6 miles for a health and
(15) fitness activity. Each camper walked 2 miles. The camp leader paid \$0.50 into a
Fun Day account for every mile walked. Write an expression to represent the total
amount of money earned from walking by counselors and campers.

16. Verify Are the expressions below equivalent? Explain.
(9)
$$\left(11w^4 \cdot 3z^9\right)\left(2w^7z^2\right) \stackrel{?}{=} 66w^{11}z^{11}$$

17. (Contests) Miguel entered a contest offering prizes to the top 3 finishers. The
(14) probability of winning 1st is 12%, the probability of winning 2nd is 18%, and the
probability of winning 3rd is 20%. What is the probability that Miguel will not win
any prize?

18. (Retailing) Use the circle graph.
(14)
   a. What is the probability that a randomly chosen person who
purchased a shirt paid \$40.00 or more?

   b. What is the probability that a randomly chosen person who
purchased a shirt paid \$30 or less?

Shirt Sales

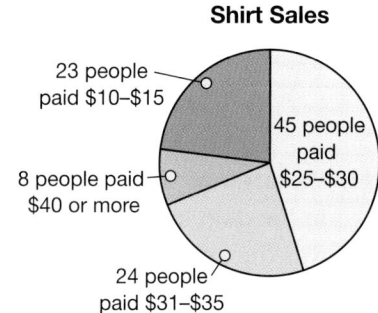

19. (Construction) To calculate the amount of fencing for a rectangular area, Kelvin
(12) uses the formula $P = 2(l + w)$. Bonnie uses the formula $P = 2(w + l)$. Will their
calculations of the perimeter be the same? Explain.

20. Write Explain how to simplify $\dfrac{4}{7} \div \left[\left(-\dfrac{3}{8}\right) \cdot \left(-\dfrac{8}{3}\right)\right]$.
(11)

21. Simplify $\frac{2}{5} \div \left(-\frac{7}{2}\right) \cdot \left(-\frac{5}{2}\right)$.
(4)

22. **Write** Explain why $k^2 \cdot m \cdot b^4 \cdot c^3$ cannot be simplified using the Product Rule
(3) of Exponents.

23. **Justify** Write the expression so there are no parentheses. Justify your change
(15) with a property. $6(ab + ef)$

24. **Generalize** Some real numbers can contain patterns within them, such as
(1) 21.12122122212222…
   a. Find a pattern in the number above. Is the pattern you found a repeating
   pattern?
   b. Is this number a rational number or an irrational number? Explain.

25. Convert 630 cubic centimeters to cubic inches. (Hint: 1 in. = 2.54 cm)
(8)

26. **Multi-Step** The temperature at 6 a.m. was 30°C. If the temperature increases by
(10) 2 degrees every half hour, what will the temperature be by 9 a.m.? What time will
   it be when the temperature is 50°C?

27. Simplify $-|10 - 7|$.
(5)

*28. (Internet Usage) The circle graph shows
(22) approximate total Internet usage in the world.
   a. The estimated number of Internet users
   worldwide is 1,154,358,778. About how
   many people in North America use the
   Internet?
   b. About how many more people use the Internet
   in Asia than in North America?

Internet Usage per Region

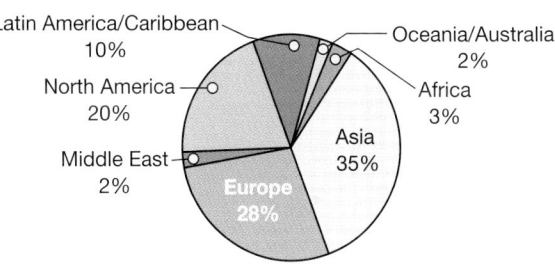

29. **Geometry** A small square park is 784 square yards. A row of trees was planted
(13) on one side of the park. One tree was planted at each corner. Then one tree was
   planted every seven yards between the corner trees. How many trees were planted
   in the row?

30. (Quality Control) Elite Style inspects 500 hair dryers manufactured and finds 495 to
(Inv 1) have no defects. There are 20,000 hair dryers in their warehouse.
   a. What is the experimental probability that a hair dryer will have no defects?
   b. Predict the number of hair dryers that will have no defects in the warehouse.

LESSON
25

Differentiating Between Relations and Functions

Warm Up

1. **Vocabulary** In the _____ (−5, 2), −5 is the _____ and 2 is the _____.
(20)

2. Simplify $(-4)^2 + 3^2 - 2^3$.
(3)

3. Find the value of y when $x = 8$.
(20)
$$5y = -3x - 6$$

4. Find the value of x when $y = -0.4$.
(24)
$$x - 8y = 1.6$$

5. **Multiple Choice** Jenny has n dollars in her savings account. If she deposits
(17) d dollars in her savings account each week, which expression represents the amount she will have in her savings account at the end of a year?
A $n + 52d$ **B** $52d - n$ **C** $n + d$ **D** $52n + d$

New Concepts

The **domain** is the set of possible values for the independent variable (input values) of a set of ordered pairs.

The **range** is the set of values for the dependent variable (output values) of a set of ordered pairs.

Math Language

In an ordered pair (*x*, *y*), *x* is the **independent variable** and *y* is the **dependent variable**.

A **relation** is a set of ordered pairs where each number in the domain is matched to one or more numbers in the range. Relations can also be represented using set notation, tables, diagrams, or equations.

Example 1   **Determining the Domain and Range of a Relation**

Give the domain and range of the relation.

$\{(2, 6), (2, 10), (8, 6), (5, 1), (4, 6), (3, 9)\}$

SOLUTION

Use a mapping diagram. Place the *x*-values in the oval on the left, and the *y*-values in the oval on the right.

The domain is all the *x*-values.

The range is all the *y*-values.

Domain: $\{2, 3, 4, 5, 8\}$

Range: $\{1, 6, 9, 10\}$

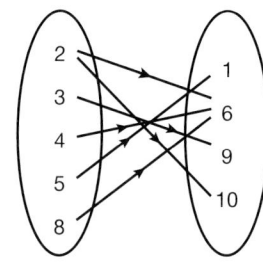

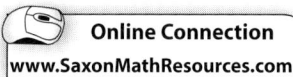
Online Connection
www.SaxonMathResources.com

A **function** is a mathematical relationship pairing each value in the domain with exactly one value in the range.

Hint

When you write the domain and range, only write 10 and 3 once.

Domain: {0, 3, 4, 8, 10}

Range: {1, 2, 3, 4, 9}

Example 2 Identifying a Set of Ordered Pairs as a Function

a. Determine whether $\{(3, 3), (10, 1), (0, 3), (8, 9), (4, 4), (10, 2)\}$ represents a function.

SOLUTION

Each domain value must map with exactly one range value.

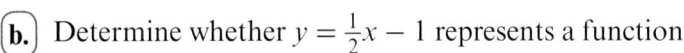

The diagram shows that the domain value of 10 maps to the range values 1 and 2.

The relation is not a function. Each domain value does not have exactly one range value.

b. Determine whether $y = \frac{1}{2}x - 1$ represents a function.

SOLUTION

No matter what value is substituted for the independent variable x, the equation outputs exactly one value for the dependent variable y.

Domain (x)	-6	0	2	5	7	10
Range (y)	-4	-1	0	$\frac{3}{2}$	$\frac{5}{2}$	4

The equation represents a function.

If a relation is graphed on a coordinate grid, the **vertical-line test** can be used to determine if the relation is a function.

Vertical-Line Test
A graph on the coordinate plane represents a function if any vertical line intersects the graph in exactly one point.

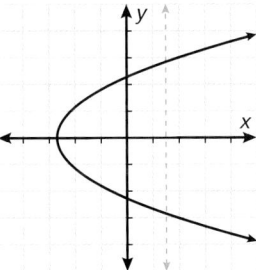

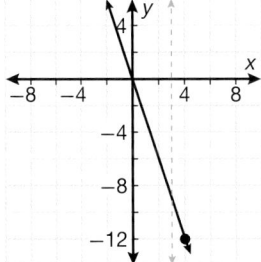

The relation is not a function. The vertical-line cuts the graph in more than one place.

The relation is a function. The vertical-line cuts the graph in exactly one place.

Example 3 | Identifying a Graph as a Function

Use the table. Graph the ordered pairs on a coordinate grid and determine whether the ordered pairs represent a function.

Domain (x)	Range (y)
-6	-4
0	-1
2	0
5	$\frac{3}{2}$
7	$\frac{5}{2}$

SOLUTION

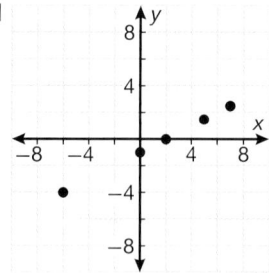

No matter what vertical line is drawn, the graph is intersected at only one point by each line. The ordered pairs represent a function.

In a function, the independent variable determines the value of the dependent variable. This means the dependent variable y is a function of the independent variable x. In terms of the variables, y is a function of x and can be written like the following example:

$$y = f(x)$$
$$y = 6x + 3$$
$$f(x) = 6x + 3$$

Example 4 | Writing a Function

a. Write $x + 2y = 5$ in function form.

SOLUTION

$x + 2y = 5$

$$y = -\frac{x}{2} + \frac{5}{2} \qquad \text{Solve for } y.$$

$$f(x) = -\frac{x}{2} + \frac{5}{2}$$

b. Food labels list the grams of fats, carbohydrates, and proteins in a single serving. Proteins convert to 4 calories per gram. Write a rule in function notation to represent the number of calories from protein.

SOLUTION

The number of calories depends on the number of grams of protein eaten.

dependent variable: number of calories

independent variable: number of grams of protein

Let p represent the number of grams of protein.

$$y = 4p$$

$$f(p) = 4p \qquad \text{Use function notation.}$$

Example 5 Application: Reading

A student reads an average of 25 pages per day while reading a 544-page novel. Write a rule in function notation to find the number of pages she has left to read at the end of any given day.

SOLUTION

Let d represent the days spent reading.

$25d$	number of pages read
$544 - 25d$	number of pages that have not been read

The number of pages left to read depends on the number of days the student has been reading.

$$y = 544 - 25d$$

$$f(d) = 544 - 25d \qquad \text{Use function notation.}$$

Math Reasoning

Write Does it make sense for d to be greater than 21? Explain.

Lesson Practice

a. Give the domain and range of the relation: $(1, 2)$; $(2, 1)$; $(4, 6)$; $(8, 5)$;
(Ex 1) $(7, 7)$; $(3, 10)$

b. Using a diagram, determine whether the ordered pairs represent a
(Ex 2) function. $\{(11, 12); (12, 1); (5, 5); (14, 10); (13, 7)\}$

c. Determine whether $y = 3x - 1$ represents a function.

d. Use the table. Graph the ordered pairs on a coordinate plane and
(Ex 3) determine whether the ordered pairs represent a function.

x	-1	0	1	-2	0
y	3	0	3	6	6

e. (Printing) A brochure costs \$0.07 per page to print. Write a rule in
(Ex 4) function notation to represent the cost of printing c copies of the brochure.

f. (Novelist) An author writes 30 pages per day. Write a function rule that
(Ex 5) the author can use to find how many pages she has left to write before reaching page 400.

Practice Distributed and Integrated

1. Solve $0.3 + 0.05y = 0.65$.
(24)

2. Verify Verify that the following solutions are correct for each equation given.
(19) **a.** $103 + x = 99$ when $x = -4$

b. $\frac{1}{2} - x = \frac{3}{4}$ when $x = -\frac{1}{4}$

*3. Make a table to determine whether $y = x + 2$ represents a function.
(25)

*4. **(Hiking)** A hiker can average 15 minutes per mile. Write a rule in function notation
(25) to describe the time it takes the hiker to walk m miles.

5. Subtract $3.16 - 1.01 - 0.11$.
(10)

*6. **Multiple Choice** Which set of ordered pairs represents a function?
(25)
 A $\{(1, 1); (2, 2); (3, 3); (4, 4)\}$

 B $\{(1, 0); (2, 1); (1, 3); (2, 4)\}$

 C $\{(1, 1); (1, 2); (1, 3); (1, 4)\}$

 D $\{(10, 1); (10, 2); (12, 3); (12, 4)\}$

*7. A square has a side length of s. Write a rule in function notation to represent the
(25) perimeter.

*8. **Generalize** If a set of ordered pairs is a function, are the ordered pairs also a relation?
(25) Explain.

*9. **Analyze** A student draws a circle on a coordinate plane. The center of the circle is
(25) at the origin. Is this circle a function or a relation? Explain.

*10. **(Photography)** A student is making a pinhole camera. What is the circumference of
(24) the pinhole in the box? Use 3.14 for π and round to the nearest hundredth.

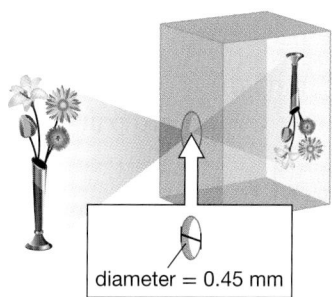

diameter = 0.45 mm

*11. **(Astronomical Unit)** An astronomical unit is the average distance from the Sun to
(8) the Earth. 1 AU (astronomical unit) is approximately equal to 93 million miles.
If Jupiter is about 5.2 AU from the Sun, about how many miles is it from
the Sun?

12. **Write** Describe a possible situation for the discrete graph.
(Inv 2)

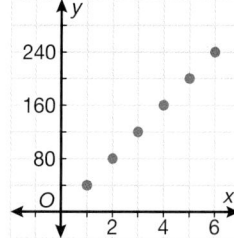

*13. **(Movie Club)** Stephen belongs to a movie club in which he pays an annual fee of
(23) $39.95 and then rents DVDs for $0.99 each. In one year, Stephen spent $55.79.
Write and solve an equation to find how many DVDs he rented.

14. **Error Analysis** Two students solve $5a + 4 = 34$. Which student is correct? Explain the error.
(23)

Student A	Student B
$5a + 4 = 34$	$5a + 4 = 34$
$\dfrac{5a + 4}{5} = \dfrac{34}{5}$	$\quad +4 \quad\ +4$
$a + \dfrac{4}{5} = \dfrac{34}{5}$	$5a = 38$
$a = \dfrac{34}{5} - \dfrac{4}{5}$	$a = \dfrac{38}{5}$
$a = \dfrac{30}{5}$	
$a = 6$	

15. **Multiple Choice** The graph shows the points scored by Michaela and Jessie during the first five basketball games of the season. What conclusion can you make from the graph?
(22)

  A Michaela is the best player on the team.

  B Michaela usually scores more points than Jessie.

  C Neither player will score more than 18 points in the next game.

  D Jessie does not play as much as Michaela.

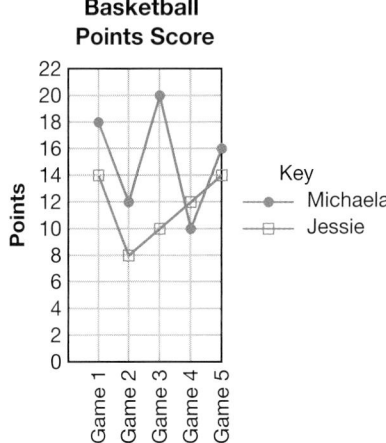

*16. **Write** Two sets of data represent the number of bottles of water and the number of bottles of juice a store sells each month. Give reasons why the following types of graphs would be appropriate to represent the data: a double-bar graph, a double-line graph, and two stem-and-leaf plots.
(22)

17. Choose an appropriate graph to display the portion of students in a class who have birthdays in each month. Explain your choice.
(22)

18. Find the value of $3z - 2(z - 1)^2 + 2$ for $z = 4$.
(9)

19. (Cooking) A recipe calls for 2.5 cups of orange juice for a batch of fruit drink. In the equation, $y = 2.5x$, y represents the number of cups of orange juice and x represents number of batches of fruit drink. Make a table when $x = 1, 2, 3$, and 4 batches of fruit drink. Then graph the ordered pair in your table.
(20)

20. **Analyze** "Three more than x" can be written as $x + 3$ or $3 + x$. Can "three less than x" be written as $x - 3$ or $3 - x$? Explain.
(17)

21. **Multi-Step** Population growth for a certain type of animal is determined by the formula $N_n = N_i 2^n$, where N_i is the initial population size and N_n is the population size after n generations. If the initial population is 45, what is the difference between the population size after the fourth generation and the population size after the sixth generation?
(16)

22. **(Architecture)** An architect is designing a very large square mall. Estimate the total
(13) area of the mall, if each side length is approximately 4890 feet.

23. **Write** True or False. The expression $12 - 8 - 2$ could be simplified using the
(12) Associative Property. Explain.

24. Solve $1\frac{1}{2}y = 6\frac{3}{4}$.
(21)

25. Solve $\frac{1}{8}m - \frac{1}{4} = \frac{3}{4}$.
(23)

26. **Verify** Determine if each statement below is true or false. If false, explain why.
(9)

    a. $\dfrac{(5 - x)^3 + 12}{(4x)} = \dfrac{41 - x}{x^3}$ for $x = 2$.

    b. $\dfrac{(5 - x)^3 + 12}{(4x)} = \dfrac{41 - x}{x^3}$ for $x = 3$.

27. **Measurement** The distance between City A and City C is 312.78 miles. City B lies on
(6) a point on a direct line between Cities A and C. If the distance between City C and
City B is 191.9 miles, what is the distance between Cities A and B?

28. **(Computer Engineering)** Eight bits, or 2^3 bits, equal one byte. How many bits are in 64,
(3) or 2^6, bytes?

29. **Geometry** The measure of the length of a rectangle is $4x - y$ feet and the
(15) width is xy. What expression would show the area of the rectangle? Explain.

30. Simplify $|-2 - 3| - 4 + (-8)$.
(6)

Solving Multi-Step Equations

Warm Up

1. **Vocabulary** The product of a number and its _____ is 1.
   (11)

2. Simplify $2x + 5y + 3x - 2y$ by adding like terms.
   (18)

3. Solve $2x + 5 = 12$. Check your solution.
   (23)

4. **Multiple Choice** Which is the solution of $3x + 6 = 33$?
   (23)

    A 13   **B** 9

    C 7   **D** 8

New Concepts

Equations that are more complex may have to be simplified before they can be solved. More than two steps may be required to solve them. If there are like terms on one side of an equation, combine them first. Then apply inverse operations and the properties of equality to continue solving the equation.

Example 1   Combining Like Terms

Solve $5x + 8 - 3x + 2 = 20$. Justify each step. Check the solution.

SOLUTION

> **Math Language**
>
> **Like terms** have the same variable(s) raised to the same power(s).

$$5x + 8 - 3x + 2 = 20$$

$5x - 3x + 8 + 2 = 20$	Commutative Property of Addition
$2x + 10 = 20$	Combine like terms.
$-10 = -10$	Subtraction Property of Equality
$2x = 10$	Simplify.
$\dfrac{2x}{2} = \dfrac{10}{2}$	Division Property of Equality
$x = 5$	Simplify.

Check Substitute 5 for x.

$$5x + 8 - 3x + 2 = 20$$
$$5(5) + 8 - 3(5) + 2 \stackrel{?}{=} 20$$
$$25 + 8 - 15 + 2 \stackrel{?}{=} 20$$
$$20 = 20 \checkmark$$

Complex equations can contain symbols of inclusion such as parentheses and brackets. Eliminate the symbols of inclusion first. Use the Distributive Property if multiplication is indicated by the symbols of inclusion. Then combine like terms on each side of the equation. Continue to solve the equation by applying inverse operations and the properties of equality.

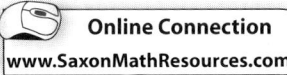
Online Connection
www.SaxonMathResources.com

Example 2 Using Distributive Property

Solve $x + 3(2x + 4) = 47$. Justify each step. Check the solution.

SOLUTION

$$x + 3(2x + 4) = 47$$
$$x + 6x + 12 = 47 \qquad \text{Distributive Property}$$
$$7x + 12 = 47 \qquad \text{Combine like terms.}$$
$$\underline{-12 = -12} \qquad \text{Subtraction Property of Equality}$$
$$7x = 35 \qquad \text{Simplify.}$$
$$\frac{7x}{7} = \frac{35}{7} \qquad \text{Division Property of Equality}$$
$$x = 5 \qquad \text{Simplify.}$$

Check Substitute 5 for x.

$$x + 3(2x + 4) = 47$$
$$5 + 3[2(5) + 4] \stackrel{?}{=} 47$$
$$5 + 3[10 + 4] \stackrel{?}{=} 47$$
$$5 + 3[14] \stackrel{?}{=} 47$$
$$47 = 47 \quad \checkmark$$

Math Reasoning

Write What is another way to eliminate the coefficient 7 from $7x$?

When equations contain symbols of inclusion and like terms, first apply the Distributive Property. Next, add like terms. Then apply inverse operations and the properties of equality to solve the equation.

Example 3 Simplifying before Solving

Solve $5x - (x - 3) - 1 = 18$. Justify each step. Check the solution.

SOLUTION

$$5x - (x - 3) - 1 = 18$$
$$5x - x + 3 - 1 = 18 \qquad \text{Distributive Property}$$
$$4x + 2 = 18 \qquad \text{Combine like terms.}$$
$$\underline{-2 = -2} \qquad \text{Subtraction Property of Equality}$$
$$4x = 16 \qquad \text{Simplify.}$$
$$\frac{1}{4} \cdot 4x = 16 \cdot \frac{1}{4} \qquad \text{Multiplication Property of Equality}$$
$$x = 4 \qquad \text{Simplify.}$$

Check Substitute 4 for x.

$$5x - (x - 3) - 1 = 18$$
$$5(4) - (4 - 3) - 1 \stackrel{?}{=} 18$$
$$20 - 1 - 1 \stackrel{?}{=} 18$$
$$18 = 18 \quad \checkmark$$

Caution

Remember to multiply by -1 when distributing a negative across parentheses.

┌─ **Example 4** **Application: Landscaping**

Jim is building a right triangular flower bed. One of the acute angles will measure twice the other acute angle. What are the measures of the two acute angles?

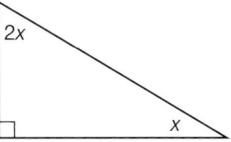

SOLUTION

$x + 2x + 90 = 180$	Sum of the angle measures
$3x + 90 = 180$	Combine like terms.
$\underline{-90 = -90}$	Subtraction Property of Equality
$3x = 90$	Simplify.
$\dfrac{3x}{3} = \dfrac{90}{3}$	Division Property of Equality
$x = 30$	Simplify.

The measures of the angles are 30° and 60°.

Lesson Practice

Solve. Justify each step. Check the solution.

a. $3x + 2 - x + 7 = 16$
(Ex 1)

b. $6(x - 1) = 36$
(Ex 2)

c. $5x - 3(x - 4) = 22$
(Ex 3)

 d. **Geometry** Juan is building a triangular shelf. He
(Ex 4) wants one angle to be a right angle and the other two angles to have the same measure. What are the measures of the angles?

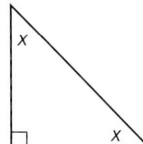

Practice Distributed and Integrated

*1. Solve for x in the equation $\frac{3}{4} + \frac{1}{2}x + 2 = 0$.
(26)

*2. **Multiple Choice** A vending machine will only accept quarters in change. What are
(25) the independent and dependent variables that describe the amount of money in change held by the vending machine?

A Independent variable: value of 1 quarter; dependent variable: number of quarters

B Independent variable: value of 1 quarter; dependent variable: value of the quarters

C Independent variable: value of the quarters; dependent variable: number of quarters

D Independent variable: number of quarters; dependent variable: value of the quarters

*3. Multiple Choice Which one of the expressions below can be simplified by combining
(18) like terms?

A $6(5x + 1)$ B $2x(3 + 8)$

C $7x + 5$ D $9x - 6y + 4$

4. A table shows temperature changes over a period of a week.
(22)   **a.** Why would a circle graph inaccurately display the data?

   b. Which type of graph would best display the data?

 *5. (Digital Technology) The average size for the memory storage of an mp3 player is
(26) 2 gigabytes (GB). The average size of an mp3 song is 5.5 megabytes (MB). About
how many songs can you store on a 2-gigabyte player if the player requires
16 megabytes for its own use? (Hint: 1gigabyte = 1024 megabytes)

 *6. Write Describe two different methods for solving $12(x + 7) = 96$.
(26)

*7. Justify Solve $-5(3x - 7) + 11 = 1$. Justify each step with an operation or property.
(26)

*8. Verify Draw the graph of a function. Check to see if your graph is truly a function.
(25)

*9. Use the graph. Determine whether the relation is a function.
(25)

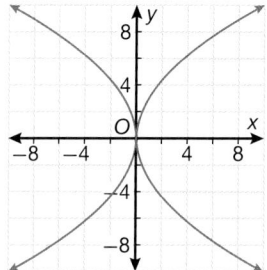

10. Solve $0.4m + 2.05 = 10.45$.
(24)

11. Error Analysis Two students solved $0.4x - 0.08 = 6.32$. Which student is correct?
(24) Explain the error.

Student A	Student B
$0.4x - 0.08 = 6.32$	$0.4x - 0.08 = 6.32$
$10(0.4x) - 100(0.08) = 100(6.32)$	$100(0.4x) - 100(0.08) = 100(6.32)$
$4x - 8 = 632$	$40x - 8 = 632$
$\underline{+8 \quad +8}$	$\underline{+8 \quad +8}$
$4x = 640$	$40x = 640$
$\dfrac{4x}{4} = \dfrac{640}{4}$	$\dfrac{40x}{40} = \dfrac{640}{40}$
$x = 160$	$x = 16$

12. Verify Is $x = 8$ a solution for $7x - 12 = 44$? Explain. If false, provide a correct
(23) solution and check.

*13. **Multi-Step** Emil cooks 64 hot dogs. He uses 5 packages of hot dogs plus 4 hot dogs
(23) left over from a meal earlier in the week. How many hot dogs are in each package?

  a. Write an equation to find the number of hot dogs in a package.

  b. Solve the equation, and then check the solution.

*14. **(Kangaroos)** A large kangaroo can travel 15 feet in each hop. Write and solve an
(21) equation to find how many hops it takes for the kangaroo to travel one mile.
  (Hint: 5,280 feet = 1 mile)

15. **Verify** Show that the graphed point is a solution to the equation $y = 2x + 9$.
(12)

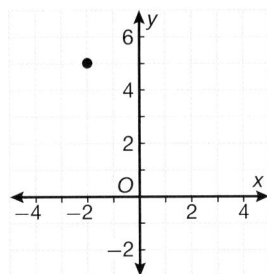

16. **Analyze** Determine whether $3p^2qd^3$ and $(2qdp \cdot -5d^2p)$ are terms that can be
(18) combined. Explain your reasoning.

17. **Probability** The probability of rain on Monday is a. It is twice as likely to
(17) rain on Tuesday. Write an expression to represent the probability of rain on
  Tuesday.

18. **(Biology)** A biologist wants to calculate the volume of a spherical cell. She uses the
(16) equation for the volume of a sphere, which is $V = \frac{4}{3}\pi r^3$. If the cell has a radius of
  2 micrometers, what is its volume? Use 3.14 for π and round to the nearest tenth.

19. **(Employment)** Jim manages a restaurant that is currently hiring employees. On
(14) Tuesday, he interviewed 2 waiters, 2 line cooks, 3 dishwashers, and 1 chef. On
  Thursday, he interviewed 2 waiters, 1 line cook, 2 dishwashers, and 3 chefs. What
  is the probability that a randomly selected person interviewed applied to be a
  waiter?

20. **Verify** Compare the following expression using $<, >, =$. Verify your answer.
(13)
  $$\sqrt{324} - \sqrt{144} \bigcirc \sqrt{400} - \sqrt{289}$$

21. Evaluate.
(7)
  $$\frac{6}{2}[5(3 + 4)]$$

22. **Model** Use a number line to model $-8 - (-4) - (-6)$. Then simplify the
(6) expression.

23. Simplify.
(4)
  $$2 \cdot (3 + 4)^2 + 15$$

24. Subtract $\dfrac{1}{4} - \dfrac{1}{3}$.
(10)

 25. Probability The probability of rolling a 4 on a six-sided number cube is $\dfrac{1}{6}$. To find
(3) the probability of rolling a 6-sided number cube and getting a 4 five times in a row, multiply the probability $\dfrac{1}{6}$ by itself five times. Write the answer using an exponent.

26. (**Investing**) To find the amount of money earned on a bank deposit that earns
(2) quarterly compounded interest, the formula $A = P\left(1 + \dfrac{r}{4}\right)^{4t}$ is used.

P = principal, (the amount originally deposited)

r = the interest rate

t = time in years.

a. How many terms are in $P\left(1 + \dfrac{r}{4}\right)^{4t}$?

b. How many variables are in $P\left(1 + \dfrac{r}{4}\right)^{4t}$?

c. What is the coefficient of t?

27. Identify the coefficient, the variable(s), and the number of terms in $\dfrac{1}{3}Bh$.
(2)

 28. Multi-Step The Noatak National Preserve in Alaska covers 6,574,481 acres. One
(8) acre is equal to 4840 square yards. What is the area of the preserve in square miles?

a. Find the area of the preserve in square yards.

b. Convert square yards to square miles. (Hint: 1 mile = 1760 yards)

29. Geometry To find the volume of a rectangular-prism shaped–
(12) sunscreen bottle, Jagdeesh uses the formula $V = lwh$. Betty uses
the formula $V = wlh$. Will the volume of the bottle be the same?
Explain.

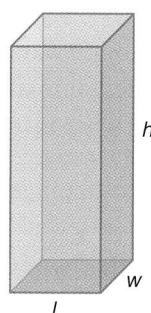

30. The spinner in a board game is divided into four equal sections colored blue, red,
(Inv 1) green, and yellow. Conduct a simulation using random numbers to determine the
number of times the spinner lands on blue in 30 spins. Use the random number
generator in a graphing calculator to simulate the spins.

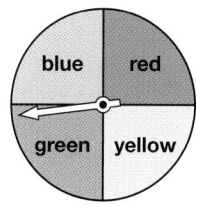

Identifying Misleading Representations of Data

1. **Vocabulary** A bar graph uses _____ to represent data.
(22)

2. True or False: A circle graph shows how data change.
(22)

3. Draw a graph that represents a flag being raised up a flagpole slowly at the
(Inv 2) beginning and quickly at the end.

4. Solve $2(2x + 3) = 24$.
(26)

New Concepts

When displaying data, components such as the scale or labels can make a graph misleading.

Example 1   **Identifying Misleading Line Graphs**

The line graph shows the number of members of a health club each month since it opened. Explain why the graph may be misleading.

Hint

When there is a large gap between data values, a graph may use a broken axis. In the graph showing memberships, the vertical axis has a broken scale.

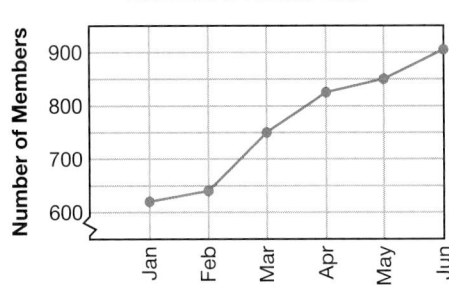

Number of Members at Renaldo's Health Club

SOLUTION Because the scale does not start at zero, the membership appears to have increased much more than it actually did.

Another characteristic that may create a misleading graph is the size of the increments in the scale.

Example 2   **Identifying Misleading Bar Graphs**

A radio station conducted a survey of music preferences of listeners. The bar graph shows the results. Explain why the graph may be misleading.

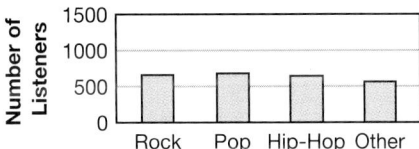

Listener Music Preferences

SOLUTION

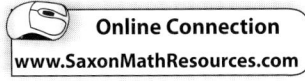

Online Connection
www.SaxonMathResources.com

The large increments of the scale make the data values appear to be closer than they actually are.

Example 3 Identifying Misleading Circle Graphs

The circle graph shows the number of some types of sandwiches a deli sells in one day. Explain why the graph may be misleading.

Sandwiches

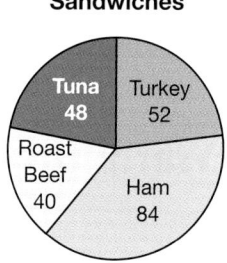

SOLUTION The title does not specify that these were the only sandwiches the deli sold, and it may not represent all categories. The deli may also have served a chicken salad or other type of sandwich, making the graph misleading.

Example 4 Application: Television Prices

An electronics store created the graph to show the average selling price of a television each year.

a. Explain why the graph may be misleading.

SOLUTION The large increments make the data values appear to be closer than they actually are.

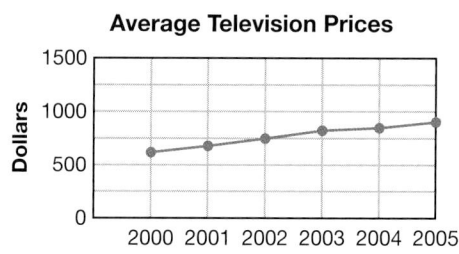

b. What conclusion might be made from the graph? Why might the store have created this graph?

SOLUTION The graph seems to show that the prices have not increased much over the past five years. The store may want it to appear as though prices have not increased significantly; when in reality they have actually increased by almost 50 percent.

c. Make a graph of the sales data that is not misleading.

SOLUTION Use a broken axis and smaller increments.

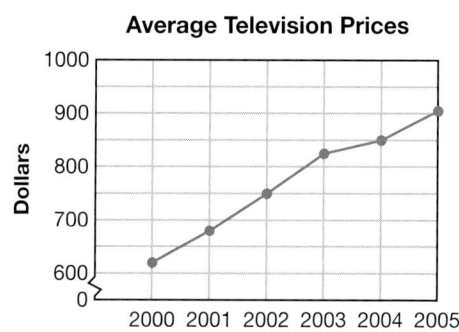

Math Reasoning

Analyze What increments could be used for the vertical axis of the graph in Example **4a** so that the graph is not misleading?

Lesson Practice

a. The graph at right shows the number of miles a car traveled each year. Explain why the graph may be misleading.
(Ex 1)

Miles Driven

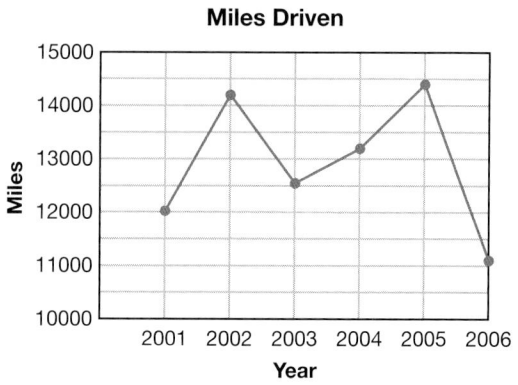

b. The graph below shows baking temperatures of various foods. Explain *(Ex 2)* why the graph may be misleading.

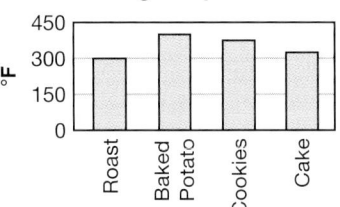

Cooking Temperatures

c. The circle graph below shows the number of some kinds of dogs that *(Ex 3)* were sold by the pet store. Explain why the graph may be misleading.

Types of Dogs Sold

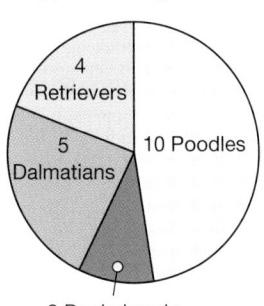

2 Dachshunds

A salesperson created the graph at right to display the number of products he sold each month.
(Ex 4)

d. Explain why the graph may be misleading.

e. What conclusion might be made from the graph? Why might the salesman have created this graph?

f. Make a graph of the sales data that is not misleading.

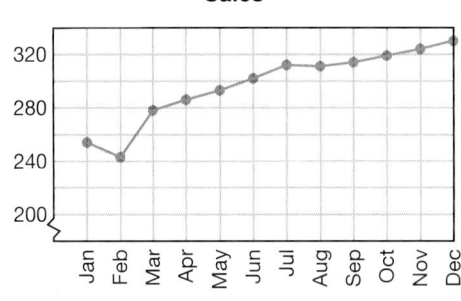

Sales

Practice   **Distributed and Integrated**

1. Simplify $(-2 + 3) \div (4 - 5 + 3)$.
(11)

Solve.

2. $0.5x - 0.2 = 0.15$
(23)

3. $\dfrac{1}{4} + \dfrac{2}{5}x + 1 = 2\dfrac{1}{4}$
(26)

4. Multiple Choice Which is the solution to the equation below?
(24)

$-0.4n + 0.305 = 0.295$

A 0.025   **B** −0.025   **C** 0.0004   **D** −0.7375

5. Analyze On a coordinate plane, a student draws a graph of two parallel lines
  (25) perpendicular to the y-axis. Does the graph represent a function?

6. Identify the property illustrated by $3 \cdot (9 \cdot 5) = (3 \cdot 9) \cdot 5$.
  (12)

*7. (**Automotive Safety**) The stopping distance d required by a moving vehicle is
  (25) dependent on the square of its speed s. Write a rule in function notation to
  represent this information.

*8. A petting zoo contains 10 species of animals. The graph shows percentages of
  (27) the 5 most numerous types of animals at the zoo. Give reasons why the circle
  graph may be misleading.

Petting Zoo

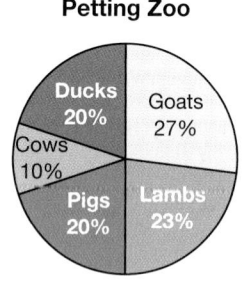

*9. Justify Is 4 a solution to the equation $5x + 8 - 3x + 4 = 20$? Justify your
  (26) answer.

*10. The bar graph shows results of a taste test of four
  (27) different brands of yogurt. True or False. Twice as many
  people preferred Brand A over Brand D.

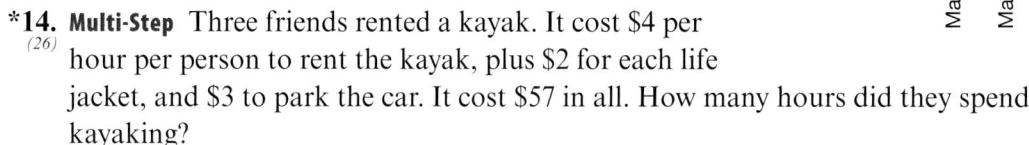

*11. Analyze Using the set of data values 125,000, 105,000, 162,000, 112,000, and
  (27) 148,000 without using a broken axis or very large intervals, how could a student
  make a reasonably sized graph of the data?

*12. (**Production**) A company has 6 machines to produce parts
  (27) for its product. A manager uses the bar graph showing
  the number of parts produced by each machine each day.
  What incorrect conclusions might the manager make
  about the efficiency of the machines?

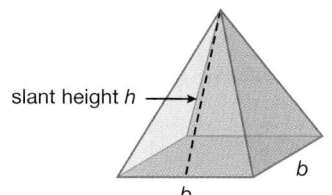

*13. True or False: Large intervals on a scale can make
  (27) changes in data appear less than they actually are. If false,
  explain why.

*14. Multi-Step Three friends rented a kayak. It cost $4 per
  (26) hour per person to rent the kayak, plus $2 for each life
  jacket, and $3 to park the car. It cost $57 in all. How many hours did they spend
  kayaking?

*15. Geometry The formula for the surface area of a square pyramid is
  (26) $S = \left(4 \cdot \frac{1}{2}bh\right) + b^2$. If the measure of b is 5 m, what is the largest slant
  height possible for the total surface area to be no more than 150 m²?

slant height h →

16. Justify What is the first step in solving $0.35 + 0.22x = 1.67$?
(24)

*17. (Phone Charges) The length of the first ten calls Tyrese made one month were 13, 28,
(22) 6, 10, 13, 22, 31, 12, 2, and 9 minutes. In a stem-and-leaf plot of the data which
digit would appear the most in the leaves column?

18. Verify Show that $-\frac{3}{4}x = 12$ and $\frac{5}{32}x = -2\frac{1}{2}$ have the same solution.
(21)

19. Graph the ordered pair $(-1, 0)$ on a coordinate plane.
(20)

20. Measurement To measure the length of a steel rod, an engineer uses a reference
(19) point a few millimeters from the end of the ruler. She then subtracts this
reference point from her final measurement of 325 mm. If the rod's length is
318 mm, what reference point did she use?

21. Convert 37 American dollars to Indian rupees. (Hint: 1 rupee = \$0.025)
(8)

22. Statistics Absolute deviation is the absolute value of the difference between a
(5) value in a data set and the mean of the data set. For the data set $\{8, 9, 11, 12, 15\}$,
the mean is 11, so the absolute deviation for the value 15 is $|15 - 11| = |4| = 4$.
What is the absolute deviation for each of the other numbers in the above data set?

23. (Fundraising) The cheerleaders made \$3 profit on each item sold in a fundraiser.
(15) They sold x calendars and y candles in total. Write and simplify an algebraic
expression to find the total profit.

24. Write A coin is tossed 8 times. What is the probability that the next time the coin
(14) is tossed the result will be heads? Explain.

25. Simplify $11 \cdot 3 + 7$.
(4)

26. Multi-Step A vending machine has q quarters and d dimes.
(9) **a.** Write an expression with variables to represent the value of the money.

b. Find the value of the change in the machine if there are 21 quarters and 13 dimes.

27. Use $<$, $>$, or $=$ to compare the expressions. $\frac{1}{3} + \frac{1}{5} \cdot \frac{2}{15} \bigcirc \left(\frac{1}{3} + \frac{1}{5}\right) \cdot \frac{2}{15}$
(7)

28. Write A man runs up and down stairs. If the number of stairs he runs up plus the
(6) number of stairs he runs down is the total number of stairs, describe his position
at the end of his run.

29. Write Show the steps for simplifying $10 \cdot 4^2 + 72 \div 2^3$.
(4)

30. (Accounting) Accountants prepare financial reports for businesses. Identify the set
(1) of numbers that best describes the numbers in a financial report. Explain your
choice.

Solving Equations with Variables on Both Sides

1. Vocabulary In the expression $-5x + 2 + 3x$, $-5x$ and $3x$ are
   _____ terms.
   (2)

2. Simplify $10 - 4(5 + 3) + 2^3$.
   (7)

Solve.

3. $2(3 - x) = 10$
   (26)

4. $-3(1 + 2x) + x = 32$
   (26)

5. Multiple Choice Which value is a solution to the equation
   $3(x - 4) - x = 30$?
   A 14   **B** 9   **C** 6   **D** 21

New Concepts

To solve an equation with variables on both sides, use inverse operations to bring the variables together on one side of the equation.

Materials

• algebra tiles

Exploration Modeling Variables on Both Sides of an Equation

Use algebra tiles to model and solve $4x + 5 = 2x + 11$.

4x + 5	2x + 11	
		Model each side of the equation.
		Add 2 −x-tiles to both sides. Remove pairs that equal zero.
		Add 5 −1-tiles to both sides. Remove the zero pairs.
		Arrange into 2 equal groups. What is the value of x?

a. Model $x + 3 = 2x - 4$. Then find the value of x.

b. Model $3x - 1 = x - 3$. Then find the value of x.

Example 1 Using Inverse Operations

Solve $6x = 4x - 10$. Justify each step. Check the solution.

SOLUTION

$$6x = 4x - 10$$

$\underline{-4x = -4x}$	Subtraction Property of Equality
$2x = -10$	Combine like terms.
$\dfrac{2x}{2} = \dfrac{-10}{2}$	Division Property of Equality
$x = -5$	

Check Substitute -5 for x in the original equation.

$$6x = 4x - 10$$
$$6(-5) \overset{?}{=} 4(-5) - 10$$
$$-30 \overset{?}{=} -20 - 10$$
$$-30 = -30 \quad \checkmark$$

Equations with variables on both sides might also contain symbols of inclusion and like terms. The first step is to apply the Distributive Property. The second step is to add like terms. Then apply inverse operations and the properties of equality to solve the equation.

Example 2 Simplifying Before Solving

Solve $5(2x + 4) - 2x = 6 + 2(3x + 12)$. Justify each step.

SOLUTION

$5(2x + 4) - 2x = 6 + 2(3x + 12)$	
$10x + 20 - 2x = 6 + 6x + 24$	Distributive Property
$10x - 2x + 20 = 6x + 6 + 24$	Commutative Property
$8x + 20 = 6x + 30$	Combine like terms.
$\underline{-6x \qquad = -6x}$	Subtraction Property of Equality
$2x + 20 = 30$	Simplify.
$\underline{-20 = -20}$	Subtraction Property of Equality
$2x = 10$	Simplify.
$\dfrac{1}{2} \cdot 2x = 10 \cdot \dfrac{1}{2}$	Multiplication Property of Equality
$x = 5$	Simplify.

An **identity** is an equation that is always true. It has infinitely many solutions. If no value of the variable makes an equation true, then the equation has no solution.

Math Language

Inverse operations undo each other. Addition and subtraction are inverse operations. Multiplication and division are inverse operations.

Math Reasoning

Write What is another way to eliminate the coefficient 2 from 2x?

Example 3 **No Solutions or Infinitely Many Solutions**

Solve each equation. Justify each step.

a. $10 - 6x = -2(3x - 5)$

SOLUTION

$10 - 6x = -2(3x - 5)$

$10 - 6x = -6x + 10$ Distributive Property

$\underline{+6x = +6x}$ Addition Property of Equality

$10 = 10$ Simplify. Always true.

Since $10 = 10$ is always true, the equation is an identity.

b. $7x - 2 = 9x - 5 - 2x$

SOLUTION

$7x - 2 = 9x - 5 - 2x$

$7x - 2 = 7x - 5$ Combine like terms.

$\underline{-7x = -7x}$ Addition Property of Equality

$-2 = -5$ Simplify. Never true.

Since $-2 = -5$ is never true, the equation has no solutions.

Math Reasoning

Analyze When the simplified equation is an identity, what values of the variable will satisfy the original equation?

Math Reasoning

Analyze When all variables are eliminated in an equation, resulting in a false statement, what values of the variable satisfy the original equation?

Example 4 **Application: Telephone Rates**

Telephone Company A charges $18.95 per month for local calls and $0.04 per minute for long-distance calls. Telephone Company B charges $21.95 per month for local calls and $0.02 per minute for long-distance calls. For what number of minutes of long-distance calls per month is the cost of the plans the same?

SOLUTION

Let $m =$ the number of minutes of long distance calls.

Company A's monthly charge $= \$18.95 + \$0.04m$

Company B's monthly charge $= \$21.95 + \$0.02m$

$18.95 + 0.04m = 21.95 + 0.02m$ Write an equation.

$\underline{-0.02m = \qquad -0.02m}$ Subtraction Property of Equality

$18.95 + 0.02m = 21.95$ Simplify.

$\underline{-18.95 \qquad = -18.95}$ Subtraction Property of Equality

$0.02m = 3.00$ Simplify.

$\dfrac{0.02m}{0.02m} = \dfrac{3.00}{0.02}$ Division Property of Equality

$m = 150$ Simplify.

The costs will be same for 150 minutes.

Solve each equation. Justify each step. Check the solution.

a. $6x = 3x + 27$
(Ex 1)

b. $2 + 3(3x - 6) = 5(x - 3) + 15$
(Ex 2)

Solve each equation. Justify each step. If the equation is an identity, write identity. If the equation has no solution, write no solution.
(Ex 3)

c. $2(x + 3) = 3(2x + 2) - 4x$

d. $3(x + 4) = 2(x + 5) + x$

e. (**Membership Rates**) A fitness center has a membership fee of \$125.
(Ex 4) Members only pay \$5 per day to work out at the center. A nonmember pays \$10 per day to work out. After how many work-out days is the total cost for members, including the membership fee, the same as the total cost for nonmembers?

1. Solve for y: $\frac{3}{4}y = 4\frac{7}{8}$.
(21)

*2. Solve for p: $3p - 4 - 6 = 2(p - 5)$.
(28)

*3. Formulate You have \$3 in bills and a certain number of nickels in one pocket. In
(28) the other pocket you have \$2 in bills and a certain number of dimes. You have the same number of dimes as nickels and the same amount of money in each pocket. Write an equation to find the number of dimes and nickels you have.

4. Error Analysis Two students used the Distributive Property to solve the same
(26) multi-step equation. Which student is correct? Explain the error.

Student A	Student B
$4x - 2(12 - x) = 18$	$4x - 2(12 - x) = 18$
$4x - 24 - x = 18$	$4x - 24 + 2x = 18$
$3x - 24 = 18$	$6x - 24 = 18$
$3x = 42$	$6x = 42$
$x = 14$	$x = 7$

*5. (**Wages**) A worker at one farm is paid \$486 for the week, plus \$0.03 for every pound
(28) of apples she picks. At another farm, a worker is paid \$490 for the week, plus \$0.02 for every pound of apples. For how many pounds of apples are the workers paid the same amount?

*6. Multiple Choice What is the value of x when $(x + 15)\frac{1}{3} = 2x - 1$?
(28)

A $\frac{18}{5}$ **B** $\frac{5}{18}$ **C** $\frac{18}{7}$ **D** $\frac{7}{18}$

*7. Error Analysis Two students solved the same multi-step equation. Which student
(28) is correct? Explain the error.

Student A	Student B
$3x - 4 = 2x - (4 + x)$	$3x - 4 = 2x - (4 + x)$
$3x - 4 = 2x - 4 + x$	$3x - 4 = 2x - 4 - x$
$3x - 4 = 3x - 4$	$3x - 4 = x - 4$
$0 = 0$	$2x = 0$
All real numbers.	$x = 0$

*8. Generalize If the equation $yx = zx$ is true, when yx is positive, $x \neq 0$, and z is
(26) a negative integer. Will x be positive or negative?

 9. Geometry The graph shows areas of several square
(27) sheets of paper.

a. About how many times greater does the
area of Sheet 4 appear to be than that of
Sheet 3?

b. The squares have side lengths of 9, 10, 8, and
11 inches. About how many times greater is the
area of Sheet 4 than the area of Sheet 3?

Area of Paper Squares

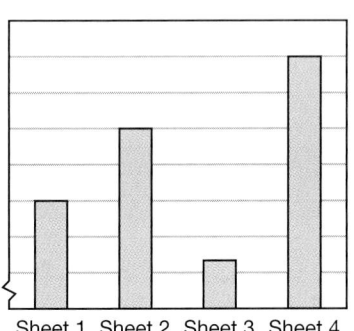

Sheet 1 Sheet 2 Sheet 3 Sheet 4

10. True or False: A broken scale can make changes in data appear less than they
(27) actually are. If false, explain why.

11. Multi-Step Average home prices in several cities are shown in the table.
(27)

City	Woodside	Reefville	Boynton	Dunston	York
Average Home Price (in thousands)	$265	$210	$320	$375	$350

a. Make a bar graph with a scale from 200 to 400. Use intervals of 40.

b. Without looking at the scale, what conclusions might the graph lead to?

c. Why might a real estate agent who sells houses only in Reefville want to show
potential clients a graph like this?

*12. Multi-Step Use the graph.
(25)
a. Give the domain and range of the relation.

b. Determine whether the relation is a function. Explain.

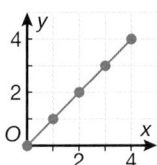

*13. Multiple Choice Use the graph shown. A conservation group
(25) has been working to increase the population of a herd of
Asian elephants. The graph shows the results of their
efforts. Which relations represent the data in the graph?

A $\{(1, 4.5), (2, 6), (3, 10), (4, 14.5)\}$

B $\{(1, 5), (2, 6), (3, 10), (4, 15)\}$

C $\{(4.5, 1), (6, 2), (10, 3), (14.5, 4)\}$

D $\{(5, 1), (6, 2), (10, 3), (15, 4)\}$

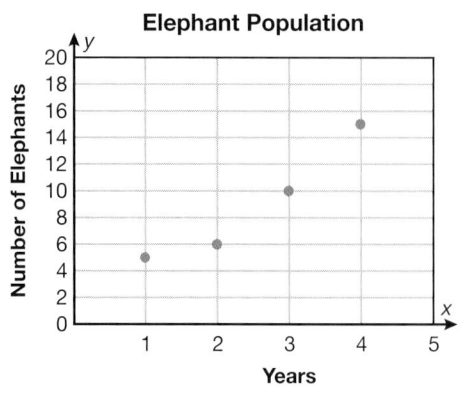

14. 0.28 of what number is 18.2?
(24)

15. (Internet Access) At a local diner, customers can enjoy wireless
(23) Internet access.

a. Write an equation that can be used to find the cost of being online
for *m* minutes.

b. Estimate You know it will require $1\frac{1}{2}$ to 2 hours to get your research
done online. About how much will it cost to do your work
at the diner?

16. Determine whether the statement is true or false. If false, explain why.
(22) A line graph can help analyze change over time.

17. Use the coordinate grid.
(20) Find the coordinates of point *K*.

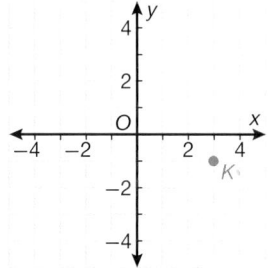

*18. Silvia had $247 in her savings account. She made a deposit into her savings
(19) account. Now, her account has $472. Write an equation that shows the amount
of money that is currently in her account. Determine how much money was
deposited.

19. (Cooking) George has already sliced 1 carrot and continues to slice 6 carrots per
(18) minute. Frank has already sliced 16 carrots and continues to slice 4 carrots
per minute.

a. Write expressions representing the number of carrots sliced by each person in
m minutes.

b. Write an expression for the total number of carrots sliced.

20. (Grades) A student raised her grade by 13 points. Write an expression to represent
(17) her new grade.

*21. **Astronomy** The gravitational force between two objects can be approximated
(6) by using $F = \frac{m_1 m_2}{d^2}$, where F is the gravitational force in newtons, m_1 is the mass
in kilograms of the first object, m_2 is the mass in kilograms of the second object,
and d is the distance between them expressed in meters. If the mass of a satellite
is 500 kilograms, the mass of a small asteroid is 1500 kilograms, and the distance
between them is 1000 meters, what is the gravitational force between the satellite
and the asteroid?

22. **Verify** Use two different methods to evaluate $8(10 - 4)$. Verify that each method
(15) gives the same result.

23. Evaluate $\sqrt{49} + 4^2$.
(13)

24. True or False: $(b + c) + d = b + (c + d)$. Justify your answer.
(12)

25. Evaluate the expression $3n^2 p^5 + 4(n - 8)^2$ for the given values $n = -3$ and $p = 1$.
(9)

26. **Write** Give a counterexample for the following statement: The set of irrational
(1) numbers is closed under subtraction.

27. **Measurement** Find the perimeter of the polygon.
(18)

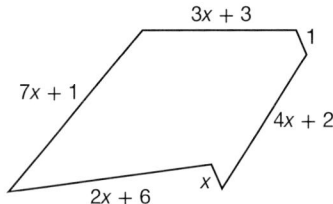

28. **Probability** A coin is tossed 3 times.
(1)
   a. What set of numbers could be used to express the different probabilities of how
the coin is tossed?

   b. Could the probability ever be a whole number? Explain.

29. **Write** When a student converts from miles to feet, will the student multiply or
(8) divide? Explain.

*30. **Write** Describe a situation that could be represented by a continuous graph.
$(Inv\ 2)$

Solving Literal Equations

Warm Up

1. Vocabulary A _____ (*constant, variable*) is a letter used to represent
(2) an unknown.

2. Evaluate the expression *rt* if $r = 4$ and $t = 7$.
(9)

3. Solve the equation $3x - 24 = 6$.
(26)

4. Solve the equation $4x + 14 = 2x + 20$.
(28)

5. Solve the equation $5x + 2 = 2x - 9$.
(28)

New Concepts

Recall when solving an equation with one variable, inverse operations are used to isolate the variable as shown below.

$2x - 6 = 14$

$\underline{+6 = +6}$ Add 6 to undo subtracting 6.

$2x = 20$ Simplify.

$\dfrac{2x}{2} = \dfrac{20}{2}$ Divide by 2 to undo multiplication.

$x = 10$ Simplify.

A **literal equation** is an equation with more than one variable. As in an equation with one variable, use inverse operations and properties of equalities to solve for a specific variable in a literal equation. The solution for the specific variable will be in the terms of the other variables and numbers.

Math Reasoning

Connect Give an example of an equation that would contain more than one variable.

Example 1 Solving for a Variable

Solve for *y*: $2x + 3y = 10$. Justify each step.

SOLUTION

$2x + 3y = 10$ Find *y* in the equation.

$\underline{-2x \quad = -2x}$ Subtract 2x to eliminate from the *y* side.

$3y = -2x + 10$ Simplify.

$\dfrac{3y}{3} = \dfrac{-2x}{3} + \dfrac{10}{3}$ Divide by 3 to eliminate the coefficient of *y*.

$y = \dfrac{-2x}{3} + \dfrac{10}{3}$ Simplify.

Online Connection
www.SaxonMathResources.com

If the variable being solved for is on both sides of the equation, the first step is to eliminate the variable on one side or the other.

Example 2 Solving for Variables on Both Sides

Solve for p: $4p + 2a - 5 = 6a + p$. Justify each step.

SOLUTION

$$4p + 2a - 5 = 6a + p$$

$\underline{-p} \qquad = \qquad \underline{-p}$		Eliminate the p on the right side.
$3p + 2a - 5 = 6a$		Combine like terms.
$\underline{-2a + 5} = \underline{-2a + 5}$		Eliminate the $2a$ and -5 from the left side.
$3p = 4a + 5$		Combine like terms.
$\dfrac{3p}{3} = \dfrac{4a}{3} + \dfrac{5}{3}$		Divide both sides by 3.
$p = \dfrac{4a}{3} + \dfrac{5}{3}$		Simplify.

A formula is a type of literal equation. Use inverse operations to isolate any variable in the formula.

Example 3 Solving a Formula for a Variable

The formula $C = \frac{5}{9}(F - 32)$ expresses Celsius temperature in terms of Fahrenheit temperature. Find the Fahrenheit temperature when the Celsius temperature is 20°.

SOLUTION

Step 1: Solve for F. Justify each step.

$$C = \frac{5}{9}(F - 32)$$

$\dfrac{9}{5} \cdot C = \dfrac{9}{5} \cdot \dfrac{5}{9}(F - 32)$	Multiplication Property of Equality
$\dfrac{9}{5}C = F - 32$	Simplify.
$\underline{+32} = \underline{+32}$	Addition Property of Equality
$\dfrac{9}{5}C + 32 = F$	Simplify.

Step 2: Substitute 20 for C.

$$\frac{9}{5}C + 32 = F$$

$$\frac{9}{5}(20) + 32 = F$$

$$36 + 32 = F$$

$$68 = F$$

20°C is equivalent to 68°F.

Hint

Remember that dividing by a fraction is the same as multiplying by the reciprocal.

Example 4 Application: Geometry

The formula for the circumference of a circle is $C = 2\pi r$. If the circle's circumference is 24 inches, what is the radius? Leave the symbol π in the answer.

SOLUTION

Step 1: Since the question asked for the radius, the first step is to solve the formula for r.

$$C = 2\pi r$$

$$\frac{C}{2\pi} = \frac{2\pi r}{2\pi} \qquad \text{Isolate the variable } r.$$

$$\frac{C}{2\pi} = r \qquad \text{Simplify.}$$

Step 2: Substitute 24 for C.

$$\frac{24}{2\pi} = r$$

$$\frac{12}{\pi} = r \qquad \text{Simplify.}$$

The radius of the circle is $\frac{12}{\pi}$ inches.

Example 5 **Application: Travel Plans**

The Ramirez family is taking a trip to the coast. They live 270 miles from the coast. They want to make the trip in $4\frac{1}{2}$ hours. Use the distance formula $d = rt$ to determine the average speed the family needs to drive.

SOLUTION

Step 1: The answer will be the speed they are driving, so solve the formula for r.

$$d = rt$$

$$\frac{d}{t} = \frac{rt}{t} \qquad \text{Divide both sides by } t.$$

$$\frac{d}{t} = r \qquad \text{Simplify.}$$

Step 2: Substitute 270 for d and 4.5 for t.

$$\frac{d}{t} = r$$

$$\frac{270}{4.5} = r$$

$$60 = r$$

The Ramirez family needs to average a speed of 60 mph to make the trip in $4\frac{1}{2}$ hours.

18. Measurement To convert between feet and inches, use the equation $i = 12f$ where i is the number of inches and f is the number of feet. Complete the table and graph the solutions.
(20)

f	i
3	
5	
8	
10	

19. Verify True or False. A repeating decimal multiplied by a variable is an irrational number. If the statement is false, give a counterexample.
(2)

20. (Astronomy) The temperature on the surface of Mars varies by 148°F. The highest temperature is about 23°F. What is that lowest temperature on the surface of Mars?
(6)

21. (Consumer Economics) A strawberry container costs $1 and the strawberries cost $2 per pound. Write an expression to represent the total cost for a container with s pounds of strawberries.
(17)

22. Simplify $x^2 - 3yx + 2yx^2 - 2xy + yx$.
(18)

23. Solve $-3y + \dfrac{1}{2} = \dfrac{5}{7}$.
(23)

24. Solve $k + 4 - 5(k + 2) = 3k - 2$.
(28)

25. Generalize The value of $z + 2$ is an odd integer. What generalizations can be made about z using this information?
(9)

26. Which expression is greater: $\dfrac{1}{3} - 1$ or $\dfrac{1}{2} - 1$.
(10)

27. Justify Simplify $(3 + 5) - 2^3$. Justify each step using the order of operations or mathematical properties.
(7)

28. Analyze Find the value of y when $x = 2$.
(6)

$$-x - (-2) = y$$

29. (Population Growth) The expression $303{,}000{,}000 \times (1.015)^t$, where t stands for years, represents the population growth of the U.S.A. Based on this expression, about how many people will live in the U.S.A. eight years from now?
(3)

30. Probability On the first street in Hidden Oaks subdivision, 5 out of 20 families own trucks.
(Inv 1)

   a. What is the probability that a randomly selected family in the subdivision owns a truck?

   b. Predict the number of truck-owning families you can expect among the 140 families living in the subdivision.

Creating a Table

Graphing Calculator Lab (*Use with Lesson 30*)

An equation describes a relationship between two quantities. Sometimes it is inconvenient to calculate a large quantity of outputs by substituting given values into the equation. Instead, use your graphing calculator to quickly make a table of values.

Find the value of y for the equation $y = 3x + 5$ when $x = 15, 45, 75, 105,$ and 135.

1. To enter the equation into the $Y =$ editor, press the `Y=` key. Then press **3** `X,T,θ,n` `+` **5.**

2. Open the Table Setup menu by pressing `2nd` `WINDOW` (TBLSET). TblStart is the value of x to start the table of values. ΔTbl is the increment by which x-values in the table should increase.

   Since the smallest value of x is 15, press **1 5** `ENTER`. Consecutive x-values increase by 30, so for ΔTbl, press **3 0** `ENTER`.

3. Press `2nd` `GRAPH` (TABLE) to view the table of values.

   From this screen's table of values, you can see that $y = 50$ when $x = 15$, $y = 140$ when $x = 45$, $y = 230$ when $x = 75$, $y = 320$ when $x = 105$, and $y = 410$ when $x = 135$.

4. Press the ⌄ key repeatedly to see larger values of x and y,

   For $x = 405$, $y = 1220$.

You can compare y-values for more than one equation for a given set of x-values. Enter equations into the [Y=] editor for Y_1, Y_2, and so on, for as many equations as you have. Then set TblStart and ΔTbl values in the Table Setup menu and press [2nd] [GRAPH TABLE] to view the table of values. Use the [◀] and [▶] keys to navigate across the equations and the [▲] and [▼] keys to scroll through values of x in the table.

Lab Practice

Use a table to find y for the equation for the given values of x. Indicate the TblStart and ΔTbl values you use.

a. $y = 2x - 2$ for $x = 2$, 5, 8, and 11

b. $y = 4x$ for $x = 1$, 8, 15, and 22

Stephanie is growing two varieties of flowers for a show taking place in three months. The height y in inches of Flower A after x months can be modeled by the equation $y = 2x + 1$. Flower B grows according to the equation $y = 3x - 2$. Stephanie will plant the flowers at the same time and monitor their height at the end of each month. If Flower A and Flower B are the same height, she will use them to make an arrangement to present at the flower show.

c. How would Stephanie simulate the growth of each flower?

d. What would Stephanie enter into the calculator to simultaneously model the growth of Flower A and Flower B?

e. What TblStart value should Stephanie use?

f. What ΔTbl value should she use?

g. How tall are Flower A and Flower B at the end of each month?

h. Will Stephanie be able to create an arrangement of Flowers A and B for the flower show? Explain.

Graphing Functions

Warm Up

1. **Vocabulary** A _____ (*relation, function*) is a set of ordered pairs where
(25) each number in the domain is matched to one or more numbers in the range.

**Determine the coordinates of each point labeled
on the coordinate grid.**

2. Point A
(20)

3. Point B
(20)

4. Point C
(20)

5. Evaluate $2x + 3$ for $x = 4$.
(9)

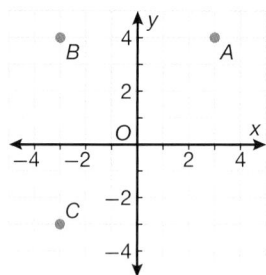

New Concepts

A **linear equation** is an equation whose graph is a line. You can use a table
of ordered pairs to graph an equation. To determine if the graph represents
a function, use the vertical line test. If a vertical line intersects the graph at
more than one point, then the graph is not a function. A **linear function** is a
function whose graph is a line. A linear function can be written in the form
$f(x) = mx + b$, where m and b are real numbers.

Example 1 Using Tables to Graph Functions

**Graphing
Calculator**

For help with creating
tables, refer to Graphing
Calculator Lab 2, p. 177.

Graph each equation using a table of values. Use a graphing calculator
to check your table. Decide whether the graph represents a function and
whether it is linear or nonlinear.

a. $y = x$

SOLUTION

x	0	1	2	3	4
y	0	1	2	3	4

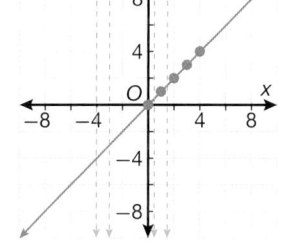

Any vertical line intersects this graph at only one point, so the graph is a
function. The graph is a line, so it is a linear function.

b. $y = x^2$

Math Reasoning

Generalize How can
values in a table be used
to tell whether data are
linear?

SOLUTION

x	-2	-1	0	1	2
y	4	1	0	1	4

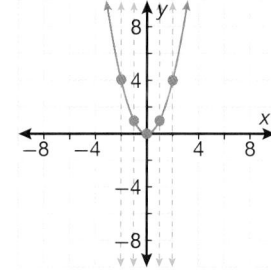

According to the vertical line test, the graph
is a function. The graph is not a line, so it is
a nonlinear function.

Example 2 Matching a Graph to a Table

Use the coordinates in each table to match each graph with one of the tables.

Table 1 Rule: $f(x) = \frac{1}{3}x + 4$

x	−3	0	3	6	9
$f(x)$	3	4	5	6	7

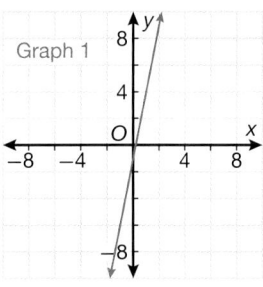

Graph 1

Table 2 Rule: $f(x) = 5x - 1$

x	−2	−1	0	1	2
$f(x)$	−11	−6	−1	4	9

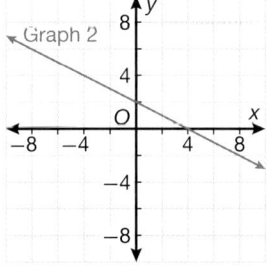

Graph 2

Table 3 Rule: $f(x) = -\frac{1}{2}x + 2$

x	−4	−2	0	2	4
$f(x)$	4	3	2	1	0

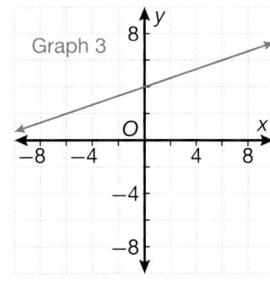

Graph 3

Math Reasoning

Analyze To match an equation to a graph, what characteristic(s) of the graph can often be most easily identified in the equation?

SOLUTION

Table 1 has the ordered pair $(0, 4)$. The graph in Graph 3 is the only graph that includes this point. The ordered pairs $(3, 5)$ and $(6, 6)$ also are on the graph. Graph 3 matches the values in Table 1.

For Table 2, look at the ordered pair $(0, -1)$. This ordered pair only occurs in Graph 1. The ordered pairs $(-1, -6)$ and $(1, 4)$ also are on the graph. Graph 1 matches the values in Table 2.

Graph 2 matches Table 3. The ordered pairs $(-4, 4)$, $(0, 2)$, and $(4, 0)$ are on Graph 2.

Example 3 Matching an Equation to a Graph

Match the three equations below to the three graphs shown.

Equation A: $y = x + 3$

Equation B: $y = |x| + 3$

Equation C: $y = \sqrt{x} + 3$

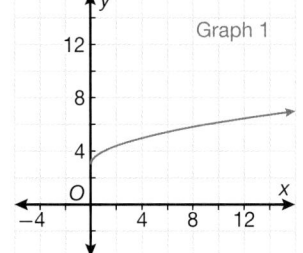

Graph 1

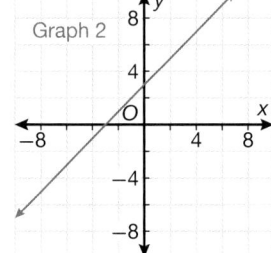

Graph 2

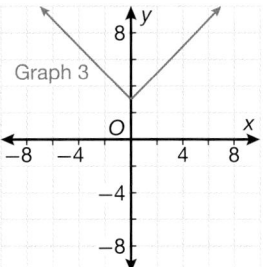

Graph 3

SOLUTION

Find three ordered pairs for each equation. Check to see which graph includes the ordered pairs.

Equation A: Substituting different values of x into $y = x + 3$ results in the following ordered pairs: $(0, 3)$, $(1, 4)$ and $(2, 5)$. Only Graph 2 includes these ordered pairs, so Equation A matches Graph 2.

Equation B: For $y = |x| + 3$, any value for x will have a positive y-value. Equation B matches Graph 3.

Equation C: For $y = \sqrt{x} + 3$, there cannot be x-values that are negative. Equation C matches Graph 1.

Example 4   Identifying the Domain and Range

Use the graphs to identify the domain and range of each function.

a.

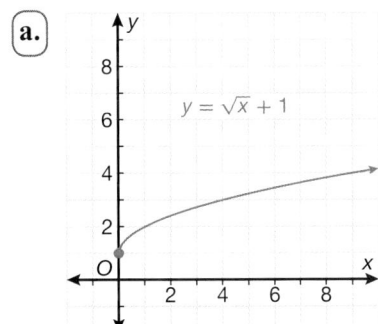

SOLUTION

The domain is $x \geq 0$ because you cannot take the square root of a negative number. By inspection of the graph, the range is $y \geq 1$.

b.

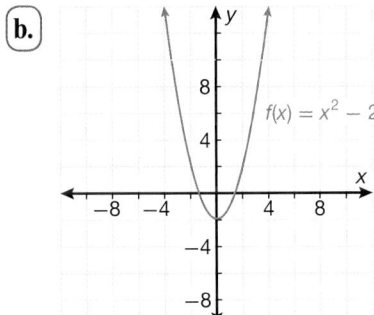

SOLUTION

By inspection of the graph, the domain is all real numbers and the range is $y \geq -2$.

Example 5 | Application: Car Wash Fundraiser

The soccer team raises money by washing cars. They charge $5 per car and spend a total of $4 on soap. The table shows the money they raise. Make a graph and use it to find the amount they raise by washing 7 cars. Write the rule in functional notation and use it to check the answer.

Math Reasoning

Verify Why is the money raised for 0 cars −$4.00?

Number of Cars Washed, x	0	1	2	3	4	5
Money Raised, $f(x)$	−4	1	6	11	16	21

SOLUTION

Use the ordered pairs to make a graph. Extend the line beyond $x = 7$. The y-value on the line is 31 when $x = 7$, so the soccer team raises $31 by washing 7 cars.

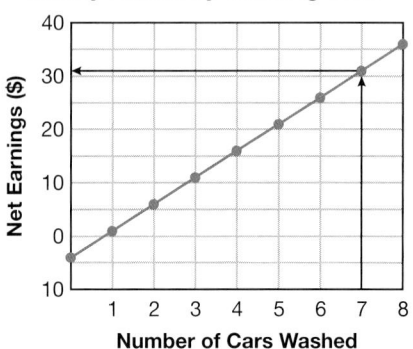

Money Raised by Washing Cars

Check the answer by evaluating the function for $x = 7$. The rule is $5 times the number of cars x minus $4, or

$f(x) = 5x − 4$.

$f(x) = 5x − 4$

$f(7) = 5(7) − 4$

$\quad\ = 35 − 4$

$\quad\ = 31$

Lesson Practice

a. Graph $y = 2x + 5$ using a table of values. Use a graphing calculator to check your table. Decide whether the graph represents a function and whether it is linear or nonlinear.
(Ex 1)

b. Graph $y = x^2 + 1$ using a table of values. Use a graphing calculator to check your table. Decide whether the graph represents a function and whether it is linear or nonlinear.
(Ex 1)

c. Match the equation $y = −2x^2$ to the correct graph.
(Ex 3)

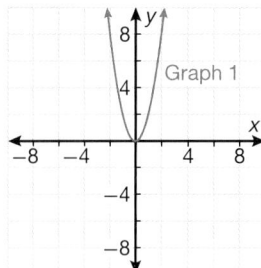

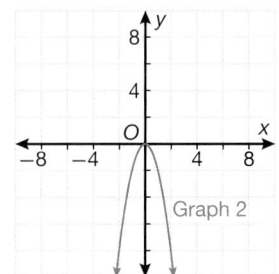

Use the coordinates in the tables to match the graph with each table.
(Ex 2)

d. $y = \dfrac{1}{3}x + 1$

x	−6	−3	0	3	6
y	−1	0	1	2	3

e. $y = 3x + 1$

x	−3	−2	0	1	2
y	−8	−5	1	4	7

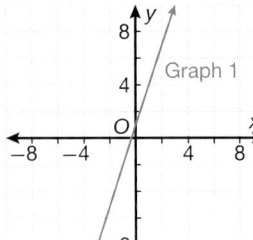
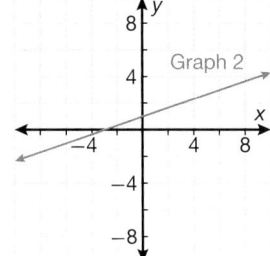

Identify the domain and range of the function shown in each graph.
(Ex 4)

f.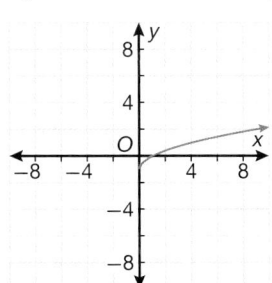

g.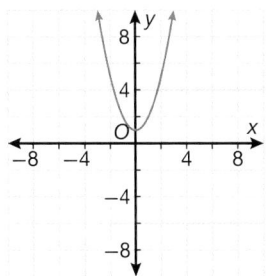

h. **Emails to Congress** The table shows the number of emails history classes
(Ex 5) send to their senators. Make a graph and use it to find how many emails were sent from 8 classes. Write the rule in function notation and use it to check your answer.

Number of Classes, x	1	2	3	4
Emails Sent, $f(x)$	30	60	90	120

Practice Distributed and Integrated

Solve.

1. $x + \dfrac{1}{2} = 2\dfrac{1}{5}$
(19)

2. $0.4x - 0.3 = -0.14$
(23)

3. $\dfrac{1}{3} + \dfrac{5}{12}x - 2 = 6\dfrac{2}{3}$
(26)

4. $\dfrac{2}{3} - \dfrac{4}{9}x + 1 = 2\dfrac{7}{9}$
(26)

*5. Solve and check $x - 4(x - 3) + 7 = 6 - (x - 4)$.
(28)

*6. Verify Is the statement below true or false? Explain.
(25)

The graph of a circle shows that the equation of the circle, $x^2 + y^2 = 1$, is a function.

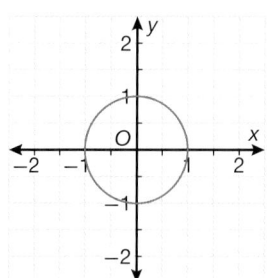

*7. **Savings** For every dollar Mirand deposits into her checking account, she deposits
(30) 1.5 times as much into her savings account, which started with $50. So, $s = 1.5c +$
50, where s is the amount in savings and c is the amount deposited in checking.
Which graph represents this equation?

Graph 1

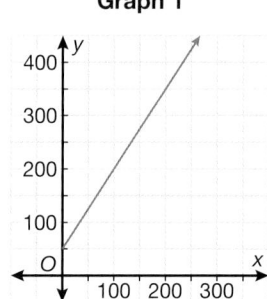

Graph 2

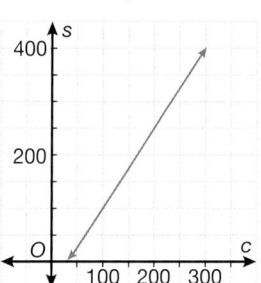

*8. Multiple Choice Which equation represents the line on the graph?
(30)
   A $y = x + 10$

   B $y - x = 10$

   C $-x = 10 + y$

   D $y = -x + 10$

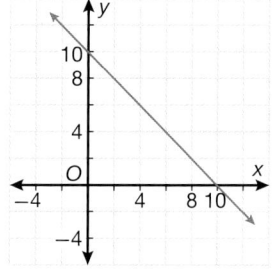

*9. Multi-Step The table shows the total number of shrubs a gardener plants after each
(30) half hour.

Time (hours)	0.5	1	1.5	2
Number of Shrubs	1	3	7	8

   a. Plot these data on a coordinate grid.

   b. Is the graph a function? Explain.

   c. Predict Can you predict the number of shrubs the gardener will plant in
     3 hours? Why or why not?

*10. Use the table to make a graph. Is the graph linear? Explain.
(30)

x	0	1	2	3
y	4	7	10	13

11. Error Analysis Two students solved $2x - y = 6$ for y. Which student is correct?
(29) Explain the error.

Student A	Student B
$2x - y = 6$	$2x - y = 6$
$2x = y + 6$	$2x = y + 6$
$2x - 6 = y$	$2x + 6 = y$

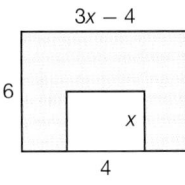

12. Geometry What is the area of the shaded part of the rectangle?
(29)

Rectangle with top side $3x - 4$, left side 6, bottom side 4, and inner square labeled x.

*13. Multi-Step Solve $\frac{x}{2} + \frac{y}{3} = 2$ for y. Find y when $x = 3$.
(29)

*14. (Consumer Math) Joel deposited money in an account that has a certain annual
(29) interest rate. Using the formula $i = prt$, or interest $=$ principal $\cdot$ rate $\cdot$ time,
how could he compute for the rate if the numeric value of the other items
was given?

15. Simplify $\dfrac{3 + 7(-3)}{-7 - 2(-3)}$.
(11)

16. Error Analysis Two students solved the same multi-step equation. Which student
(28) is correct? Explain the error.

Student A	Student B
$2x - 4(3x + 6) = -6(2x + 1) - 4$	$2x - 4(3x + 6) = -6(2x + 1) - 4$
$2x - 12x + 6 = -12x + 1 - 4$	$2x - 12x - 24 = -12x - 6 - 4$
$-10x + 6 = -12x - 3$	$-10x - 24 = -12x - 10$
$2x = -9$	$2x = 14$
$x = -4\frac{1}{2}$	$x = 7$

17. Measurement On a map, 1 centimeter represents 50 kilometers. The actual distance
(21) between two cities is 675 kilometers. Find the distance between the two cities on
the map.

*18. Multiple Choice What would make the graph of basketball scores less
(27) misleading?

A Using a broken scale on the horizontal axis

B Using a broken scale on the vertical axis

C Using larger intervals

D Using smaller intervals

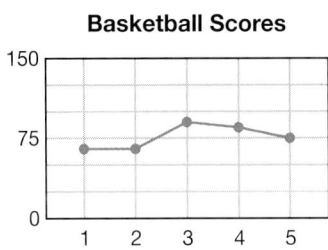

Basketball Scores

19. **Generalize** What effect do large intervals have on the appearance of a graph?
(27)

*20. (Sales) The circle graph shows the amounts of orange juice and fruit
(27) punch sold each month. Explain why this graph is misleading and
determine what may be a more appropriate graph to compare
the sales of the two beverages.

Fruit Juice Sales

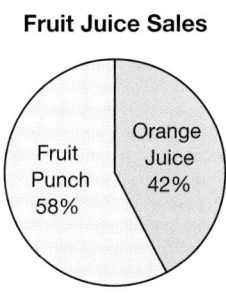

21. **Model** Make a stem-and-leaf plot of the following temperatures in Woodmont:
(22)
72°F, 74°F, 63°F, 62°F, 63°F, 78°F, 65°F, 51°F, 53°F, 53°F, 61°F, 80°F.

22. (Hair Growth) Hair grows approximately half an inch each month.
(12) John's hair is 2 inches long. Let m be the number of months. The
formula $h = 2 + 0.5m$ calculates the length John's hair will be in
m months if he does not cut it. Complete the table and graph the
solutions.

m	h
4	
6	
10	
20	

23. A television remote has a key for each of the channels 0 through 9. If one key is
(14) chosen at random, what is the chance that channel 5 is chosen? Write your answer
as a percent.

24. **Multi-Step** Todd has 18 boxes of cards with x cards in each box. He divides the cards
(12) equally with 5 friends. The expression $18x \div 6$ represents the number of cards each
person has. Simplify the expression and justify each step.

25. **Justify** Evaluate $5.2 - 1.6 + 4.08 + 8$. Justify each step.
(10)

26. **Generalize** In unit analysis, you often need to apply unit ratios multiple times to
(8) convert to the desired units. For example, $4518 \text{ cm}^2 \cdot \frac{1 \text{ m}}{100 \text{ cm}} \cdot \frac{1 \text{ m}}{100 \text{ cm}} = 0.4518 \text{ m}^2$
converts from square centimeters to square meters. State a general rule for
applying a unit ratio the correct number of times to perform a unit conversion.

27. **Justify** Evaluate $3 + \left(\frac{5 - 2}{4} + 2^2 \right)$. Justify each step.
(7)

28. (Consumer Economics) A gym charges \$2 a visit for the first 15 visits in a month.
(4) After that, the cost is reduced to $\frac{1}{4}$ of the price per visit. Use the expression
$15 \cdot \$2 + (23 - 15) \cdot \frac{1}{4} \cdot \$2$ to show how much someone will pay if they go to
this gym 23 times in a month.

29. **Analyze** Given the equations $a = (1.01)^x$ and $b = (0.99)^x$, which value, a or b,
(3) grows smaller as the exponent x grows larger?

30. **Write** Write a possible situation that could be represented by the graph at the right.
(Inv 2)

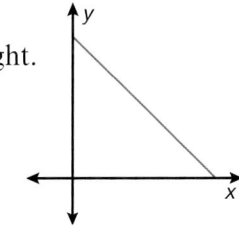

Analyzing the Effects of Bias in Sampling, Surveys, and Bar Graphs

Math Language

A **population** is a group that someone is gathering information about.

A **sample** is part of a population.

A sample is **random** if every member of the population has an equal chance of being chosen.

Online Connection
www.SaxonMathResources.com

To gather complete and accurate information about a particular population, researchers need to collect data from all of the population's members.

Sampling It is not always practical to survey every individual in the population, so researchers use data from the sample to draw conclusions about the entire population. The table below identifies five sampling methods.

	Sampling Method	Example
Simple Random	Select a group at random from the larger population.	Draw names of people to survey from a hat.
Stratified Random	Separate a population into smaller groups that have a certain characteristic. Then survey at random within each group.	Separate a herd of cows by breed; then survey a random sample from each breed.
Systematic Random	After calculating the required sample size, survey every nth member.	Choose the number 5 at random. Survey every 5th person.
Convenience	Select individuals from the population based on easy availability and/or accessibility.	Survey the first five people who arrive at a local mall.
Voluntary	Sample individuals who self-select into a survey by responding to a general appeal.	A news program asks viewers to participate in an online poll.

Luggage Survey A luggage company wants to know the most popular backpack color among high school students. Company representatives record the color of backpacks carried by boys in the cafeteria during lunch. Since the survey excludes high school girls, the sample is biased. It does not include some members of the population.

Analyze Give a reason why the sampling method may be biased.

1. A chef asks the first four customers who order the new cheese sauce if they like it.

2. At a convention of science teachers, attendees are asked to identify what their favorite subject was in high school.

3. A librarian sends questionnaires about library usage to families with children.

(**Zoo Survey**) Researchers for an advertising campaign survey people to find out why they like to visit the zoo.

4. Give an example of an unbiased sample for this survey.

5. Describe a systematic sampling method.

6. Justify Would it be biased to only survey families with children? Explain.

(**Biased Questions**) Occasionally, researchers ask biased questions that force the person being questioned to respond with a particular answer. For instance, "Didn't you eat enough?" uses a negative question, which indicates that the person who is being questioned has eaten enough.

Write Create one biased and one non-biased question for each survey.

7. A restaurant owner polls ten patrons on whether they enjoyed the chef's special.

8. A music store questions five customers about their listening habits.

(**Marketing**) Advertisers may accidentally or intentionally present data in a misleading way. Consider these graphs of the data collected from a survey of pet owners.

Graph A: This could be misleading because of the break in the graph. It appears that the number of people who have dogs is much greater than those who have cats, birds, or fish.

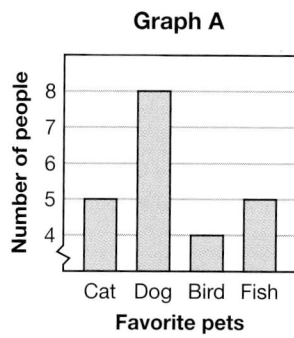

Graph B: This could be misleading because there are no labels on the vertical axis. It is not possible to determine whether each grid represents 1 person or 100 people.

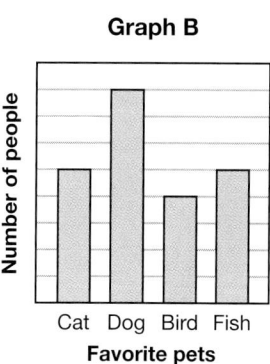

Graph C: This is not misleading. The vertical scale starts at 0 and the intervals are equal.

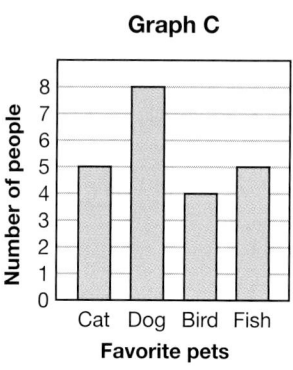

Your school district is discussing the possibility of requiring students to wear school uniforms. Your class was chosen to select the colors for the uniforms. They will be either blue or white. Each student should indicate a color preference.

Materials
• paper bag
• small squares of blue paper
• large squares of white paper

9. Record the results in a table.

10. Make a bar graph of the data.

11. Draw a set of axes. Label the horizontal axis with the uniform colors. Label the vertical axis with the number of students.

12. Draw two bars, each with a height equal to the number of people who chose the color.

Create a biased bar graph of the data.

13. Draw a set of axes. Label the horizontal axis with the uniform colors.

14. Use the colored squares of paper to create a blue or white column. If 5 students chose blue, then build a bar with 5 blue squares.

15. **Analyze** What is the difference between the two graphs you created?

Investigation Practice

Managers of an apartment complex want to know what visitors to the complex think of the complex and the management office employees. They survey every fifth person who signs a lease.

a. What is the population?

b. Identify the sample.

c. Which of the following is the sampling method used?

   A random   **B** systematic

   C stratified   **D** voluntary

d. What is a possible bias for this survey?

e. The approximate areas of four different oceans are listed below. Create a graph of the data that is misleading. Then redraw your graph so it is not misleading.

Ocean	Approximate area (million mi²)
Arctic	5
Indian	27
Atlantic	30
Pacific	60

Proportions are used to represent many real-world situations that require finding a missing value. Using the cross products is an efficient method for solving the proportions.

Example 4 Solving Multi-Step Proportions

a. The ratio of boys to girls in a math class is 3:2. The class has 25 students in all. How many boys and how many girls are in the class?

SOLUTION

The ratio of boys to girls is 3 to 2. There are 3 boys in each group of 5 students.

$$\frac{\text{number of boys}}{\text{total in group}} = \frac{3}{5} \qquad \text{Write a ratio.}$$

Write and solve a proportion. Let b represent the number of boys in the class.

$$\frac{3}{5} = \frac{b}{25} \qquad \text{There are } b \text{ boys to 25 students.}$$

$$3 \cdot 25 = 5 \cdot b \qquad \text{Write the cross products.}$$

$$5b = 75 \qquad \text{Simplify.}$$

$$b = 15 \qquad \text{Solve.}$$

There are 15 boys in the class. So, there are $25 - 15$ or 10 girls in the class.

b. On the map, Albany to Jamestown measures 12.6 centimeters, Jamestown to Springfield measures 9 centimeters, and Springfield to Albany measures 4.75 centimeters. What is the actual distance from Albany to Jamestown to Springfield and back to Albany?

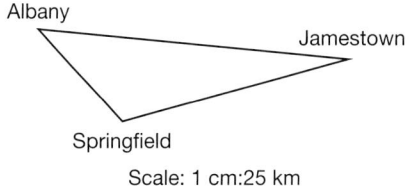

Scale: 1 cm:25 km

SOLUTION

$$12.6 + 9 + 4.75 = 26.35 \text{ cm} \qquad \text{Find the total distance on the map.}$$

$$\frac{26.35 \text{ cm}}{x \text{ km}} = \frac{1 \text{ cm}}{25 \text{ km}} \qquad \text{Set up a proportion using the map scale.}$$

$$26.35 \cdot 25 = 1 \cdot x \qquad \text{Write the cross products.}$$

$$658.75 = x \qquad \text{Solve.}$$

The actual distance is 658.75 kilometers.

Proportions are frequently used to solve problems involving variations of the distance formula $d = rt$.

$$\text{rate} = \frac{\text{distance}}{\text{time}} \quad \text{or} \quad \text{time} = \frac{\text{distance}}{\text{rate}}$$

Example 5 **Application: Trucking**

Mr. Jackson drove a truck 300 miles in 6 hours. If he drives at a constant speed, how long will it take him to drive 450 miles?

SOLUTION

Let x represent the number of hours it will take to drive 450 miles.

$$rate = \frac{distance}{time}$$

$$\frac{300 \text{ miles}}{6 \text{ hours}} = \frac{450 \text{ miles}}{x \text{ hours}}$$ Set up a proportion.

$$300 \cdot x = 450 \cdot 6$$ Write cross products.

$$300x = 2700$$ Solve.

$$x = 9$$

Mr. Jackson will drive 450 miles in 9 hours.

Lesson Practice

a. Which is the better buy: 8 boxes for $4.96 or 5 boxes for $3.25?
(Ex 1)

b. A chemist raised the temperature of a liquid 45°F in 1 minute. What is this amount in degrees Fahrenheit per second?
(Ex 2)

c. Jamie typed 20 pages of a document in 2 hours. How many pages did she type in 1 minute?
(Ex 2)

Solve each proportion.
(Ex 3)

d. $\dfrac{c}{7} = \dfrac{3}{21}$ **e.** $\dfrac{5}{n+2} = \dfrac{10}{16}$

f. The ratio of blue chips to red chips in a bag is 5:7. The bag has 60 chips in all. How many blue chips and how many red chips are in the bag?
(Ex 4)

g. A map shows a 5.5-inch distance between Orange City and Newtown, and a 3.75-inch distance from Newtown to Westville. The scale on the map is 1 inch:100 miles. What is the actual distance, if you drive from Orange City via Newtown to Westville?
(Ex 4)

h. If Jeff walks 4 miles in 48 minutes, how far can he walk in 72 minutes?
(Ex 5)

Practice   Distributed and Integrated

Simplify.

1. $7 - 4 - 5 + 12 - 2 - |-2|$
(10)

2. $-6 \cdot 3 + |-3(-4 + 2^3)|$
(11)

Solve.

3. $-0.05n + 1.8 = 1.74$
(24)

4. $-y - 8 + 6y = -9 + 5y + 2$
(28)

*5. Multiple Choice What is the value of x when $2x - 4.5 = \frac{1}{2}(x + 3)$?
(28)
   A 9   **B** 2.4   **C** 2   **D** 4

6. Solve for y: $4 + 2x + 2y - 3 = 5$.
(29)

7. Simplify $4k(2c - a + 3m)$.
(15)

Evaluate.

8. $3x^2 + 2y$ when $x = -2$ and $y = 5$
(16)

9. $2(a^2 - b)^2 + 3a^3b$ when $a = -3$ and $b = 2$
(16)

*10. If 10 boxes of cereal sell for $42.50, what is the unit price?
(31)

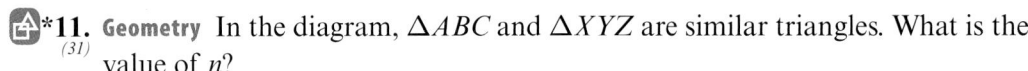 ***11. Geometry** In the diagram, $\triangle ABC$ and $\triangle XYZ$ are similar triangles. What is the
(31)   value of n?

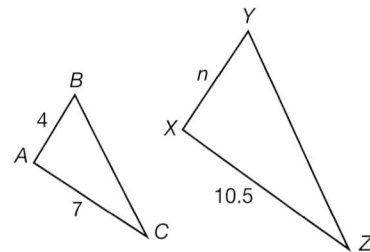

*12. Predict An estimate of the number of tagged foxes to the total number of foxes in
(31)   a forest is 3:13. A forest warden recorded 21 tagged foxes. About how many foxes
   are in the forest?

13. Multi-Step A skydiver falls at a rate given by $s = 1.05\sqrt{w}$, where s is the falling
(13)   speed in feet per second and w is the weight of the skydiver with gear in pounds.
   What is the approximate falling speed of a 170-pound man with 40 pounds of
   gear? (Round to the nearest whole number.)

14. Copy and complete the table for $y = x^2 + 2$. Then use the table to graph the
(30)   equation.

x	-3	-1	0	1	3
y	11	3	2		

*15. (**Shopping**) Glenn buys 4 computers for $2800. How much will
(31)   6 computers cost?

16. Probability A spinner is divided into 5 sections labeled *A* through *E*. The bar graph
(22) shows the results of 50 spins. What is the experimental probability that the next
spin will land on *A* or *D*?

Spin Results

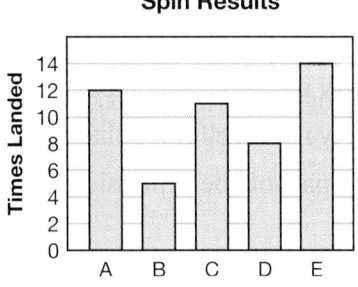

17. Mileage The table shows how far a car travels for each gallon of gasoline it uses.
(30)

Number of Gallons, *x*	1	2	3	4
Miles Traveled, *f(x)*	33	66	99	132

a. Use the table to make a graph.

b. Write a rule for the function.

c. How far will the car travel using 10 gallons of gasoline?

18. Multi-Step Students are paid *d* dollars per hour for gardening and *g* dollars per hour
(18) for babysitting and housework. Sally babysat for 6 hours and mowed lawns for 3
hours. Her brother weeded gardens for 5 hours and mopped floors for 1 hour.
a. Write an expression to represent the amount each student earned.

b. Write expressions for the total amount they earned together.

c. If they are paid $5 an hour for gardening and $4 an hour for babysitting and
housework, how much did they earn together?

*19. Carpentry A carpenter has propped a board up against a wall. The wall, board,
(26) and ground form a right triangle. What will be the measures of the three angles?

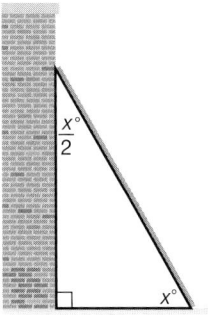

20. Give the domain and range of the relation.
(25)

$$\{(12, 2); (11, 10); (18, 0); (19, 1); (13, 4)\}$$

*21. Use a graphing calculator to make a table of values for $f(x) = x^2 - 1$.
(30) Graph the function and determine the domain and range.

Example 1 **Simplifying Expressions with Negative Exponents**

Simplify each expression. All variables represent nonzero real numbers.

a. x^{-3}

SOLUTION

$$x^{-3} = \frac{1}{x^3}$$ Write with only positive exponents.

b. $\dfrac{y^{-4}}{x^2}$

SOLUTION

$$\frac{y^{-4}}{x^2} = \frac{1}{x^2 \cdot y^4} = \frac{1}{x^2 y^4}$$ Write with only positive exponents.

c. $\dfrac{1}{w^{-4}}$

SOLUTION

$$\frac{1}{w^{-4}} = w^4$$ Write with only positive exponents.

Example 2 **Evaluating Expressions with Negative and Zero Exponents**

Evaluate each expression for $a = -2$ and $b = -3$.

a. $a^2 b^0$

SOLUTION

$a^2 b^0$

$= a^2 \cdot 1$ Simplify using the Zero Exponent Property.

$= a^2$ Multiplicative Identity

$= (-2)^2$ Substitute -2 for a.

$= 4$ Simplify.

b. $3b^{-3} \cdot b$

SOLUTION

$3b^{-3} \cdot b$

$= 3b^{-2}$ Product Property of Exponents

$= \dfrac{3}{b^2}$ Simplify using the Negative Exponent Property.

$= \dfrac{3}{(-3)^2}$ Substitute -3 for b. Then simplify.

$= \dfrac{3}{9} = \dfrac{1}{3}$ Simplify.

Caution

When working through problems, you may incorrectly replace b^0 with 0 instead of 1.

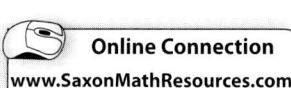

Online Connection
www.SaxonMathResources.com

The Quotient Property of Exponents is used when dividing algebraic expressions. This property states that to divide two algebraic expressions with the same base, subtract their exponents.

Quotient Property of Exponents
If m and n are real numbers and $x \neq 0$, then

$$\frac{x^m}{x^n} = x^{m-n} = \frac{1}{x^{n-m}}$$

$$\frac{5^4}{5^2} = 5^{4-2} = 5^2 = 25 \qquad \frac{5^2}{5^4} = \frac{1}{5^{4-2}} = \frac{1}{5^2} = \frac{1}{25}$$

Example 3 Using the Quotient Property of Exponents

Simplify each expression. All variables represent nonzero real numbers.

Math Reasoning

Analyze Why is $\frac{x^5}{x} = x^4$?

a. $\dfrac{x^7}{x^3}$

SOLUTION

$$\frac{x^7}{x^3}$$

$$= x^{7-3} \qquad \text{Quotient Property of Exponents}$$

$$= x^4 \qquad \text{Simplify.}$$

b. $\dfrac{x^3}{x^{-7}}$

SOLUTION

$$\frac{x^3}{x^{-7}}$$

$$= x^{3-(-7)} \qquad \text{Quotient Property of Exponents}$$

$$= x^{10} \qquad \text{Simplify.}$$

Math Reasoning

Analyze Use the Quotient Property of Exponents to show another method for simplifying $\frac{x^{-5}}{x}$.

c. $\dfrac{x^{-5}y^6z}{z^{-3}y^2x}$

SOLUTION

$$\frac{x^{-5}y^6z}{z^{-3}y^2x}$$

$$= x^{-5-1}y^{6-2}z^{1-(-3)} \qquad \text{Quotient Property of Exponents}$$

$$= x^{-6}y^4z^4 \qquad \text{Simplify.}$$

$$= \frac{y^4z^4}{x^6} \qquad \text{Write with only positive exponents.}$$

Example 4   Application: The Intensity of Sound

Math Reasoning

Write Which value is greater, 10^{-2} or 10^1? Explain.

The intensity of sound can be measured in watts per square meter. The table below lists intensity levels for some common sounds.

Intensity of Sound

Watts/Square Meter	Common Sound
10^3 to 10^7	Rocket Liftoff
10^0 to 10^2	Jet Liftoff
10^{-2} to 10^0	Loud Music
10^{-6} to 10^{-4}	Vacuum Cleaner
10^{-9} to 10^{-6}	Regular Speech
10^{-10} to 10^{-9}	Soft Whisper

How many times more intense is the sound of a rocket liftoff at 10^3 watts per square meter than that of regular speech at 10^{-7} watts per square meter?

Express the answer in exponential and standard form.

Math Language

10^{10} is in **exponential form**. 10,000,000,000 is in **standard form**.

SOLUTION

$\dfrac{10^3}{10^{-7}}$ Write a ratio to compare the sound intensities.

$= 10^{3-(-7)}$ Quotient Property of Exponents

$= 10^{10}$ Simplify the exponent.

$= 10{,}000{,}000{,}000$ Simplify.

The sound of a rocket liftoff is 10^{10} or 10,000,000,000 times more intense than that of regular speech.

Lesson Practice

Simplify each expression. All variables represent nonzero real numbers.
(Ex 1)

a. x^{-5} b. $\dfrac{p^{-8}}{q^4}$ c. $\dfrac{1}{d^{-8}}$

Evaluate each expression for $a = 4$, $b = 6$, and $c = 3$.
(Ex 2)

d. $a^0 b c^2$ e. $4a^{-2}$

Simplify each expression. All variables represent nonzero real numbers.
(Ex 3)

f. $\dfrac{x^{10}}{x^4}$ g. $\dfrac{x^9}{x^{-2}}$ h. $\dfrac{xy^{-3}z^5}{y^2 x^2 z}$

i. Refer to the table in Example 4. How many times more intense is
(Ex 4) the sound of a jet liftoff at 10^1 watts per square meter than that of a vacuum cleaner at 10^{-5} watts per square meter? Express the answer in exponential and standard form.

Simplify.

*1. $y^0 \dfrac{y^6}{y^5}$
(32)

*2. $\dfrac{m^3 p^2 q^{10}}{m^{-2} p^4 q^{-6}}$
(32)

Solve.

3. $9x - 2 = 2x + 12$
(28)

*4. $3y - y + 2y - 5 = 7 - 2y + 5$
(28)

5. $2y + 3 = 3(y + 7)$
(28)

6. $5(r - 1) = 2(r - 4) - 6$
(28)

 *7. **Geometry** Express the ratio of the area of the circle to the area of the square.
(32)

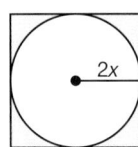

2x

8. The sum of twice a number and 17 is 55. Find the number.
(17)

*9. **Error Analysis** Two students solved the proportion $\frac{3}{8} = \frac{x}{4}$. Which student is correct?
(31) Explain the error.

Student A	**Student B**
$\dfrac{3}{8} = \dfrac{x}{4}$	$\dfrac{3}{8} = \dfrac{x}{4}$
$3 \cdot x = 8 \cdot 4$	$8 \cdot x = 3 \cdot 4$
$x = 10\dfrac{2}{3}$	$x = 1\dfrac{1}{2}$

*10. (Health) The circle graph shows the prevalence of all listed types of allergies among
(27) people who suffer from allergies. What about the graph may lead someone to an inaccurate conclusion?

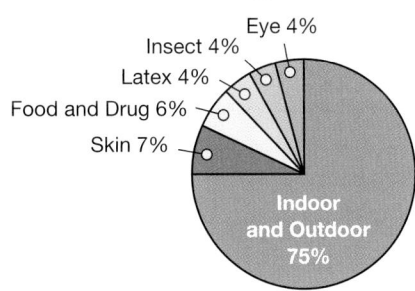

Allergy Prevalence

Eye 4%
Insect 4%
Latex 4%
Food and Drug 6%
Skin 7%
Indoor and Outdoor 75%

11. **Write** Why is it best to combine like terms in an equation, such as
(26) $3n + 9 - 2n = 6 - 2n + 12$, before attempting to isolate the variable?

12. **Verify** Is $n = 9$ a solution for $-28 = -4n + 8$? Explain. If false, provide a correct
(23) solution and check.

13. The table lists the ordered pairs from a relation. Determine whether the relation
$_{(25)}$ represents a function. Explain why or why not

Domain (x)	Range (y)
1	5
0	6
2	4
1	8
3	3

14. If there are 60 dozen pencils in 12 cartons, how many are in 1 carton?
$_{(31)}$

15. Multi-Step How many seconds are in 1 day?
$_{(31)}$

16. (Roller Coasters) The table shows the number of roller coasters in several countries.
$_{(22)}$ Suppose one student displays the data in a bar graph, and another student makes a
circle graph of the data. Compare the information that each type of display shows.

Roller Coasters Worldwide

Country	Japan	United Kingdom	Germany	France	China	South Korea	Canada	United States
Number	240	160	108	65	60	54	51	624

17. If there are 720 pencils in 6 cartons, how many dozen pencils are in 10 cartons?
$_{(31)}$

18. Multi-Step How many centimeters are in 1 kilometer?
$_{(31)}$

*19. (Geography) On a map, Brownsville and Evanstown are 2.5 inches apart. The scale
$_{(31)}$ on the map is 1 inch:25 miles. How far apart are the two towns?

20. Copy and complete the table for $y = |x| + 10$. Then use the table to graph the
$_{(30)}$ equation. Is the graph of the equation a function?

x	-3	-2	-1	0	1	2
y						

*21. Multiple Choice Which expression is simplified?
$_{(32)}$

A $\dfrac{6xy^2}{z^0}$ **B** $\dfrac{6x^3y^{-2}}{z}$ **C** $\dfrac{6x^3y^2}{z}$ **D** $\dfrac{6x^3y^2z}{z}$

*22. (Chemistry) An electron has a mass of 10^{-28} grams and a proton has a mass of
$_{(32)}$ 10^{-24} grams. How many times greater is the mass of a proton than the mass
of an electron?

23. Multi-Step A border is being built along two sides of a triangular garden. The third
(17) side is next to the house.

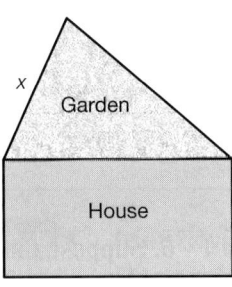

    a. The second side of the garden is 4 feet longer than first side. Write an
expression for the length of the second side.

    b. If the total amount of border is 28 feet, how long are the sides of the garden
that are not next to the house?

24. Multi-Step The temperature of a liquid is 72°F. The first step of a set of instructions
(19) requires that a scientist cools the liquid by 15°F. The second step requires that she
warms it until it reaches 85°F. By how many degrees will she warm the liquid in
the second step?

25. Analyze Megan and Molly have an age gap of 6 years. Megan is older. If Molly is
(29) 8 years old, then how old is Megan?

26. (Fuel Costs) It cost Rayna $73.25 to fill her truck with gas, not including tax.
(24) The gasoline tax is $0.32 per gallon. If the price for gasoline including tax is
$3.25 per gallon, how many gallons of gas did she buy?

    a. Write an equation to represent the problem.

    b. How many gallons of gas did she buy?

27. Expand the expression $(5p - 2c)4xy$ by using the Distributive Property.
(15)

Solve each proportion.

28. $\dfrac{7}{x} = \dfrac{1}{0.5}$
(31)

*29. $\dfrac{1}{x} = \dfrac{-3}{x + 2}$
(31)

30. Multi-Step How far Sam bikes in two hours depends on the rate at which he rides.
(20) His distance is represented by the equation $y = 25x$, where x is the time in hours
and y is the distance in miles.

    a. Copy and complete the table and graph the solutions.

x	1	2	3	4	5
y					

    b. Connect the points. What do you notice?

    c. Predict If Sam rides at the same rate, how long will it take him to ride 80 miles?

Example 3 | Calculating the Probability of Dependent Events

Natalia has two squares and three circles in a bag.

a. Find the probability of drawing a circle, keeping it, and then drawing another circle without the use of a tree diagram.

SOLUTION

For the first draw, the bag has 5 shapes and 3 are circles.

$$P(\text{1st circle}) = \frac{3}{5}$$

For the second draw, a circle has been removed. There is one less circle and one less shape.

$$P(\text{2nd circle}) = \frac{2}{4}$$

To find the probability of these two events, multiply their probabilities.

$$P(\text{1st circle}) \cdot P(\text{2nd circle}) = \frac{3}{5} \cdot \frac{2}{4} = \frac{6}{20} = \frac{3}{10}$$

b. Find the probability of drawing a square, keeping it, and then drawing a circle.

SOLUTION

For the first draw, the bag has 5 shapes and 2 are squares.

$$P(\text{square}) = \frac{2}{5}$$

For the second draw, a square has been removed. There is one less shape, but the number of circles is the same.

$$P(\text{circle}) = \frac{3}{4}$$

To find the probability of these two events, multiply their probabilities.

$$P(\text{square}) \cdot P(\text{circle}) = \frac{2}{5} \cdot \frac{3}{4} = \frac{6}{20} = \frac{3}{10}$$

Odds are another way of describing the likelihood of an event. Odds are expressed as a ratio, usually written with a colon. Odds can be calculated for something or against something happening.

Definition of Odds
Odds of an event: A ratio expressing the likelihood of an event.
Assume that all outcomes are equally likely, and that there are m favorable and n unfavorable outcomes.
The odds for the event are $m{:}n$.　　　　The odds against the event are $n{:}m$.

Example 4 Calculating Odds

A bag contains 6 red marbles, 2 yellow marbles, and 1 blue marble.

a. What are the odds of drawing a red marble?

SOLUTION

Look at the favorable outcomes and the unfavorable outcomes.

There are 6 red marbles (favorable outcomes).

There are 3 marbles that are not red (unfavorable outcomes).

The odds of drawing a red marble are 6:3 or 2:1.

b. What are the odds against drawing a blue marble?

SOLUTION

Look at the favorable and the unfavorable outcomes.

There are 8 marbles that are not blue (unfavorable outcome).

There is 1 blue marble (favorable outcome).

The odds against drawing a blue marble are 8:1.

Hint

The sum of the favorable and unfavorable outcomes should be the same as the total possible outcomes.

Example 5 Solving Multi-Step Problems Involving Probability

Isaac has 6 blue and 4 white shirts in his closet. There are also 2 pairs of navy pants and 3 pairs of khaki pants in his closet.

a. What is the probability Isaac will choose khaki pants and a white shirt from his closet?

SOLUTION

$$P(\text{khaki pants}) = \frac{3}{5}$$

$$P(\text{white shirt}) = \frac{4}{10} = \frac{2}{5}$$

$$P(\text{khaki pants and white shirt}) = \frac{3}{5} \cdot \frac{2}{5} = \frac{6}{25}$$

b. Assume that after the pants and shirt are worn, they are put in the laundry hamper. What is the probability that he will choose khaki pants and a white shirt from the closet to wear the next day?

SOLUTION

$$P(\text{khaki pants}) = \frac{2}{4} = \frac{1}{2}$$

$$P(\text{white shirt}) = \frac{3}{9} = \frac{1}{3}$$

$$P(\text{khaki pants and white shirt}) = \frac{1}{2} \cdot \frac{1}{3} = \frac{1}{6}$$

Identify each set of events as independent or dependent.

a. A card is chosen from a deck of cards, replaced, and then a second card
(Ex 1) is chosen.

b. A marble is drawn from a bag, kept, and then a second marble is drawn.
(Ex 1)

c. A coin is flipped, and a number cube is rolled.
(Ex 1)

d. A spinner is spun and the result is recorded. Then the spinner is spun a
(Ex 1) second time.

e. A coin is flipped and a six-sided number cube is tossed. Make a tree
(Ex 2) diagram showing all possible outcomes. What is the probability of
landing on tails and on an even number?

A bag contains 4 red blocks and 3 blue blocks.
(Ex 3)

f. Find the probability of drawing a red block, keeping it, and then
drawing another red block.

g. Find the probability of drawing a blue block, keeping it, and then
drawing a red block.

Use the spinner to answer the problems.
(Ex 4)

h. What are the odds of spinning black?

i. What are the odds against spinning gray?

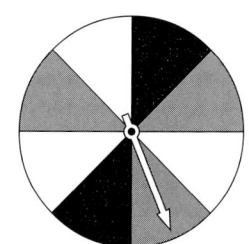

Campers select one inside activity and one outside activity
daily. There are 5 inside activities and 8 outside activities.
(Ex 5)

j. What is the probability of choosing pottery and
horseback riding on the first day?

k. Inside activities can be repeated, but outside activities cannot be repeated.
What is the probability of choosing pottery and swimming the second day?

> **Caution**
>
> The outside events are dependent, so the total number of outcomes changes.

Solve.

1. $-5v = 6v + 5 - v$
(28)

2. $-3(b + 9) = -6$
(26)

3. $-22 = -p - 12$
(26)

4. $-\frac{2}{5} = -\frac{1}{3}m + \frac{3}{5}$
(26)

5. $\frac{2}{x} = \frac{30}{-6}$
(31)

6. $\frac{x - 4}{6} = \frac{x + 2}{12}$
(31)

Simplify.

7. $\frac{y^6 x^5}{y^5 x^7}$
(32)

*8. $\frac{w^{-5}z^{-3}}{w^{-3}z^2}$
(32)

9. $\frac{4x^2 z^0}{2x^3 z}$
(32)

*10. Model There are 10 little marbles and 4 big marbles in a bag. A big marble is drawn
(33) and not replaced. Draw a picture that represents how the contents of the bag
change between the first draw and the second draw.

*11. Write Explain the difference between probability and odds.
(33)

*12. True or False: Two rolls of a number cube are independent events.
(33)

*13. Is the set of whole numbers closed under subtraction? Explain.
(1)

*14. Multiple Choice A bag contains 3 blue stones, 5 red stones, and 2 white stones.
(33) What is the probability of picking a blue stone, keeping it, and then picking a
white stone?

A $\dfrac{3}{50}$ **B** $\dfrac{1}{15}$ **C** $\dfrac{3}{28}$ **D** $\dfrac{1}{2}$

15. (Stock Market) The value of an investor's stock changed by $-1\frac{3}{4}$ points last week.
(11) This week the value changed by 3 times as much. How much did the value of the
investor's stock change this week?

*16. Predict What is the probability of rolling a 3 twice in a row on a six-sided number
(33) cube?

17. Write Give an example of a situation in which someone may want to use large
(27) intervals on a graph to persuade people to come to a certain conclusion.

*18. Analyze Simplify $x^3 \cdot x^{-3}$. What is the mathematical relationship between x^n and x^{-n}?
(32)

19. (Time) A nanosecond is 10^{-9} times as fast as 1 second and a microsecond is
(32) 10^{-6} times as fast as 1 second. How much faster is the nanosecond than the
microsecond?

20. Convert 30 quarts per mile to gallons per mile.
(31)

*21. Error Analysis Two students solved the proportion $\frac{5}{9} = \frac{c}{45}$. Which student is correct?
(31) Explain the error.

Student A	Student B
$\dfrac{5}{9} = \dfrac{c}{45}$	$\dfrac{5}{9} = \dfrac{c}{45}$
$9c = 225$	$9c = 225$
$c = 25$	$c = 2025$

*22. (Vehicle Rental) One moving company charges $19.85 plus $0.20 per mile to rent a
(28) van. The company also rents trucks for $24.95 plus $0.17 per mile. At how many
miles is the price the same for renting the vehicles?

23. If a set of ordered pairs is not a relation, can the set still be a function? Explain.
(25)

24. Write Explain how to find the solution of $0.09n + 0.2 = 2.9$.
(24)

25. (Keeping Cool) The British thermal unit (BTU) is a unit of energy used globally in
(21) air conditioning industries. The number of BTUs needed to cool a room depends
on the area of the room. To find the number of BTUs recommended for any size
room, use the formula $B = 377lw$, where B is the number of BTUs, l is the length
of the room, and w is the width of the room. The room you want to cool uses the
recomended number of 12,252.5 BTUs and is 5 meters wide. Find the area of the
room.

26. Multi-Step A quarterback throws the ball approximately 30 times per game. He
(20) has already thrown the ball 125 times this season. The equation $y = 30x + 125$
predicts how many times he will have thrown the ball after x more games.

x	y
2	
3	
4	
5	

a. Copy and complete the table using a graphing calculator and then graph the
solutions.

b. When will he have thrown the ball more than 300 times?

27. (Marathons) A marathon is 26.2 miles long. In order to qualify for the Boston
(21) Marathon, Jill must first complete a different marathon within $3\frac{2}{3}$ hours. Her
average speed in the last marathon she completed was 7.8 miles per hour. Did she
qualify for the Boston Marathon? Explain.

28. Geometry The rectangles shown are similar.
(31)

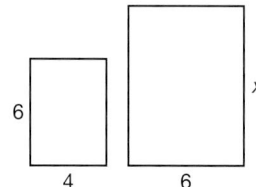

a. Find the ratio of the side lengths of the smaller rectangle to the larger
rectangle.

b. Find the longer side length of the larger rectangle using proportions.

29. Jack is building a square pen for his dog. If he wants the area of the pen to be
(13) 144 square feet, how long should he make each side of the pen?

30. True or False: Whole numbers include negative numbers.
(1)

LESSON
34

Recognizing and Extending Arithmetic Sequences

Warm Up

1. **Vocabulary** Any quantity whose value does not change is called
(2) a _____.

Simplify.

2. $7.2 - 5.8 - (-15)$
(6)

3. $-0.12 - (-43.7) - 73.5$
(6)

4. $6(-2.5)$
(11)

5. $(-15)(-4.2)$
(11)

New Concepts

Sequences of numbers can be formed using a variety of patterns and operations. A **sequence** is a list of numbers that follow a rule, and each number in the sequence is called a **term of the sequence**. Here are a few examples of sequences:

> **Math Language**
>
> The symbol "…" is an **ellipsis** and is read "and so on." In mathematics, the symbol means the pattern continues without end.

1, 3, 5, 7, …

7, 4, 1, −2, …

2, 6, 18, 54, …

1, 4, 9, 16, …

In the above examples, the first two sequences are a special type of sequence called an arithmetic sequence. An **arithmetic sequence** is a sequence that has a constant difference between two consecutive terms called the **common difference.**

To find the common difference, choose any term and subtract the previous term. In the first sequence above, the common difference is 2, while in the second sequence, the common difference is −3.

$$1, \quad 3, \quad 5, \quad 7, \dots \qquad\qquad 7, \quad 4, \quad 1, \quad -2, \dots$$
$$+2 \quad +2 \quad +2 \qquad\qquad\qquad -3 \quad -3 \quad -3$$

If the sequence does not have a common difference, then it is not arithmetic.

Example 1 **Recognizing Arithmetic Sequences**

Determine if each sequence is an arithmetic sequence. If yes, find the common difference and the next two terms.

a. 7, 12, 17, 22, …

SOLUTION Since $12 - 7 = 5$, $17 - 12 = 5$, and $22 - 17 = 5$, the sequence is arithmetic with a common difference of 5. The next two terms are $22 + 5 = 27$ and $27 + 5 = 32$.

b. 3, 6, 12, 24, …

SOLUTION Since $6 - 3 = 3$ and $12 - 6 = 6$, there is no common difference and the sequence is not arithmetic.

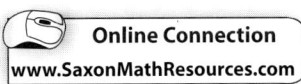

Online Connection
www.SaxonMathResources.com

The first term of a sequence is denoted as a_1, the second term as a_2, the third term a_3, and so on. The nth term of an arithmetic sequence is denoted a_n. The term preceding a_n is denoted a_{n-1}. For example, if $n = 6$, then the term preceding a_6 is a_{6-1} or a_5.

Term Number (n)	Term	Sequence Pattern	Description
1	1st or a_1	7	a_1
2	2nd or a_2	$(7) + 4$	$a_1 + d$
3	3rd or a_3	$(7 + 4) + 4$	$a_2 + d$
4	4th or a_4	$(7 + 4 + 4) + 4$	$a_3 + d$
5	5th or a_5	$(7 + 4 + 4 + 4) + 4$	$a_4 + d$
n	n^{th} or a_n	$a_{n-1} + 4$	$a_{n-1} + d$

Math Reasoning

Generalize Give an example of an arithmetic sequence. State the first 4 terms and the common difference.

Arithmetic sequences can be represented using a formula.

Arithmetic Sequence Formula

Use the formula below to find the next term in a sequence.

$$a_n = a_{n-1} + d$$

a_1 = first term

d = common difference

n = term number

In the arithmetic sequence 7, 11, 15, 19, ..., $a_1 = 7$, $a_2 = 11$, $a_3 = 15$, and $a_4 = 19$. The common difference is 4.

Example 2 **Using a Recursive Formula**

Use a recursive formula to find the first four terms of an arithmetic sequence where $a_1 = -2$ and the common difference $d = 7$.

SOLUTION

$a_n = a_{n-1} + d$	Write the formula.
$a_n = a_{n-1} + 7$	Substitute 7 for d.
$a_1 = -2$	Write the first term.
$a_2 = -2 + 7 = 5$	Find the second term.
$a_3 = 5 + 7 = 12$	Find the third term.
$a_4 = 12 + 7 = 19$	Find the fourth term.

The first four terms of the sequence are -2, 5, 12, and 19.

A rule for finding any term in an arithmetic sequence can be developed by looking at a different pattern in the sequence 7, 11, 15, 19, ...

Term	Term Number (n)	Sequence Pattern	Description
1st or a_1	1	7	a_1
2nd or a_2	2	$7 + 4 = 7 + (1)4$	$a_1 + (1)d$
3rd or a_3	3	$7 + 4 + 4 = 7 + (2)4$	$a_1 + (2)d$
4th or a_4	4	$7 + 4 + 4 + 4 = 7 + (3)4$	$a_1 + (3)d$
5th or a_5	5	$7 + 4 + 4 + 4 + 4 = 7 + 4(4)$	$a_1 + (4)d$
n^{th} or a_n	n	$7 + (n - 1)4$	$a_1 + (n - 1)d$

Finding the nth Term of an Arithmetic Sequence

$$a_n = a_1 + (n - 1)d$$

a_1 = first term d = common difference

Example 3 Finding the nth Term in Arithmetic Sequences

a. Use the rule $a_n = 6 + (n - 1)2$ to find the 4th and 11th terms of the sequence.

SOLUTION

4th term:

$$a_4 = 6 + (4 - 1)2$$
$$= 6 + (3)2$$
$$= 6 + 6$$
$$= 12$$

11th term:

$$a_{11} = 6 + (11 - 1)2$$
$$= 6 + (10)2$$
$$= 6 + 20$$
$$= 26$$

b. Find the 10th term of the sequence 3, 11, 19, 27, ...

SOLUTION

$a_1 = 3$ and the common difference $d = 11 - 3 = 8$

$a_n = 3 + (n - 1)8$ Write the rule, substituting for a, and d.

$a_{10} = 3 + (10 - 1)8$ Substitute the value for n.

$a_{10} = 75$ Simplify using the order of operations.

c. Find the 10th term of the sequence $\frac{1}{4}, \frac{3}{4}, \frac{5}{4}, \frac{7}{4}, ...$

SOLUTION

$a_1 = \frac{1}{4}$ and $d = \frac{3}{4} - \frac{1}{4} = \frac{2}{4} = \frac{1}{2}$

$a_n = \frac{1}{4} + (n - 1)\frac{1}{2}$ Write the rule, substituting for a, and d.

$a_{10} = \frac{1}{4} + (10 - 1)\frac{1}{2}$ Substitute the value for n.

$a_{10} = \frac{19}{4}$ Simplify using the order of operations.

Math Reasoning

Verify Is the sequence $-1, -5, -9, -13, \ldots$ an arithmetic sequence?

Example 4 **Application: Seating for a Reception**

The first table at a reception will seat 9 guests while each additional table will seat 6 more guests.

a. Write a rule to model the situation.

SOLUTION $a_1 = 9$ and $d = 6$. The rule is $a_n = 9 + (n - 1)6$.

b. Use the rule to find how many guests can be seated with 10 tables.

SOLUTION

$a_n = 9 + (n - 1)6$

$a_{10} = 9 + (10 - 1)6$

$a_{10} = 63$

63 guests can be seated with 10 tables.

Lesson Practice

Determine if each sequence is an arithmetic sequence. If yes, find the common difference and the next two terms.
(Ex 1)

a. $7, 6, 5, 4, \ldots$

b. $10, 12, 15, 19, \ldots$

c. Use a recursive formula to find the first four terms of an arithmetic sequence where $a_1 = -3$ and the common difference $d = 4$.
(Ex 2)

d. Use the rule $a_n = 14 + (n - 1)(-3)$ to find the 4th and 11th terms of an arithmetic sequence.
(Ex 3)

e. Find the 10th term of the sequence $1, 10, 19, 28, \ldots$.
(Ex 3)

f. Find the 11th term of the sequence $\frac{2}{3}, 1, 1\frac{1}{3}, 1\frac{2}{3}, \ldots$.
(Ex 3)

Flowers are purchased to put on tables at a reception. The head table needs to have 12 flowers and the other tables need to have 6 flowers each.
(Ex 4)

g. Write a rule to model the situation.

h. Use the rule to find the number of flowers needed for 15 tables.

Practice   Distributed and Integrated

Solve each proportion

1. $\frac{2}{10} = \frac{x}{-20}$
(31)

2. $\frac{32}{4} = \frac{x + 4}{3}$
(31)

*3. (**Construction**) An amphitheater with tiered rows is being constructed. The first row will have 24 seats and each row after that will have an additional 2 seats. If there will be a total of 15 rows, how many seats will be in the last row?
(34)

*4. Use a graphing calculator to complete the table of values
(30) for the function $f(x) = 2x^2 - 5$. Graph the function.

x	y
-2	
-1	
0	
1	
2	

*5. Solve $y = x + \frac{z}{3}$ for z.
(29)

Solve each equation. Check your answer.

6. $4x + 2 = 5(x + 10)$
(28)

7. $2\left(n + \frac{1}{3}\right) = \frac{3}{2}n + 1 + \frac{1}{2}n - \frac{1}{3}$
(28)

8. A bead is drawn from a bag, kept, and then a second bead is drawn. Identify
(33) these events as independent or dependent.

*9. Justify Is the sequence $0.3, -0.5, -1.3, -2.1, \ldots$ an arithmetic sequence? Justify
(34) your answer.

 *10. Write Explain why the sequence $2, 4, 8, 12, 16, \ldots$ is not an arithmetic sequence.
(34)

*11. Multiple Choice In the rule for the nth term of an arithmetic sequence
(34) $a_n = a_1 + (n - 1)d$, what does d represent?

  A the number of terms   **B** the first term

  C the nth term   **D** the common difference

*12. Is the sequence $7, 14, 21, 28, \ldots$ an arithmetic sequence? If it is, then find the
(34) common difference and the next two terms. If it is not, then find the next two
terms.

13. Statistics A poll is taken and each person is asked two questions.
(33) The results are shown in the table. What is the probability
that someone answered "yes" to both questions?

	Question 1	Question 2
Yes	55	30
No	45	70

14. Predict A number cube labeled 1–6 is rolled two times. What is the probability of
(33) rolling a 2 and then a 3?

*15. Geometry A rectangle with perimeter 10 units has a length of 3 units and a width
(34) of 2 units. Additional rectangles are added as shown below.

$P = 10$ units $P = 16$ units $P = 22$ units $P = 28$ units

  a. Write a rule for the perimeter of n rectangles.

  b. Use the rule to find the perimeter of 12 rectangles.

*16. Work uniforms include pants or a skirt, a shirt, and a tie or a vest. There are
(33) 3 pairs of pants, 5 skirts, 10 shirts, 2 ties, and 1 vest in a wardrobe.

  a. What is the probability of choosing a pair of pants, a shirt, and a tie?

  b. The pants and shirt from the previous day must be washed, but the tie returns
to the wardrobe. What is the probability of choosing pants, a shirt, and a tie the
next day?

17. Evaluate the expression $d = 6 \cdot \frac{1}{c^{-2}}$ for $c = 2$.
(32)

18. (Physical Science) The wavelengths of microwaves can range from 10^{-3} m to 10^{-1} m.
(32) Express the range of wavelengths using positive exponents.

19. Multiple Choice Ms. Markelsden baked 36 cookies in 45 minutes. How many cookies
(31) can she bake in 3 hours?

    A 45 cookies   **B** 81 cookies

    C 64 cookies   **D** 144 cookies

20. Does $y = x^2 + 2$ represent a function? Explain how you know.
(30)

21. (Architecture) A model of a building is 15 inches tall. In the scale drawing, 1 inch
(31) represents 20 feet. How tall is the building?

*22. Generalize Given $\frac{2}{b} = \frac{1}{a}$, where a and b are positive numbers, write an equation
(31) that shows how to find a.

23. The line graph at right shows the costs of tuition at a
(27) university over the past 5 years. How might this graph be
misleading?

24. Write The equation $x + 5 = x - 5$ has no solution. Explain
(28) why it has no solution.

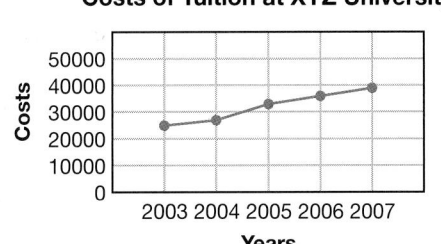

Costs of Tuition at XYZ University

25. Verify Solve $16x + 4(2x - 6) = 60$ for x. Check your answer.
(26)

26. True or False: Any irrational number divided by an irrational number will be
(1) an irrational number. Explain your answer.

27. (Savings) Hector has $400 in his savings account. Each week he deposits his $612.50
(23) paycheck and takes out $250 to live on for the week. If he wants to buy a car for
$5500, about how many months will it take him to save up for the car?

28. Multi-Step Jamal is riding his bike at a rate of about 8 miles per hour. How many
(31) hours will it take Jamal to ride 50 miles?

29. (Car Rental) A family rented a car that cost $45 per day plus $0.23 per mile. If the
(24) family rented the car for 7 days and paid $395.50 altogether, how many miles did
they drive?

30. Error Analysis Two students determine whether the ordered pairs in the table
(25) represent a function. Which student is correct? Explain the error.

	Student A		Student B
	(7, 12) and (7, 10) The x-values are the same, so it is not a function.		All the y-values are different, so it is not a function.

x	y
7	10
−2	−3
7	12
5	4

Locating and Using Intercepts

Warm Up

1. Vocabulary A pair of numbers that can be used to locate a point on a
(20) coordinate plane is called a(n) _____.

Evaluate.

2. $3x + 14; x = -9$
(16)

3. $7.5w - 84.3; w = 15$
(16)

Solve.

4. $7x - 18 = -74$
(23)

5. $57 + 19y = -76$
(23)

New Concepts

Math Language

An **ordered pair** can be
used to locate a point on
a coordinate plane.

Linear equations can be graphed by making a table of ordered pairs that
satisfy the equation and then graphing the corresponding points (x, y).
An ordered pair or set of ordered pairs that satisfy an equation is called the
solution of a linear equation in two variables. When an equation is in standard
form, the linear equation can be graphed another way.

Standard Form of a Linear Equation
The **standard form of a linear equation** is $Ax + By = C$, where A, B, and C are real numbers and A and B are not both zero.

The x-coordinate of the point where the graph of an equation intersects the
x-axis is called the x-**intercept.** The y-coordinate of the point where the graph
of an equation intersects the y-axis is called the y-**intercept.** The coordinate
pairs $(x, 0)$ and $(0, y)$ that satisfy a linear equation are two solutions of the
linear equation in two variables.

Example 1 **Finding x- and y-Intercepts**

Find the x- and y-intercepts for $3x + 4y = 24$.

SOLUTION

To find the intercepts, make a table. Substitute 0 for y and solve for x.
Substitute 0 for x and solve for y.

$$3x + 4y = 24$$
$$3x + 4(0) = 24$$
$$3x = 24$$
$$\frac{3x}{3} = \frac{24}{3}$$
$$x = 8$$

$$3x + 4y = 24$$
$$3(0) + 4y = 24$$
$$4y = 24$$
$$\frac{4y}{4} = \frac{24}{4}$$
$$y = 6$$

x	y
8	0
0	6

The x-intercept is 8. The y-intercept is 6.

Online Connection
www.SaxonMathResources.com

At a school play, student tickets are $5 and adult tickets are $8. Let x be the number of student tickets sold. Let y be the number of adult tickets sold. The equation $5x + 8y = 400$ shows that one drama club member raised $400 from ticket sales. Find the intercepts and explain what each means.

SOLUTION

Substitute 0 for y and solve for x. Then substitute 0 for x and solve for y.

$$5x + 8y = 400 \qquad\qquad 5x + 8y = 400$$
$$5x + 8(0) = 400 \qquad\qquad 5(0) + 8y = 400$$
$$5x = 400 \qquad\qquad 8y = 400$$
$$\frac{5x}{5} = \frac{400}{5} \qquad\qquad \frac{8y}{8} = \frac{400}{8}$$
$$x = 80 \qquad\qquad y = 50$$

The x-intercept is 80. The y-intercept is 50.

The x-intercept shows that if the drama club member sold no adult tickets, 80 student tickets were sold. The y-intercept shows that if no student tickets were sold, 50 adult tickets were sold.

Lesson Practice

a. Find the x- and y-intercepts for $-6x + 9y = 36$.
(Ex 1)

b. Graph $4x + 7y = 28$ using the x- and y-intercepts.
(Ex 2)

c. Find the x- and y-intercepts on the graph.
(Ex 3)

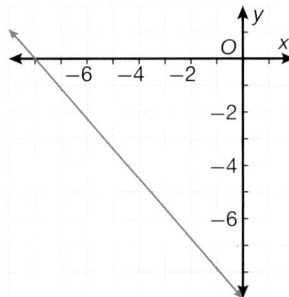

d. Write $4y = 12x - 12$ in standard form. Then graph the equation using the x- and y-intercepts.
(Ex 4)

e. (**Athletics**) Hirva jogs 6 miles per hour and bikes 12 miles per hour. The equation $6x + 12y = 24$ shows that she has gone a total of 24 miles. Find the intercepts and explain what each means.
(Ex 5)

Solve.

1. $\dfrac{-2.25}{x} = \dfrac{9}{6}$
(31)

*2. $\dfrac{y+2}{y+7} = \dfrac{11}{31}$
(31)

3. $2(f+3) + 4f = 6 + 6f$
(28)

4. $3x + 7 - 2x = 4x + 10$
(28)

Evaluate each expression for the given value of the variable.

5. $(m+6) \div (2-5)$ for $m = 9$
(9)

6. $-3(x + 12 \cdot 2)$ for $x = -8$
(9)

Simplify by combining like terms.

7. $10y^3 + 5y - 4y^3$
(18)

8. $10xy^2 - 5x^2y + 3y^2x$
(18)

9. Identify the subsets of real numbers to which the number $\sqrt{7}$ belongs.
(1)

*10. Find the x- and y-intercepts for $5x + 10y = -20$.
(35)

*11. Find the x- and y-intercepts for $-8x + 20y = 40$.
(35)

*12. Write Explain how knowing the x- and y-intercepts is helpful in graphing a linear
(35) equation.

*13. Multiple Choice What is the x-intercept for the equation $15x + 9y = 45$?
(35)   **A** $(0, 3)$ **B** $(3, 0)$ **C** $(5, 0)$ **D** $(0, 5)$

*14. (**Fishery**) A Pacific salmon can swim at a maximum speed of 8 miles per hour. The
(35) function $y = 8x$ describes how many miles y the fish swims in x hours. Graph the
function. Use the graph to estimate the number of miles the fish swims in 2.5 hours.

15. Determine if the sequence 34, 29, 24, 19, … is an arithmetic sequence or not. If yes,
(34) find the common difference and the next two terms. If no, find the next two terms.

16. Error Analysis Two students are finding the common difference for the arithmetic
(34) sequence 18, 15, 12, 9, …. Which student is correct? Explain the error.

Student A	Student B
$18 - 15 = 3$	$15 - 18 = -3$
$15 - 12 = 3$	$12 - 15 = -3$
$12 - 9 = 3$	$9 - 12 = -3$

*17. Geometry A right triangle is formed by the origin and the x- and y-intercepts of
(35) $14x + 7y = 56$. Find the area of the triangle.

18. Data Analysis The table shows the weights of a newborn baby who was 7.5 lb at birth.
(34)

Week Number	Weight (lb)
1	9
2	10.5
3	12
4	13.5

  a. Write a recursive formula for the baby's weight gain.

  b. If the pattern continues, how much will the baby weigh after 7 weeks?

*19. Multi-Step Use the arithmetic sequence $-65, -72, -79, -86, \ldots$.
(34)

  a. What is the value of a_1?

  b. What is the common difference d?

  c. Write a rule for the nth term of the sequence.

20. Write A coin is flipped and lands on heads. It is flipped again and lands on tails. Identify these events as independent or dependent.
(33)

21. (Economics) You have agreed to a babysitting job that will last 14 days. On the first day, you earn \$25, but on each day after that you will earn \$15. How much will you earn if you babysit for 7 days?
(34)

22. Probability A bag holds 5 red marbles, 3 white marbles, and 2 green marbles. A marble is drawn, kept out, and then another marble is drawn. What is the probability of drawing two white marbles?
(33)

*23. Multiple Choice Which of the following expressions is the simplified solution
(32) of $\frac{m^3 n^{-10} p^5}{m n^0 p^{-2}}$?

  A $\dfrac{m^3 p^3}{n^{10}}$ **B** $\dfrac{m^3 p^7}{n^{10}}$ **C** $\dfrac{m^2 p^3}{n^9}$ **D** $\dfrac{m^2 p^7}{n^{10}}$

*24. Verify Is the statement $4^{-2} = -16$ correct? Explain your reasoning.
(32)

25. Convert 45 miles per hour to miles per minute.
(31)

26. Rewrite the following question so it is not biased: Would you rather buy a brand new luxury SUV or a cheap used car?
(Inv 3)

27. Identify the independent variable and the dependent variable: money earned, hours worked.
(20)

28. (Temperature) Use the formula $F = \frac{9}{5} C + 32$ to find an equivalent Fahrenheit temperature when the temperature is $-12°C$.
(23)

29. (Homework) A student has to write a book report on a book that contains 1440 pages. Suppose she plans to read 32 pages per day. Using function notation, express how many pages remain after reading for d days.
(25)

30. (Soccer) For every hour a player practices soccer, he must drink 8 fluid ounces of liquid to stay hydrated. Write an equation describing this relation and determine whether it is a function.
(25)

Writing and Solving Proportions

1. Vocabulary A _____ is a comparison of two quantities using division.
(31)

Solve.

2. $\dfrac{13}{52} = \dfrac{x}{36}$
(31)

3. $\dfrac{42}{56} = \dfrac{63}{w}$
(31)

4. $15x - 37 = 143$
(23)

5. $78 + 22y = -230$
(23)

New Concepts

Proportions are frequently used to solve problems in mathematics. Proportional reasoning can be applied in many situations, including reading and drawing maps, architecture, and construction. Solving problems in these situations requires knowledge of similar figures.

Reading Math

The ~ symbol indicates similar figures and reads "is similar to." The ≅ symbol indicates congruent figures and reads "is congruent to."

If two geometric objects or figures are **similar,** they have the same shape but are not necessarily the same size. The triangles below are similar.

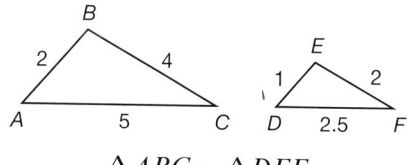

$$\triangle ABC \sim \triangle DEF$$

When two figures are similar, they have sides and angles that correspond. Corresponding sides and angles are found using the order of the letters in the similarity statement. In the triangles above, $\angle A$ and $\angle D$ correspond, $\angle B$ and $\angle E$ correspond, and $\angle C$ and $\angle F$ correspond. Corresponding angles of similar figures are **congruent,** or have the same measure.

$$\angle A \cong \angle D \qquad \angle B \cong \angle E \qquad \angle C \cong \angle F$$

Reading Math

$\overline{AB}$ is read "segment AB."

Sides of similar figures also correspond. In the example above, $\overline{AB}$ and $\overline{DE}$ correspond, $\overline{BC}$ and $\overline{EF}$ correspond, and $\overline{AC}$ and $\overline{DF}$ correspond. Corresponding sides of similar figures do not have to be congruent. However, they do have to be in proportion. The ratio of the all pairs of corresponding sides must be the same.

$$\frac{AB}{DE} = \frac{BC}{EF} = \frac{AC}{DF}$$

In the example above, the ratio of the sides of $\triangle ABC$ to $\triangle DEF$ is 2 to 1. This ratio, which can also be written as $\frac{2}{1}$ or 2:1, is called the scale factor of $\triangle ABC$ to $\triangle DEF$.

$$\frac{AB}{DE} = \frac{BC}{EF} = \frac{AC}{DF} = \frac{2}{1}$$

A **scale factor** is the ratio of a side length of a figure to the side length of a similiar figure. The scale factor of $\triangle DEF$ to $\triangle ABC$ is 1 to 2.

g. Find the ratio of the volumes. How does this ratio compare to the scale factor?

Ratios of the Perimeter, Area, and Volume of Similar Figures

If two similar figures have a scale factor of $\frac{a}{b}$, then the ratio of their perimeters is $\frac{a}{b}$, the ratio of their areas is $\frac{a^2}{b^2}$, and the ratio of their volumes is $\frac{a^3}{b^3}$.

Example 4 Application: Changing Dimensions

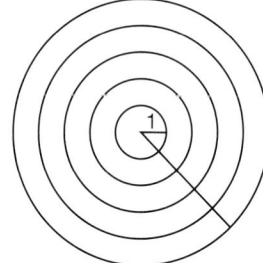

A dartboard is composed of concentric circles. The radius of the smallest inner circle is 1 inch, and with each consecutive circle, the radius increases by 1 inch.

Math Language

Perimeter is the distance around a closed plane figure. **Circumference** is the distance around a circle.

a. What is the ratio of the circumference of the two inner circles to the circumference of the outermost circle?

SOLUTION

$$\frac{\text{circumference of two inner circles}}{\text{circumference of outermost circle}} = \frac{2\pi(2)}{2\pi(5)} = \frac{2}{5}$$

b. What is the ratio of the area of the two inner circles to the area of the outermost circle?

SOLUTION

$$\frac{\text{area of two inner circles}}{\text{area of outermost circle}} = \frac{\pi(2)^2}{\pi(5)^2}$$

$$= \frac{4\pi}{25\pi}$$

$$= \frac{4}{25}$$

Math Reasoning

Verify Use Example 3 to show that if similar figures have a scale factor of $\frac{a}{b}$, then the ratio of their areas is $\frac{a^2}{b^2}$.

Lesson Practice

a. $\triangle ABC \sim \triangle LKM$. Find m$\angle K$ and m$\angle C$.
(Ex 1)

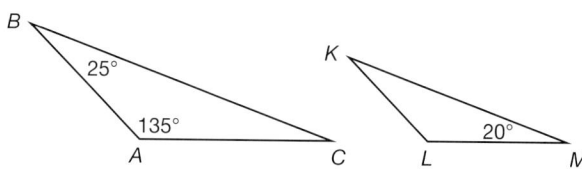

b. The figures are similar. Find the scale factor. Then use the scale factor to find x.
(Ex 1)

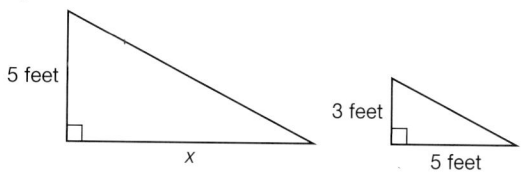

22
(33)

23
(18)

24.
(20)

25.
(23)

26.
(23)

27.
(32)

28.
(26)

29.
(27)

30.
(28)

c. The side of a building casts
(Ex 2) a shadow 21 meters long. A
statue that is 5 meters tall casts
a shadow 4 meters long. The
triangles are similar. How tall
is the building?

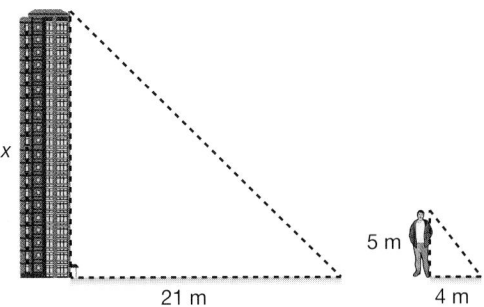

d. The scale drawing of the kitchen tabletop has dimensions 5 inches by
(Ex 3) 2.5 inches. If the scale factor of the drawing to the actual table is
1 in.:18 in., what are the dimensions of the actual table?

e. Small toy cars are constructed using a scale factor of 1 in.:64 in. What is
(Ex 4) the ratio of the areas of the toy car and the actual car?

Practice   Distributed and Integrated

Solve each proportion.

*1. $\dfrac{3}{4} = \dfrac{x}{100}$
(36)

*2. $\dfrac{5.5}{x} = \dfrac{1.375}{11}$
(36)

Simplify each expression.

3. $2^2 + 6(8 - 5) \div 2$
(4)

4. $\dfrac{(3 + 2)(4 + 3) + 5^2}{6 - 2^2}$
(4)

5. $\dfrac{14 - 8}{-2^2 + 1}$
(4)

6. The point (3, 5) is graphed in which quadrant of a coordinate plane?
(20)

7. True or False: The set of ordered pairs below defines a function.
(25)

$$\{(1, 3), (2, 3), (3, 3), (4, 3)\}$$

*8. The triangles at right are similar. Find the missing length.
(36)

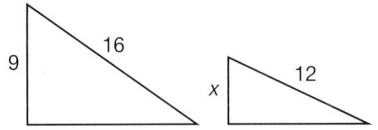

*9. Multiple Choice One triangle has side lengths 3, 5, and 6. A similar triangle has
(36) side lengths 18, 15, and 9. Which of the following ratios is the scale factor of the
triangles?

   A $\dfrac{1}{6}$
   B $\dfrac{1}{3}$
   C $\dfrac{1}{5}$
   D $\dfrac{2}{3}$

*10. (Landscaping) A landscaping company needs to measure the height of a tree. The
(36) tree casts a shadow that is 6 feet long. A person who is 5 feet tall casts a shadow
that is 2 feet long.

a. Draw a picture to represent the problem.

b. Use your picture to find the height of the tree.

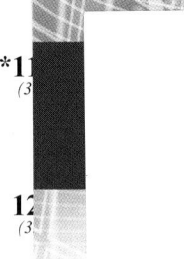

*11
(3

12
(3

*13
(3(

14
(3:

15
(3:

*16
(3:

17
(3:

18
(34

*19
(34

*20.
(33,

21.
(31)

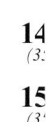

To divide numbers in scientific notation, divide the coefficients, and then divide the powers. If the result is not in scientific notation, adjust it so that it is.

Example 3 **Dividing Numbers in Scientific Notation**

Find the quotient. Write the answer in scientific notation.

$$\frac{1.2 \times 10^3}{9.6 \times 10^6}$$

SOLUTION

$$\frac{1.2 \times 10^3}{9.6 \times 10^6}$$

$$= \frac{1.2}{9.6} \times \frac{10^3}{10^6} \qquad \text{Divide the coefficients and divide the powers.}$$

$$= 0.125 \times 10^{-3} \qquad \text{Simplify.}$$

Notice that this number is not in scientific notation. There is not one nonzero digit before the decimal point. Move the decimal to the right one place and subtract one from the exponent.

$$0.125 \times 10^{-3} = 1.25 \times 10^{-4}$$

> **Hint**
>
> When you divide powers with like bases, keep the base the same and subtract the exponents.
>
> $\frac{10^3}{10^6} = 10^{3-6}$

Example 4 **Comparing Expressions with Scientific Notation**

Compare. Use $<$, $>$, or $=$.

$$\frac{7.2 \times 10^6}{3.6 \times 10^4} \bigcirc \frac{1.05 \times 10^7}{3.5 \times 10^5}$$

SOLUTION

$$\frac{7.2 \times 10^6}{3.6 \times 10^4} \qquad\qquad \frac{1.05 \times 10^7}{3.5 \times 10^5}$$

$$= \frac{7.2}{3.6} \times \frac{10^6}{10^4} \qquad\qquad = \frac{1.05}{3.5} \times \frac{10^7}{10^5}$$

$$= 2 \times 10^2 = 200 \qquad = 0.3 \times 10^2 = 30$$

Since $200 > 30$, then $\dfrac{7.2 \times 10^6}{3.6 \times 10^4} > \dfrac{1.05 \times 10^7}{3.5 \times 10^5}$.

Example 5 **Application: Speed of Light**

The speed of light is 3×10^8 meters per second. If Earth is 1.47×10^{11} meters from the sun, how many seconds does it take light to reach Earth from the sun? Write the answer in scientific notation.

SOLUTION Divide the earth's distance from the sun by the speed of light.

$$\frac{1.47 \times 10^{11}}{3 \times 10^8} = 0.49 \times 10^3$$

$$= 4.9 \times 10^2 \qquad \text{Write the answer in scientific notation.}$$

It takes light about 4.9×10^2 seconds to reach the earth from the sun.

228

Lesson Practice

Write each number in scientific notation.
(Ex 1)

    a. $1{,}234{,}000.$ **b.** $0.0306.$

    c. Find the product. Write the answer in scientific notation.
(Ex 2)

$$(5.82 \times 10^3)(6.13 \times 10^{11})$$

    d. Find the quotient. Write the answer in scientific notation.
(Ex 3)

$$\frac{(7.29 \times 10^{-2})}{(8.1 \times 10^{-6})}$$

    e. Compare. Use $<$, $>$, or $=$.
(Ex 4)

$$\frac{4.56 \times 10^9}{3 \times 10^5} \bigcirc \frac{5.2 \times 10^8}{1.3 \times 10^5}.$$

    f. (**Astronomy**) The speed of light is 3×10^8 meters per second. If Mars is
(Ex 5) 2.25×10^{11} meters from the Sun, how many seconds does it take light to reach Mars from the Sun? Write the answer in scientific notation.

Practice   Distributed and Integrated

Simplify each expression.

1. $18 \div 3^2 - 5 + 2$ **2.** $7^2 + 4^2 + 3$ **3.** $3[-2(8 - 13)]$
(4)   *(4)*   *(4)*

Simplify each expression by combining like terms.

4. $13b^2 + 5b - b^2$ **5.** $-3(8x + 4) + \frac{1}{2}(6x - 24)$
(18)   *(18)*

*6. Write 7.4×10^{-9} in standard notation.
(37)

*7. Write Explain how to recognize if a number is in scientific notation.
(37)

*8. Write Explain why anyone would want to use scientific notation.
(37)

*9. Multiple Choice What is $(3.4 \times 10^{10})(4.8 \times 10^5)$ in scientific notation?
(37)   **A** 1.632×10^{15} **B** 1.632×10^{16} **C** 16.32×10^{15} **D** 16.32×10^{16}

*10. (**Physiology**) The diameter of a red blood cell is about 4×10^{-5} inches. Write this
(37) number in standard notation.

11. The triangles shown are similar. Find the missing length.
(36)

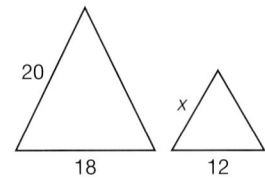

12. A student's final grade is determined by adding four test grades and dividing by
(26) 4. The student's first three test grades are 79, 88, and 94. What must the student make on the last test to get a final grade of 90?

*13. Graph $50x - 100y = 300$ using the x- and y-intercepts.
(35)

14. Geometry A square has side lengths of 3 centimeters. Another square has side
(36) lengths of 6 centimeters.

   a. What is the scale factor of the sides of the smaller square to the larger
   square?

   b. What is the perimeter of each square?

   c. What is the ratio of the perimeter of the smaller square to the perimeter of the
   larger square?

   d. What is the area of each square?

   e. What is the ratio of the area of the smaller square to the area of the larger
   square?

*15. Error Analysis In the figures at right, $\angle A$ and $\angle F$ correspond. Two students
(36) are finding the measure of $\angle F$. Which student is correct? Explain
the error.

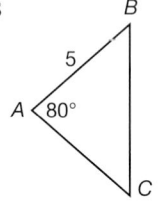 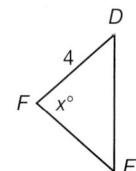

Student A	Student B
$\dfrac{5}{4} = \dfrac{80}{x}$	$m\angle A = m\angle F$
$5x = 320$	$80° = m\angle F$
$x = 64$	
$m\angle F = 64°$	

16. (Architecture) A room is 10 feet by 12 feet. If the scale of the blueprints to the room
(36) is 1 inch to 2 feet, find the dimensions of the room on the blueprints.

*17. Measurement What is the ratio of the area of the smaller circle to the area of the
(36) larger circle?

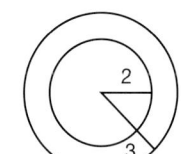

18. Verify Verify that the sequence $4, 2\frac{2}{3}, 1\frac{1}{3}, 0, \ldots$ is an arithmetic sequence.
(34)

19. A piece of fruit is chosen from a box, eaten, and then a second piece of fruit is
(33) chosen. Identify these events as independent or dependent.

20. Predict An estimate of the number of tagged foxes to the total number of foxes
(31) in a forest is 3 to 13. A forest warden noted 21 tagged foxes during a trip in the
forest. Write a proportion to indicate the total number of foxes that might be in
the forest.

21. Multiple Choice In the rule for the nth term of arithmetic sequence
(34) $a_n = a_1 + (n - 1)d$, what does a_1 represent?

   A the number of terms   **B** the first term

   C the nth term   **D** the common difference

*22. (Physical Science) The wavelengths of ultraviolet light can range from 10^{-9} meter to
(32) 10^{-7} meter. Express the range of wavelengths using positive exponents.

23. **Estimate** Between which two whole numbers is the solution to $\frac{13}{14} = \frac{x}{10}$?
(31)

24. (Dog Breeds) The table shows the number of dogs of the top five breeds registered
(27) with the American Kennel Club in 2006. Describe how the data could be displayed
in a potentially misleading way.

Breed	Labrador Retriever	Yorkshire Terrier	German Shepherd	Golden Retriever	Beagle
Number	123,760	48,346	43,575	42,962	39,484

25. Choose an appropriate graph to display a survey showing what type of sport
(22) most people like. Explain your answer.

26. (Exercising) A weightlifter averages 2 minutes on each exercise. Each workout
(25) includes a 20-minute swim. Write a rule in function notation to describe the time it
takes to complete w exercises and the swim.

27. **Estimate** Using the order of magnitude, estimate the value of 89,678 multiplied
(3) by 11,004,734.

28. **Justify** Solve for x: $7x + 9 = 2(4x + 2)$. Justify each step.
(29)

*29. An oceanographer wants to convert measurements that are above and below sea
(30) level from yards to feet. He takes measurements of depths and heights in yards
and feet.

yards	-679	-125	32	79
feet	-2037	-375	96	237

    a. Formulate Use the table to write a formula to convert from yards to feet.

    b. Predict Use the formula to convert 27.5 yards to feet.

    c. Write a formula to convert yards to inches.

30. **Multi-Step** A rectangle has a perimeter of $38 + x$ centimeters. The rectangle has a
(28) length of $3x - 2$ centimeters and a width of x centimeters. What is the length of
the rectangle?

    a. Substitute the dimensions of the rectangle into the perimeter formula
       $P = 2w + 2l$.

    b. Solve for x.

    c. Find the length of the rectangle.

Simplifying Expressions Using the GCF

Warm Up

1. **Vocabulary** When two or more quantities are multiplied, each is a
   ₍₂₎ _____ (**term, factor**) of the product.

Simplify.

2. $2x(3x - 5)$
₍₁₆₎

3. $-3x^2y(4x^2 - 7xy)$
₍₁₆₎

4. $\dfrac{x^5}{x^{-3}}$
₍₃₂₎

5. $\dfrac{1}{-(-4)^3}$
₍₃₂₎

New Concepts Simplifying expressions that contain numbers often requires knowledge of prime numbers and factors. Recall that a prime number is a whole number that is only divisible by itself and 1.

$$2 = 1 \cdot 2 \qquad 5 = 1 \cdot 5 \qquad 13 = 1 \cdot 13 \qquad 19 = 1 \cdot 19$$

All whole numbers other than 1 that are not prime are composite numbers.

Math Reasoning

Formulate Find all of the prime numbers that are less than 100.

Composite numbers have whole-number factors other than 1 and the number itself. They can be written as a product of prime numbers, which is called the prime factorization of a number.

$$4 = 2 \cdot 2 \qquad 6 = 2 \cdot 3 \qquad 8 = 2 \cdot 2 \cdot 2$$

Several methods can be used to find the prime factorization of a number. The process requires breaking down the composite numbers until all the factors are prime numbers.

The prime factorization for the number 24 can be found in at least three ways.

$$24 = 2 \cdot 12$$
$$= 2 \cdot 2 \cdot 6$$
$$= 2 \cdot 2 \cdot 2 \cdot 3$$

```
        24
       /  \
      4    6
     / \  / \
    2  2 2   3
```

```
2 | 24
2 | 12
2 | 6
3 | 3
    1
```

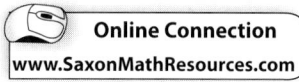

Online Connection
www.SaxonMathResources.com

It does not matter which method is used to find a prime factorization. The final product, however, must consist of only prime numbers. The factors are usually written in ascending order.

Example 1 Finding the Prime Factorization of a Number

Find the prime factorization of each number.

a. 120

SOLUTION

Method 1: List the factors and then the prime factors.

$$120 = 2 \cdot 60$$
$$= 2 \cdot 2 \cdot 30$$
$$= 2 \cdot 2 \cdot 2 \cdot 15$$
$$= 2 \cdot 2 \cdot 2 \cdot 3 \cdot 5$$

Method 2: Use a factor tree.

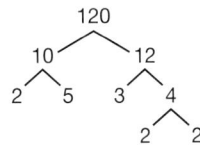

The prime factors are 2, 2, 2, 3, and 5.

Method 3: Use division by primes.

$$
\begin{array}{r|l}
2 & 120 \\
\hline
2 & 60 \\
\hline
2 & 30 \\
\hline
3 & 15 \\
\hline
5 & 5 \\
\hline
 & 1
\end{array}
$$

The prime factors are 2, 2, 2, 3, and 5.

The prime factorization of $120 = 2 \cdot 2 \cdot 2 \cdot 3 \cdot 5$.

b. 924

SOLUTION

$$924 = 2 \cdot 462$$
$$= 2 \cdot 2 \cdot 231$$
$$= 2 \cdot 2 \cdot 3 \cdot 77$$
$$= 2 \cdot 2 \cdot 3 \cdot 7 \cdot 11$$

The prime factorization of $924 = 2 \cdot 2 \cdot 3 \cdot 7 \cdot 11$.

Prime factorization can be used when determining the **greatest common factor (GCF) of monomials,** which is the product of the greatest integer that divides without a remainder into the coefficients and the greatest power of each variable that divides without a remainder into each term.

Finding the GCF means finding the largest monomial that divides without a remainder into each term of a polynomial.

> **Hint**
>
> One method for finding the prime factorization of a number is to divide out all 2's first, then all 3's, then all 5's, and so on, if they are factors.

Example 2 — Determining the GCF of Algebraic Expressions

Find the GCF of each expression.

a. $6a^2b^3 + 8a^2b^2c$

SOLUTION

Write the prime factorization for both terms.

$$6a^2b^3 = 2 \cdot 3 \cdot a \cdot a \cdot b \cdot b \cdot b \qquad\qquad 8a^2b^2c = 2 \cdot 2 \cdot 2 \cdot a \cdot a \cdot b \cdot b \cdot c$$

Find all factors that are common to both terms.

$$6a^2b^3 = 2 \cdot 3 \cdot a \cdot a \cdot b \cdot b \cdot b$$
$$8a^2b^2c = 2 \cdot 2 \cdot 2 \cdot a \cdot a \cdot b \cdot b \cdot c$$

Each term has one factor of 2, two factors of a and two factors of b, so the GCF of $6a^2b^3$ and $8a^2b^2c$ is $2 \cdot a \cdot a \cdot b \cdot b = 2a^2b^2$.

b. $8c^4d^2e - 12c^3d^4e^2$

SOLUTION

$$8c^4d^2e = 2 \cdot 2 \cdot 2 \cdot c \cdot c \cdot c \cdot c \cdot d \cdot d \cdot e$$
$$12c^3d^4e^2 = 2 \cdot 2 \cdot 3 \cdot c \cdot c \cdot c \cdot d \cdot d \cdot d \cdot d \cdot e \cdot e$$

The GCF is $4c^3d^2e$.

Finding the GCF of a polynomial allows you to factor it and to write the polynomial as a product of factors instead of the sum or difference of monomials.

Factoring a polynomial is the inverse of the Distributive Property. Using the Distributive Property will "undo" the factoring of the GCF.

Example 3 — Factoring a Polynomial

Factor each polynomial completely.

a. $6x^3 + 8x^2 - 2x$

SOLUTION

Find the GCF of the terms. The GCF is $2x$.

Write each term of the polynomial with the GCF as a factor.

$$6x^3 + 8x^2 - 2x = 2x \cdot 3x^2 + 2x \cdot 4x - 2x \cdot 1$$
$$2x(3x^2 + 4x - 1)$$

Check

$$2x(3x^2 + 4x - 1)$$
$$2x(3x^2) + 2x(4x) - 2x(1) \qquad \text{Use the Distributive Property.}$$
$$6x^3 + 8x^2 - 2x \qquad\qquad\quad \text{Multiply each term by the GCF.}$$

The factored polynomial is the same as the original polynomial.

Hint

You can also divide each term by the GCF.
$$\frac{6x^3}{2x} = 3x^2$$

Caution

To completely factor a polynomial, you must factor out the greatest common factor, not just a common factor.

b. $9x^4y^2 - 9x^6y$

SOLUTION

The GCF of the polynomial is $9x^4y$.

$$9x^4y^2 - 9x^6y = 9x^4y \cdot y - 9x^4y \cdot x^2$$

The factored polynomial is $9x^4y\,(y - x^2)$.

Fractions can be simplified if the numerator and denominator contain common factors. This is because the operations of multiplication and division undo each other.

numeric fractions: $\dfrac{4}{10} = \dfrac{2}{5}$ and $\dfrac{8}{4} = \dfrac{2}{1}$ or 2

algebraic fractions: $\dfrac{4x}{10} = \dfrac{2x}{5}$ and $\dfrac{8x}{4} = 2x$

Notice that there is no addition or subtraction involved in the fractions above. Simplifying fractions with addition or subtraction in the numerator follows similar rules to adding or subtracting numeric fractions. A fraction can only be simplified if the numerator and the denominator have common factors.

Example 4 Simplifying Algebraic Fractions

Simplify each expression.

a. $\dfrac{3p + 3}{3}$

SOLUTION

$$\dfrac{3p + 3}{3}$$

$$= \dfrac{\cancel{3}(p + 1)}{\cancel{3}} \qquad \text{Factor out the GCF.}$$

$$= p + 1 \qquad \text{Simplify.}$$

b. $\dfrac{5x - 25x^2}{5xy}.$

SOLUTION

$$\dfrac{5x - 25x^2}{5xy}$$

$$= \dfrac{\cancel{5x}(1 - 5x)}{\cancel{5x}y} \qquad \text{Factor out the GCF.}$$

$$= \dfrac{1 - 5x}{y} \qquad \text{Simplify.}$$

Math Reasoning

Write Explain why you cannot reduce the fraction $\dfrac{5x - 2}{5}$.

Example 5 Application: Finding the Height of an Object

The formula $h = -16t^2 + 72t + 12$ can be used to represent the height of an object that is launched into the air from 12 feet off the ground with an initial velocity of 72 feet/second. Rewrite the formula by factoring the right side using the GCF and making the t^2-term positive.

SOLUTION

The GCF of the monomials is 4. To keep the t^2-term positive, factor out -4. So $h = -4(4t^2 - 18t - 3)$.

Lesson Practice

Find the prime factorization of each number.
(Ex 1)

   a. 100   **b.** 51

Find the GCF of each expression.
(Ex 2)

   c. $24m^3n^4 + 32mn^5p$ **d.** $5p^2q^5r^2 - 10pq^2r^2$

Factor each polynomial completely.
(Ex 3)

   e. $8d^2e^3 + 12d^3e^2$ **f.** $12x^4y^2z - 42x^3y^3z^2$

Factor each expression completely.
(Ex 4)

   g. $\dfrac{6x + 18}{6}$ **h.** $\dfrac{18x + 45x^3}{9x}$

   i. The formula $h = -16t^2 + 60t + 4$ can be used to find the height of an
(Ex 5) object that is launched into the air from 4 feet off the ground with an initial velocity of 60 feet/second. Rewrite the formula by factoring the right side of the equation using the GCF and making the t^2-term positive.

Practice Distributed and Integrated

Solve each equation for the variable indicated.

   1. $6 = hj + k$ for j
(29)
                     2. $\dfrac{a + 3}{b} = c$ for a
(29)

Draw a graph that represents each situation.

   3. A tomato plant grows taller at a steady pace.
(Inv 2)

   4. A tomato plant grows at a slow pace, and then grows rapidly with more sun and
(Inv 2) water.

   5. A tomato plant grows slowly at first, remains a constant height during a dry spell,
(Inv 2) and then grows rapidly with more sun and water.

Find each unit rate.

   6. Thirty textbooks weigh 144 pounds.   **7.** Doug makes \$43.45 in 5.5 hours.
(31)   *(31)*

8. Write 2×10^6 in standard notation.
(37)

9. Solve $\dfrac{p}{3} = \dfrac{18}{21}$.
(31)

*10. Find the prime factorization of 140.
(38)

*11. **Multiple Choice** Which of the following expressions is the correct simplification
(38) of $\dfrac{10x + 5}{5}$?

    A $2x + 5$ **B** $2x + 1$ **C** $10x + 1$ **D** $5x$

*12. (**Free Fall**) The function $h = 40 - 16t^2$ can be used to find the height of an object
(38) as it falls to the ground after being dropped from 40 feet in the air. Rewrite the
equation by factoring the right side.

*13. **Write** Explain how the Distributive Property and factoring a polynomial are related.
(38)

*14. **Generalize** Explain why the algebraic fraction $\dfrac{6(x - 1)}{6}$ can be reduced, and why
(38) the fraction $\dfrac{6x - 1}{6}$ cannot be reduced.

15. (**Biology**) The approximate diameter of a DNA helix is 0.000000002 meters.
(37) Write this number in scientific notation.

16. **Measurement** A nanosecond is one-billionth of a second. Write this number in
(37) scientific notation.

17. Write 78,000,000 in scientific notation.
(37)

*18. **Geometry** A square has side length 6.04×10^{-5} meters. What is its area?
(37)

*19. The triangles are similar. Find the missing length.
(36)

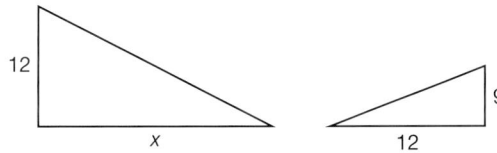

20. **Multi-Step** An adult brain weighs about 3 pounds.
(37)
    a. There are about 100 billion brain cells in the brain. Write this number in
    scientific notation.

    b. Divide the weight of an adult brain by the number of cells and find how many
    pounds one brain cell weighs. Write the answer in scientific notation.

*21. **Analyze** Find the x- and y-intercepts for $y = 12x$ and explain how they relate to the
(35) graph of the equation.

22. (**Fundraising**) The math club has a carwash to raise money. Out of the first 40 vehicles,
(33) 22 are SUVs and 18 are cars. What are the odds against the next one being a car?

*23. **Justify** Explain why the statement $3^{-2} = -6$ is false.
(32)

24. Analysis A bookstore wants to show the number of different types of books that
(Inv 3) were sold on a given day. Why is this graph misleading?

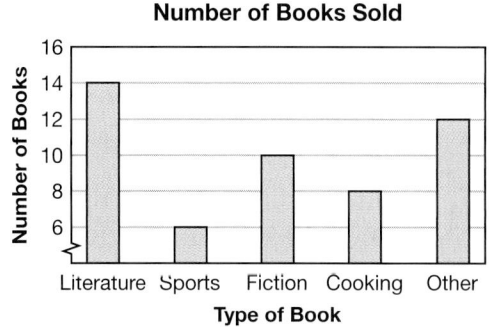

Number of Books Sold

*25. Determine if the sequence $\frac{5}{4}, 2, \frac{11}{4}, \frac{7}{2}, \ldots$ is an arithmetic sequence. If yes, find the
(34) common difference and the next two terms.

26. Multiple Choice Which equation is in standard form?
(35)
   A $y - 6 = 3(x + 4)$ **B** $y = -6x + 13$

   C $10y = 12y + 25$ **D** $9x + 11y = 65$

27. How is the value 30 represented in a stem-and-leaf plot?
(22)

28. (Pool Charges) Barton Springs Pool charges $2 a visit plus a membership fee of $20.90
(28) a month. Blue Danube Pool charges $2.95 a visit, with no membership fee. At what
number of visits per month will the total fees for each pool be the same?

29. (Stock Market) On a day of heavy trading, one share of ABC Industries' stock
(26) originally decreased by $5 only to increase later in the day by twice the original
value. The stock ended the day at $43 a share. What was the starting price of
one share?

30. Multi-Step The table shows the total number of shrubs a gardener planted after
(30) each half hour.

Time (hr)	0.5	1	1.5	2
Number of Shrubs	1	3	7	8

   a. Plot this data on a coordinate grid.

   b. Determine if the graph is a function. Explain.

   c. Predict Can you predict the number of shrubs the gardener will plant
      in 3 hours? Why or why not?

LESSON 39

Using the Distributive Property to Simplify Rational Expressions

Warm Up

1. **Vocabulary** The set of _____ numbers includes all rational and irrational numbers.
(1)

Simplify.

2. $-3x^2y\,(4x^2y^{-1} - xy)$
(15)

3. $mn(2x - 3my + 5ny)$
(15)

4. $\dfrac{5x - 25x^2}{5x}$
(38)

5. Factor. $3a^2b^3 - 6a^4b + 12ab$
(38)

New Concepts

A **rational expression** is an expression with a variable in the denominator. Rational expressions can be treated just like fractions. As with fractions, the denominator cannot equal zero. Therefore, any value of the variable that makes the denominator equal to zero is not permitted.

Math Reasoning

Write Why isn't division by zero allowed?

Variables stand for unknown real numbers. So, all properties that apply to real numbers also apply to rational expressions. The Distributive Property can be used to simplify rational expressions.

Example 1 **Distributing Over Addition**

Simplify $\dfrac{x^2}{y^2}\left(\dfrac{x^2}{y} + \dfrac{3y^3}{m}\right)$.

SOLUTION

Hint

When multiplying powers, add the exponents. When dividing powers, subtract the exponents.

$$\dfrac{x^2}{y^2}\left(\dfrac{x^2}{y} + \dfrac{3y^3}{m}\right)$$

$$= \left(\dfrac{x^2}{y^2} \cdot \dfrac{x^2}{y}\right) + \left(\dfrac{x^2}{y^2} \cdot \dfrac{3y^3}{m}\right) \qquad \text{Multiply } \dfrac{x^2}{y^2} \text{ by each term inside the parentheses.}$$

$$= \dfrac{x^4}{y^3} + \dfrac{3x^2y^3}{y^2m} \qquad \text{Simplify.}$$

$$\dfrac{x^4}{y^3} + \dfrac{3x^2y}{m}; \; y \neq 0, \, m \neq 0$$

Note that $y \neq 0$ and $m \neq 0$ because either value would make the denominator equal to zero.

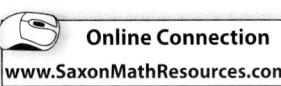
Online Connection
www.SaxonMathResources.com

Math Reasoning

Justify Why can the final expression not be simplified further?

Example 2   Distributing Over Subtraction

Simplify $\dfrac{m}{z}\left(\dfrac{axp}{mk} - 2m^4p^4\right)$.

SOLUTION

$$\dfrac{m}{z}\left(\dfrac{apx}{mk} - 2m^4p^4\right)$$

$$= \dfrac{mapx}{zmk} - \dfrac{m \cdot 2m^4p^4}{z} \qquad \text{Distribute } \dfrac{m}{z}.$$

$$= \dfrac{apx}{zk} - \dfrac{2m^5p^4}{z}; z \neq 0, k \neq 0, m \neq 0 \qquad \text{Simplify.}$$

Note that $z \neq 0$, $k \neq 0$, and $m \neq 0$ because any of those values would make a denominator equal to zero. Although there is not an m in the denominator of the final expression, there is one in the denominator of the original expression; that is why $m \neq 0$.

When simplifying an expression with negative exponents, the final expression should not have negative exponents.

Example 3   Simplifying with Negative Exponents

Simplify each expression.

a. $\dfrac{b^3}{d^{-3}}\left(\dfrac{2b^2}{d} - \dfrac{f^{-3}d}{b}\right)$

SOLUTION

$$\dfrac{b^3}{d^{-3}}\left(\dfrac{2b^2}{d} - \dfrac{f^{-3}d}{b}\right)$$

$$= \dfrac{b^3 \cdot 2b^2}{d^{-3} \cdot d} - \dfrac{b^3 \cdot f^{-3}d}{d^{-3}b} \qquad \text{Distribute } \dfrac{b^3}{d^{-3}}.$$

$$= \dfrac{2b^5}{d^{-2}} - \dfrac{b^3f^{-3}d}{d^{-3}b} \qquad \text{Product Property of Exponents}$$

$$= 2b^5d^2 - \dfrac{b^2d^4}{f^3}; d \neq 0, b \neq 0, f \neq 0 \qquad \text{Simplify.}$$

b. $\dfrac{n^{-1}}{m}\left(\dfrac{mx}{cn^{-3}p^{-5}} + 5n^{-4}p^{-5}\right)$

SOLUTION

$$\dfrac{n^{-1}}{m}\left(\dfrac{mx}{cn^{-3}p^{-5}} + 5n^{-4}p^{-5}\right)$$

$$= \dfrac{n^{-1}mx}{mcn^{-3}p^{-5}} + \dfrac{n^{-1} \cdot 5n^{-4}p^{-5}}{m} \qquad \text{Distribute } \dfrac{n^{-1}}{m}.$$

$$= \dfrac{n^{-1}x}{cn^{-3}p^{-5}} + \dfrac{5n^{-5}p^{-5}}{m} \qquad \text{Simplify.}$$

$$= \dfrac{n^2xp^5}{c} + \dfrac{5}{mn^5p^5}; c \neq 0, m \neq 0, n \neq 0, p \neq 0 \qquad \text{Simplify.}$$

Simplify each expression.

a. $\dfrac{ab}{c^2}\left(\dfrac{axb}{c} + 2bx - \dfrac{4}{c^2}\right)$

SOLUTION

$\dfrac{ab}{c^2}\left(\dfrac{axb}{c} + 2bx - \dfrac{4}{c^2}\right)$

$= \dfrac{ab \cdot axb}{c^2 \cdot c} + \dfrac{ab \cdot 2bx}{c^2} - \dfrac{ab \cdot 4}{c^2 \cdot c^2}$ \qquad Distribute $\dfrac{ab}{c^2}$.

$= \dfrac{a^2b^2x}{c^3} + \dfrac{2ab^2x}{c^2} - \dfrac{4ab}{c^4}; c \neq 0$ \qquad Simplify.

b. $\dfrac{g^2h}{d^2}\left(\dfrac{g^{-2}xh}{d^{-1}} - 2h^4x^{-1} + \dfrac{9}{d^{-3}}\right)$

SOLUTION

$\dfrac{g^2h}{d^2}\left(\dfrac{g^{-2}xh}{d^{-1}} - 2h^4x^{-1} + \dfrac{9}{d^{-3}}\right)$

$= \dfrac{g^0xh^2}{d} - \dfrac{2h^5x^{-1}g^2}{d^2} + \dfrac{9g^2h}{d^{-1}}$ \qquad Distribute $\dfrac{g^2h}{d^2}$.

$= \dfrac{xh^2}{d} - \dfrac{2h^5g^2}{xd^2} + 9dg^2h; d \neq 0$ and $x \neq 0$ \qquad Simplify.

Hint

When a variable has no exponent, it is implied that the exponent is 1.

Any variable or number raised to the 0 power equals 1.

─ **Example** 5 **Application: Furniture**

A tabletop that is in the shape of a trapezoid has height $\dfrac{a^2c}{b}$, and bases $\dfrac{b^3}{c}$ and $\dfrac{da}{c^2}$. The area of the tabletop is represented by the expression $\dfrac{a^2c}{2b}\left(\dfrac{b^3}{c} + \dfrac{da}{c^2}\right)$. Simplify the expression.

SOLUTION

$\dfrac{a^2c}{2b}\left(\dfrac{b^3}{c} + \dfrac{da}{c^2}\right)$

$= \dfrac{a^2cb^3}{2bc} + \dfrac{a^2c \cdot da}{2bc^2}$ \qquad Distribute.

$= \dfrac{a^2b^3c}{2bc} + \dfrac{a^3cd}{2bc^2}$ \qquad Multiply.

$= \dfrac{a^2b^2}{2} + \dfrac{a^3d}{2bc}$ \qquad Simplify.

The area of the tabletop can be represented by the simplified expression $\dfrac{a^2b^2}{2} + \dfrac{a^3d}{2bc}$ where b and $c \neq 0$.

Hint

The formula for the area of a trapezoid is $A = \dfrac{1}{2}h(b_1 + b_2)$.

Simplify each expression.

a. $\dfrac{r^2}{q}\left(\dfrac{r^2}{q^3} + \dfrac{7q^3}{w}\right)$
(Ex 1)

b. $\dfrac{t}{z}\left(\dfrac{uay}{tq} - 2t^3y^2\right)$
(Ex 2)

c. $\dfrac{j^{-2}}{m}\left(\dfrac{j^{-3}}{m^{-2}} + \dfrac{9m^3}{k}\right)$
(Ex 3)

d. $\dfrac{n^{-2}}{z}\left(\dfrac{v^{-2}cb}{nv^{-1}} - 4n^5b^{-3}\right)$
(Ex 3)

e. $\dfrac{fs}{d^4}\left(\dfrac{fhs}{d} + 2sk - \dfrac{7}{d^6}\right)$
(Ex 4)

f. $\dfrac{zx}{w^{-2}}\left(\dfrac{zd^{-2}x}{w} + 5tz - \dfrac{2}{w^{-4}}\right)$
(Ex 4)

g. (Painting) A rectangular canvas is to be painted. The area of the canvas
(Ex 5) with length $\left(\dfrac{t^{-3}}{y^{-2}} + \dfrac{z^{-4}}{y^5t}\right)$ and width $\dfrac{t^2y}{z}$ is represented by the expression
$\dfrac{t^2y}{z}\left(\dfrac{t^{-3}}{y^{-2}} + \dfrac{z^{-4}}{y^5t}\right)$ where t, y and $z \neq 0$. Simplify the expression.

Math Reasoning

Generalize For problem **f**, which variable in the numerator cannot equal zero? Explain.

Practice   Distributed and Integrated

Solve each equation. Check your answer.

1. $4\left(y + \dfrac{3}{2}\right) = -18$
(26)

2. $x - 4 + 2x = 14$
(26)

3. True or False: The set of integers is closed under division. If false, give a
(1) counterexample.

Translate words into algebraic expressions.

4. the sum of a and 3
(17)

5. 2.5 more than k
(17)

6. 3 less than x
(17)

7. 2 more than the product of 3 and y
(17)

*8. Simplify $\dfrac{d^2}{s^2}\left(\dfrac{d^2}{s} + \dfrac{9s^3}{h}\right)$.
(39)

*9. Write Why isn't division by zero allowed?
(39)

*10. Justify Simplify $\dfrac{x^{-2}}{n^{-1}}(2x^{-4} + n^{-3})$ and explain each step.
(39)

*11. Multiple Choice Simplify $\dfrac{g^{-2}s}{b^2}\left(\dfrac{g^{-3}s^{-1}}{b^{-1}} + \dfrac{4}{b^3}\right)$ where b, g and $s \neq 0$.
(39)

A $\dfrac{4g^{-5}s^{-1}}{b^4}$

B $\dfrac{g^{-5}s^{-1}}{b} + \dfrac{4g^{-2}s}{b^5}$

C $\dfrac{g^{-5}}{b} + \dfrac{4g^{-2}s}{b^5}$

D $\dfrac{1}{bg^5} + \dfrac{4s}{b^5g^2}$

*12. Simplify the expression $\dfrac{w^2 p}{t}\left(\dfrac{4}{w^4} - \dfrac{t^2}{p^5}\right)$.
(39)

*13. Find the prime factorization of 918.
(38)

*14. Error Analysis Two students factor the polynomial $16x^4y^2z + 28x^3y^4z^2 + 4x^3y^2z$ as
(38) shown below. Which student is correct? Explain the error.

Student A	**Student B**
$4x^3y^2z(4x + 7y^2z)$	$4x^3y^2z(4x + 7y^2z + 1)$

15. Geometry The area of a rectangle is represented by the polynomial $6a^2b + 15ab$.
(38) Find two factors that could be used to represent the length and width of the
rectangle.

16. Multiple Choice Complete the following statement: The side lengths of similar
(36) figures _____.

A must be congruent **B** cannot be congruent

C are in proportion **D** must be whole numbers

17. Multi-Step Use the expression $24x^2y^3 + 18xy^2 + 6xy$.
(38) **a.** What is the GCF of the polynomial?

b. Use the GCF to factor the polynomial completely.

*18. Probability The probability that a point selected at random is in the shaded
(38) region of the figure is represented by the fraction $\dfrac{\text{area of shaded rectangle}}{\text{area of entire rectangle}}$. Find the
probability. Write your answer in simplest form.

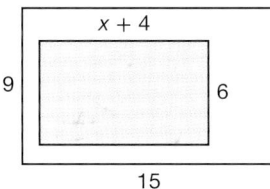

*19. Analyze In order to double the volume of water in a fish tank, is it necessary
(36) to double the length, width, and height of the tank? If yes, explain why. If no,
explain how to double the volume of water.

*20. Graph $27x + 9y = 54$ using the x- and y-intercepts.
(35)

*21. Fundraising For a fundraiser, the science club sold posters for \$5 and mugs
(35) for \$8. The equation $5x + 8y = 480$ shows that they made \$480. Find the
x- and y-intercepts.

22. Entertainment A contestant is in the bonus round of a game show where
(34) she can win \$1500 for answering the first question correctly and then an
additional \$500 for each correct response to each of the next five questions.
If she answers all of the questions correctly, how much money will she
receive when she answers the sixth question?

23. Write 0.00608 in scientific notation.
(37)

24. **Error Analysis** Two students write 1.32×10^{-5} in standard form. Which student is
(37) correct? Explain the error.

Student A	Student B
0.00000132	0.0000132

25. **Verify** Show that $4\frac{3}{4}$ is the solution to $\frac{1}{n-1} = \frac{4}{15}$.
(31)

26. Evaluate the expression $\dfrac{x^2 y^{-2}}{z^2}$ if $x = 3$, $y = 4$, and $z = -2$.
(32)

27. **Analyze** The odds of winning a CD in a raffle are 3:7. Explain how to find the
(33) probability of not winning a CD.

28. (Stamp Collecting) The table shows some collectible stamps with their estimated
(25) values. Explain whether the ordered pairs, such as (2, $2) and (2, $3), will be a
function.

Number	Stamp	Value (low)	Value (high)
1	11¢ President Hayes (1931)	$2	$4
2	14¢ American Indian (1931)	$2	$3
3	4¢ President Taft (1930)	$1	$3
4	1¢ Benjamin Franklin (1911)	$5	$50

29. (Salaries) In an interview with a potential employee, an
(27) employer shows a line graph displaying the average salary
of employees over several years. Explain why the graph is
potentially misleading and why the employer might have
shown this graph.

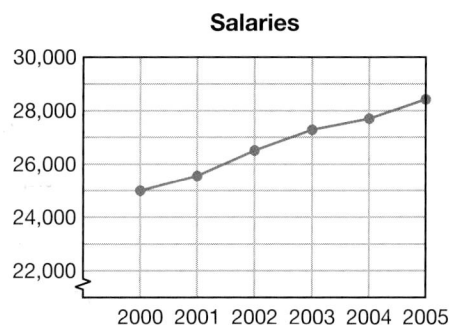

30. **Formulate** Write a rule for the table in function notation.
(30)

g	2	4	6	8	10
$f(g)$	1.5	2.5	3.5	4.5	5.5

Simplifying and Evaluating Expressions Using the Power Property of Exponents

Warm Up

1. Vocabulary The _____ is the number that tells how many times the
(3)
base of a power is used as a factor.

Simplify.

2. $(4x^2y^3)(5x^4y^4)$
(3)

3. $\dfrac{24x^3y^6}{36x^5y^3}$
(32)

4. $(-3)^2 - 3^2$
(11)

5. Compare: $4^2 + \sqrt{36} \bigcirc -(-3)^2 + \sqrt{25}$. Use >, <, or =.
(13)

New Concepts

Previous lessons have explored expressions involving exponents. Several rules and definitions have been developed.

$$x^0 = 1 \qquad\qquad x^m \cdot x^n = x^{m+n}$$

$$x^1 = x \qquad\qquad x^{-n} = \frac{1}{x^n}$$

$$\frac{x^m}{x^n} = x^{m-n}$$

There is another property of exponents that involves raising a power to a power.

Exploration · Raising a Power to a Power

This Exploration shows how to raise a power to a power.

The expression $(2^4)^3$ means to use 2^4 as a factor three times.

$$(2^4)^3 = 2^4 \cdot 2^4 \cdot 2^4 = 2^{12}$$

Simplify.

a. $(3^2)^3$ **b.** $(4^5)^2$ **c.** $(7^2)^4$

d. Are there any patterns? What conclusions can you draw from the patterns?

The expression $(a^2)^3$ means to use a^2 as a factor three times.

$$(a^2)^3 = a^2 \cdot a^2 \cdot a^2 = a^6$$

Simplify.

e. $(a^3)^5$ **f.** $(b^6)^2$

g. $(d^4)^4$

h. Using the results from **a** through **g** above, write a rule for raising a power to a power.

Hint

Write in a 1 if there is no exponent for variables or numbers. For example, $4 = 4^1$ and $x = x^1$.

Math Reasoning

Generalize Use the meaning of powers and exponents to explain why $(a^2)^3 = a^6$.

Online Connection
www.SaxonMathResources.com

Solve each proportion.

1. $\dfrac{3}{12} = \dfrac{-24}{m}$
(31)

2. $\dfrac{-4}{0.8} = \dfrac{2}{x-1}$
(31)

3. $\dfrac{5}{12} = \dfrac{1.25}{k}$
(31)

4. True or False: All whole numbers are integers. If false, give a counterexample.
(1)

*5. Simplify $(4^4)^5$ using exponents.
(40)

*6. Multiple Choice Which expression simplifies to $-24x^4y^3$?
(40)

 A $(-2x^2y)^2(6y)$ **B** $-2(x^2y)^2(6y)$

 C $-(2x^2y)^2(6y)$ **D** $(-2xy)^3(3)$

7. Simplify $\dfrac{e^3}{r^5}\left(\dfrac{e^2}{4r} + \dfrac{r^9}{k}\right)$.
(39)

*8. (Cooking) Use the formula $A = \pi r^2$ for the area of a circle. A 6-inch pizza covers
(40) an area of $\pi(6)^2 = 36\pi$ square inches. What happens to the area of the pizza if you double the radius and make a 12-inch pizza?

*9. Verify Is the statement $(a + b)^n = a^n + b^n$ true? Verify your answer with a numeric
(40) example.

*10. Generalize When do you know to add exponents and when to multiply exponents?
(40)

11. (Painting) A rectangular top on a bench is to be painted.
(39) Its area is $\dfrac{wd^{-3}}{c}\left(\dfrac{d}{w^{-4}} + \dfrac{c^{-2}}{wd}\right)$. Simplify.

12. Simplify $\dfrac{a^2}{d^2}\left(\dfrac{a^{-2}x}{d^{-1}} - \dfrac{2x}{d^{-3}}\right)$ where d and $a \neq 0$.
(39)

*13. Geometry The equation of an ellipse is $\dfrac{wx^2}{g^2} + \dfrac{gy^2}{w^2} = 1$. To enlarge the ellipse, the
(39) left side is multiplied by $\dfrac{g^5}{w^{-2}}$. This expression is $\dfrac{g^5}{w^{-2}}\left(\dfrac{wx^2}{g^2} + \dfrac{gy^2}{w^2}\right)$. Simplify.

14. The trim around a window has a total length of $\dfrac{rt}{w^3}\left(\dfrac{rty}{w} + 2ty - \dfrac{8}{w^2}\right)$.
(39) **a.** Simplify the expression.

 b. Identify the variables that cannot equal zero.

*15. Find the GCF of $4xy^2z^4 - 2x^2y^3z^2 + 6x^3y^4z$.
(38)

16. Error Analysis Two students are simplifying the fraction $\dfrac{3x-6}{9}$ as shown below.
(38) Which student is correct? Explain the error.

Student A	Student B
$\dfrac{3x-6}{9} = \dfrac{\cancel{3}(x-2)}{\cancel{9}_3} = \dfrac{x-2}{3}$	$\dfrac{\cancel{3}x-6}{\cancel{9}_3} = \dfrac{x-\cancel{6}^2}{\cancel{3}} = x-2$

*17. (**Shipping**) A shipping container is in the shape of a rectangular box that has
$_{(38)}$ a length of $10x + 15$ units, a width of $5x$ units, and a height of 2 units.

   a. Write an expression that can be used to find the volume of the box.

   b. Factor the expression completely.

18. 0.78 of 250 is what number?
$_{(24)}$

19. Give the domain and range of $\{(4, 9); (4, 7); (2, 4); (5, 12); (9, 4)\}$.
$_{(25)}$

20. The heights of 8 trees were 250, 190, 225, 205, 180, 240, 210, and 220 feet. How
$_{(27)}$ could a misleading graph make you think the trees are all very similar in size?

   a. Make a bar graph of the data using a broken axis.

   b. Make a bar graph of the data using large increments.

   c. Compare the two graphs.

21. Justify Without changing the number to standard form, explain how you can tell
$_{(37)}$ that $-10 < 1 \times 10^{-4}$.

*22. Multiple Choice What is $\frac{1.6 \times 10^7}{6.4 \times 10^2}$ in scientific notation?
$_{(37)}$

   A 2.5×10^4 **B** 0.25×10^5 **C** 2.5×10^6 **D** 4×10^5

23. (**Astronomy**) The diameter of the moon is approximately 3,480,000 meters.
$_{(37)}$ Write this distance in scientific notation.

24. The rectangles below are similar. Find the missing length.
$_{(36)}$

*25. (**Drama**) The cost of presenting a play was \$110. Each ticket was sold for \$5.50.
$_{(35)}$ The equation $11x - 2y = 110$ shows how much money was made after ticket sales.
Graph this equation using the intercepts.

26. Justify Is the sequence 0.2, 2, 20, 200, … an arithmetic sequence? Justify your
$_{(34)}$ answer.

27. There are 2 yellow stickers and 4 purple stickers. Make a tree diagram showing all
$_{(33)}$ possible outcomes of drawing two stickers. How many possible ways are there to
draw a purple sticker, keep it, and then draw another purple sticker?

28. In a stem-and-leaf plot, which digit of the number 65 would be a leaf?
$_{(22)}$

29. Measurement How many inches are there in 18 yards?
$_{(31)}$

30. Analyze The rule for negative exponents states that for every nonzero
$_{(32)}$ number x, $x^{-n} = \frac{1}{x^n}$. Explain why the base, x, cannot be zero.

Using Deductive and Inductive Reasoning

Math Language

A **premise** is the foundation for an argument. It is used as evidence for the conclusion. A **conclusion** is an opinion or decision that logically follows the premise.

There are two basic kinds of reasoning: deductive and inductive. **Deductive reasoning** bases a conclusion on laws or rules. **Inductive reasoning** bases a conclusion on an observed pattern. Both types of reasoning can be used to support or justify conclusions.

All fruit have seeds. An apple is a fruit.

The two statements form an argument. The first statement is the premise, and the second statement is the conclusion. In deductive reasoning, if the argument is solid, the conclusion is guaranteed. In inductive reasoning, if the argument is solid, the conclusion is supported but not guaranteed. Consider the following examples:

Daryl	Aliya
According to Newton's First Law, every object will remain in uniform motion in a straight line unless compelled to change its state by the action of an external force. So, if I kick a ball, it will travel forward at a constant speed until it hits the wall.	In the past, I've noticed that every time I kick a soccer ball, it travels forward at a constant speed until it hits the wall. The next time I kick a ball, it will keep going until it hits the wall.

Daryl's reasoning is deductive because it is based on his knowledge of Newton's First Law of Motion. Aliya reasons inductively, basing her conclusions on her observations.

Identify the type of reasoning used. Explain your answer.

1. Premise: A student has earned a score of 100 on the last five math tests.
   Conclusion: The student will earn a score of 100 on the next math test.

2. Premise: The measures of three angles of a rectangle are all 90°.
   Conclusion: The measure of the fourth angle is 90°.

3. Premise: A number pattern begins with 3, 5, 7, 9, 11, ….
   Conclusion: The next number in the pattern will be 13.

Each premise and conclusion above can be written as one sentence. For instance, the second set could be restated as, "If the measures of three angles of a rectangle are all 90°, then the measure of the fourth angle is 90°." This is called a conditional statement. A **conditional statement** is a logical statement that can be written in "if-then" form.

A conditional statement is made up of two parts: a hypothesis and a conclusion. The **hypothesis** is the condition. It follows the word "if." The **conclusion** is the judgment. It follows the word "then." A conditional statement can either be true or false.

Online Connection
www.SaxonMathResources.com

Hint

If a conditional statement is true and you apply it to a situation in which the hypothesis is true, then you can state that the conclusion is true by deductive reasoning.

✎ **Write** Use the given hypothesis to write a true or false conditional statement.

4. Write a true conditional statement: If you stay in the sun too long, ….

5. Write a true conditional statement: If a student has a temperature higher than 101 degrees, ….

6. Write a false conditional statement: If a number is divisible by 5, ….

The statement "If a figure has four sides, then it is a square" is false. It is not true because a rectangle has four sides, but a rectangle is not a square. An example that contradicts a statement is called a counterexample. One counterexample is sufficient to show that a statement is false.

Provide a counterexample for each statement.

7. The sum of a positive number and a negative number is negative.

8. If a student is a teenager, then she is 14 years old.

Investigation Practice

Identify the type of reasoning used. Explain your answer.

a. My friend has an allergic reaction when he eats peanuts.

b. If a driver sees a red light, she should stop.

Use the given hypothesis to write a true or false conditional statement.

c. Write a true conditional statement: If it rains today, ….

d. Write a false conditional statement: If $x = 2$, ….

Use the diagram to write a counterexample for each statement.

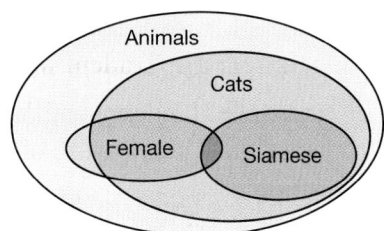

e. If an animal is a cat, then it is Siamese.

f. All female cats are Siamese.

Finding Rates of Change and Slope

Warm Up

1. Vocabulary A _____ (*literal, linear*) equation is an equation whose
(30) graph is a straight line.

2. Find the range of the function $f(x) = 2x + 3$ for the domain $\{0, 1, 2\}$.
(25)

Name the quadrant on the coordinate plane in which the following points are located:

3. $(3, -5)$ **4.** $(-3, -5)$ **5.** $(-5, 3)$
(20)   (20)   (20)

New Concepts

A **rate of change** is a ratio that compares the change in one quantity with the change in another. For example, the speed of a car is a rate of change that compares the distance and the time traveled.

Exploration **Analyzing a Graph**

Arvand leaves his house and jogs to Cory's house. Later they walk to a local pizza shop. The graph shows the distance Arvand traveled between the time he left home and when he arrived at the pizza shop.

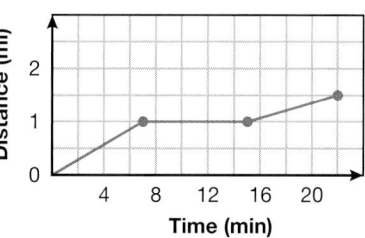

a. When was Arvand traveling the fastest?

b. How long was Arvand at Cory's house? How can you tell?

c. Compare the graph during the times Arvand was jogging to Cory's and when they were walking to the pizza shop.

Example 1 **Determining Rate of Change from a Graph**

A car travels on a highway at a constant speed. The graph shows the relationship between the distance traveled and the time traveled. Find the rate of change.

SOLUTION Choose two points on the graph and find the ratio of the change in distance to the change in time.

$$\frac{\text{change in distance}}{\text{change in time}} = \frac{120 - 60}{2 - 1}$$

$$= 60$$

The rate of change is 60 miles per hour.

Hint

You can use any two points on the line to determine the rate of change.

Online Connection
www.SaxonMathResources.com

Example 2   Determining Rate of Change from a Table

A shop charges a fee for renting kayaks. What is the rate of change for the rental fees?

Time (hours)	2	4	6	8
Cost	$32.50	$60.50	$88.50	$116.50

SOLUTION Notice that the costs increase the same amount every 2 hours. Choose two sets of values from the table to find the ratio of the change in cost to the change in time.

$$\frac{\text{change in cost}}{\text{change in time}} = \frac{60.5 - 32.5}{4 - 2} = \frac{28}{2}$$

The rate of change is $14 per hour.

Math Reasoning

Predict The rate of change is $14 per hour. How much would it cost to rent a kayak for 10 hours?

Slope of a Line

The **slope** of a line is a rate of change. It is equal to the ratio of the vertical change (rise) to the horizontal change (run).

$$\text{slope} = \frac{\text{rise}}{\text{run}}$$

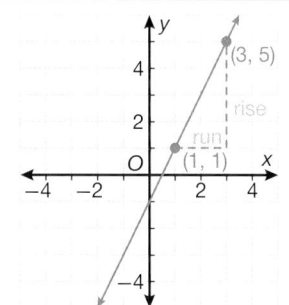

Example 3   Determining Slope from a Graph

Find the slope of each line.

a.

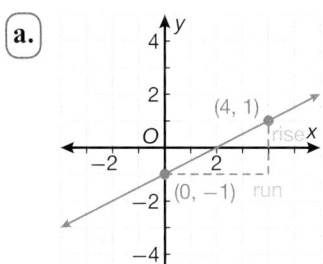

SOLUTION Find the ratio of the rise to the run.

$$\text{slope} = \frac{\text{rise}}{\text{run}} = \frac{2}{4}$$

$$= \frac{1}{2}$$

b.

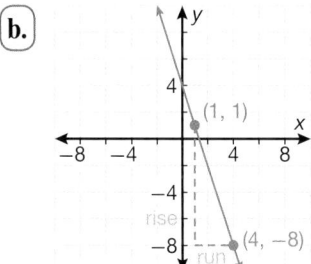

SOLUTION Find the ratio of the rise to the run.

$$\text{slope} = \frac{\text{rise}}{\text{run}} = \frac{-9}{3}$$

$$= -3$$

A line with a positive slope rises from left to right. A line with a negative slope falls from left to right. There are two other cases to consider: horizontal and vertical lines.

Horizontal and Vertical Lines

The graph of the equation $y = c$, where c is a constant, is a horizontal line. The slope of a horizontal line is 0.

The graph of the equation $x = c$, where c is a constant, is a vertical line. The slope of a vertical line is undefined.

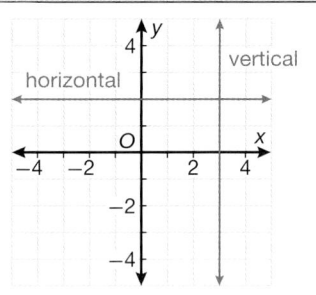

Example 4 **Graphing Horizontal and Vertical Lines**

a. Find the slope of the horizontal line.

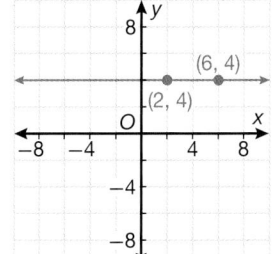

SOLUTION Find the ratio of the rise to the run.

$$\text{slope} = \frac{\text{rise}}{\text{run}} = \frac{4 - 4}{6 - 2}$$

$$= \frac{0}{4}$$

The slope is 0 because 0 divided by any nonzero number is 0.

b. Find the slope of the vertical line.

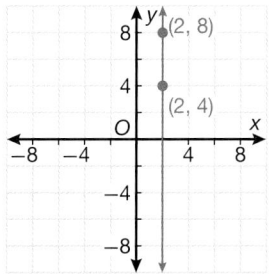

SOLUTION Find the ratio of the rise to the run.

$$\text{slope} = \frac{\text{rise}}{\text{run}} = \frac{8 - 4}{2 - 2}$$

$$= \frac{4}{0}$$

The slope is undefined because any number divided by 0 is undefined.

Example 5 **Application: Cooking**

The graph and table show the relationship between the number of servings a salsa recipe makes and the ounces of black beans used to make this recipe.

Servings	4	6	10	18
Black Beans (oz)	10	15	25	45

a. Use the table or graph to find the slope of the line.

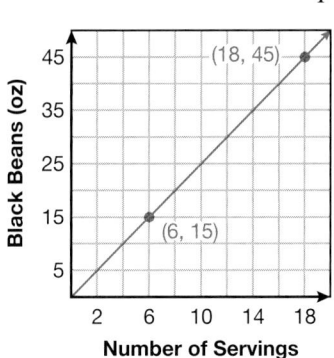

Hint

Notice that the value of the rate of change is equal to the slope of the line.

SOLUTION Find the ratio of the change in amount of beans to the change in servings.

$$\frac{\text{change in amount of beans}}{\text{change in servings}} = \frac{15 - 10}{6 - 4} = \frac{5}{2}$$

The slope is $\frac{5}{2}$.

b. What does the rate of change mean in this example?

SOLUTION Explain how the variables are related in this ratio.

For every 5 ounces of black beans, 2 servings of salsa can be made.

Lesson Practice

a. Use the graph to find the rate of change.
(Ex 1)

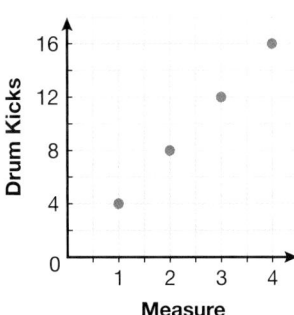

b. Use the table to find the rate of change.
(Ex 2)

Miles	3	5	7	9
Feet	15,840	26,400	36,960	47,520

Find the slope of each line.

c.
(Ex 3)

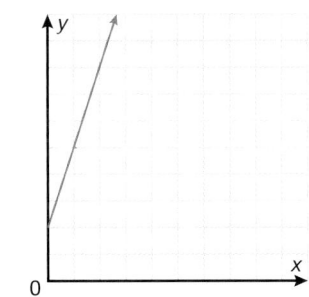

d.
(Ex 3)

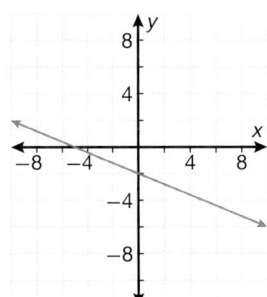

e. Find the slope of the horizontal line that passes through the points (5, 3) and (8, 3).
(Ex 4)

f. Find the slope of the vertical line that passes through the points (6, 5) and (6, 10).
(Ex 4)

(Music) The table shows the number of times Iliana kicked her bass drum during each measure in a song.

Measure	1	2	3	4
Drum Kicks	4	8	12	16

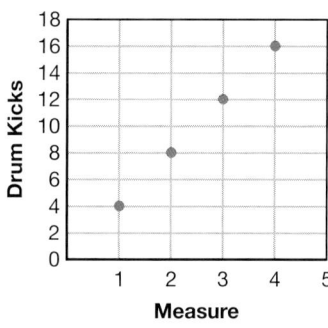

g. Use the table or graph to find the slope of the line.
(Ex 5)

h. What does the rate of change mean in this problem?
(Ex 5)

Practice   Distributed and Integrated

Solve each equation. Check your answer.

1. $-2(b + 5) = -6$
(26)

2. $4(y + 1) = -8$
(26)

3. $\dfrac{5}{8} = 2m + \dfrac{3}{8}$
(26)

Find the slope of the line.

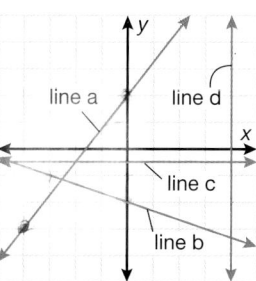

*4. line a
(41)

*5. line b
(41)

*6. line c
(41)

*7. line d
(41)

8. Write 110,400 in scientific notation.
(37)

*9. **Multiple Choice** Which of the following expressions is the GCF of
(38) $45a^3b^4c^2 + 30a^2bc^3$?

   A $15a^2bc^2$ **B** $5a^2bc^2$ **C** $3a^3b^4c^3$ **D** $15a^3b^4c^3$

10. **Verify** Is $2x(5x^3 + 6x^2 - 3x)$ completely factored? Explain why or why not. If no,
(38) factor the polynomial completely.

*11. (Finances) The graph shows the amount of money Siobhan has in her bank account
(41) over time. What is the rate of change in her balance over time?

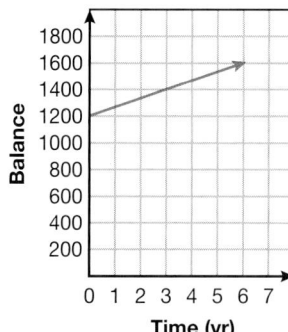

*12. **Analyze** At some point on Mindy's mountain climbing trip, a graph relating her
(41) distance up the mountain over her climbing time shows a line with a negative slope. Why might this be?

13. Simplify $(b^3)^5$ using exponents.
(40)

14. **Error Analysis** Two students simplify the expression $(-2x^7)^5$ as shown below. Which
(40) student is correct? Explain the error.

Student A	Student B
$(-2x^7)^5 = -10x^{35}$	$(-2x^7)^5 = -32x^{35}$

*15. **Geometry** Use the formula $A = s^2$ to find the area of the square.
(40)

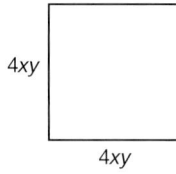

4xy

4xy

16. **Multi-Step** There are 10 millimeters in a centimeter. Therefore, there are 10^3 cubic
(40) millimeters in one cubic centimeter.

a. There are 10^2 centimeters in a meter. How many cubic centimeters are in
one cubic meter?

b. How many cubic millimeters are in one cubic meter?

17. (Packing) The sides of a box in the shape of a cube are $5ab$ inches long. What is the
(40) volume of the box?

Simplify

18. $\dfrac{fr}{d^3}\left(\dfrac{fsr}{d^2} + 3fs - \dfrac{8}{d}\right)$
(39)

*19. $\dfrac{rt^{-2}}{g^{-3}h}\left(\dfrac{tg^4}{r^3h^{-2}} - \dfrac{r^3h}{g^{-2}r^{-2}}\right)$.
(39)

*20. (Woodworking) You are making furniture for a miniature dollhouse with a scale of
(36) 1 in.:12 in. If an actual chair measures 3 feet high, what will be the height of the
chair in the dollhouse?

21. Find the x- and y-intercepts on the graph.
(35)

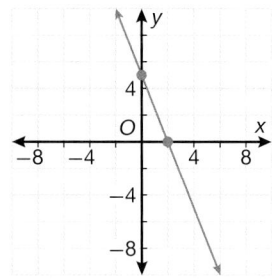

22. **Measurement** The formula $F = \frac{9}{5}C + 32$ calculates the number of degrees
(35) Fahrenheit from the degrees Celcius. Write this formula in standard form.

23. Write a recursive formula for the arithmetic sequence 8, 19, 30, 41,…. Then find
(34) the next two terms of the sequence.

24. **Write** Explain the difference between dependent and independent events.
(33)

25. (**Cooking**) To make two batches of cookies, Ralph needs $\frac{3}{4}$ cup molasses. How many
(31) cups would he need to make 6 batches of cookies?

26. (**Painting**) It will cost $2.50 per square foot to paint the walls of a storage shed.
(25) Write a rule in function notation to describe the cost of painting x square feet of
outside wall space.

27. The two parabolas have the same shape but different orientations. Determine
(25) whether each parabola is a function.

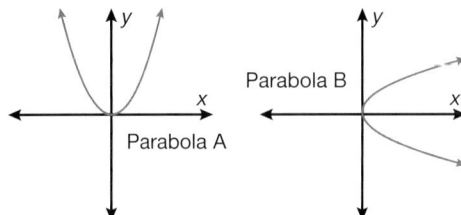

Parabola B

Parabola A

28. Multi-Step A physicist wants to find the kinetic energy of a ball that has a mass of
(16) 2.5 kg and travels a distance of 5.8 meters in 2.5 seconds. The formula for kinetic
energy is $E_K = \frac{1}{2}mv^2$, where m is the mass of the object and v is the object's velocity.
The formula for velocity is $v = \frac{d}{t}$, where d is distance traveled and t is the amount
of time. What are the velocity and the kinetic energy of the ball?

29. Multi-Step Two cars travel the same distance. Car 1 travels at 50 mph and Car 2 at
(28) 65 mph. If it takes Car 1 one more hour to travel than Car 2, how far did the cars
travel? Remember, $d = rt$.

a. Write an expression to represent the distance Car 2 travels.

b. Write an expression to represent the distance Car 1 travels.

c. Use these expressions to find the time Car 2 traveled.

d. Use this information to determine the distance traveled.

30. Multi-Step The length of a rectangle is 5 inches less than 3 times the width.
(23) The perimeter of the rectangle is 14 inches. Find the length and width of the
rectangle.

LESSON 42

Solving Percent Problems

Warm Up

1. **Vocabulary** Two equivalent ratios form a _____.
(31)

Solve the equation.

2. $3x + 8 = 32$
(23)

3. $-6y - 7 = 29$
(23)

4. A team's ratio of wins to losses in football games is 5 to 4. If the team wins
(36) 25 games, how many games did the team lose?

5. The ratio of white marbles to black marbles is 7 to 10. There are
(36) 136 marbles in the bag. How many marbles are white?

New Concepts

A **percent** is a ratio that compares a number to 100. For example, 50% is the ratio $\frac{50}{100}$. There are three components that form a percent statement: the whole is the total amount; the percent is a rate that quantifies an amount measured with respect to the whole; the percentage is a number that represents a percent of the whole.

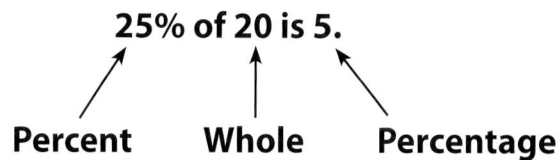

25% of 20 is 5.

Percent   **Whole**   **Percentage**

If two of the components are known, then the third component can be determined.

Example 1   Using an Equation to Find a Percentage

a. What number is 25% of 50?

SOLUTION

$c = 0.25 \cdot 50$ Change the percent to its decimal form.

$= 12.5$ Multiply the percent by the whole.

Check 25% is $\frac{25}{100}$ or $\frac{1}{4}$. So, $\left(\frac{1}{4}\right)(50) = 12.5$.

b. What number is 125% of 64?

SOLUTION

$n = 1.25 \cdot 64$ Change the percent to its decimal form.

$= 80$ Multiply the percent by the whole.

Check 125% is $\frac{125}{100}$ or $\frac{5}{4}$. So, $\left(\frac{5}{4}\right)(64) = 80$

Online Connection
www.SaxonMathResources.com

A percent statement can be set up as a proportion. One ratio compares the part of a quantity to the whole quantity. The other ratio is the percent rate written in the form of a ratio.

$$\frac{\text{part}}{\text{whole}} = \text{percent rate}$$

For example, 10% of 50 is 5 can be written as a proportion.

Part

$$\text{Whole} \longrightarrow \frac{5}{50} = \frac{10}{100} \longleftarrow \textbf{Percent}$$

Example 2 Using a Proportion

(a.) What number is 125% of 48?

SOLUTION

Set up a proportion to find the percentage.

$$\frac{c}{48} = \frac{125}{100} \qquad \text{Write a proportion.}$$

$$6000 = 100c \qquad \text{Cross multiply.}$$

$$60 = c \qquad \text{Solve for } c.$$

60 is 125% of 48.

Check 125% is $\frac{5}{4}$. So, $\left(\frac{5}{4}\right)(48) = 60$.

(b.) 15 is what percent of 45?

SOLUTION

Set up a proportion to find the percent.

$$\frac{15}{45} = \frac{x}{100} \qquad \text{Write a proportion.}$$

$$45x = 1500 \qquad \text{Cross multiply.}$$

$$x = 33.\overline{3} \qquad \text{Solve for } x.$$

15 is $33\frac{1}{3}\%$ of 45.

Check $33\frac{1}{3}\%$ is $\frac{1}{3}$. So, $\left(\frac{1}{3}\right)(45) = 15$.

> **Caution**
>
> When setting up a proportion, make sure you know which is the part and which is the whole.

Example 3 Application: Calculating Wages

Ana receives $1153.84 in gross earnings every two weeks. However, 28.07% of the gross earnings is removed for taxes and other deductions. Using an equation, determine the net pay.

Hint

Gross earning is the amount of money earned by a worker before any deductions, like taxes, are taken out. Net pay is actual amount of money a worker receives after deductions.

SOLUTION First, find the total amount of money that will be deducted. Then subtract the deductions from the gross earnings to determine that net pay.

$$28.07\% \cdot \$1153.84 = d$$

$$0.2807 \cdot \$1153.84 = d$$

$$\$323.88 \approx d$$

Now $323.88 of deductions is subtracted from the gross earnings.

$$\text{(gross earnings)} - \text{(deductions)} = \text{(net pay)}$$

$$\$1153.84 \quad - \quad \$323.88 \quad = \$829.96$$

The amount that Ana receives in net pay is $829.96.

Check Use estimation. Since about 30% is deducted from about $1200, then she receives about 70% of $1200 in net pay. Use an equation to find 70% of $1200.

$$(0.70)(\$1200) = \$840$$

$829.96 is a reasonable answer because $829.96 is about $840.

Example 4 Application: Finances

Dominic earns $9.25 an hour working part-time. The circle graph shows how he divides his earnings. This month Dominic has worked a total of 54 hours.

Find the amount of Dominic's earnings that will be put into savings this month.

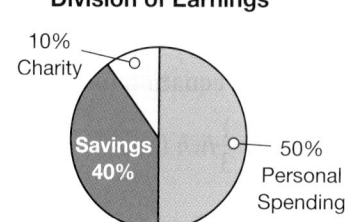

Division of Earnings

10% Charity
Savings 40%
50% Personal Spending

Math Reasoning

Why is it necessary to determine the total amount earned first?

SOLUTION Find the total amount that Dominic earned this month. Then find 40% of the total amount earned.

$$(\$9.25)(54) = \$499.50 \qquad \text{Multiply the rate by the hours.}$$

Dominic earned $499.50 this month. Now find 40% of $499.50 to determine how much money will be put into savings. Set up a proportion to find the percentage.

$$\frac{c}{\$499.50} = \frac{40}{100} \qquad \text{Write a proportion.}$$

$$40 \cdot \$499.50 = 100c \qquad \text{Cross multiply.}$$

$$\frac{\$19{,}980}{100} = \frac{100c}{100} \qquad \text{Divide both sides by 100.}$$

$$\$199.80 = c \qquad \text{Solve for } c.$$

Dominic puts $199.80 into savings this month.

Example 3   Application: Moving Objects

The expression $3.5t + 0.7t^2$ represents the distance a moving object travels through time t. The expression $1.4t^2$ represents the distance the same object moves from rest with twice the acceleration.

Simplify $\dfrac{3.5t + 0.7t^2}{1.4t^2}$.

SOLUTION

$1.4t^2$	Identify the denominator.
$t \neq 0$	Determine undefined values.
$\dfrac{3.5t + 0.7t^2}{1.4t^2} = \dfrac{0.7t(5 + t)}{1.4t^2}$	Factor the numerator.
$= \dfrac{0.7t(5 + t)}{0.7t(2t)}$	Factor the denominator.
$= \dfrac{5 + t}{2t}$	Simplify.

The simplified expression is $\dfrac{5 + t}{2t}$, $t \neq 0$.

Math Reasoning

Analyze Determine the undefined value for the rational expression $\frac{3.5t + 0.7t^2}{1.4t^2}$. What is its meaning in the context of the problem?

Lesson Practice

Determine the values for which each rational expression is undefined.
(Ex 1)

  a. $\dfrac{16x - 7}{5x}$ **b.** $\dfrac{1 + 3x}{x + 8}$ **c.** $\dfrac{11 - x}{6x - 42}$

Simplify each rational expression. Determine undefined values.
(Ex 2)

  d. $\dfrac{7x - 27}{5x}$ **e.** $\dfrac{3x^2 - 3x}{9x^2 + 15x}$ **f.** $\dfrac{4x + 28}{3x^2 + 21x}$

A package is needed that uses the least amount of material to hold the greatest volume of product. A container in the shape of a right circular cylinder has a surface area of $S = 2\pi rh + 2\pi r^2$ and a volume of $V = \pi r^2 h$.

  g. Simplify $\dfrac{2\pi rh + 2\pi r^2}{\pi r^2 h}$.

Practice   Distributed and Integrated

Evaluate each function for the given input value.

  1. $f(x) = -2x$ for $x = -5$
  (30)

                                     2. $h(x) = 3x - 1$ for $x = 7$
                                     (30)

Find the indicated term of each arithmetic sequence.

  3. $a_n = 16 + (n - 1)(-0.5)$, 15th term
  (34)

  4. $-8, -6, -4, -2, \ldots$, 100th term
  (34)

Identify the values that make the rational expressions below undefined.

*5. $\dfrac{25}{x + 10}$
(43)

*6. $\dfrac{12 + 3x}{5 - x}$
(43)

7. What is 14% of 120?
(42)

8. What is 75% of 60?
(42)

9. A school needs to raise $2700. A nearby store promises to donate twice the
(23) amount the students raise. How much money do the students need to raise?

10. Ann-Marie has $2.55 in nickels and dimes. She has $1.80 in dimes. How many
(24) nickels does Ann-Marie have?

    a. Write an equation to represent the situation.

    b. How many nickels does she have?

11. **Error Analysis** Two students use the diagram to determine whether the
(25) relation is a function. Which student is correct? Explain the error.

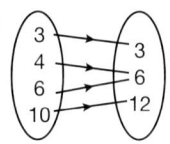

Student A	Student B
$\{(3, 3), (4, 6), (6, 6), (10, 12)\}$ The y-values are not all different; y equals 6 twice. So, it is not a function.	$\{(3, 3), (4, 6), (6, 6), (10, 12)\}$ All the x-values are different, so it is a function.

12. **Write** Explain how you can use a graph to tell whether a relation is a function.
(30)

13. ⟨**Geography**⟩ A map shows a 2.5-inch distance between Brownsville and Evanstown.
(31) The scale on the map is 1 inch:25 miles. How far apart are the two towns?

*14. **Multiple Choice** Which of the following rational expressions is undefined at $x = -6$?
(43)

    A $\dfrac{x - 6}{12x + 72}$
        B $\dfrac{x}{2(x + 12)}$

    C $\dfrac{x + 6}{72 - 12x}$
       D $\dfrac{2x + 12}{x}$

*15. ⟨**Digital Signal Processing**⟩ In digital signal processing, electronic signals are often
(43) represented as rational expressions. The rational expression $\dfrac{3z^2 + 2.7z}{(z + 0.9)(z - 0.9)}$ models a digital signal. What is the simplified form of this signal representation?

*16. **Analyze** Given the rational expression $\dfrac{8x}{2x + 16}$, for what values of x would its
(43) reciprocal be undefined?

17. ⟨**Phone Numbers**⟩ A student forgets the last two digits of her friend's phone number.
(33) She does remember that the digits are different. What is the probability of guessing the last two digits correctly on the first try?

18. **Multi-Step** In an arithmetic sequence, $a_1 = 17$ and $d = 10$.
(34)
    a. Write a rule for the nth term of the sequence.

    b. Use the rule to find the fourth and eleventh terms of the sequence.

19. **Verify** Verify that $5x + 6y = -12$ is the standard form of the equation
(35)
$y = -\frac{5}{6}x - 2$.

20. Name the corresponding sides and angles of the two similar
(36)
triangles shown at right.

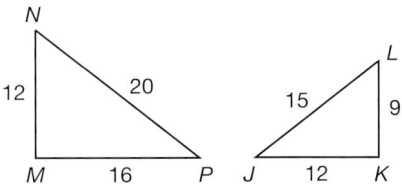

*21. Multiply $(1.6 \times 10^{-5})(2.2 \times 10^3)$ and write the answer in scientific notation.
(37)

22. (Packaging) The bottom of a rectangular box has a length of $6x + 4$ inches and a
(38)
width of $8x$ inches.

a. Write an expression that can be used to find the area of the bottom of the box.

b. Factor the expression completely.

*23. **Multiple Choice** Simplify $(10g^3h^{-4})^2 (3gh^6)^3$.
(40)

    A $2700g^9h^{10}$ **B** $180g^9h^{10}$ **C** $180g^5h^7$ **D** $2700g^{18}h^{16}$

24. **Formulate** Multiply $(8x^3)(2x)^{-3}$. What is true about $(8x^3)$ and $(2x)^{-3}$?
(40)
(Hint: Simplify the expression.)

25. Simplify $\dfrac{k}{g}\left(\dfrac{rtw}{nk} - 5k^2w^6\right)$.
(39)

*26. **Probability** $P(A) = \dfrac{r^2}{t}$, $P(B) = \dfrac{t}{s}$, and $P(C) = \dfrac{s^2}{rt}$. $P(A$ and $(B$ or $C))$ is represented
(39)
by the expression $\dfrac{r^2}{t}\left(\dfrac{t}{s} + \dfrac{s^2}{rt}\right)$. Simplify.

27. Use the table to find the rate of change.
(41)

Tables	3	5	7	9
Guests	36	60	84	108

*28. **Multi-Step** A plant in Selena's garden will eventually reach a height of 134.4
(42)
centimeters. Today the plant measures 42 centimeters in height. What percent of
the present height of Selena's plant is the final height of the plant?

a. Write a proportion to solve the problem.

b. Find the solution.

c. Choose a method with which to check your work and determine the
reasonability of your solution.

29. (Restoration) At the beginning of 1999, the Leaning Tower of Pisa leaned 14.5 feet
(42)
past center and was in danger of falling over. Engineers tried removing dirt from
the side of the tower opposite from the direction in which it leans, and were able to
reduce the lean by about 10%. About how far past center did the tower lean after
the dirt was removed?

*30. **Geometry** Two similar triangles are shown at right. The
(42)
sides on the larger triangle are 130% of those on the
smaller triangle. What is the length of side x?

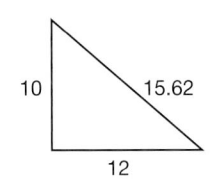 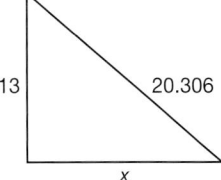

Finding Slope Using the Slope Formula

Warm Up

1. Vocabulary The _____ of a line is the steepness of the line.
(41)

Name the coordinates of each point.
(20)

2. W

3. X

4. Y

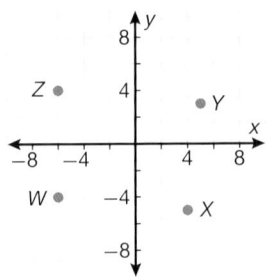

5. Use the table to find the rate of
(41) change.

Servings	2	4	8	12
Corn (oz)	8	16	32	48

New Concepts Any two ordered pairs on a line can be used to determine the slope of the line. The **slope** is a measure of the steepness of a line. The slope m of a line containing points (x_1, y_1) and (x_2, y_2) is $m = \dfrac{y_2 - y_1}{x_2 - x_1}$.

Math Reasoning

Write Describe the formula for slope using only words.

┌─ **Example 1** **Determining Slope from Two Points**

Determine the slope of the line that contains the given points.

a. $(2, 4)$ and $(6, 6)$

SOLUTION

$$m = \frac{y_2 - y_1}{x_2 - x_1} \quad \text{slope formula}$$

$$= \frac{6 - 4}{6 - 2} \quad \text{Substitute } x\text{- and } y\text{-values.}$$

$$= \frac{1}{2} \quad \text{Simplify.}$$

The slope of the line is $\frac{1}{2}$.

b. $(-4, 4)$ and $(4, -2)$

SOLUTION

$$m = \frac{y_2 - y_1}{x_2 - x_1}$$

$$= \frac{(-2) - 4}{4 - (-4)}$$

$$= -\frac{3}{4}$$

The slope of the line is $-\frac{3}{4}$.

Math Reasoning

Analyze When is the slope an improper fraction?

c. $(0, -5)$ and $(5, 10)$

SOLUTION

$$m = \frac{y_2 - y_1}{x_2 - x_1} \quad \text{slope formula}$$

$$= \frac{10 - (-5)}{5 - 0} \quad \text{Substitute } x\text{- and } y\text{-values.}$$

$$= 3 \quad \text{Simplify.}$$

The slope of the line is 3.

d. $(-6, 5)$ and $(3, -13)$

SOLUTION

$$m = \frac{y_2 - y_1}{x_2 - x_1}$$

$$= \frac{(-13) - 5}{3 - (-6)}$$

$$= -2$$

The slope of the line is -2.

Online Connection
www.SaxonMathResources.com

22. Determine the slope of the line containing the two points $(2, -9)$ and $(4, -25)$.
(44)

23. Formulate Translate "the sum of $\frac{1}{2}$ an unknown and the opposite of 4 is less than 6."
(45)

24. Multiple Choice Marshall deposits $45 into his savings account every month. His current balance is $215. After how many months will his balance exceed $500? Write an inequality to represent the situation.
(45)

    A $45w + 215 > 500$ **B** $45w + 500 \leq 215$

    C $45w + 215 \leq 500$ **D** $45w + 500 > 215$

25. Write $\sqrt[6]{m}$ with a fractional exponent.
(46)

*26. Multiple Choice Which expression is equal to $-15^{\frac{1}{4}}$?
(46)

    A $\sqrt[4]{-15}$ **B** $-\sqrt[4]{15}$

    C $\dfrac{1}{\sqrt[4]{-15}}$ **D** $-\dfrac{1}{\sqrt[4]{15}}$

27. Find the percent of increase or decrease from an original price of $500 to a new price of $400.
(47)

*28. Error Analysis Student A and Student B computed the percent of increase of the price of gasoline in Idaho at $3.25 in June 2007, from the nationwide average of $3.07. Which student is correct? Explain the error.
(47)

Student A	Student B
$\dfrac{\$3.25 - \$3.07}{\$3.07} = \dfrac{\$0.18}{\$3.07}$	$\dfrac{\$3.07 - \$3.25}{\$3.25} = -\dfrac{\$0.18}{\$3.25}$
≈ 0.06	≈ -0.06
$= 6\%$	$= -6\%$

*29. Geometry Draw a similar figure whose perimeter is 75% more than the perimeter of the square below.
(47)

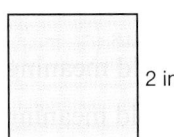

2 in.

30. Analyze Determine if the premise and the conclusion use inductive or deductive reasoning. Explain your choice.
(Inv 4)

Premise: The light turned on the last 50 times the switch was flipped.

Conclusion: The light will turn on the next time the switch is flipped.

Graphing Linear Functions

While the graph of an equation can be drawn by hand, this method may be time-consuming. Also, it can be difficult to read exact values on a hand-drawn graph. A graphing calculator quickly creates an accurate graph of an equation.

Graph the line $y = 2x + 7$.

1. Enter the equation into the Y= editor. Press the Y= key. Then press 2 X,T,θ,n + 7.

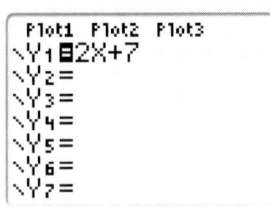

2. Press ZOOM and choose **6: ZStandard** to view the graph of the equation in the standard viewing window.

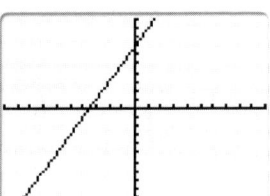

3. Place the cursor on the y-intercept by pressing TRACE. The cursor will automatically appear on the y-intercept the first time the function is traced. The coordinates of the cursor are located at the bottom of the screen. The y-intercept for the line $y = 2x + 7$ is $(0, 7)$.

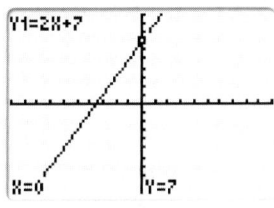

4. While the cursor is tracing the y-intercept, press ENTER. This will center the viewing window on the y-intercept.

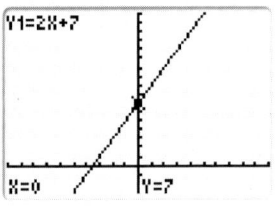

5. Press ZOOM and select **5: ZSquare**. The graph now appears to have a steeper incline. This is the most accurate picture of the graph of $y = 2x + 7$.

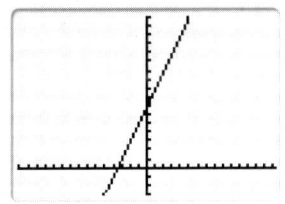

Online Connection
www.SaxonMathResources.com

Example 3 Writing an Inequality from a Graph

Write an inequality for each graph.

a. (number line with open circle at −1, marks at −3, −1, 1)

SOLUTION

endpoint: −1   inequality: >

$k > -1$

b. (number line with closed circle at 25, marks at 5, 15, 25, 35, 40)

SOLUTION

endpoint: 25   inequality: ≥

$n \geq 25$

c. (number line with open circle at 3/4, marks at 0, 1/4, 1/2, 3/4, 1)

SOLUTION

endpoint: $\frac{3}{4}$ inequality: <

$r < \frac{3}{4}$

d. (number line with closed circle at 150, marks at 120, 150, 180)

SOLUTION

endpoint: 150   inequality: ≤

$z \leq 150$

Example 4 Application: Practice Time

Marie does not take a break until she has practiced playing the violin for at least half an hour.

a. Write an inequality to represent the number of hours that Marie must practice before she takes a break.

SOLUTION Let h represent the number of hours that Marie practices. The phrase "at least" can be represented with ≥.

$h \geq 0.5$

b. Graph the solution set of the inequality.

SOLUTION Identify the endpoint (0.5), determine if the circle is open or closed (closed), and the direction in which the arrowhead points (to the right).

> **Math Reasoning**
>
> **Analyze** Although the graph of an inequality for a problem-solving situation includes a wide range of values, the problem will create some restrictions. What restrictions would be placed on this problem?

Lesson Practice

a. Determine which of the values $\{-2, 0, 5, 11\}$ are part of the solution set
(Ex 1) of the inequality $3x + 4 < 19$.

Graph each inequality.

b. $u > -2$
(Ex 2)

c. $t \geq 2.5$
(Ex 2)

d. $y \le 3\frac{1}{3}$
(Ex 2)

e. $0 > v$
(Ex 2)

Write an inequality for each graph.

f.
(Ex 3)
$-1 \quad 0 \quad 1 \quad 2 \quad 3$

g.
(Ex 3)
$8 \quad 10 \quad 12 \quad 14 \quad 16$

h.
(Ex 3)
$30 \quad 40 \quad 50 \quad 60$

i.
(Ex 3)
$-1 \quad 0 \quad 1$

j. (Chemistry) The boiling point of a liquid is the temperature at which it
(Ex 4) changes into a gas. The boiling point of water under normal atmospheric conditions is 100°C. Write an inequality to represent the temperatures for which water is a gas. Graph the solution set of the inequality.

Practice   Distributed and Integrated

Factor the greatest common factor.

1. $6k^5m^2 - 2k^3m - km$
(38)

2. $mx^4y^2 - m^2x^3y^3 + 5m^2x^6y^2$
(38)

Simplify.

3. $\left(\dfrac{2x}{3y^4}\right)^3$
(40)

4. $(2x^3y^2)^4$
(40)

5. True or False: The set of whole numbers is closed under subtraction. If false, give a counterexample.
(1)

6. Determine the slope of the line shown in the graph.
(44)

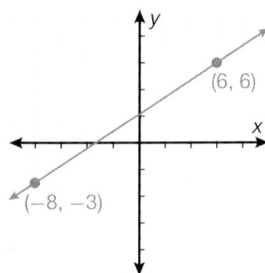

7. Write $5x - 2 = 6y$ in standard form.
(35)

8. Write the expression $\sqrt[4]{y}$ with a fractional exponent.
(46)

9. Probability 7 cards labeled P, E, R, C, E, N, and T are in a jar. Find the probability of picking a P and then an E if the card drawn is not replaced.
(33)

a. A trainer made a box-and-whisker plot of the number of seconds her
(Ex 1) clients could stand on a balance pod. Use the interquartile range to identify outliers.

Number of Seconds on Balance Pod

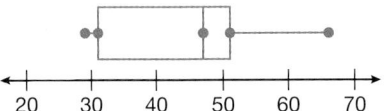

b. Make a box-and-whisker plot to display the data of scores on some state
(Ex 2) tests: 411, 507, 387, 475, 507, 477, 484, 605, 496, 504, 529, 585, 459, 586, 508, 589. Half the tests are between which scores?

c. A coach records the number of yards run by his players.
(Ex 3)

$$1, 22, 18, 34, 37, 89, 44, 43, 19, 28, 27, 23, 19, 21$$

Display the data using a box-and-whisker plot. Identify any outliers.

The populations of the 17 largest U.S. cities in 2005 are listed in millions.

0.7, 2, 0.9, 2.8, 1.5, 0.7, 1.3, 0.8, 0.7, 0.6, 0.8, 1.2, 3.8, 1.5, 0.7, 8.1, 0.9

d. Identify any outliers.
(Ex 4)

e. Use a graphing calculator to make a box-and-whisker plot of this data
(Ex 4) with and without the outlier. Which plot represents the data better?

Solve each equation. Check your answer.

1. $\dfrac{1}{2} + \dfrac{3}{8}x - 5 = 10\dfrac{1}{2}$
(26)

2. $0.02x - 4 - 0.01x - 2 = -6.3$
(24)

3. $x - 5x + 4(x - 2) = 3x - 8$
(28)

Simplify.

4. $\dfrac{2x^2 - 10x}{2x}$
(38)

5. $\dfrac{b^2}{d^{-3}}\left(\dfrac{db^{-2}}{4} - \dfrac{3f^{-3}d^2}{b^{-2}}\right)$
(39)

*6. (**Chemistry**) Avogadro's number is represented by 6.02×10^{23}. Writing this number
(40) as a product, which value would have to be in the exponent of the expression
$(6.02 \times 10^{15})(10^{-})^2$?

7. Multi-Step The formula to convert degrees Fahrenheit to degrees Celsius is
(41) $C = \dfrac{5}{9}(F - 32)$.

    a. On a separate sheet of paper, make a table of the equivalent Celsius temperature to −4, 32, 50, and 77 degrees Fahrenheit.

    b. Use the table to make a graph of the relationship.

    c. Find the slope of the graph.

Hint

Don't forget to first put the numbers in order from least to greatest.

*8. A class makes a box-and-whisker plot to show how many children are in each
(54) family. Identify the median, upper and lower quartiles, upper and lower extremes,
and the interquartile range.

Children per Family

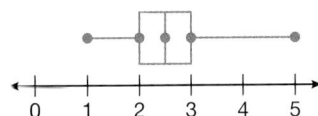

*9. A doctor makes a box-and-whisker plot to show the number of patients she
(54) sees each day. Identify the median, upper and lower quartiles, upper and lower
extremes, and the interquartile range.

Patients per Day

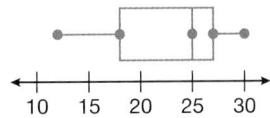

*10. Formulate Create a data set that meets the following criteria: lower extreme 62,
(54) lower quartile 70, median 84, upper quartile 86, and upper extreme 95.

*11. Multiple Choice Using a box-and-whisker plot, which information can you
(54) gather?

    A the mode   **B** the range

    C the mean   **D** the number of data values

*12. (**Astronomy**) The planets' distances (in millions of miles) from the sun are as follows:
(54)

$$36, 67, 93, 142, 484, 887, 1765, \text{ and } 2791$$

Make a box-and-whisker plot of these distances and determine if any planet's
distance is an outlier.

13. Find the percent of increase or decrease to the nearest percent from the original
(47) price of $2175.00 to the new price of $2392.50.

*14. Choose an appropriate measure of central tendency to represent the data set. Justify
(48) your answer.

    12 quiz scores (in percents): 86, 92, 88, 100, 86, 94, 92, 78, 90, 96, 94, 84.

*15. (**Manufacturing**) A skateboard factory has 467 skateboards in stock. The factory can
(49) produce 115 skateboards per hour. Write a linear equation in slope-intercept form
to represent the number of skateboards in inventory after so many hours if no
shipments are made.

16. Write an inequality for the graph below.
(50)

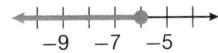

17. (Automotive Maintenance) The following chart shows the wear on a particular brand
(44) of tires every 10,000 miles. What is the average rate of wear for this brand of tires?

Mileage	Tread Depth
10,000	20 mm
20,000	16 mm
30,000	12 mm
40,000	8 mm

18. The diagram shows types of transportation. Use the diagram to determine if each
(Inv 4) statement is true or false. If the statement is false, provide a counterexample.

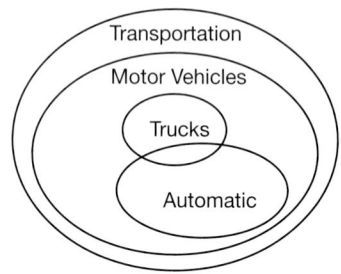

a. If a vehicle is a truck, then the vehicle is an automatic.

b. All trucks are motor vehicles.

19. Write Explain the difference between $\sqrt{-1}$ and $\sqrt{1}$.
(46)

20. Write Explain why $\frac{2g}{2g+6}$ cannot be simplified to $\frac{1}{6}$.
(51)

21. Multiple Choice Which expression is not equivalent to $3rd^{-1} - \frac{6}{r^{-1}d}$?
(51)

   A $-3rd^{-1}$ **B** $\frac{-3r}{d}$ **C** $\frac{-3d}{r}$ **D** $\frac{-3}{r^{-1}d}$

***22.** (Telecommunications) Jane bought a prepaid phone card that had 500 minutes. She
(52) used about 25 minutes of calling time per week. Write and graph an equation
to approximate her remaining calling time y (in minutes) after 9 weeks.

23. Find the slope of the line that passes through $(1, 6)$ and $(3, -4)$.
(52)

24. Describe a line that has a slope of 0 and passes through the point $(-1, 1)$.
(52)

25. Write an equation in slope-intercept form of a line that passes through the
(52) points $(14, -3)$ and $(-6, 9)$.

26. Error Analysis Students were asked to find the sum of the polynomials vertically.
(53) Which student is correct? Explain the error.

Student A	Student B
$-6x^3 - 3x^2 + 5$	$-6x^3 - 3x^2 + 5$
$+\ \ 2x^3 - x\ \ - 7$	$+\ \ \ \ 2x^3\ \ - x - 7$
$-4x^3 - 4x^2 - 2$	$-4x^3 - 3x^2 - x - 2$

27. Geometry Write a polynomial expression for the perimeter of the triangle. Simplify the
(53) polynomial and give your answer in standard form.

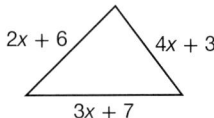

28. Measurement The length of the sidewalk that runs in front of Trina's house is
(53) $3x - 16$ and the width is $5x + 21$. Find the perimeter of the sidewalk.

***29. Multi-Step** The table shows the amounts that Doug and Jane plan to deposit in
(53) their savings account. Their savings account has the same annual growth rate g.

Date	1/1/04	1/1/05	1/1/06	1/1/07
Doug	$300	$400	$200	$25
Jane	$375	$410	$50	$200

a. On January 1, 2007, the value of Doug's account D can be modeled by
$D = 300g^3 + 400g^2 + 200g + 25$, where g is the annual growth rate. Find a
model for Jane's account J on January 1, 2007.

b. Find a model for the combined amounts of Doug and Jane's account on
January 1, 2007.

30. Find the sum of $(9x^3 + 12) + (16x^3 - 4x + 2)$ using a horizontal format.
(53)

Calculating the Intersection of Two Lines

Graphing Calculator Lab (*Use with Lesson 55*)

A graphing calculator can be used to find the intersection of two lines. Find the intersection of $y = 2x - 5$ and $2y + 3x = 6$.

Caution

Equations entered into the Y = Editor should be solved for *y*.

1. Enter the equations into the **Y = Editor**.

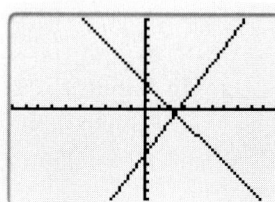

Graphing Calculator Tip

For help with graphing equations, refer to Graphing Calculator Lab 3 on page 305.

2. Graph the equations in a standard viewing window.

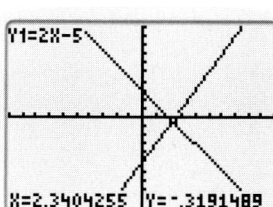

3. Approximate the intersection by tracing the line. Trace one of the lines by pressing `TRACE`. The ⌄ and ⌃ keys are used to move the cursor to another line. The ◂ and ▸ keys are used to move the cursor along a line. Use the keys to move the cursor to the intersection. The coordinates of the cursor are displayed at the bottom of the screen. The approximate intersection point of $y = 2x - 5$ and $2y + 3x = 6$ is about $(2.3, -0.3)$.

4. Calculate the exact intersection.

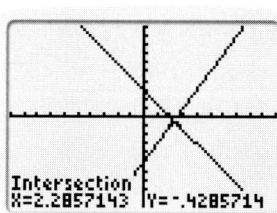

Press **2nd** **TRACE** (CALC) and select **5:Intersection.**
At the prompt "First Curve?," press **ENTER**
to select the first line. At the next prompt,
"Second Curve?," press **ENTER** to select the
second line. Use the ◄ and ► keys to move
the cursor near the intersection. At the
prompt "Guess?," press **ENTER**. The solution is
displayed as a decimal at the bottom of
the screen.

5. Change to the x- and y-coordinates to
   fractions. Press **2nd** [QUIT] to return
   to the home screen. Press **X,T,θ,n** and
   ENTER, and then press **MATH** and select
   1:>Frac. Press **ENTER**. Press **ALPHA** [Y] and
   ENTER, and then press **MATH** and select
   1:>Frac. Press **ENTER**.

```
X▸Frac
           16/7
Y▸Frac
           -3/7
■
```

Lab Practice

a. Use the trace feature to find the approximate intersection of
   $y = -2x + 3$ and $y = 0.5x + 1$.

b. Use the intersection feature to find the exact intersection of
   $y = -2x + 3$ and $y = 0.5x + 1$.

c. Use the graphing calculator to find the intersection of $y = -2x + 2$
   and $3y - 4x = 12$.

d. Use the intersection feature to find the exact intersection of
   $y = -\frac{3}{2}x - 5$ and $y = \frac{1}{3}x + 5$.

e. Use the graphing calculator to find the intersection of $y = 4x - 1$ and
   $2y + x = 2$.

Example 3 Identifying the LCM of Three Monomials

Find the LCM of $6p^2s^3$, $2m^2s^2$, and $8m^3p$.

SOLUTION

Write each expression as a product of prime numbers.

$6p^2s^3 = 2 \cdot 3 \cdot p \cdot p \cdot s \cdot s \cdot s$

$2m^2s^2 = 2 \cdot m \cdot m \cdot s \cdot s$

$8m^3p = 2 \cdot 2 \cdot 2 \cdot m \cdot m \cdot m \cdot p$

In the LCM, the factor 2 will appear three times and the factor 3 will appear one time.

$$2 \cdot 2 \cdot 2 \cdot 3$$

No one variable appears in all three expressions. The most the variable m appears is three times. The most the variable p appears is two times. The most the variable s appears is three times.

$\text{LCM} = 2 \cdot 2 \cdot 2 \cdot 3 \cdot m \cdot m \cdot m \cdot p \cdot p \cdot s \cdot s \cdot s$

The LCM is $24m^3p^2s^3$.

Example 4 Identifying the LCM of Polynomials

a. Find the LCM of $(3x + 1)$ and $(2x + 9)$.

SOLUTION

The binomials are prime. Their only factors are 1 and themselves. The LCM, then, is the product of the binomials.

The LCM is $(3x + 1)(2x + 9)$.

b. Find the LCM of $(7x^2 + 21x)$ and $(6x + 18)$.

SOLUTION

Factor each binomial, if possible.

The GCF of the terms in $(7x^2 + 21x)$ is $7x$. Factor it.

$(7x^2 + 21x) = 7 \cdot x(x + 3)$

The GCF of the terms in $(6x + 18)$ is 6. Factor it.

$(6x + 18) = 6(x + 3) = 2 \cdot 3(x + 3)$

$(x + 3)$ is a common factor, appearing one time in each binomial. The numbers 2, 3, and 7 are also factors, appearing one time. The variable x is also a factor.

$\text{LCM} = 2 \cdot 3 \cdot 7 \cdot x(x + 3)$

The LCM is $42x(x + 3)$.

c. Find the LCM of $(60x^3 + 24x)$ and $(45x^4 + 18x^2)$.

SOLUTION

Factor each binomial, if possible.

The GCF of the terms in $(60x^3 + 24x)$ is $12x$. Factor it.

$(60x^3 + 24x) = 2 \cdot 2 \cdot 3 \cdot x(5x^2 + 2)$

The GCF of the terms in $(45x^4 + 18x^2)$ is $9x^2$. Factor it.

$(45x^4 + 18x^2) = 3 \cdot 3 \cdot x \cdot x(5x^2 + 2)$

$(5x^2 + 2)$ is a common factor, appearing one time in each binomial. The numbers 2, 3, and the variable x are also factors, appearing at most two times.

$\text{LCM} = 2 \cdot 2 \cdot 3 \cdot 3 \cdot x \cdot x(5x^2 + 2)$

The LCM is $36x^2(5x^2 + 2)$.

Caution

Terms in parentheses are grouped and cannot be separated during factoring. The grouped terms make one factor.

Example 5 Application: Scheduling

A math test is given every 9 days. A history test is given every 14 days. A science test is given every 18 days. How many days into the school year will all three tests be given on the same day?

SOLUTION

Understand The frequency of the tests is a regular pattern. At some point the patterns will overlap and all three tests will be given on the same day.

Plan Math tests are given on days that are multiples of 9. History tests are given on days that are multiples of 14. Science tests are given on days that are multiples of 18. If the LCM of 9, 14, and 18 is found, it will show the day that all three tests will be given.

Solve Write each number as a product of prime numbers.

$$9 = 3 \cdot 3$$
$$14 = 2 \cdot 7$$
$$18 = 3 \cdot 3 \cdot 2$$

In the LCM, the factor 2 will appear one time, the factor 3 will appear two times, and the factor 7 will appear one time.

$$\text{LCM} = 2 \cdot 3 \cdot 3 \cdot 7$$
$$\text{LCM} = 126$$

So, all three tests will be given 126 days into the school year.

Check List the multiples of each number to 126.

9: 9, 18, 27, 36, 45, 54, 63, 72, 81, 90, 99, 108, 117, 126

14: 14, 28, 42, 56, 70, 84, 98, 112, 126

18: 18, 36, 54, 72, 90, 108, 126

The least multiple that appears in each list is 126. ✓

Math Reasoning

Predict If a school year is 180 days long, how many times will a student have a math and science test on the same day?

*12. Geometry The length of a rectangular pool is four times the width. A
(58) four-foot-wide deck surrounds the pool. Write a polynomial expression for the
area of the pool and deck. Use the Distributive Property and write your answer in
standard form.

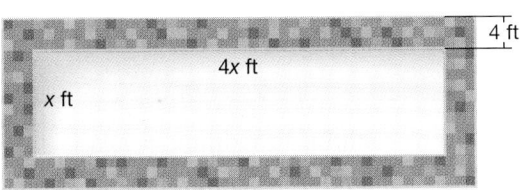

*13. Multi-Step Henry has a game that includes a number cube. The side length of the
(58) cube is $(5x + 1)$ inches. Find the volume of the number cube.

a. Find the area of the base. Multiply the length times the width.

b. Find the volume by multiplying the product found in part **a** by the height.

*14. Measurement Tim has a garden in the shape of a right triangle. The triangle has a
(58) base of $6x^2 + 8x + 12$ feet and a height of $(x - 1)$ feet. What is the area of Tim's
garden?

$(x - 1)$ ft

$(6x^2 + 8x + 12)$ ft

15. Find the product of $4x(x^2 + 2x - 9)$.
(58)

16. Write an equation of the line in slope-intercept form. The slope is 2; the
(49) y-intercept is -1.

17. What is the degree of $12x^4x^3 + 6xy + 41x^2y^3$?
(53)

18. (Baseball) The percentage of games won is used to determine a team's standing in
(54) the league. In the American League, the following percentages were recorded:

$$0.604, 0.540, 0.505, 0.465, 0.380, 0.600, 0.584, 0.505, 0.446,$$
$$0.430, 0.580, 0.545, 0.475, 0.451$$

Make a box-and-whisker plot of these percentages and determine if there is an
outlier.

*19. Estimate The cost of a chain is directly proportional to its length. Use the
(56) graph to estimate the cost of a chain that is 18 inches long.

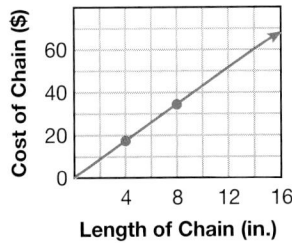

20. Multiple Choice Which point represents the same direct variation as $(3, -9)$?
(56)
   A $(4, -8)$ **B** $(4, -7)$ **C** $(4, -12)$ **D** $(4, -16)$

21. Find the LCM of $16c^6$ and $24c^3$.
(57)

*22. (Games) Every $20x^3y$ turns, you win $500. Every $12xy^3c$ turns, you get to roll again.
(57) How many turns do you take before you win $500 and get to roll again on the same turn?

23. Find the LCM of $300d^2$ and $90d^4$.
(57)

24. **Formulate** The equations $y = 3x - 24$ and $y = 24x + 9$ define two lines. Write a
(43) rational expression that represents the ratio of the first line to the second line. Simplify the expression, if possible.

25. Determine the slope of the line that goes through the points $(-1, 1)$ and $(1, -1)$.
(44)

26. (Biology) Write a counterexample for the following statement: If an animal has
(Inv 4) wings, then the animal is an insect.

27. **Multi-Step** A canister of oatmeal has a height of 7 inches. Its volume is
(46) 28π cubic inches.

    a. Write an equation you can use to find the radius of the cylinder.

    b. Find the radius of the canister.

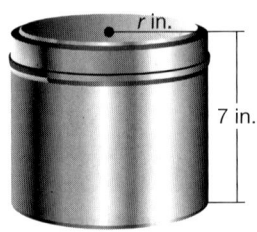

28. (Astronomy) The relative gravity on Jupiter is 2.34. This means that the weight of an
(49) object on Jupiter is 2.34 times greater than its weight on Earth. Identify the slope and the y-intercept of the equation representing this relationship and then write an equation for the situation in slope-intercept form.

29. **Verify** Write the converse of the following statement: If a number is an integer,
(Inv 5) then it is a rational number. Give an example to show that the converse is false.

30. **Write** What is an excluded value for a rational expression? Why is it excluded?
(51)

*11. Multi-Step Joseph lives 5 miles from the school and Maya lives 2 miles from the
(63) school. If Joseph walks from his house in an opposite direction from the school
at a speed of 4 miles per hour, and Maya walks from her house in an opposite
direction from the school at a speed of 6 miles per hour, after how long will they
be the same distance from the school? What is that distance?

*12. Multiple Choice If y varies inversely as x, and $y = 9$ when $x = 12$, what is y when
(64) $x = 4$?

    A 3   **B** 5.3   **C** 27   **D** 108

13. (Recycling) Use the table to compare the mean value of the amount of waste
(48) generated in the United States to the mean value of the amount of materials
recovered for recycling from 1960 to 2005. Write a statement based on this
comparison.

Generation and Materials Recovery of Municipal Solid Waste, 1960–2005
(in millions of tons)

Activity	1960	1970	1980	1990	2000	2003	2004	2005
Generation	88.1	121.1	151.6	205.2	237.6	240.4	247.3	245.7
Materials Recovery	5.6	8.0	14.5	33.2	69.1	74.9	77.7	79.0

14. Multi-Step A model sailboat calls for trim around the largest sail. The sail
(51) is triangular with side lengths $\dfrac{8}{2a^2 + 3a}$ centimeters, $\dfrac{5a + 1}{2a^2 + 3a}$ centimeters, and
$\dfrac{3a + 3}{2a^2 + 3a}$ centimeters. How much trim will be used?

Find each of the statistical measures below using the data in the plot.

Annual Base Salary
at Marketing Associates

Stem	Leaves
2	1, 1, 2, 2, 3, 3, 3, 6, 8
3	0, 1, 2, 6, 6, 9
4	2, 5, 8
5	3, 5, 7
6	4, 8

Key: 3| 1 means $31,000

15. median   **16.** mode
(62)   (62)

17. range   **18.** relative frequency of $22,000
(62)   (62)

19. (Health) To calculate a personal body mass index, students first had to report
(54) their weight in pounds. Make a box-and-whisker plot of the weights below and
determine if there is an outlier.

        140, 145, 170, 157, 130, 155, 190, 180, 175, 120, 116, 118, 112, 103

20. Identify Statement 2 as the converse, inverse, or contrapositive of Statement 1.
(Inv 5) Then indicate the truth value of each statement.

    Statement 1: If a figure is a rhombus, then it is not a rectangle.

    Statement 2: If a figure is a rectangle, then it is not a rhombus.

⊙*21. Statistics The standard deviation is the square root of the variance of a set of data.
(61) If the variance of a set of data is 24, what is the standard deviation in simplest form?

22. Justify There are two different ways to write $\sqrt{\frac{75}{45}}$ in simplest form. Find both and
(61) then explain why each is correct.

*23. Error Analysis Two students solved the following systems of equations. Which
(63) student is correct? Explain the error.

Student A	Student B
$2x + 11y = 13$	$2x + 11y = 13$
$2x + 9y = 11$	$2x + 6y = 8$
$20y = 24$	$5y = 5$
$y = 1.2$	$y = 1$
$(-0.1, 1.2)$	$(1, 1)$

24. Geometry The areas of two similar rectangles add up to 39 square
(63) units. Twice the area of Rectangle A plus one-third the area
of Rectangle B equals 33 square units. What are the areas of
Rectangles A and B?

25. Graph $9x - 1.5y + 12 = 0$ using slope-intercept form.
(49)

26. Solve the following system of linear equations: $-3x + 2y = -6$.
(63) $$-5x - 2y = 22$$

27. Multi-Step Use the system of linear equations to answer the problems below.
(55)
$$2x - y = 14$$
$$x + 4y = -2$$

  a. Graph the system.

  b. Determine the solution.

  c. Check your answer by using substitution.

28. (Boyle's Law) In chemistry, Boyle's Law states that the volume of a sample of gas is
(64) inversely related to its pressure if the temperature remains constant. Jameka recorded
the pressure of a sample of gas inside a 450-cubic millimeter container to be 95 kPa. If
the pressure increased to 475 kPa, what would the new volume of the gas be?

29. Write Describe a proportional situation that is represented by the equation $y = 6x$.
(56)

30. Generalize How would you describe the location of a graphed inverse variation
(64) based on the constant?

Writing Equations of Parallel and Perpendicular Lines

Warm Up

1. **Vocabulary** The _____ form for the equation of a line is $y - y_1 = m(x - x_1)$, where m is the slope and (x_1, y_1) is a point on the line.
(52)

Find the slope and y-intercept.

2. $2x + y = -5$ **3.** $-9x + 3y = 12$
(49)   *(49)*

4. Write an equation in slope-intercept form for a line that passes through the
(52) point $(0, -5)$ and has a slope of $\frac{2}{3}$.

New Concepts

Parallel lines are lines that are in the same plane but do not intersect.

Slopes of Parallel Lines

Two nonvertical lines are parallel if they have the same slope and are not the same line.

Any two vertical lines are parallel.

Example The equations $y = 2x + 7$ and $y = 2x - 1$ have the same slope, 2, and different y-intercepts. The graphs of the two lines are parallel.

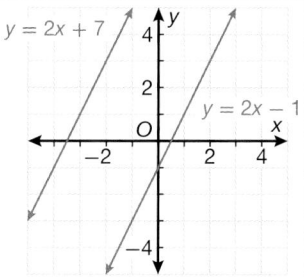

Example 1   Determining if Lines are Parallel

Determine if the equations represent parallel lines.

$$y = -\frac{4}{3}x + 5 \text{ and } 4x + 3y = 6$$

Math Reasoning

Analyze Will one ordered pair ever satisfy the equations of a pair of parallel lines? Explain.

SOLUTION

Write both equations in the slope-intercept form $y = mx + b$.

$$y = -\frac{4}{3}x + 5 \qquad \text{The first equation is already in slope-intercept form.}$$

Write the second equation in slope-intercept form by solving for y.

$$4x + 3y = 6$$
$$\underline{-4x \qquad = -4x}$$
$$3y = -4x + 6$$
$$\frac{3y}{3} = -\frac{4x}{3} + \frac{6}{3}$$
$$y = -\frac{4}{3}x + 2$$

Since both lines have the same slope but have different y-intercepts, the two lines are parallel.

Online Connection
www.SaxonMathResources.com

Example 2 Writing Equations of Parallel Lines

Write an equation in slope-intercept form for the line that passes through $(-1, 1)$ and is parallel to a line with equation $y = 2x - 1$.

SOLUTION

Determine the slope of the parallel line. Then substitute the slope and the point into the point-slope formula.

The slope of the line $y = 2x - 1$ is 2. Any line parallel to the given line has a slope of 2.

Substitute $m = 2$ and the point $(-1, 1)$ into the point-slope formula. Write the equation in slope-intercept form.

$$y - y_1 = m(x - x_1)$$
$$y - 1 = 2(x + 1) \qquad \text{Substitute the slope and point into the equation.}$$
$$y - 1 = 2x + 2 \qquad \text{Distributive Property}$$
$$y = 2x + 3 \qquad \text{Add 1 to both sides.}$$

The equation of the line is $y = 2x + 3$.

Perpendicular lines are two lines that intersect at right angles.

Slopes of Perpendicular Lines
Any two lines are perpendicular if their slopes are negative reciprocals of each other. A vertical and horizontal line are also perpendicular. 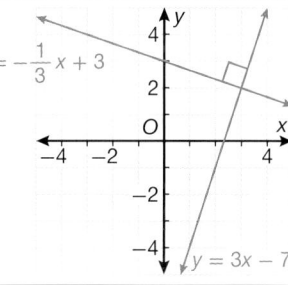 **Example** The slope of $y = 3x - 7$ is 3. The slope of $y = -\frac{1}{3}x + 3$ is $-\frac{1}{3}$. Since the slopes are negative reciprocals, the lines are perpendicular.

Example 3 Determining if Lines are Perpendicular

Determine if the lines passing through the given points are perpendicular.

line *1*: $(-5, 4)$ and $(-3, 0)$ line *2*: $(-2, -2)$ and $(-4, -3)$

SOLUTION

Find the slope of each line.

$$m_1 = \frac{y_2 - y_1}{x_2 - x_1} \qquad\qquad\qquad m_2 = \frac{y_2 - y_1}{x_2 - x_1}$$
$$= \frac{0 - 4}{-3 - (-5)} \qquad\qquad\qquad = \frac{-3 - (-2)}{-4 - (-2)}$$
$$= \frac{-4}{2} \qquad\qquad\qquad\qquad = \frac{-1}{-2}$$
$$= -2 \qquad\qquad\qquad\qquad = \frac{1}{2}$$

Since -2 is the negative reciprocal of $\frac{1}{2}$, the lines are perpendicular.

Example 4 **Writing Equations of Perpendicular Lines**

Write an equation in slope-intercept form for the line that passes through $(-2, -3)$ and is perpendicular to a line with equation $y = -3x + 1$.

SOLUTION

The slope of $y = -3x + 1$ is -3. Any line perpendicular to the given line has a slope of $\frac{1}{3}$, which is a negative reciprocal of -3.

Substitute $m = \frac{1}{3}$ and the point $(-2, -3)$ into the point slope formula. Write the equation in slope-intercept form.

$$y - y_1 = m(x - x_1)$$

$$y - (-3) = \frac{1}{3}(x - (-2)) \qquad \text{Substitute the slope and point into the equation.}$$

$$y + 3 = \frac{1}{3}x + \frac{2}{3} \qquad \text{Simplify.}$$

$$y = \frac{1}{3}x - 2\frac{1}{3} \qquad \text{Subtract 3 from both sides and simplify.}$$

Example 5 **Application: Coordinate Geometry**

Use the slopes of the line segments to show that LMN is a right triangle.

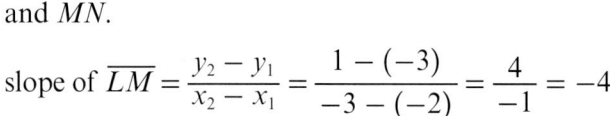

SOLUTION

LMN is a right triangle if $\overline{LM}$ is perpendicular to $\overline{MN}$. Find the slope of $\overline{LM}$ and $\overline{MN}$.

$$\text{slope of } \overline{LM} = \frac{y_2 - y_1}{x_2 - x_1} = \frac{1 - (-3)}{-3 - (-2)} = \frac{4}{-1} = -4$$

$$\text{slope of } \overline{MN} = \frac{y_2 - y_1}{x_2 - x_1} = \frac{-3 - (-2)}{-2 - 2} = \frac{-1}{-4} = \frac{1}{4}$$

The slopes of $\overline{LM}$ and $\overline{MN}$ are negative reciprocals, so the two sides are perpendicular. Therefore, LMN is a right triangle because it contains a right angle.

Lesson Practice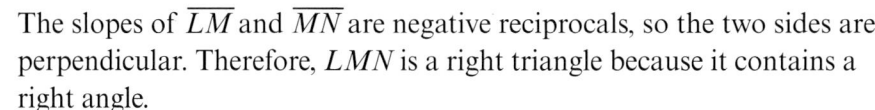

a. Determine if the equations represent parallel lines.
(Ex 1)

$$y = \frac{2}{3}x + 5\frac{1}{3} \text{ and } \frac{3}{2}x + y = 1$$

b. Write an equation in slope-intercept form for the line that passes
(Ex 2) through $(-3, 2)$ and is parallel to a line with equation $y = \frac{4}{7}x + \frac{5}{7}$.

c. Determine if the lines passing through the points are perpendicular.
(Ex 3)
line 1: $(-2, 2)$ and $(2, -4)$ *line 2:* $(3, 6)$ and $(5, 3)$.

d. Write an equation in slope-intercept form for the line that passes *(Ex 4)* through $(-1, 3)$ and is perpendicular to a line with equation $y = \frac{4}{7}x + \frac{5}{7}$.

e. **Geometry** Use the slopes of the line segments to *(Ex 5)* show that ABC is a right triangle.

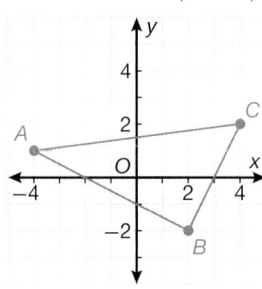

Simplify.

1. $\sqrt{360}$ *(61)*

2. $\sqrt{252}$ *(61)*

3. $\sqrt{384}$ *(61)*

Find the product using the FOIL method.

4. $(x^2 + 5)^2$ *(58)*

5. $(x - 2)(x - 9)$ *(58)*

6. Graph the inequality $c \geq -5$. *(50)*

7. **Justify** Explain how you find the LCM of $2(x - 5)^3$ and $3(x - 5)^7$. *(57)*

8. **Multiple Choice** The key of a stem-and-leaf plot shows $2|9 = 2.9$ cm. What is the *(62)* value of a data point with a leaf of 4 and a stem of 7?

   A 4.7 cm   **B** 7.4 cm   **C** 47 cm   **D** 74 cm

*9. (Sports) The results in seconds for the men's 50-meter freestyle swimming finals at *(62)* the NCAA Division II Championship in 2007 are listed below. Create a stem-and-leaf plot to organize the data.

$$20.43, 20.32, 20.36, 20.39, 20.67, 20.68, 20.68, 20.81, 20.62,$$
$$20.97, 21.07, 21.24, 21.25, 21.31, 21.45, 21.56$$

10. **Multi-Step** The cost of parking at a concert is \$22 for the first 2 hours and \$4 for *(52)* each additional hour. Write an equation that models the total cost y of parking a car in terms of the number of additional hours x. Using the linear equation, find the total cost of parking for 9 hours.

11. **Error Analysis** Two students attempted to write an inverse variation equation *(64)* relating x and y when $x = 5$ and $y = 10$. Which student is correct? Explain the error.

Student A	Student B
$y = \dfrac{50}{x}$	$y = 2x$

*12. Measurement Giao wants to construct a picture frame made of wooden pieces that
(63) are 7 centimeters and 3 centimeters in length. He needs 20 pieces, and the total
perimeter of the frame needs to be 108 centimeters. If Giao cuts eight 3-centimeter
pieces first and is left with 0.8 meter of wood, will he have enough wood to cut
the 7-centimeter pieces? Explain.

Solve each system of linear equations by the method indicated.

13. Use graphing.
(55)
$$2x - y = 3$$
$$3x + y = 2$$

14. Use elimination.
(63)
$$5x + 7y = 41$$
$$3x + 7y = 47$$

15. Use substitution.
(59)
$$5x - 2y = 22$$
$$9x + y = 12$$

16. (Banking) Ryan and Kathy both have savings accounts. Ryan has $12 in his account
(55) and plans to add $3 each week to it. Kathy does not have any money in her
account, but plans to add $5 each week. How many weeks will it take until Ryan and
Kathy have the same amount of money?

*17. Multi-Step The results for the women's 3-meter diving finals at the NCAA Division II
(62) Championship in 2007 are listed below.

499.15, 429.15, 409.75, 405.90, 395.65, 382.15, 353.20, 351.75,
342.30, 333.75, 328.20, 325.75, 315.20, 302.85, 292.90, 277.90

a. Write Explain how to determine the intervals to create a histogram for the data.
Identify the intervals.

b. Create a histogram for this data using the intervals from part **a.**

c. Is a histogram or a stem-and-leaf plot a better display for this data?
Explain.

18. Write the equation of the graphed line in slope-intercept form.
(49)

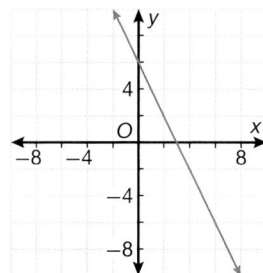

19. (Investing) Trey is making an investment of $(x - 11)$ dollars. The rate of interest
(60) on the investment is $(x - 11)$ percent. What is the interest gained after one year?
(Hint: interest = principle × rate × time; $i = prt$)

20. (Construction) The school is constructing a new gym. They want a 12-foot-wide tile
(60) border around the outside edge of the square court, and the total side length is $7x$.
Write a polynomial for the area of the court, not including the tile border.

7x

12 feet

21. Find the LCM of $16c^6$ and $24c^3$.
(57)

*22. ⟮**Games**⟯ Every $20x^3y$ turns, you win \$500. Every $12xy^3c$ turns, you get to roll again.
(57) How many turns do you take before you win \$500 and get to roll again on the same turn?

23. Find the LCM of $300d^2$ and $90d^4$.
(57)

24. Formulate The equations $y = 3x - 24$ and $y = 24x + 9$ define two lines. Write a
(43) rational expression that represents the ratio of the first line to the second line. Simplify the expression, if possible.

25. Determine the slope of the line that goes through the points $(-1, 1)$ and $(1, -1)$.
(44)

26. ⟮**Biology**⟯ Write a counterexample for the following statement: If an animal has
(Inv 4) wings, then the animal is an insect.

27. Multi-Step A canister of oatmeal has a height of 7 inches. Its volume is
(46) 28π cubic inches.

    a. Write an equation you can use to find the radius of the cylinder.

    b. Find the radius of the canister.

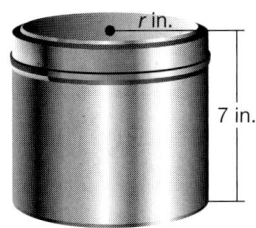

28. ⟮**Astronomy**⟯ The relative gravity on Jupiter is 2.34. This means that the weight of an
(49) object on Jupiter is 2.34 times greater than its weight on Earth. Identify the slope and the y-intercept of the equation representing this relationship and then write an equation for the situation in slope-intercept form.

29. Verify Write the converse of the following statement: If a number is an integer,
(Inv 5) then it is a rational number. Give an example to show that the converse is false.

30. Write What is an excluded value for a rational expression? Why is it excluded?
(51)

Finding Special Products of Binomials

Warm Up

1. Vocabulary Which polynomial is a trinomial?
(53)

A $3x^3 + 5$ **B** $7x^2 + 5 \cdot 4x$

C $4x^2 + 6x - 9$ **D** $2x^3 + 5x^2 + 3x - 8$

Simplify.
(58)

2. $(2x + 3)(3x - 5)$

3. $(3x + 7)(5x + 6)$

4. $(3x - 2)(3x^2 - x + 7)$

New Concepts

> **Exploration**   Multiplying Binomials

Square the following binomials

Hint

To square a binomial multiply it by itself.

1. $(2t + 2)^2$

2. $(4y + 3)^2$

3. $(a + b)^2$

4. $(t - 5)^2$

5. $(2x - 3)^2$

6. $(a - b)^2$

7. Describe a pattern for $(a + b)^2$ and $(a - b)^2$.

Multiply the following binomials

8. $(3x + 4)(3x - 4)$

9. $(x + 6)(x - 6)$

10. $(a + b)(a - b)$

11. Describe a pattern for $(a + b)(a - b)$.

The square of a binomial $(a + b)^2$ or $(a - b)^2$ results in a perfect-square trinomial. Trinomials of the form $a^2 + 2ab + b^2$ and $a^2 - 2ab + b^2$ are **perfect-square trinomials** because they are the product of a factor times itself.

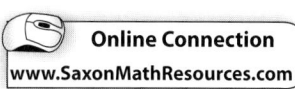
Online Connection
www.SaxonMathResources.com

The product of a sum and difference of two binomials $(a - b)(a + b) = a^2 - b^2$ produces the difference of two squares.

Special Product of Binomials	
Square of a Binomial	
Pattern	**Example**
$(a + b)^2 = a^2 + 2ab + b^2$	$(x + 5)^2 = x^2 + 10x + 25$
$(a - b)^2 = a^2 - 2ab + b^2$	$(2x - 4)^2 = 4x^2 - 16x + 16$
Sum and Difference	
Pattern	**Example**
$(a + b)(a - b) = a^2 - b^2$	$(3x - 2)(3x + 2) = 9x^2 - 4$

Example 1 Squaring Binomials in the Form $(a + b)^2$

a. Find the product: $(x + 2)^2$.

SOLUTION

$(a + b)^2 = a^2 + 2ab + b^2$ Write the pattern.

$(x + 2)^2 = (x)^2 + 2(x)(2) + 2^2$ Apply the pattern.

$\qquad = x^2 + 4x + 4$ Simplify.

b. Find the product: $(2x + 4)^2$.

SOLUTION

$(a + b)^2 = a^2 + 2ab + b^2$ Write the pattern.

$(2x + 4)^2 = (2x)^2 + 2(2x)(4) + 4^2$ Apply the pattern.

$\qquad = 4x^2 + 16x + 16$ Simplify.

Example 2 Squaring Binomials in the Form $(a - b)^2$

a. Find the product: $(x - 8)^2$.

SOLUTION

$(a - b)^2 = a^2 - 2ab + b^2$ Write the pattern.

$(x - 8)^2 = (x)^2 - 2(x)(8) + (8)^2$ Apply the pattern.

$\qquad = x^2 - 16x + 64$ Simplify.

b. Find the product: $(2x - 7)^2$.

SOLUTION

$(a - b)^2 = a^2 - 2ab + b^2$ Write the pattern.

$(2x - 7)^2 = (2x)^2 - 2(2x)(7) + (7)^2$ Apply the pattern.

$\qquad = 4x^2 - 28x + 49$ Simplify.

Caution

$(x - 5)^2 \neq x^2 + 25$

Remember to either use the pattern for squaring binomials or use the FOIL method.

$(x - 5)^2 = (x - 5)(x - 5)$
$\qquad = x^2 - 10x + 25$

Example 3 **Finding Products in the Form** $(a + b)(a - b)$

a. Find the product: $(x + 3)(x - 3)$.

SOLUTION

$$(a + b)(a - b) = a^2 - b^2 \qquad \text{Write the pattern.}$$
$$(x + 3)(x - 3) = (x)^2 - (3)^2 \qquad \text{Apply the pattern.}$$
$$= x^2 - 9 \qquad \text{Simplify.}$$

b. Find the product: $(5x + 4)(5x - 4)$.

SOLUTION

$$(a + b)(a - b) = a^2 - b^2 \qquad \text{Write the pattern.}$$
$$(5x + 4)(5x - 4) = (5x)^2 - (4)^2 \qquad \text{Apply the pattern.}$$
$$= 25x^2 - 16 \qquad \text{Simplify.}$$

Example 4 **Mental Math**

a. Use mental math to find 39^2. To use mental math, remember to use the special, product patterns.

SOLUTION

$$(40 - 1)^2 \qquad \text{Write } 39^2 \text{ as a square of binomial.}$$
$$= 40^2 - 2(40)(1) + (1)^2 \qquad \text{Apply the pattern.}$$
$$= 1600 - 80 + 1$$
$$= 1521 \qquad \text{Simplify.}$$

b. Use mental math to find the product of $16 \cdot 24$. To use mental math, remember to use the special product patterns.

SOLUTION

$$(20 - 4)(20 + 4) = 20^2 - 4^2 \qquad \text{Write } 16 \cdot 24 \text{ as the product of the difference and the sum.}$$
$$= 400 - 16 \qquad \text{Simplify.}$$
$$= 384$$

Example 5 **Application: Gardening**

Roberto has a garden in the shape of a parallelogram. It has a height of $(x - 2)$ and a base length of $(x + 2)$. Find the area of Roberto's garden.

Math Reasoning

Write How could Roberto check his work?

SOLUTION

$$A = bh$$
$$= (x - 2)(x + 2) \qquad \text{Write as the product of difference and sum.}$$
$$= (x)^2 - (2)^2$$
$$= x^2 - 4 \qquad \text{Simplify.}$$

Find each product.

a. $(x + 9)^2$ *(Ex 1)*

b. $(3x + 5)^2$ *(Ex 1)*

c. $(x - 1)^2$ *(Ex 2)*

d. $(8x - 6)^2$ *(Ex 2)*

e. $(x + 8)(x - 8)$ *(Ex 3)*

f. $(3x + 2)(3x - 2)$ *(Ex 3)*

g. Use mental math to find 28^2. *(Ex 4)*

h. Use mental math to find the product of $58 \cdot 62$. *(Ex 4)*

i. George is pouring a rectangular cement slab for his house. The length is $(x - 6)$ and the width is $(x + 6)$. Find the area of George's new slab. *(Ex 5)*

Practice Distributed and Integrated

Simplify.

1. $(3k + 2k^2 - 4) - (k^2 + k - 6)$ *(53)*

2. $(-2m + 1) + (6m^2 - m - 2)$ *(53)*

3. $(x + 4)(x - 5)$ *(58)*

4. $(x + 2)(6x^2 + 4x + 5)$ *(58)*

Find the square of each binomial.

*5. $(3t - 1)^2$ *(60)*

*6. $(3t + 1)^2$ *(60)*

*7. (Painting) Dat is painting a picture for his grandmother. He wants a 3-inch-wide blue border around the square painting. Write a special product and simplify to find the area of the picture including the border. *(60)*

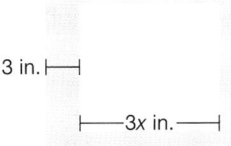

3 in. ⊢—⊣

⊢—3x in.—⊣

8. Solve the linear system by substitution. *(59)*

$$y = 2x - 9$$

$$8x - 6y = 34$$

*9. **Multiple Choice** Which of the following quadratic expressions is the product of $(6x + 7)^2$? *(60)*

A $36x^2 + 42x + 49$

B $12x^2 + 84x + 49$

C $36x^2 + 84x + 49$

D $36x + 84x + 49$

10. Solve the linear system by substitution.
(59)

$$y = 2x - 4$$
$$y = x + 5$$

*11. Write How can you check your work when finding a product of two binomials using special-product patterns?
(60)

*12. Verify Tell whether the statement $(9x + 8)(9x + 8) = 81x^2 + 64$ is true or false. If false, explain why.
(60)

*13. Measurement The perimeter of a rectangle is 78 feet. The length is 3 feet more than 3 times the width. Find the dimensions of the rectangle.
(59)

14. Error Analysis Two students are in the process of finding the solution to the system of equations. Which student is correct? Explain the error.
(59)

$$x + 4y = 19$$
$$6x + 5y = 38$$

Student A	Student B
$x = -4y + 19$	$x = -4y + 19$
$6(-4y + 19) + 5y = 38$	$6(-4y + 19) + 5y = 38$
$-24y + 114 + 5y = 38$	$-24y + 19 + 5y = 38$
$-19y = -76$	$-19y = 19$
$y = \dfrac{76}{19} = 4$	$y = -1$

15. (Installation) A contractor is installing some special light bulbs for two floors in a building. For the first floor, she purchased 5 natural-light bulbs and 2 ceiling bulbs at a cost of $23. For the second floor, she purchased 3 natural-light bulbs and 4 ceiling bulbs at a cost of $25. How much does each type of bulb cost?
(55)

*16. Multi-Step The sum of 4 times a girl's age and 7 times a boy's age is 169. The boy is 1 year older than twice the age of the girl. Find how old each will be 10 years from now.
(59)

*17. Geometry The perimeter of a rectangle is 24 centimeters. The length is 4 centimeters less than 7 times the width. Find the dimensions of the rectangle.
(59)

18. Data-Analysis Display the data using a box-and-whisker plot titled "Average Monthly Rainfall in Cloudcroft, NM (in inches)". Identify any outliers.
(54)

1.68, 1.90, 1.54, 0.84, 1.35, 2.21, 6.10, 6.04, 3.11, 1.78, 1.58, 2.33

19. Verify Show that $12f^4$ is the LCM of $6f^4$ and $4f^2$.
(57)

20. Multiple Choice What is the LCM of $(4x^4 - 14x^3)$ and $(6x^2 - 21x)$?
(57)

A $6x^3(2x - 7)$ **B** $6x^4(2x - 7)$

C $6(2x^4 - 7x^3)(2x^2 - 7x)$ **D** $(4x^4 - 14x^3)(6x^2 - 21x)$

21. Tell whether the set of ordered pairs (2, 8), (4, 16), and (7, 28) represents a direct
(56) variation.

22. (Tennis) A tennis court's dimensions can be represented by a width of $4x + 25$ feet
(58) and a length of $2x + 15$ feet. Write a polynomial for the area of the court.

23. Determine the slope of the line graphed below.
(44)

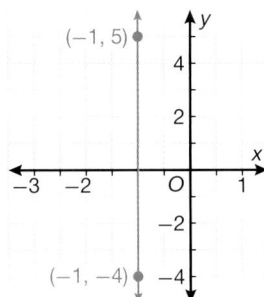

*24. Find the product of $(x + 2)(x + 9)$ using the FOIL method.
(58)

25. Translate the inequality $x - 2.5 > 4.7$ into words.
(45)

26. (Hobby) Eleanor has more than twice as many football trading cards as José.
(45) Eleanor has 79 trading cards. What is the greatest number of trading cards José
might have?

27. **Multi-Step** The varsity football team started summer training with 85 players.
(47) 10 players dropped out after 1 week of training, and then 7 players dropped out
after 2 weeks.
   a. What was the percent of decrease for the first week? What was the percent of
   decrease for the second week?

   b. What was the total percent of decrease for the 2 weeks of summer training?

28. (Law Enforcement) Arnold is using the graph to represent a speed limit of 45 miles
(50) per hour. What restrictions should also be placed on the graph?

29. Before painting, the edges around a rectangular light fixture must be taped. The
(51) length of the fixture is $\frac{2a}{3a - 2}$ yards, and the width is $\frac{a - 2}{3a - 2}$ yards. How much tape
is needed?

30. **Justify** Identify the slope and y-intercept of the line $y = x - 4$. Explain.
(52)

Transforming Linear Functions

A **family of functions** share common characteristics. A **parent function** is the simplest function in a family of functions. The parent function for a linear function is $f(x) = x$. Functions in the family are transformations of the parent function. The graph of $f(x) = x$ is shown below.

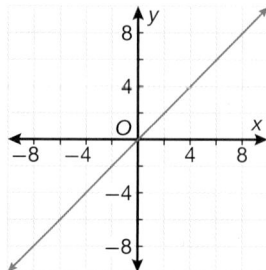

A **translation** shifts every point in a figure the same distance in the same direction. A translation can be thought of as a slide. A translation of a linear function is also referred to as a vertical change.

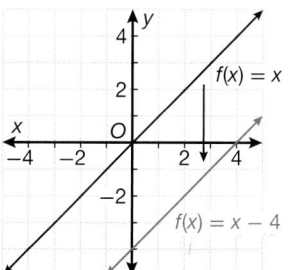

1. Graph $f(x) = x$, $f(x) = x + 3$, and $f(x) = x - 2$ on the same coordinate grid.

2. **Generalize** Compare the graphs of $f(x) = x + 3$ and $f(x) = x - 2$ to the parent function. Use the y-intercept in your comparison.

A vertical stretch or compression changes the rate of change of a linear equation.

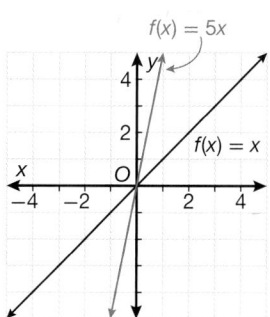

3. Graph $f(x) = x$, $f(x) = 3x$, and $f(x) = \frac{1}{3}x$ on the same coordinate grid.

4. **Generalize** Discuss how the slope of a line is related to the steepness of a line.

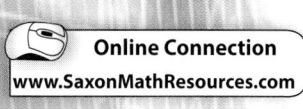

5. **Predict** Will the graph of $f(x) = \frac{2}{3}x$ be steeper than the graph of the parent function? Explain.

A **reflection** produces a mirror image across a line. A reflection can be thought of as a flip.

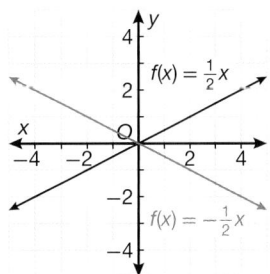

6. Graph $f(x) = 4x$ and $f(x) = -4x$ on the same coordinate plane.

7. **Generalize** Discuss how the slope of a line is related to the reflection of a line.

Some functions involve more than one transformation of the parent function.

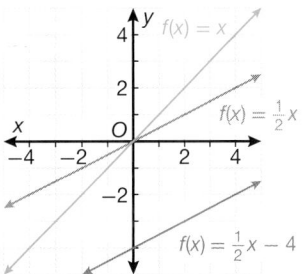

8. Graph $f(x) = x$ and $f(x) = 3x + 2$ on the same coordinate plane.

9. **Write** Describe the transformations from the graph of $f(x) = x$ to the graph of $f(x) = 3x + 2$.

Investigation Practice

Graph each function on a coordinate plane with the parent function $f(x) = x$. Then describe the transformation.

a. $f(x) = x + 4$

b. $f(x) = -x$

c. $f(x) = \frac{1}{2}x$

d. $f(x) = 4x - 2$

Simplifying Radical Expressions

Warm Up

1. **Vocabulary** The _____ of x is the number whose square is x.
(13)

Simplify.

2. $\sqrt{36}$
(13)

3. $\sqrt{81}$
(13)

4. $\sqrt{\dfrac{1}{4}}$
(46)

5. $\sqrt{54}$ is between which two consecutive integers?
(13)

New Concepts

A **radical expression** is an expression containing a radical. Radical expressions can be simplified using the Product of Radicals Rule.

Product Property of Radicals
If a and b are non-negative real numbers, then
$\sqrt{a}\,\sqrt{b} = \sqrt{ab}$ and $\sqrt{ab} = \sqrt{a}\,\sqrt{b}.$

Factoring a radicand into perfect squares is one way to determine if a radical expression can be simplified.

Example 1 Simplifying With Perfect Squares

Simplify using perfect squares.

Math Language

A **perfect square** is a number that is the square of an integer.

(a.) $\sqrt{225}$

SOLUTION

$\sqrt{225}$

$= \sqrt{9 \cdot 25}$ Find the perfect squares that are factors of 225.

$= \sqrt{9} \cdot \sqrt{25}$ Product of Radicals Rule

$= 3 \cdot 5$ Simplify the perfect squares.

$= 15$ Multiply.

(b.) $\sqrt{72}$

SOLUTION

$\sqrt{72}$

$= \sqrt{9 \cdot 4 \cdot 2}$ Find the perfect squares that are factors of 72.

$= \sqrt{9} \cdot \sqrt{4} \cdot \sqrt{2}$ Product of Radicals Rule

$= 3 \cdot 2\sqrt{2}$ Simplify.

$= 6\sqrt{2}$ Multiply.

Online Connection
www.SaxonMathResources.com

If a is equal to the area of a square, then $\sqrt{a}$ is the length of a side of the square. The formula for the area of a square is side length × side length, which can be written as $\sqrt{a} \cdot \sqrt{a} = a$.

a. Use the formula for the area of a square to write the area of a square that is 4 units squared.

b. Simplify the formula for the area of a square that is 4 units² using the Product of Radicals Rule.

c. Simplify the product formed by the radicand.

d. **Verify** Find the square root to show whether the equation is true.

The product of the square root of the area and the square root of the same area is equal to the area. This rule can be applied to all non-negative real numbers.

e. **Generalize** Write a rule for simplifying the expression $\sqrt{x} \cdot \sqrt{x}$, where x is a non-negative real number.

f. Simplify $\sqrt{4} \cdot \sqrt{4}$ using the Product of Radicals Rule.

g. Simplify the radicand using the Product Property of Exponents.

h. **Generalize** Write a rule for simplifying the expression $\sqrt{x^2}$, where x is a non-negative real number.

Another way to simplify radical expressions is by factoring the radicand into prime numbers.

Example **2** **Simplifying With Prime Factors**

Simplify using prime factorization.

$\sqrt{180}$

SOLUTION

$\sqrt{180}$

$= \sqrt{2 \cdot 2 \cdot 3 \cdot 3 \cdot 5}$ Find the prime factorization.

$= \sqrt{2} \cdot \sqrt{2} \cdot \sqrt{3} \cdot \sqrt{3} \cdot \sqrt{5}$ Product Property of Radicals

$= 2 \cdot 3\sqrt{5}$ Simplify.

$= 6\sqrt{5}$ Multiply.

Example 3 Simplifying With Powers of Ten

Simplify using powers of ten.

a. $\sqrt{10{,}000}$

SOLUTION Write the radicand as a power of ten. Then simplify.

$$\sqrt{10{,}000}$$
$$=\sqrt{10^4} \qquad\qquad\qquad \text{Write the radicand as a power of ten.}$$
$$=\sqrt{10^2 \cdot 10^2} \qquad\qquad \text{Find factors that are perfect squares.}$$
$$=\sqrt{10^2} \cdot \sqrt{10^2} \qquad\quad \text{Product Property of Radicals}$$
$$= 10 \cdot 10 \qquad\qquad\quad \text{Simplify.}$$
$$= 100 \qquad\qquad\qquad \text{Multiply.}$$

b. $\sqrt{100{,}000}$

SOLUTION Write the radicand as a power of ten. Then simplify.

$$\sqrt{100{,}000}$$
$$=\sqrt{10^5} \qquad\qquad\qquad\qquad \text{Write the radicand as a power of ten.}$$
$$=\sqrt{10^2 \cdot 10^2 \cdot 10^1} \qquad\qquad \text{Find factors that are perfect squares.}$$
$$=\sqrt{10^2} \cdot \sqrt{10^2} \cdot \sqrt{10^1} \qquad \text{Product Property of Radicals}$$
$$= 10 \cdot 10 \cdot \sqrt{10} \qquad\qquad\;\; \text{Simplify.}$$
$$= 100 \sqrt{10} \qquad\qquad\qquad\; \text{Multiply.}$$

Math Reasoning

Generalize Find a pattern in the square roots of powers of ten.

The rules of radicals and exponents apply to variable expressions.

Example 4 Simplifying With Variables

Simplify. All variables represent non-negative real numbers.

a. $\sqrt{81x^4y^3}$

SOLUTION Use the Product Property of Radicals. Then simplify.

$$\sqrt{81x^4y^3}$$
$$=\sqrt{81} \cdot \sqrt{x^4} \cdot \sqrt{y^3} \qquad \text{Product Property of Radicals}$$
$$= 9 \cdot x^2 \cdot y \sqrt{y} \qquad\qquad \text{Simplify.}$$
$$= 9x^2y\sqrt{y} \qquad\qquad\qquad \text{Multiply.}$$

b. $\sqrt{162r^4s^8}$

SOLUTION Use the Product Property of Exponents

$$= \sqrt{162r^4s^8}$$
$$= \sqrt{162} \cdot \sqrt{r^4} \cdot \sqrt{s^8} \qquad\qquad\qquad \text{Product Property of Radicals}$$
$$= \sqrt{81} \cdot \sqrt{2} \cdot \sqrt{r^2} \cdot \sqrt{r^2} \cdot \sqrt{s^4} \cdot \sqrt{s^4} \qquad \text{Find factors that are perfect squares.}$$
$$= 9 \cdot \sqrt{2} \cdot r^2 \cdot s^4 \qquad\qquad\qquad\qquad \text{Simplify.}$$
$$= 9r^2s^4\sqrt{2} \qquad\qquad\qquad\qquad\qquad \text{Multiply.}$$

Example 5 Application: Length of a Square Room

Idriana has a square bedroom. The area measures 48 square meters. Find the length of one side of Idriana's bedroom by simplifying $\sqrt{48 \text{ m}^2}$ using prime factorization.

SOLUTION

$$s = \sqrt{48 \text{ m}^2} \qquad \text{Simplify.}$$
$$= \sqrt{2 \cdot 2 \cdot 2 \cdot 2 \cdot 3 \text{ m}^2} \qquad \text{Product of Radicals Rule}$$
$$= 2 \cdot 2\sqrt{3} \text{ m} \qquad \text{Simplify.}$$
$$= 4\sqrt{3} \text{ m} \qquad \text{Multiply.}$$

The length of one side of Idriana's bedroom is $4\sqrt{3}$ m.

Lesson Practice

Simplify using perfect squares.
(Ex 1)

   a. $\sqrt{75}$ **b.** $\sqrt{63}$

   c. Simplify $\sqrt{363}$ using prime factorization.
(Ex 2)

   d. Simplify. $\sqrt{1,000,000}$ using powers of ten.
(Ex 3)

Simplify. All variables represent non-negative real numbers.

   e. $\sqrt{90b^2c^4}$.   **f.** $\sqrt{25x^3y^7}$.
(Ex 4)   *(Ex 4)*

   g. Find the length of one side of a square room with an area of 80 square meters.
(Ex 5)

Practice   Distributed and Integrated

Simplify.

  *1. $\sqrt{12}$ ***2.** $\sqrt{200}$
(61)   *(61)*

Evaluate.

  3. $x^{\frac{1}{4}}$ when $x = -16$ **4.** $x^{\frac{1}{3}}$ when $x = 343$
(46)   *(46)*

  5. Write What does FOIL stand for in the term FOIL method?
(58)

  6. (**Basketball**) A basketball court is $\frac{144x}{x+3}$ feet long and $\frac{432}{x+3}$ feet wide. A team runs laps around the court. How far have they run after one lap?
(51)

  7. Error Analysis Students were asked to use the sum and difference pattern to find the product of $(x-8)(x+8)$. Which student is correct? Explain the error.
(60)

Student A	Student B
$(x-8)(x+8)$	$(x-8)(x+8)$
$= x^2 - 8^2$	$= x^2 - 8^2$
$= x^2 - 64$	$= x^2 + 64$

8. Multiple Choice A rectangular picture is twice as long as it is wide. The picture has (58) a 4-inch-wide mat around the picture. Let x represent the picture's width. Which product gives the area of the picture and mat?

A $(2x)(x)$ **B** $(2x + 4)(x + 2)$

C $(2x + 8)(x + 8)$ **D** $(-2x + 6)(6 + 2)$

Solve the systems by the method given.

*9. Use a graphing calculator to solve.
(55)

$$-5x + 8y = 7$$
$$3y = -2x - 9$$

10. Use substitution to solve.
(59)

$$2x - 3y = 3$$
$$x = 4y - 11$$

11. (World Records) In 2005, power-plant employees built the world's largest igloo in
(46) Quebec, Canada. The igloo is approximately in the shape of a half sphere and has a volume of about 1728π cubic feet. What is the igloo's approximate diameter? (Hint: The formula for the volume of a sphere is $V = \frac{4}{3}\pi r^3$.)

12. Multi-Step The following data shows the attendance at seven home games for a high
(48) school football team: 5846, 6023, 5921, 7244, 6832, 6496, 7012.

a. Find the mean attendance value for the data set.

b. Suppose the stadium was almost filled to capacity for the homecoming game and that the data value 11,994 is now added to the data set. How does this outlier affect the mean of the data?

Simplify.

13. $(4b - 3)^2$ **14.** $(-2x + 5)^2$
(60)   (60)

*15. (Fundraising) At a school fundraiser, students charge $10 to wash a car and
(59) $20 to wash an SUV. They make $1700 by washing 105 vehicles. How many of each kind do they wash?

16. Multi-Step Use these points (1, 3) and (2, 8) to answer the problems below.
(52) **a.** Find the slope of the line that passes through the points.

b. Graph the line.

c. Write the equation of the line in point-slope form.

d. Write the equation of the line in slope-intercept form.

e. Fill in the missing coordinates of the points $(x, -3)$ and $(-2, y)$.

17. (Physics) An object's weight on the moon varies directly with its weight on Earth. A
(56) 60-pound dog would weigh 9 pounds on the moon. How much would a 25-pound dog weigh on the moon?

18. Multiple Choice Which point is a solution of to the linear system?
(59)

$$y - 5x = 3$$
$$3x + 8y = 24$$

A $(1, 8)$ **B** $(0, 0)$ **C** $(0, 3)$ **D** $(4, 1.5)$

*19. Write Explain how to simplify $\sqrt{18a^2}$, $a \geq 0$.
(61)

*20. Geometry A triangle has a length of $(x - 4)$ inches and a height of $(x + 4)$ inches.
(60) What is the area of the triangle?

21. Analyze What polynomial can be added to $x^2 + 5x + 1$ to get a sum of $4x^2 - 3$?
(53)

Find the LCM.

22. 21, 33, 13   **23.** 8, 32, 12
(57)   (57)

*24. Multi-Step Laura is building on to her new pool house. Write an expression for the
(60) area of the non-shaded region. Find the area.

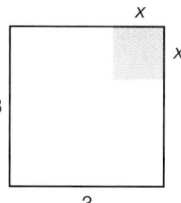

   a. Find the area of the large square.

   b. Find the area of the smaller square.

   c. Write an expression for the area of the non-shaded region.

*25. Measurement Alan is building a square patio. He wants an 8-inch-wide border
(60) of flowers around his patio, and the total length of one side is $8x$. Write a
polynomial that represents the area of the floor of the patio not including the
border of flowers.

*26. Multi-Step The area of a circle is 20π cm². How long is the radius?
(61)
   a. Write an expression that can be used to find the length of the radius
       of a circle if given the area, A.

   b. Use the expression to find the length of the radius.

Translate each inequality into a sentence.

27. $\dfrac{n}{7} + 3 \geq 5$ **28.** $3g - 4 < -2$
(45)   (45)

*29. Circular Motion The tangential velocity of an object in circular motion can be
(61) found using the expression $\sqrt{ar}$, where a is the centripetal acceleration and r is the
path radius of the circle. What is the tangential velocity of an object with a path
radius of 15 cm and a centripetal acceleration of 60 cm/s²?

30. Make a box-and-whisker plot of the data below and title it "Shoe Sizes."
(54)

$$5, 10, 6, 7, 6.5, 7, 7, 8.5, 6.5, 8, 9, 7.5, 7$$

Drawing Histograms

Graphing Calculator Lab (*Use with Lesson 62*)

A histogram is a vertical bar graph that organizes data into equally sized intervals. This makes it easy to see where the majority of data values fall in a measurement scale. Given a set of data, you can make a histogram with a graphing calculator.

A teacher has test scores for her class and wants to know how many students earned higher than 70 points. Use the data to make a histogram.

30, 33, 33, 34, 55, 56, 63, 65, 67, 71, 80, 82, 85, 88, 89, 90, 90, 97

Graphing Calculator Tip

For help with entering data into a list, see the graphing calculator keystrokes in Lab 4.

1. Enter the data into List 1.

2. Press 2nd $\overset{\text{STAT PLOT}}{\text{Y=}}$ and select **1:Plot1...** to open the plot setup menu.

3. Press ENTER to turn Plot1 **On** and then press the ⌄ key once and the ▷ key twice to select the type at the end of the first row. Press ENTER. The setting for **Xlist** should be L1 and **Freq** should be 1. If the **Xlist** setting is not L1, press the ⌄ key once and then 2nd $\overset{\text{LIST}}{\text{STAT}}$ ENTER.

4. Create a histogram by pressing ZOOM and selecting **9:ZoomStat.**

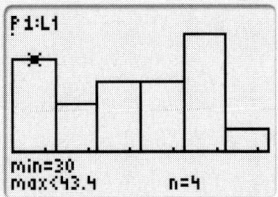

Press TRACE. The first interval has a minimum value of 30 and a maximum value of 43.4. To count the students who earned a score higher than 70 points, the intervals need to be graphed in multiples of 10 points.

5. Press WINDOW to change the intervals and window settings.

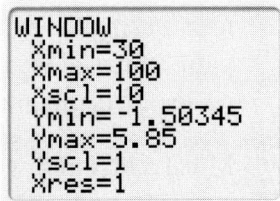

The lowest test score is 30, so press ENTER to accept **Xmin=30.** Since the test scores do not exceed 100 points, press **1 0 0** ENTER. To use intervals of 10 points, set **Xscl** by pressing **1 0** ENTER.

Online Connection
www.SaxonMathResources.com

6. Press GRAPH to view the histogram in the new window.

7. Use TRACE and then use the ◀ and ▶ keys to view the statistical values. The "min=" and "max<" provide minimum and maximum values for each interval. The "n=" gives the number of test scores in the interval.

One student earned a score in the 70's, five students earned a score in the 80's, and three earned a score of at least 90 points. Therefore, of the 18 students, nine earned a score above 70 points on the test.

Lab Practice

The data list the results of a words-per-minute typing test.

39, 41, 42, 47, 47, 50, 53, 55, 55, 57, 60, 62, 64, 68, 70, 71

a. Use a graphing calculator to make a histogram of the data using intervals of 5 words per minute.

b. According to the data, how many people type between 55 and 65 words per minute?

The histogram shows the ages of all members of a local orchestra.

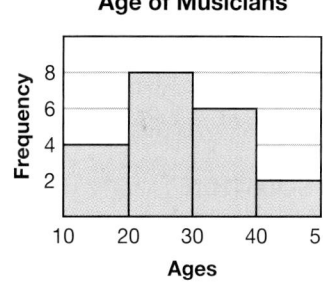

Age of Musicians

c. How many musicians in the orchestra could be teenagers?

   A 2 **B** 4

   C 6 **D** 8

d. Analyze The orchestra's conductor wants to give a prize to musicians in the age group that attends the most rehearsals. Based on the histogram, is he correct to give the prize to musicians who are between 20 and 29 years old? Explain.

Displaying Data in Stem-and-Leaf Plots and Histograms

Warm Up

1. Vocabulary The sum of the values in a data set divided by the number of data values gives the _____.
(48)

  A mean   **B** median   **C** mode   **D** range

Find the mean, median, mode, and range.

2. 5, 3, 7, 6, 2, 4, 5, 8
(48)

3. 12, 15, 20, 16, 14, 13
(48)

New Concepts

A **stem-and-leaf plot** is a data display that uses some digits as "stems" and others as "leaves". The "stems" have a greater place value than the "leaves." Stem-and-leaf plots are helpful in organizing data and displaying it to show the distribution of values.

$$\text{stem} \longrightarrow \quad 2 \quad 3 \quad \longleftarrow \text{leaf}$$

The digits other than the last digit are the stem. The last digit of a number is the leaf.

Example 1   Making a Stem-and-Leaf Plot

The high temperatures in degrees Fahrenheit for April 2007 in New Orleans, Louisiana, are shown. Create a stem-and-leaf plot of the data.

70, 83, 84, 77, 66, 67, 53, 55, 64, 69, 82, 78, 80, 81, 66,

71, 75, 76, 80, 78, 78, 81, 83, 83, 82, 81, 80, 85, 87, 87

SOLUTION

Step 1: There are two place values in each temperature in the data set, tens and ones. Organize the data by each tens value. Write each place-value group in ascending order. Include any values that repeat.

50's: 53, 55

60's: 64, 66, 66, 67, 69

70's: 70, 71, 75, 76, 77, 78, 78, 78

80's: 80, 80, 80, 81, 81, 81, 82, 82, 83, 83, 83, 84, 85, 87, 87

Step 2: Use the tens digit of each group as the stem of a row on a stem-and-leaf plot. Write each ones digit as the leaf for the corresponding tens digit.

Step 3: Create a key to show how to read each entry in the plot.

$$8\,|\,5 = 85°F$$

High Temperatures (°F)
April 2007 for New Orleans, LA

Stem	Leaves
5	3, 5
6	4, 6, 6, 7, 9
7	0, 1, 5, 6, 7, 8, 8, 8
8	0, 0, 0, 1, 1, 1, 2, 2, 3, 3, 3, 4, 5, 7, 7

Key: 5 | 3 = 53°F

Stem-and-leaf plots are used to show the distribution of data. In the stem-and-leaf plot for Example 1, there is an unequal distribution of temperatures in the 80's. This may not have been as obvious when the data was in a continuous list. When organizing the data by place values, it becomes easier to identify unequal distributions.

Stem-and-leaf plots are used to find measures of central tendency and other statistical measures because the actual data points are included in the plot. One of the many statistical measures that are helpful is relative frequency. In an experiment, the number of times an event happens divided by the total number of trials is the **relative frequency** of that event.

Example 2   Analyzing a Stem-and-Leaf Plot

Use the stem-and-leaf plot from Example 1 to find the following statistical measures.

a. median

SOLUTION

To find the median, find the middle value(s). For these data there are two middle values. The 15th and 16th values are 78 and 80. Find the average of 78 and 80.

$$\frac{78 + 80}{2} = \frac{158}{2} = 79$$

The median of the data is 79°F.

b. mode

SOLUTION

The mode is the value or values that occur most frequently. There are 4 values that occur 3 times: 78, 80, 81, and 83. These are the modes.

c. range

SOLUTION

The range is the difference between the greatest and least value in the set. The greatest data value is 87; the least data value is 53. The range is 34°F.

d. relative frequency of 80

SOLUTION

The data value 80 occurs 3 times. There are a total of 30 data values.

$$\frac{3}{30} = \frac{1}{10} = 0.10 = 10\%$$

Caution

The data must be in order before finding the middle value(s).

Hint

Relative frequency can be expressed as a fraction, a decimal, or a percent.

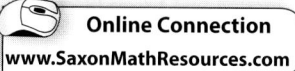
Online Connection
www.SaxonMathResources.com

Another display that can be used to show the distribution of numeric data is a histogram. A **histogram** is a bar graph that displays the frequency of data in equal intervals. Each bar must be the same width and should touch the bar(s) next to it.

Example 3 Making a Histogram

Create a histogram of the data from Example 1.

SOLUTION

The data from Example 1 are already organized into four intervals of 10. Create a graph showing the intervals and the number of data points in each interval.

**High Temperatures April 2007
New Orleans, LA**

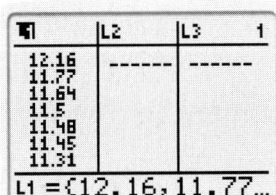

Example 4 Application: Sports

The list below shows the results in meters of the first round triple jump from the 2007 NCAA women's outdoor track championships. Create a histogram of the data using a graphing calculator.

12.16, 11.77, 11.64, 11.50, 11.48, 11.45, 11.31, 10.94, 10.98, 9.88,
12.08, 11.58, 11.41, 11.5, 11.34, 11.24, 11.22, 11.13, 10.76

SOLUTION

Graphing Calculator Tip

Lists can be created using the home screen or using the STAT screen. Lists can only be edited in the STAT screen.

Step 1: Enter the data into a list in the calculator.

Step 2: Change the window settings to select intervals and to correctly view the data plot.

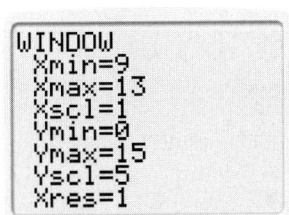

Step 3: On the STAT PLOT screen, select the histogram plot. Labels are not shown on the screen.

**Triple Jump Results NCAA 2007
Women's Outdoor Championship**

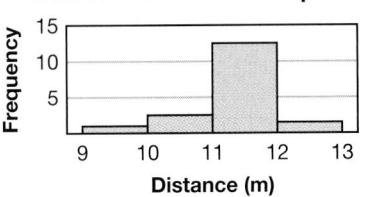

a. The list shows the low temperatures in degrees Fahrenheit in New
(Ex 1) Orleans for the first 15 days of April 2007. Create a stem-and-leaf plot
of the data.

65, 70, 69, 61, 56, 52, 43, 42, 51, 60, 63, 52, 60, 54, 50

b. Create a histogram of the data in problem **a.**
(Ex 3)

c. Use the stem-and-leaf plot to find the median, mode, and range of the
(Ex 2) low temperatures the last 15 days of April 2007 in New Orleans, LA.

Low Temperatures (°F) Last 15 Days
April 2007 for New Orleans, LA

Stem	Leaves
4	5
5	4, 6, 7, 8, 9, 9
6	0, 3, 3, 4, 4, 8, 8
7	1

Key: 5 | 6 = 56°F

d. Use the stem-and-leaf plot in problem **c** to find the relative frequency
(Ex 2) of 64.

e. Create a histogram of the data in problem **c** using a graphing calculator.
(Ex 4)

Find each of the following statistical measures using the data in the plot below.

Service Club Ages
of Members

Stem	Leaves
2	5, 6
3	0, 2, 3, 4, 4, 4, 8, 9
4	1, 1, 2, 6, 7
5	2, 5, 7
6	0, 4

Key: 5| 6 means 56 years old

*1. median
(62)

*2. mode
(62)

*3. range
(62)

*4. relative frequency of 41
(62)

Simplify.

5. $\sqrt{88}$
(61)

*6. $\sqrt{720}$
(61)

7. $\sqrt{180}$
(60)

8. Write Explain in your own words how to graph the equation $y = -\frac{1}{3}x + 2$.
(49)

*9. Error Analysis Students were asked to find the product $(2n - 5)^2$ using the square of a binomial pattern. Which student is correct? Explain the error.
₍₆₀₎

Student A	Student B
$(2n - 5)^2$	$(2n - 5)^2$
$= (2n)^2 - 2(2n)(5) + (5)^2$	$= (2n)^2 - 5^2$
$= 4n^2 - 20n + 25$	$= 4n^2 - 25$

10. Analyze The solution to a system of equations is $(4, 6)$. One equation in the system is $2x + y = 14$. One term in the other equation is $3x$. What could the equation be?
₍₅₉₎

11. Multiple Choice Which system of equations has a solution of $(2, -2)$?
₍₅₉₎

A $x + y = 0$
  $2x - 3y = -2$

B $5x - 3y = 16$
  $4x + 9y = 10$

C $9x - 2y = 22$
  $3x + 6y = -6$

D $x + 2y = -2$
  $2x + y = -2$

Multiply.

12. $-4(x^2 + 4x - 1)$
₍₅₈₎

13. $(b - 8)^2$
₍₆₀₎

14. $\left(x + \dfrac{1}{2}\right)\left(x + \dfrac{1}{4}\right)$
₍₆₀₎

15. (Consumer Math) Consumers spend $95 million on Father's Day cards and $152 million on Mother's Day cards. What is the amount of increase or decrease from Mother's Day to Father's Day cards? What percentage of the combined total do consumers spend on Mother's Day cards?
₍₄₇₎

*16. Geometry The stem-and-leaf plot shows the diameters of a shipment of bicycle tires to a bicycle shop. Find the circumference of the tire with the median diameter in the data set. Use 3.14 for pi.
₍₆₂₎

**Diameters of
Bicycle Tires**

Stem	Leaves
1	5, 5, 6, 7, 7, 8, 9, 9
2	0, 0, 0, 1, 2, 2, 4

Key: 1|5 means 15 inches

17. Solve the following system by graphing: $y = x + 6$
₍₅₅₎
$$y + 3x = 6.$$

18. Write Explain what the whiskers in a box-and-whisker plot represent.
₍₅₄₎

*19. (Fundraising) The amount of money raised for a charity event by the homerooms at Jefferson High School are shown below. Create a stem-and-leaf plot of the data.
₍₆₂₎

$150, $125, $134, $129, $106, $157, $108, $135, $144, $149

20. (**Commerce**) The weekly profit, p, in dollars at Bill's TV repair shop can be estimated by
_(52)_ the equation $p = 30n - 400$, where n is the number of TVs repaired in a week. Graph
the equation and predict the profit for a week if 50 TVs are repaired.

Evaluate.

21. Evaluate $\sqrt[4]{x^2}$ when $x = 9$.
_(46)_

22. Evaluate $\sqrt[3]{x^6}$ when $x = 2$.
_(46)_

23. Write an equation for a direct variation that includes the point $(10, -90)$.
_(56)_

24. Multi-Step Levi deposits \$500 into a savings account that earns interest
_(53)_ compounded annually. Let r be the annual interest rate. After two years, the
balance from the first deposit is given by the polynomial $500 + 1000r + 500r^2$.
A year after making the first deposit, Levi makes another deposit. A year later,
the balance from the second deposit is $600 + 600r$.
 a. Find the balance of the accounts combined in terms of r after 2 years.
 b. Find the balance after two years when $r = 0.03$.

Find the missing number.

25. original price: \$68
_(47)_

new price: _____

29% increase

26. original price: _____
_(47)_

new price: \$98.60

15% decrease

27. (**Triathlon Training**) Training for a triathlon involves running, swimming, and biking.
_(57)_ The athlete runs every $(2r - 2s)$ days, swims every $(4r^2 - 4rs)$ days, and bikes every
$(8rs - 8s^2)$ days. When would the athlete have all three activities on the same day?

28. Multiple Choice Which of the following is not equivalent to $\sqrt{2800}$?
_(61)_ **A** $10\sqrt{28}$ **B** $2\sqrt{700}$ **C** $20\sqrt{7}$ **D** $40\sqrt{7}$

*29. (**Gardening**) Isaac is planting a square flower garden. He wants a 10-inch-wide
_(60)_ brick border around the outside edge of the garden. The total side length is $9x$.
Write a special product that represents the area of the garden not including the
brick border. Simplify.

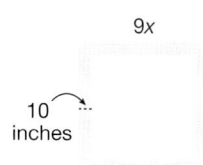

9x

10 inches

*30. Coordinate Geometry Lucia drew a square on grid paper that has an area of 25 units^2.
_(61)_ What points could she have plotted?

Solving Systems of Linear Equations by Elimination

1. Vocabulary The graph of a _____ equation is a straight line.
(30)

Simplify.

2. $3(4x - 5)$
(15)

3. $4(7y + 12)$
(15)

4. $ky^2k^3k^2y^5$
(3)

5. $xy - 3xy^2 + 5y^2x - 4xy$
(18)

New Concepts

It is not always practical to isolate one of the variables in a system of linear equations in order to solve by substitution. Sometimes it is easier to eliminate one of the variables by combining the two equations using addition or subtraction.

Example **1** **Adding Equations**

Solve the system by elimination and check the answer.

$$5x + 2y = 9$$
$$-5x + 6y = 7$$

SOLUTION

The two equations have equal and opposite coefficients for one of the variables, so add the equations to eliminate that variable.

$$5x + 2y = 9$$
$$\underline{-5x + 6y = 7}$$
$$8y = 16 \qquad \text{Add equations and combine like terms.}$$
$$y = 2 \qquad \text{Divide both sides by 8.}$$

Substitute 2 for y in one of the original equations and solve for x.

$$5x + 2(2) = 9 \qquad \text{Substitute 2 for } y \text{ in the first equation.}$$
$$5x + 4 = 9 \qquad \text{Multiply.}$$
$$5x = 5 \qquad \text{Subtract 4 from both sides.}$$
$$x = 1 \qquad \text{Divide both sides by 5.}$$

The solution is $(1, 2)$.

Check Substitute $(1, 2)$ for x and y in both of the original equations.

$-5x + 6y = 7$	$5x + 2y = 9$
$-5(1) + 6(2) \overset{?}{=} 7$ Substitute.	$5(1) + 2(2) \overset{?}{=} 9$
$-5 + 12 \overset{?}{=} 7$ Multiply.	$5 + 4 \overset{?}{=} 9$
$7 = 7$ ✓ Add.	$9 = 9$ ✓

Caution

Be sure to list the values for x and y in the correct order, (x, y).

Online Connection
www.SaxonMathResources.com

Example 2 Subtracting Equations

Solve the system by elimination. $7x + 3y = -5$

$$2x + 3y = 5$$

SOLUTION

$7x + 3y = -5$	Both equations have the same positive
$2x + 3y = \underline{5}$	coefficient for one of the variables.
$5x = -10$	Subtract the equations and combine like terms.
$x = -2$	Divide both sides by 5.

Substitute -2 for x in one of the original equations and solve for y.

$2x + 3y = 5$	
$2(-2) + 3y = 5$	Substitute -2 for x in the second equation.
$-4 + 3y = 5$	Multiply.
$3y = 9$	Add 4 to both sides.
$y = 3$	Divide both sides by 3.

The solution is $(-2, 3)$.

Sometimes it may be necessary to first multiply one or both of the equations by a number in order to have opposite coefficients.

Example 3 Multiplying One Equation

Solve the system by elimination. $5y = 8x - 2$

$$4x - 3y = -2$$

SOLUTION

$-8x + 5y = -2$	Write the first equation in standard form.
$8x - 6y = -4$	Multiply the second equation by 2.
$-y = -6$	Add the equations and combine like terms.
$y = 6$	Simplify.

Substitute 6 for y in one of the original equations and solve for x.

$5y = 8x - 2$	
$5(6) = 8x - 2$	Substitute 6 for y in the first equation.
$30 = 8x - 2$	Multiply.
$32 = 8x$	Add 2 to both sides.
$4 = x$	Divide both sides by 8.

The solution is $(4, 6)$.

Hint

Subtracting is the same as adding the opposite.

Hint

Make sure both equations are in standard form in order to easily combine like terms.

Example 4 Multiplying Two Equations

Solve the system $4x - 3y = 15$ by elimination.
$$6x + 5y = -25$$

Math Reasoning

Write Is there another way to solve Example 4 by elimination? Explain.

SOLUTION

Multiply the first equation by 3 and the second equation by -2 to get opposite coefficients for the variable x.

$$3(4x - 3y = 15) \quad \rightarrow \quad 12x - 9y = 45$$
$$-2(6x + 5y = -25) \quad \rightarrow \quad -12x - 10y = 50$$

$$\begin{aligned} 12x - 9y &= 45 \\ -12x - 10y &= 50 \\ \hline -19y &= 95 \end{aligned}$$ Add the equations and combine like terms.

$$y = -5$$ Divide both sides by -19.

Substitute -5 for y in one of the original equations and solve for x.

$$6x + 5y = -25$$
$$6x + 5(-5) = -25$$ Substitute -5 for y in the second equation.
$$6x - 25 = -25$$ Multiply.
$$6x = 0$$ Add 25 to both sides.
$$x = 0$$ Divide both sides by 6.

The solution is $(0, -5)$.

Example 5 Application: Coin Collecting

Carlos has 32 Buffalo nickels, some with dates and some without dates. Buffalo nickels without dates are worth \$0.15, and dated Buffalo nickels are worth \$0.75. If Carlos's collection of Buffalo nickels is worth \$10.80, how many of the coins have dates on them?

SOLUTION Write and solve a system of linear equations.

$$u + d = 32$$
$$0.15u + 0.75d = 10.80$$

Multiply the first equation by -15 and the second equation by 100 to get opposite coefficients for the variable x.

$$-15(u + d = 32) \quad \rightarrow \quad -15u + (-15d) = -480$$
$$100(0.15u + 0.75d = 10.80) \quad \rightarrow \quad 15u + 75d = 1080$$

$$\begin{aligned} -15u + (-15d) &= -480 \quad &\text{Distributive Property} \\ 15u + 75d &= 1080 \quad &\text{Distributive Property} \\ \hline 60d &= 600 \quad &\text{Add the equations and combine like terms.} \\ d &= 10 \quad &\text{Divide both sides by 60.} \end{aligned}$$

Carlos has 10 Buffalo nickels with dates.

a. Solve the system by elimination and check the answer.
(Ex 1)

$$7x - 4y = -3$$
$$-3x + 4y = -1$$

Solve each system by elimination.

b. $11x + 6y = 21$
(Ex 2) $11x + 4y = 25$

c. $-2x + 5y = 6$
(Ex 3) $6x - 2y = 34$

d. $-8x - 3y = 26$
(Ex 4) $-5x - 2y = 16$

e. **Box Office Sales** A movie theater sells 540 tickets to a matinee showing of
(Ex 5) a new animated feature. A child matinee ticket costs \$5.50 and an adult matinee ticket costs \$6.00. If the movie theater made \$3060 for that showing, how many adult tickets were sold?

Practice **Distributed and Integrated**

Simplify.

1. $\sqrt{256}$
(61)

2. $\sqrt{108}$
(61)

3. $\sqrt{294}$
(61)

4. $\left(\dfrac{r^{-3} t^{\frac{1}{2}} e}{r g^4 t^{\frac{3}{2}}} \right)^2$
(40)

5. **Sports** A sports court has area $\dfrac{t^3 n^{-2} s}{f^7 t b^5} \left(\dfrac{t^{-2}}{n s^3} - \dfrac{f^6 t^{-1}}{b} \right)$. Simplify.
(39)

6. Find the range for these 6 house sizes in a neighborhood (in square feet):
(48)

$$1450, 1500, 2800, 1630, 1500, 1710$$

7. Tell whether the set of ordered pairs (5, 12), (3, 7.2), and (7, 16.8) represents a
(56) direct variation.

Find the LCM.

8. $2t^3 s v^5$, $6v^3 t^4$, and $10v^8 s^4$
(57)

9. $14dv^3$, $7s^2 v$, and $28s^7 v^5$
(57)

10. **Multiple Choice** Which of the following polynomials is equal to $(x + 5)(x - 5)$?
(60)
A $x^2 - 25$ **B** $x^2 + 25$ **C** $x^2 - 5x + 25$ **D** $x^2 - 10x + 25$

*11. **Landscaping** Nasser wants to plant a 4-foot-high Yoshino Cherry tree near a
(63) 7-foot-high Snowdrift Crabapple tree. If the cherry tree grows at a rate of 16 inches a year and the crabapple tree grows at a rate of 13 inches per year, when will the two trees be the same height?

Solve each system of linear equations using the method indicated.

12. Solve by substitution: $6x - 2y = 12$.
(59)
$$y = -5x + 10$$

*13. Solve by elimination: $6x + 4y = 22$
(63)
$$-6x + 2y = -16$$

*14. Verify Solve the system of linear equations by graphing: $\begin{array}{l} -x + y = 4 \\ 2x + y = 1 \end{array}$ Check your
(55)
answer with a graphing calculator.

15. City Planning The city manager wants to build a rectangular walking
(53)
track around the town's park. Below is a sketch of the new park.
Write a polynomial expression for the perimeter of the rectangle.
Simplify the polynomial.

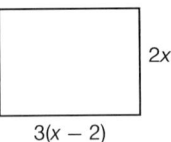

$2x$

$3(x - 2)$

*16. Multiple Choice Which ordered pair is a solution of the system of equations?
(63)
$$9x - 3y = 20$$
$$3x + 6y = 2$$

A $\left(-\dfrac{2}{3}, 2\right)$ **B** $\left(2, \dfrac{2}{3}\right)$ **C** $\left(2, -\dfrac{2}{3}\right)$ **D** $\left(-2, \dfrac{2}{3}\right)$

*17. Verify After solving a system of linear equations by elimination, how could you
(63)
algebraically check your solution?

18. Multi-Step A group of 30 white-tailed deer all had 2 antler points at 1.5 years. At
(54)
4.5 years, their points were counted again.

Number of Points at 4.5 years	2	3	4	5	6	7	8	9
Number of Deer	1	0	4	3	7	4	10	1

a. Make a box-and-whisker plot for the data set at 4.5 years.

b. Can you predict how many points a deer would have at 4.5 years old if you
know that it had 2 points at 1.5 years?

*19. Geometry Main Market Square in Krakow, Poland has an area of 40,000 m². Find
(61)
the length of one side of the square.

20. Football A football field's dimensions can be represented by a width of $3x + 15$ feet
(58)
and a length of $x + 10$ feet. Write a polynomial expression for the area of the field.

Find the missing number.

21. original price: $1527
(47)
new price: _____
38% decrease

22. original price: $25,720
(47)
new price: _____
1.5% increase

23. original price: $10.25
(47)
new price: _____
215% increase

24. Write Write the two patterns for the square of a binomial.
(60)

25. (City Planning) A city is planning to build a new park in a shape of a square in the business district. It has a side length of $2x + 6$ feet. Find the area of this park.
(58)

***26. Multiple Choice** Which of the following expressions is the simplest form of $\sqrt{76g^6}$?
(61)
   A $2g^3\sqrt{19}$ **B** $2g^4\sqrt{19}$ **C** $6g^3\sqrt{2}$ **D** $6g^4\sqrt{2}$

***27. Error Analysis** Two students used the stem-and-leaf plot to find the mode height of the basketball players at their school. Which student is correct? Explain the error.
(62)

Heights of Players on Team		Student A	Student B
Stem	Leaves	The mode is 185 cm.	The mode is 170 cm.
16	5, 7		
17	1, 5, 6, 8, 8, 9		
18	4, 5, 5, 5		
19	2, 7		
20	1		

Key: 16| 5 means 165 cm

***28. Write** Explain how to solve the system of linear equations.
(63)

$$3x - 2y = 10$$

$$-\frac{9}{2}x + 3y = -15$$

29. What must be true about the coefficient of a linear function if that function experiences a vertical stretch of the parent function?
(Inv 6)

***30. Probability** The histogram displays the number of hours students in Helene's homeroom average at their part-time jobs. What is the probability that a student randomly selected from the homeroom works 5–10 hours per week?
(62)

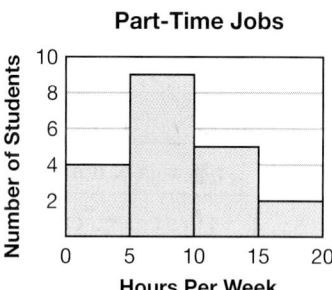

Part-Time Jobs

In a direct variation, if there is at least one known value for an x- and y-pair, the constant of variation, k, can be determined. The same holds true for an inverse variation; if at least one known value for an x- and y-pair exists, the constant of variation can be determined.

Example 3 Graphing an Inverse Variation

Write an inverse variation relating x and y when $y = 8$ and $x = 3$. Then graph the relationship.

SOLUTION

Find k.

$k = xy$

$k = 3(8)$ Substitute in the values for x and y.

$\quad = 24$ Multiply.

$y = \dfrac{24}{x}$ Substitute 24 for k in the inverse variation equation.

The inverse variation relating x and y is $y = \dfrac{24}{x}$.

Use the equation to make a table of values.

x	-6	-4	-2	0	2	4	6
y	-4	-6	-12	Undefined	12	6	4

Plot the points. Then connect them with a smooth curve.

Check Use a graphing calculator to graph the equation $y = \dfrac{24}{x}$ and to verify that your graph is correct.

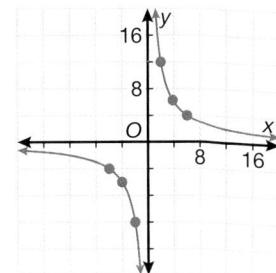

Example 4 Application: Truck Transportation

A truck driver is delivering goods from one state to another. Her speed is inversely related to her travel time. If she is traveling at 55 miles per hour, it will take her 13 hours to reach her destination. How long will it take her if she travels at 65 miles per hour?

SOLUTION Use the product rule for inverse variation to solve.

$x_1 y_1 = x_2 y_2$

$55 \cdot 13 = 65 \cdot y_2$ Substitute 55 for x_1, 13 for y_1, and 65 for x_2.

$715 = 65 y_2$ Multiply.

$11 = y_2$ Divide both sides by 65.

It will take the truck driver 11 hours if she travels at 65 miles per hour.

Tell whether each relationship is an inverse variation. Explain.
(Ex 1)

a. $4y = x$ **b.** $3xy = 9$

c. If y varies inversely as x and $y = 3.5$ when $x = 20$, find x when $y = 10$.
(Ex 2)

d. Write an inverse variation relating x and y when $x = 8$ and $y = \frac{1}{2}$. Then graph the relationship.
(Ex 3)

e. Sierra found an inverse relationship between her hourly pay rate and the number of hours she must work to earn a set amount. If she works 7 hours for $8 an hour, how long will she work at $10 an hour to earn the same amount?
(Ex 4)

Practice   **Distributed and Integrated**

Find the LCM.

1. $8mn^4$ and $12m^5n^2$
(57)

2. $\frac{1}{2}wx^3$ and $\frac{1}{4}w^2x^6$
(57)

Tell whether each equation shows inverse variation. Write "yes" or "no".

*3. $y = \dfrac{x}{11}$
(64)

*4. $y = \dfrac{3}{x}$
(64)

*5. Estimate If y varies inversely as x and $y = 24$ when $x = 99$, estimate the value of y when $x = 50$.
(64)

6. What is the minimum and maximum number of books read over the summer by 10 students: 10, 9, 8, 10, 1, 8, 11, 20, 9, 10?
(48)

7. (**Budgeting**) The cost of a cell phone plan includes a monthly fee plus a charge per minute. The charge for 200 minutes is $50. The charge for 350 minutes is $57.50. How much is the monthly fee and how much is the charge per minute?
(59)

Find the product.

8. $(b + 2)^2$
(60)

9. $(x - 8)(x + 2)$ Use the FOIL method.
(58)

*10. Multi-Step Darius drew a square on grid paper that covers 121 cm^2.
(61)

    a. Write an expression to find the side length.

    b. Substitute known values into the equation.

    c. Find the side length.

    d. In which unit is the side length measured?

*11. Multi-Step Joseph lives 5 miles from the school and Maya lives 2 miles from the
(63) school. If Joseph walks from his house in an opposite direction from the school
at a speed of 4 miles per hour, and Maya walks from her house in an opposite
direction from the school at a speed of 6 miles per hour, after how long will they
be the same distance from the school? What is that distance?

*12. Multiple Choice If y varies inversely as x, and $y = 9$ when $x = 12$, what is y when
(64) $x = 4$?

    A 3   **B** 5.3   **C** 27   **D** 108

13. (Recycling) Use the table to compare the mean value of the amount of waste
(48) generated in the United States to the mean value of the amount of materials
recovered for recycling from 1960 to 2005. Write a statement based on this
comparison.

**Generation and Materials Recovery of Municipal Solid Waste, 1960–2005
(in millions of tons)**

Activity	1960	1970	1980	1990	2000	2003	2004	2005
Generation	88.1	121.1	151.6	205.2	237.6	240.4	247.3	245.7
Materials Recovery	5.6	8.0	14.5	33.2	69.1	74.9	77.7	79.0

14. Multi-Step A model sailboat calls for trim around the largest sail. The sail
(51) is triangular with side lengths $\dfrac{8}{2a^2 + 3a}$ centimeters, $\dfrac{5a + 1}{2a^2 + 3a}$ centimeters, and
$\dfrac{3a + 3}{2a^2 + 3a}$ centimeters. How much trim will be used?

Find each of the statistical measures below using the data in the plot.

**Annual Base Salary
at Marketing Associates**

Stem	Leaves
2	1, 1, 2, 2, 3, 3, 3, 6, 8
3	0, 1, 2, 6, 6, 9
4	2, 5, 8
5	3, 5, 7
6	4, 8

Key: 3| 1 means $31,000

15. median
(62)

16. mode
(62)

17. range
(62)

18. relative frequency of $22,000
(62)

19. (Health) To calculate a personal body mass index, students first had to report
(54) their weight in pounds. Make a box-and-whisker plot of the weights below and
determine if there is an outlier.

    140, 145, 170, 157, 130, 155, 190, 180, 175, 120, 116, 118, 112, 103

20. Identify Statement 2 as the converse, inverse, or contrapositive of Statement 1.
(Inv 5) Then indicate the truth value of each statement.

    Statement 1: If a figure is a rhombus, then it is not a rectangle.

    Statement 2: If a figure is a rectangle, then it is not a rhombus.

*21. Coordinate Geometry What kind of quadrilateral is the figure $WXYZ$? Justify
(65) your answer.

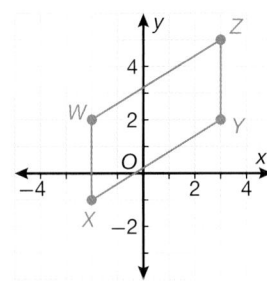

22. State whether the equation $5xy = 40$ shows inverse variation. Write "yes" or "no".
(64)

*23. Write If line a is parallel to line b, could you find a line that makes lines a and b a
(65) reflection of each other? Explain.

*24. Analyze How many parallel lines can be found for the line $y = 2x + 1$?
(65)

*25. Find the slope of a line that is parallel to the line $6x + 3y = 36$.
(65)

*26. Multi-Step Draw a coordinate grid, and number it from -5 to $+5$ along the x- and
(65) y-axis. Will a line passing through the points $(-4, 0)$ and $(4, 2)$ be parallel to
$y = -\frac{1}{4}x - 3$?

    a. Model Graph the points $(-4, 0)$ and $(4, 2)$.

    b. Find the equation for the line that passes through both points.

    c. Justify Is the line $y = -\frac{1}{4}x - 3$ parallel to the line you graphed? Explain.

*27. Error Analysis Two students solved the given system of equations. Which
(63) student is correct? Explain the error.

Student A	Student B
$3y = 2x + 8$	$3y = 2x + 8$
$8x = -2y + 24$	$8x = -2y + 24$
$11x = 32$	$14y = 56$
$x = 2\frac{10}{11}; \left(2\frac{10}{11}, 4\frac{20}{33}\right)$	$y = 4; (2, 4)$

28. (**Paralympics**) Suki is training in her wheelchair for the 100-meter race at the next
(63) Paralympics. In her initial acceleration phase, she averages a speed of 2.7 meters
per second. At her maximum speed phase, she averages a speed of 6.6 meters per
second. If she finishes a practice race in 18.1 seconds, how many meters long (to
the nearest tenth of a meter) is her initial acceleration phase?

*29. Geometry The height h of a cylinder varies inversely with the area of the base B
(64) when the volume is constant. If the height of a cylinder is 6 centimeters when the
area of the base is 12 square centimeters, what is the area of the base of the
cylinder at right with the same volume?

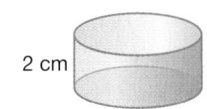
2 cm

30. Multi-Step Tyson often rides his bike 8 miles to visit a friend. His speed varies
(64) inversely with the time it takes to cover that distance. Today he rode at 16 mph to
get to his friend's house, and then he rode at a rate of 12 mph to get home. How
much longer did it take him to get home than to get to his friend's house?

Solving Inequalities by Adding or Subtracting

Warm Up

1. Vocabulary A(n) _____ is a mathematical statement comparing quantities that are not equal.
(45)

Solve.

2. $x + 13 = 21$
(19)

3. $-26 + x = -9$
(19)

Graph.

4. $x < 2$
(50)

5. $x \geq -3$
(50)

New Concepts

Recall that you can add or subtract the same number from both sides of an equation and it remains a true statement. The same is true for inequalities. The Addition Property of Inequality states that when the same number is added to both sides of an inequality, the statement remains true.

Addition Property of Inequality
For any real numbers a, b, and c:
If $a < b$, then $a + c < b + c$.   If $a \leq b$, then $a + c \leq b + c$.
If $a > b$, then $a + c > b + c$.   If $a \geq b$, then $a + c \geq b + c$.

Example 1 Using the Addition Property of Inequality

Solve the inequality $x - 10 < -6$ and graph the solution on a number line.

SOLUTION

$$x \quad 10 < -6$$
$$\underline{+10 \quad +10} \qquad \text{Addition Property of Inequality}$$
$$x < 4 \qquad \text{Simplify.}$$

The solution includes all values less than, but not including, 4.

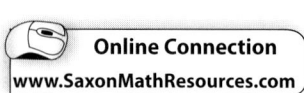

The solution to the inequality is $x < 4$.

Inequalities have an infinite number of solutions. This makes it impossible to check all the solutions. The endpoint and the direction of the inequality can be checked. For example, the solution in Example 1 can be checked using the steps on the following page.

Reading Math

An open circle on the graph of an inequality means that the value is not part of the solution.

Online Connection
www.SaxonMathResources.com

Step 1: Check the endpoint.

The endpoint should be a solution of the related equation $x - 10 = -6$.

$$x - 10 = -6$$

$$4 - 10 \overset{?}{=} -6 \qquad \text{Substitute 4 for } x.$$

$$-6 = -6 \ \checkmark \qquad \text{Simplify.}$$

Step 2: Check the inequality symbol.

Substitute a number less than 4 for x in the original inequality. The number chosen should be a solution of the inequality.

$$x - 10 < -6$$

$$2 - 10 \overset{?}{<} -6 \qquad \text{Substitute a number less than 4 for } x.$$

$$-8 < -6 \ \checkmark \qquad \text{Simplify.}$$

Since the endpoint and the direction of the inequality are correct, the solution of $x - 10 < -6$ is $x < 4$.

> ### Example 2 Checking Solutions
>
> Solve the inequality $x - 3 \geq 5$. Then graph and check the solution.
>
> **SOLUTION**
>
> $$x - 3 \geq 5$$
> $$\underline{+3 \quad +3} \qquad \text{Addition Property of Inequality}$$
> $$x \geq 8 \qquad \text{Simplify.}$$
>
>
> **Check** The endpoint and direction of the inequality symbol should be checked to verify the solution.
>
> Check the endpoint.
>
> $$x - 3 = 5$$
> $$8 - 3 \overset{?}{=} 5$$
> $$5 = 5 \ \checkmark$$
>
> Check the direction of the inequality. Choose a number greater than 8.
>
> $$x - 3 \geq 5$$
> $$9 - 3 \overset{?}{\geq} 5$$
> $$6 \geq 5 \ \checkmark$$

Reading Math

A closed circle on the graph of an inequality means that the value is part of the solution.

Just as you can add the same number to both sides of an inequality, you can also subtract the same number from each side. When equal quantities are subtracted from both sides of an inequality, the inequality remains true.

<table>
<tr><th colspan="2">Subtraction Property of Inequality</th></tr>
<tr><td colspan="2">For any real numbers a, b, and c:</td></tr>
<tr><td>If $a < b$, then $a - c < b - c$.</td><td>If $a \leq b$, then $a - c \leq b - c$.</td></tr>
<tr><td>If $a > b$, then $a - c > b - c$.</td><td>If $a \geq b$, then $a - c \geq b - c$.</td></tr>
</table>

Example 3 Using Subtraction

Solve the inequality $x + 2 > 3$. Then graph and check the solution.

SOLUTION

$$x + 2 > 3$$
$$\underline{-2 \quad -2} \qquad \text{Subtraction Property of Inequality}$$
$$x > 1 \qquad \text{Simplify.}$$

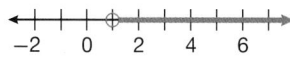

$$-2 \quad 0 \quad 2 \quad 4 \quad 6$$

The solution is $x > 1$.

Check

Check the endpoint.   Check the direction of the inequality.

$$x + 2 = 3 \qquad\qquad\qquad x + 2 > 3$$
$$1 + 2 \overset{?}{=} 3 \qquad\qquad\qquad 2 + 2 \overset{?}{>} 3$$
$$3 = 3 \ \checkmark \qquad\qquad\qquad 4 > 3 \ \checkmark$$

The solution of $x + 2 > 3$ is $x > 1$.

Example 4 Application: Travel

An airline allows a suitcase that weighs no more than 50 pounds when it is full. Jared's empty suitcase weighs 5 pounds. How much weight can Jared pack in his suitcase? Write an inequality to solve the problem. Check your solution.

SOLUTION

Write an inequality to represent the situation. Then solve the inequality.

$$x + 5 \leq 50$$
$$x \leq 45 \qquad \text{Subtract 5 from both sides.}$$

Jared can pack no more than 45 pounds.

Check

Check the endpoint.   Check the direction of the inequality.

$$x + 5 = 50 \qquad\qquad\qquad x + 5 \leq 50$$
$$45 + 5 \overset{?}{=} 50 \qquad\qquad\qquad 44 + 5 \overset{?}{\leq} 50$$
$$50 = 50 \ \checkmark \qquad\qquad\qquad 49 \leq 50 \ \checkmark$$

Hint

To check an inequality solution, try substituting in numbers that are part of the solution set.

a. Solve the inequality $x - \frac{1}{2} > 3$ and graph the solution on a number line.
(Ex 1)

Solve each inequality. Then graph and check the solution.

b. $z - 2 \geq \frac{1}{2}$
(Ex 2)

c. $y + 1.1 \leq 3.2$
(Ex 3)

d. Rebecca wants to crochet a scarf that is at least 4.4 feet long. So far, she has completed 2.5 feet. How much more does Rebecca intend to crochet? Write an inequality to solve the problem. Check your solution.
(Ex 4)

Practice Distributed and Integrated

Simplify the rational expression, if possible.

1. $\dfrac{11p}{6s^4} + \dfrac{p}{6s^4}$
(51)

2. $\dfrac{4x}{5w^4} - \dfrac{5x}{5w^4}$
(51)

3. $\dfrac{7y}{3x^4 + 1} + \dfrac{5y}{3x^4 + 1}$
(51)

Solve the inequality.

*4. $z + 10 \geq 3$
(66)

*5. $x - 4 \leq 9$
(66)

6. Graph the inequality $z \leq 1\frac{2}{3}$.
(50)

 7. Write Explain the difference between $x > 5$ and $x \geq 5$.
(66)

8. Define a linear function that has shifted upward 3 units.
(Inv 6)

9. (Sports) In June 2000, the Russian Alexander Popov set a new world record of 21.64 seconds in men's freestyle swimming. Create the graph of an inequality that represents the times that could beat Popov's record. Explain any restrictions on the graph.
(50)

10. Geometry In two similar triangles, the lengths of the sides of the larger triangle are directly proportional to the lengths of the corresponding sides of the smaller triangle. Find the length of x.
(56)

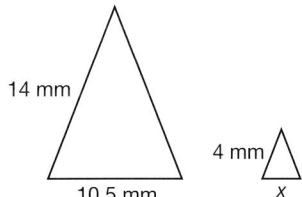

11. Multi-Step The total enrollment P and the female enrollment F of membership in a scholarship program (in thousands) can be modeled by the equations below, where t is the number of years since it was instituted.
(53)

$$P = 2387.74t + 155{,}211.46 \qquad F = 1223.58t + 79{,}589.03$$

a. Find a model that represents the male enrollment M in the scholarship program.

b. For the year 2010, the value of P is projected to be 298,475.86 and the value of F is projected to be 153,003.83. Use these figures to project the male enrollment in 2010.

*12. Multiple Choice What is the solution to $3z + 2 \leq z - 4 + 2 + z$?
(66)

    A $z \leq -4$ **B** $z \leq 0$ **C** $z \leq 3$ **D** $z \leq 4$

*13. Coordinate Geometry Find a line that is both a line of symmetry for the
(65) figure and also a perpendicular bisector of two of the sides.

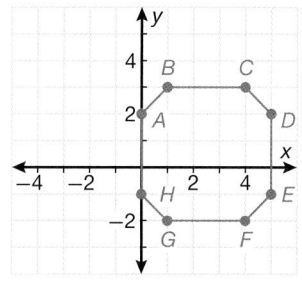

14. Multi-Step In a student poll about yearbook covers, every 12th student likes
(57) blue, every 16th student likes red, and every 28th student likes white.

    a. How many students are polled before one student likes red, white, and blue?

    b. If 1200 students are polled, how many like red, white, and blue?

15. Solve the system of equations by substitution.
(59)

$$x = 10y - 2$$
$$2x - 18y = 8$$

*16. Velocity The tangential velocity of an object in circular motion can be found using
(61) the expression $\sqrt{\frac{Fr}{m}}$, where F is the centripetal force, r is the radius of the circle, and
m is the mass of the object. What is the tangential velocity of an object with a path
radius of 2 m, a centripetal force of 60 kgm/s^2, and a mass of 3 kg?

17. Multiple Choice Which system of equations has a solution of $y = 5$?
(63)

    A $2x + 5y = 16$ **B** $2x + 5y = 19$

        $2x + y = -4$ $x - 5y = -13$

    C $2x + 5y = -4$ **D** $2x + 5y = 11$

       $-2x + y = -8$ $x - 5y = -17$

18. Justify Explain the steps that are used to solve this system of linear equations by
(63) elimination.

$$2x + 6y = 4$$
$$3x - 7y = 6$$

*19. Coordinate Geometry What kind of quadrilateral is *EFHG*? Justify your answer.
(65)

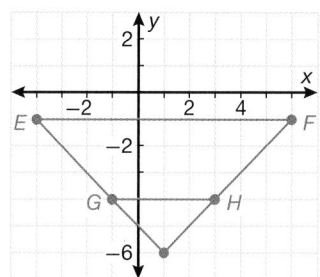

20. Error Analysis Two students are using the product rule below to find the missing
value. Which student is correct? Explain the error.
(64)

If y varies inversely as x and $y = 0.2$ when $x = 100$, find y when $x = 4$.

Student A	Student B
$x_1 y_2 = x_2 y_1$	$x_1 y_1 = x_2 y_2$
$100 \cdot y_2 = 4 \cdot 0.2$	$100 \cdot 0.2 = 4 \cdot y_2$
$100 y_2 = 0.8$	$20 = 4 y_2$
$y_2 = 0.008$	$5 = y_2$

21. Write a direct-variation equation relating x and y when $x = 5$ and $y = 30$.
(56)

22. Write an inverse-variation equation relating x and y when $x = 4$ and $y = 20$.
(64)

Multiply.

23. $(2x - 3)(2x - 3)$ **24.** $(t - 12)(t + 12)$ **25.** $(y^3 - 4)^2$
(60)   *(60)*   *(60)*

26. Justify Find the product of $(2y + 4)(3y + 5)$ using the Distributive Property.
(58) Then find the product using the FOIL method. Show that the answers are the
same using either method.

27. (Life Expectancy) For most mammals, there is an inverse relationship between life
(64) span and heart rate. Use the table below to write an inverse-variation equation to
represent this relationship. Then find the life span in years, rounded to the nearest
tenth, of a hamster with an average heart rate of 450 beats per minute.

Animal	Heart Rate (beats per minute)	Life Span (in minutes)
Guinea Pig	280	3,571,429
Rabbit	205	4,878,049
Dog	115	8,695,952
Rat	328	3,048,780

*28. Coordinate Geometry Show that PQR is a right triangle.
(65)

*29. Justify True or False: The lines represented by $y = \frac{x}{3} - 1$ and $-4 = 12x + 4y$
(65) are parallel. Explain.

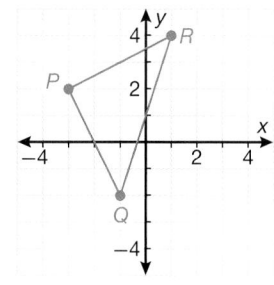

*30. (Running) John plans to run at least 5 miles more this week than he ran last week.
(66) He ran 25 miles last week. Write and solve an inequality describing the number of
miles John plans to run this week.

Solving and Classifying Special Systems of Linear Equations

Warm Up

1. **Vocabulary** A(n) _____ of linear equations is a set of linear
(55)
equations with the same variables.

Find the slope and *y*-intercept.

2. $y = 4x - 7$ **3.** $6x - 2y = 18$
(49)   (49)

4. Find the slope of a line parallel to $15x + 3y = 24$.
(65)

5. Find the slope of a line perpendicular to $x + 4y = 7$.
(65)

New Concepts

Systems of linear equations can be classified by their common solutions. If no common solution exists, the system consists of **inconsistent equations.** The graphs of inconsistent equations never intersect. Therefore, since parallel lines never intersect, the graphs of inconsistent equations are the graphs of parallel lines.

Example 1   Solving Inconsistent Systems of Equations

Caution

Be sure to isolate a variable before using it to solve by substitution.

Solve.

$$-3x + y = -4$$
$$y = 3x$$

SOLUTION

Use substitution.

$y = 3x - 4$ Isolate *y*.

$y = 3x$

$3x = 3x - 4$ Substitute 3*x* for *y* in the first equation.

$0 = -4$ Subtract 3*x* from both sides of the equation.

The statement is false. This means the system has no solution, so it is an inconsistent system.

Other systems of equations, known as **dependent systems,** can have an infinite number of solutions. The equations of a dependent system are called **dependent equations,** and they have identical solution sets. Since they have identical solution sets, the equations are the same.

Two methods can be used to solve dependent systems algebraically. One method shows that the equations are identical. The other method shows that the variables in dependent systems can be assigned any value. So, both equations have infinitely many solutions—an infinite set of ordered pairs.

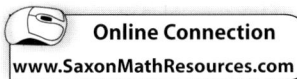

Online Connection
www.SaxonMathResources.com

Example 2 Solving Dependent Systems of Equations

Solve.

$$x + 3y = 6$$

$$\frac{1}{3}x + y = 2$$

SOLUTION Write the equations in slope-intercept form.

Method 1: $x + 3y = 6 \longrightarrow y = -\frac{1}{3}x + 2$

$$\frac{1}{3}x + y = 2 \longrightarrow y = -\frac{1}{3}x + 2$$

The equations are identical. Since the graphs would be the same line, there are infinitely many solutions. Any ordered pair (x, y) that satifies the equation $y = -\frac{1}{3}x + 2$.

SOLUTION

Method 2: $x + 3y = 6$

$$\frac{1}{3}x + y = 2$$

$$y = 2 - \frac{1}{3}x \qquad \text{Isolate } y \text{ in the second equation.}$$

$$x + 3\left(2 - \frac{1}{3}x\right) = 6 \qquad \text{Substitute } 2 - \frac{1}{3}x \text{ for } y \text{ in the first equation.}$$

$$x + 6 - x = 6 \qquad \text{Distribute.}$$

$$6 = 6 \qquad \text{Simplify.}$$

All variables have been eliminated. The last equation is true, $6 = 6$. This means that the original equations are true for all values of the variables. There are infinitely many solutions—an infinite set of ordered pairs.

Math Reasoning

Analyze What is characteristic of systems of equations that are dependent?

A consistent system will have at least one common solution. An independent system will have exactly one solution. An independent system is also a consistent system. The graphs of the equations of an independent system will intersect at one point. Systems of linear equations can be classified into three different categories based on the number of solutions.

Systems of Linear Equations		
Consistent and Independent	**Consistent and Dependent**	**Inconsistent**
Exactly One Solution	Infinitely Many Solutions	No Solution
The graphed lines intersect at a single point.	The graphed lines are the same line. The line is the solution.	The lines are parallel and do not intersect.

Example 3 Classifying Systems of Equations

Determine if each system of equations is consistent and independent, consistent and dependent, or inconsistent.

a.
$$x - \frac{1}{4}y = \frac{3}{4}$$
$$2x + y = 1$$

Math Reasoning

Write Why is there only one solution for a system of independent and consistent equations?

SOLUTION

Solve the system of equations.

$$x - \frac{1}{4}y = \frac{3}{4} \quad \longrightarrow \quad y = 4x - 3$$

$$2x + y = 1 \quad \longrightarrow \quad y = -2x + 1$$

Use substitution.

$$y = 4x - 3$$
$$y = -2x + 1$$

$$-2x + 1 = 4x - 3 \qquad \text{Substitute } y = -2x + 1 \text{ in the first equation.}$$

$$\frac{2}{3} = x \qquad \text{Solve for } x.$$

Substitute $\frac{2}{3}$ for x in one of the original equations and solve for y.

$$2\left(\frac{2}{3}\right) + y = 1 \qquad \text{Substitute } \frac{2}{3} \text{ for } x \text{ in the second equation.}$$

$$y = -\frac{1}{3} \qquad \text{Solve for } y.$$

The solution is $\left(\frac{2}{3}, -\frac{1}{3}\right)$. There is exactly one solution, so the system is consistent and independent.

Check Graph the lines and verify the solution.

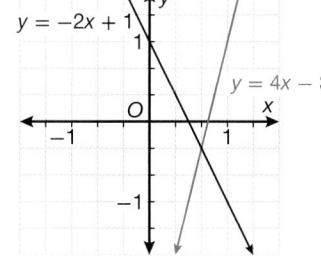

b.
$$3x + y = 2$$
$$y = -3x - 4$$

SOLUTION Write the equations in slope-intercept form.

$$3x + y = 2 \quad \longrightarrow \quad y = -3x + 2$$
$$y = -3x - 4$$

The two equations have the same slope and different y-intercepts. The lines are parallel, so there is no solution. The system is inconsistent.

Check Graph the lines and verify the solution.

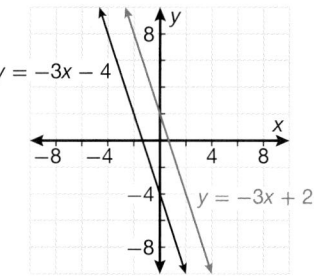

Example 4 | Application: Jogging

Brandon started jogging at a rate of 4 miles per hour. After he jogged 1 mile, his friend Anton started jogging on the same path at a pace of 4 miles per hour. If they continue to jog at the same rate, will Anton ever catch up with Brandon? Explain.

SOLUTION Write a system of equations to represent the situation.

$$y = 4x + 1$$

$$y = 4x$$

The two equations have the same slope and different y-intercepts. The lines are parallel, so there are no solutions.

The boys are jogging at the same rate. Brandon had jogged 1 mile before Anton started. Anton will never catch up with Brandon.

Lesson Practice

Solve.

a. $y = \dfrac{1}{2}x + \dfrac{1}{2}$
(Ex 1)

$y = \dfrac{1}{2}x + 7$

b. $x + y = 10$
(Ex 2)

$-x - y = -10$

Determine if the system of equations is consistent and independent, consistent and dependent, or inconsistent.
(Ex 3)

c. $4y = 4x + 4$

$-4y = -4x - 4$

d. $-2x + y = 3$

$y = -x - 2$

e. An emergency-road-service company offers different plans to its
(Ex 4) customers. Plan X offers service calls for $22 each. Plan Y offers a rate of $40 per month with an additional charge of $12 for each service call. For one month, how many service calls would it take for Plan Y to cost the same as Plan X? Explain.

Practice   Distributed and Integrated

Find the product.

1. $(2b - 3)^2$
(60)

2. $(-b^3 + 5)^2$
(60)

Simplify.

3. $\sqrt{25x^4}$
(61)

4. $\sqrt{144x^6y}$
(61)

5. Simplify the rational expression $\frac{3x}{y^2} + xy^{-2}$, if possible.
(51)

6. In three hours, James read 18 pages of his history book. In four hours, he read
(52) 21 pages. Write the equation of the line that passes through the two points that represent the data in the problem. Use the equation to predict how many pages James will read in six hours.

Solve the inequality.

7. $z - 3 \geq 10$
(66)

8. $z - 5 < -2$
(66)

9. (Hobbies) The stem-and-leaf plot shows the number of
(62) cards each member of a baseball card enthusiasts' club has. What is the mode(s) of the data?

Cards in Collection

Stem	Leaves
30	9
31	1, 4, 5, 7, 7, 9
32	0, 1, 4, 4, 4, 7, 8
33	5, 6
34	2, 8, 9
35	0, 4, 6, 6, 6, 7,

Key: 31| 5 means 315 cards

10. (Transportation) Two subway trains run through a station. One train goes through
(57) the station every 44 minutes and the other train goes through the station every 28 minutes. If they just went through the station at the same time, how many minutes will it be until the next time they are both at the station at the same time?

11. Multi-Step A bank teller receives several deposits in one day. She tallies how
(54) many of each amount she receives.
  a. Make a box-and-whisker plot for the set of data.

  b. List the lower extreme, lower quartile, median, upper quartile, and upper extreme of the data.

Amount	Tally
$25	4
$50	2
$60	6
$75	3
$80	7
$100	5

*12. Identify Statement 2 as the converse, inverse, or contrapositive of Statement 1.
(Inv 5) Then indicate the truth value of each statement.

  Statement 1: If a figure is not a polygon, then it is not a square.

  Statement 2: If a figure is a polygon, then it is a square.

13. Error Analysis Two students solve the inequality $x + 2 < 3$. Which student is correct?
(66) Explain the error.

Student A	Student B
$x + 2 < \quad 3$ $\underline{+2 \quad +2}$ $x < 5$	$x + 2 < \quad 3$ $\underline{-2 \quad -2}$ $x < 1$

*14. (**Sports**) The ages of the players of the Eastern Conference team during the 2007
(62) All-Star Game are listed below. Create a histogram of the data.

$$25, 30, 24, 26, 30, 29, 21, 25, 33, 28, 34, 25$$

15. Multi-Step Find the volume of a toy building block that it is in the shape of a cube
(58) with a side length of $(2x + 2)$ inches.
    a. Find the area of the base. Find the product of the length and the width.

    b. Find the volume by multiplying the product found in part **a** by the height.

16. Verify Show that $(20, 15)$ is a solution to the system of equations.
(59)

$$5x - 2y = 70$$
$$3x + 4y = 120$$

*17. Coordinate Geometry For the figure at right, find two lines that are both a
(65) line of symmetry and a perpendicular bisector of the sides.

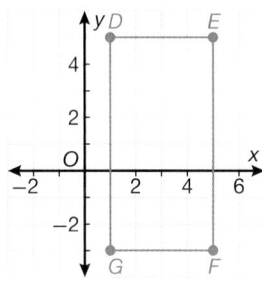

*18. (**Job Hunting**) Claudio is looking for a new job in sales. He interviews with
(63) Company A and they offer him a base salary of $32,000 plus a 1.5% bonus on his
total sales for the year. When he interviews with Company B, they offer him a base
salary of $26,000 plus a 3% bonus on his total sales for the year. How much would
Claudio have to sell to make the same amount at each job?

*19. Analyze If an equation is multiplied by a number, a system of equations is formed
(67) that has infinitely many solutions. Classify the system formed by adding a number
to a given equation.

Determine if the lines are parallel or perpendicular.

20. $y = 3x + 12$ and $y + 9 = 3x$
(65)

Solve each system of linear equations.

21. $2x - 3y = -17$ ***22.** $y = x - 5$
(63) $\quad 2x - 9y = -47$ (67) $\quad\quad y = -2x + 1$

23. Multiple Choice If y varies inversely as x, and $y = 7.5$ when $x = 5$, what is the value
(64) of k?
    A 0   **B** 0.67   **C** 1.5   **D** 37.5

24. Write Will the graph of an inverse variation ever cross the x-axis? Explain.
(64)

25. Probability A teacher allows students to draw from a bag of various prizes, four
(64) of which are new graphing calculators. If there are 24 students and each student
chooses 3 items, what is the probability that the first student will choose a
graphing calculator on his or her first draw?

26. 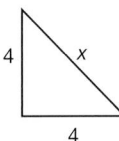 **Geometry** The triangle inequality states that the sum of the lengths of any two sides
(66) of a triangle must be greater than the length of the third side. Write an inequality
for the length of the third side of the triangle.

*27. Multi-Step Mr. Sanchez is planning a business trip. He estimates that he will have
(66) to drive 55 miles on one highway, 48 miles on another, and then 72 more miles to
arrive at his destination. He starts with 25,000 miles on his car's odometer and
later finds that his estimate was high.

a. Write an inequality to represent the odometer reading at the end of the trip.

b. Solve the inequality.

c. The inequality only considers the greatest amount the odometer could read.
Write and solve an inequality for the least it could read.

*28. Error Analysis Two students checked the graph of a system of equations to see if it
(67) was consistent and independent, consistent and dependent, or inconsistent. Which
student is correct? Explain the error.

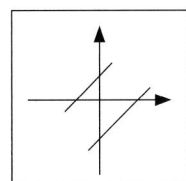

	Student A		**Student B**
	consistent and dependent		inconsistent

*29. (**Newspaper Delivery**) Mauricio and Aliyya are comparing their newspaper delivery
(67) speeds. Mauricio can deliver $y = 65x + 15$ papers per hour. Aliyya can deliver
$13x - \frac{1}{5}y = -3$ papers per hour. Who delivers faster?

*30. Verify Wanda determined that the system of equations below has one solution in
(67) common. Find the common solution and check your answer.

$$2y = 4x + 1$$
$$y = 8x - 7$$

Mutually Exclusive and Inclusive Events

Warm Up

1. Vocabulary Events where the outcome of one event does not affect the probability of the other event are called _____.
(33)

Find the probability for one roll of a number cube.

2. P(less than 4)
(14)

3. P(multiple of 3)
(14)

Simplify.

4. $\dfrac{2}{3} + \dfrac{1}{6}$
(SB3)

5. $\dfrac{3}{4} - \dfrac{1}{3}$
(SB3)

New Concepts

Probability describes the possibility of an event happening. In some cases, the events cannot happen at the same time. For example, when someone tosses a fair coin, there are two possible outcomes: heads or tails. Both outcomes cannot occur at the same time. Two events that cannot both occur in the same trial or experiment are **mutually exclusive events,** or disjoint events.

Math Reasoning

Write Give an example of mutually exclusive events.

Probability of Mutually Exclusive Events
If A and B are mutually exclusive events, then
$P(A \text{ or } B) = P(A) + P(B)$

Example 1 Finding the Probability of Mutually Exclusive Events

What is the probability of rolling either a sum of 6 or a sum of 11 using two different number cubes?

Roll of Cube 2

Roll of Cube 1	1	2	3	4	5	6
1	2	3	4	5	6	7
2	3	4	5	6	7	8
3	4	5	6	7	8	9
4	5	6	7	8	9	10
5	6	7	8	9	10	11
6	7	8	9	10	11	12

SOLUTION

Make a table of possible outcomes. Using two number cubes, it is not possible to roll both a sum of 6 and a sum of 11 at the same time.

Find the probability of each event and add them.

$P(A \text{ or } B) = P(A) + P(B)$

$P(6 \text{ or } 11) = P(6) + P(11)$

$$= \frac{5}{36} + \frac{2}{36}$$

$$= \frac{7}{36}$$

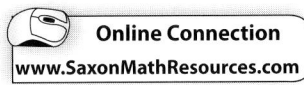
Online Connection
www.SaxonMathResources.com

The probability of rolling either a sum of 6 or a sum of 11 is $\frac{7}{36}$.

In some instances it is possible for two events to occur at the same time. Two events are **inclusive events,** or joint events, if they can both occur at the same time.

Math Reasoning

Write Give an example of inclusive events.

Probability of Inclusive Events
If A and B are inclusive events, then
$P(A \text{ or } B) = P(A) + P(B) - P(A \text{ and } B)$

Example 2 **Finding the Probability of Inclusive Events**

What is the probability of rolling at least one odd number or a sum of 8 using two number cubes?

SOLUTION

Determine if the events are inclusive. List the possible outcomes for each event below.

rolling at least one odd number outcomes:

$(1, 1), (1, 2), (1, 3), (1, 4), (1, 5), (1, 6), (3, 1), (3, 2), (3, 3), (3, 4), (3, 5),$
$(3, 6), (5, 1), (5, 2), (5, 3), (5, 4), (5, 5), (5, 6), (2, 1), (4, 1), (6, 1), (2, 3),$
$(4, 3), (6, 3), (2, 5), (4, 5), (6, 5)$

rolling a sum of 8 outcomes:

$(2, 6), (6, 2), (3, 5), (5, 3), (4, 4)$

rolling at least one odd number and a sum of 8 outcomes:

$(3, 5), (5, 3)$

$$P(A \text{ or } B) = P(A) + P(B) - P(A \text{ and } B)$$
$$P(\text{odd or } 8) = P(\text{odd}) + P(8) - P(\text{odd and } 8)$$
$$= \frac{27}{36} + \frac{5}{36} - \frac{2}{36}$$
$$= \frac{30}{36}$$
$$= \frac{5}{6}$$

The probability of rolling either an odd number or a sum of 8 is $\frac{5}{6}$.

Example 3 **Application: Survey**

Briceson needs to randomly call 125 people from the state of Wyoming to conduct a short survey. The following data correspond to estimated values from 2005 describing the state's populace. Briceson assumes that everyone who is employed is younger than 75.

Total Population	Employed People	People 75 and Older
510,000	291,000	29,000

How many people can he expect to call who are either employed or are 75 or older?

SOLUTION

Probability can be used to determine the number of people.

The events are mutually exclusive.

$$P(A \text{ or } B) = P(A) + P(B)$$

$$P(\text{employed or} \geq 75) = P(\text{employed}) + P(\geq 75)$$

$$= \frac{291}{510} + \frac{29}{510}$$

$$= \frac{32}{51}$$

Briceson can expect 32 out of 51 people to be employed or to be at least 75 years old. Multiply the probability by the 125 people.

$$125 \cdot \frac{32}{51}$$

$$= \frac{4000}{51}$$

$$\approx 78$$

Briceson can expect to call about 78 people who are either employed or 75 or older.

Math Reasoning

Verify Why is $\frac{4000}{51}$ rounded to the nearest whole number in Example 3?

Example 4 **Application: Digital Music**

Natalia has music from a variety of different artists on her MP3 player. There are 26 rock artists, 18 pop artists, 19 country artists, 10 alternative artists, and 7 crossover artists. The music by the crossover artists Natalia chose is on the pop and country charts. If Natalia's music player randomly selects the next artist, what is the probability that the artist will be singing a pop or country song?

SOLUTION

Find the total number of outcomes.

$$26 + 18 + 19 + 10 + 7 = 80$$

The events are inclusive events because the crossover artists are considered to be both country and pop artists.

$$P(A \text{ or } B) = P(A) + P(B) - P(A \text{ and } B)$$

$$P(\text{pop or country}) = P(\text{pop}) + P(\text{country}) - P(\text{pop and country})$$

$$= \frac{25}{80} + \frac{26}{80} - \frac{7}{80}$$

$$= \frac{11}{20}$$

There is an $\frac{11}{20}$ chance that the music player will choose a pop or country song next.

a. What is the probability of rolling either a sum of 2 or a sum of 10 using two number cubes?
(Ex 1)

b. What is the probability of rolling at least one even number or a sum of 3 using two number cubes?
(Ex 2)

c. A digital music player randomly selects a song from a group of 12 rock, 12 pop, 5 country, and 3 alternative artists. What is the probability that the music player selects either a rock or alternative song?
(Ex 3)

d. Angelina uses Briceson's data from Example 3. She is planning to call 200 people from Wyoming. She assumes that 10,000 of the people who are 75 or older are also employed.
(Ex 4)

Total Population	Employed People	People 75 and Older
510,000	291,000	29,000

How many people would Angelina expect to call that are either employed or are 75 or older?

Practice   Distributed and Integrated

Determine the degree of each polynomial.

1. $14x^2y^3z^4$
(53)

2. $12q^2r + 4r - 10q^2r^6$
(53)

3. $5x^4z^3 + 4xz$
(53)

Simplify.

4. $\sqrt{\dfrac{1}{48}}$
(61)

5. $\sqrt{\dfrac{4}{25x^4}}$
(61)

Tell whether each of the following equations shows inverse variation. Write "yes" or "no".

6. $y = \dfrac{5}{x}$
(64)

7. $y = \dfrac{1}{2}x$
(64)

Solve each inequality.

8. $x + 1 > 1.1$
(66)

9. $x - 2.3 \le 7.6$
(66)

Find the probability of the following events.

*10. rolling a sum of 7 or a sum of 11 with two number cubes
(68)

*11. rolling a sum of 1 or a sum of 13 with two number cubes
(68)

12. Probability A caterer is sorting silverware. There are 75 knives, 50 forks, and
(7) 75 spoons. Twenty of the forks and 30 of the spoons have red handles. If a piece of silverware is chosen at random, what is the probability that it will be a fork or have a red handle? Write and solve an expression to find the probability.

13. A car rental company charges a flat rate of $50 and an additional $.10 per mile to
(52) rent an automobile. Write an equation to model the total charge y in terms of x
number of miles driven. Predict the cost after 100 miles driven.

14. (Chemistry) When Liquid A has a temperature of 0°F, Liquid B has a temperature
(52) of -8°F. When Liquid A has a temperature of 4°F, Liquid B has a temperature of
-9°F. Write an equation of a line that passes through the two points that represent
the data in this problem. Use the equation to predict the temperature of Liquid B
if Liquid A has a temperature of -4°F.

*15. Use the following system to answer the problems below.
(55)
$$x = y + 2$$
$$2x = y$$

   a. Graph the system.

   b. Determine the solution. Verify the solution using your graphing calculator.

16. (Carpentry) Jorge is adding a rectangular family room onto his house. The
(58) dimensions of the room can be represented by a width of $(x + 6)$ feet and a length
of $(2x + 5)$ feet. Write a polynomial expression for the area A of the new room.

17. Multi-Step The sum of 6 times a boy's age and 5 times a girl's age is 150. The girl is
(59) 2 years less than twice the boy's age. Find how old each was 5 years ago.

18. Justify True or False: $(a + b)(a + b) = a^2 + b^2$. Justify by giving an example.
(60)

19. (Craft Fair) Celine sells her hand-painted chairs and tables at a local craft fair. She
(63) is selling her chairs for $30 a piece and her tables for $60 a piece. At the end of the
day, she noted that she had sold 20 items for a total of $780. How many chairs did
Celine sell? how many tables?

20. Error Analysis Two students want to find the equation of the line perpendicular to
(65) $y = -\frac{1}{5}x + 4$ that passes through $(1, -3)$. Which student is correct? Explain the error.

Student A	Student B
$y = 5x + b$	$y = 5x + b$
$1 = 5(-3) + b$	$-3 = 5(1) + b$
$1 = -15 + b$	$-3 = 5 + b$
$+15 \quad +15$	$-5 \quad -5$
$16 = b$	$-8 = b$
$y = 5x + 16$	$y = 5x - 8$

21. Multi-Step Draw a coordinate grid, numbering from -6 to $+6$ along the x- and
(65) y-axis. Will a line that passes through the points $(0, -4)$ and $(5, -2)$ be
perpendicular to the line that passes through the points $(-2, 5)$ and $(0, 1)$?

   a. Model Line 1 passes through the points $(0, -4)$ and $(5, -2)$. Line 2 passes
   through the points $(-2, 5)$ and $(0, 1)$. Graph the lines.

   b. Write an equation for both lines.

   c. Justify Are the lines perpendicular? Explain.

22. (**Discounts**) A new pet store is selling dog food for $2 off. Another pet store is selling
(66) dog food for $14.99. Write and solve an inequality to represent the highest original
price, before the discount, that will make the dog food at the new pet store cheaper.

23. Error Analysis Two students solve and graph the inequality $x - 5 \leq -8$. Which
(66) student is correct? Explain the error.

Student A

Student B

Find the common solution for each system of equations.

24. $y = \dfrac{3}{4}x + 3$
(67)
$y = x$

25. Multi-Step Two satellite radio companies are offering different plans. One
(67) offers a flat fee of $15 per month for all stations. The second charges a rate of
$y = \$10 + \$1.5x$, where x is the number of additional stations. Do the plans
ever cost the same amount?

  a. How many stations can a consumer purchase from the second company before
  exceeding the flat fee of $15?

  b. Classify the system of equations for the plans offered by both companies.

  c. How is the classification of the equations misleading given the problem situation?

  d. Do the plans ever cost the same amount?

26. Geometry Two secants to a circle are shown at right. Classify the system formed by
(67) the equations for these two lines.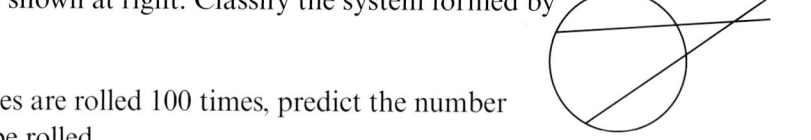

*27. Predict If two standard number cubes are rolled 100 times, predict the number
(68) of times that a sum of 7 or 11 will be rolled.

*28. Multiple Choice Which one of the following situations describes mutually
(68) exclusive events?

  A rolling doubles or a sum of 4 with two number cubes

  B choosing an odd number or a multiple of 3

  C tossing a coin heads-up or rolling a 2 with a number cube

  D rolling two 5s or a sum of 12 with two number cubes

*29. (**Weather Forecasting**) On a winter day in Maine, there was a 30% chance of only
(68) freezing rain, a 45% chance of only rain, and a 25% chance of only snow. What
was the chance of getting only freezing rain or snow?

*30. Analyze Given two possible events, A and B, will the probability of either A or B
(68) occurring be higher if they are inclusive events or mutually exclusive events?

Adding and Subtracting Radical Expressions

Warm Up

1. Vocabulary Terms that have the same variable(s) raised to the same power(s) are called _____.
<small>(18)</small>

Simplify.

2. $3s + 4t + 8s - 7t$
<small>(18)</small>

3. $9wv - 4m + 13m - 17wv$
<small>(18)</small>

4. $\sqrt{72}$
<small>(61)</small>

5. $\sqrt{50}$
<small>(61)</small>

New Concepts

Combining radicals is similar to combining like terms. When combining radical expressions, use like radicals. **Like radicals** have the same radicand and index. **Unlike radicals** have different radicands and/or index numbers.

> **Math Language**
>
> A **radicand** is the number or expression under a radical symbol.

Example 1   **Combining Like Radicals**

Simplify. All variables represent non-negative real numbers.

a. $2\sqrt{7} + 4\sqrt{7}$

SOLUTION

Add the like radicals together.

$$2\sqrt{7} + 4\sqrt{7} = (2 + 4)\sqrt{7} \qquad \text{Combine coefficients of like radicals.}$$
$$= 6\sqrt{7}$$

b. $4\sqrt{xy} - 6\sqrt{xy}$

SOLUTION

Subtract the like radicals.

$$4\sqrt{xy} - 6\sqrt{xy} = (4 - 6)\sqrt{xy} \qquad \text{Combine coefficients of like radicals.}$$
$$= -2\sqrt{xy}$$

c. $6\sqrt{2} + 8\sqrt{11}$

SOLUTION

No simplification is possible since the radicands are not alike.

d. $\dfrac{2\sqrt{5q}}{7} + \dfrac{3\sqrt{5q}}{7} - \dfrac{4\sqrt{3r}}{7}$

SOLUTION

$$\dfrac{2\sqrt{5q}}{7} + \dfrac{3\sqrt{5q}}{7} + \dfrac{4\sqrt{3r}}{7}$$

$$= \dfrac{(2 + 3)\sqrt{5q}}{7} - \dfrac{4\sqrt{3r}}{7} \qquad \text{Combine the like radicals.}$$

$$= \dfrac{5\sqrt{5q} - 4\sqrt{3r}}{7} \qquad \text{Simplify.}$$

> **Online Connection**
> www.SaxonMathResources.com

It is not always apparent that radicals are alike until they are simplified. All radicals should be simplified before trying to identify like radicals.

Example 2 Simplifying Before Combining

Simplify. All variables represent non-negative real numbers.

(a.) $3\sqrt{8m^3} + 2\sqrt{2m} + 4\sqrt{2m}$

SOLUTION

$3\sqrt{8m^3} + 2\sqrt{2m} + 4\sqrt{2m}$

$= 3\sqrt{4 \cdot m^2 \cdot 2m} + 2\sqrt{2m} + 4\sqrt{2m}$ Factor the first radicand.

$= 3\sqrt{4} \cdot \sqrt{m^2} \cdot \sqrt{2m} + 2\sqrt{2m} + 4\sqrt{2m}$ Product Property of Radicals

$= 6m\sqrt{2m} + 2\sqrt{2m} + 4\sqrt{2m}$ Simplify $3\sqrt{4} \cdot \sqrt{m^2}$.

$= (6m + 2 + 4)\sqrt{2m}$ Factor out $\sqrt{2m}$.

$= (6m + 6)\sqrt{2m}$ Simplify.

(b.) $c\sqrt{75c} - \sqrt{27c^3}$

SOLUTION

$c\sqrt{75c} - \sqrt{27c^3}$

$= c\sqrt{25} \cdot \sqrt{3c} - \sqrt{9} \cdot \sqrt{c^2} \cdot \sqrt{3c}$ Factor the radicands.

$= 5c\sqrt{3c} - 3c\sqrt{3c}$ Simplify each expression.

$= (5c - 3c)\sqrt{3c}$ Factor out $\sqrt{3c}$.

$= 2c\sqrt{3c}$ Simplify.

> **Hint**
>
> Use the **Product Property of Radicals.** If $a \geq 0$ and $b \geq 0$, then $\sqrt{ab} = \sqrt{a} \cdot \sqrt{b}$.

Example 3 Application: Finding the Perimeter of a Triangle

Find the perimeter of a right triangle if the lengths of the two legs are $4\sqrt{9}$ inches and $2\sqrt{64}$ inches, and the hypotenuse is $2\sqrt{100}$ inches.

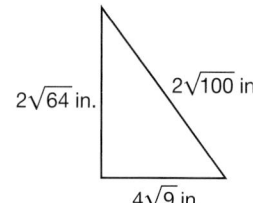

$2\sqrt{64}$ in. $2\sqrt{100}$ in $4\sqrt{9}$ in.

SOLUTION

The perimeter is the distance around the figure.

$P = 4\sqrt{9} + 2\sqrt{64} + 2\sqrt{100}$

$P = 4\sqrt{3^2} + 2\sqrt{8^2} + 2\sqrt{10^2}$ Factor each radicand.

$P = 4 \cdot 3 + 2 \cdot 8 + 2 \cdot 10$ Simplify each radical.

$P = 12 + 16 + 20$ Multiply.

$P = 48$ Add.

The perimeter is 48 inches.

┌─ **Example 4** **Application: Finding the Perimeter of a Swimming Pool**

A rectangular swimming pool has a length of $\sqrt{800}$ feet and a width of $\sqrt{648}$ feet. What is its perimeter?

SOLUTION

Understand The length and width of a rectangle are given. Find the perimeter.

Plan Use the formula for perimeter and the length and width of the pool to write an equation.

Solve Perimeter $= l + l + w + w$

$P = \sqrt{800} + \sqrt{800} + \sqrt{648} + \sqrt{648}$

$P = \sqrt{20^2 \cdot 2} + \sqrt{20^2 \cdot 2} + \sqrt{18^2 \cdot 2} + \sqrt{18^2 \cdot 2}$ Factor each radicand.

$P = 20\sqrt{2} + 20\sqrt{2} + 18\sqrt{2} + 18\sqrt{2}$ Simplify each radical.

$P = 76\sqrt{2}$ feet   Add.

Check Square each simplified radical expression to make sure the radicals were simplified correctly.

$\left(20\sqrt{2}\right)^2$ $\left(18\sqrt{2}\right)^2$

$\stackrel{?}{=} 20\sqrt{2} \cdot 20\sqrt{2}$ $\stackrel{?}{=} 18\sqrt{2} \cdot 18\sqrt{2}$

$\stackrel{?}{=} 400 \cdot 2$ $\stackrel{?}{=} 324 \cdot 2$

$= 800$ ✓ $= 648$ ✓

The dimensions of the rectangular swimming pool are $\sqrt{800}$ and $\sqrt{648}$. So, the solution is correct.

Hint

Perimeter is the distance around a figure. Add the length of all 4 sides to find the perimeter of the pool.

Lesson Practice

Simplify. All variables represent non-negative real numbers.

a. $9\sqrt{5} + 8\sqrt{5}$
(Ex 1)

b. $11\sqrt{ab} - 23\sqrt{ab}$
(Ex 1)

c. $5\sqrt{7} + 3\sqrt{2}$
(Ex 1)

d. $\dfrac{3\sqrt{2x}}{5} + \dfrac{2\sqrt{2x}}{5} - \dfrac{\sqrt{2x}}{5}$
(Ex 1)

e. $4\sqrt{3c^2} - 8\sqrt{2c^2}$
(Ex 2)

f. $-11\sqrt{10a} + 3\sqrt{250a} + \sqrt{160a}$
(Ex 2)

g. Find the perimeter of a right triangle if the lengths of the two legs
(Ex 3) are $\sqrt{12}$ meters and $\sqrt{48}$ meters, and if the hypotenuse is $2\sqrt{15}$ meters.

h. A rectangular garden is $\sqrt{27a^2}$ feet wide and $\sqrt{75a^2}$ feet long. What is
(Ex 4) its perimeter?

Add.

*1. $-6\sqrt{2} + 8\sqrt{2}$
(69)

*2. $-4\sqrt{7} - 5\sqrt{7}$
(69)

*3. $2\sqrt{3} + 5\sqrt{3}$
(69)

Determine the degree.

4. $9x$
(53)

5. $-3x^2 + 2x + 16$
(53)

6. $xy + 2$
(53)

Find the probability of the events described below.

*7. rolling a sum of 2 or a sum of 12 with two number cubes
(68)

8. rolling a sum greater than 1
(68)

9. **(Volleyball)** A volleyball is hit upward from a height of 1.4 meters. The expression
(53) $-4.3t^2 + 7.7t + 1.4$ can be used to find the height (in meters) of the volleyball at time t. The ball was hit from a moving platform that has a height (in meters) of $-3t^2 + 5t + 6$. What is the combined height?

10. Display the data using a box-and-whisker plot titled "Hours a Candle Burns".
(54) Identify any outliers.

$$4, 12, 3, 5, 7, 9, 4, 8, 3, 18, 5, 8, 4$$

11. **Multi-Step** The number of miles represented on a map varies directly with the
(56) number of inches on the map. In Texas, the distance from Austin to San Antonio is 79 miles; on a map, it is 5 inches.
a. Write the equation that represents this relationship.
b. Graph this relationship.
c. Estimate how far Waco is from Austin if they are $6\frac{1}{2}$ inches apart on a map.

12. **(Produce Purchase)** Bananas are $0.10 and apples are $0.25. The total cost for 35 pieces
(59) of fruit is $6.80. How many of each fruit were purchased?

13. **Multi-Step** Luke is building a new fence around his property.
(60) Write an expression for the area of the shaded region.
a. Find the area of the smaller square.
b. Write an expression for the area of the larger square using special products.
c. Simplify part **b.**
d. Write an expression for the area of the shaded region.

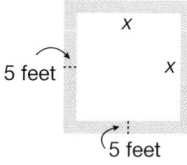

5 feet

x

x

5 feet

14. **Generalize** Use examples to explain why $\sqrt{x} \cdot \sqrt{x} = -x$ for all negative values of x.
(61)

15. Solve the system of linear equations given below.
(63)
$$6x + 15y = 15$$
$$7x - 3y = -3$$

16. (**Prom Night**) Jamal and his friends want to rent a limousine for prom night. The
(64) cost per person varies inversely with the number of people renting the limousine.
If 4 people rent the limousine, it will cost them $180 each. How much would it
cost per person if 12 people rented the limousine?

Determine if the lines are parallel or perpendicular.

17. $y = -\frac{3}{2}x + 8\frac{1}{2}$ and $y - \frac{2}{3}x = 0$
(65)

18. Data Analysis Rachel will receive an A in math for the semester if the mean of her
(66) test scores is at least 90. If her first two test scores are as shown in the table, write
an inequality for the score Rachel needs on her third test to receive an A for the
semester.

Test	Grade
Test 1	85
Test 2	95
Test 3	?

19. Analyze Graph the inequalities $x + 5 > 3$ and $x - 6 \leq -8$ on the same number line.
(66) What is true about their combined solutions?

20. Multiple Choice Which graph represents the solution to $x + 6 \geq 2x - 12$?
(66)

A ![number line from -12 to -4, filled point at -6 with arrow left]
 −12 −10 −8 −6 −4

B ![number line from 12 to 20, filled point at 18 with arrow left]
 12 14 16 18 20

C ![number line from -12 to -4, filled point at -6 with arrow right]
 −12 −10 −8 −6 −4

D ![number line from -20 to -12, filled point at -18 with arrow right]
 −20 −18 −16 −14 −12

21. Find the common solution for the system of equations given below.
(67)
$$-\frac{1}{4}x + y = -2$$
$$-x + 4y = -8$$

22. Error Analysis Two students found a common solution for a system of equations.
(67) Which student is correct? Explain the error.

Student A	Student B
$y = -5x - 2$	$y = -5x - 2$
$6y = -30x - 12$	$6y = -30x - 12$
$-6y = +30x + 12$	$-6y = +30x + 12$
$\underline{6y = -30x - 12}$	$\underline{6y = -30x - 12}$
$0 = 0$	$0 = 0$
Solution:	Solution:
$y = -5x - 2$	$(0, 0)$

*23. (**Sanitation**) A garbage truck is on time with its collections if it maintains an average
(67) rate of $y = 75x + 5$. Currently, the truck is running at a rate of $\frac{1}{5}y - 15x = 1$.
Is the garbage truck on schedule?

24. Error Analysis Two students found the probability of choosing either a black 2 or a
(68) king from a deck of cards. Which student is correct? Explain the error.

Student A	Student B
$P(A \text{ or } B) = \dfrac{2}{52} + \dfrac{4}{52}$	$P(A \text{ or } B) = \dfrac{2}{52} \cdot \dfrac{4}{52}$
$= \dfrac{6}{52}$	$= \dfrac{8}{2704}$
$= \dfrac{3}{26}$	$= \dfrac{1}{338}$

*25. Multi-Step Miranda baked several casseroles: 36 servings of chicken casserole,
(68) 24 servings of pasta casserole, 30 servings of beef casserole, and 28 servings of
vegetarian casserole. She gives 1 serving to her brother. What is the probability
that he will get a pasta casserole or a vegetarian casserole?

a. What is the probability that the serving will be pasta?

b. What is the probability that the serving will be vegetarian?

c. What is the probability that the serving will be pasta or vegetarian?

26. If a circle is made into the spinner shown,
(68) what is the probability of landing on either a
black space or a space worth 10 points?

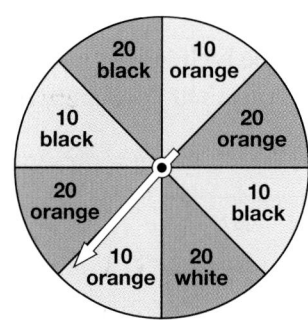

27. Analyze True or False: For the set of integers, $\sqrt{x^n}$ can be simplified when $x \geq 0$
(69) and $n \geq 2$. Justify your answer.

*28. Error Analysis Ms. Nguyen asks her students if they can combine the radicals in the
(69) expression $\sqrt{13x} + \sqrt{23x} - \sqrt{33x}$. Student A says it is possible. Student B says
that the radicals in the expressions $\sqrt{13x} + \sqrt{23x} - \sqrt{33x}$ do not combine. Which
student is correct? Explain the error.

*29. Estimate Estimate the sum of $\sqrt{51} + \sqrt{63} + \sqrt{83} + \sqrt{104}$.
(69)

*30. (Great Pyramid) Each of the four sides of the base of the
(69) Great Pyramid measures 756 feet. If a scale model is
made with the measurement of $\sqrt{756}$ inches for each
side of the base, how many inches is the perimeter of
the base of the scale model of the pyramid rounded
to the nearest whole number?

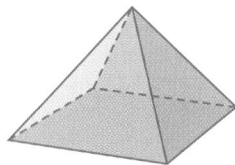

Solving Inequalities by Multiplying or Dividing

Warm Up

1. Vocabulary The _____ of an inequality in one variable is a value or
$^{(50)}$ set of values that satisfies the inequality.

Solve.

2. $12x = -84$ $\qquad$ **3.** $-7x = -91$
$^{(21)}$ $\qquad\qquad\qquad\quad$ $^{(21)}$

Graph each inequality.

4. $x > -1$ $\qquad\qquad\qquad$ **5.** $x \leq 4$
$^{(50)}$ $\qquad\qquad\qquad\qquad\quad$ $^{(50)}$

New Concepts

When multiplying an inequality by a positive value, the order of the
inequality does not change.

Math Language

The **order of the inequality** refers to the direction of the inequality symbol. If $x > 2$ is rewritten $x < 2$, then the order of the inequality has changed.

$$5 > 3, \text{ so } 5(2) > 3(2) \qquad 8 < 12, \text{ so } 8(4) < 12(4)$$

Multiplication Property of Inequality for $c > 0$
For every real number a and b, and $c > 0$: $\qquad\qquad$ If $a > b$, then $ac > bc$. $\qquad$ If $a < b$, then $ac < bc$. $\qquad\qquad$ This property is also true for $\geq$ and $\leq$.

Example 1 **Multiplying by a Positive Number**

Solve, graph, and check the solution for the inequality $\frac{1}{2}x \leq 8$.

SOLUTION

Solve the inequality.

$$\frac{1}{2}x \leq 8$$

$(2)\frac{1}{2}x \leq 8(2)$ $\qquad$ Multiplication Property of Inequality for $c > 0$

$\qquad x \leq 16$ $\qquad$ Simplify.

Graph the solution on a number line.

Hint

When checking the direction of an inequality, any value in the solution set can be substituted. Generally, it is best to select a value that can be easily computed.

Check

Check the endpoint. $\qquad\qquad\qquad$ Check the direction of the inequality.

$$\frac{1}{2}x \overset{?}{=} 8 \qquad\qquad\qquad\qquad \frac{1}{2}x \overset{?}{\leq} 8$$

$$\frac{1}{2}(16) \overset{?}{=} 8 \qquad\qquad\qquad\qquad \frac{1}{2}(14) \overset{?}{\leq} 8$$

$$8 = 8 \ \checkmark \qquad\qquad\qquad\qquad\qquad 7 \leq 8 \ \checkmark$$

Both statements are true, so the solution is correct.

Online Connection
www.SaxonMathResources.com

When solving an equation, the equality symbol never changes. Each transformation results in an equation equivalent to the previous equation. Multiplying an inequality by a positive value is similar to solving an equation because the symbol of inequality does not change, regardless of the operations required to solve the statement. However, when multiplying an inequality by a negative value, the order of the inequality does change.

$$5 > 3, \text{ so } 5(-2) < 3(-2) \text{ because } -10 < -6.$$

$$8 < 12, \text{ so } 8(-4) > 12(-4) \text{ because } -32 > -48.$$

Multiplication Property of Inequality for $c < 0$
For every real number a and b, and $c < 0$:
If $a > b$, then $ac < bc$.
If $a < b$, then $ac > bc$.
This property is also true for $\geq$ and $\leq$.

Example 2   **Multiplying by a Negative Number**

Solve, graph, and check the solution for the inequality $\frac{-x}{5} < 5$.

SOLUTION

Solve the inequality.

$$\frac{-x}{5} < 5$$

$$(-5)\frac{-x}{5} > 5(-5) \qquad \text{Multiplication Property of Inequality for } c < 0$$

$$x > -25 \qquad \text{Simplify.}$$

Graph the solution on a number line.

Check

Check the endpoint.

$$\frac{-x}{5} \stackrel{?}{=} 5$$

$$\frac{-(-25)}{5} \stackrel{?}{=} 5$$

$$\frac{25}{5} \stackrel{?}{=} 5$$

$$5 = 5 \ \checkmark$$

Check the direction of the inequality.

$$\frac{-x}{5} \stackrel{?}{<} 5$$

$$\frac{-(-20)}{5} \stackrel{?}{<} 5$$

$$\frac{20}{5} \stackrel{?}{<} 5$$

$$4 < 5 \ \checkmark$$

Both statements are true, so the solution is correct.

When dividing an inequality by a positive value, the order of the inequality does not change.

$$6 > 4, \text{ so } \frac{6}{2} > \frac{4}{2}. \qquad 8 < 12, \text{ so } \frac{8}{4} < \frac{12}{4}.$$

Division Property of Inequality for $c > 0$

For every real number a and b, and $c > 0$:

If $a > b$, then $\frac{a}{c} > \frac{b}{c}$.   If $a < b$, then $\frac{a}{c} < \frac{b}{c}$.

This property is also true for $\geq$ and $\leq$.

Example 3   **Dividing by a Positive Number**

Solve, graph, and check the solution for the inequality $18 > 3r$.

SOLUTION

Solve the inequality.

$18 > 3r$

$\dfrac{18}{3} > \dfrac{3r}{3}$ Division Property of Inequality for $c > 0$

$6 > r$ Simplify.

Graph the solution on a number line.

Check

Check the endpoint.   Check the direction of the inequality.

$18 \overset{?}{=} 3r$ $18 \overset{?}{>} 3r$

$18 \overset{?}{=} 3(6)$ $18 \overset{?}{>} 3(5)$

$18 = 18$ ✓ $18 > 15$ ✓

Both statements are true so the solution is correct.

Caution

When the variable is on the right side of the inequality, be careful to read the inequality symbol correctly. $6 > r$ means that r is less than 6.

When dividing an inequality by a negative value, the order of the inequality changes.

$$6 > 4, \text{ so } \frac{6}{-2} < \frac{4}{-2}. \qquad 8 < 12, \text{ so } \frac{8}{-4} > \frac{12}{-4}.$$

Division Property of Inequality for $c < 0$

For every real number a and b, and $c < 0$:

If $a > b$, then $\frac{a}{c} < \frac{b}{c}$.   If $a < b$, then $\frac{a}{c} > \frac{b}{c}$.

This property is also true for $\geq$ and $\leq$.

Example 4 Dividing by a Negative Number

Solve, graph, and check the solution for the inequality $-4m \geq 7$.

SOLUTION

Solve the inequality.

$$-4m \geq 7$$

$$\frac{-4m}{-4} \leq \frac{7}{-4} \qquad \text{Division Property of Inequality for } c < 0$$

$$m \leq -1\frac{3}{4} \qquad \text{Simplify. Write the solution as a mixed number.}$$

Graph the solution on a number line.

Check

Check the endpoint.

$$-4m \stackrel{?}{=} 7$$

$$-4\left(-1\frac{3}{4}\right) \stackrel{?}{=} 7$$

$$7 = 7 \quad \checkmark$$

Check the direction of the inequality.

$$-4m \stackrel{?}{\geq} 7$$

$$-4(-2) \stackrel{?}{\geq} 7$$

$$8 \geq 7 \quad \checkmark$$

Both statements are true, so the solution is correct.

Math Reasoning

Connect Solving inequalities is exactly the same as solving equations. Do you agree or disagree with the statement? Explain.

Example 5 Application: Business

An employment agency charges a company 15% of the salary for every position filled. What salary must a company pay a new employee for the employment agency to earn a commission of at least $6000?

SOLUTION

Write and solve an inequality.

$$0.15s \geq 6000$$

$$\frac{0.15s}{0.15} \geq \frac{6000}{0.15} \qquad \text{Division Property of Inequality for } c > 0$$

$$s \geq 40,000 \qquad \text{Simplify.}$$

Any salary of $40,000 or more will earn a commission of at least $6000.

Check

Check the endpoint.

$$0.15s \stackrel{?}{=} 6000$$

$$0.15(40,000) \stackrel{?}{=} 6000$$

$$6000 = 6000 \quad \checkmark$$

Check the direction of the inequality.

$$0.15s \stackrel{?}{\geq} 6000$$

$$0.15(50,000) \stackrel{?}{\geq} 6000$$

$$7500 \geq 6000 \quad \checkmark$$

Math Reasoning

Analyze When solving word problems with inequalities, think about what restrictions exist on the solution set. What are restrictions for this business application?

Solve, graph, and check the solution for each inequality.

a. $\frac{1}{3}n < 2$ (Ex 1)

b. $\frac{-x}{4} < 8$ (Ex 2)

c. $6w \leq 57$ (Ex 3)

d. $\frac{1}{2} \geq -4a$ (Ex 4)

e. Barney earns a 4% commission on what he sells. How much does he need to sell to earn at least a $750 commission every month? (Ex 5)

Practice Distributed and Integrated

Find the probability of the following events.

1. tossing a coin heads-up or rolling a 3 with a number cube (68)

2. tossing a coin tails-up or rolling a number less than 4 on a number cube (68)

3. tossing a coin tails-up and rolling a number greater than 6 on a number cube (33)

Solve the inequality.

4. $y - 2 < \frac{1}{2}$ (66)

5. $y + \frac{3}{2} < \frac{1}{4}$ (66)

Add.

*6. $18\sqrt{3y} + 8\sqrt{3y}$ (69)

7. $\sqrt{3x} + 2\sqrt{3x}$ (69)

8. Write an inverse variation equation relating x and y when $x = 18$ and $y = 4.5$. (64)

9. Determine if the inequality symbol needs to be reversed, and then solve. (70)

$$-2a \geq -5$$

*10. A team scores 56, 42, 60, 43, 51, 22, 44, 55, and 49 points. (54)
   a. Identify any outliers.

   b. On the same screen of the graphing calculator, make one box-and-whisker plot of these data without identifying any outliers, and make another box-and-whisker plot that does identify any outliers.

   c. How many points would you expect the team to score in the next game? Explain your answer.

11. (Ages) The ages at a family party are recorded. (54)

$$5, 30, 33, 42, 36, 40, 1, 44, 29, 61, 82, 63, 29, 38, 6, 11$$

Make a box-and-whisker plot of these ages and determine if there is an outlier.

*12. Use the graphing calculator to determine the solution to the following system. (55)

$$x + y = -2$$
$$y = 4x - 7$$

13. **Multi-Step** Balls are printed in a pattern. Every 18th ball has stripes, every 15th ball
(57) has polka dots, and every 30th ball has stars.

   a. How many balls are printed before there is a ball that has stripes, polka dots, and stars?

   b. How many balls have been printed at that point that have only two of the designs?

14. (Building) Jason is building a square deck around his home. His home is also in
(60) the shape of a square. He wants the deck to be 9 feet wide around the outer edge
of his house. The house has a total side length of $8x$. Write a special product
and simplify to find the area of the house including the deck.

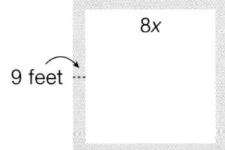

9 feet

15. (Golden Rectangle) The length of a golden rectangle is equal to $x + x\sqrt{5}$. If $x = \sqrt{5}$,
(61) what is the length of the golden rectangle?

16. **Multi-Step** The data below show the number of customers served each day for
(62) a month at a diner.

    80, 86, 105, 109, 127, 148, 137, 148, 141, 140, 135, 146, 90, 95, 101, 83,

       114, 148, 127, 86, 85, 91, 141, 136, 82, 148, 127, 149, 80, 86

   a. Create a stem-and-leaf plot of the data.

   b. **Analyze** Describe the distribution of the data. What conclusions can be drawn
from this?

17. Solve the following system using the elimination method.
(63)

$$-8x - 5y = -52$$
$$4x + 3y = 28$$

18. (Decibel Levels) The relationship between the intensity of sound (W/m²) and the
(64) distance from the source of the sound is represented by the equation $I = \frac{k}{d^2}$. If you
sit only 1 meter away from the stage at a rock concert, the intensity of sound is
about 0.1 W/m². If Vanessa does not want the sound intensity to be any more than
0.0001 W/m², how close to the stage can she sit?

*19. **Coordinate Geometry** Prove that $ABCD$ is a rectangle.
(65)

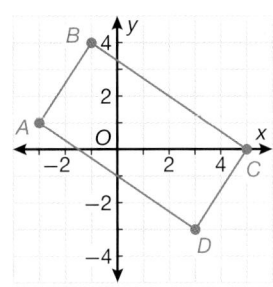

20. **Multiple Choice** Which one of the following systems has only one common
(67) solution?

   A $y = 21x + 6$ **B** $5x - 2y = 0$ **C** $-y = 13x - 6$ **D** $x - 7y = 14$

      $y = -7x$ $\frac{5}{2}x - y = 0$ $-2y = 26x + 9$ $\frac{1}{4}x - \frac{7}{4}y = \frac{7}{2}$

21. Write What kind of system is formed by two equations where one equation is a multiple of the other? Explain.
(67)

22. Error Analysis Two students found the probability of choosing either a black card or a face card from a deck of cards. Which student is correct? Explain the error.
(68)

Student A	Student B
$P(A \text{ or } B) = \frac{26}{52} + \frac{12}{52}$	$P(A \text{ or } B) = \frac{26}{52} + \frac{12}{52} - \frac{6}{52}$
$= \frac{38}{52}$	$= \frac{32}{52}$
$= \frac{19}{26}$	$= \frac{8}{13}$

*23. (Fantasy Football) In fantasy football, virtual teams are built by choosing from a pool of real players. In one pool of players, 72 play only defense, 65 play only offense, 8 play both, and 27 are on special teams. If at least one player must be chosen at random, what is the probability that the player will play either offense or special teams?
(68)

24. Geometry One side of a square measures $2\sqrt{9}$ meters. What is its perimeter?
(69)

*25. What must be true about the coefficient of a linear function if that function experiences a vertical compression of the parent function?
(Inv 6)

26. Multi-Step A flag displayed in the school measures $6\sqrt{4}$ feet by $5\sqrt{4}$ feet. If the school decides to display 8 flags, what is the total measurement of the sides of all the flags?
(69)

*27. Multiple Choice Which graph shows the solution set of $5f > -10$?
(70)

*28. Write Explain in your own words how to solve the inequality $-\frac{2}{5}g \le 6$.
(70)

*29. Analyze Kyle wants to spend at most $100 for birthday presents for the 4 other members of his family this year. He plans to spend the same amount on each person. Write and solve an inequality to represent the situation. What restrictions exist on the solution set?
(70)

*30. (Cooking) Marianna can afford to buy at most 20 pounds of ground turkey. Write and solve an inequality to determine the number of burgers she can make if each patty uses $\frac{1}{3}$ pound of ground turkey.
(70)

Comparing Direct and Inverse Variation

Many situations involve direct or inverse variation. The formula $d = r \cdot t$, which relates distance, speed, and time, can represent either direct or inverse variation depending on the variable that is held constant.

A direct variation is a relationship between two variables whose ratio is constant. The equation $y = kx$, where k is a nonzero constant called the constant of variation, shows direct variation between variables x and y.

Identify the constant of variation, given that y varies directly with x. Then write the equation of variation.

1. y is 10 when x is 2. **2.** y is 3 when x is 6.

The equation of direct variation can be written equivalently as $\frac{y}{x} = k$.

(**Distance**) Alex walks 3 miles per hour. If he walks at that rate for twice as long, he will travel twice as far. The ratio of the distance and time is always the same.

3. Identify the constant of variation.

4. Model Write an equation of direct variation that relates Alex's time to his distance traveled.

In inverse variation, when x increases, y decreases. An inverse variation describes a relationship between two variables whose product is a constant. The equation $xy = k$, where k is a nonzero constant, defines an inverse variation between x and y.

Identify the constant of variation, given that y varies inversely with x. Then write the equation of variation.

5. y is 1 when x is 3. **6.** y is 4 when x is $\frac{1}{2}$.

The equation of inverse variation can be written equivalently as $y = \frac{k}{x}$.

Notice the difference between the equations for inverse and direct variation. Inverse variation is the quotient of k and x, whereas direct variation is the product of k and x.

(**Rate**) Alex lives 4 miles from school. If he walks at a slower rate than normal, it will take him longer to reach his destination. In other words, the more time he spends walking home, the slower he is actually walking. This situation represents inverse variation.

7. Identify the constant of variation.

8. Model Write an equation of inverse variation that relates Alex's time to his rate of speed.

Graph the functions on a graphing calculator and complete the table.

	Direct or Inverse Variation	Linear or Not Linear	x– Intercept
9. $y = 3x$			
10. $y = x$			

11. What are the differences between the graph of a direct variation and an inverse variation?

Math Reasoning

Analyze Why will the graph of the inverse function never reach the x-axis as x increases?

Formulate Make a graph to determine whether the data show variation. If so, indicate the type of variation and write an equation of variation.

12. The table shows the force F, in Newtons, needed to move a rock a distance d, in meters, along the ground.

Distance	1	2	3	4	5
Force	600	300	200	150	120

13. The table shows an employee's pay p per number of hours worked h.

Hours Worked (h)	1	2	3	4	5
Pay (p)	$8.50	$17.00	$25.50	$34.00	$42.50

Investigation Practice

Identify the constant of variation. Then write the equation of variation.

a. y varies directly with x; $y = 14$ when $x = 2$.

b. w varies inversely with z; $w = -8$ when $z = 3$.

c. A recipe calls for 3 tomatoes to make 9 servings of salsa. Write an equation of variation where t represents the number of tomatoes and s represents the number of salsa servings. If Alex has 5 tomatoes, how many servings can he make?

d. The table compares the pressure P in atmospheres to the volume of oxygen V in liters at 0°C. Make a graph to determine whether the data show direct or inverse variation. If so, find the equation of variation.

Pressure	25	50	100	200	500
Volume	2.80	1.40	0.70	0.35	0.14

Finding the Line of Best Fit

Graphing Calculator Lab (*Use with Lesson 71*)

A graphing calculator is often the easiest and most accurate method for making a scatter plot from a data set and then finding the equation of the line of best fit.

The following table gives the total number *y* in billions of movie admissions for *x* years after 1993.

Year (*x*)	1	2	3	4	5	6	7	8	9	10
Admissions (*y*)	1.29	1.26	1.34	1.39	1.48	1.47	1.42	1.49	1.63	1.57

Find a line of best fit for the data. According to the model, about how many billion movie admissions were there in 2004 ($x = 11$)?

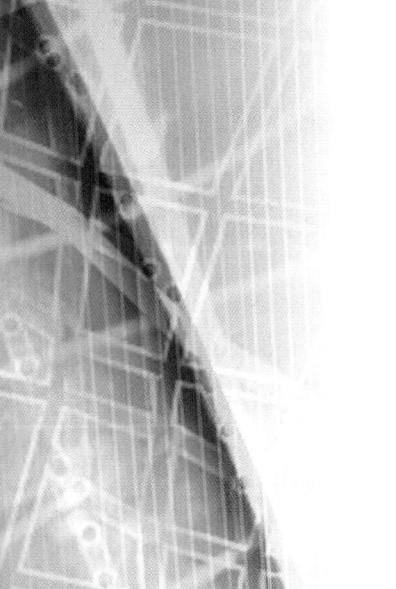
1. Press **STAT** and choose **1:Edit.** Clear any old data by pressing the ⬆ key until the list name is selected. Press **CLEAR** and then **ENTER**.

2. Enter the *x*-values as L1. Use the ▶ key to move to the next column and enter the *y*-values as L2.

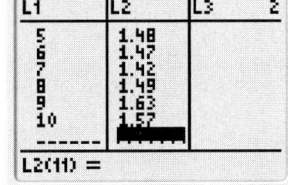

3. Press **2nd** **Y=** (STAT PLOT) and select **1:Plot1...** to open the plot setup menu.

4. Press **ENTER** to turn **Plot1 On.** Then press the ⬇ key once and then **ENTER** to select the first **Type**.

5. The default settings for **Xlist:** and **Ylist:** are L1 and L2, respectively. If these are not the current settings, then move the cursor next to **Xlist:**. Press **2nd** **STAT**. Select the list of independent variables, **1:L1.** To change the **Ylist:** setting, press **2nd** **STAT** and select **2:L2,** the list of dependent variables.

6. Create a scatter plot by pressing **ZOOM** and selecting **9:ZoomStat.**

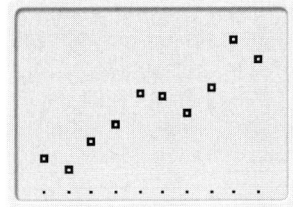

7. Find the linear regression for the scatter plot. Press **STAT** and the ▶ key to highlight the **CALC** menu. Select **4:LinReg(ax+b).**

8. Set the parameters for the linear regression. Press **2nd** **STAT** (LIST) and choose **1:L1.** Then press **,** **2nd** **STAT** (LIST) and choose **2:L2.**

9. To view the line of best fit with the scatter plot, press **,** **VARS** and the ▶ key to highlight Y-VARS. Then press **ENTER** twice to select Y1 as the destination for the equation.

10. Press **ENTER**. To write the equation of the line of best fit, the values of a and b are 0.036 and 1.236, respectively. The equation for the line of best fit is $y = 0.036x + 1.236$.

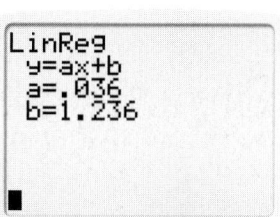

11. Press **GRAPH** to view the line of best fit with the scatter plot.

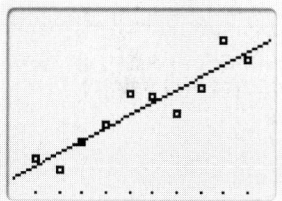

12. Predict the value of y when $x = 11$. Since $x = 11$ is outside the viewing window, press **WINDOW** and the ▼ key and type **11.**

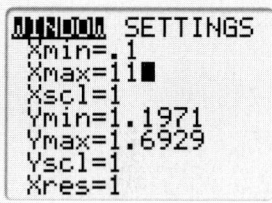

13. Press **2nd** **TRACE** (CALC) and select **1:value.** Type **11** and press **ENTER**. When $x = 11$, the value of y is 1.632.

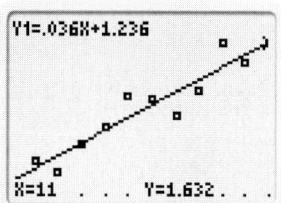

Therefore, according to the line of best fit, there would be about 1.632 billion movie admissions in the year 2004.

Lab Practice

The table gives solar energy cell capacity y in megawatts for x years after 1989. Use a graphing calculator to create a scatter plot and to graph the line of best fit for the data. What is an equation for the line of best fit? Use the model to predict the solar-energy cell capacity in 1996 ($x = 7$).

Year (x)	1	2	3	4	5	6
Capacity (y)	13.8	14.9	15.6	21.0	26.1	31.1

Making and Analyzing Scatter Plots

Warm Up

1. Vocabulary The constant m in the _____ form $y = mx + b$ is the slope of the line.
(49)

2. The equation of a line is $y = -2x + 6$. What is the slope of the line?
(49)

3. Write the equation $x - 2y = 4$ in slope-intercept form.
(49)

4. Write an equation in slope-intercept form for a line with slope $= \frac{3}{8}$ and y-intercept $= -4$.
(49)

New Concepts

One type of graph that relates two sets of data with plotted ordered pairs is called a **scatter plot.** Scatter plots are considered discrete graphs because their points are separate and disconnected. The points on scatter plots sometimes form a linear pattern. In these situations, a line can be drawn to model the pattern, which is called a trend line. A **trend line** is a line on a scatter plot, which shows the relationship between two sets of data.

Example 1 Graphing a Scatter Plot and a Trend Line

Use the data in the table.

x	1	2	3	4	5	6
y	4	10	12	18	23	29

a. Make a scatter plot of the data. Then draw a trend line on the scatter plot.

SOLUTION Plot the points on a coordinate plane. Then draw a straight line as near to as many of the points as possible.

b. Find an equation for the trend line.

SOLUTION Use two points on or near the trend line to write an equation for the line.

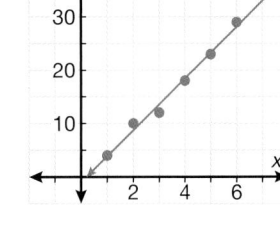

$$m = \frac{y_2 - y_1}{x_2 - x_1}$$

$$= \frac{29 - 4}{6 - 1}$$ Find the slope of the line; use (1, 4) and (6, 29).

$$= 5$$

$(y - y_1) = m(x - x_1)$ Write the equation for the line.

$(y - 4) = 5(x - 1)$ Substitute $m = 5$ and (1, 4) for (x_1, y_1).

$y = 5x - 1$ Solve for y.

> **Caution**
>
> A trend line does not have to go through any of the points on the scatter plot. It has to be drawn equally as close to one point as to another so that it models the approximate slope of the points.

> **Math Reasoning**
>
> **Predict** Using the table, the graph, or the equation from Example 1, what do you think would be a reasonable y-value for an x-value of 7?

> **Online Connection**
> www.SaxonMathResources.com

Trend lines may vary. However, a trend line that shows the linear relationship of a scatter plot the most accurately is called the line of best fit. The equation of the line of best fit can be calculated on a graphing calculator. The line of best fit is also referred to as the regression line.

Example 2   Calculating a Line of Best Fit

The table shows the averages for homework grades and test scores for nine students. Use a graphing calculator to find the equation of the line of best fit.

Homework Grades and Test Scores

Average Homework Grade	75	85	94	88	91	95	76	84	90
Average Test Scores	83	87	95	93	88	91	83	80	92

Graphing Calculator Tip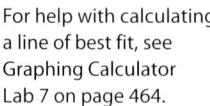

For help with calculating a line of best fit, see Graphing Calculator Lab 7 on page 464.

SOLUTION

Step 1: Enter the data into your graphing calculator by pressing `STAT` `ENTER` to EDIT the data. Enter the average homework grades into L1 and the average test scores into L2. Then return to the home screen.

Step 2: Calculate the equation for the line of best fit by pressing `STAT` ▶ to access the CALC menu. Then press `4` to choose LinReg $(ax + b)$. Type in L_1, L_2 and press `ENTER` to calculate the values used for writing the equation.

Hint

The calculator uses the variable a instead of m to represent the slope in the slope-intercept form of a line.

Step 3: Round the values for a and b to the nearest thousandth and write the equation for the line of best fit in slope-intercept form:
$y = 0.558x + 39.792$

Two sets of data may be related to each other. A correlation is a measure of the strength and direction of the association between data sets or variables. When the points tightly cluster in a linear pattern, then the correlation is strong.

Data can be positively correlated or negatively correlated. There is a positive correlation when the data values for both variables increase. There is a negative correlation when the data values for one variable increase while the data values for the other variable decrease.

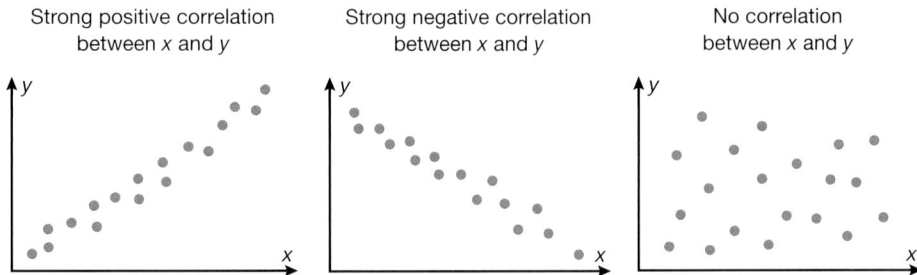

Strong positive correlation between x and y | Strong negative correlation between x and y | No correlation between x and y

The direction of the association can be determined for scatter plots that have correlation. If the slope of the trend line is positive, then there is a positive correlation between the data values. If the slope of the trend line is negative, then there is a negative correlation between the data values.

Factor each trinomial.

a. $x^2 + 3x + 2$
(Ex 1)

b. $x^2 - 10x + 16$
(Ex 1)

c. $x^2 + 4x - 12$
(Ex 2)

d. $x^2 - 5x - 36$
(Ex 2)

e. $x^2 + 9xy + 20y^2$
(Ex 3)

f. $x^2 - xy - 12y^2$
(Ex 3)

g. $12x + 20 + x^2$
(Ex 4)

h. $7x + x^2 - 44$
(Ex 4)

i. Evaluate $x^2 + x - 6$ and its factors for $x = 4$.
(Ex 5)

Practice   Distributed and Integrated

1. Solve the inequality $x + 2 + 3 > 6$. Then graph and check the solution.
(66)

Find the probability of the following events.

2. choosing a vowel or a consonant from the alphabet
(68)

3. rolling a sum that is a multiple of 4 or a set of doubles with two number cubes
(68)

Factor.

*4. $x^2 + 11x + 24$
(72)

*5. $k^2 - 3k - 40$
(72)

*6. $m^2 + 9m + 20$
(72)

*7. $x^2 + 33 + 14x$
(72)

*8. Error Analysis Two students are factoring the following trinomial. Which student is
(72) correct? Explain the error.

$$x^2 - 5x - 6$$

Student A	Student B
$(-6)(1) = -6$	$(-6)(-1) = -6$
$(-6) + 1 = -5$	$(-6) - (-1) = -5$
$x^2 - 5x - 6 = (x + 1)(x - 6)$	$x^2 - 5x - 6 = (x - 1)(x - 6)$

*9. (Baking) The area of the sheet-cake pans at a bakery are described by the trinomial
(72) $x^2 + 15x + 54$. What are the dimensions of a pan if $x = 11$?

*10. Analyze How many possible pairs of number factors does c have in the following
(72) trinomial?

$$x^2 + bx + 36$$

*11. Model These tiles represent the trinomial $x^2 + x - 6$.
₍₇₂₎

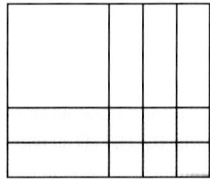

What does each of the shaded rectangles represent?

12. Make a scatter plot from the data in
₍₇₁₎ the table.

x	5	10	15	20	25	30
y	11	13	16	20	21	25

13. Error Analysis Two students are describing a trend line for a scatter plot but have
₍₇₁₎ different definitions. Which student is correct? Explain the error.

Student A	Student B
A trend line is a line on a scatter plot that goes through two data points and indicates a trend in the data.	A trend line is a line on a scatter plot that models the slope of the data points and indicates a trend in the data.

*14. Geometry Ten groups of students were given different circular objects. They
₍₇₁₎ measured the circumference and the diameter of the object. The table shows the results for each group.

Diameter (in.)	4	3.75	8	6.25	5.5	5	7	1.5	3	9
Circumference (in.)	12.1	12	25	19	16	16	21	4.5	9.5	28

a. Make a scatter plot of the data and draw a trend line.

b. Write an equation that models the data.

c. How does your equation compare to the formula for the circumference of a circle, $C = \pi d$?

15. Multi-Step Use the scatter plot.
₍₇₁₎
a. Use the trend line to estimate the corresponding y-value for an x-value of 18.

b. Use the trend line to estimate the x-value for a y-value of 50.

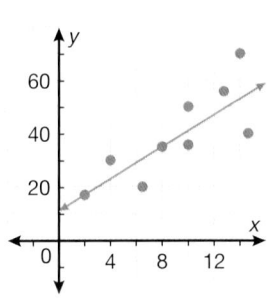

16. Write Can a perfect square have a negative square root? Explain.
₍₆₉₎

19. Multiple Choice A _____ is a graph made up of separate, disconnected points.
(71)
 A discrete graph **B** continuous graph **C** trend graph **D** linear graph

20. Determine if the inequality symbol in the expression $-\frac{2}{3}c \le 6$ needs to be
(70) reversed, and then solve.

21. If a square measures $\sqrt{144}$ inches on one side, what is the perimeter of the square?
(69)

22. Determine the probability of rolling a sum of 9 or an odd number with two
(68) number cubes.

23. Multi-Step The library charges a late fee based on the number of days a book is
(67) overdue. The equation for the fee is $y = \$0.25d + \$0.05$.
 a. What is the fee for a book that is 10 days overdue?

 b. Thirty days is the maximum number of days for which the library charges.
  What is the maximum amount the library charges?

 c. Classify the system of equations for the library fee and $y = \$7.55$.

24. Justify If a, b, x, and y are all greater than 0 and $x > a$ and $y < b$, how does
(66) $\frac{x}{y}$ compare to $\frac{a}{b}$? Justify your answer.

*25. Predict Use the trend line to predict the corresponding y-value for an x-value of 40.
(71)

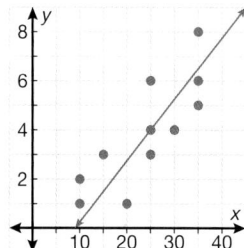

26. Justify True or False: The lines represented by $y = \frac{x}{4} - 2$ and $4y = x + 8$ are
(65) parallel. Explain.

27. (Construction) To build Ariane's house will take a constant number of individual
(64) work days. If a construction crew of 15 people can build the house in 20 days, how
many people does it take to finish the house in 5 days?

28. Multi-Step A container has a square base. The area is 800 cm^2. The size of a book is
(61) 25 cm by 30 cm. Can the book lie flat on the base of the container?
 a. Find the side length of the container.

 b. Compare the side length with the dimensions of the book.

 c. Use the comparison to determine if the book will fit.

29. Solve the system by substitution: $3x + y = 13$.
(59)
$$2x - 4y = 4$$

30. Sue purchases a rectangular billboard sign for her new business. The length can
(58) be represented by $6x^2 + 6x + 6$ and the width is $(x + 8)$. What is the area of Sue's
new billboard?

Factoring Trinomials: $ax^2 + bx + c$

Warm Up

1. Vocabulary A _____ is a polynomial with three terms.
(53)

Factor.

2. $x^2 + 3x - 10$
(72)

3. $x^2 - x - 42$
(72)

Simplify.

4. $(4x + 5)(3x - 2)$
(58)

5. $(2x + 5)^2$
(60)

New Concepts

Recall that a pattern is used when factoring trinomials of the form $x^2 + bx + c$. A pair of numbers is found whose product is c and whose sum is b. When a trinomial takes the form $ax^2 + bx + c$, the pattern no longer works. When the leading coefficient a is not equal to 1 another pattern emerges.

> **Example** **1**   **Factoring when b and c are Positive**
>
> Factor completely.
>
> $2x^2 + 7x + 5$
>
> **SOLUTION**
>
> Since $2x^2$ is the product of $(2x)$ and (x), write $(2x\quad)(x\quad)$.
>
> The third term of the trinomial, 5, is the product of the last terms in the binomials. List the pairs of numbers that result in a product of 5.
>
> $\qquad (1)(5) \qquad\qquad (5)(1) \qquad\qquad (-1)(-5) \qquad\qquad (-5)(-1)$
>
> Because the middle term, $7x$, is positive, eliminate the pairs of negative numbers. Check each of the other pairs to see which gives you $7x$.
>
> $(2x + 1)(x + 5) \qquad\qquad (2x + 5)(x + 1)$
>
> $\qquad\quad 1x \qquad\qquad\qquad\qquad\quad 5x$
>
> $\qquad \dfrac{+10x}{11x} \qquad\qquad\qquad \dfrac{+2x}{7x}$
>
> So, $2x^2 + 7x + 5 = (2x + 5)(x + 1)$.
>
> **Check** Use FOIL to "undo" the factoring.
>
> $(2x + 5)(x + 1) \overset{?}{=} 2x^2 + 2x + 5x + 5$
>
> $\qquad\qquad\qquad\quad = 2x^2 + 7x + 5 \; \checkmark$

Hint

When c is positive, the second term in both binomials will have the same sign (negative or positive) depending on the sign of b.

Online Connection
www.SaxonMathResources.com

Example 4 **Application: Carpeting**

Chavez wants to find the area of a rectangular throw rug. The rug has a side length of $8 + \sqrt{5}$ feet and a width of $2 + \sqrt{2}$ feet. What is the area of the rug?

SOLUTION

$$A = lw$$
$$= \left(8 + \sqrt{5}\right)\left(2 + \sqrt{2}\right)$$
$$= 16 + 8\sqrt{2} + 2\sqrt{5} + \sqrt{10}$$

The area of the rug is $\left(16 + 8\sqrt{2} + 2\sqrt{5} + \sqrt{10}\right)$ square feet.

Lesson Practice

Simplify. All variables represent non-negative real numbers.

a. $\sqrt{5}\sqrt{3}$
(Ex 1)

b. $3\sqrt{7} \cdot 2\sqrt{3}$
(Ex 1)

c. $\left(3\sqrt{6}\right)^2$
(Ex 1)

d. $3\sqrt{3x} \cdot \sqrt{2x}$
(Ex 1)

e. $\sqrt{7}\left(2 + \sqrt{4}\right)$
(Ex 2)

f. $\sqrt{5}\left(\sqrt{4} - \sqrt{3}\right)$
(Ex 2)

g. $\left(5 + \sqrt{9}\right)\left(4 - \sqrt{6}\right)$
(Ex 3)

h. $\left(4 - \sqrt{7}\right)^2$
(Ex 3)

i. The square dance floor at the local community building is being replaced. The floor's side length is $32 + \sqrt{13}$ feet. What is the area of the dance floor?
(Ex 4)

> **Caution**
>
> $\left(4 - \sqrt{7}\right)^2 \neq 16 + \sqrt{49}$
>
> Remember to either use the square of a binomial pattern, the Distributive Property, or the FOIL method when squaring a binomial.

Practice   Distributed and Integrated

Solve.

1. $\dfrac{5}{6} \leq -2p$
(70)

2. $|x + 4| = 5$
(74)

Factor.

3. $12x^2 - 25x + 7$
(75)

4. $x^2 + 10x - 39$
(72)

5. $5z^2 + 2z - 7$
(75)

6. $3x^2 + 25x - 18$
(75)

Simplify.

*7. $4\sqrt{3} \cdot 6\sqrt{6} \cdot 3\sqrt{3} \cdot 2\sqrt{2}$
(76)

8. $-17\sqrt{7s} - 4\sqrt{7s}$
(69)

*9. $\left(4\sqrt{5}\right)^2$
(76)

*10. $3\sqrt{2} \cdot 4\sqrt{12} - 6\sqrt{54}$
(76)

11. $\sqrt{\dfrac{x^3}{60}}$
(61)

12. Use mental math to find the product of $17 \cdot 23$.
(60)

*13. (City Parks) The City Works Department wants to build a new fence around the town's park. Write an expression for the area of the figure at right. Find the area.
(76)

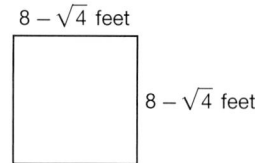

$8 - \sqrt{4}$ feet

$8 - \sqrt{4}$ feet

*14. Justify Explain how to find the product of $\sqrt{2}\left(\sqrt{3} - \sqrt{8}\right)$.
(76)

*15. Write Find two radical expressions that when multiplied together equal a perfect square.
(76)

*16. Multiple Choice Which expression is not equivalent to $\sqrt{48}$?
(76)
  A $\sqrt{3 \cdot 16}$ **B** $16\sqrt{3}$ **C** $\sqrt{4^2 \cdot 3}$ **D** $4\sqrt{3}$

17. (Vacation) The cost of a vacation, in dollars, is represented by the expression $46x^2 - 9x + 95$, where x is the number of nights. What is the cost of a 3-night vacation?
(9)

18. Error Analysis Two students factor $5x^2 - 6x - 8$. Which student is correct? Explain the error.
(75)

Student A	Student B
$(5x + 4)(x - 2)$	$(5x - 4)(x + 2)$

*19. Geometry The sum of the squares of the two legs of a right triangle is $16x^2 - 40x + 25$. Factor the expression, and then take the square root to find the expression that represents the length of the hypotenuse.
(75)

20. Multi-Step The area of a rectangular ottoman is represented by $2x^2 + 3x - 27$ square inches.
(75)
  a. Evaluate the expression for $x = 12$.
  b. Factor the expression completely.

21. Error Analysis Two students are solving $|3x| = 6$. Which student is correct? Explain the error.
(74)

Student A	Student B
$\begin{array}{ll} \multicolumn{2}{c}{|3x| = 6} \\ 3x = 6 & 3x = -6 \\ 3x - 3 = 6 - 3 & 3x - 3 = -6 - 3 \\ x = 3 & x = -9 \end{array}$ The solution set of $\|3x\| = 6$ is $\{6, -6\}$.	$\begin{array}{ll} \multicolumn{2}{c}{|3x| = 6} \\ 3x = 6 & 3x = -6 \\ \dfrac{3x}{3} = \dfrac{6}{3} & \dfrac{3x}{3} = \dfrac{-6}{3} \\ x = 2 & x = -2 \end{array}$ The solution set of $\|3x\| = 6$ is $\{2, -2\}$.

*22. (Household Security) A window guard is designed to be placed directly into windows that are 27 inches wide. The guard can be compressed or expanded with a tension spring to fit windows that are three inches narrower or wider than the standard width. Write and solve an absolute-value equation for the maximum and minimum width of windows in which the guard is designed to fit.
(74)

23. Multiple Choice Which inequality describes the graph?
(73)

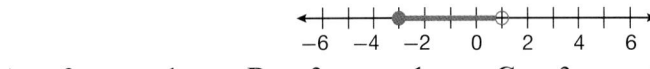

A $-3 < x < 1$ **B** $-3 \leq x < 1$ **C** $-3 < x \leq 1$ **D** $-3 \leq x \leq 1$

24. Analyze What are the solutions to the compound inequality $x > 3$ OR $x < 5$? Explain
(73) your answer.

*25. (Climate) The heat index displays apparent air temperatures in relation to the
(71) actual air temperature. The table shows the apparent air temperature for different
humidity levels given that the actual air temperature is 85°.

Humidity Level (percent)	10	20	30	40	50	60	70	80	90	100
Apparent Air Temperature (°F)	80	82	84	86	88	90	93	97	102	108

a. Use the data to make a scatter plot.

b. Do the data values show a positive correlation, a negative correlation, or
no correlation?

26. Data Analysis Use the values from the table to draw a scatter plot.
(71)

x	1	2	3	4	5	6
y	6	11	19	24	28	34

27. Analyze A book has 12 chapters about flying birds, 5 chapters about flying
(68) insects, 4 chapters about land insects, and 4 chapters about land mammals. If
the probability of picking a chapter about certain types of animals is $\frac{8}{25}$, what
type of animal is the chapter about?

28. Multi-Step A new exercise facility recently opened up. Its initial promotional rate
(67) for new members, represented by $y = \$20 + \$6x$, includes a monthly fee plus an
additional amount for x services.
a. How many services do new members receive before paying the same amount as
a regular fee of $32?

b. Write an equation describing the regular rate for the facility.

c. Classify the system of equations for the promotional and regular facility rates.

29. (Snowfall) In 1947, Mount Locke, Texas, had 23.5 inches of snow—its greatest yearly
(66) snowfall. The greatest monthly snowfall recorded was 20.5 inches, which occurred
in January, 1958. Since the record wasn't broken in 1958, how many more inches of
snow could Mount Locke, Texas, have had that year?

30. Multi-Step The sum of Kaleigh and Dwayne's ages is 30. Three times Kaleigh's
(63) age minus twice Dwayne's age equals 5. How old is César if he is five years
younger than Kaleigh?

Solving Two-Step and Multi-Step Inequalities

Warm Up

1. *Vocabulary* A(n) _____ is a mathematical statement with two
(21) equivalent expressions.

Solve and graph.

2. $x - \dfrac{1}{3} > 2$
(66)

3. $x + 2.1 < 4.3$
(66)

4. $\dfrac{1}{2}x \le -3$
(70)

5. $-5x \ge 10$
(70)

New Concepts

Two-step and multi-step inequalities require more than one inverse operation
to isolate the variable.

Reading Math

$<$ less than
$\le$ less than or equal to
$>$ greater than
$\ge$ greater than or equal to

> ### Example 1 Solving Two-Step Inequalities
>
> Solve each inequality and graph the solutions.
>
> **a.** $8m - 12 \le -36$
>
> **SOLUTION**
>
> $8m - 12 \le -36$
>
> $\qquad 8m \le -24$ Add 12 to both sides.
>
> $\qquad m \le -3$ Divide both sides by 8.
>
> To graph the solutions, place a closed circle on -3 and shade the number
> line to the left of the closed circle.
>
>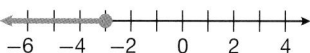
>
> **b.** $9 - 3m > 21$
>
> **SOLUTION**
>
> $9 - 3m > 21$
>
> $\qquad -3m > 12$ Subtract 9 from both sides.
>
> $\qquad m < -4$ Divide both sides by -3 and reverse the direction
> of the inequality sign.
>
> To graph the solutions, place an open circle on -4 and shade the number
> line to the left of the open circle.
>
>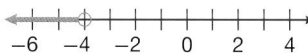

Math Reasoning

Write Why is an inequality graphed on a number line?

Before using inverse operations to isolate the variable, simplify each side
of an inequality. Simplify by using the order of operations, distributing,
combining like terms, or multiplying by the LCM of the denominators.

Example 2 Solving Multi-Step Inequalities

Solve each inequality and graph the solutions.

a. $-8 + (-11) < -7d - 12$

SOLUTION

$$-8 + (-11) < -7d - 12$$

$$-19 < -7d - 12 \qquad \text{Simplify the left side.}$$

$$-7 < -7d \qquad \text{Add 12 to both sides.}$$

$$1 > d \qquad \text{Divide both sides by } -7 \text{ and reverse the direction of the inequality sign.}$$

Place an open circle on 1. Shade the numbr line to the left of the circle.

b. $-6(4 - x) \geq -12^2$

SOLUTION

$$-6(4 - x) \geq -12^2$$

$$-24 + 6x \geq -144 \qquad \text{Simplify both sides.}$$

$$6x \geq -120 \qquad \text{Add 24 to both sides.}$$

$$x \geq -20 \qquad \text{Divide by 6.}$$

Place a closed circle on -20. Shade the number line to the right of the circle.

c. $\dfrac{3}{4}y + \dfrac{1}{2} < \dfrac{7}{10}$

SOLUTION

$$\frac{3}{4}y + \frac{1}{2} < \frac{7}{10}$$

$$\frac{3(\overset{5}{\cancel{20}})}{\cancel{4}}y + \frac{1(\overset{10}{\cancel{20}})}{\cancel{2}} < \frac{7(\overset{2}{\cancel{20}})}{\cancel{10}} \qquad \text{Multiply by the LCM, 20.}$$

$$15y + 10 < 14 \qquad \text{Simplify.}$$

$$15y < 4 \qquad \text{Subtract 10 from both sides.}$$

$$y < \frac{4}{15} \qquad \text{Divide both sides by 15.}$$

Since $\frac{4}{15}$ is a little less than $\frac{1}{3}$ the distance between 0 and 1, estimate that distance on the number line. Place an open circle on $\frac{4}{15}$. Then shade the number line to the left of the open circle.

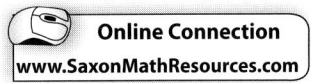

Online Connection
www.SaxonMathResources.com

Example 3   Application: Loans

A student borrows $55 from his parents. They agree to subtract $3 from the loan for each hour he works in the yard. To find the number of hours, x, he needs to work before he owes less than $30, solve the inequality $55 - 3x < 30$.

SOLUTION

$$55 - 3x < 30$$

$$-3x < -25 \qquad \text{Subtract 55 from both sides.}$$

$$x > \frac{25}{3} \qquad \text{Divide both sides by } -3.$$

$$x > 8\frac{1}{3} \qquad \text{Simplify.}$$

He must work more than $8\frac{1}{3}$ hours.

Caution

Remember to change the direction of the inequality symbol when multiplying or dividing both sides by a negative number.

Hint

Explain the meaning of the solution after solving a real-world problem.

Lesson Practice

Solve each inequality and graph the solutions.

a. $4x + 29 \le 25$
(Ex 1)

b. $-36 - 7k < 6$
(Ex 1)

c. $-18 + (-3) < -4f + 11$
(Ex 2)

d. $-5(10 - 5p) > (-10)^2$
(Ex 2)

e. $\frac{1}{12}y + \frac{2}{3} \ge \frac{5}{6}$
(Ex 2)

f. (**Athletics**) A student runs a quarter-mile in 180 seconds. She improves
(Ex 3) her time by 5 seconds each week. To find the number of weeks w needed for her time to be at most 150 seconds, solve the inequality $180 - 5t \le 150$.

Practice   Distributed and Integrated

Use the stem-and-leaf plot to find the following statistical measures.

1. Find the median.
(62)

2. Find the mode.
(62)

Average Milk Production

Stem	Leaves
3	5, 7
4	1, 6, 7, 7, 7, 8, 8, 9, 9
5	0, 2, 3, 6
6	1, 1

Key: 6 | 1 means 61 pounds

3. Factor the expression $6x^2 - 10x - 4$ completely.
(75)

4. Solve $9 > 0.3r$.
(70)

*5. Solve $5 + 4x > 37$, and then graph the solution.
(77)

Solve.

*6. $\dfrac{x}{-3} - 2 \le 1$
(77)

*7. $-3x + 2 \le 1$
(77)

*8. $\dfrac{x}{5} - 4 > 9$
(77)

9. $-5 < r - 6 < -2$
(73)

Simplify.

10. $4\sqrt{3}x\,\sqrt{4}x$
(76)

11. $\sqrt{400g^6}$
(61)

*12. **Generalize** Describe how solving inequalities is different from solving equations.
(77)

*13. **Multiple Choice** What is the solution to $6 - 7y < 48$?
(77)
   A $y < -6$ **B** $y > -6$ **C** $y > -48$ **D** $y < -48$

*14. (**Hobbies**) Building ships in a bottle is Jeff's favorite hobby. He has \$42 to purchase
(77) two ship kits and two bottles. Each ship kit is \$18. To find how much he can spend
on each bottle, solve the inequality $2(18) + 2b \le 42$.

15. (**Body Surface Area**) Physicians can estimate the body surface area of an adult
(76) (in square meters) using the formula $x = \sqrt{\dfrac{HW}{3125}}$ called BSA, where H is height in
inches and W is weight is pounds. Find the BSA of a person who is $\sqrt{5184}$ inches tall
and weighs $\sqrt{32{,}400}$ pounds. Round to the nearest whole number.

16. The brightness of a photograph is represented by the expression $12x^2 - 2x - 4$.
(75) Factor this expression completely.

17. **Error Analysis** Students were asked to find the product of $\sqrt{75} \cdot \sqrt{2}$. Which student is
(76) correct? Explain the error.

Student A	Student B
$\sqrt{75} \cdot \sqrt{2}$	$\sqrt{75} \cdot \sqrt{2}$
$\sqrt{150}$	$\sqrt{150}$
$5\sqrt{6}$	$5\sqrt{30}$

*18. **Multi-Step** A tsunami is a big ocean wave that can be caused by underwater
(76) volcanic eruptions, earthquakes, or hurricanes. The equation $S = \sqrt{g \cdot d}$ models
the speed of a tsunami, where g is the acceleration due to gravity, which is
9.8 meters/second^2, and where d is the depth of the ocean in meters.
   a. Suppose a tsunami begins in the ocean at a depth of 1000 meters. What is the
speed of the tsunami?
   b. Suppose a tsunami begins in the ocean at a depth of 2000 meters. What is the
speed of the tsunami?

*19. **Geometry** A triangle has a base of $3 + \sqrt{15}$ inches and a height of $5 - \sqrt{20}$ inches.
(76) Find the area.

20. **Error Analysis** Two students factor $15x^2 + 16x - 15$. Which student is correct? Explain
(75) the error.

	Student A		Student B
	$(3x + 5)(5x - 3)$		$(3x - 5)(5x + 3)$

21. **Multiple Choice** Solve $|x - 3| + 2 = 0$.
(74)
    A $\{5, 1\}$ **B** $\{4, -1\}$ **C** $\{1\}$ **D** $\varnothing$

22. **Write** Why is there no solution for the absolute-value equation $|x + 11| + 3 = 1$?
(74)

23. (**Weaving**) The area of rugs designed by a weaver are described by the trinomial
(72) $x^2 + 30x - 400$. What are the dimensions of a rug if x is 40?

24. State whether the data show a positive correlation, a negative correlation,
(71) or no correlation.

*25. **Measurement** A manufacturing company is making screws that have a
(73) width of 4 millimeters. Each screw must be made so that the actual width
is ± 0.03 millimeters of the desired width. Write a compound inequality to
represent this situation.

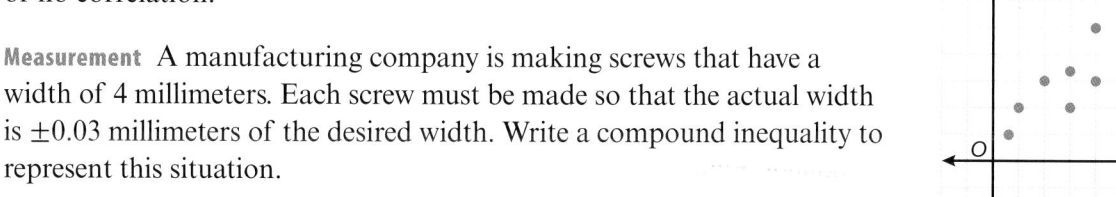

26. **Verify** Verify that $3gh\sqrt{275g^7h^9}$ can be simplified to $15g^4h^5\sqrt{11gh}$.
(69)

27. **Multi-Step** Gwynedd's piggy bank contains 57 quarters, 24 dimes, 35 nickels,
(68) and 60 pennies. Gwynedd turns her piggy bank over and one coin falls out.
What is the probability that the coin will be worth more than 5 cents?
a. What is the probability that the coin is a quarter or dime?

b. What is the probability that the coin is a quarter or worth more than 5 cents?

c. Explain how the previous two answers are related.

28. (**Cell Phones**) Two different cell phone service plans are represented by the given
(67) equations. Classify this system of equations.

$$p = 6x + 24$$
$$p = 8x + 20$$

29. **Multi-Step** Anya has a number of square bricks with a side length of 1 foot that
(64) she wants to use to create a rectangular patio in her backyard. At first, she
arranges them so the rectangle is 12 bricks long by 3 bricks wide, but then she
decides she does not like that arrangement. How can Anya arrange the bricks if
she would rather have a square-shaped patio?

30. **Error Analysis** Two students simplified the expression as shown. Which student is
(61) correct? Explain the error.

	Student A		Student B
	$\sqrt{80y^2z^2} = 16yz\sqrt{5}$		$\sqrt{80y^2z^2} = 4yz\sqrt{5}$

Graphing Rational Functions

Warm Up

1. **Vocabulary** A _____ expression is an expression where the
(39) denominator contains a variable and the value of the variable cannot
make the denominator equal to zero.

2. True or False: The graph of the equation $x = -2$ is a vertical line.
(30)

3. True or False: The graph of the equation $y = -x$ is a horizontal line.
(30)

4. Determine when the expression $\frac{x+7}{3x}$ is undefined.
(43)

New Concepts

A **rational function** is a function whose rule can be given as a rational
expression. This means that a rational function has a variable in the
denominator. Rational functions, like rational expressions, are undefined
when the denominator is equal to zero.

A value of a variable for which an expression or a function is undefined is
called an **excluded value.** For the function $y = \frac{7}{x+2}$, -2 is an excluded value;
this is because when $x = -2$, the function is undefined.

Example 1 Determining Excluded Values

Find the excluded values.

$$y = \frac{m-4}{3m-12}$$

SOLUTION

Simplify the denominator by factoring out the GCF.

$3m - 12 = 3(m - 4)$ The GCF is 3.

Set the denominator equal to zero and solve for m.

$3(m - 4) = 0$ Set the denominator equal to zero.

$\dfrac{3(m-4)}{3} = \dfrac{0}{3}$ Divide both sides by 3.

$m - 4 = 0$ Simplify.

$\underline{+4 \quad +4}$ Add 4 to both sides.

$m = 4$ Simplify.

The denominator equals zero when $m = 4$, so 4 is an excluded value.

$$m \neq 4$$

Math Reasoning

Verify Show that
$m = 4$ without factoring
out the GCF.

Reading Math

$x \neq 6$ is read, "x is not
equal to 6" or "x cannot
equal 6".

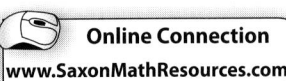
Online Connection
www.SaxonMathResources.com

Rational functions are discontinuous functions. **Discontinuous functions** are functions that have a break or jump in the graph. A break or jump in the graph can be due to an asymptote. An **asymptote** is a boundary line that the graph of a function approaches but never touches or crosses.

Caution

Students may draw asymptotes as solid lines. However, asymptotes are usually shown with dashed lines because asymptotes are not part of the graph of the rational function.

When a graph of a rational function has a vertical asymptote, then there is an excluded value for the function. To determine where vertical asymptotes occur, find the excluded values for the function. Rational functions also have horizontal asymptotes. When the function is in the form $y = \frac{a}{x-b} + c$, the vertical asymptote occurs at $x = b$ and the horizontal asymptote occurs at $y = c$.

Example 2 Determining Asymptotes

Identify the asymptotes.

(a.) $y = \dfrac{2}{x-8}$

SOLUTION

$$y = \frac{2}{x-8} \qquad \text{a rational function in the form } y = \frac{a}{x-b} + c,$$
$$\text{where } a = 2, b = 8, \text{ and } c = 0$$

Since $b = 8$, the equation of the vertical asymptote is $x = 8$.

Since $c = 0$, the equation of the horizontal asymptote is $y = 0$.

(b.) $y = \dfrac{4}{x+10} + 3$

SOLUTION

$$y = \frac{4}{x+10} + 3 \qquad \text{a rational function in the form } y = \frac{a}{x-b} + c,$$
$$\text{where } a = 4, b = -10, \text{ and } c = 3$$

$$y = \frac{4}{x - (-10)} + (3)$$

Since $b = -10$, the equation of the vertical asymptote is $x = -10$.

Since $c = 3$, the equation of the horizontal asymptote is $y = 3$.

Hint

When $c = 0$ in the rational function $y = \frac{a}{x-b} + c$, the horizontal asymptote is the x-axis.

Hint

Compare the equation of the given rational function to $y = \frac{a}{x-b} + c$ to determine the correct sign of the asymptotes.

The parent function for rational functions is $y = \frac{1}{x}$.

By identifying the asymptotes from the form $y = \frac{a}{x-b} + c$ and plotting a few points, the rational function can be graphed.

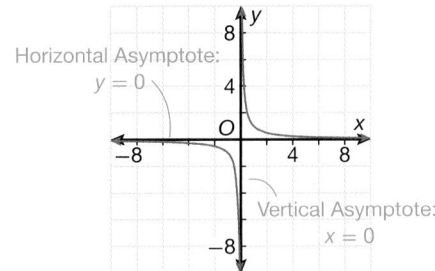

Example 3 **Graphing Using Asymptotes**

Identify the asymptotes and graph each function.

$$y = \frac{1}{x-4} - 2$$

SOLUTION

Step 1: Identify the vertical and horizontal asymptotes.

$$y = \frac{1}{x-4} - 2 \qquad a = 1, b = 4, \text{ and } c = -2$$

The equation of the vertical asymptote is $x = 4$.

The equation of the horizontal asymptote is $y = -2$.

Step 2: Graph the asymptotes using dashed lines.

Step 3: Make a table of values.

x	0	2	3	5	6
y	$-2\frac{1}{4}$	$-2\frac{1}{2}$	-3	-1	$-1\frac{1}{2}$

Step 4: Plot the points and connect them with smooth curves.

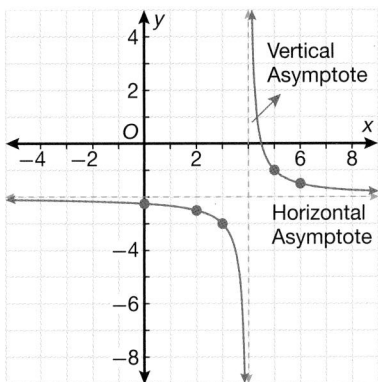

┌─ **Example 4** Application: Soccer

The Soccer Administration plans to have 64 regular players on a team. The players will be divided equally among the coaches. There will be one backup player placed on each team at the beginning of the season in addition to the regular players. The number of players on each team, y, is given by $y = \frac{64}{x} + 1$, where x is the number of coaches.

a. Determine the vertical and horizontal asymptotes of the function.

SOLUTION

$$y = \frac{64}{x} + 1 \qquad a = 64, b = 0, \text{ and } c = 1$$

The equation of the horizontal asymptote is $y = 1$.

The equation of the vertical asymptote is $x = 0$.

b. If there are 4 coaches, how many players will each team have?

SOLUTION

$$y = \frac{64}{x} + 1$$

$$y = \frac{64}{4} + 1 \qquad \text{Replace } x \text{ with 4.}$$

$$y = 17 \qquad \text{Divide 64 by 4 and then add } 16 + 1.$$

There will be 17 players on each team.

Hint

When a rational function has no value for b in $y = \frac{a}{x-b} + c$, the vertical asymptote is the y-axis or $x = 0$.

Lesson Practice

Find the excluded values.
(Ex 1)

a. $y = \dfrac{4}{6m}$

b. $y = \dfrac{6m}{m+2}$

c. $y = \dfrac{m-3}{4m-8}$

Identify the asymptotes.
(Ex 2)

d. $y = \dfrac{4}{x+1}$

e. $y = \dfrac{2}{x+7} + 6$

Identify the asymptotes and graph each function.

f. $y = \dfrac{6}{x+4}$
(Ex 3)

g. $y = \dfrac{1}{x-6} - 5.$
(Ex 3)

A golf instructor has a budget of \$5500 to buy new demonstration clubs. He will receive 5 free clubs when he places his order. The number of clubs, y, that he can buy is given by $y = \dfrac{5500}{x} + 5$, where x is the price per club.
(Ex 4)

h. Determine the vertical and horizontal asymptotes of the function.

i. If each club costs \$100, how many clubs will he receive?

Solve each system of linear equations.

1. $3x - 2y = 17$
(63)
$-4x - 3y = 17$

2. $y = 2x + 4$
(63)
$-x - 3y = 9$

Factor.

3. $x^2 + 10xy + 21y^2$
(72)

4. $-30 - 13x + x^2$
(72)

***5.** Find the excluded values for $y = \frac{4}{7m}$.
(78)

***6.** Find the excluded values for $y = \frac{m - 2}{3m + 9}$.
(78)

***7.** Find the vertical asymptote for $y = \frac{5}{x - 3} + \frac{2}{5}$.
(78)

8. Solve $3 - 9m < 30$ and graph the solution.
(77)

9. Use the Distributive Property to find the product of $5(\sqrt{4} + \sqrt{36})$.
(76)

***10.** (Awards) Jason plans to buy 20 prizes for the next school carnival and to divide
(78) them equally between the winners of the school trivia contest. There will also be
an additional 6 prizes given to each winner at the awards assembly. The number of
prizes for each winner, y, is given by $y = \frac{20}{x} + 6$, where x is the number of winners.
Find the asymptotes and graph the function.

***11. Verify** Show that the value $y = 5$ will not satisfy the function $y = \frac{1}{x} + 5$.
(78)

***12. Justify** What are the equations of the asymptotes in the graph of
(78)
$y = \frac{2.3}{x + 1.9} + 0.3$?

***13. Multiple Choice** What is the vertical asymptote for the rational function $y = \frac{6.1}{x + 1.5} + 3.1$?
(78)
    A $x = 3.1$ **B** $x = 1.5$

    C $x = -1.5$ **D** $x = 6.1$

***14.** (Budgeting) You have $30 to spend at the mall and your mother gives you an
(77) additional $15. You must buy a new shirt that is on sale for $12. You also would
like to purchase 3 CDs. To find the maximum amount you can spend on each CD,
solve the inequality $30 + 15 \geq 12 + 3c$.

15. Error Analysis Two students solve $8p - 7 \leq 3p + 18$. Which student is correct?
(77) Explain the error.

Student A	Student B
$8p - 7 \leq 3p + 18$	$8p - 7 \leq 3p + 18$
$5p - 7 \leq 18$	$-7 \leq -5p + 18$
$5p \leq 25$	$-25 \leq -5p$
$p \leq 5$	$5 \leq p$

16. Geometry The triangle inequality theorem states that the sum of any two sides of a
(77) triangle must be greater than the third side. A triangle has sides $4g + 10$, $3g - 13$,
and 46 as the longest side. Therefore, $(4g + 10) + (3g - 13) > 46$. Solve for g.

17. Multi-Step You can hike the trails at 2.5 miles per hour. You break for 1 hour to rest
(77) and eat lunch. You want to hike at least 15 miles. To find the number of hours you
will hike, solve the inequality $2.5(h - 1) \geq 15$.

18. Error Analysis Students were asked to find the product of $\sqrt{2}(7 + \sqrt{14})$. Which
(76) student is correct? Explain the error.

Student A	Student B
$\sqrt{2}(7 + \sqrt{14})$	$\sqrt{2}(7 + \sqrt{14})$
$\sqrt{14} + \sqrt{28}$	$7\sqrt{2} + \sqrt{28}$
$\sqrt{14} + 2\sqrt{7}$	$7\sqrt{2} + 2\sqrt{7}$

*19. (Art) Michael is submitting his first painting to the county fair art show. His
(76) painting has a side length of $7 + \sqrt{32}$ inches and a width of $9 + \sqrt{50}$ inches.
What is the area of Michael's painting?

20. Verify Show that $10x^2 - 11xy - 6y^2 = (2x - 3y)(5x + 2y)$.
(75)

21. Multiple Choice Which expression is the factored form of $20x^2 + 49x + 9$?
(75)
   A $(10x + 3)(2x + 3)$

   B $(20x + 3)(x + 3)$

   C $(5x + 1)(4x + 9)$

   D $(5x + 9)(4x + 1)$

22. Measurement The area of a rectangular tray is represented by $4x^2 - 16x + 16$
(75) square inches. Evaluate the expression for $x = -3$.

23. Solve $|n| = 12$.
(74)

24. (Dining) A restaurant offers discounted meals to children 12 years old and under or
(73) to senior citizens who are at least 65 years old. Write a compound inequality that
represents this situation.

25. State whether the data show a positive correlation, a negative correlation, or no
(71) correlation.

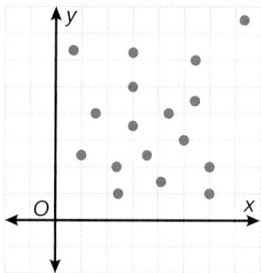

26. Verify Solve the inequality $\frac{n}{5} \leq -3$. Then select several values of n to substitute
(70) into the inequality to verify the answer.

27. Multi-Step The larger square has an area of $216x^2$ and the smaller square has an area
(69) of $125x^2$. What is the combined perimeter of the two squares?

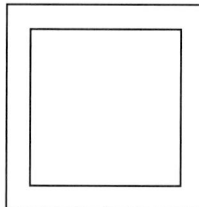

28. (**Game Play**) Derek is playing a board game with three number cubes. What is the
(68) probability of Derek rolling three of a kind or a sum that is an odd number?

29. Multiple Choice What slope would the line parallel to $3x - y = -3$ have?
(65)

  A $-\frac{1}{3}$ **B** $\frac{1}{3}$

  C 3   **D** -3

30. Create a histogram to display the following data representing average daily
(62) milk production (in gallons) of seventeen dairies: 49, 41, 50, 47, 35, 47, 61,
49, 60, 46, 53, 48, 37, 47, 56, 52, 48. Use 35–39 as the starting interval.

Factoring Trinomials by Using the GCF

Warm Up

1. **Vocabulary** A _____ is the sum or difference of monomials.
(53)

Factor.

2. $x^2 + 3x - 10$
(72)

3. $-13p + p^2 + 36$
(72)

4. $-11x - 21 + 2x^2$
(75)

5. $5x^2 - 13x - 6$
(75)

New Concepts

The terms of a polynomial that is factored completely will have no common factors other than 1. To factor completely, begin by factoring out the greatest common factor, or GCF.

Example **1** **Factoring Trinomials with Positive Leading Coefficients**

Factor completely.

a. $x^4 + 5x^3 + 6x^2$

SOLUTION

Find the GCF of the terms. In this case, x^2 is the GCF.

$x^4 + 5x^3 + 6x^3$

$x^2(x^2 + 5x + 6)$ Factor out the GCF.

Find two numbers that have a product of 6 and a sum of 5.

$2 \cdot 3 = 6$ and $2 + 3 = 5$

$x^2(x^2 + 5x + 6) = x^2(x + 2)(x + 3)$

So, $x^4 + 5x^3 + 6x^2 = x^2(x + 2)(x + 3)$.

b. $4x^3 - 4x^2 - 80x$

SOLUTION

The GCF of the terms is $4x$.

$4x^3 - 4x^2 - 80x$

$4x(x^2 - x - 20)$ Factor out the GCF.

Find two numbers that have a product of -20 and a sum of -1.

$4 \cdot -5 = -20$ and $4 + (-5) = -1$

$4x(x^2 - x - 20) = 4x(x + 4)(x - 5)$

So, $4x^3 - 4x^2 - 80x = 4x(x + 4)(x - 5)$.

When the leading coefficient is negative, factor out a -1.

> **Caution**
>
> Include the GCF in the final factored form. The factored form equals the original trinomial if its factors are multiplied.

> **Math Language**
>
> The **leading coefficient** is the coefficient of the term with the greatest degree.

Factor completely.

a. $p^5 + 13p^4 + 12p^3$
(Ex 1)

b. $6n^4 - 6n^3 - 12n^2$
(Ex 1)

c. $-r^2 + r + 30$
(Ex 2)

d. $-5d^3 - 25d^2 - 20d$
(Ex 2)

e. $y^3x + 3y^2x - 54yx$
(Ex 3)

f. $5bx^3 - 5bx^2 - 60bx$
(Ex 3)

g. $18fh - 240h + 6f^2h$
(Ex 4)

h. (**Construction**) A box is to be built in the shape of a rectangular prism. Its
(Ex 5) volume is represented by the expression $90x^3 + 450x^2 + 540x$. Factor the
expression completely.

Practice Distributed and Integrated

Assuming that y varies inversely as x, find the missing value.

1. If $y = 6$ and $x = 9$, what is y when $x = 12$?
(64)

Solve each system of linear equations.

2. $5x = 2y + 10$
(63)
$\quad -3y = -2x + 4$

3. $x - y = 2$
(63)
$\quad y + 2x = 1$

4. Solve the compound inequality $3b - 2 < -8$ OR $4b + 3 > 11$.
(73)

Factor.

5. $x^2 - 4x - 45$
(72)

*6. $k^4 + 6k^3 + 8k^2$
(79)

7. $5x^2 + 3x - 2$
(75)

*8. $2x^3 + 16x^2 + 30x$
(79)

*9. $abx^2 - 5abx - 24ab$
(79)

10. $15mx^2 + 9mx - 6m$
(79)

11. Find the excluded values for $y = \dfrac{9m}{m + 3}$.
(78)

12. Solve $16 + (-6) \geq 2(d + 4)$ and graph the solution.
(77)

*13. **Write** Can you factor out the GCF after factoring a trinomial?
(79)

*14. **Justify** When asked to factor $3x^2 + 45x + 132$, one student writes $3(x + 4)(x + 11)$.
(79) Another student writes $3(x + 11)(x + 4)$. Show that both answers are correct.
Explain your answer.

*15. **Multiple Choice** Which expression is factored completely?
(79)
A $2(5x - 10)(x - 5)$ **B** $10(x^2 - 7x + 10)$

C $5(2x - 4)(x - 5)$ **D** $10(x - 5)(x - 2)$

*16. **Physics** An object is thrown from inside a hole. Its height after x seconds
$^{(79)}$ is represented by the expression $-16x^2 + 32x - 16$. Factor the expression
completely.

17. **Error Analysis** Students were asked to find the vertical asymptote of the expression
$^{(78)}$ $y = \dfrac{1}{x+2} + 8$. Which student is correct? Explain the error.

Student A	Student B
$x = -2$	$y = 8$

*18. **Multi-Step** A band teacher has a budget of $50,000 to buy new instruments. He
$^{(78)}$ will receive 1 free instrument when he places his order. The number of
instruments, y, that he can get is given by $y = \dfrac{50,000}{x} + 1$, where x is the
price per instrument.
 a. What is the horizontal asymptote of this rational function?

 b. What is the vertical asymptote?

 c. If the price per instrument is $1000, how many instruments will he receive?

19. **Party Planning** A party planner has a budget of $1350.00 to buy a steak dinner for
$^{(78)}$ the entire guest list for a company retirement party. The planner will receive
15 free dinners when she places the order. The number of steak dinners, y, that the
planner can buy is given by $y = \dfrac{1350}{x} + 15$, where x is the price per steak dinner.
 a. What is the horizontal asymptote of this rational function?

 b. What is the vertical asymptote?

 c. If the price per dinner is $25, how many dinners will the planner receive?

*20. **Geometry** Write a rational function that shows the relationship between
$^{(78)}$ the side lengths of the similar triangles shown.

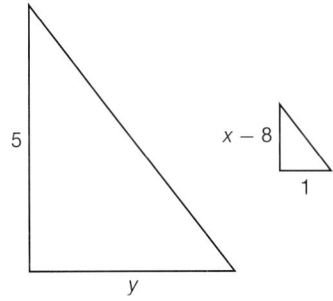

21. **Automotive Care** Steve's car is really dirty and is almost on empty. He has $20. A car
$^{(77)}$ wash is $7 and gas is $3 per gallon. To find how many gallons of gas he can buy with
a car wash, solve the inequality $7 + 3g \le 20$.

22. **Error Analysis** Two students solve $3h + 15 > 6$. Which student is correct? Explain
$^{(77)}$ the error.

Student A	Student B
$3h + 15 > 6$	$3h + 15 > 6$
$3h > -9$	$3h > -9$
$h < -3$	$h > -3$

23. **Write** Explain the process for multiplying binomials with radicals.
$^{(76)}$

24. Multiple Choice Between which two numbers does $\sqrt{124}$ fall on a number line?
  (76)
  A 9 and 11   **B** 8 and 11   **C** 12 and 14   **D** 11 and 13

25. Measurement Lou is building a square sandbox. The sandbox has a side length of
  (76) $6\sqrt{36}$ inches. What is the area of the sandbox?

26. (Fine Arts) In an antique shop, a painting is inclined on a display easel at an angle
  (74) of 65°. The angle of inclination can be increased or decreased by a maximum of 8°
  from the present setting by an adjustment screw. Write and solve an absolute-value
  equation for the maximum and minimum angles of inclination for the easel.

27. Write Describe the characteristics of the trend line for scatter plots with a positive
  (71) correlation, a negative correlation, and no correlation.

28. Multi-Step The video store charges $4.80 per rental of a DVD. The store spends
  (70) $5100 on expenses each month. How many videos does the store have to rent to
  make more money than it spends on expenses?
  a. What are the total expenses of the store?

  b. Write an inequality to show how many DVDs need to be rented to make a
  profit.

  c. Solve the inequality.

  d. How many DVDs need to be rented a month to make a profit?

29. (Sewing) Deandra wants to put trimming around a rectangular tablecloth that
  (69) measures $2\sqrt{49}$ feet by $\sqrt{81}$ feet. How many feet of trimming will Deandra need?

*30. Multi-Step A fitness center has a small elevator for members to use and to move
  (66) fitness equipment. The elevator has a maximum capacity of 750 pounds.
  a. Troy weighs 185 pounds. Write an inequality representing how much more
  weight the elevator can carry if Troy uses the elevator.

  b. Alicia needs to move weight equipment to the second floor. She has four
  75-pound weights, four 50-pound weights, four 25-pound weights, and six
  20-pound weights. Will she be able to bring all of the weights up in one elevator
  trip? Explain.

Calculating Frequency Distributions

Warm Up

1. **Vocabulary** A _____ is a value that describes the center of a data set
(48) and includes the mean, median, and mode.

Find the theoretical probability of each outcome.

2. flipping one coin and having it land tails up
(14)

3. randomly choosing a yellow marble from a bag of 3 yellow marbles and
(14) 7 blue marbles

4. rolling a 1 on a number cube labeled 1–6
(14)

5. randomly choosing the letter A from the letters in MATH
(14)

New Concepts

Discrete events have a finite number of outcomes. A **compound event** is an
event consisting of two or more simple events. A simple event could be
tossing heads on a coin. A compound event could be tossing heads and then
tails on a coin.

A **frequency distribution** shows the number of observations falling into
several ranges of data values. Tables, graphs, tree diagrams, and lists are used
to show frequency distributions.

> **Math Reasoning**
>
> **Analyze** Why is rolling cubes with a sum of 7 more likely than rolling any other sum?

Exploration **Displaying Frequency Distributions**

The likelihood of a particular sum when two number cubes are rolled, is
determined by the number of different sums that can be made with the two
cubes.

a. Make a table or tree diagram to show the different possible sums, or
outcomes.

b. Complete the table showing the probability of each sum, or outcome.

Sum	2	3	4	5	6	7	8	9	10	11	12
Probability											

> **Math Language**
>
> **Frequency** is how often something happens.

c. Roll two differently colored number cubes 50 times. Use a frequency
table to record the number of times each outcome occurs.

Sum	2	3	4	5	6	7	8	9	10	11	12
Frequency											

d. Use a bar graph to display your results.

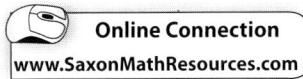

Online Connection
www.SaxonMathResources.com

e. Based on the theoretical probabilities you calculated, are your results
what you expected?

Example 1 Using Experimental Probability

A baseball player bats multiple times in a season. The table shows the results of each at bat. Make a bar graph that shows the frequency distribution of the data. Find the experimental probability of each outcome.

Out	Walk	Single	Double	Triple	Home Run
30	36	20	9	3	1

SOLUTION

Understand A player bats multiple times. Make a bar graph showing the number of times each outcome occurs. Then state the probability of each outcome.

Plan Calculate the total number of times at bat. Then find the probability of each outcome. Make a bar graph. Let each bar represent an outcome. The height of the bars will show the frequency of each outcome.

Solve The total number of times at bat is $30 + 36 + 20 + 9 + 3 + 1 = 99$.

$$P(\text{out}) = \frac{30}{99} = \frac{10}{33} \qquad\qquad P(\text{walk}) = \frac{36}{99} = \frac{4}{11}$$

$$P(\text{single}) = \frac{20}{99} \qquad\qquad P(\text{double}) = \frac{9}{99} = \frac{1}{11}$$

$$P(\text{triple}) = \frac{3}{99} = \frac{1}{33} \qquad\qquad P(\text{home run}) = \frac{1}{99}$$

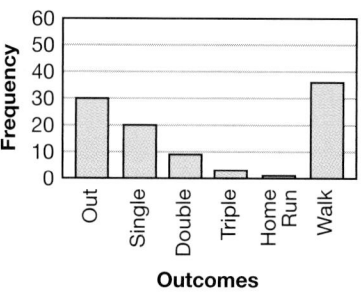

Results of At Bat

Check To check the probabilities, the numerators should match the data in the table. Each denominator is 99. Make sure fractions are reduced correctly.

To check the graph, make sure the heights of the bars match the data in the table. The sum of the heights of the bars should be 99, the total number of times at bat.

Hint

Probability is
number of favorable outcomes
÷ total number of outcomes.
Use this to write the ratio for each result. For example, for outs, write the ratio of 30 to 99 because the player was out 30 times in 99 at bats.

Caution

In a bar graph, the bars do not touch each other. All of the bars are the same width. Their heights may differ.

Example 2   Representing Data with a Table

A student spins the spinner and flips a fair coin.

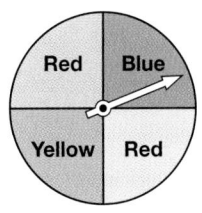

a. Make a table to show the possible outcomes in this experiment.

SOLUTION

The column headings are the possible colors for the spinner. Since there are two red sections on the spinner, there are two red columns.

The row headings are the possible sides of a coin, heads and tails.

The table is completed by recording all possible outcomes of a spin and a flip. Abbreviate the outcomes.

	Red	Blue	Red	Yellow
Heads	RH	BH	RH	YH
Tails	RT	BT	RT	YT

b. Find the theoretical probability of each possible outcome.

SOLUTION

The table shows that there are 8 possible outcomes.

$$P(\text{RH}) = \frac{2}{8} = \frac{1}{4} \qquad P(\text{BH}) = \frac{1}{8} \qquad P(\text{YH}) = \frac{1}{8}$$

$$P(\text{RT}) = \frac{2}{8} = \frac{1}{4} \qquad P(\text{BT}) = \frac{1}{8} \qquad P(\text{YT}) = \frac{1}{8}$$

Example 3   **Representing Data with a Graph**

Suppose that eleven cards each contain one letter from the word MISSISSIPPI.

a. Make a bar graph to represent the frequency distribution for all possible outcomes.

SOLUTION

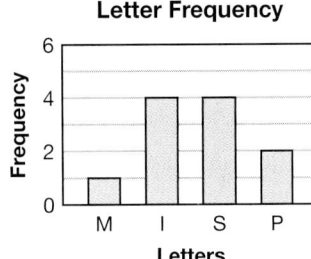

b. Find the theoretical probability of each outcome.

SOLUTION

$$P(\text{M}) = \frac{1}{11} \qquad P(\text{I}) = \frac{4}{11} \qquad P(\text{S}) = \frac{4}{11} \qquad P(\text{P}) = \frac{2}{11}$$

Math Language

A **fair coin** has an equally likely chance of coming up heads or tails on the toss of the coin.

Math Reasoning

Justify Why is the probability of spinning "red" $\frac{1}{2}$?

Reading Math

P(RH) is the probability of spinning "red" and landing on "heads."

Hint

Although some letters are on more than one card, there will be only one bar on the graph for each letter.

a. (**Bowling**) A man bowls five games. He keeps track of how many pins
(Ex 1) he knocks down on the first try of each turn. Make a bar graph that
shows the frequency distribution of the data. Find the experimental
probability of each outcome.

Number of Pins	0	1	2	3	4	5	6	7	8	9	10
Frequency	1	0	0	4	1	2	0	6	17	8	11

A student flips two coins.
(Ex 2)

    b. Make a table to show the possible outcomes in this experiment.

    c. Find the theoretical probability of each outcome.

**A toddler tears off the labels on several soup cans. There were 6 cans of
vegetable soup, 3 cans of tomato soup, 2 cans of potato soup, and 1 can of clam
chowder. One can is randomly chosen to open.**
(Ex 3)

    d. Make a bar graph to show the frequency distribution for all possible
outcomes.

    e. Find the theoretical probability of each outcome.

Practice   Distributed and Integrated

1. Write an equation for a line that passes through $(-1, 4)$ and is parallel to
(65) $2y + 10x = -36$.

Assuming that y varies inversely as x, find the missing value for each problem.

2. If $y = 108$ and $x = 3$, what is x when $y = 3$?
(64)

3. If $y = 56$ and $x = 7$, what is x when $y = 4$?
(64)

4. Find the horizontal asymptote: $y = \dfrac{7}{x+5}$.
(78)

5. Find the horizontal asymptote: $y = \dfrac{3}{2x+3} - 5$.
(78)

Solve.

6. $11|x| = 55$
(74)

7. $x - 5 \geq 0$ OR $x + 1 < -2$
(73)

Factor.

*8. $c^{12} + 11c^{11} + 24c^{10}$
(79)

9. $42x^4 + 77x^3 - 70x^2$
(79)

*10. $-3m^2 - 30m - 48$
(79)

*11. $(x-1)x^2 + 7x(x-1) + 10(x-1)$
(79)

*12. A student rolls a number cube, numbered 1−6, and spins the spinner.
Make a table of the possible outcomes.
₍₈₀₎

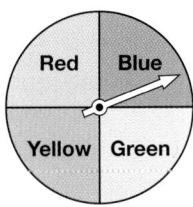

*13. Generalize Explain when you would choose a graph or a table to show a frequency distribution.
₍₈₀₎

14. Multiple Choice Which expression represents the probability of getting a 4 or 5 on three number cubes, numbered 1−6, and heads on four coins?
₍₈₀₎

A $P = \dfrac{4}{6} \cdot \dfrac{5}{6} \cdot \dfrac{4}{2}$ **B** $P = \dfrac{1}{6} \cdot \dfrac{1}{6} \cdot \dfrac{1}{2}$

C $P = \left(\dfrac{1}{6}\right)^2 \cdot \left(\dfrac{1}{2}\right)^4$ **D** $P = \left(\dfrac{1}{3}\right)^3 \cdot \left(\dfrac{1}{2}\right)^4$

*15. (**Chemistry**) Experiments in a chemistry lab either succeed or fail. They also can be characterized as chemical or physical reactions. Make a table to show all the possible outcomes.
₍₈₀₎

*16. Probability A bag contains 3 red marbles and 7 blue marbles. A marble is drawn and replaced. Use an equation to show the probability of drawing 3 red marbles in a row.
₍₈₀₎

17. (**Physics**) An object is thrown from a tower. The expression $-16x^2 + 32x + 48$ represents its height after x minutes. Factor this expression completely.
₍₇₉₎

18. Error Analysis Two students factor $2x^2 - 2x - 12$. Which student is correct? Explain the error.
₍₇₉₎

Student A	Student B
$(2x + 4)(x - 3)$	$2(x + 2)(x - 3)$

*19. Geometry A square has area $9m^4 - 54m^3 + 81m^2$ square inches. What is its side length?
₍₇₉₎

20. Multi-Step The volume of a rectangular cereal box is represented by the expression $3x^3 + 3x^2 - 18x$.
₍₇₉₎
  a. Factor the expression completely.

  b. What are the dimensions of the box?

21. Error Analysis Students were asked to find the excluded values for $\dfrac{5m}{m + 3}$. Which student is correct? Explain the error.
₍₇₈₎

Student A	Student B
$m + 3 \neq 0$	$m + 3 \neq 0$
$m \neq 3$	$m \neq -3$
$m \neq 3$	$m \neq -3$

*22. **Bakery** Erica plans to buy 100 cookies for the parent-teacher conference and
(78) to divide them equally among the number of parents attending. There will also
be an additional dozen cookies given to each parent at the end of school party.
The number of cookies for each parent, y, is given by $y = \frac{100}{x} + 12$, where x is
the number of parents. Find the asymptotes and graph the function.

23. **Analyze** Explain why you would not reverse the inequality sign for $6x < -42$ and
(77) why you would for $-6x < 42$.

24. **Multiple Choice** What is the solution to $5 - 3(2 - m) \geq 29$?
(77)   **A** $m \leq -10$ **B** $m \geq -10$ **C** $m \leq 10$ **D** $m \geq 10$

25. Use the Distributive Property to find the product of $\sqrt{4}(3 + \sqrt{6})$.
(76)

26. **Softball** The speed of a pitched ball is represented by the expression $9x^2 - 36x - 13$.
(75) Factor the expression completely.

27. **Justify** Why would you eliminate the factor pair $(5)(9z^2)$ in determining the
(72) binomial factors of $x^2 + 18xz + 45z^2$?

28. **Multi-Step** Use the table of values.
(71)

x	40	100	120	20	80	60
y	80	161	196	34	141	105

  a. Enter the data into a graphing calculator and find an equation for the line of
  best fit.

  b. How can you tell if there is a positive or negative correlation for the data from
  the equation?

29. **Real Estate** A realtor gets 6.5% commission for each house sold. Write and solve
(70) an inequality to find the house prices that will give the realtor a commission of at
least $20,000.

30. **Multi-Step** Two trains leave the rail yard at the same time. One travels east and the
(67) other west. The distance in miles traveled by the westbound train is $d = 40t + 12$.
The distance in miles traveled by the eastbound train is $\frac{1}{4}d = 10t + 3$.
  a. Classify these two equations.

  b. After a time of 10 hours, which train will have traveled farther?

Identifying and Writing Joint Variation

Joint variation occurs when a quantity varies directly as the product of two or more other quantities. When y varies jointly with a set of variables, y is directly proportional to each variable taken one at a time. For example, if $y = kxz$ where k is the constant of variation and $k \neq 0$, then y varies jointly with x and z.

The equation $b = 3ac$ is a joint variation in which b varies jointly with a and c. The table of values below illustrates the relationship between the variables. Use the table to complete the statements that follow.

a	b	c
1	3	1
2	6	1
1	6	2
2	12	2

1. Doubling a causes b to change by a factor of _____.

2. _____ c causes b to change by a factor of two.

3. The statements above are true because b is _____ proportional to a, and b is directly proportional to _____.

4. Doubling both _____ and _____ causes _____ to quadruple.

In each case, you must hold one variable constant to calculate changes in the other two variables.

If you know y varies jointly with x and z and also know one set of values, you can use the equation $y = kxz$ to find the equation of variation.

Suppose y varies jointly with x and z. Find y when $x = 8$ and $z = 3$, given that $y = 20$ when $x = 5$ and $z = 2$.

5. **Model** Set up an equation in the form $y = kxz$ using the given values.

6. What is the value of k?

7. Use the value of k to write an equation of joint variation that relates x, y, and z.

8. Find y when $x = 8$ and $z = 3$.

Online Connection
www.SaxonMathResources.com

Example 4 | Application: Dog Breeds

The table shows the average number of American Kennel Club registrations (rounded to the nearest 100) for Bernese mountain dogs and rottweilers.

American Kennel Club Registrations, 2002–2006

Breed	2006 Registrations	Average Yearly Change
Bernese Mountain Dogs	3700	300
Rottweilers	14,700	−1900

If the trend continues, in which year will the number of registered Bernese mountain dogs be equal to or exceed the number of registered rottweilers?

SOLUTION

Write an expression for the number of registered dogs for y years after 2006.

Bernese mountain dogs: $3700 + 300y$

rottweilers: $14,700 - 1900y$

$3700 + 300y \geq 14,700 - 1900y$	Write an inequality.
$3700 + 2200y \geq 14,700$	Add 1900y to both sides.
$2200y \geq 11,000$	Subtract 3700 from both sides.
$y \geq 5$	Divide both sides by 2200.

The solution $y \geq 5$ does not answer the question. The variable y represents the years after 2006.

$2006 + 5 = 2011$

If the trend continues, the number of Bernese mountain dogs registered will be equal to or exceed the number of rottweilers registered in 2011.

Math Reasoning

Analyze In the year 2011, how does the number of rottweilers compare to the number of Bernese mountain dogs? Explain.

Lesson Practice

Solve and graph each inequality.

a. $4x - 8 > -2x + 4$
(Ex 1)

b. $-\dfrac{3a}{5} + \dfrac{7}{10} \geq \dfrac{2a}{5} - \dfrac{9}{10}$
(Ex 1)

c. $4(x - 1) - 2x \leq 6 - 5(x + 2)$
(Ex 2)

Determine whether each inequality is always true, sometimes true, or never true. If it is sometimes true, identify the solution set.
(Ex 3)

d. $x + 5 + 3x > 4x + 19$

e. $x + 5 > x - 3$

f. The table shows the average number of cell phone minutes used by Ara and Lexi.
(Ex 4)

User	January Average	Average Change, January–May
Ara	4000	500
Lexi	12,000	−500

If the trend continues, in which month will Ara's average minutes be equal to or greater than Lexi's?

Factor completely.

1. $w^2 - 13w + 36$
(72)

2. $-q^2 + q + 42$
(79)

3. $30x^2 - 7xy - 2y^2$
(75)

4. $x^2 - 11 + 6x - 44$
(72)

Solve.

5. $|x - 3| = 14$
(74)

6. $|x + 4| = 7.5$
(74)

7. $-5 - \dfrac{n}{8} \geq -6$
(77)

8. $12 - 3d \leq -3$
(77)

Solve and graph. Then check the solution.

*9. $6v + 5 > -2v - 3$
(81)

10. $y + 4.5 < 10$
(66)

Write an equation for each of the lines described.

11. a line that passes through $(1, -2)$ and is perpendicular to $y = 2x + 6$
(65)

12. a line that passes through $(6, 5)$ and is parallel to $y = -x + 4$
(65)

13. Multi-Step To win a game, Alvaro needs to spin a black section or the number 10.
(68)

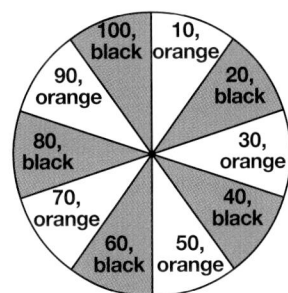

a. What is the probability of spinning a black section?

b. What is the probability of spinning a 10?

c. Are the events inclusive or mutually exclusive?

d. What is the probability of Alvaro hitting a black section or the number 10?

14. (Employment) The table below shows the number of people employed in the United
(71) States. Make a scatter plot of the data.

U.S. Employment (in millions)

Year	1970	1975	1980	1985	1990	1995	2000
Employment (in millions)	79	86	99	107	119	125	137

15. Verify Show that 2 is a solution of the compound inequality $x < 3$ OR $x > 6$.
(73)

16. (Gardening) Debra is planting a square garden. The side length is $8 + \sqrt{8}$ inches.
(76) Write an expression to find the area of the garden, and then find the area.

17. Measurement To find the values of x for which the triangle
(77) would have a perimeter of more than 81 units, solve the inequality
$x + (x + 13) + (2x + 12) > 81$.

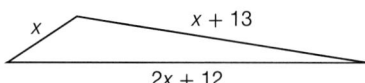

*18. Write How do changes to the value of b affect the graph of $y = \dfrac{a}{x - b} + c$?
(78)

*19. Two number cubes are rolled and their values are added. One number cube is
(80) labeled 1–6. The other has two of each of the numbers 1, 2, and 3. The possible
outcomes are displayed in the table.

What is the theoretical probability of each possible sum?

Cube 1

		1	2	3	4	5	6
Cube 2	**1**	2	3	4	5	6	7
	2	3	4	5	6	7	8
	3	4	5	6	7	8	9
	1	2	3	4	5	6	7
	2	3	4	5	6	7	8
	3	4	5	6	7	8	9

20. Multiple Choice What is the horizontal asymptote for the rational expression
(78) $y = \dfrac{7}{x - 2} + 4$?

   A $y = -2$ **B** $y = 4$ **C** $y = -4$ **D** $y = 7$

21. (**Football**) A football is kicked into the air. In the expression $-5t^2 + 25t - 30$,
(79) t represents the time when the ball is 30 feet in the air. Factor the expression
completely.

22. Error Analysis Two students factor $9m^2x^3 + 81mx^3 + 126x^3$. Which student is correct?
(79) Explain the error.

Student A	**Student B**
$9m^2x^3 + 81mx^3 + 126x^3$ $= 9x^3(m^2 + 9m + 14)$ $= 9x^3(m + 2)(m + 7)$	$9m^2x^3 + 81mx^3 + 126x^3$ The GCF is $9x^3$. Factor out $9x^3$. $m^2 + 9m + 14$ $= (m + 2)(m + 7)$

*23. (**Games**) Two number cubes are rolled and their values are added. Find the
(80) probability that the sum is less than or equal to 7.

*24. Geometry Students made five tetrahedrons, a three-dimensional figure with four
(80) triangular faces, and labeled the faces 1–4. Use an equation to find the probability
that all five tetrahedrons land on 3.

*25. Error Analysis Two students find the probability of rolling two number cubes and
(80) getting a sum less than 6. Which student is correct? Explain the error.

Student A	Student B
$\dfrac{10}{36} = \dfrac{5}{18}$	$\dfrac{15}{36} = \dfrac{5}{12}$

26. Multi-Step A game has two spinners. After spinning both spinners, the sum of the
(80) spins is found.

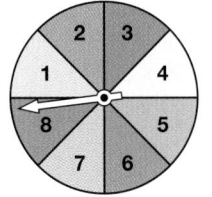 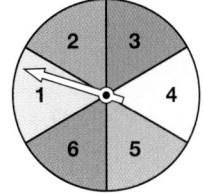

a. Make a table of all possible outcomes.

b. What is the probability that the sum is greater than 8?

*27. Multiple Choice What is the first step in solving the inequality
(81) $2(x + 5) > x + 12$?

A Combine the variables.

B Use the Addition Property of Inequality.

C Apply the Distributive Property.

D Use the Multiplication Property of Inequality.

*28. (Travel) A car rental company charges $40 a day with no additional mileage fees.
(81) Another company charges $24 each day plus $0.16 per mile. How many miles
would have to be driven in one day for the first company to offer the better deal?

*29. Write Explain how to solve the inequality $2x + 5 > -3(x - 15)$. Identify the
(81) solution.

*30. Estimate During their freshman year, Malcolm averaged 17.3 points per game
(81) and Frederico averaged 15.2 points per game. In their sophomore year, Malcolm
averaged 19.1 points per game and Frederico averaged 18.4 points per game.
If the trend continues, in which years will Frederico have a better average than
Malcolm?

Solving Multi-Step Compound Inequalities

Warm Up

1. **Vocabulary** A(n) _____ is made up of two inequalities combined
   (73) with the word *and* or *or*.

Solve each inequality.

2. $8x > 6x - 12$
   (81)

3. $-1 -(-7) \leq 3(y - 6)$
   (77)

4. $x - 2 < -7$ OR $2x \geq 11$
   (73)

5. **Multiple Choice** Which compound inequality is equivalent to $6 \leq -2x < 22$?
   (73)
   A $-11 < x \leq -3$ **B** $-11 > x \geq -3$

   C $8 \leq x < 24$ **D** $-24 < x \leq -8$

New Concepts

Inequalities can be solved in two or more steps using inverse operations. A compound inequality is made of two inequalities joined by the word AND or OR.

$$-2 < x \text{ AND } x \leq 5 \qquad x \leq -4 \text{ OR } x \geq 1$$

Hint

The term AND indicates that the solution must satisfy both inequalities. The term OR indicates that the solution must satisfy either inequality.

Example **1**   **Solving Multi-Step Compound Inequalities**

Solve and graph each inequality.

a. $4x - 7 < 3$ OR $2x - 19 > -7$

SOLUTION Isolate the variable in both inequalities.

$4x - 7 < 3$ OR $2x - 19 > -7$

$\underline{+7 \quad +7} \qquad \underline{+19 \quad +19}$ Addition Property of Inequality

$4x < 10$ OR $2x > 12$ Simplify.

$\dfrac{4x}{4} < \dfrac{10}{4}$ OR $\dfrac{2x}{2} > \dfrac{12}{2}$ Division Property of Inequality

$x < 2\dfrac{1}{2}$ OR $x > 6$ (number line: 0 1 2 3 4 5 6 7)

b. $-9 \leq 3x - 4 + 2x \leq 11$

SOLUTION Isolate the variable between the inequality signs.

$-9 \leq 3x - 4 + 2x \leq 11$

$\underline{+4} \qquad \underline{+4} \qquad \underline{+4}$ Addition Property of Inequality

$-5 \leq 3x + 2x \leq 15$ Simplify.

$\dfrac{-5}{5} \leq \dfrac{5x}{5} \leq \dfrac{15}{5}$ Division Property of Inequality

$-1 \leq x \leq 3$ (number line: -2 0 2 4)

Caution

Be sure to perform inverse operations on all three parts of the compound inequality.

Example 2 Simplifying Before Solving Inequalities

Solve the inequality. Justify each step.

a. $-15 \le 3(2x - 1) \le 39$

SOLUTION

$-15 \le 3(2x - 1) \le 39$	
$-15 \le 6x - 3 \le 39$	Distributive Property
$\underline{ +3 \qquad +3 \quad +3}$	Addition Property of Inequality
$-12 \le 6x \le 42$	Simplify.
$\frac{1}{6} \cdot -12 \le \frac{1}{6} \cdot 6x \le \frac{1}{6} \cdot 42$	Multiplication Property of Inequality
$-2 \le x \le 7$	Simplify.

b. $-12 \ge -6b - 18$ OR $-2(4 - b) \ge 10$

SOLUTION

$-12 \ge -6b - 18$ OR $-2(4 - b) \ge 10$	
$-12 \ge -6b - 18$ OR $-8 + 2b \ge 10$	Distributive Property
$\underline{+18 \qquad\quad +18 \qquad +8 \qquad\quad +8}$	Addition Property of Inequality
$6 \ge -6b$ OR $2b \ge 18$	Simplify.
$\frac{6}{-6} \le \frac{-6b}{-6}$ OR $\frac{2b}{2} \ge \frac{18}{2}$	Division Property of Inequality
$-1 \le b$ OR $b \ge 9$	Simplify.

Example 3 Application: Zoology

Zoologists randomly choose 5 zebras out of a herd of 20. Four zebras weigh 540 pounds, 550 pounds, 520 pounds, and 530 pounds, respectively. What could the weight of the fifth zebra be if the average weight of all 5 zebras is to be between 500 and 600 pounds?

SOLUTION Set up a compound inequality representing the situation and solve.

> **Hint**
>
> To find the mean (average) of a set of data, divide the sum of the data by the number of data in the set.

Minimum Weight	**Mean Weight**	**Maximum Weight**
greater than or equal to 500	$\dfrac{540 + 550 + 520 + 530 + x}{5}$	less than or equal to 600

$$500 \le \frac{540 + 550 + 520 + 530 + x}{5} \le 600$$

$$500 \cdot 5 \le \frac{2140 + x}{5} \cdot 5 \le 600 \cdot 5$$

$$2500 \le 2140 + x \le 3000$$
$$\underline{-2140 \quad -2140 \qquad\quad -2140}$$
$$360 \le x \le 860$$

The fifth zebra's weight could be between 360 lb and 860 lb, inclusive.

Online Connection
www.SaxonMathResources.com

Solve and graph each inequality.
(Ex 1)

   a. $2x + 9 < 8$ OR $3x + 3 > 12$.

   b. $24 \le 2x + 8 < 36$.

Solve the inequality. Justify each step.
(Ex 2)

   c. $6 \le 2(x + 12) < 12$

   d. $-16 > 2(x - 2)$ OR $27 < 3(x + 2)$

   e. Of 4 babies born in a hospital in 1 night, 3 have weights of 5.2 pounds,
(Ex 3)   6.3 pounds, and 7.5 pounds, respectively. What could be the weight of the fourth baby if the average of all their weights fall within 6 and 8 pounds?

Practice   Distributed and Integrated

Factor completely.

  1. $2x^2 + 9xy + 7y^2$
(75)

  2. $-4m^2 + 8mn + 5n^2$
(75)

Find the product.

  3. $\left(\sqrt{3} - 12\right)^2$
(76)

  4. $\left(2x + \sqrt{3}\right)\left(2x - \sqrt{3}\right)$
(76)

Find the excluded values.

  5. $\dfrac{m - 6}{2m - 10}$
(78)

  6. $\dfrac{y + 4}{-2y - 6}$
(78)

Solve the inequality. Then graph and check the solution.

  7. $2z - 6 \le z$
(66)

  8. Solve and graph $2x + 9 > -x + 18$.
(81)

Determine if the following systems of equations are consistent and independent, consistent and dependent, or inconsistent.

  9. $y = 10x - 2$
(67) $y = 10x + 8$

  10. $y = 3x$
(67) $2y = 6x$

11. Multi-Step The perimeter of a square area rug is 48 feet. What is the length of each
(69) side? Express your answer as a radical number.

12. (**Quilting**) A quilter uses a series of rectangular patterns to design quilt blocks. The
(72) area of the quilt block can be represented by the trinomial $(x^2 + 7x + 12)$ cm^2. If he plans a quilt block with x having a value of 20 centimeters, what is the dimension of the longer side of the block?

13. Multi-Step A real number is less than 12 or is greater than 15.
(73)
   a. Write a compound inequality that represents the situation.

   b. Graph the solution.

14. Estimate What is the lesser value of q in the solution set of $|q - 24.9| = 5.1$?
(74)

15. (Cell Phones) You pay $10 a month plus $0.30 per minute for your cell phone. You budget $20 each month for your bill. To find the maximum minutes you can use your phone, solve the inequality $10 + 0.3m \le 20$.
(77)

16. Probability Write a rational function that expresses the following probability. Find the probability y of randomly choosing a red marble out of a bag full of x number of marbles that contains only one red marble.
(78)

17. Verify Show that $-8u^5y + 56u^4y - 80u^3y = -8u^3y(u - 5)(u - 2)$.
(79)

18. Multiple Choice Which expression is the complete factored form of $3x^6 + 6x^5 - 45x^4$?
(79)

  A $3x^4(x - 3)(x + 5)$ **B** $x^4(3x - 9)(x + 5)$

  C $x^4(x - 3)(3x - 15)$ **D** $(3x - 9)(x^5 + 5x^4)$

*19. Use the graph to find the theoretical probability of receiving each grade.
(80)

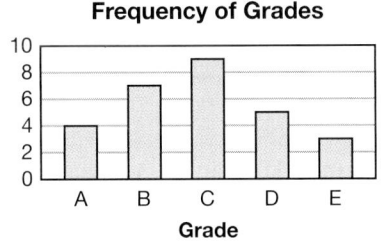

Frequency of Grades

20. (Biology) A Punnett square shows the probability distribution for genes. A short pea plant contributes two short genes, labeled "t." A tall pea plant contributes two tall genes, labeled "T." The plant will be short if it inherits the combination "tt." "TT" means the plant will be tall. The combination "Tt" also results in a tall plant. What is the probability that this plant will be short? Explain your answer.
(80)

	T	**T**
t	Tt	Tt
t	Tt	Tt

*21. Error Analysis Two students use an equation to find the probability of getting heads on four coins and rolling a 2 or 3 on two number cubes labeled 1–6. Which student is correct? Explain the error.
(80)

Student A	**Student B**
$P(4 \text{ heads and two 2 or 3}) =$	$P(4 \text{ heads and two 2 or 3}) =$
$\left(\dfrac{1}{2}\right)^4 \cdot \left(\dfrac{1}{6} \cdot \dfrac{1}{6}\right)^2 = \dfrac{1}{20{,}736}$	$\left(\dfrac{1}{2}\right)^4 \cdot \left(\dfrac{1}{3}\right)^2 = \dfrac{1}{144}$

*22. Multi-Step Veejay is throwing a party. It costs $75 to rent a skating arena plus $3 per person to rent skates. It costs $100 to rent a bowling alley plus $2 per person to rent bowling shoes. How many people would Veejay have to invite to his party for the bowling alley to cost more than the skating arena?
(81)

  a. Write an inequality to answer.

  b. Solve the inequality.

  c. Explain the correct domain of the solution set.

23. **(Music)** Amber normally listens to 1 new CD and 7 old CDs every day. She starts
(81) to listen to 2 more new CDs each day and 1 less old CD each day. How many days
will it take her to listen to more new CDs than old CDs?

*24. **Geometry** The length of a rectangle is greater than its width. The length is $4x + 7$
(81) and the width is $5x - 2$. What does the value of x have to be for this statement to
be true?

*25. **Error Analysis** Two students are told to write an inequality that is a contradiction.
(81) Which student is correct? Explain the error.

Student A	Student B
$-2 + x > x + 3$	$2x + 24 < 3x + 24$

*26. Solve the inequality. Justify your steps.
(82) $-17 > -2x - 7$ OR $27 > 3(x + 6)$

*27. **Multiple Choice** What is the solution to $32 < 7x + 11 < 39$?
(82) **A** $21 > x > 28$ **B** $3 < x > 4$

  C $3 < x < 4$ **D** $3 > x > 4$

*28. **(Cholesterol Levels)** An average level of HDL, a type of good cholesterol, for a
(82) person is usually no more than 60, and an unhealthy level is lower than 40.
A doctor sees 4 patients and tests their HDL levels. The first 3 levels are 45, 52,
and 60. What can the fourth patient's HDL level be if the average of all four
patients' levels fall in the average, but not unhealthy, range of levels?

*29. **Formulate** Half of Mr. Rubenstein's math class studied for the test and the other
(82) half did not. Everyone who studied for the test got a score no lower than 90;
everyone who did not study got a score lower than 70. Write the scores of the class
as an inequality.

*30. **Estimate** Felipe wants to earn a grade between 90 and 100 in math. There are
(82) 4 major tests over the year, which are averaged to determine his final grade. Felipe
scored 94, 88, and 91 on the first 3 tests. What must he score on the last test for his
average grade to fall between 90 and 100? Round his scores to solve.

Factoring Special Products

Warm Up

1. Vocabulary A trinomial that is the square of a binomial is
(60) called a(n) _____.

Factor.

2. $3x^4 - 12x$
(38)

3. $48y^2 + 16y^3 - 56y^5$
(38)

Multiply.

4. $(2b - 3)^2$
(60)

5. $(3x + 7)(3x - 7)$
(60)

New Concepts

Look for a pattern in the products.

Math Reasoning

Verify How can you check the products of these binomials?

$(x + 1)^2 = (x + 1)(x + 1) = x^2 + 2x + 1$ → $x^2 + 2 \cdot 1x + 1^2$

$(x + 2)^2 = (x + 2)(x + 2) = x^2 + 4x + 4$ → $x^2 + 2 \cdot 2x + 2^2$

$(x + 3)^2 = (x + 3)(x + 3) = x^2 + 6x + 9$ → $x^2 + 2 \cdot 3x + 3^2$

$(x - 1)^2 = (x - 1)(x - 1) = x^2 - 2x + 1$ → $x^2 - 2 \cdot 1x + (-1)^2$

$(x - 2)^2 = (x - 2)(x - 2) = x^2 - 4x + 4$ → $x^2 - 2 \cdot 2x + (-2)^2$

The pattern is:

Square the first term in the binomial.

Square the second term in the binomial.

Multiply the product of both terms by 2.

Recall that a perfect-square trinomial is a polynomial that is the square of a binomial. The trinomial has the form $a^2 + 2ab + b^2$ or $a^2 - 2ab + b^2$. When squaring binomials use the following patterns:

$$(a + b)^2 = a^2 + 2ab + b^2$$

$$(a - b)^2 = a^2 - 2ab + b^2$$

Use the same patterns to factor perfect-square trinomials.

Perfect-Square Trinomials
The factored form of a perfect-square trinomial is:
$a^2 + 2ab + b^2 = (a + b)^2$ **Example:** $x^2 + 12x + 36 = (x + 6)^2$
$a^2 - 2ab + b^2 = (a - b)^2$ **Example:** $x^2 - 12x + 36 = (x - 6)^2$

Online Connection
www.SaxonMathResources.com

Example 1 Factoring Perfect-Square Trinomials

Determine whether each polynomial is a perfect-square trinomial. If it is, factor the trinomial.

a. $x^2 + 6x + 9$

SOLUTION

$x^2 + 6x + 9$

$= x^2 + 2 \cdot 3x + 3^2$ Write in perfect-square trinomial form.

$= (x + 3)^2$ It is a perfect-square trinomial.

b. $x^2 - 2x + 4$

SOLUTION

$x^2 - 2x + 4$

$\neq x^2 - 2 \cdot 1x + 2^2$ This is not equivalent to the perfect-square trinomial form. It is not a perfect-square trinomial.

c. $36x^2 - 48x + 16$

SOLUTION

$36x^2 - 48x + 16$

$= 4(9x^2 - 12x + 4)$ Factor out 4.

$= 4[(3x)^2 - 2 \cdot (3x)(2) + 2^2]$ Write in perfect-square trinomial form.

$= 4(3x - 2)^2$ It is a perfect-square trinomial.

Example 2 Application: Cell Phone Towers

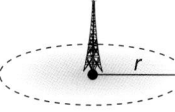

A cellular phone tower's signal covers a circular area with a radius r in miles. The strength of the signal is increased, and now covers an area of $\pi r^2 + 10\pi r + 25\pi$ square miles. By how much did the radius of the coverage area increase?

SOLUTION

Factor the expression for the new coverage area.

$\pi r^2 + 10\pi r + 25\pi$

$= \pi(r^2 + 10r + 25)$ Factor π out of the expression.

$= \pi(r^2 + 2 \cdot 5r + 5^2) = \pi(r + 5)^2$ Write in perfect-square trinomial form.

The radius of the new circle is $r + 5$.

The radius of the coverage area increased by 5 miles.

> **Hint**
>
> The original area covered by the phone tower signal was πr^2.

Look for a pattern in the products.

$$(x+1)(x-1) = x^2 - 1 \quad \longrightarrow \quad (x \cdot x) - 1x + 1x - (1 \cdot 1) = x^2 - 1^2$$
$$(x+2)(x-2) = x^2 - 4 \quad \longrightarrow \quad (x \cdot x) - 2x + 2x - (2 \cdot 2) = x^2 - 2^2$$
$$(x+3)(x-3) = x^2 - 9 \quad \longrightarrow \quad (x \cdot x) - 3x + 3x - (3 \cdot 3) = x^2 - 3^2$$
$$(a+b)(a-b) = a^2 - b^2 \quad \longrightarrow \quad (a \cdot a) - ab + ab - (b \cdot b) = a^2 - b^2$$

The pattern can be used to factor the difference of two squares.

Difference of Two Squares
The factored form of a difference of two squares is:
$a^2 - b^2 = (a+b)(a-b)$ **Example:** $x^2 - 49 = (x+7)(x-7)$

Example 3 Factoring the Difference of Two Squares

Determine whether each binomial is the difference of two squares. If so, factor the binomial.

a. $4x^2 - 25$

SOLUTION

$4x^2 - 25$

$= (2 \cdot 2)(x \cdot x) - (5 \cdot 5)$ Factor each term.

$= (2x)^2 - 5^2$ Write as a difference of two squares.

$= (2x + 5)(2x - 5)$ Factor.

b. $9m^4 - 16n^6$

SOLUTION

$9m^4 - 16n^6$

$= (3 \cdot 3)(m^2 \cdot m^2) - (4 \cdot 4)(n^3 \cdot n^3)$ Factor each term.

$= (3m^2)^2 - (4n^3)^2$ Write as a difference of two squares.

$= (3m^2 + 4n^3)(3m^2 - 4n^3)$ Factor.

c. $x^2 - 8$

SOLUTION

$x^2 - 8$

$= (x \cdot x) - (4 \cdot 2)$ Factor each term.

$= x^2 - 8$ This is not a difference of two squares.

d. $-64 + z^8$

SOLUTION

$-64 + z^8 = z^8 - 64$ Write terms in descending order.

$= (z^4 \cdot z^4) - (8 \cdot 8)$ Factor each term.

$= (z^4)^2 - 8^2$ Write as a difference of two squares.

$= (z^4 + 8)(z^4 - 8)$ Factor.

Hint

Use exponent rules.
$m^4 = m^{2+2} = m^2 \cdot m^2$
$n^6 = n^{3+3} = n^3 \cdot n^3$

Example 4 Application: Garden Planning

Ganesh is designing a square border around a square pond. The area of the pond is 225 square feet. Use the difference of two squares to write an expression that represents the area of the border.

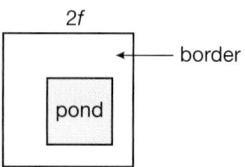

SOLUTION

Area of larger square:

$$A = lw$$
$$= (2f)(2f)$$

Area of pond:

$$A = lw$$
$$225 = (15)(15)$$

Find the difference between the area of the square surrounding the pond and the area of the pond.

$(2f)^2 - (15)^2$ Write as a difference of two squares.

$= (2f - 15)(2f + 15)$ Factor.

The area of the border is $(2f - 15)(2f + 15)$ ft².

Lesson Practice

Determine whether the polynomial is a perfect-square trinomial. If so, factor the trinomial.
(Ex 1)

a. $x^2 + 14x + 49$

b. $6n^4 - 12n^2 + 6$

c. $3g^2 + 9g + 9$

d. A radio tower's signal covers a circular area with a radius r in miles.
(Ex 2) The strength of the signal is increased, and now covers an area of $\pi r^2 + 12\pi r + 36\pi$ square miles. By how much did the radius of the coverage area increase?

Determine whether the binomial is the difference of two squares. If so, factor the binomial.
(Ex 3)

e. $25x^2 - 4$ **f.** $9b^2 - 100a^2$

g. $x^2 - 14$ **h.** $-81 + x^{10}$

i. A square border is designed around a square pool.
(Ex 4) Use the difference of two squares to write and factor an expression that represents the area of the border.

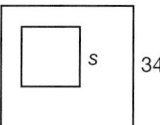

Find the product.

1. $(7 + \sqrt{6})(4 - \sqrt{9})$
(76)

2. $(x + \sqrt{12})(x - \sqrt{3})$
(76)

Solve.

*3. $\dfrac{-b}{4} + \dfrac{3}{8} \geq \dfrac{3b}{4} - \dfrac{5}{8}$
(81)

4. $11h + 9 \leq 5h - 21$
(81)

Factor completely.

5. $3x^5 - 3x^4 - 216x^3$
(79)

6. $-12x^3 - 48x$
(79)

Determine whether the polynomial is a perfect-square trinomial or a difference of two squares. Then factor the polynomial.

*7. $x^2 + 10x + 25$
(83)

*8. $x^2 + 12x + 36$
(83)

9. **Geometry** Show that TUV is a right triangle.
(65)

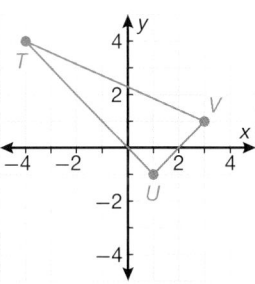

*10. **Analyze** The expression $-7x + 2y$ is one factor of a difference of two squares.
(83) What is the expanded polynomial?

11. **Hiking** Raul and his friends are hiking a 4-mile trail. After 2 hours of hiking,
(66) they turn off of the path to find a spot for lunch, and then hike back to the trail and continue to the end. Write an inequality to represent x, the total distance they hiked.

Determine if the following systems are consistent and independent, consistent and dependent, or inconsistent.

12. $y = 2x + 5$
(67) $y - 2x = 1$

13. $3y = 2x + 4$
(67) $3x = 4.5y - 6$

14. Find the probability of rolling a sum of 10 or a set of doubles with two
(68) number cubes.

15. **Multi-Step** The local bank offers a savings account with a 3% annual interest rate.
(70) Alfred wants to earn at least $60 in interest. How much should he deposit?

   a. Write an inequality to represent the situation.

   b. Solve the inequality.

   c. How much should he deposit?

   d. Graph the solution.

16. (Food Packaging) The label of a certain cheese states that it weighs 8 ounces. The
(73) actual weight of the product sold is allowed to be 0.2 ounces above or below that.
Write a compound inequality that represents this situation.

17. **Multi-Step** Solve $\frac{|x+3|}{4} = 6$.
(74)

   a. Isolate the absolute-value expression.

   b. Use the definition of absolute value to rewrite the absolute-value
   equation as two equations.

   c. What is the solution set?

18. **Generalize** Explain how you know if the second terms of binomial factors are
(75) both positive, both negative, or have opposite signs.

19. (Consumerism) A preschool has a budget of $1000 to buy new outside toys. They will
(78) receive 1 free toy when they place the order. The number of toys, y, that they can
get is given by $y = \frac{1000}{x} + 1$, where x is the price per toy.

   a. What is the horizontal asymptote of this rational function?

   b. What is the vertical asymptote?

   c. If the price per toy is $5, how many toys will they receive?

20. **Measurement** The length of the hypotenuse of a right triangle is found by adding
(79) the squares of the two legs and then taking the square root. The sum of the
squares of the legs is $16m^6 + 320m^5 + 1600m^4$. Find the length of the hypotenuse
by factoring.

21. **Verify** The table shows that the theoretical
(80) probability of landing on heads two times
when flipping two coins is $\frac{1}{4}$. Use an equation
to show that the probability is correct.

	Tails	Heads
Tails	TT	TH
Heads	HT	HH

22. **Multiple Choice** Using the table, what is the
(80) probability of rolling an even number and
spinning a yellow or a green?

   A $\frac{1}{3}$ **B** $\frac{1}{6}$

   C $\frac{1}{18}$ **D** $\frac{1}{1944}$

	Red	Yellow	Green
1	1R	1Y	1G
2	2R	2Y	2G
3	3R	3Y	3G
4	4R	4Y	4G
5	5R	5Y	5G
6	6R	6Y	6G

*23. **Write** Describe how factoring can help find $45^2 - 15^2$.
(83)

*24. Error Analysis Beth claims that the inequality $12x + 67 \geq 52 + 5x + 15$ is always
(81) true for any value of x. Is Beth correct? Explain the error.

25. (Finances) Chad works 20 hours each week. Juan works 10 hours and makes an
(81) additional $50 in tips each week. They both get paid the same amount per hour.
How much money do they each have to earn per hour for Chad to make more
money than Juan?

26. Error Analysis Two students solve the following compound inequality. Which
(82) student is correct? Explain the error.

Student A	Student B
$10 < -2x + 2 < 16$	$10 < -2x + 2 < 16$
$-4 < x < -7$	$-4 > x > -7$

*27. Multi-Step Yvonne learns that a refrigerator should be kept at a temperature of no
(82) more than 40°F but warmer than 32°F.
  a. Write an expression to show the possible range of proper refrigerator
  temperatures.

  b. Yvonne tests the temperatures of some refrigerators at an appliance store.
  The first 4 temperatures are 35°, 40°, 20°, and 45°. What should the last
  temperature be if the average of the temperatures is within the proper
  temperature range?

*28. Justify Solve the inequality $28 < 2(x + 3) < 42$ and justify each step.
(82)

*29. Multiple Choice Which expression is a perfect-square trinomial?
(83)
  A $9x^2 + 49$ **B** $64x^2 - 100$

  C $6x^2 + 48x - 96$ **D** $49x^2 - 28x + 4$

*30. (Home Improvement) A square storage shed sits in the corner of a square deck that
(83) has a side length of s feet. The shed has a side length of 8 feet. Harper wants to
apply a coat of paint to the deck. Write and factor an expression to find the area
of the deck Harper will paint, not including the storage shed.

Identifying Quadratic Functions

---

1. **Vocabulary** The equation $f(x) = 7x^2 - 3x + 1$ is written in _____
(25) (**expanded, function**) notation.

Evaluate.

2. $6x^3$ for $x = 2$
(9)

3. $x^2 - 4x + 3$ for $x = -3$
(9)

4. $500 - 7x^2$ for $x = -10$
(9)

5. **Multiple Choice** Solve $7x - y = 2 + 6x$ for y.
(29)

   A $y = \dfrac{7x - 2}{6}$ **B** $y = x - 2$ **C** $y = -x$ **D** $y = 13x + 2$

New Concepts A function pairs each value in the domain with exactly one value in the range. A **quadratic function** is a function that can be written in the form $f(x) = ax^2 + bx + c$, where a is not equal to 0. So, quadratic functions must have a quadratic term, but they may also have a linear and/or a constant term.

Math Language

The table shows ways to describe the **domain** and **range**.

Domain	Range
x-values	y-values
Independent variable	Dependent variable
x	$f(x)$

$$f(x) = ax^2 + bx + c, \text{ where } a \neq 0$$

quadratic term   linear term   constant term

All quadratic functions consist of a polynomial expression with a degree of exactly 2. The degree of a polynomial is the same as the term with the greatest degree. The polynomial can be named by its highest degree.

Polynomial	Degree	Name Using Degree
$3x + 2$	1	Linear
$x^2 + 4x - 5$	2	Quadratic
$2x^3 - x^2 + 1$	3	Cubic

A quadratic function can be written in many ways; however, there is a standard way to write a quadratic function.

Math Language

Quadratic comes from the Latin word *quadratus*, which means "square."

Standard Form of a Quadratic Function
The **standard form of a quadratic function** is $f(x) = ax^2 + bx + c$, where a, b, and c are real numbers and $a \neq 0$.

If a function cannot be written in the standard form of a quadratic function, then the function is not quadratic.

Example 1 Identifying Quadratic Functions

Determine whether each function represents a quadratic function.

a. $y + 7x = 4x^2 - 6$

SOLUTION

$y + 7x = 4x^2 - 6$

$y = 4x^2 - 7x - 6$ Solve for y.

It is a quadratic function because it can be written in the standard form of a quadratic equation.

b. $y = 5 + 2x$

SOLUTION

$y = 5 + 2x$

Since there is no quadratic term, it is not a quadratic function.

c. $-2x^3 + y = -5x^3 + x^2$

SOLUTION

$-2x^3 + y = -5x^3 + x^2$

$y = -3x^3 + x^2$ Add $2x^3$ to both sides.

Since there is a cubic term, it is not a quadratic function.

Math Reasoning

Write What type of function is related to the equation $y = 5 + 2x$? Describe the graph that represents the equation.

The graph of $f(x) = x^2$ is known as the quadratic parent function. Graph the parent function by making a table of values. Plot the points and connect them with a smooth U-shaped curve called a **parabola.**

x	-4	-2	0	2	4
y	16	4	0	4	16

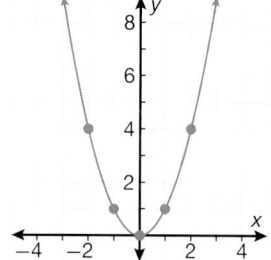

Math Reasoning

Analyze Compare the widths of the graphs representing $f(x) = x^2$ and $f(x) = -3x^2$.

Example 2 Graphing Quadratic Functions Using a Table

Use a table to graph the function.

$f(x) = -3x^2$

SOLUTION

Plot the points in a coordinate plane and draw a smooth curve through the points.

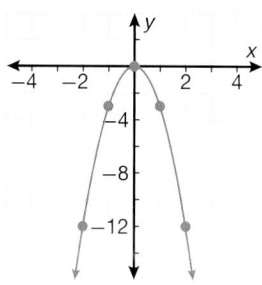

x	-2	-1	0	1	2
y	-12	-3	0	-3	-12

Online Connection
www.SaxonMathResources.com

The direction of a parabola can be determined by value of the coefficient of the quadratic term.

Direction of a Parabola
For a quadratic function in standard form, $y = ax^2 + bx + c$:
If $a < 0$, the parabola opens downward.
If $a > 0$, the parabola opens upward.

Example 3 **Determining the Direction of a Parabola**

Determine whether the graph of each function opens upward or downward.

a. $f(x) = 3x^2 + 8$

SOLUTION

$f(x) = 3x^2 + 8$ $\qquad a = 3$

The graph opens upward because $a > 0$.

b. $f(x) = 3x - x^2 + 5$

SOLUTION

$f(x) = 3x - x^2 + 5$

$f(x) = -x^2 + 3x + 5$ $\qquad$ Write in standard form.

Since $a = -1$, $a < 0$ and the graph opens downward.

Example 4 **Application: Free Fall**

A pebble is dropped from a 256-foot-tall cliff. The equation $256 - h = 16t^2$ can be used to find the height h of the pebble after falling for t seconds. Find the height of the pebble after falling for 2 seconds.

SOLUTION

Understand Determine the height of the pebble using the function

$256 - h = 16t^2$. Define the variables in the function.

$h =$ height in feet $\qquad t =$ time in seconds

Plan Solve the equation for height h, and then find h when $t = 2$.

Solve Solve the equation for height h.

$256 - h = 16t^2$

$\qquad h = -16t^2 + 256$

Find h when $t = 2$.

$h = -16t^2 + 256$

$\quad = -16(2)^2 + 256$

$\quad = 192$ feet

The height of the pebble after falling for 2 seconds is 192 feet.

Check Make a table of values. Choose positive values for the number of seconds t.

t	0	1	2	3	4
h	256	240	192	112	0

From the table the range is $0 \le h \le 256$ and the answer was 192 feet, so the answer is reasonable.

Lesson Practice

Determine whether each function represents a quadratic function.
(Ex 1)

a. $4 - y = x - 2x^2 - 3$

b. $x = -x^2 + y$

c. $4 = y$

Use a table of values to graph the function.
(Ex 2)

d. $f(x) = 4x^2 - 3$

x	-2	-1	0	1	2
y					

Determine whether the graph of each function opens upward or downward.
(Ex 3)

e. $f(x) = 2x^2 - 4$

f. $f(x) = 2x - 5x^2$

g. An acorn falls from a 16-foot-tall oak tree. The equation
(Ex 4) $h = -16t^2 + 16$ can be used to find the height h of the acorn after falling for t seconds. Find the height of the acorn after falling for 0.5 seconds.

Practice Distributed and Integrated

Determine whether the polynomial is a perfect-square trinomial or a difference of two squares. Then factor the polynomial.

1. $q^2 + 18q + 81$
(83)

*2. $36x^2 - 144$
(83)

Simplify.

3. $\sqrt{12} + \sqrt{48} - \sqrt{27}$
(69)

4. $\sqrt{18} + \sqrt{32} + \sqrt{50}$
(69)

Solve. Graph the solution.

5. $2p + 7 > p - 10$
(77)

6. $16 < 2x + 8$ OR $15 > 7x + 1$
(82)

*7. Rewrite $x + 15x^2 - y = 4$ in the standard form of a quadratic function, if
(84) possible.

Find the probability of the following events.

8. spinning a blue section or a letter *B*
(68)

9. spinning a gray section or a letter *D*
(68)

10. spinning a white section or a letter *C*
(68)

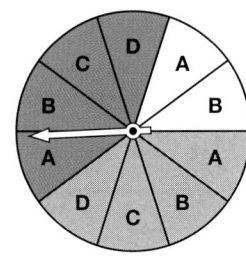

11. (Computer Electronics) The failure rate for desktop computers is 5% for the first year
(68) of use. For notebooks it is 15%. If you purchase both a new computer and a notebook, what is the probability that either one will fail in the first year?

12. Multi-Step Use the scatter plot.
(71)
  a. Using two points on the line, find an equation for the trend line.

  b. Does the graph show a positive correlation, a negative correlation, or no correlation?

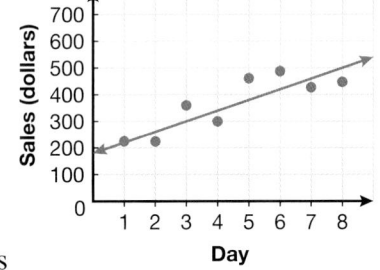

13. (Entertainment) People are often employed by amusement parks to
(74) predict the ages and weights of patrons. For a fee, one guesser claims she can predict a patron's weight within three pounds of the correct weight. If the guess is incorrect, the patron receives a prize. Write and solve an absolute-value equation for the maximum and minimum values of a correct guess for a person weighing 162 pounds.

14. Multi-Step The success rate on an exam is represented by $72x^2 - 156x + 72$.
(79)
  a. Evaluate the expression for $x = 2$.

  b. Factor the expression completely.

15. Verify Show that $\sqrt{14} \cdot \sqrt{21} = 7\sqrt{6}$.
(76)

16. Find the vertical asymptote: $y = \dfrac{1.6}{x + 2.5 + 7.8}$.
(78)

17. (Baseball) A pop fly is hit into the infield. In the expression $-5t^2 + 40t - 35$,
(79) t represents the time that the ball was 37 meters high. Factor the expression completely.

18. One student is selected from a school committee that has 12 seniors, 8 juniors,
(80) 10 sophomores, and 4 freshmen. Make a graph showing the frequency distribution.

19. Data Analysis Use the frequency distribution from the table to make a bar graph.
(80)

	Pasta Salad	Cucumber Salad	Caesar Salad	Carrot Salad
Number	12	16	22	10

*20. The value of *a* varies jointly with *b* and *c*. What is the constant of variation if
(Inv 8) $a = 18$, $b = 2$, and $c = 3$? Write an equation expressing the given relationship.

21. Model Graph the solution for $2(x + 9) - 14 > 3x + 7 + 2x$.
(81)

22. Multiple Choice What is the justification for subtracting 11 from all parts of the inequality $32 < 7x + 11 < 39$?
(82)

A Combine the variable.

B Addition Property of Inequality

C Distributive Property of Inequality

D Multiplication Property of Inequality

23. (Health Checks) A borderline unhealthy cholesterol level is between 200 and 240.
(82) Five patients come to the doctor with borderline cholesterol levels. The first 4 have levels of 210, 230, 225, and 235. What could the fifth patient's level be if the average of all the patients' levels are within the borderline unhealthy range?

*24. Error Analysis Ms. Cho asks two students to factor the polynomial only if it is a
(83) perfect-square trinomial. Which student is correct? Explain the error.

Student A	Student B
$x^2 + 8x - 16 = (x - 4)^2$	$x^2 + 8x - 16$ is not a perfect-square trinomial.

*25. Multi-Step A cylindrical thermos has a radius of r. Beneath the outer surface
(83) is an insulating layer. The volume, in cubic centimeters, that the thermos can hold is given by the expression $30\pi r^2 - 60\pi r + 30\pi$.

a. Factor the polynomial representing the volume of the thermos.

b. How thick is the insulating layer?

c. What is the height of the thermos?

Insulating Layer

*26. Geometry The surface area of a cube is given by the expression
(83) $6x^2 + 36x + 54$. What is the length of one side in terms of x?

*27. Multiple Choice Which function does the table of values
(84) represent?

x	-2	-1	0	1	2
y	6	6	4	0	-6

A $y = x + 8$

B $y = -x^2 + 12$

C $y = x^2 + 2$

D $y = -x^2 - 3x + 4$

*28. Formulate Write the equation of a function with degree 1 and of a function with
(84) degree 2.

*29. Generalize What is the relationship of the graph of $y = x^2$ to the graph of
(84) $y = -x^2$?

*30. (Water Fountains) A circular fountain sits in front of a city library. A pool of water
(84) surrounds a sculpture that sits on a circular platform in the middle. The radius of the sculpture is half the radius of the entire fountain. Write an equation to represent the area of the pool. Is the equation a quadratic function?

Solving Problems Using the Pythagorean Theorem

Warm Up

1. (13) **Vocabulary** The square of an integer is a _____ (*perfect square, radical expression*).

Simplify.

2. (13) $\sqrt{625}$ **3.** (13) $\sqrt{196}$ **4.** (61) $\sqrt{216}$

Estimate to the nearest tenth.

5. (13) $\sqrt{389}$

New Concepts

The Pythagorean Theorem states an important relationship among the lengths of the sides of any right triangle.

Math Language

The **hypotenuse** of a right triangle is the side opposite the right angle. The **legs** are the sides that form the right angle.

Pythagorean Theorem	
If a triangle is a right triangle with legs of lengths a and b and hypotenuse of length c, then $$a^2 + b^2 = c^2.$$	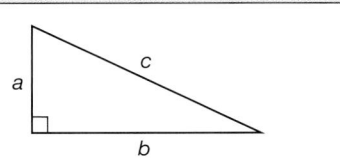

Exploration Justifying the Pythagorean Theorem

The legs of the four blue congruent triangles form a square. The gray quadrilateral is also a square.

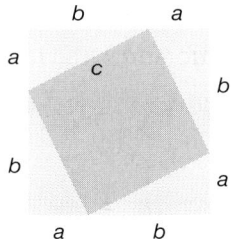

1. Explain why $(a + b)^2$ represents the area of the outer square formed by the blue triangles.

2. What area does the expression $\frac{1}{2}ab$ represent?

3. Write an algebraic expression for the area of the gray square.

4. Use the expressions from problems **1**, **2**, and **3** to translate the statement below into an equation.

Area of outer square = Area of 4 triangles + Area of gray square

5. Show that the equation you wrote in problem **4** simplifies to $a^2 + b^2 = c^2$.

Online Connection
www.SaxonMathResources.com

Example 1   Calculating Missing Side Lengths

Use the Pythagorean Theorem to find the missing side lengths.

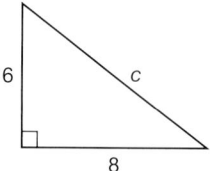

a. Find side length c.

SOLUTION

$a^2 + b^2 = c^2$	Pythagorean Theorem
$8^2 + 6^2 = c^2$	Substitute 8 for a and 6 for b.
$64 + 36 = c^2$	Simplify.
$100 = c^2$	Add.
$\sqrt{100} = c$	Take the square root of each side.
$10 = c$	Simplify. Because c is a length, c cannot be negative.

The side length c is 10.

b. Find side length t to the nearest tenth.

SOLUTION

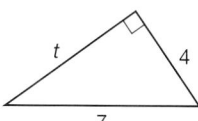

$a^2 + b^2 = c^2$	Pythagorean Theorem
$4^2 + t^2 = 7^2$	Substitute 4 for a, t for b, and 7 for c.
$16 + t^2 = 49$	Simplify.
$t^2 = 33$	Subtract 16 from each side.
$t = \sqrt{33}$	Take the positive square root of each side.
$t \approx 5.7$	Estimate; round to the nearest tenth.

c. Find side length k.

SOLUTION

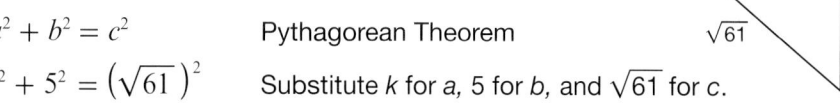

Hint

Recall that $(\sqrt{a})^2 = a$ for $a \geq 0$.

$a^2 + b^2 = c^2$	Pythagorean Theorem
$k^2 + 5^2 = \left(\sqrt{61}\right)^2$	Substitute k for a, 5 for b, and $\sqrt{61}$ for c.
$k^2 + 25 = 61$	Simplify.
$k^2 = 36$	Subtract 25 from each side.
$k = \sqrt{36}$	Take the positive square root of each side.
$k = 6$	Simplify.

d. Find side length m in simplest radical form.

SOLUTION

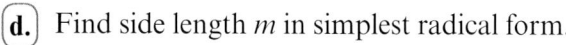

$a^2 + b^2 = c^2$	Pythagorean Theorem
$12^2 + 8^2 = m^2$	Substitute 12 for a, 8 for b, and m for c.
$208 = m^2$	Simplify the left side.
$\sqrt{208} = m$	Take the positive square root of each side.
$4\sqrt{13} = m$	Simplify the square root.

The **Converse of the Pythagorean Theorem** is also true; that is, if a triangle has side lengths a, b, and c that satisfy the equation $a^2 + b^2 = c^2$, then the triangle is a right triangle with legs of lengths a and b and hypotenuse of length c.

Pythagorean Triples

A **Pythagorean triple** is a group of three nonzero whole numbers a, b, and c that represent the lengths of the sides of a right triangle. Two triangles whose side lengths are Pythagorean triples are shown below.

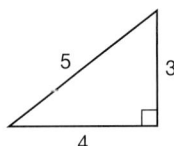 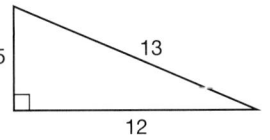

Example 2 Determining a Right Triangle

Determine whether the given side lengths form a Pythagorean triple.

a. 9, 40, 41

SOLUTION

Check whether 9, 40, and 41 satisfy the converse of the Pythagorean Theorem.

$$9^2 + 40^2 \overset{?}{=} 41^2 \qquad \text{Substitute 9, 40, and 41 into } a^2 + b^2 = c^2.$$
$$81 + 1600 \overset{?}{=} 1681 \qquad \text{Simplify.}$$
$$1681 = 1681 \;\checkmark \qquad \text{The equation is true.}$$

Because 9, 40, and 41 are three nonzero whole numbers that satisfy $a^2 + b^2 = c^2$, they form a Pythagorean triple.

b. 8, 10, 12

SOLUTION

Check whether 8, 10, and 12 satisfy the converse of the Pythagorean Theorem.

$$8^2 + 10^2 \overset{?}{=} 12^2 \qquad \text{Substitute 8, 10, and 12 into } a^2 + b^2 = c^2.$$
$$64 + 100 \overset{?}{=} 144 \qquad \text{Simplify.}$$
$$164 \neq 144 \qquad \text{The equation is false.}$$

Because 8, 10, and 12 do not satisfy $a^2 + b^2 = c^2$, they do not form a Pythagorean triple.

c. 7, 11, $\sqrt{170}$

SOLUTION

Because $\sqrt{170}$ is not a nonzero whole number, the lengths 7, 11, and $\sqrt{170}$ do not form a Pythagorean triple.

Hint

Remember that since the hypotenuse is the longest side, the greatest number is subsituted for c.

Math Reasoning

Verify Show that the lengths 7, 11, and $\sqrt{170}$ determine a right triangle, even though they do not form a Pythagorean triple.

Example 3 **Application: Length of a Ladder**

The ladder in the diagram satisfies the "1 in 4 rule," a rule of thumb for the safe use of ladders. This rule states that when the bottom of a ladder is positioned x feet from the base of a building, the top of the ladder should reach a point $4x$ feet off the ground. Find the length of the ladder in the diagram. Round your answer to the nearest tenth of a foot.

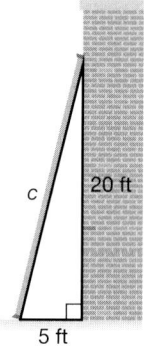

SOLUTION

The ladder is the hypotenuse of a right triangle. The lengths of the legs of the triangle are 5 feet and 20 feet. Use the Pythagorean Theorem to find the length c of the ladder.

$a^2 + b^2 = c^2$

$5^2 + 20^2 = c^2$ Substitute 5 for a and 20 for b.

$425 = c^2$ Simplify the left side.

$\sqrt{425} = c$ Take the positive square root of each side.

$5\sqrt{17} = c$ Simplify the square root.

$20.6 \approx c$ Estimate; round to the nearest tenth.

The length of the ladder is 20.6 feet.

Lesson Practice

Use the Pythagorean Theorem to find the missing side lengths.
(Ex. 1)

a. Find side length c.

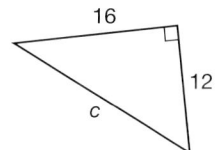

b. Find side length m to the nearest tenth.

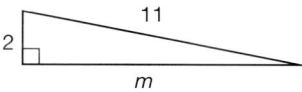

c. Find side length r.

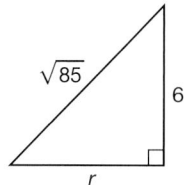

d. Find side length s in simplest radical form.

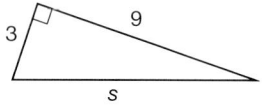

Determine whether the given side lengths form a Pythagorean triple.
(Ex. 2)

   e. $5, 9, 11$ **f.** $8, 15, 17$ **g.** $4, \sqrt{65}, 13$

   h. (**Length of a Ladder**) A ladder leaning against a building satisfies the "1 in
(Ex 3)   4 rule" for the safe use of ladders. The bottom of the ladder is 8 ft from
the base of the building. The top of the ladder touches the building
32 feet above the ground. Find the length of the ladder to the nearest
tenth.

Practice   Distributed and Integrated

Simplify.

  1. $3\sqrt{45} - \sqrt{5}$
(69)

  2. $\dfrac{p^{-1}}{w}\left(\dfrac{wx}{cp^{-2}q^{-4}} + 5pq^{-3}\right)$
(39)

Factor completely.

  3. $-3t^3 - 27t^2 - 24t$
(79)

  4. $4x^4 - 16x^2$
(79)

  5. $2x^2 + 14 - 9x - x^2$
(72)

Determine whether the polynomial is a perfect-square trinomial or a difference of two squares. Then factor the polynomial.

  6. $3g^2 - 12$
(83)

  7. $9x^2 - 24x + 16$
(83)

Write the equations in the standard form of a quadratic function, if possible.

  8. $4 + y = -8 + 16x$
(84)

  9. $y + x^2 = 3x^2 - 10x + 12$
(84)

Solve.

  10. $0.7 + 0.05y = 0.715$
(24)

  11. $\dfrac{1}{2} + \dfrac{3}{4}x = \dfrac{1}{6}x + 2$
(28)

  12. Find the solution of $-1.2x \geq -4.8$. Then graph the solution set.
(70)

  13. Write an equation for a line that passes through $(1, 5)$ and is parallel to $y = -3\frac{1}{2}x - 9$.
(65)

  14. (**Gardening**) Niko wants to build a fence around his garden. If his garden measures
(69) $2\sqrt{4}$ feet by $\sqrt{25}$ feet, how many feet of fencing does Niko need?

  15. Verify Show that the solution to $\dfrac{x}{-5} + 6 \leq 10$ is $x \geq -20$.
(77)

*16. Use the Pythagorean Theorem to find the missing side length. Give the answer in
(85) simplest radical form.

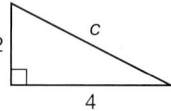

17. Find the vertical asymptote: $y = \dfrac{2.4}{x + 4.5} + 6.9$.
(78)

18. Given that y varies inversely with x, identify the constant of variation when
(Inv 7) $x = 4$ and $y = 2$.

19. Statistics In 2005 the population of North Dakota was about 635,000—a decrease
(81) of about 7000 from five years earlier. The population of Wyoming in 2005 was
509,000—an increase of about 15,000 from five years earlier. If this trend continues,
around what year will Wyoming's population exceed North Dakota's?

*20. (**Sail Dimensions**) A main sail can be modeled by a right triangle whose sides are
(85) called the leach edge, the luff edge, and the foot. If the luff edge measures 27.5 feet
and the foot measures 10 feet, use the Pythagorean Theorem to estimate the length
of the leach edge to the nearest foot.

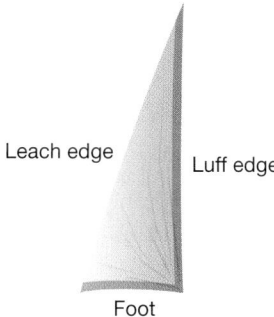

*21. Multi-Step In cooking school, Larissa learns that some foods should never be
(82) kept in the "danger zone": the temperature at which bacteria grow the fastest,
potentially causing food poisoning. She learns that the danger zone is 5°C to 60°C.

   a. Write an inequality that shows the temperatures that are in the danger zone in
     degrees Celsius.

   b. Find an inequality that shows the temperatures that are in the danger zone in
     degrees Fahrenheit by substituting the expression $\frac{5}{9}(f - 32)$ for the variable
     used in the inequality from part a, and then solve for f.

   c. Write an inequality to show at what temperature food should be kept in degrees
     Fahrenheit.

22. Verify Solve the inequality $24 < 2x + 6 < 36$. Check to make sure that the
(82) equation really is an AND inequality.

*23. **Error Analysis** Two students factor the polynomial. Which student is correct? Explain
(83) the error.

Student A	Student B
$25x^2 - 36 = (5x - 6)^2$	$25x^2 - 36 = (5x - 6)(5x + 6)$

*24. (Tires) A truck's tire has an outside radius of r inches. The area of the side of the tire,
(83) not including the inside rim, is $\pi r^2 - 81\pi$ inches. What is the diameter of the rim?

25. **Geometry** Graph the quadratic function representing the total surface area of a
(84) cube with side length x.

*26. **Write** Explain why the Pythagorean Theorem cannot be used to find the missing
(85) side length c.

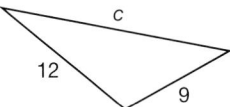

*27. **Formulate** One leg of a right triangle is twice the length of the other leg. The length
(85) of the hypotenuse is $\sqrt{45}$ centimeters. Let x represent the length of the shorter leg.
Use the Pythagorean Theorem to write and solve an equation to find the length of
the legs.

*28. **Multiple Choice** What is the perimeter of the triangle to the nearest inch?
(85)

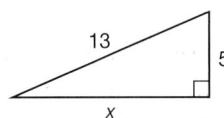

  A 212 inches   **B** 30 inches   **C** 32 inches   **D** 12 inches

*29. (Grades) The grade a student earns on a project is represented by $6x^2 - 11x - 35$,
(75) where x is the number of hours spent working on the project.
a. Factor the polynomial.

b. What grade is earned when a student works 4 hours on the project?

*30. **Multi-Step** Write an expression for the area of the square. Then find the
(76) area.

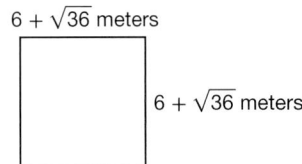

Calculating the Midpoint and Length of a Segment

1. **Vocabulary** In an ordered pair, the _____ (*x-coordinate, y-coordinate*)
(20) indicates the distance up or down from the origin.

Simplify.

2. $-3.8 - 5.5$
(6)

3. $(-6 - (-3))^2$
(4)

4. When viewed from the side, a
(85) skateboard landing ramp looks like
a right triangle. What is the actual
length of a ramp that is 2 feet tall if
the base is 4 feet long? Round your
answer to the nearest tenth.

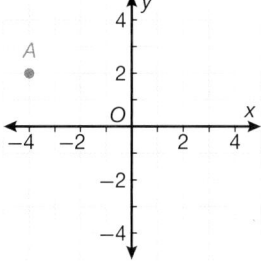

5. **Multiple Choice** Identify the coordinates of point *A*.
(20)

A $(4, 2)$ **B** $(-4, 2)$

C $(2, -4)$ **D** $(4, -2)$

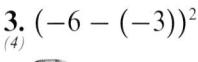

New Concepts

The Pythagorean Theorem is used to find distances that are difficult to measure directly.

Example **1**   **Calculating Distance Using the Pythagorean Theorem**

Math Reasoning

Analyze A crow flies directly from *P* to *Q*. How much farther does the car travel than the crow?

The diagram shows a grid of city streets.
A car travels from point *P* to point *Q* by
moving east to point *R* and then south to
point *Q*. What is the direct distance (in
city blocks) from point *P* to point *Q*?

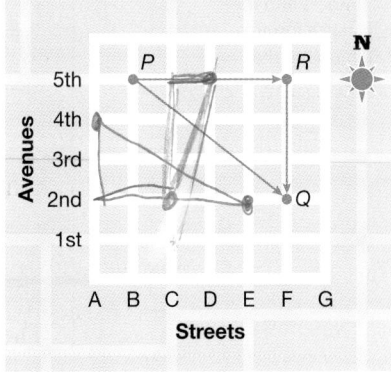

SOLUTION To find the direct distance
(in city blocks) from *P* to *Q*, use the
Pythagorean Theorem, written in the
form $(PQ)^2 = (PR)^2 + (RQ)^2$.

$(PQ)^2 = (PR)^2 + (RQ)^2$ Pythagorean Theorem

$(PQ)^2 = 4^2 + 3^2$ Substitute 4 for *PR* and 3 for *RQ*.

$\sqrt{(PQ)^2} = \sqrt{4^2 + 3^2}$ Take the positive square root of each side.

$\sqrt{(PQ)^2} = \sqrt{25}$ Simplify under the radical.

$PQ = 5$ Simplify the square root.

Online Connection
www.SaxonMathResources.com

The direct distance from point *P* to point *Q* is 5 city blocks.

The Pythagorean Theorem can also be used to find the distance between two points in a coordinate plane. In the diagram for Example 1, let 1st Ave. be the x-axis and let A St. be the y-axis; then P is $(1, 4)$ and Q is $(5, 1)$. The lengths PR and RQ are found by subtracting coordinates.

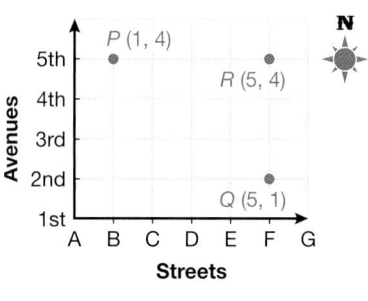

$$(PQ)^2 = (PR)^2 + (RQ)^2$$

$$\sqrt{(PQ)^2} = \sqrt{(PR)^2 + (RQ)^2}$$

$$\sqrt{(PQ)^2} = \sqrt{|5 - 1|^2 + |1 - 4|^2}$$

$$\sqrt{(PQ)^2} = \sqrt{4^2 + 3^2}$$

$$\sqrt{(PQ)^2} = \sqrt{16 + 9}$$

$$\sqrt{(PQ)^2} = \sqrt{25}$$

$$PQ = 5$$

Hint

Use absolute value when subtracting the coordinates so that the lengths *PR* and *RQ* will be positive numbers.

This method of finding the distance between two points leads to the distance formula.

The Distance Formula

The distance d between two points (x_1, y_1) and (x_2, y_2) is

$$d = \sqrt{(x_2 - x_1)^2 + (y_2 - y_1)^2}.$$

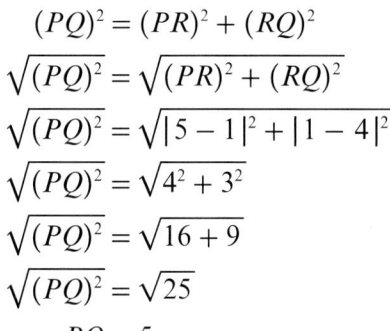

Example 2 Finding the Distance Between Two Points

Find the distance between $(3, -2)$ and $(6, 4)$.

SOLUTION Use the distance formula. Substitute $(3, -2)$ for (x_1, y_1) and $(6, 4)$ for (x_2, y_2).

$$d = \sqrt{(x_2 - x_1)^2 + (y_2 - y_1)^2}$$

$$= \sqrt{(6 - 3)^2 + (4 - (-2))^2} \qquad \text{Substitute.}$$

$$= \sqrt{3^2 + 6^2} \qquad \text{Simplify inside parentheses.}$$

$$= \sqrt{9 + 36} \qquad \text{Simplify powers.}$$

$$= \sqrt{45} \qquad \text{Add.}$$

$$= 3\sqrt{5} \qquad \text{Simplify the radical.}$$

The distance between $(3, -2)$ and $(6, 4)$ is $3\sqrt{5}$.

Caution

Be careful when substituting negative numbers into the distance formula. Remember that

$$(4 - (-2)) = 4 + 2.$$

Example 3 Classifying Polygons

Determine whether quadrilateral $ABCD$ is a rhombus.

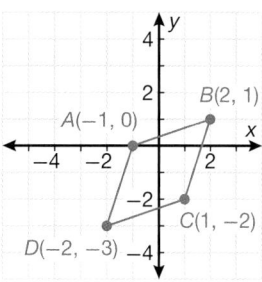

Math Language

A **rhombus** is a quadrilateral with four congruent sides.

Trend lines may vary. However, a trend line that shows the linear relationship of a scatter plot the most accurately is called the line of best fit. The equation of the line of best fit can be calculated on a graphing calculator. The line of best fit is also referred to as the regression line.

Graphing Calculator Tip

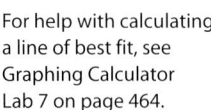

For help with calculating a line of best fit, see Graphing Calculator Lab 7 on page 464.

Example 2 Calculating a Line of Best Fit

The table shows the averages for homework grades and test scores for nine students. Use a graphing calculator to find the equation of the line of best fit.

Homework Grades and Test Scores

Average Homework Grade	75	85	94	88	91	95	76	84	90
Average Test Scores	83	87	95	93	88	91	83	80	92

SOLUTION

Step 1: Enter the data into your graphing calculator by pressing [STAT] [ENTER] to EDIT the data. Enter the average homework grades into L1 and the average test scores into L2. Then return to the home screen.

Step 2: Calculate the equation for the line of best fit by pressing [STAT] [▶] to access the CALC menu. Then press [4] to choose LinReg $(ax + b)$. Type in L_1, L_2 and press [ENTER] to calculate the values used for writing the equation.

Step 3: Round the values for a and b to the nearest thousandth and write the equation for the line of best fit in slope-intercept form:

$$y = 0.558x + 39.792$$

Hint

The calculator uses the variable a instead of m to represent the slope in the slope-intercept form of a line.

Two sets of data may be related to each other. A correlation is a measure of the strength and direction of the association between data sets or variables. When the points tightly cluster in a linear pattern, then the correlation is strong.

Data can be positively correlated or negatively correlated. There is a positive correlation when the data values for both variables increase. There is a negative correlation when the data values for one variable increase while the data values for the other variable decrease.

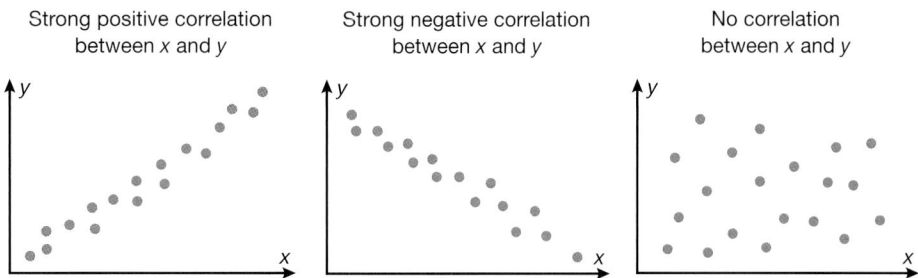

The direction of the association can be determined for scatter plots that have correlation. If the slope of the trend line is positive, then there is a positive correlation between the data values. If the slope of the trend line is negative, then there is a negative correlation between the data values.

Example 3 Identifying Correlations

State whether there is a positive correlation, a negative correlation, or no correlation between the data values.

a.

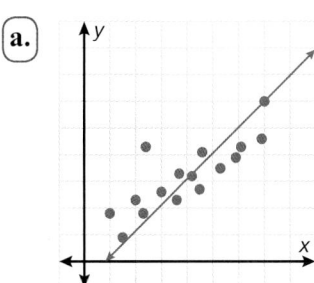

SOLUTION As the trend line rises from left to right, there is a positive correlation. Both sets of data values are increasing.

b.

x	10	9	8	7	6	5	4	3	2
y	60	63	72	75	77	81	83	89	92

SOLUTION Negative correlation: As x-values decrease the $y =$ values increase.

c. height and shoe size

SOLUTION Positive correlation: Taller people tend to have larger feet.

d. date of birth and shoe size

SOLUTION No correlation: date of birth and shoe size are not related to each other.

Example 4 Matching Situations to Scatter Plots

Match each situation with the scatter plot that models it best.

a. number of trucks on the road and number of days in a month

b. time spent driving and distance traveled

c. number of months you own a car and the value of the car

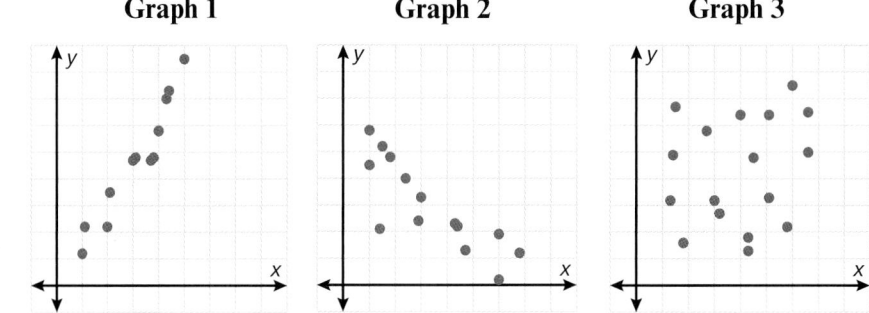

Graph 1   Graph 2   Graph 3

SOLUTION

a. Graph 3, as there is no correlation between the number of trucks on the road and the number of days in a month

b. Graph 1, as there is a positive correlation between time spent driving and distance traveled

c. Graph 2, as there is a negative correlation between the age of a car and its value

Estimations and predictions can be determined when there is a correlation, or a trend, between data values. Interpolation is a process of determining data points between given data points. Extrapolation is a process of determining data points that are beyond the given data points.

Example 5 Application: Population Growth

The table shows the population of the United States from the year 1960 through the year 2000.

U. S. Population

Year	1960	1965	1970	1975	1980	1985	1990	1995	2000
Population (in millions)	180	194	205	215	228	238	250	267	282

Math Reasoning

Analyze Why might a prediction determined by an equation for the line of best fit, be better than a prediction determined by a trend line?

a. Draw a scatter plot and a trend line for the data.

SOLUTION Plot the points with the year on the horizontal axis and the population on the vertical axis. Draw a straight line as near to as many of the points as possible.

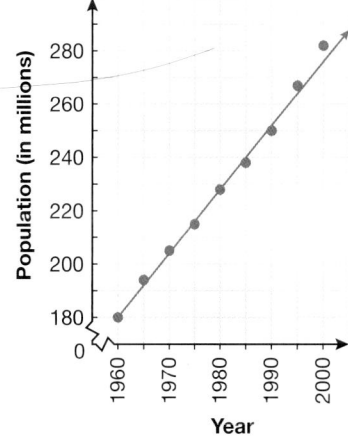

b. Use the trend line to make a prediction for the population in the year 2005.

SOLUTION From the graph, the population in the year 2005 will be about 290 million people.

c. Find the equation for a line of best fit using a graphing calculator. Round the values for a and b to the nearest thousandth.

SOLUTION Use the LinReg $(ax + b)$ feature on a graphing calculator to compute the values for the line of best fit.

The equation for the line of best fit is $y = 2.467x - 4655.222$.

d. Use the equation for the line of best fit to estimate the population in the year 2005. Round the answer to the nearest million.

SOLUTION

$y = 2.467x - 4655.222$

$y = 2.467(2010) - 4655.222$

$y \approx 291$ million

Use the data in the table.
(Ex 1)

x	1	2	3	4	5	6
y	14	27	43	53	70	85

a. Make a scatter plot from the data in the table. Then draw a trend line on the scatter plot.

b. Find an equation for the trend line.

c. Use a graphing calculator to find the equation of the line of best fit for the data in the table.
(Ex 2)

x	10	12	14	16	18	20
y	25	28	30	35	36	40

State whether there is a *positive correlation*, a *negative correlation*, or *no correlation* between the data values.
(Ex 3)

d.

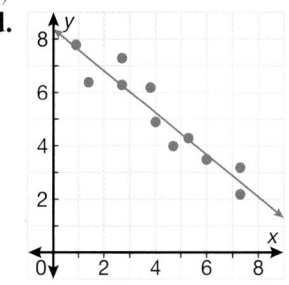

e.

x	2	5	6	8	9	11	13	16	20
y	10	12	13	15	17	20	21	24	26

f. the outdoor temperature and the number of sweaters sold in a store

g. hair color and height

Match each situation with the scatter plot that models it best.
(Ex 4)

h. time spend exercising and calories burned.

i. the number of dishes washed and the number of ounces of detergent remaining in a bottle.

j. the population of a country and the number of states in the country.

Graph 1	**Graph 2**	**Graph 3**

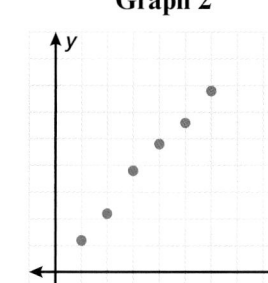
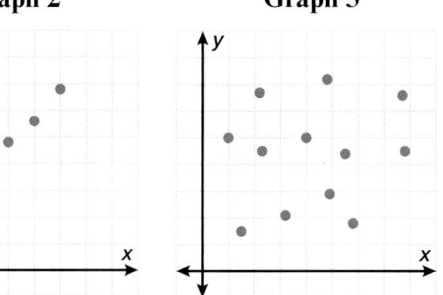

The table shows the number of people employed in agriculture in the United States from the year 1940 to the year 2000.

U. S. Agricultural Employment

Year	1940	1950	1960	1970	1980	1990	2000
Employment (in millions)	9.5	7.2	5.5	3.5	3.4	3.2	2.5

k. Draw a scatter plot and a trend line for the data.
(Ex 5)

l. Use the trend line to make a prediction for the population in the year 2010.
(Ex 5)

m. Find the equation for a line of best fit using a graphing calculator. Round the values for a and b to the nearest thousandth.
(Ex 5)

n. Use the equation for the line of best fit to estimate the population in the year 2010. Round the answer to the nearest half million.
(Ex 5)

Practice   Distributed and Integrated

1. Make a scatter plot from the data in the table.
(71)

x	1	2	3	4	5	6
y	26	24	21	14	9	5

Is the ordered pair (5, 2) a solution to the following systems?

2. $y = 7 - x$
(55)
$$y = \frac{1}{5}x + 1$$

3. $5y - x = 5$
(55)
$$y = 2x - 8$$

Subtract.

4. $31\sqrt{5} - 13\sqrt{5}$
(69)

*5. $\sqrt{27} - \sqrt{12}$
(69)

Find the common solution for each system of equations.

6. $-y = x + 8$
(67)
$$y = -x + 1$$

*7. $6y - x = 12$
(67)
$$y = \frac{1}{6}x + 2$$

Write an inverse variation equation relating x and y.

8. $x = \frac{2}{3}, y = 33$
(64)

9. $x = 6, y = 14$
(64)

*10. Error Analysis Two students solved the inequality $14 < -0.2k$ as shown below.
(70) Which student is correct? Explain the error.

Student A	Student B
$14 < -0.2k$	$14 < -0.2k$
$\dfrac{14}{0.2} > \dfrac{-0.2}{-0.2}k$	$\dfrac{14}{-0.2} > \dfrac{-0.2}{-0.2}k$
$70 > k$	$-70 > k$

*11. Multiple Choice When one set of data values increases as the other set of data values
(71) decreases, what type of correlation does this represent?

A positive   **B** negative   **C** constant   **D** none

*12. (**Elections**) The table shows the voter turnout for National Federal Elections.
(71)

U.S. Voter Turnout (in millions)

Year	1990	1992	1994	1996	1998	2000	2002	2004
Number of Voters (in millions)	68	104	75	96	73	106	80	122

a. Use the data to make a scatter plot.

b. Does the scatter plot show any trend in the data?

*13. Generalize If a scatter plot shows a negative correlation, what can you say about
(71) the relationship between the two sets of data values?

14. Error Analysis Student A and Student B combine the radicals. Which student is
(69) correct? Explain the error.

Student A	**Student B**
$8\sqrt{4y^2z^3} - 3yz\sqrt{49z}$	$8\sqrt{4y^2z^3} - 3yz\sqrt{49z}$
$= 8 \cdot 2yz\sqrt{z} - 3yz \cdot 7\sqrt{z}$	$= 8 \cdot 4yz\sqrt{z} - 3yz \cdot 7\sqrt{z}$
$= 16yz\sqrt{z} - 21yz\sqrt{z}$	$= 32yz\sqrt{z} - 21yz\sqrt{z}$
$= -5yz\sqrt{z}$	$= 11yz\sqrt{z}$

*15. (**Biking**) Randy biked $\sqrt{27}$ miles on the bike trail. He backtracked $\sqrt{3}$ miles, and
(69) then proceeded $\sqrt{12}$ miles to finish the trail. How far is Randy from his starting
point?

16. Multiple Choice Which of the following situations describes inclusive events?
(68)

A rolling a sum of 5 or a sum of 4 with two number cubes

B rolling a sum of 3 or a factor of 6 with two number cubes

C rolling two 5's or a sum of 8 with two number cubes

D rolling two 4's or a sum of 9 with two number cubes

17. Write If a fair coin is used, what is the probability that one toss will result in either
(68) heads or tails? Explain why your answer makes sense.

*18. (**Nutrition**) Each day Paolo tries to consume at least 40 grams of protein. One day
(66) he has two soy shakes, each with 15 grams of protein, as well as a bowl of peanuts,
containing 5 grams of protein. Write an inequality describing how much more
protein Paolo should consume that day.

19. Line 1 passes through the points $(2, -6)$ and $(4, 6)$. Line 2 passes through the
(65) points $(0, 1)$ and $(6, 0)$. Are the lines parallel or perpendicular?

20. Data Analysis Use the table of values to draw a scatter plot.
(71)

x	72	60	65	50	56	69
y	32	31	30	28	28	38

21. Determine if the inequality symbol in the inequality $11b < 5$ needs to be reversed, and then solve.
(70)

*22. Geometry JoAnna is making a banner the shape of an equilateral triangle. She has
(70) 36 inches of cording to put around the banner. Write and solve an inequality to find the range of measures of one side of the banner.

23. Multi-Step A company spends 2% of its sales on marketing. How much money does
(70) the company need to earn to spend at least $250,000 on marketing?

  a. Write an inequality to represent the situation.

  b. Solve the inequality.

  c. How much money is needed to spend $250,000 on marketing?

24. Generalize How would you choose which variable to eliminate when solving a
(63) system of linear equations?

25. Use the table to determine if there is a positive correlation, a negative correlation,
(71) or no correlation between the data sets.

x	3	6	10	13	15	17
y	100	88	73	62	51	38

26. Write Is it possible to determine the mode of a data set using a histogram?
(62) Explain.

27. (Pendulum) The period of a pendulum is equal to $2\pi\sqrt{\frac{l}{g}}$, where l is the length of
(61) the pendulum and g is the acceleration due to gravity. If the length of the pendulum is 40 m and the acceleration due to gravity is 10 m/s^2, what is the period of the pendulum?

*28. (Demography) The population of Fremont, California in 2005 was 200,770 and
(55) increased by 921 people by 2006. The population of Amarillo, Texas in 2005 was 183,106 and increased by 2419 people by 2006.

  a. Write a system of linear equations to represent the population of these cities assuming that they continued to grow at these yearly rates. Let x be the number of years after 2005 and y be the population.

  b. Use a graphing calculator to solve the system of equations. At what year would the populations be equal?

29. Write an equation for a direct variation that includes the point $(6, 42)$.
(56)

30. Multi-Step A cereal box is in the shape of a rectangular prism. Find the volume of
(58) a cereal box that has a width of $(2x + 2)$ inches, a length of $(5x + 1)$ inches, and a height of $(6x + 4)$ inches.

  a. Multiply the length times the width.

  b. Multiply the height times the product found in part **a.**

Factoring Trinomials: $x^2 + bx + c$

Warm Up

1. **Vocabulary** A polynomial with two terms is a _____.
(53)

Simplify.

2. $(5x + 3)(2x - 4)$
(58)

3. $(5x - 6)^2$
(60)

4. $(x + 1)(x^2 + 3)$
(58)

New Concepts

The polynomial $x^2 + bx + c$ is a trinomial. Like numbers, some trinomials can be factored. One way to learn how to factor a trinomial is to model the terms of a trinomial with algebra tiles.

Math Reasoning

Generalize Why is $x^2 + bx + c$ classified as a trinomial?

Exploration **Representing Trinomials with Algebra Tiles**

The following tiles represent terms in the trinomial $x^2 + 3x + 2$.

The tiles that represent some trinomials can be placed side by side to form rectangles. The tiles can be arranged to form a rectangle that has the dimensions $(x + 2)$ and $(x + 1)$.

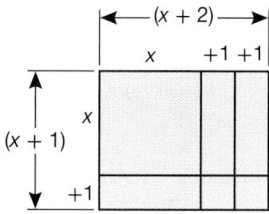

The area of the rectangle formed by the tiles can be represented as $(x + 2)(x + 1)$. By simplifying the product, the result will be the trinomial $x^2 + 3x + 2$. The binomials $x + 2$ and $x + 1$ are the factors of $x^2 + 3x + 2$.

a. **Model** Draw the tiles that represent the trinomial $x^2 + 4x + 3$.

b. Arrange the tiles into a rectangle.

c. **Analyze** What are the dimensions of the rectangle?

d. **Formulate** Use the dimensions of the rectangle to calculate the area of the rectangle.

Online Connection
www.SaxonMathResources.com

e. **Analyze** What are the factors of $x^2 + 4x + 3$?

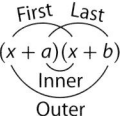
Tiling is a method for modeling the factoring of trinomials, but it is a slow method for finding the factors. Thinking about how factors are multiplied leads to a quicker method.

Binomials can be multiplied using the FOIL method. In each case, the product is a trinomial.

This procedure can be reversed to factor a trinomial into the product of two binomials. There is a pattern for factoring trinomials that are written in the standard form $ax^2 + bx + c$; that is, when $a = 1$.

1. The last term of the trinomial, c, is the product of the last terms of the binomials.

2. The coefficient of the middle term, b, is the sum of the last terms of the binomials.

Example 1 **Factoring when c is Positive**

Factor each trinomial.

a. $x^2 + 9x + 18$

SOLUTION

In this trinomial, b is 9 and c is 18. Because b is positive, it must be the sum of two positive numbers that are factors of c.

Three pairs of positive numbers have a product of 18.

$(1)(18) = 18$ $\qquad$ $(2)(9) = 18$ $\qquad$ $(3)(6) = 18$

Only one pair of these numbers has a sum of 9.

$(1) + (18) = 19$ $\qquad$ $(2) + (9) = 11$ $\qquad$ $(3) + (6) = 9$

The constant terms in the binomials are 3 and 6.

$x^2 + 9x + 18 = (x + 3)(x + 6)$

The factored form of $x^2 + 9x + 18$ is $(x + 3)(x + 6)$.

b. $x^2 - 5x + 4$

SOLUTION

In this trinomial, b is -5 and c is 4. Because b is negative, it must be the sum of two negative numbers that are factors of c.

Two pairs of negative numbers have a product of 4.

$(-1)(-4) = 4$ $\qquad$ $(-2)(-2) = 4$

Only one pair of these numbers has a sum of -5.

$(-1) + (-4) = -5$ $\qquad$ $(-2) + (-2) = -4$

The constant terms in the binomials are -1 and -4.

$x^2 - 5x + 4 = (x - 1)(x - 4)$

The factored form of $x^2 - 5x + 4$ is $(x - 1)(x - 4)$.

Example **2** **Factoring when c is Negative**

Factor each trinomial.

a. $x^2 + 3x - 10$

SOLUTION

In this trinomial, b is 3 and c is -10.

Four pairs of positive and negative numbers have a product of -10.

$(-1)(10)$ $(1)(-10)$ $(-2)(5)$ $(2)(-5)$

The sum of only one of these pairs is 3.

$(-1) + 10 = 9$ $1 + (-10) = -9$ $(-2) + 5 = 3$ $2 + (-5) = -3$

The constant terms in the binomials are -2 and 5. So,

$x^2 + 3x - 10 = (x - 2)(x + 5)$

b. $x^2 - 7x - 8$

SOLUTION

In this trinomial, $b = -7$ and $c = -8$.

Four pairs of positive and negative numbers have a product of -8.

$(-1)(8)$ $(1)(-8)$ $(-2)(4)$ $(2)(-4)$

The sum of only one of these pairs is -7.

$(-1) + 8 = 7$ $1 + (-8) = -7$ $(-2) + 4 = 2$ $2 + (-4) = -2$

The constant terms in the binomial are 1 and -8. So,

$x^2 - 7x - 8 = (x + 1)(x - 8)$

Example **3** **Factoring with Two Variables**

Factor each trinomial.

a. $x^2 + 5xy + 6y^2$

SOLUTION In this trinomial, b and c have values of $5y$ and $6y^2$, respectively. Because both b and c are positive, b must be the sum of two positive terms that are factors of c.

Six pairs of positive terms have a product of $6y^2$.

$(1y^2)(6)$ $(1y)(6y)$ $(1)(6y^2)$ $(2y^2)(3)$ $(2y)(3y)$ $(2)(3y^2)$

Eliminate pairs of terms that contain y^2 because their sums cannot yield a term containing y. For example, $(1y^2)(6)$ has the sum $(y^2 + 6)$.

Only the pair $2y$ and $3y$ has a sum of $5y$, which is the value of b. So,

$x^2 + 5xy + 6y^2 = (x + 2y)(x + 3y)$

Math Reasoning

Analyze How can the absolute value of the factors of c be used to find the last terms of the binomial factors?

Reading Math

The middle term of the trinomial is written $2xy$, not $2yx$, even though $2y$ is the value of b in the trinomial $x^2 + bx + c$.

---

b. $x^2 + 2xy - 3y^2$

SOLUTION

In this trinomial, b is $2y$ and c is $-3y^2$.

Four pairs of positive and negative terms have a product of $-3y^2$.

$$(-1)(3y^2) \qquad (1)(-3y^2) \qquad (-1y)(3y) \qquad (1y)(-3y)$$

Only the pair $-1y$ and $3y$ has a sum of $2y$, which is the value of b. So,

$$x^2 + 2xy - 3y^2 = (x - y)(x + 3y)$$

Hint

The terms of a trinomial are written in standard form when the terms contain descending powers of the variable.

Example 4 **Rearranging Terms before Factoring**

Factor the trinomial.

$-21 - 4x + x^2$

SOLUTION

Write the trinomial in the standard form as $x^2 - 4x - 21$, where b is -4 and c is -21.

Four pairs of numbers have a product of -21.

$$(1)(-21) \qquad (-1)(21) \qquad (3)(-7) \qquad (-3)(7)$$

Only the pair 3 and -7 has a sum of -4. So,

$$x^2 - 4x - 21 = (x + 3)(x - 7)$$

Example 5 **Evaluating Trinomials**

Evaluate $x^2 + 5x - 14$ and its factors for $x = 3$.

SOLUTION

In this trinomial, b is 5 and c is -14.

The number pair -2 and 7 has a sum of 5 and a product of -14.

So, $x^2 + 5x - 14 = (x - 2)(x + 7)$

Now evaluate $x^2 + 5x - 14$ and $(x - 2)(x + 7)$ for $x = 3$.

Trinomial	Factors
$x^2 + 5x - 14$	$(x - 2)(x + 7)$
$= (3)^2 + 5(3) - 14$	$= (3 - 2)(3 + 7)$
$= 9 + 15 - 14$	$= (1)(10)$
$= 10$	$= 10$

The results are the same. The trinomial is equal to the product of its binomial factors.

Factor each trinomial.

a. $x^2 + 3x + 2$
(Ex 1)

b. $x^2 - 10x + 16$
(Ex 1)

c. $x^2 + 4x - 12$
(Ex 2)

d. $x^2 - 5x - 36$
(Ex 2)

e. $x^2 + 9xy + 20y^2$
(Ex 3)

f. $x^2 - xy - 12y^2$
(Ex 3)

g. $12x + 20 + x^2$
(Ex 4)

h. $7x + x^2 - 44$
(Ex 4)

i. Evaluate $x^2 + x - 6$ and its factors for $x = 4$.
(Ex 5)

Practice Distributed and Integrated

1. Solve the inequality $x + 2 + 3 > 6$. Then graph and check the solution.
(66)

Find the probability of the following events.

2. choosing a vowel or a consonant from the alphabet
(68)

3. rolling a sum that is a multiple of 4 or a set of doubles with two number cubes
(68)

Factor.

*4. $x^2 + 11x + 24$
(72)

*5. $k^2 - 3k - 40$
(72)

*6. $m^2 + 9m + 20$
(72)

*7. $x^2 + 33 + 14x$
(72)

*8. Error Analysis Two students are factoring the following trinomial. Which student is
(72) correct? Explain the error.

$$x^2 - 5x - 6$$

Student A	Student B
$(-6)(1) = -6$	$(-6)(-1) = -6$
$(-6) + 1 = -5$	$(-6) - (-1) = -5$
$x^2 - 5x - 6 = (x + 1)(x - 6)$	$x^2 - 5x - 6 = (x - 1)(x - 6)$

*9. (Baking) The area of the sheet-cake pans at a bakery are described by the trinomial
(72) $x^2 + 15x + 54$. What are the dimensions of a pan if $x = 11$?

*10. Analyze How many possible pairs of number factors does c have in the following
(72) trinomial?

$$x^2 + bx + 36$$

*11. Model These tiles represent the trinomial $x^2 + x - 6$.
(72)

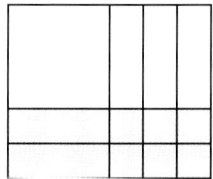

What does each of the shaded rectangles represent?

12. Make a scatter plot from the data in the table.
(71)

x	5	10	15	20	25	30
y	11	13	16	20	21	25

13. Error Analysis Two students are describing a trend line for a scatter plot but have different definitions. Which student is correct? Explain the error.
(71)

Student A	**Student B**
A trend line is a line on a scatter plot that goes through two data points and indicates a trend in the data.	A trend line is a line on a scatter plot that models the slope of the data points and indicates a trend in the data.

*14. Geometry Ten groups of students were given different circular objects. They measured the circumference and the diameter of the object. The table shows the results for each group.
(71)

Diameter (in.)	4	3.75	8	6.25	5.5	5	7	1.5	3	9
Circumference (in.)	12.1	12	25	19	16	16	21	4.5	9.5	28

a. Make a scatter plot of the data and draw a trend line.

b. Write an equation that models the data.

c. How does your equation compare to the formula for the circumference of a circle, $C = \pi d$?

15. Multi-Step Use the scatter plot.
(71)
a. Use the trend line to estimate the corresponding y-value for an x-value of 18.

b. Use the trend line to estimate the x-value for a y-value of 50.

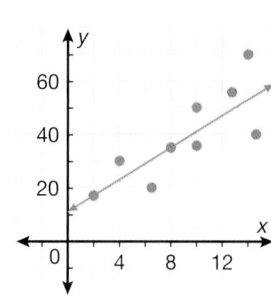

16. Write Can a perfect square have a negative square root? Explain.
(69)

17. (Air Traffic Control) An airplane approaching from the north is flying along a flight
(67) path of $y = 6x + 2$. The airport runway lies on the path $\frac{1}{2}y = 3x + 1$. Will the
airplane be able to land on the runway if it continues on its current path? Explain.

18. **Coordinate Geometry** The triangle shown at right is formed by the
(67) intersection of three lines. The lines can be paired to form three separate
systems of two equations. Classify these systems.

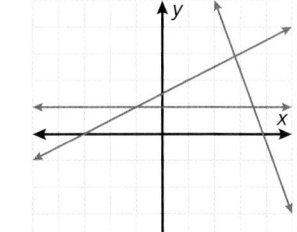

19. Determine if the lines described are parallel or perpendicular.
(65)

Line 1 passes through the points $(-6, 3)$ and $(6, 1)$.

Line 2 passes through the points $(-6, -2)$ and $(6, -4)$.

20. **Model** Make a table that relates the length and width of a rectangle with a constant
(64) area of 100 square feet.

*21. **Multi-Step** Yoon has a number of dimes and quarters she wants to put into rolls.
(63) She has 124 coins in all that add up to $20.50. If a roll of quarters is equal to
ten dollars, how many extra quarters does she have that will not fill up a roll?

22. Find the LCM of $(5x - 9)$ and $(3x + 8)$.
(57)

23. **Multiple Choice** Simplify $20\sqrt{7} - 12\sqrt{7} + 2\sqrt{7}$.
(69) **A** $10\sqrt{7}$ **B** $18\sqrt{7}$ **C** $34\sqrt{7}$ **D** $-12\sqrt{7}$

24. (Hobbies) Enrique recorded his personal best times in minutes for
(62) completing different levels of a computer game in the stem-and leaf
plot shown. What is his median time for completing a level?

Personal Best Times
for Completing Levels
of Computer Game

Stem	Leaves
0	8, 9
1	1, 2, 3, 3, 8, 9
2	2, 2, 5, 6
3	0, 3
4	1

25. **Multi-Step** The sum of two numbers is 36. Their difference is 8. Find
(59) each of the numbers. What is their product?

26. Write an equation for a direct variation that includes the point
(56) $(13, 13)$.

27. (Physics) The distance an object travels in a certain amount of time is directly
(56) proportional to its rate of travel. An object travels 105 meters at a rate of
3 meters per second. How far will an object travel if it travels at 5 meters per
second for the same amount of time?

28. Solve $2 < -4a$.   **29.** Solve $\frac{-1}{3} < \frac{-1}{9}p$.
(70)   (70)

30. (Real Estate) Donna and James have to pay 20% of the cost of a house as a down
(70) payment. They have $35,000 saved for the down payment. Write and solve an
equation to determine the range for the sale price of a house they can make a
down payment on.

Solving Compound Inequalities

Warm Up

1. Vocabulary A(n) _____ is a mathematical statement comparing quantities that are not equal.
(45)

Solve.

2. $x + 7 < 0$
(66)

3. $x - 3 \geq -5$
(66)

4. $-x \geq 5$
(70)

5. $\dfrac{-x}{4} \leq 3$
(70)

New Concepts

Sometimes inequalities are described using two inequalities instead of just one. In these instances, a compound inequality is written to represent the situation. A **compound inequality** is two inequalities combined with the word AND or OR. A **conjunction** is a compound inequality that uses the word AND.

The statement $x \geq -3$ AND $x \leq 5$ is a conjunction. Because the word "AND" connects the two inequalities, the conjunction can also be written $-3 \leq x \leq 5$.

The graph of a conjunction is the intersection of the graphs of the two inequalities. That is, it includes all points common to both inequalities. For example, consider the graph of $x \geq -3$ AND $x \leq 5$.

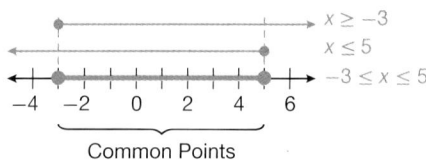

Reading Math

Read $-3 \leq x \leq 5$ as "x is greater than or equal to -3 and less than or equal to 5," or as "x is between -3 and 5, inclusive."

Example 1 Writing and Graphing Conjunctions

Write and graph a compound inequality to represent the statement.

a. all real numbers that are greater than 1 and less than 4

SOLUTION

$x > 1$ AND $x < 4$ or $1 < x < 4$

b. The winds of a hurricane range from 75 miles per hour to 200 miles per hour.

SOLUTION

$x \geq 75$ AND $x \leq 200$ or $75 \leq x \leq 200$

Math Language

The phrase **"less than"** and "is less than" are often confused. For example, "six less than x" is translates to $x - 6$ while "six is less than x" translates to $6 < x$.

Online Connection
www.SaxonMathResources.com

19. **Multiple Choice** A _____ is a graph made up of separate, disconnected points.
(71)
  A discrete graph   **B** continuous graph   **C** trend graph   **D** linear graph

20. Determine if the inequality symbol in the expression $-\frac{2}{3}c \leq 6$ needs to be
(70) reversed, and then solve.

21. If a square measures $\sqrt{144}$ inches on one side, what is the perimeter of the square?
(69)

22. Determine the probability of rolling a sum of 9 or an odd number with two
(68) number cubes.

23. **Multi-Step** The library charges a late fee based on the number of days a book is
(67) overdue. The equation for the fee is $y = \$0.25d + \$0.05$.
  a. What is the fee for a book that is 10 days overdue?

  b. Thirty days is the maximum number of days for which the library charges.
   What is the maximum amount the library charges?

  c. Classify the system of equations for the library fee and $y = \$7.55$.

24. **Justify** If a, b, x, and y are all greater than 0 and $x > a$ and $y < b$, how does
(66) $\frac{x}{y}$ compare to $\frac{a}{b}$? Justify your answer.

***25.** **Predict** Use the trend line to predict the corresponding y-value for an x-value of 40.
(71)

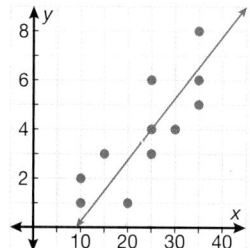

26. **Justify** True or False: The lines represented by $y = \frac{x}{4} - 2$ and $4y = x + 8$ are
(65) parallel. Explain.

27. (Construction) To build Ariane's house will take a constant number of individual
(64) work days. If a construction crew of 15 people can build the house in 20 days, how
many people does it take to finish the house in 5 days?

28. **Multi-Step** A container has a square base. The area is 800 cm². The size of a book is
(61) 25 cm by 30 cm. Can the book lie flat on the base of the container?
  a. Find the side length of the container.

  b. Compare the side length with the dimensions of the book.

  c. Use the comparison to determine if the book will fit.

29. Solve the system by substitution: $3x + y = 13$.
(59)
$$2x - 4y = 4$$

30. Sue purchases a rectangular billboard sign for her new business. The length can
(58) be represented by $6x^2 + 6x + 6$ and the width is $(x + 8)$. What is the area of Sue's
new billboard?

Factoring Trinomials: $ax^2 + bx + c$

Warm Up

1. **Vocabulary** A _____ is a polynomial with three terms.
(53)

Factor.

2. $x^2 + 3x - 10$
(72)

3. $x^2 - x - 42$
(72)

Simplify.

4. $(4x + 5)(3x - 2)$
(58)

5. $(2x + 5)^2$
(60)

New Concepts

Recall that a pattern is used when factoring trinomials of the form $x^2 + bx + c$. A pair of numbers is found whose product is c and whose sum is b. When a trinomial takes the form $ax^2 + bx + c$, the pattern no longer works. When the leading coefficient a is not equal to 1 another pattern emerges.

Example 1 Factoring when *b* and *c* are Positive

Factor completely.

$2x^2 + 7x + 5$

SOLUTION

Since $2x^2$ is the product of $(2x)$ and (x), write $(2x \quad)(x \quad)$.

The third term of the trinomial, 5, is the product of the last terms in the binomials. List the pairs of numbers that result in a product of 5.

$$(1)(5) \qquad (5)(1) \qquad (-1)(-5) \qquad (-5)(-1)$$

Because the middle term, $7x$, is positive, eliminate the pairs of negative numbers. Check each of the other pairs to see which gives you $7x$.

$(2x + 1)(x + 5) \qquad (2x + 5)(x + 1)$

$\qquad 1x \qquad\qquad\qquad 5x$

$\qquad +10x \qquad\qquad +2x$
$\qquad \overline{11x} \qquad\qquad \overline{7x}$

So, $2x^2 + 7x + 5 = (2x + 5)(x + 1)$.

Check Use FOIL to "undo" the factoring.

$(2x + 5)(x + 1) \overset{?}{=} 2x^2 + 2x + 5x + 5$
$\qquad\qquad\qquad = 2x^2 + 7x + 5 \ \checkmark$

> **Hint**
>
> When *c* is positive, the second term in both binomials will have the same sign (negative or positive) depending on the sign of *b*.

> **Online Connection**
> www.SaxonMathResources.com

Example 5 Rearranging Before Factoring

Factor completely.

a. $-17x + 5 + 12x^2$

SOLUTION

Before factoring, rearrange the terms so that they are in descending order according to the exponent.

$12x^2 - 17x + 5$

The first term, $12x^2$, can be factored as $(12x)(x)$, $(6x)(2x)$, and $(4x)(3x)$.

The last term, 5, can be factored as $(-5)(-1)$ and $(-1)(-5)$.

Check each pair to see which results in the middle term, $-17x$.

Possibilities	Middle Term
$(12x - 5)(x - 1)$	$-17x$ ✓
$(12x - 1)(x - 5)$	$-61x$
$(6x - 5)(2x - 1)$	$-16x$
$(6x - 1)(2x - 5)$	$-32x$
$(4x - 5)(3x - 1)$	$-19x$
$(4x - 1)(3x - 5)$	$-23x$

So, $12x^2 - 17x + 5 = (12x - 5)(x - 1)$.

b. $-2 - 7x + 4x^2$

SOLUTION

Rearrange the terms in the expression to $4x^2 - 7x - 2$.

The first term, $4x^2$, can be factored as $(4x)(x)$ and $(2x)(2x)$.

The last term, -2, can be factored as $(-2)(1)$, $(-1)(2)$, $(2)(-1)$, and $(1)(-2)$.

Check each pair to see which results in the middle term, $-7x$.

Possibilities	Middle Term
$(4x - 2)(x + 1)$	$2x$
$(4x - 1)(x + 2)$	$7x$
$(4x + 2)(x - 1)$	$-2x$
$(4x + 1)(x - 2)$	$-7x$ ✓
$(2x - 2)(2x + 1)$	$-2x$
$(2x - 1)(2x + 2)$	$2x$
$(2x + 2)(2x - 1)$	$2x$
$(2x + 1)(2x - 2)$	$-2x$

So, $4x^2 - 7x - 2 = (4x + 1)(x - 2)$.

Factor completely.

a. $9x^2 + 38x + 8$
(Ex 1)

b. $10x^2 - 23x + 12$
(Ex 2)

c. $3x^2 + 5x - 2$
(Ex 3)

d. $6x^2 - 5x - 4$
(Ex 3)

e. $6x^2 + 11xy + 4y^2$
(Ex 4)

f. $-13x + 14x^2 + 3$
(Ex 5)

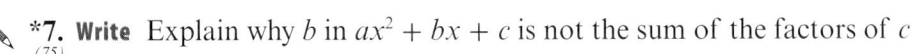

Practice Distributed and Integrated

Factor completely.

*1. $6x^2 + 13x + 6$
(75)

*2. $3x^2 - 14x - 5$
(75)

*3. $18 - 15x + 2x^2$
(75)

*4. $-15 + 7x + 2x^2$
(75)

Simplify.

5. $22c\sqrt{de} - 9\sqrt{de}$
(69)

6. $8\sqrt{7} - 4\sqrt{11} - 3\sqrt{7} + 7\sqrt{11}$
(69)

*7. Write Explain why b in $ax^2 + bx + c$ is not the sum of the factors of c.
(75)

*8. Justify Show that $7x^2 - 12x + 10$ is prime (cannot be factored).
(75)

*9. Multiple Choice Evaluate $2x^2 - 10x + 14$ if $x = -2$.
(75)
    A 2   **B** 10   **C** 42   **D** 50

*10. For a situation that represents a direct variation, what does the graph of that situation
(Inv 7) look like?

11. Solve $|z| = 5$.
(74)

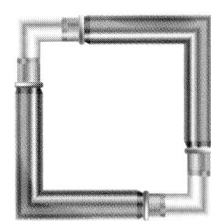

12. Geometry Sliding-glass tubes form a square with a perimeter of 36 inches.
(74) Both the length and width of the square can be changed by ± 1.5 inches.
    a. Write an absolute-value equation to find the greatest and least perimeter of
        the square.

    b. What are the greatest and least perimeters?

*13. Multi-Step Given the equation $|x + 2| + 6 = 17$, answer the questions below.
(74)
    a. Isolate the absolute value expression.

    b. Use the definition of absolute value to rewrite the absolute-value equation as two equations.

    c. What is the solution set?

*14. (Physics) A steel bar at a temperature of 300°C has the length L. If the temperature
(74) of the bar is raised or lowered 100°C, its length will increase or decrease by 0.12%, respectively. Write an absolute-value equation for the maximum and minimum lengths of the bar when it is heated to 400°C or cooled to 200°C.

15. Solve the compound inequality $-14 \le -3x + 10 \le -5$.
(73)

16. Error Analysis Two students graph the compound inequality $-2 < x < 1$ as shown.
(73) Which student is correct? Explain the error.

Student A	Student B
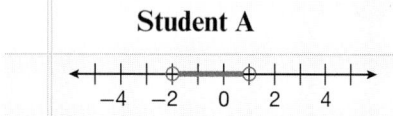	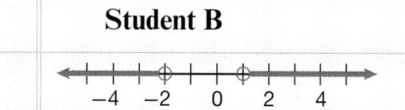

17. (Temperature) The predicted high temperature for the day is 88°F and the predicted
(73) low temperature for the day is 65°F. Write a compound inequality that shows the range of temperatures predicted for the day.

18. Multiple Choice Which binomial is a factor of $x^2 + 5x - 6$?
(72)
    A $x + 1$ **B** $x + 2$ **C** $x + 3$ **D** $x + 6$

19. Verify Show that 2 is a solution of the compound inequality $x < 3$ OR $x > 6$.
(73)

20. Use the scatter plot and the trend line to write an equation of the line.
(71)

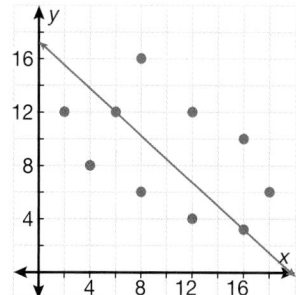

21. Measurement Tyrone bought 24 quarts of juice for a party. He plans to serve the
(70) juice in $\frac{1}{4}$-quart cups. How many servings can he plan to make with the juice he has available?

22. (Fitness) To make the swim team, Maria needs to swim 10 laps in under 8 minutes.
(70) Write and solve an inequality to find the maximum average time per lap she could swim to still make the team.

23. Suppose Carrie walks home from school at a rate of 4 miles per hour. Write an
(Inv 7) equation that relates Carrie's time to the distance traveled home. Is this a direct or indirect variation? What represents the constant of variation?

24. Find the probability of choosing an odd number card from a pack of cards
(68) numbered 1 through 9 or the number 1.

25. (Web Authoring) A company designs web sites and charges a fee of $y = \$250 + \$50w$.
(67) The charge includes a base fee of $250, plus a weekly fee based on the number of weeks the client requires full support. If the equation $y = 800$ represents the amount a company pays, for how many weeks do they receive full support?

26. Analyze The equation $y = 4$ describes a horizontal line with zero slope. The
(67) equation $x = 4$ describes a vertical line with infinite slope. Classify the system formed by these two equations.

27. Multi-Step Charlene is shopping for used DVDs. She buys some DVDs from Bin A
(66) that cost $7 each and some from Bin B that cost $5 each. Charlene has $45.
  a. Write an inequality representing the situation. (Hint: You must use two different variables to represent DVDs from each bin.)
  b. Can Charlene buy 4 DVDs from Bin A and 4 from Bin B?
  c. Charlene decides to buy 3 DVDs from Bin A. How many can she choose from Bin B?

28. Multi-Step The amounts of measurable rain (in inches) per day recorded
(62) for Seattle in July 2007 are listed below.

$$0.06, 0.04, 0.01, 0.28, 0.01, 0.15, 0.21, 0.38, 0.30, 0.10$$
  a. Create a histogram of the data.
  b. Is this the best representation of the data for the entire month? Why or why not?

29. Find the product: $(4y - 4)(4y + 4)$.
(60)

30. Solve the system of equations by substitution.
(59)
$$5x + 3y = 1$$
$$8x + 4y = 4$$

Multiplying Radical Expressions

Warm Up

1. Vocabulary A _____ is an expression that contains a radical.
(61)

Simplify.

2. $\sqrt{50{,}000}$
(61)

3. $\sqrt{108}$
(61)

4. $2\sqrt{8} - 3\sqrt{32}$
(69)

5. $2\sqrt{18} + 4\sqrt{300} - \sqrt{72}$
(69)

New Concepts

Math Reasoning

Generalize Why must a and b be greater than or equal to zero when finding $\sqrt{a} \cdot \sqrt{b}$?

Product Property of Radicals
The square root of a product equals the product of the square roots of the factors. $$\sqrt{ab} = \sqrt{a} \cdot \sqrt{b} \text{ where } a \geq 0 \text{ and } b \geq 0.$$

This means, for example, that $\sqrt{(8)(2)}$ is the same as $\sqrt{8} \cdot \sqrt{2}$.

Example 1 Simplifying Radical Expressions

Simplify. All variables represent non-negative real numbers.

a. $\sqrt{8}\sqrt{2}$

SOLUTION

$\sqrt{8}\sqrt{2} = \sqrt{16}$ Use the Product Property of Radicals.

$\quad\quad = 4$ Simplify.

b. $6\sqrt{2} \cdot 4\sqrt{3}$

SOLUTION

$6 \cdot 4\sqrt{2 \cdot 3}$ Use the Product Property of Radicals.

$= 24\sqrt{6}$ Simplify.

c. $\left(6\sqrt{3}\right)^2$

SOLUTION

$\left(6\sqrt{3}\right)^2$

$= (6)^2\left(\sqrt{3}\right)^2$ Power of a Product Property

$= 36\sqrt{9}$ Square each factor.

$= 36 \cdot 3$ Simplify.

$= 108$ Multiply.

Online Connection
www.SaxonMathResources.com

d. $2\sqrt{6x} \cdot \sqrt{4x}$

SOLUTION

$$2\sqrt{6x} \cdot \sqrt{4x}$$
$$= 2\sqrt{24x^2} \qquad \text{Multiply.}$$
$$= 4x\sqrt{6} \qquad \text{Simplify.}$$

Example 2 Applying the Distributive Property

Simplify.

a. $\sqrt{2}(3 + \sqrt{6})$

SOLUTION

$$\sqrt{2}(3 + \sqrt{6})$$
$$= 3\sqrt{2} + \sqrt{12} \qquad \text{Use the Distributive Property.}$$
$$= 3\sqrt{2} + 2\sqrt{3} \qquad \text{Simplify.}$$

b. $\sqrt{2}(\sqrt{6} - \sqrt{9})$

SOLUTION

$$\sqrt{2}(\sqrt{6} - \sqrt{9})$$
$$= \sqrt{12} - \sqrt{18} \qquad \text{Use the Distributive Property.}$$
$$= 2\sqrt{3} - 3\sqrt{2} \qquad \text{Simplify.}$$

Example 3 Multiplying Binomials with Radicals

Simplify.

a. $(4 + \sqrt{9})(2 - \sqrt{6})$

SOLUTION

$$(4 + \sqrt{9})(2 - \sqrt{6})$$
$$= 8 - 4\sqrt{6} + 2\sqrt{9} - \sqrt{54} \qquad \text{Use the Distributive Property or FOIL.}$$
$$= 8 - 4\sqrt{6} + 6 - 3\sqrt{6} \qquad \text{Simplify the radicals.}$$
$$= 14 - 7\sqrt{6} \qquad \text{Simplify by combining like terms.}$$

b. $(6 - \sqrt{3})^2$

SOLUTION

$$(6 - \sqrt{3})^2$$
$$= 36 - 12\sqrt{3} + \sqrt{9} \qquad \text{Use the square of a binomial pattern.}$$
$$= 39 - 12\sqrt{3} \qquad \text{Simplify the radical and combine like terms.}$$

Example 4   Application: Carpeting

Chavez wants to find the area of a rectangular throw rug. The rug has a side length of $8 + \sqrt{5}$ feet and a width of $2 + \sqrt{2}$ feet. What is the area of the rug?

SOLUTION

$$A = lw$$
$$= \left(8 + \sqrt{5}\right)\left(2 + \sqrt{2}\right)$$
$$= 16 + 8\sqrt{2} + 2\sqrt{5} + \sqrt{10}$$

The area of the rug is $\left(16 + 8\sqrt{2} + 2\sqrt{5} + \sqrt{10}\right)$ square feet.

Lesson Practice

Simplify. All variables represent non-negative real numbers.

a. $\sqrt{5}\sqrt{3}$
(Ex 1)

b. $3\sqrt{7} \cdot 2\sqrt{3}$
(Ex 1)

c. $\left(3\sqrt{6}\right)^2$
(Ex 1)

d. $3\sqrt{3x} \cdot \sqrt{2x}$
(Ex 1)

e. $\sqrt{7}\left(2 + \sqrt{4}\right)$
(Ex 2)

f. $\sqrt{5}\left(\sqrt{4} - \sqrt{3}\right)$
(Ex 2)

g. $\left(5 + \sqrt{9}\right)\left(4 - \sqrt{6}\right)$
(Ex 3)

h. $\left(4 - \sqrt{7}\right)^2$
(Ex 3)

i. The square dance floor at the local community building is being replaced. The floor's side length is $32 + \sqrt{13}$ feet. What is the area of the dance floor?
(Ex 4)

> **Caution**
>
> $\left(4 - \sqrt{7}\right)^2 \neq 16 + \sqrt{49}$
>
> Remember to either use the square of a binomial pattern, the Distributive Property, or the FOIL method when squaring a binomial.

Practice   Distributed and Integrated

Solve.

1. $\dfrac{5}{6} \leq -2p$
(70)

2. $|x + 4| = 5$
(74)

Factor.

3. $12x^2 - 25x + 7$
(75)

4. $x^2 + 10x - 39$
(72)

5. $5z^2 + 2z - 7$
(75)

6. $3x^2 + 25x - 18$
(75)

Simplify.

*7. $4\sqrt{3} \cdot 6\sqrt{6} \cdot 3\sqrt{3} \cdot 2\sqrt{2}$
(76)

8. $-17\sqrt{7s} - 4\sqrt{7s}$
(69)

*9. $\left(4\sqrt{5}\right)^2$
(76)

*10. $3\sqrt{2} \cdot 4\sqrt{12} - 6\sqrt{54}$
(76)

11. $\sqrt{\dfrac{x^3}{60}}$
(61)

SOLUTION Use the distance formula to find the length of each side of $ABCD$.

$$AB = \sqrt{(x_2 - x_1)^2 + (y_2 - y_1)^2}$$
$$= \sqrt{(2 - (-1))^2 + (1 - 0)^2}$$
$$= \sqrt{3^2 + 1^2}$$
$$= \sqrt{9 + 1}$$
$$= \sqrt{10}$$

$$BC = \sqrt{(x_2 - x_1)^2 + (y_2 - y_1)^2}$$
$$= \sqrt{(2 - 1)^2 + (1 - (-2))^2}$$
$$= \sqrt{1^2 + 3^2}$$
$$= \sqrt{1 + 9}$$
$$= \sqrt{10}$$

$$CD = \sqrt{(x_2 - x_1)^2 + (y_2 - y_1)^2}$$
$$= \sqrt{(1 - (-2))^2 + (-2 - (-3))^2}$$
$$= \sqrt{3^2 + 1^2}$$
$$= \sqrt{9 + 1}$$
$$= \sqrt{10}$$

$$AD = \sqrt{(x_2 - x_1)^2 + (y_2 - y_1)^2}$$
$$= \sqrt{(-1 - (-2))^2 + (0 - (-3))^2}$$
$$= \sqrt{1^2 + 3^2}$$
$$= \sqrt{1 + 9}$$
$$= \sqrt{10}$$

$ABCD$ is a quadrilateral with four congruent sides, so $ABCD$ is a rhombus.

The **midpoint** of a line segment is the point that divides the segment into two equal-length segments. You can find the coordinates of the midpoint of a line segment by using the midpoint formula.

The Midpoint Formula

The midpoint M of the line segment with endpoints (x_1, y_1) and (x_2, y_2) is

$$M = \left(\frac{x_1 + x_2}{2}, \frac{y_1 + y_2}{2}\right).$$

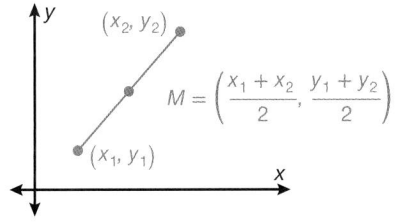

Example 4 **Finding the Midpoint of a Segment**

Find the midpoint of the line segment with the given endpoints.

$(3, 5)$ and $(7, -2)$

SOLUTION Use the midpoint formula. Substitute $(3, 5)$ for (x_1, y_1) and $(7, -2)$ for (x_2, y_2).

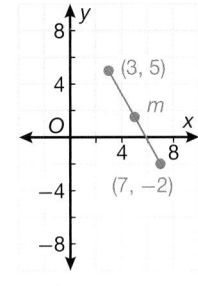

$$M = \left(\frac{x_1 + x_2}{2}, \frac{y_1 + y_2}{2}\right)$$

$$= \frac{3 + 7}{2}, \frac{5 + (-2)}{2} \qquad \text{Substitute.}$$

$$= \left(\frac{10}{2}, \frac{3}{2}\right) \qquad \text{Simplify.}$$

$$= \left(5, \frac{3}{2}\right) \qquad \text{Simplify.}$$

The midpoint of the line segment with endpoints $(3, 5)$ and $(7, -2)$ is $\left(5, \frac{3}{2}\right)$.

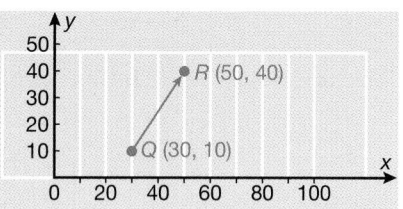

Example 5 Application: Football

A coordinate plane can be used to model positions of players on a football field.

A quarterback is on the 30-yard line at (30, 10). He throws a pass to his receiver who is on the 50-yard line at (50, 40). Find the length of the pass as a radical in simplest form. Then use a calculator to estimate the length to the nearest yard.

SOLUTION Use the distance formula to find the distance between the quarterback and his receiver. Substitute (30, 10) for (x_1, y_1) and (50, 40) for (x_2, y_2).

$d = \sqrt{(x_2 - x_1)^2 + (y_2 - y_1)^2}$ Distance formula

$ = \sqrt{(50 - 30)^2 + (40 - 10)^2}$ Substitute.

$ = \sqrt{20^2 + 30^2}$ Simplify inside parentheses.

$ = \sqrt{400 + 900}$ Simplify powers.

$ = \sqrt{1300}$ Add.

$ = 10\sqrt{13} \approx 36$ Simplify. Use a calculator to approximate.

The pass is about 36 yards long.

Math Reasoning

Analyze If the pass is intercepted midway between the quarterback and the receiver, what are the coordinates of the player who intercepts the pass?

Lesson Practice

a. Use the diagram of city streets from Example 1. What is the direct distance (in city blocks) from the corner of C St. and 2nd Ave. to the corner of D St. and 5th Ave.? Give your answer in simplest radical form. Use a calculator to approximate the answer to the nearest whole city block.
(Ex 1)

b. Find the distance between the points $(-3, -2)$ and $(4, 2)$.
(Ex 2)

c. Determine whether quadrilateral $PQRS$ is a rhombus.
(Ex 3)

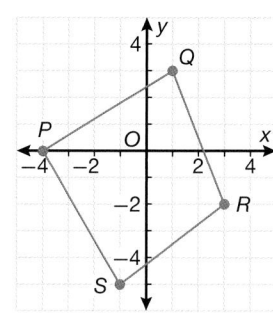

d. Find the midpoint of the line segment with endpoints $(-2, 3)$ and $(4, 7)$.
(Ex 4)

e. (**Football**) Use a coordinate plane like the one shown in Example 5. A quarterback is on the 20-yard line at (20, 33). He throws a pass to his receiver, who is on the opponent's 58-yard line at (58, 15). Find the length of the pass as a radical in simplest form. Then use a calculator to estimate the length to the nearest yard.
(Ex 5)

Solve and graph the solution set.

1. $15y < 60$
(70)

2. $16 < 6x + 10$ OR $-16 > 6x - 10$
(82)

Factor completely.

3. $-2g^2 - 8g + 90$
(79)

4. $20b^2 + 21b - 5$
(75)

5. $-13w^2 + 38w - 25$
(79)

Write each equation in the standard form of a quadratic function, if possible.

6. $y - 14x = -20x^2$
(84)

7. $x - 5x = -2x^2 + 7$
(84)

*8. Find the distance between $(4, -1)$ and $(7, 3)$ using the distance formula.
(86)

9. (Personal Finance) George's credit card company offers 4% cash back on all
(70) purchases. Write and solve an inequality to determine how many charges he needs to make in one year to earn at least $100 cash back.

10. Use the table to determine if there is a positive correlation, a negative correlation,
(71) or no correlation between the data sets.

x	2	4	6	8	10	12
y	12	25	40	51	61	75

11. Multi-Step A real number is at most 13 and at least 5.
(73) **a.** Write two separate inequalities to describe the problem.

  b. Write the two inequalities as one compound inequality.

  c. Graph the compound inequality.

12. (Carpentry) Louis is building a new rectangular room onto his house. The room has
(76) a side length of $3 + \sqrt{15}$ feet and a width of $4 + \sqrt{36}$ feet. What is the area of Louis's new room?

13. Multi-Step The temperature in Texas has never been above 120 degrees Fahrenheit.
(77) Describe this using Celsius temperature by solving the inequality $120 \geq \frac{9}{5}C + 32$.

14. Write How do changes to the value of c affect the graph of $y = \frac{a}{x - b} + c$?
(78)

15. A sandwich maker chooses a meat and a vegetable at random to put on a sandwich.
(80) There are three meats: turkey, ham, and chicken. There are 5 vegetables: lettuce, tomato, cucumber, onion, and peppers. Make a table of the possible outcomes.

16. (Hobbies) Kelly goes to a local store that has a monthly fee of $5 and rents games
(81) there for $1.75 a week. An online company has no monthly fee but rents games for $2.25 a week. How many games would Kelly have to rent per month for the local store to be the better deal?

17. Measurement One square has an area of 16 square units and another square has an area of 36 square units. A third square has an area greater than that of the smaller square and less than that of the larger square. What are the possible lengths of the sides of the third square?
(82)

18. Multiple Choice What is the factored form of $32x^2 - 50y^2$?
(83)

A $2(4x + 5y)^2$ **B** $2(4x - 5y)^2$

C $2(4x + 5y)(4x - 5y)$ **D** $2(16x + 25y)(16x - 25y)$

*19. Verify Rewrite the expression $y^2 - x^2 - 8x - 41$ as a difference of two squares minus a perfect-square polynomial to show that $y^2 - x^2 - 8x - 41 = (y + 5)(y - 5) - (x + 4)^2$.
(83)

20. Error Analysis Two students are asked if the equation $7x^2 + 24 = y - 6x(2 - 3x^2)$ is a quadratic function. Which student is correct? Explain the error.
(84)

Student A	Student B
$y = -18x^3 + 7x^2 + 12x + 24$ no	$y = 10x^2 + 12x + 24$ yes

21. Economics A company has developed a new product. To determine the selling price, the company uses the function $y = -55x^2 + 1500x$ to predict the profit for selling the product for x dollars. Does the graph of this function open upward or downward? Explain why this might be given the context of the situation.
(84)

22. Use the Pythagorean Theorem to find the missing side length. Give the answer in simplest radical form.
(85)

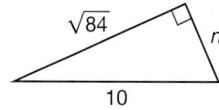

*23. Geometry A right isosceles triangle is a right triangle whose legs are equal in length.
(85)

   a. Find the length of the hypotenuse of a right isosceles triangle with leg lengths of 3.

   b. Find the length of the hypotenuse of a right isosceles triangle with leg lengths of 5.

   c. Formulate Use the results of parts **a** and **b** to suggest a formula for the hypotenuse of a right isosceles triangle with legs of length a.

*24. Error Analysis Two students use the Pythagorean Theorem to find length p. Which student is correct? Explain the error.
(85)

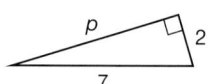

Student A	Student B
$2^2 + 7^2 = p^2$ $4 + 49 = p^2$ $53 = p^2$ $\sqrt{53} = p$	$2^2 + p^2 = 7^2$ $4 + p^2 = 49$ $p^2 = 45$ $p = \sqrt{45}$ $p = 3\sqrt{5}$

*25. Use the diagram of city streets from Example 1 on page 563. What is the
(86) direct distance (in city blocks) from the corner of A St. and 4th Ave. to the corner
of E St. and 2nd Ave.? Give your answer in simplest radical form and to the nearest
tenth of a city block.

*26. Multi-Step Marisol is flying a kite as shown in the diagram.
(85) **a.** Use the Pythagorean Theorem to find the length h.

b. How high is the kite off of the ground?

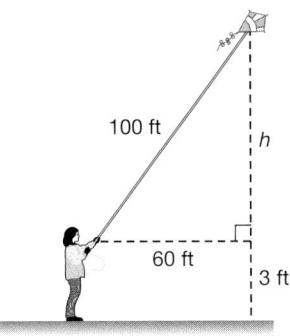

100 ft h

60 ft

3 ft

*27. Write To find the distance between $(5, 3)$ and $(-2, 9)$, Dan lets $(x_1, y_1) = (5, 3)$ in
(86) the distance formula. Dawn lets $(x_1, y_1) = (-2, 9)$. Explain why Dan and Dawn
will get the same result.

*28. Justify Is the triangle with vertices at $(-3, 3)$, $(1, 0)$, and $(4, 4)$ a right triangle?
(86) Justify your answer.

*29. Multiple Choice Which points are not endpoints of a line segment with midpoint
(86) $(7, -3)$?

A $(1, 2)$ and $(13, -8)$ **B** $(5, 0)$ and $(9, -5)$

C $(2, -9)$ and $(12, 3)$ **D** $(4, -2)$ and $(10, -4)$

*30. ⬡**Baseball** A baseball diamond is a square that is 90 feet long on each side. Use
(86) a coordinate grid to model positions of players on the field; place home plate
at $(0, 0)$, first base at $(90, 0)$, second base at $(90, 90)$, and third base at $(0, 90)$.
An outfielder located at $(50, 300)$ throws to the third-baseman. How long is the
throw? Round you answer to the nearest foot.

Factoring Polynomials by Grouping

Warm Up

1. **Vocabulary** For the terms in a polynomial, the product of the greatest integer that divides evenly into the coefficients and the greatest power of each variable that divides evenly into each term is the _____.
(38)

Factor each polynomial completely.

2. $90k^4 + 15k^3$
(38)

3. $x^2 - 8x + 15$
(72)

4. $4n^2 + 5n - 21$
(75)

5. $81x^2 - 64y^2$
(83)

New Concepts

Polynomials can be factored by grouping. When a polynomial has four terms, make two groups and factor out the greatest common factor from each group.

Hint

Factoring is the opposite of multiplying. Check the answer by multiplying. The product should be the original polynomial.

Example 1 **Factoring Four-Term Polynomials**

Factor $2x^2 + 4xy + 7x + 14y$. Check your answer.

SOLUTION

$2x^2 + 4xy + 7x + 14y$

$= (2x^2 + 4xy) + (7x + 14y)$ Group terms that have a common factor.

$= 2x(x + 2y) + 7(x + 2y)$ Factor out the GCF of each binomial.

$= (x + 2y)(2x + 7)$ Factor out $(x + 2y)$.

Check

$(x + 2y)(2x + 7)$

$\overset{?}{=} 2x^2 + 7x + 4xy + 14y$ Multiply using FOIL.

$= 2x^2 + 4xy + 7x + 14y$ ✓   Commutative Property

The product is the original polynomial.

Example 2 **Rearranging before Grouping**

Factor $3y^2 - 8y^3 - 8y + 3$. Check your answer.

SOLUTION

Use the Commutative and Associative Properties to rearrange terms to form two binomials with common factors.

$3y^2 - 8y^3 - 8y + 3$

$= 3y^2 + 3 - 8y^3 - 8y$ Group terms that have a common factor.

$= (3y^2 + 3) - (8y^3 + 8y)$ Group into two binomials.

$= 3(y^2 + 1) - 8y(y^2 + 1)$ Factor out the GCF of each binomial.

$= (y^2 + 1)(3 - 8y)$ Factor out $(y^2 + 1)$.

Hint

When rearranging terms, make sure the negative sign is distributed properly.

Online Connection
www.SaxonMathResources.com

Check

$(y^2 + 1)(3 - 8y)$

$\stackrel{?}{=} 3y^2 - 8y^3 + 3 - 8y$ Multiply using FOIL.

$= 3y^2 - 8y^3 - 8y + 3$ ✓ Commutative Property

The product is the original polynomial.

Example 3   **Factoring with the Greatest Common Factor**

Factor $45a^3b - 15a^3 + 15a^2b - 5a^2$. Check your answer.

SOLUTION

$= 45a^3b - 15a^3 + 15a^2b - 5a^2$

$= 5a^2(9ab - 3a + 3b - 1)$ Factor out the GCF.

$= 5a^2[(9ab - 3a) + (3b - 1)]$ Group into two binomials.

$= 5a^2[(3a)(3b - 1) + 1(3b - 1)]$ Factor out the GCF of each binomial.

$= 5a^2[(3b - 1)(3a + 1)]$ Factor out $(3b - 1)$.

Check

$5a^2[(3b - 1)(3a + 1)]$

$\stackrel{?}{=} 5a^2[9ab + 3b - 3a - 1]$ Multiply using FOIL.

$\stackrel{?}{=} 45a^3b + 15a^2b - 15a^3 - 5a^2$ Distributive Property

$= 45a^3b - 15a^3 + 15a^2b - 5a^2$ ✓ Commutative Property

The product is the original polynomial.

Example 4   **Factoring with Opposites**

Factor $3a^2b - 18a + 30 - 5ab$ completely. Check your answer.

SOLUTION

$3a^2b - 18a + 30 - 5ab$

$= (3a^2b - 18a) + (30 - 5ab)$ Group into two binomials.

$= 3a(ab - 6) + 5(6 - ab)$ Factor the GCF from each binomial.

$= 3a(ab - 6) + 5(-1)(ab - 6)$ Take the opposite by multiplying by –1.

$= 3a(ab - 6) - 5(ab - 6)$ Simplify.

$= (ab - 6)(3a - 5)$ Factor out $(ab - 6)$.

Check

$(ab - 6)(3a - 5)$

$\stackrel{?}{=} 3a^2b - 5ab - 18a + 30$ Multiply using FOIL.

$= 3a^2b - 18a + 30 - 5ab$ ✓ Commutative Property

The product is the original polynomial.

Math Reasoning

Verify Show that $5(6 - ab)$ is equivalent to $-5(ab - 6)$.

A trinomial of the form $ax^2 + bx + c$ can also be factored by grouping. The trinomial is expressed as a polynomial with four terms so that it can be factored by grouping.

To express trinomials in the form $ax^2 + bx + c$ with four terms, first identify a, b, and c. For example, in the trinomial $2x^2 + 11x + 15$, $a = 2$, $b = 11$, and $c = 15$. Then, to factor a trinomial such as $2x^2 + 11x + 15$ by grouping, use the steps shown below.

Step 1: Find the product of ac.

$$2 \cdot 15 = 30$$

Step 2: Find two factors of ac with a sum equal to b.

$$6 \cdot 5 = 30 \text{ and } 6 + 5 = 11$$

Step 3: Write the trinomial using the sum. Replace $11x$ with $6x + 5x$.

$$2x^2 + 11x + 15 = 2x^2 + 6x + 5x + 15$$

Step 4: Factor by grouping.

$$2x^2 + 11x + 15$$
$$= 2x^2 + 6x + 5x + 15$$
$$= (2x^2 + 6x) + (5x + 15)$$
$$= 2x(x + 3) + 5(x + 3)$$
$$= (x + 3)(2x + 5)$$

Example 5 **Factoring a Trinomial**

Factor each trinomial by grouping.

a. $x^2 - 7x - 44$

SOLUTION

$ac = 1 \cdot -44 = -44$; Factors of -44 with a sum of -7 are -11 and 4.

$$x^2 - 7x - 44$$

$= x^2 - 11x + 4x - 44$	Replace $-7x$ with $-11x$ and $4x$.
$= (x^2 - 11x) + (4x - 44)$	Group into two binomials.
$= x(x - 11) + 4(x - 11)$	Factor out the GCF of each binomial.
$= (x - 11)(x + 4)$	Factor out $(x - 11)$.

b. $6k^2 - 17k + 10$

SOLUTION

$ac = 6 \cdot 10 = 60$; Factors of 60 with a sum of -17 are -5 and -12.

$$6k^2 - 17k + 10$$

$= 6k^2 - 12k - 5k + 10$	Replace $-17k$ with $-12k$ and $-5k$.
$= (6k^2 - 12k) - (5k - 10)$	Group into two binomials.
$= 6k(k - 2) - 5(k - 2)$	Factor out the GCF of each binomial.
$= (k - 2)(6k - 5)$	Factor out $(k - 2)$.

Caution

Remember to change the signs of terms within the parentheses when factoring out negative 1.

Factor completely. Check your answer.

a. $3y^2 + 6yz + 4y + 8z$
(Ex 1)

b. $3y^2 - 4y^3 + 3 - 4y$
(Ex 2)

c. $99x^3y - 33x^3 + 33x^2y - 11x^2$
(Ex 3)

d. $3a^2b - 4ab + 20 - 15a$
(Ex 4)

Factor each trinomial by grouping.
(Ex 5)

e. $x^2 - 4x - 77$

f. $6a^2 - 1a - 15$

Practice   Distributed and Integrated

Factor.

1. $x^2 + 3xy - 54y^2$
(72)

*2. $64a^2b - 16a^3 + 18a^2b - 9$
(87)

Solve.

3. $2g + 9 - 4g < 5 + 6g - 2$
(81)

4. $6(k - 5) > 3k - 26$
(81)

Use an equation to find the probability of the event.

5. rolling 4 on two number cubes and a coin landing on heads
(80)

6. rolling a number less than 4 on two number cubes and a coin landing on heads
(80)

Determine whether the polynomial is a perfect-square trinomial or a difference of two squares. Then factor the polynomial.

7. $100 - c^6$
(83)

8. $4x^2 + 20x + 25$
(83)

Find the distance between the given points. Give the answer in simplest radical form.

9. $(1, 3)$ and $(4, 7)$
(86)

*10. $(2, -1)$ and $(6, 3)$
(86)

11. Which situation would most likely be represented by a negative correlation: hours
(71) of practice and your golf score, hours of practice and the number of baskets you make in basketball, or hours of practice and the cost of a computer? Hint: In golf, the lower the score, the better.

12. (Entertainment) The table shows the average ticket price for a movie. Make a scatter
(71) plot from the data.

Year	1990	1995	2000	2001	2002	2003	2004	2005
Ticket Price (dollars)	4.23	4.35	5.40	5.65	5.80	6.03	6.21	6.41

13. Multi-Step A grower ships fruit to a processing plant in 50-pound cases. The plant
(74) will not accept cases that differ from this weight by more than ±0.5 pound.

    a. Write an absolute-value equation to find the minimum and maximum weights
of the cases that the processing plant will accept.

    b. What are the maximum and minimum acceptable weights?

14. (**Hiking**) Heidi can hike the mountains at 2 miles per hour. She has already hiked
(77) 5 miles and wants to be sure to turn around before she hikes more than 9 miles. To
find the number of hours she can hike before she needs to turn around, solve the
inequality $2m + 5 \leq 9$.

15. Multi-Step The local public library has a budget of $3000 to buy new children's
(78) books. The library will receive 100 free books when it places its order. The number
of books, y, that they can get is given by $y = \frac{3000}{x} + 100$, where x is the price
per book.

    a. What is the horizontal asymptote of this rational function?

    b. What is the vertical asymptote?

    c. If the price per book is $20, how many books will the library receive?

16. Generalize How do you know when a trinomial is factored completely?
(79)

17. (**Painting Job**) Marco paints walls and charges a $20 set-up fee. He charges at
(82) least $60 per big wall, and for small walls he charges no more than $40 per wall.
He has just completed a job painting either all big walls or all small walls. His
invoice states that he received $2420 in payment. How many walls could he have
painted?

18. Measurement A map has a scale 1 cm:500 m. A circular pond on the map has an
(83) area of $9x^2\pi - 6x\pi + \pi$ square centimeters. What is the actual diameter of the
pond?

19. Multiple Choice The graph of which function opens downward?
(84)

    A $-8y + 3x^2 = 4 + 7x$ **B** $-12x^2 + 15y = 18$

    C $-y + 36x = x^2 + 40$ **D** $-15 + 9y = 45x^2 - 3x$

*20. Write Explain how to graph a quadratic function such as $y + 28x - 3 = 50x^2 + 7$.
(84)

21. Use the Pythagorean Theorem to find the missing side length.
(85) Give the answer in simplest radical form.

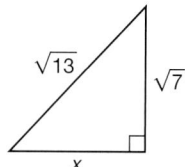

*22. Do the lengths 10, $5\sqrt{5}$, and 15 form a right triangle?
(85)

23. (**Art**) Theresa is painting on a triangular canvas. The lengths of the sides of the
(85) canvas are 24 inches, 32 inches, and 42 inches. Is her canvas a right triangle?

*24. Error Analysis Two students use the distance formula to find the length of the line
(86)   segment with endpoints $(-1, 6)$ and $(4, -2)$. Which student is correct?
Explain the error.

Student A	Student B
$d = \sqrt{(4 + 1)^2 + (-2 - 6)^2}$	$d = \sqrt{(4 - 1)^2 + (-2 - 6)^2}$
$d = \sqrt{25 + 64}$	$d = \sqrt{9 + 64}$
$d = \sqrt{89}$	$d = \sqrt{73}$

*25. Geometry A midsegment of a triangle is a line segment joining the midpoints of
(86)   two sides of the triangle. A triangle has vertices at $P = (3, 2)$, $Q = (3, 8)$, and
$R = (7, 6)$.
a. Find the endpoints M and N of the midsegment that joins sides $\overline{PQ}$ and $\overline{QR}$.

b. Verify Show that the length of the midsegment $\overline{MN}$ is half the length
of $\overline{PR}$.

26. Multi-Step Use a coordinate plane to model the following situation in a football
(86)   game: A quarterback is on the 25 yard line at $(25, 10)$; he has two receivers, one at
$(30, 40)$ and the other at $(50, 20)$.
a. Find the quarterback's distance to the receiver at $(30, 40)$. Give your answer to
the nearest yard.

b. Find the quarterback's distance to the receiver at $(50, 20)$. Give your answer to
the nearest yard.

c. Which receiver is closer to the quarterback?

*27. Multi-Step The area of a right triangle is $x^2 + 2x$. The base, b, equals $x + 2$. What is
(87)   the length of the height, h?
a. Write the formula for the area of a triangle given the base and height.

b. Set the area equal to the product of the base and the height.

c. Factor.

d. Divide by the length of the base to find the length of the height.

*28. Write Is a binomial also a polynomial? Explain.
(87)

*29. Formulate Write an expression to show the price of 2 discounted books when the
(87)   first one is $20 + n$ and each one after that is $(20 + n)(n - 5)$.

*30. (Cost) The baseball team gets new uniforms. The first group of 5 costs $y^2 + 5$
(87)   dollars, and after that, each group of 5 costs $y + 1$ dollars. How much do the
uniforms cost if the team buys 15?

Multiplying and Dividing Rational Expressions

Warm Up

1. **Vocabulary** A _____ (*radical, rational*) expression has at least one variable in its denominator.
   (39)

Simplify. Assume that no denominator is equal to zero.

2. $x^6 x^2$
   (3)

3. $\dfrac{8b^4}{12b^9}$
   (32)

4. $\dfrac{12y^4 - 18y^3}{28y^2 - 42y}$
   (43)

5. Factor $x^2 - 14x + 24$.
   (72)

New Concepts

Multiplying and dividing rational expressions follows the same procedure as multiplying and dividing fractions.

Math Language

A **polynomial** is a monomial or a sum or difference of monomials.

Multiplying Rational Expressions	Dividing Rational Expressions
If a, b, c, and d are nonzero polynomials, $\dfrac{a}{b} \cdot \dfrac{c}{d} = \dfrac{ac}{bd}$.	If a, b, c, and d are nonzero polynomials, $\dfrac{a}{b} \div \dfrac{c}{d} = \dfrac{a}{b} \cdot \dfrac{d}{c} = \dfrac{ad}{bc}$.

Example 1 Multiplying Rational Expressions

Find each product.

(a.) $\dfrac{6x^4 y}{21xy^3} \cdot \dfrac{7x^2 y^2}{3x^3 y^2}$

SOLUTION

Hint

Remember, when multiplying powers, find the sum of the exponents.

$$x^a \cdot x^b = x^{a+b}$$

When dividing powers, subtract the exponents.

$$\frac{x^a}{x^b} = x^{a-b}$$

$\dfrac{6x^4 y}{21xy^3} \cdot \dfrac{7x^2 y^2}{3x^3 y^2}$

$= \dfrac{42x^6 y^3}{63x^4 y^5}$ Multiply the numerators and denominators.

$= \dfrac{2x^2}{3y^2}$ Simplify.

(b.) $\dfrac{6x^2}{5y^4} \cdot \dfrac{3x}{7y^2}$

SOLUTION

$\dfrac{6x^2}{5y^4} \cdot \dfrac{3x}{7y^2}$

$= \dfrac{18x^3}{35y^6}$ Multiply the numerators and denominators.

Online Connection
www.SaxonMathResources.com

There are no common factors, so the product does not simplify any further.

Example 2 Multiplying a Rational Expression by a Polynomial

Multiply $\dfrac{9}{3x-15} \cdot (x^2 - 2x - 15)$. Simplify your answer.

SOLUTION

Math Reasoning

Justify How did you decide what binomials to factor the trinomial into?

$$\dfrac{9}{3x-15} \cdot (x^2 - 2x - 15)$$

$$= \dfrac{9}{3x-15} \cdot \dfrac{(x^2 - 2x - 15)}{1} \quad \text{Write the polynomial with a denominator of 1.}$$

$$= \dfrac{9}{3(x-5)} \cdot \dfrac{(x-5)(x+3)}{1} \quad \text{Factor the trinomial.}$$

$$= \dfrac{\overset{3}{\cancel{9}}}{\underset{1}{\cancel{3}(\cancel{x-5})}} \cdot \dfrac{(\cancel{x-5})(x+3)}{1} \quad \text{Divide out like factors.}$$

$$= 3(x + 3) \quad \text{Simplify.}$$

$$= 3x + 9 \quad \text{Distribute.}$$

There is more than one way to find the product of two rational expressions. The factors can be multiplied first before being simplified. Another way to solve the problem would be to simplify each expression first, and then to multiply, simplifying again if necessary.

Example 3 Multiplying Rational Expressions Containing Polynomials

Multiply $\dfrac{8m^2n + 2mn}{2m} \cdot \dfrac{15}{24mn + 6n}$. Simplify your answer.

SOLUTION

Method 1: Multiply first.

$$\dfrac{8m^2n + 2mn}{2m} \cdot \dfrac{15}{24mn + 6n}$$

$$= \dfrac{15(8m^2n + 2mn)}{2m(24mn + 6n)}$$

$$= \dfrac{120m^2n + 30mn}{48m^2n + 12mn}$$

$$= \dfrac{30mn(4m + 1)}{12mn(4m + 1)}$$

$$= \dfrac{\overset{5}{\cancel{30mn(4m+1)}}}{\underset{2}{\cancel{12mn(4m+1)}}}$$

$$= \dfrac{5}{2}$$

Method 2: Factor first.

$$\dfrac{8m^2n + 2mn}{2m} \cdot \dfrac{15}{24mn + 6n}$$

$$= \dfrac{2mn(4m + 1)}{2m} \cdot \dfrac{15}{6n(4m + 1)}$$

$$= \dfrac{2mn(\overset{1}{\cancel{4m+1}})}{\cancel{2m}} \cdot \dfrac{\overset{5}{\cancel{15}}}{\underset{2}{\cancel{6n}}(\underset{1}{\cancel{4m+1}})}$$

$$= \dfrac{5}{2}$$

Example 4 Dividing Rational Expressions

Find each quotient.

a. $\dfrac{5st^4}{4s^2t} \div \dfrac{15s^2t}{2s^3t^2}$

SOLUTION

$\dfrac{5st^4}{4s^2t} \div \dfrac{15s^2t}{2s^3t^2}$

$= \dfrac{5st^4}{4s^2t} \cdot \dfrac{2s^3t^2}{15s^2t}$ Write as multiplication by the reciprocal.

$= \dfrac{10s^4t^6}{60s^4t^2}$ Multiply the numerators and denominators.

$= \dfrac{t^4}{6}$ Simplify.

b. $\dfrac{9r^2 - 12r}{27} \div (3r - 4)$

SOLUTION

$\dfrac{9r^2 - 12r}{27} \div (3r - 4)$

$= \dfrac{9r^2 - 12r}{27} \div \dfrac{(3r - 4)}{1}$ Write the polynomial with a denominator of 1.

$= \dfrac{9r^2 - 12r}{27} \cdot \dfrac{1}{(3r - 4)}$ Write as multiplication by the reciprocal.

$= \dfrac{3r(3r - 4)}{27} \cdot \dfrac{1}{(3r - 4)}$ Factor.

$= \dfrac{\overset{1}{\cancel{3}}r\cancel{(3r-4)}}{\underset{9}{\cancel{27}}} \cdot \dfrac{1}{\cancel{(3r-4)}}$ Divide out like factors.

$= \dfrac{r}{9}$ Simplify.

c. $\dfrac{x^2 + 4x + 3}{x^2} \div \dfrac{x + 3}{x}$

SOLUTION

$\dfrac{x^2 + 4x + 3}{x^2} \div \dfrac{x + 3}{x}$

$= \dfrac{x^2 + 4x + 3}{x^2} \cdot \dfrac{x}{x + 3}$ Write as multiplication by the reciprocal.

$= \dfrac{\cancel{(x+3)}(x + 1)}{x^{\cancel{2}1}} \cdot \dfrac{\overset{1}{\cancel{x}}}{\cancel{(x+3)}}$ Factor. Divide out like factors.

$= \dfrac{x + 1}{x}$ Simplify.

Example **5** **Application: Profit**

A business makes a profit of $\dfrac{x^4}{100x^2 + 100x}$ dollars for each item sold.
If $x^2 + 5x + 4$ items are sold, what is the total profit in terms of x?

SOLUTION

Multiply the profit for each item sold by the amount of items sold.

$$\frac{x^4}{100x^2 + 100x} \cdot (x^2 + 5x + 4)$$

$$= \frac{x^4}{100x^2 + 100x} \cdot \frac{x^2 + 5x + 4}{1} \qquad \text{Write the polynomial with a denominator of 1.}$$

$$= \frac{x^4}{100x(x + 1)} \cdot \frac{(x + 4)(x + 1)}{1} \qquad \text{Factor.}$$

$$= \frac{x^{4^{3}}}{100x\cancel{(x + 1)}} \cdot \frac{(x + 4)\cancel{(x + 1)}}{1} \qquad \text{Divide out like factors.}$$

$$= \frac{x^3(x + 4)}{100} \qquad \text{Simplify.}$$

Lesson Practice

Find each product.
(Ex 1)

a. $\dfrac{4z^5q^8}{14qz^7} \cdot \dfrac{14qz^4}{3q^4z}$

b. $\dfrac{5x^2}{7y^4} \cdot \dfrac{4x^2}{9y^3}$

Multiply. Simplify your answer.

c. $\dfrac{6}{2x - 18} \cdot (x^2 - 6x - 27)$
(Ex 2)

d. $\dfrac{8m + 6m^2n}{12} \cdot \dfrac{8m}{24m + 8mn}$
(Ex 3)

Find each quotient.
(Ex 4)

e. $\dfrac{8j^2k^7}{15k^7j^4} \div \dfrac{6j^3k}{5kj^6}$

f. $\dfrac{x^2 + 7x + 12}{x + 5} \div (x + 3)$

g. $\dfrac{x^2 + 5x + 6}{x + 2} \div \dfrac{x + 3}{y^2}$

h. (**Profits**) Tran makes a profit of $\dfrac{x^2}{20x^2 + 10x}$ for each ticket he sells.
(Ex 5) What is his profit in terms of x if he sells $x^2 + 9x + 20$ tickets?

1. Solve $6(x + 2) - 4x > 2 + x + 2$.
(81)

2. Solve and graph the inequality $4 \geq 2(x + 3)$ OR $23 < 8x + 7$.
(82)

Rewrite the equation in the standard form of a quadratic function, if possible.

3. $x(y - 2x) = 18x^2$
(84)

4. $2(y - 2x) = 6x^2$
(84)

Find the distance between the given points. Give the answer in simplest radical form.

5. $(-4, -5)$ and $(2, -3)$
(86)

6. $(3, -2)$ and $(1, 0)$
(86)

Find the midpoint of the line segment with the given endpoints.

7. $(-4, -5)$ and $(2, -3)$
(86)

8. $(3, -2)$ and $(1, 0)$
(86)

Find the product or quotient.

*9. $\dfrac{2y^2 + 10y}{y + 5} \cdot \dfrac{2x}{2x^3}$
(88)

*10. $\dfrac{6y}{x} \div \dfrac{x + y}{3y}$
(88)

*11. $\dfrac{7x}{y} \div \dfrac{4}{y}$
(88)

Factor.

12. $7x - 60 + x^2$
(72)

13. $64a^3b - 32a^3 + 16a^2b - 8a^2$
(87)

14. (**Woodworking**) To inlay designs on the top of chest, a crafter uses a series of
(72) patterns. The patterns are represented by the trinomial $x^2 + 4x - 21$. What are the dimensions of the patterns?

15. Write a compound inequality that describes the graph.
(73)

16. (**Athletic Directing**) An athletic director has a budget of \$700 to buy uniforms. He
(78) will receive 5 free uniforms when he places his order. The number of uniforms, y, that he can get is given by $y = \frac{700}{x} + 5$, where x is the price per uniform.
a. What is the horizontal asymptote of this rational function?
b. What is the vertical asymptote?
c. If the price per uniform is \$50, how many uniforms will he receive?
d. Can the athletic director receive only 5 uniforms? Why or why not?

17. Multi-Step The area of a triangular sail in square feet is represented by the
(79) equation $\frac{1}{2}x^2 + \frac{7}{2}x + 5$.
a. Factor this expression completely in terms of the area of a triangle.
b. Let $x = 3$. What is the area of the sail in square feet?

18. Write Why is making tables and graphs a good way to show probability distribution?
(80)

19. (Paving) A new restaurant is opening in a square building with a side length of
(83) s feet. A parking lot surrounds the building in the form of a larger square. The restaurant sits in the middle of the lot. The plot of land on which the restaurant and parking lot lie has an area of $9s^2 + 54s + 81$ square feet. How far does the parking lot extend from the building?

*20. Analyze The figure shows the first four right triangles in the *Wheel of*
(85) *Theodorus* (named after a fifth-century Greek philosopher).

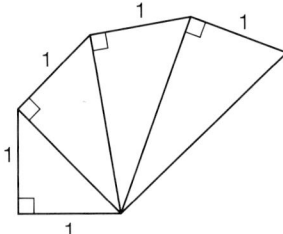

    a. Find the length of the hypotenuse of each of the four triangles.

    b. Predict Suppose the pattern of the triangles is continued until the figure contains 10 triangles. Predict what the length of the hypotenuse of the tenth triangle will be.

21. Multiple Choice Which lengths represent the lengths of the sides of a right
(85) triangle?

    A $3, 4, 6$ **B** $\sqrt{13}, 5, 12$

    C $\sqrt{15}, 7, 8$ **D** $6, 8, 12$

22. Error Analysis Students A and B find the midpoint of the line segment with
(86) endpoints $P = (12, -5)$ and $Q = (-2, 3)$. Student A says that the x-coordinate of the midpoint is $\frac{12 - (-2)}{2} = \frac{14}{2} = 7$. Student B says that the x-coordinate of the midpoint is $\frac{12 + (-2)}{2} = \frac{10}{2} = 5$. Which student is correct? Explain the error.

23. (Software) A game designer is working on a computer basketball game. On the
(86) computer screen, the coordinates of the corners of the court are $(20, 20)$, $(20, 70)$, $(114, 70)$, and $(114, 20)$. Find the length of a diagonal of the court to the nearest tenth of a unit.

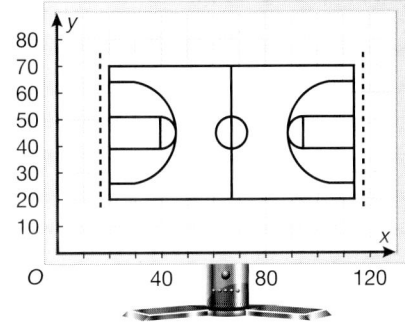

*24. Measurement Malik is adding 5 feet to the length of a screened-in porch. If the
(87)   porch is originally a square room with area x^2 and the new area measures
       50 square feet, what are the dimensions of the new porch?

*25. Geometry A rectangle has a length of $12x^2 + 3y$ and a width of $6x^2 + y$.
(87)   What is its area? What is the simplest way to express the area?

26. Multiple Choice What is the result of a complete factoring of $25x^2 - 81$?
(87)   **A** $25(x + 9)(x - 9)$

       B $5x \cdot 5x - 81$

       C $5^2 x^2 - 9^2$

       D $(5x + 9)(5x - 9)$

*27. Generalize What is the method for multiplying and dividing exponents when working
(88)   with rational expressions?

*28. Multiple Choice Multiply $\dfrac{y^2 + 6y + 5}{y^2} \cdot \dfrac{y}{y + 1}$.
(88)

   A $\dfrac{y + 5}{y^2}$ **B** $\dfrac{y + 5}{y}$

   C $\dfrac{(y + 1)(y + 5)}{y^2}$ **D** $y(y + 5)$

*29. (Murals) Lucy paints murals. She charges \$10.00 per square foot. If she paints a
(88)   mural that is $c^2 + 7c + 10$ ft by $\dfrac{1}{c + 5}$ ft, how much does Lucy charge for painting
       the mural?

30. Multi-Step The area of a square patio is represented by $81x^2 - 36x + 4$ square feet.
(75)   **a.** Factor the expression completely.

       b. Why do you think this expression is called a perfect square?

Characteristics of Parabolas

A zero of a function is an *x*-value where $f(x) = 0$. You can find the zeros of a parabola using a hand-drawn graph or algebraically using the equation. You can use a graphing calculator to compute approximate values, of any *x*-intercepts and the maximum or minimum of the parabola.

Find any *x*-intercepts and the maximum or minimum of the parabola $y = -2x^2 + 4x - 2$.

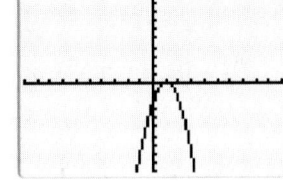

1. Enter the equation $y = -2x^2 + 4x - 2$ into the **Y=** editor.

2. Press **ZOOM** **6:ZStandard** to graph the equation.

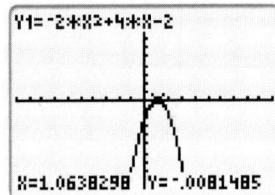

3. Press **TRACE** and then use the ◀ and ▶ keys to move along the curve to the approximate *x*-intercept. The coordinates appear at the bottom of the screen. The *x*-intercept occurs close to the point $(1.064, -0.008)$.

4. Find more accurate coordinates of the *x*-intercept.

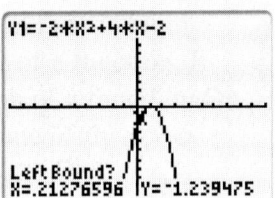

   Press **2nd** **TRACE** (CALC) and select **2:zero**.

   Use the ◀ key to trace along the curve to a point to the left of the *x*-intercept and then press **ENTER**.

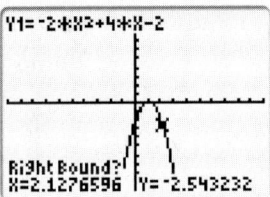

   Press the ▶ key to trace along the curve to a point to the right of the *x*-intercept and then press **ENTER**.

   Press the ◀ key to trace to a point near the *x*-intercept and then press **ENTER**.

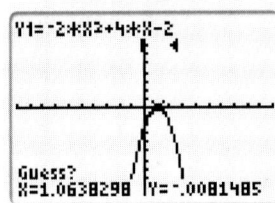

   The approximate coordinates appear at the bottom of the screen. The *x*-intercept of the parabola occurs of about the point $(1, 0)$.

   For this parabola, the *x*-intercept is also the maximum of the function.

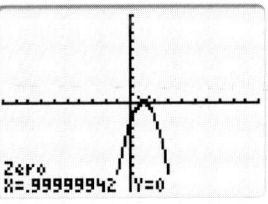

Graphing Calculator Tip

For help with entering an equation into the **Y =** **editor**, see the Graphing Calculator Lab 3 on page 305.

Online Connection
www.SaxonMathResources.com

Example 3 Subtracting with Unlike Denominators

Subtract. Simplify your answers.

$$\frac{x + 3}{x - 4} - \frac{2}{x^2 + x - 20}$$

SOLUTION

$$\frac{x + 3}{x - 4} - \frac{2}{x^2 + x - 20}$$

$$= \frac{x + 3}{x - 4} - \frac{2}{(x - 4)(x + 5)} \qquad \text{Factor the denominators.}$$

$$= \frac{x + 3}{x - 4}\left(\frac{x + 5}{x + 5}\right) - \frac{2}{(x - 4)(x + 5)} \qquad \text{Write each expression using the LCD.}$$

$$= \frac{x^2 + 8x + 15}{(x - 4)(x + 5)} - \frac{2}{(x - 4)(x + 5)} \qquad \text{Multiply.}$$

$$= \frac{x^2 + 8x + 13}{(x - 4)(x + 5)} \qquad \text{Subtract.}$$

The numerator cannot be factored; the expression is in simplified form.

Example 4 Simplifying with Opposite Denominators

Add. Simplify your answer.

$$\frac{8}{v - 4} + \frac{v - 7}{4 - v}$$

SOLUTION

The denominators are opposites. Multiplying either denominator by -1 will make both denominators the same.

$$\frac{8}{v - 4} + \frac{v - 7}{4 - v}$$

$$= \frac{8}{v - 4}\left(\frac{-1}{-1}\right) + \frac{v - 7}{4 - v} \qquad \text{Multiply the numerator and denominator by } -1.$$

$$= \frac{-8}{4 - v} + \frac{v - 7}{4 - v} \qquad \text{Simplify.}$$

$$= \frac{-8 + v - 7}{4 - v} \qquad \text{Add numerators.}$$

$$= \frac{v - 15}{4 - v} \qquad \text{Combine like terms.}$$

Hint

A plane flying into a headwind is going against the wind, and is therefore slower. A plane with a tailwind is flying with the wind, and is therefore faster.

Example 5 Application: Transportation

A plane flies 2000 miles with a headwind and makes the return trip with a tailwind. Write and simplify an expression for the total time of the round-trip flight assuming that the wind speed w remains constant and the plane's rate averages 500 miles per hour.

SOLUTION

Rearrange the distance formula $t = \frac{d}{r}$, and use it to write expressions for the time of each flight. Then add the expressions.

$$\text{time going} = \frac{2000}{500 - w} \qquad \text{time returning} = \frac{2000}{500 + w}$$

$$\text{total time} = \frac{2000}{500 - w} + \frac{2000}{500 + w}$$

$$= \frac{2000}{500 - w}\left(\frac{500 + w}{500 + w}\right) + \frac{2000}{500 + w}\left(\frac{500 - w}{500 - w}\right)$$

$$= \frac{1{,}000{,}000 + 2000w}{(500 - w)(500 + w)} + \frac{1{,}000{,}000 - 2000w}{(500 - w)(500 + w)}$$

$$= \frac{2{,}000{,}000 + 2000w - 2000w}{(500 - w)(500 + w)} = \frac{2{,}000{,}000}{(500 - w)(500 + w)}$$

Math Reasoning

Estimate About how long is the round-trip flight if the wind speed is 50 mph?

The expression $\frac{2{,}000{,}000}{(500 - w)(500 + w)}$, where w is the wind speed, represents the time of the round-trip flight.

Lesson Practice

Add or subtract. Simplify your answers.

a. *(Ex 1)* $\dfrac{4mn}{24m} + \dfrac{11mn}{24m}$

b. *(Ex 1)* $\dfrac{7y - 2}{y + 6} - \dfrac{y - 38}{y + 6}$

c. *(Ex 1)* $\dfrac{d^4 + 2d^3}{d^2 - 5d - 36} + \dfrac{2d^3}{d^2 - 5d - 36}$

d. *(Ex 2)* $\dfrac{-3p}{6p^2} + \dfrac{2p^3}{p^4}$

e. *(Ex 3)* $\dfrac{x}{x + 3} - \dfrac{3}{x^2 + 5x + 6}$

f. *(Ex 4)* $\dfrac{-1}{t^4 - 2} + \dfrac{t + 9}{2 - t^4}$

g. *(Ex 5)* A kayaker paddles 5 miles one way against the current and then makes the return trip with the current. Write and simplify an expression for the total time of the kayaking trip, assuming that the rate of the current remains constant and that the kayaker's paddling rate averages 1.5 miles per hour.

Practice   Distributed and Integrated

Find the distance between the given points. Give the answer in simplest radical form.

1. *(86)* $(-3, -1)$ and $(4, 2)$

2. *(86)* $(1, 1)$ and $(9, 1)$

Factor completely.

3. *(75)* $12 + 17x + 6x^2$

4. *(75)* $21t + 4t^2 - 49$

Determine whether the polynomial is a perfect-square trinomial or a difference of two squares. Then factor the polynomial.

5. *(83)* $9x^4 + 42x^2y + 49y^2$

6. *(83)* $x^6 + 16x^3 + 64$

Some absolute-value inequalities have variable expressions inside the absolute-value symbols. The expression inside the absolute-value symbols can be positive or negative.

The inequality $|x + 1| < 3$ represents all numbers whose distance from -1 is less than 3.

The inequality $|x + 1| > 3$ represents all numbers whose distance from -1 is greater than 3.

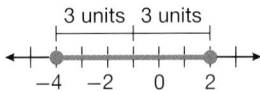

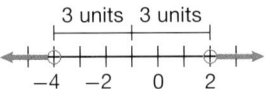

Rules for Solving Absolute-Value Inequalities
For an inequality in the form $|K| < a$, where K represents a variable expression and $a > 0$, solve $-a < K < a$ or $K > -a$ AND $K < a$.
For an inequality in the form $|K| > a$, where K represents a variable expression and $a > 0$, solve $K < -a$ OR $K > a$.
Similar rules are true for $|K| \le a$ or $|K| \ge a$.

Example 3 Solving Inequalities with Operations Inside Absolute-Value Symbols

Solve each inequality. Then graph the solution.

a. $|x - 5| \le 3$

SOLUTION

Use the rules for solving absolute-value inequalities to write a compound inequality.

$|x - 5| \le 3$

$\quad x - 5 \ge -3 \quad$ AND $\quad x - 5 \le 3 \qquad$ Write the compound inequality.

$\quad \underline{+5 \quad +5} \qquad\qquad \underline{+5 \quad +5} \qquad$ Addition Property of Inequality

$\quad\quad x \ge 2 \quad$ AND $\qquad x \le 8 \qquad$ Simplify.

Now graph the inequality.

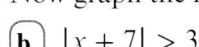

b. $|x + 7| > 3$

SOLUTION

Use the rules for solving absolute-value inequalities to write a compound inequality.

$|x + 7| > 3$

$\quad x + 7 < -3 \quad$ OR $\quad x + 7 > 3 \qquad$ Write the compound inequality.

$\quad \underline{-7 \quad -7} \qquad\qquad \underline{-7 \quad -7} \qquad$ Subtraction Property of Inequality

$\quad\quad x < -10 \quad$ OR $\qquad x > -4 \qquad$ Simplify.

Now graph the inequality.

Example 4 Solving Special Cases

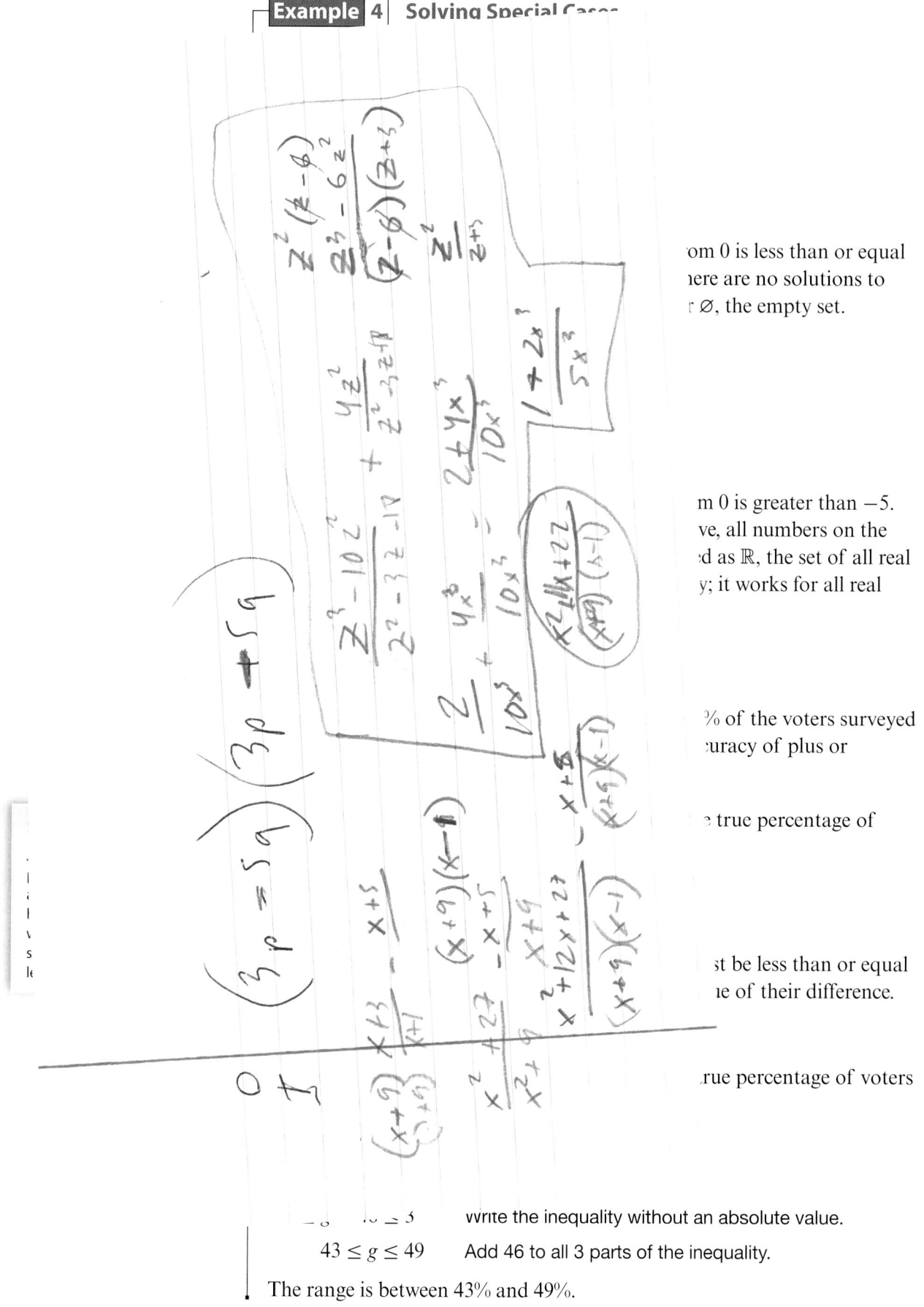

...om 0 is less than or equal
...here are no solutions to
...r ∅, the empty set.

...m 0 is greater than −5.
...ve, all numbers on the
...d as $\mathbb{R}$, the set of all real
...y; it works for all real

...% of the voters surveyed
...curacy of plus or

...e true percentage of

...st be less than or equal
...le of their difference.

...rue percentage of voters

$-\ 6\ ... \le 3$ Write the inequality without an absolute value.

$43 \le g \le 49$ Add 46 to all 3 parts of the inequality.

The range is between 43% and 49%.

a. Solve and graph the inequality $|x| < 12$.
(Ex 1)

b. Solve and graph the inequality $|x| > 19$.
(Ex 1)

c. Solve and graph the inequality $|x| + 2.8 \leq 10.4$.
(Ex 2)

d. Solve and graph the inequality $\dfrac{|x|}{-5} < -1$.
(Ex 2)

e. Solve and graph the inequality $|x - 10| \leq 12$.
(Ex 3)

f. Solve and graph the inequality $|x + 12| > 18$.
(Ex 3)

g. Solve the inequality $|x| + 21 \leq 14$.
(Ex 4)

h. Solve the inequality $|x| + 33 > 24$.
(Ex 4)

(**Industry**) A machine part must be 15 ± 0.2 cm in diameter.
(Ex 5)

i. Write an inequality to show the range of acceptable diameters.

j. Solve the inequality to find the actual range for the diameters.

Practice   Distributed and Integrated

1. Find the axis of symmetry for the graph of the equation $y = -\frac{1}{2}x^2 + x - 3$.
(89)

Add or subtract.

2. $\dfrac{6rs}{r^2s^2} + \dfrac{18r}{r^2s^2}$
(90)

3. $\dfrac{b}{2b + 1} - \dfrac{6}{b - 4}$
(90)

Factor.

4. $-4y^4 + 8y^3 + 5y^2 - 10y$
(87)

5. $3a^2 - 27$
(83)

6. $4x^2 + 6x - 4$
(75)

7. $9x^2 - 2x + 32$
(75)

*8. Solve and graph the inequality $|x| < 96$.
(91)

*9. Write Explain what $|x| \geq 54$ means on a number line.
(91)

*10. Justify When solving an absolute-value inequality, a student gets $|x| \geq -5$. Justify
(91) that any value for x makes this inequality true.

*11. Multiple Choice Which inequality is represented by the graph?
(91)

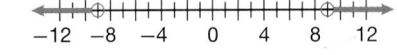

$$-12 \quad -8 \quad -4 \quad 0 \quad 4 \quad 8 \quad 12$$

A $|x| < 9$ **B** $|x| > 9$ **C** $|x| \leq 9$ **D** $|x| < -9$

*12. (**Track**) A runner finishes a sprint in 8.54 seconds. The timer's accuracy is plus or
(91) minus 0.3 seconds. Solve and graph the inequality $|t - 8.54| \leq 0.3$.

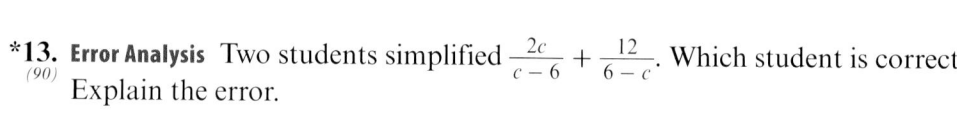

*13. **Error Analysis** Two students simplified $\frac{2c}{c-6} + \frac{12}{6-c}$. Which student is correct?
(90) Explain the error.

Student A	Student B
$\dfrac{2c - 12}{c - 6}$	$\dfrac{2c + 12}{c - 6}$
$\dfrac{2(c - 6)}{c - 6} = 2$	$\dfrac{2(c + 6)}{c - 6} = -2$

*14. **Multi-Step** A farmer has a rectangular plot of land with an area of $x^2 + 22x + 72$
(90) square meters. He sets aside x^2 square meters for grazing and $2x - 8$ square meters
for a chicken coop.
  a. Write a simplified expression for the total fraction of the field the farmer has
  set aside.

  b. Estimate About what percent of the field has the farmer set aside if $x = 30$?

15. **Geometry** Write a simplified expression for the total fraction
(90) of the larger rectangle that the triangle and smaller rectangle
cover.

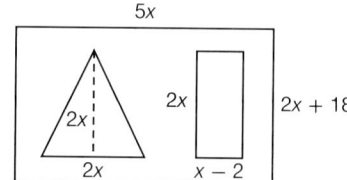

16. Find the product of $\left(\sqrt{4} - 6\right)^2$.
(76)

17. **Analyze** Why is it necessary to understand factoring when dealing with rational
(88) expressions?

18. **Multi-Step** The base of triangle ABC is $x^2 + y$. The height is $\frac{4x + 2xy}{x^3 + xy}$. What is the
(88) area of triangle ABC?
  a. Multiply the base of the triangle by its height.

  b. Multiply the product from part **a** by $\frac{1}{2}$.

*19. **Error Analysis** Two students tried to find the axis of symmetry for the equation
(89) $y = 8x + 2x^2$. Which student is correct? Explain the error.

Student A	Student B
$x = \dfrac{-b}{2a} = \dfrac{-2}{2(8)} = \dfrac{-2}{16} = -\dfrac{1}{8}$	$x = \dfrac{-8}{2(2)} = \dfrac{-8}{4} = -2$

*20. **Space** If it were possible to play ball on Jupiter, the function $y = -13x^2 + 39x$
(89) would approximate the height of a ball kicked straight up at a velocity of
39 meters per second, where x is time in seconds. Find the maximum height the
ball reaches and the time it takes the ball to reach that height. (Hint: Find the time
the ball reaches its maximum height first.)

21. **Measurement** The coordinates of two landmarks on a city map are $A(5, 3)$ and
(86) $B(7, 10)$. Each grid line represents 0.05 miles. Find the distance between
landmarks A and B.

Example 3 **Dividing a Polynomial Using Long Division**

Divide using long division.

$$(-25x + 3x^2 + 8) \div (x - 8)$$

SOLUTION

$$(-25x + 3x^2 + 8) \div (x - 8)$$

$x - 8\overline{)(3x^2 - 25x + 8)}$

Write in long-division form with expressions in standard form.

$$\begin{array}{r} 3x \\ x - 8\overline{)3x^2 - 25x + 8x} \end{array}$$

Divide the first term of the dividend by the first term of the divisor to find the first term of the quotient.

$$\begin{array}{r} 3x \\ x - 8\overline{)3x^2 - 25x + 8} \\ \underline{3x^2 - 24x} \end{array}$$

Multiply the first term of the quotient by the binomial divisor. Write the product under the dividend. Align like terms.

$$\begin{array}{r} 3x \\ x - 8\overline{)3x^2 - 25x + 8} \\ -(3x^2 - 24x) \\ \hline -x + 8 \end{array}$$

Subtract the product from the dividend. Then bring down the next term in the dividend.

$$\begin{array}{r} 3x - 1 \\ x - 8\overline{)3x^2 - 25x + 8} \\ \underline{-3x^2 + 24x} \\ -x + 8 \\ -(-x + 8) \\ \hline 0 \end{array}$$

Repeat the steps to find each term of the quotient.

The remainder is 0.

The quotient is $(3x - 1)$ remainder 0.

Check Multiply the quotient and the divisor.

$$(3x - 1)(x - 8)$$
$$= 3x^2 - 24x - x + 8$$
$$= 3x^2 - 25x + 8$$

The divisor is not always a factor of the dividend. When it is not, the remainder will not be 0. The remainder can be written as a rational expression using the divisor as the denominator.

Example 4 **Long Division with a Remainder**

Divide using long division.

$$(2x^2 - 9 - 7x) \div (-4 + x)$$

Caution

Be sure to put the divisor and dividend in descending order before dividing.

SOLUTION

$$(2x^2 - 9 - 7x) \div (-4 + x)$$

$$x - 4\overline{)2x^2 - 7x - 9}$$ Write in long-division form with expressions in standard form.

$$\begin{array}{r} 2x \\ x - 4\overline{)2x^2 - 7x - 9} \end{array}$$ Divide the first term of the dividend by the first term of the divisor to find the first term of the quotient.

$$\begin{array}{r} 2x \\ x - 4\overline{)2x^2 - 7x - 9} \\ 2x^2 - 8x \end{array}$$ Multiply the first term of the quotient by the binomial divisor. Write the product under the dividend. Align like terms.

$$\begin{array}{r} 2x \\ x - 4\overline{)2x^2 - 7x - 9} \\ -(2x^2 - 8x) \\ \hline x - 9 \end{array}$$ Subtract the product from the dividend. Then bring down the next term in the dividend.

$$\begin{array}{r} 2x + 1 \\ x - 4\overline{)2x^2 - 7x - 9} \\ -(2x^2 - 8x) \\ \hline x - 9 \\ -(x - 4) \\ \hline -5 \end{array}$$ Repeat the steps to find each term of the quotient.

The quotient is $2x + 1 - \dfrac{5}{x - 4}$.

Example 5   **Dividing a Polynomial with a Zero Coefficient**

Divide $(-2x + 5 + 3x^3) \div (-3 + x)$.

SOLUTION

$$(-2x + 5 + 3x^3) \div (-3 + x)$$

$$(3x^3 - 2x + 5) \div (x - 3)$$ Write each polynomial in standard form.

$$x - 3\overline{)3x^3 + 0x^2 - 2x + 5}$$ Write in long division form. Use $0x^2$ as a placeholder for the x^2-term.

$$\begin{array}{r} 3x^2 + 9x + 25 \\ x - 3\overline{)3x^3 + 0x^2 - 2x + 5} \\ -(3x^3 - 9x^2) \\ \hline 9x^2 - 2x \\ -(9x^2 - 27x) \\ \hline 25x + 5 \\ -(25x - 75) \\ \hline 80 \end{array}$$

$3x^3 \div x = 3x^2$

Mulitply $3x^2(x - 3)$. Then subtract.

Bring down $-2x$. $9x^2 \div x = 9x$

Multiply $9x(x - 3)$. Then subtract.

Bring down 5. $25x \div x = 25$

Multiply $25(x - 3)$. Then subtract.

The remainder is 80.

The quotient is $3x^2 + 9x + 25 + \dfrac{80}{x - 3}$.

┌─ Example 6 │ **Application: Length of a Garden**

Jim wants to find the length of the rectangular garden outside his office. The area is $(x^2 - 11x + 30)$ square feet. The width is $(x - 6)$ feet. What is the length of the garden?

SOLUTION

Hint

To find the length, solve the formula for the area of a rectangle, $A = lw$, for the length.

$$l = \frac{A}{w} \qquad \text{Solve for } l.$$

$$= \frac{x^2 - 11x + 30}{(x - 6)} \qquad \text{Evaluate for } A \text{ and } w.$$

$$= \frac{(x - 6)(x - 5)}{(x - 6)} \qquad \text{Factor the numerator.}$$

$$= \frac{\cancel{(x - 6)}\,(x - 5)}{\cancel{(x - 6)}} \qquad \text{Divide out common factors.}$$

$$= (x - 5) \qquad \text{Simplify.}$$

The length of the garden is $(x - 5)$ feet.

Lesson Practice

Divide each expression.

a. $(7x^4 + 7x^3 - 84x^2) \div 7x^2$
(Ex 1)

b. $(x^2 - 10x + 25) \div (x - 5)$
(Ex 2)

c. $(3x^2 - 14x - 5) \div (5 - x)$
(Ex 2)

Divide using long division.

d. $(8x^2 + x^3 - 20x) \div (x - 2)$
(Ex 3)

e. $(-3x^2 + 6x^3 + x - 33) \div (-2 + x)$
(Ex 4)

f. $(6x + 5x^3 - 8) \div (x - 4)$.
(Ex 5)

g. Carlos wants to find the width of his rectangular deck. The area is $(x^2 - 10x + 24)$ square feet and the length is $(x - 4)$ feet. What is the width?
(Ex 6)

Practice   Distributed and Integrated

1. Find the distance between $(-3, 2)$ and $(9, -3)$. Give the answer in simplest radical form.
(86)

2. Solve $\frac{5}{16}y + \frac{3}{8} \geq \frac{1}{2}$, and graph the solution.
(77)

Factor.

3. $2x^2 + 12x + 16$
(79)

4. $3x^3 - 5x^2 - 9x + 15$
(87)

*5. Find the quotient: $\dfrac{4x^3 + 42x^2 - 2x}{2x}$.
(93)

6. Find the axis of symmetry for the graph of the equation $y = x^2 - 2x$.
(89)

Simplify.

7. $\dfrac{\dfrac{7x^4}{4x + 18}}{\dfrac{3x^2}{6x + 27}}$
(92)

*8. $\dfrac{\dfrac{1}{x^3}}{\dfrac{1}{x^3} + \dfrac{1}{x^3}}$
(92)

*9. Write Explain how to check that $(5x + 6)$ is the correct quotient of
(93) $(15x^2 + 13x - 6) \div (3x - 1)$.

*10. Justify Show that the quotient of $(x^2 - 4) \div (x + 2)$ can be found using two
(93) different methods.

*11. (Swimming) The city has decided to open a new public pool. The area of the new
(93) rectangular pool is $(x^2 - 16x + 63)$ square feet and the width is $(x - 7)$ feet.
What is the length?

*12. Multiple Choice Simplify $\dfrac{x^3 - 7x + 3x^2 - 21}{x + 3}$.
(93)

    A $x^2 - 7$ **B** $x^3 - 7$

    C -3 **D** $\dfrac{x^2 - 7}{2x}$

*13. Error Analysis Students were asked to simplify $\dfrac{\dfrac{6x^2 - 6x}{8x^2 + 8x}}{\dfrac{3x - 3}{4x^2 + 4x}}$. Which student is correct?
(92) Explain the error.

Student A	Student B
$\dfrac{6x^2 - 6x}{8x^2 + 8x} \cdot \dfrac{4x^2 + 4x}{3x - 3}$	$\dfrac{6x^2 - 6}{8x^2 + 8x} \cdot \dfrac{4x^2 + 4x}{3x - 3}$
$= \dfrac{6x(x - 1)}{8x(x + 1)} \cdot \dfrac{4x(x + 1)}{3(x - 1)}$	$= \dfrac{6x(x - 1)}{8x(x + 1)} \cdot \dfrac{4x(x + 1)}{3(x - 1)}$
$= x$	$= \dfrac{24x^2}{24x}$

14. Multi-Step Brent rode his scooter $\dfrac{8x^2 - 48x}{24x^5}$ minutes to get to baseball practice that
(92) was $\dfrac{7x - 42}{4x^2}$ miles away.

    a. Find his rate in miles per minute.

    b. If the rate is divided by $\frac{1}{x}$, what is the new rate?

*15. Geometry The area of a parallelogram is $\dfrac{m + n}{5}$ square inches and the height is
(92) $\dfrac{m^2 + n^2}{15}$ inches. What is the length of the base?

16. Solve and graph the inequality $|x| > 84$.
(91)

Graph each function.

a. $y = x^2 - 4x + 7$
(Ex 1)

b. $y = 2x^2 - 16x + 24$
(Ex 2)

c. $y = 2x^2 - 9$
(Ex 3)

Find the zeros of each function.

d. $y = x^2 + 10x + 25.$
(Ex 4)

e. $y = 3x^2 - 21x + 30.$
(Ex 4)

f. $y = -\frac{1}{2}x^2 - 1$
(Ex 4)

g. (Ex 5) $\boxed{\text{Scoccer}}$ The height of a soccer ball that is kicked can be modeled by the function $f(x) = -8x^2 + 24x$, where x is the time in seconds after it is kicked. Find the time it takes the ball to reach its maximum height.

Practice   Distributed and Integrated

1. Find the zeros of the function shown.
(89)

2. Add $\dfrac{25}{16x^2 y} + \dfrac{xy}{32y^5}$.
(90)

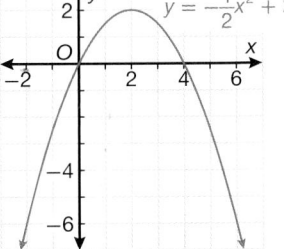

$y = -\frac{1}{2}x^2 + 2x$

*3. Solve the equation $\dfrac{10|x|}{3} + 18 = 4$ and graph the solution.
(94)

4. Solve $-0.3 + 0.14n = 2.78$.
(24)

5. Solve $\dfrac{6}{x - 3} = \dfrac{3}{10}$.
(31)

6. Find the LCD of $\dfrac{6}{x + 6} - \dfrac{12}{x^2 + 8x + 12}$.
(95)

7. The table lists the ordered pairs from a relation. Determine whether they form a function.
(25)

Domain (x)	Range (y)
10	15
11	17
8	11
9	13
5	5

8. Simplify $\dfrac{\dfrac{-x^5}{21x + 3}}{\dfrac{5x^9}{28x + 4}}$.
(92)

*9. Graph the function $y = x^2 - 2x - 8$.
(96)

*10. Write Explain how to reflect a point across the axis of symmetry to get a second point on the parabola.
(96)

*11. Justify Show that the vertex of $y = 4x^2 - 24x + 9$ is $(3, -27)$.
(96)

*12. Multiple Choice Which function has the vertex $(6, -160)$?
(96)
    A $y = 6x^2 - 72x + 56$ **B** $y = 2x^2 - 8x + 48$

    C $y = 3x^2 + 42x - 12$ **D** $y = 5x^2 - 5x + 43$

*13. (Diving) A diver moves upward with an initial velocity of 10 feet per second.
(96) How high will he be 0.5 seconds after diving from a 6-foot platform? Use
$h = -16t^2 + vt + s$.

14. Multiple Choice Find the LCD of $\dfrac{3}{2x - 10}$ and $\dfrac{5x}{2x^2 - 4x - 30}$.
(95)
    A $2(x - 5)(x + 3)$ **B** $(x - 5)(x + 3)$

    C $(x + 5)(x - 3)$ **D** $\dfrac{2}{(x - 5)(x + 3)}$

*15. Geometry One side of a triangle is $\dfrac{2}{x + 2}$ yards and two sides are each $\dfrac{-5}{3x + 6}$ yards.
(95) Find the perimeter of the triangle.

*16. Measurement Carrie measured a distance of $\dfrac{3x^2}{9x - 18}$ yards and Jessie
(95) measured a distance of $\dfrac{4x - 5}{x^2 - 4}$ yards. How much longer is Carrie's
measurement than Jessie's?

17. (Banking) The dollar amount in a student's banking account is represented by the
(91) absolute-value inequality $|x - 200| \leq 110$. Solve the inequality and graph the
solution.

18. Generalize Why is a place holder needed for missing variables in a polynomial
(93) dividend?

19. Multiple Choice Simplify $(-5x + 2x^2 - 3) \div (x - 3)$.
(93)
    A $2x - 1$ **B** $2x + 1$ **C** $\dfrac{x - 2}{2x}$ **D** $\dfrac{x^2 - 3}{5x}$

*20. (Physics) A family is going to see friends that live in two different towns. They will
(94) have to travel 100 miles plus or minus 10 miles to see either of them. They want
to spend 2 hours in the car. What are the minimum and maximum rates that they
need to go?

*21. Error Analysis Two students graph the solution to the equation $|2x + 10| = 8$.
(94) Which student is correct? Explain the error.

Student A	Student B
$\{-9, -1\}$	$\{-9, -1\}$

22. (Art) Jeremy's picture frame has an area of $x^2 - 18x + 80$ square inches. He has
(90) two square pictures in it, one measuring $\frac{1}{4}x$ inch on each side and the other
measuring $\frac{1}{2}x$ inch on each side. Write a simplified expression for the total fraction
of the frame covered by pictures.

j. Nila has plans to attend the school bookfair and she wants to spend
(Ex 5) no more than \$25. Each book series costs \$15 and each book costs \$5.
Write an inequality to describe the total cost of the books Nila can buy
and graph the inequality.

Practice   Distributed and Integrated

Simplify.

1. $\dfrac{30x^{-2}y^{12}}{6y^{-5}}$
(32)

2. $\sqrt{0.09q^2r} + q\sqrt{0.04r}$
(69)

3. $\dfrac{16g^4}{2g+3} - \dfrac{81}{2g+3}$
(90)

4. Find the range of the data set that includes the ages of 9 members of a chess club:
(48) 23, 7, 44, 31, 18, 27, 35, 39, 66.

5. Find the product $(4x^2 + 8)(2x - 7)$ using the FOIL method.
(58)

*6. Add $\dfrac{9}{9x - 36} + \dfrac{-24}{3x^2 - 48}$.
(95)

*7. Jim ran a total of $\dfrac{x}{x^2 + 2x + 1}$ miles in the gym and $\dfrac{x+2}{x+1}$ miles outside. How
(95) many more miles did he run inside?

8. Find the quotient of $(x^2 - 14x + 49) \div (x - 7)$.
(93)

Solve and graph the inequality.

9. $13 \le 2x + 7 < 15$
(82)

10. $\dfrac{|x|}{6} > 8$
(91)

11. Determine if the inequality $3x - 4x \ge 6 - x + 8$ is never, sometimes, or always
(81) true. If it is sometimes true, identify the solution set.

*12. Determine if the ordered pair $(2, 6)$ is a solution of the inequality $y > 3x - 2$.
(97)

*13. Graph the function. $y = x^2 + 2x - 24$
(96)

*14. Write What points on a graph of an inequality satisfy the inequality? Explain.
(97)

*15. Generalize How do you know which half-plane to shade for the graph of a linear
(97) inequality?

*16. Multiple Choice Which inequality represents the graph on the coordinate plane?
(97)

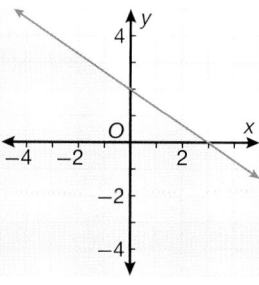

A $y \geq -\frac{2}{3}x + 2$ **B** $y \leq -\frac{2}{3}x + 2$

C $y \leq \frac{2}{3}x + 2$ **D** $y < -\frac{2}{3}x + 2$

17. (Football) Tickets for the school football game cost five dollars for adults and
(97) three dollars for students. In order to buy new helmets, at least $9000 worth of tickets must be sold. Write an inequality that describes the total number of tickets that must be sold in order to buy new helmets.

*18. Error Analysis Two students find the vertex for $y = x^2 - 6x + 19$. Which student is
(96) correct? Explain the error.

Student A	Student B
$\frac{-b}{2a} = \frac{6}{2} = 3$	$\frac{-b}{2a} = \frac{6}{2} = 3$
The vertex is $(3, 0)$.	$3^2 - 6(3) + 19 = 10$
	The vertex is $(3, 10)$.

*19. Geometry The area of a rectangle is 48 square inches. The length is three times
(96) the width. Find the width of the rectangle by finding the positive zero of the function $y = 3w^2 - 48$.

*20. Multi-Step The height y of a golf ball in feet is given by the function $y = -16x^2 + 49x$.
(96) **a.** What is the y-intercept?

b. What does this y-intercept represent?

c. What answer does the equation give for the height of the ball after 5 seconds?

d. What does that height mean?

*21. (Commuting) Jeff traveled $\frac{1}{2x^2 - 4x}$ miles for his job on Monday and $\frac{1}{x^3 - 2x^2}$ miles for
(95) his job on Tuesday. How many more miles did he travel on Tuesday?

22. Multiple Choice Add $\frac{3y + 2}{y + z} + \frac{4}{2y + 2z}$.
(95)

A $\frac{3y + 4}{y + z}$ **B** $\frac{y + 4}{y + z}$

C $\frac{6y}{4mn}$ **D** $\frac{3y - 4}{y - z}$

'hat -11 is a solution to the inequality $|3x| - 2 = 31$.

'olve $4|x - 8| = 12$.

B $\{11, -11\}$

D $\{-20, 20\}$

.e Riding Ron rode his bike for $\dfrac{10}{45x^2 + 4x - 1}$ minutes to get to his grandmother's house that was $\dfrac{1}{45x - 5} + \dfrac{2x}{25x + 5}$ miles away. Find his rate in miles per minute.

26. **Carpentry** A carpenter uses a measuring tape with an accuracy of $\pm\dfrac{1}{32}$ inches. He
(91) measures the height of a bookshelf to be $95\dfrac{5}{8}$ inches. Solve the inequality $\left| x - 95\dfrac{5}{8} \right| \le \dfrac{1}{32}$ to find the range of the height of the bookshelf.

27. **Generalize** How are the number of zeros of a function related to the location of the
(89) vertex of the function's parabola?

28. **Probability** The probability of winning a certain game is $\dfrac{2x^4y^2}{15xy^3}$. The probability
(88) of winning a different game is $\dfrac{5x^2y}{8x^3y^2}$. What is the probability of winning both games?

29. **Rate** An orange juice machine squeezes juice out of $x^2 + 30x$ oranges every hour.
(88) How much time in days will it take to squeeze 3000 oranges?

30. **Multi-Step** A circle has a radius of x. Another circle has a radius of $3x$.
(84) **a.** Write equations for the areas of both circles.

b. Graph both functions in the same coordinate plane.

c. Compare the graphs.

Solving Quadratic Equations by Factoring

Warm Up

1. Vocabulary A _____ is an x-value for the function where $f(x) = 0$.
(89)

Factor.

2. $x^2 + 3x - 88$
(72)

3. $6x^2 - 7x - 5$
(75)

4. $4x^2 + 28x + 49$
(83)

5. $12x^2 - 27$
(83)

New Concepts

A root of an equation is the solution to an equation. A quadratic equation can have zero, one, or two roots. The roots of a quadratic equation are the x-intercepts, or zeros, of the related quadratic function.

To find the roots of a quadratic equation, set the equation equal to 0. If the quadratic expression can be factored, the equation can be solved using the Zero Product Property.

Math Language

The **roots** of a quadratic equation are the values of x that make $ax^2 + bx + c = 0$.

Zero Product Property
If the product of two quantities equals zero, at least one of the quantities equals zero.

Math Reasoning

Analyze What is the difference between a quadratic function and a quadratic equation?

Example 1 Using the Zero Product Property

Solve.

$(x - 4)(x + 5) = 0$

SOLUTION

By the Zero Product Property, one or both of these factors must be equal to 0. To find the solutions, set each factor equal to zero and solve.

| $x - 4 = 0$ | $x + 5 = 0$ | Set each factor equal to zero. |
| $x = 4$ | $x = -5$ | Solve each equation for x. |

Check Substitute each solution into the original equation to show it is true.

$$(x - 4)(x + 5) = 0 \qquad\qquad (x - 4)(x + 5) = 0$$
$$(4 - 4)(4 + 5) \overset{?}{=} 0 \qquad\qquad (-5 - 4)(-5 + 5) \overset{?}{=} 0$$
$$0 \cdot 9 \overset{?}{=} 0 \qquad\qquad -9 \cdot 0 \overset{?}{=} 0$$
$$0 = 0 \;\checkmark \qquad\qquad 0 = 0 \;\checkmark$$

The solution set is $\{-5, 4\}$.

Online Connection
www.SaxonMathResources.com

Example 5 Solving Quadratic Equations with Missing Terms

Solve.

a. $18x^2 = 8x$

SOLUTION

$18x^2 - 8x = 0$ Set the equation equal to zero.

$2x(9x - 4) = 0$ Factor out the GCF.

$2x = 0$ $9x - 4 = 0$ Set each factor equal to zero.

$x = 0$ $x = \dfrac{4}{9}$ Solve each equation for x.

Check

$$18x^2 = 8x$$
$$18 \cdot (0)^2 \overset{?}{=} 8(0)$$
$$0 = 0 \checkmark$$

$$18x^2 = 8x$$
$$18\left(\dfrac{4}{9}\right)^2 \overset{?}{=} 8\left(\dfrac{4}{9}\right)$$
$$18\left(\dfrac{16}{81}\right) \overset{?}{=} 8\left(\dfrac{4}{9}\right)$$
$$\dfrac{32}{9} = \dfrac{32}{9} \checkmark$$

The solution set is $\left\{0, \dfrac{4}{9}\right\}$.

b. $4x^2 - 25 = 0$

SOLUTION

$4x^2 - 25 = 0$ Set the equation equal to 0.

$(2x - 5)(2x + 5) = 0$ Factor.

$2x - 5 = 0$ $2x + 5 = 0$ Set each factor equal to zero.

$2x = 5$ $2x = -5$ Solve each equation for x.

$x = 2.5$ $x = -2.5$

Check

$$4x^2 - 25 = 0$$
$$4(2.5)^2 - 25 \overset{?}{=} 0$$
$$4(6.25) - 25 \overset{?}{=} 0$$
$$25 - 25 \overset{?}{=} 0$$
$$0 = 0 \checkmark$$

$$4x^2 - 25 = 0$$
$$4 \cdot (-2.5)^2 - 25 \overset{?}{=} 0$$
$$4(6.25) - 25 \overset{?}{=} 0$$
$$25 - 25 \overset{?}{=} 0$$
$$0 = 0 \checkmark$$

The solution set is $\{-2.5, 2.5\}$.

a. Solve $(x - 3)(x + 7) = 0$.
(Ex 1)

Find the roots.

b. $x^2 + 3x - 18 = 0$
(Ex 2)

c. $2x^2 + 13x + 15 = 0$
(Ex 2)

Solve.

d. $5x^2 - 20x = 10x - 45$
(Ex 3)

e. $45x^2 = 27x$
(Ex 5)

f. $25x^2 - 16 = 0$
(Ex 5)

g. (Architecture) A rectangular pool has an area of 360 square feet. The
(Ex 4) length is 6 feet more than three times the width. Find the dimensions of the pool.

Practice   Distributed and Integrated

Solve and graph the inequality.

1. $11 < 2(x + 5) < 20$
(82)

2. $|x| + 1.5 \leq 7.6$
(91)

3. Determine whether the polynomial $-121 + 9x^2$ is a perfect-square trinomial or a
(83) difference of two squares. Then factor the polynomial.

4. Graph the function $y = 2x^2 + 8x + 6$.
(96)

5. The number of Apples A and Oranges O grown in a certain fruit orchard can
(53) be modeled by the given expressions where x is the number of years since the trees were planted. Find a model that represents the total number of apples and oranges grown in this orchard.

$$A = 15x^3 + 17x - 20$$
$$O = 20x^3 + 11x - 4$$

6. Write an equation for a line that passes through $(1, 2)$ and is perpendicular
(65) to $y = -\frac{3}{4}x + 2\frac{3}{4}$.

7. Solve the equation $\frac{4|x|}{9} + 3 = 11$ and graph the solution.
(94)

Simplify.

8. $\dfrac{\dfrac{3x + 6}{7x - 7}}{\dfrac{5x + 10}{14x - 14}}$
(92)

9. $(5xyz)^2(3x^{-1}y)^2$
(40)

*10. Determine if the ordered pair $(5, 5)$ is a solution of the inequality $y < -5x + 4$.
(97)

*11. Write Explain the Zero Product Property in your own words.
(98)

Hint

For help with graphing quadratic functions, see Graphing Calculator Lab 8: Characteristics of Parabolas on p. 583.

Example 2 **Solving Quadratic Equations Using a Graphing Calculator**

Solve each equation by graphing the related function on a graphing calculator.

a. $-6x - 9 = x^2$

SOLUTION

Write the equation in standard form.

$-x^2 - 6x - 9 = 0$

Graph the related function

$f(x) = -x^2 - 6x - 9$.

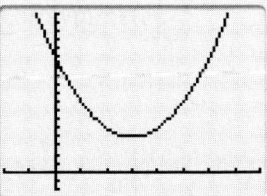

The graph appears to have an x-intercept at -3.

Use the Table function to determine the zeros of this function.

The solution is -3.

b. $-6x = -x^2 - 13$

SOLUTION

Write the equation in standard form.

$x^2 - 6x + 13 = 0$.

Graph the related function $f(x) = x^2 - 6x + 13$.

The graph opens upward and does not intersect the x-axis.

There is no solution.

c. $-3x^2 + 5x = -7$

Round to the nearest tenth.

SOLUTION

Write the equation in standard form.

$-3x^2 + 5x + 7 = 0$

Graph the related function
$f(x) = -3x^2 + 5x + 7$.

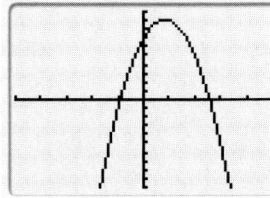

The graph appears to have x-intercepts at 3 and -1.

Use the Zero function to determine the zeros of this function. Round to the nearest tenth.

The solutions are $x = 2.6$ and -0.9.

Example 3   Application: Physics

Hint

The time t is plotted on the x-axis. The height h is plotted on the y-axis.

Gill drops a baseball from the top of a platform 64 feet off the ground. The height of the baseball is described by the quadratic equation $h = -16t^2 + 64$, where h is the height in feet and t is the time in seconds. Find the time t when the ball hits the ground.

SOLUTION

Graph the related function $h(t) = -16t^2 + 64$ on a graphing calculator.

Height h is zero when the ball hits the ground. Use the Zero function of the graphing calculator to determine the zeros of this function.

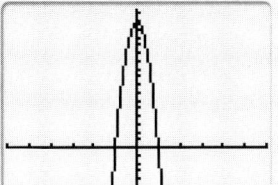

There are two zeros for the given parabola: $t = 2$ and $t = -2$. Only values greater than or equal to zero are considered. So, $t = 2$ is the only solution.

The baseball hits the ground in 2 seconds.

Lesson Practice

Solve each equation by graphing the related function.
(Ex 1)

   a. $3x^2 - 147 = 0$

   b. $5x^2 + 6 = 0$

   c. $x^2 - 10x + 25 = 0$

Solve each equation by graphing the related function on a graphing calculator.

   d. $x^2 + 64 = 16x$
(Ex 2)

   e. $x^2 + 4 = 2x$
(Ex 2)

   f. Round to the nearest tenth: $-7x^2 + 3x = -7$.
(Ex 2)

   g. Marcus shot an arrow while standing on a platform. The path of its
(Ex 3) movement formed a parabola given by the quadratic equation $h = -16t^2 + 2t + 17$, where h is the height in feet and t is the time in seconds. Find the time t when the arrow hits the ground. Round to the nearest hundredth.

Practice   Distributed and Integrated

Solve.

   1. $x(2x - 11) = 0$
(98)

   2. $\dfrac{12}{x - 6} = \dfrac{4}{x}$
(99)

*3. Generalize Using the path of a ball thrown into the air as an example, describe in
(100) mathematical terms each part of the graph the path of the ball creates.

*4. Generalize What does the graph of a quadratic equation look like when there is no
(100) solution? one solution? two solutions?

5. Given that y varies directly with x, identify the constant of variation such that
(Inv 7) when $x = 15$, $y = 30$.

 *6. (**Basketball**) Ramero shoots a basketball into the air. The ball's movement forms a
(100) parabola given by the quadratic equation $h = -16t^2 + 7t + 7$, where h is the height
in feet and t is the time in seconds. Find the maximum height of the path the
basketball makes and the time t when the basketball hits the ground. Round to the
nearest hundredth.

*7. **Multiple Choice** What is the equation of the axis of symmetry of the parabola
(100) defined by $y = \frac{1}{4}(x - 4)^2 + 5$?

    A $x = 1$ **B** $x = 4$ **C** $x = 5$ **D** $x = -4$

*8. Solve $-7x^2 - 10 = 0$ by graphing.
(100)

*9. Solve $\dfrac{6}{x} = \dfrac{8}{x + 7}$.
(99)

10. A deck of ten cards has 5 red and 5 black cards. Cards are replaced in the deck
(80) after each draw. Use an equation to find the probability of drawing a black card
twice and rolling a 6 on a number cube.

 11. **Geometry** The altitude of the right triangle divides the hypotenuse into segments
(99) of lengths x units and 5 units. To find x, solve the equation $\frac{x + 5}{6} = \frac{6}{x}$.

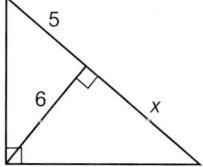

*12. **Multi-Step** Henry starts working a half-hour before Martha. He can complete the
(99) job in 4 hours. Martha can complete the same job in 3 hours.

    a. Let t represent the total time they work together. In terms of t, how long does
    Henry work?

    b. Use an equation to find how long they work together to complete the job.

    c. How long does Henry work?

13. Find the quotient of $\dfrac{a^2 + 10a - 24}{a - 2}$.   **14.** Simplify $\sqrt{49y^5}$.
(93)   *(61)*

15. (**Profit**) An entrepreneur makes \$3 profit on each object sold. She would like to
(94) make \$270 plus or minus \$30 total. What is the minimum and maximum number
of objects she needs to sell?

 16. **Data Analysis** A student knows there will be 4 tests that determine her semester
(94) grade. She wants her average to be an 85, plus or minus 5 points. What is the
minimum and maximum number of points she needs to earn during the semester?

17. Solve the equation $|10x| - 3 = 87$.
(94)

18. (**Exercise**) Tom ran a total of $\dfrac{7x}{x^2 + 3x - 18}$ miles in August and $\dfrac{2x + 1}{7x + 42}$ miles in
(95) September. How many more miles did he run in August?

19. Graph the function $y = 5x^2 - 10x + 5$.
(96)

*20. **Verify** A boundary line is a vertical line. The inequality contains a $<$ symbol.
(97) Which half-plane should be shaded on the graph?

21. Multiple Choice Which point does not satisfy the inequality $x + 2y < 5$?
(97)

A $(0, 0)$ **B** $(2, 1)$ **C** $(3, -4)$ **D** $(-1, 3)$

*22. (Ages) A boy is b years old. His father is 23 years older than the boy. The product
(98) of their ages is 50. How old is each person?

*23. Error Analysis Two students find the roots of $3x^2 - 6x = 24$. Which student is
(98) correct? Explain the error.

Student A	Student B
$3x^2 - 6x = 24$	$3x^2 - 6x = 24$
$3x(x - 2) = 24$	$3x^2 - 6x - 24 = 0$
$3x = 0 \qquad x - 2 = 0$	$3(x^2 - 2x - 8) = 0$
$x = 0 \qquad\quad x = 2$	$3(x - 4)(x + 2) = 0$
	$x - 4 = 0 \qquad x + 2 = 0$
	$x = 4 \qquad\quad x = -2$

24. Does the graph of $y + 2x^2 = 12 + x$ open upward or downward?
(84)

25. Do the side lengths 18, 80, and 82 form a Pythagorean triple?
(85)

26. Multi-Step The volume of a prism is $3x^3 + 12x^2 + 9x$. What are the possible
(87) dimensions of the prism?

    a. Factor out common terms.

    b. Factor completely.

    c. Find the dimensions.

27. (Travel) The Jackson family drove 480 miles on Saturday and 300 miles on Sunday.
(90) Their average rate on Sunday was 10 miles per hour less than their rate was on
Saturday. Write a simplified expression that represents their total driving time.

28. Multi-Step At the carnival, a man says that he will guess your weight within
(91) 5 pounds.

    a. You weigh 120 pounds. Write an absolute-value inequality to show the range of
acceptable guesses.

    b. Solve the inequality to find the actual range of acceptable guesses.

29. Verify If the numerator of a rational expression is a polynomial and the
(92) denominator of the rational expression is a different polynomial, will factoring
the polynomials always provide a way to simplify the expression? Verify your
answer by giving an example.

30. If a 9% decrease from the original price resulted in a new price of $227,500,
(47) what was the original price?

Transforming Quadratic Functions

A quadratic function is a function that can be written in the form $f(x) = ax^2 + bx + c$, where a is not equal to 0.

In Investigation 6, linear functions were graphed as transformations of the parent function $f(x) = x$. Similarly, you can graph a quadratic function as a transformation of the quadratic parent function $f(x) = x^2$.

Parameter Changes

Complete the table of values for $f(x) = x^2$ and graph the quadratic parent function.

x	$f(x)$
-3	
-2	
-1	
0	
1	
2	
3	

As is the case for the linear parent function, the quadratic parent function $f(x) = x^2$ can be written as $f(x) = ax^2$, where $a = 1$. The graph changes when other values are substituted for a.

1. Graph $y = x^2$ and $y = 2x^2$ on the same set of axes. Compare the two graphs.

2. Graph $y = x^2$ and $y = \frac{1}{2}x^2$ on the same set of axes. Compare the two graphs.

3. Graph $y = x^2$ and $y = -x^2$ on the same set of axes. Compare the two graphs.

4. **Generalize** What is the effect of a on the graph of $y = ax^2$?

5. **Predict** How will the graph of $f(x) = \frac{2}{3}x^2$ change in relation to the quadratic parent function?

6. **Predict** How will the graph of $f(x) = -4x^2$ change in relation to the quadratic parent function?

The graph of a function of the form $f(x) = ax^2$ always crosses the y-axis at $(0, 0)$. When $c \neq 0$, the graph of the function $f(x) = ax^2 + c$ does not pass through the point $(0, 0)$.

7. Graph the quadratic parent function and the function $f(x) = x^2 + 1$ on the same set of axes. Compare the two graphs.

8. Graph the quadratic parent function and the function $f(x) = x^2 - 2$ on the same set of axes.

9. Predict How will the graph of $f(x) = x^2 + 7$ compare to the graph of the quadratic parent function?

Combinations of Parameter Changes

 Predict How will each graph compare to the graph of the quadratic parent function? Verify your answer with a graphing calculator.

10. $f(x) = -x^2 + 2$

11. $f(x) = \frac{1}{2}x^2 - 3$

Investigation Practice

 **Describe how the graph for the given values of a and c changes in relation to the graph of the quadratic parent function. Verify your answer with a graphing calculator.**

a. $f(x) = ax^2 + c$ for $a = 2$ and $c = 1$

b. $f(x) = ax^2 + c$ for $a = -3$ and $c = -2$

c. $f(x) = ax^2 + c$ for $a = \frac{1}{2}$ and $c = 2$

d. $f(x) = ax^2 + c$ for $a = -\frac{1}{2}$ and $c = -1$

Write an equation for the transformation described. Then graph the original function and the graph of the transformation on the same set of axes.

e. Shift $f(x) = 2x^2 - 4$ up 2 units.

f. Shift $f(x) = 3x^2 + 5$ down 4 units and open it downward.

Solving Multi-Step Absolute-Value Inequalities

Warm Up

1. Vocabulary A(n) _____ is a mathematical statement comparing
(45)
quantities that are not equal.

Simplify.

2. $|-8 + 5| - 7$
(7)

3. $|2 \cdot -6| + 14$
(7)

Solve.

4. $3x - 7 > 17$
(77)

5. $-5x + 12 \geq 37$
(77)

New Concepts

Recall that an absolute-value inequality is solved by first isolating the absolute-value expression. Then the inequality is written as a compound inequality with no absolute-value symbols. The compound inequality uses AND when the absolute-value inequality is a "less than" inequality. The compound inequality uses OR when the absolute-value inequality is a "greater than" inequality.

Caution

The absolute-value expression must be isolated to apply the rules:

AND ←→ "less than"

OR ←→ "greater than"

Example 1 Solving Multi-Step Absolute-Value Inequalities

Solve and graph each inequality.

a. $2|x| + 3 < 11$

SOLUTION

Isolate $|x|$ and then write the inequality as a compound inequality.

$2|x| + 3 < 11$

$\quad \underline{-3 \quad -3}$ Subtraction Property of Inequality

$2|x| < 8$ Combine like terms.

$\dfrac{2|x|}{2} < \dfrac{8}{2}$ Division Property of Inequality

$|x| < 4$ Simplify.

$x > -4$ and $x < 4$ Write as a compound inequality.

The compound inequality can also be written as $-4 < x < 4$.

Online Connection
www.SaxonMathResources.com

b. $\dfrac{|x|}{5} - 4 > -2$

SOLUTION

$$\dfrac{|x|}{5} - 4 > -2$$

$\dfrac{|x|}{5} > 2$ Add 4 to each side.

$|x| > 10$ Multiply each side by 5.

$x < -10$ OR $x > 10$ Write as a compound inequality.

$$\begin{array}{cccccccc} -30 & -20 & -10 & 0 & 10 & 20 & 30 \end{array}$$

c. $-10|x| + 54 \geq -21$

SOLUTION

$$-10|x| + 54 \geq -21$$

$-10|x| \geq -75$ Subtract 54 from each side.

$|x| \leq 7.5$ Divide each side by -10.

$-7.5 \leq x \leq 7.5$ Write as a compound inequality.

$$\begin{array}{cccccccccccc} -10 & -8 & -6 & -4 & -2 & 0 & 2 & 4 & 6 & 8 & 10 \end{array}$$

Algebraic expressions within the absolute-value symbols may have one or more operations on the variable. So, after the absolute-value expression is isolated, solving the resulting compound inequality requires additional steps.

Example 2   **Solving Inequalities with One Operation Inside Absolute-Value Symbols**

Solve and graph the inequality.

$|x + 5| - 1 > 7$

SOLUTION

Isolate the absolute-value expression $|x + 5|$. Then write it as a compound inequality.

$$|x + 5| - 1 > 7$$

$|x + 5| > 8$ Add 1 to each side.

$x + 5 < -8$ OR $x + 5 > 8$ Write as a compound inequality.

Solve each part of the compound inequality for x.

$x < -13$ OR $x > 3$ Subtract 5 from each side of the two inequalities.

$$\begin{array}{ccccc} -20 & -10 & 0 & 10 & 20 \end{array}$$

Hint

Reverse the direction of the inequality symbol when dividing each side of an inequality by a negative number.

Math Reasoning

Verify For Example 3a, choose an *x*-value between −15 and 27. Show that it is a solution of the original inequality.

Solve and graph each inequality.

a. $\left| \dfrac{x}{3} - 2 \right| + 12 \le 19$

SOLUTION

$$\left| \dfrac{x}{3} - 2 \right| + 12 \le 19$$

$\left| \dfrac{x}{3} - 2 \right| \le 7$ Subtract 12 from each side.

$\dfrac{x}{3} - 2 \ge -7$ AND $\dfrac{x}{3} - 2 \le 7$ Write as a compound inequality.

$\dfrac{x}{3} \ge -5$ AND $\dfrac{x}{3} \le 9$ Add 2 to each side of the two inequalities.

$x \ge -15$ AND $x \le 27$ Multiply each side by 3 in both inequalities.

$-15 \le x \le 27$

b. $|2x + 1| + 5 \ge 8$

SOLUTION

$|2x + 1| + 5 \ge 8$

$|2x + 1| \ge 3$ Subtract 5 from each side.

$2x + 1 \le -3$ OR $2x + 1 \ge 3$ Write as a compound inequality.

$2x \le -4$ OR $2x \ge 2$ Subtract 1 from each side of both inequalities.

$x \le -2$ OR $x \ge 1$ Divide each side by 2 in both inequalities.

Example 4   **Application: Basketball**

NCAA rules require that the circumference c of a basketball used in an NCAA men's basketball game vary no more than 0.25 inch from 29.75 inches. Write and solve an absolute-value inequality that models the acceptable circumferences. What is the least acceptable circumference?

SOLUTION

Hint

Look for a value that varies by some amount. The absolute-value expression will be =, ≥, or ≤ the amount by which the value varies.

The expression $|c - 29.75|$ represents the difference between the actual circumference and 29.75 inches. The absolute-value bars ensure that the difference is a positive number. The difference can be no more than 0.25 inches, so the acceptable circumference is modeled $|c - 29.75| \le 0.25$.

$|c - 29.75| \le 0.25$

$-0.25 \le c - 29.75 \le 0.25$ Write a compound inequality.

$29.5 \le c \le 30$ Add 29.75 to each side.

The least acceptable circumference is 29.5 inches.

Solve and graph each inequality.

a. $5|x| + 6 < 31$
(Ex 1)

b. $\dfrac{|x|}{7} - 3 \geq 1$
(Ex 1)

c. $-4|x| + 9 > -1$
(Ex 1)

d. $|x - 9| + 3 \leq 10$
(Ex 2)

e. $\left|\dfrac{x}{2} + 5\right| - 9 < -2$
(Ex 3)

f. $|5x - 5| - 12 > -2$
(Ex 3)

g. (Basketball) NCAA rules require that the weight w of a basketball used
(Ex 4) in an NCAA men's basketball game vary no more than 1 ounce from 21 ounces. Write and solve an absolute-value inequality that models the acceptable weights. What is the largest acceptable weight?

Practice   Distributed and Integrated

*1. Solve and graph the inequality $7|x| - 4 \geq 3$.
(101)

*2. Error Analysis Two students solve the inequality $|x - 4| + 2 \leq 6$. Which student is
(101) correct? Explain the error.

Student A	Student B
$|x - 4| + 2 \leq 6$	$|x - 4| + 2 \leq 6$
$|x - 4| \leq 4$	$-6 \leq x - 4 + 2 \leq 6$
$-4 \leq x - 4 \leq 4$	$-6 \leq x - 2 \leq 6$
$0 \leq x \leq 8$	$-4 \leq x \leq 8$

*3. Write Describe the three steps needed to solve the inequality $\dfrac{|x|}{2} + 11 \leq 16$.
(101)

4. Simplify $\dfrac{pt^{-2}}{m^3}\left(\dfrac{p^{-2}wt}{4m^{-1}} + 6t^4w^{-1} - \dfrac{w}{m^{-3}}\right)$.
(39)

*5. Analyze Suppose that a, b, and c are all positive integers. Will the solution of
(101) the inequality $-a|x - b| \geq -c$ be a compound inequality that uses AND or a compound inequality that uses OR?

*6. (Oven Temperature) Liam's oven's temperature t varies by no more than 9°F from the
(101) set temperature. Liam sets his oven to 475°F. Write an absolute-value inequality that models the possible actual temperatures inside the oven. What is the highest possible temperature?

*7. Error Analysis Students were asked if a quadratic equation could have more than
(100) one solution. Which student is correct? Explain the error.

Student A	Student B
yes; A quadratic equation can have two solutions. When a parabola crosses the x-axis twice, there are two solutions.	no; A quadratic equation cannot cross the x-axis more than once. So, there can only be one solution.

*8. Multi-Step Shaw hits a tennis ball into the air. Its movement forms a parabola given
(100) by the quadratic equation $h = -16t^2 + 2t + 9$, where h is the height in feet and t is
the time in seconds.

a. Find the maximum height of the arc the ball makes in its flight. Round to the
nearest tenth.

b. Find the time t when the ball hits the ground. Round to the nearest hundredth.

c. Find the time t when the ball is at its maximum height. Round to the nearest
hundredth.

9. Find the LCM of $(6w^3 - 48w^5)$ and $(9w - 72w^3)$.
(57)

*10. Geometry A boy spills a cup of juice on the sidewalk. As time increases, the
(100) area of the spill changes. The area of the spill is given by the function
$A = -2t^2 + 5t + 125$, where A is the area in square feet and t is the time in
seconds. Find the time when the area is 60 square feet. Round to the nearest
hundredth.

11. Solve $x^2 + 9 = -6x$ by graphing.
(100)

12. Solve the equation $|8x| + 4 = 28$.
(94)

13. (Traveling) Mia walked $\frac{4}{r-2}$ miles to her neighbors' house on Monday and walked
(95) $\frac{r^2}{2-r}$ miles on Tuesday to go see her grandmother. How many miles total did she
walk on Monday and Tuesday?

14. Subtract $\frac{5}{x-3} - \frac{2}{x-2}$.
(95)

15. (Soccer) A soccer ball on the ground is passed with an initial velocity of 62 feet per
(96) second. What is its height after 3 seconds? Use $h = -16t^2 + vt + s$.

16. Measurement A girl is 24 years younger than her mother. The product of their
(96) ages is 81. Find the mother's age by finding the positive zero of the function
$y = x^2 - 24x - 81$.

17. Determine if the ordered pair $(-7, 2)$ is a solution of the inequality $y \le 3$.
(97)

18. Verify Show that $\frac{3}{4}$ is a solution to $(4x - 3)(5x + 7) = 0$.
(98)

19. Multiple Choice What are the roots of the equation $0 = x^2 - 10x - 39$?
(98)   **A** $0, 39$ **B** $10, 0$ **C** $3, -13$ **D** $13, -3$

*20. Solve and check: $\frac{x}{11} = \frac{6}{x-5}$.
(99)

21. Does the graph of $-8x^2 - 12 = 3 - y$ open upward or downward?
(84)

22. (**Office Management**) Maria can complete all the copies in 1 hour. It takes Lachelle
(99) 2 hours. How long will it take them if they use two identical copiers and work together?

23. **Error Analysis** Two students solve $\frac{x-8}{x+2} = \frac{x-6}{3x+6}$. Which student is correct? Explain
(99) the error.

Student A	Student B
$(x-8)(3x+6) = (x+2)(x-6)$	$(x-8)(3x+6) = (x+2)(x-6)$
$3x^2 - 18x - 48 = x^2 - 4x - 12$	$3x^2 - 18x - 48 = x^2 - 4x - 12$
$2x^2 - 14x - 36 = 0$	$2x^2 - 14x - 36 = 0$
$2(x-9)(x+2) = 0$	$2(x-9)(x+2) = 0$
$\{9\}$	$\{-2, 9\}$

24. Do the side lengths 3, $3\sqrt{3}$, and 6 form a Pythagorean triple?
(85)

25. Let $P = (-2, 1)$, $Q = (0, 2)$, $R = (1, -2)$, and $S = (-1, -3)$. Use the distance
(86) formula to determine whether $PQRS$ is a rhombus.

26. **Multi-Step** Find the product of $\frac{5x^2y^2}{3x^3y^3} \cdot \frac{9xy^2}{25xy^3}$ using two different methods.
(88)
   a. Solve the expression by multiplying first and then simplifying.

   b. Solve the expression by simplifying each factor and then multiplying.

   c. Explain which method you prefer.

27. (**Road Trip**) Carlos tracks the mileage for a road trip on his car's odometer. The
(91) total distance is 974.6 miles plus or minus 0.1 miles. Solve and graph the inequality $|x - 974.6| \leq 0.1$.

28. **Multi-Step** Amy skipped for $\frac{3x-6}{9x}$ hours to get to her grandmother's house that
(92) was $\frac{2x^2 - 4x}{7x^3}$ miles away.
   a. Find her rate in miles per hour.

   b. If the rate is divided by $\frac{1}{x^2}$, what is the new rate?

29. How do you write a remainder of 5 for a division problem that has a divisor of
(93) $(3x^2 + 7x + 8)$?

*30. What is the parent quadratic function defined to be? What is the shape of its
(Inv 10) graph and where is it located on the coordinate system?

Simplify. All variables represent non-negative numbers.

a. $\sqrt{\dfrac{5}{3}}$ *(Ex 1)*

b. $\sqrt{\dfrac{11}{x}}$ *(Ex 2)*

c. $\dfrac{\sqrt{6x^6}}{\sqrt{27x}}$ *(Ex 3)*

d. $\dfrac{3}{5 - \sqrt{6}}$ *(Ex 4)*

e. $\dfrac{3}{\sqrt{7} - 1}$ *(Ex 4)*

Practice   Distributed and Integrated

*1. Simplify $\dfrac{35}{\sqrt{7}}$.
(103)

2. Solve $\dfrac{8}{x - 1} = \dfrac{x}{7}$.
(99)

*3. Error Analysis Two students simplified the following expression. Which student is
(103) correct? Explain the error.

Student A	Student B
$\dfrac{1}{3 + \sqrt{2}}$	$\dfrac{1}{3 + \sqrt{2}}$
$\dfrac{1}{3 + \sqrt{2}} \cdot \dfrac{3 - \sqrt{2}}{3 - \sqrt{2}}$	$\dfrac{1}{3 + \sqrt{2}} \cdot \dfrac{\sqrt{2}}{\sqrt{2}}$
$\dfrac{3 - \sqrt{2}}{7}$	$\dfrac{\sqrt{2}}{3\sqrt{2} + 2}$

*4. (**Skydiving**) A 150-pound skydiver reaches terminal velocity after free-falling for a
(103) number of seconds. The formula for the terminal velocity V of a skydiver
(in feet per second) can be estimated by the formula $V = \sqrt{\dfrac{2W}{0.0063}}$, where W equals
the weight of the skydiver in pounds. Write a rational expression for the terminal
velocity of the skydiver.

5. What is 400% of 40? Use a proportion to solve.
(42)

*6. Write Is $\dfrac{2\sqrt{3}}{\sqrt{2}}$ in simplest form? Explain.
(103)

*7. Predict If $2 \div \sqrt{2}$ is $\sqrt{2}$, and $3 \div \sqrt{3}$ is $\sqrt{3}$, what is a good prediction of what the
(103) quotient of $239 \div \sqrt{239}$ might be?

8. Multi-Step The area of a square is $9x^2$. The length of one of its sides plus 32 is 47.
(102)
   a. What is the length of one of its sides?

   b. What is the area of the square?

   c. What is x?

*9. (**Time and Distance**) A stone is dropped from a height of 450 feet. Use the equation
(102) $25t^2 - 450 = 0$ to find how many seconds it takes for the stone to hit the ground.

10. Solve $\begin{array}{l} 4x + 2y = 22 \\ 6x - 5y = 9 \end{array}$ by substitution.
(59)

*11. Verify True or False: $5x^2 + 125 = 0$; $x = \pm 5$. If the answer is false, provide the
(102) correct answer.

Solve and graph the inequality.

12. $-6|x| + 20 \geq 2$
(101)

13. $14x + 2y > 6$
(97)

*14. Error Analysis Two students solve the inequality $-12|x| - 15 > -39$. Which student
(101) is correct? Explain the error.

Student A	Student B
$-12\|x\| - 15 > -39$	$-12\|x\| - 15 > -39$
$-12\|x\| > -24$	$12\|x\| + 15 < 39$
$\|x\| > 2$	$12\|x\| < 24$
$x < -2 \text{ OR } x > 2$	$\|x\| < 2$
	$-2 < x < 2$

*15. Geometry Find the length of the line segment that is the graph of the
(101) inequality $\left|\frac{x}{7} + 6\right| - 5 \leq 4$.

*16. (**Tennis**) The diameter d of a tennis ball should vary no more than $\frac{1}{16}$ inch
(101) from $2\frac{5}{16}$ inches. Write and solve an absolute-value inequality that models the
acceptable diameters. What is the greatest acceptable diameter?

17. Graph the function $y = 10x^2 - 20$.
(96)

18. (**Soccer**) The height h in meters of a kicked soccer ball is represented by the
(98) function $h = -5t^2 + 20t$, where t stands for the number of seconds after the ball
is kicked. When is the ball on the ground?

19. Data Analysis A teacher graphed the test grades. He found that the distribution
(98) formed a parabola. Solve the equation $0 = x^2 - 170x + 7000$ to find its roots.

20. Write What are the other names for the x-intercepts of a function?
(100)

21. Multiple Choice What is the equation of the parabola that passes through the points
(100) $(0, 2)$, $(-2, 6)$, and $(6, 14)$?

A $y = x^2 - x + 2$ **B** $y = -\frac{1}{2}x^2 - x + 2$

C $y = \frac{1}{2}x^2 + x - 2$ **D** $y = \frac{1}{2}x^2 - x + 2$

3. Translate the inequality $3z + 4 < 10$ into a sentence.
(45)

*4. **Multiple Choice** Which of the following radical equations will require the use of
(106) division to isolate the radical?

    A $\sqrt{x} - 12 = 2$ **B** $\sqrt{x} + 12 = 13$

    C $\dfrac{\sqrt{x}}{7} = 5$ **D** $14\sqrt{x} = 70$

*5. **Verify** Solve $\sqrt{x - 1} = \sqrt{3x + 2}$. Check your answer.
(106)

*6. **Justify** Solve $\dfrac{\sqrt{x}}{4} = 32$. Justify your answer.
(106)

*7. Find the common ratio of the geometric sequence $18, -9, 4\frac{1}{2}, -2\frac{1}{4}, \ldots$.
(105)

*8. Find the 6th term in the geometric series that has a common ratio of 2 and an
(105) initial term of 5.

9. **Multi-Step** Leila drops a ball from a height of 1 meter. The height of each bounce is
(105) 75% of the previous height.

    a. What is the ball's height after the first bounce?

    b. What rule can be used to find the ball's height after n bounces?

    c. What is the height of the sixth bounce? Round your answer to the nearest
    hundredth.

10. **Geometry** Each unit square in the figure represents 5 square feet. If the pattern
(105) continues, what will the area of the ninth figure be?

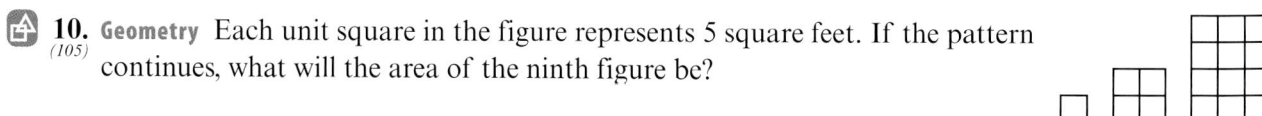

*11. (**Botany**) The growth of an ivy plant in feet can be described by $2\sqrt{x - 4}$. How
(106) many days x will it take for the ivy to reach a length of 20 feet?

12. Solve $\begin{array}{l} -5x + 4y = -37 \\ 3x - 6y = 33 \end{array}$.
(63)

*13. (**Fractals**) Fractals are geometric patterns that repeat themselves
(105) at smaller scales. The pattern shows fractals of equilateral
triangles. How many unshaded triangles will be in the sixth
figure?

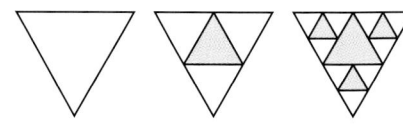

*14. Solve $x^2 + 9x = 4.75$ by completing the square.
(104)

15. **Error Analysis** Two students started solving the equation $2x^2 + 20x = -18$ as shown
(104) below. Which student is correct? Explain the error.

Student A	Student B
$2x^2 + 20x = -18$	$2x^2 + 20x = -18$
$x^2 + 10x = -9$	$x^2 + 10x = -18$
$x^2 + 10x + 25 = -9 + 25$	$x^2 + 10x + 25 = -18 + 25$
$(x + 5)^2 = 16$	$(x + 5)^2 = 7$

*16. (Business) The marketing group for a cosmetics company determined that the
(104) expression $u^2 - 0.8u$ represents the profit for every 1000 units u of mascara sold.
How many units need to be sold to have a profit margin of $0.33?

Solve each equation. Check your answer.

17. $\dfrac{60}{4x} + \dfrac{45}{5x} = 3$
(99)

*18. $\sqrt{x} = 9$
(106)

19. (Egg Toss) Tyrese and Jamcka were playing an egg-toss game. The egg's
(100) movement through the air formed a parabola given by the quadratic equation
$h = -16t^2 + 9t + 4$, where h is the height in feet and t is the time in seconds. Find
the maximum height of the path the egg makes and the time t when the egg hits
the ground. Round to the nearest hundredth.

20. Solve $x^2 - 16 = 0$ by graphing.
(100)

21. (Tennis) The weight w of a tennis ball should vary no more than $\frac{1}{12}$ ounce from $2\frac{1}{12}$
(101) ounces. Write an absolute-value inequality that models the acceptable weights.
What is the least acceptable weight?

22. **Multiple Choice** Which is the simplest form of $\dfrac{18\sqrt{7}}{3\sqrt{28}}$?
(103)

    A $\dfrac{3}{2}$ **B** 3 **C** $\dfrac{6\sqrt{7}}{\sqrt{28}}$ **D** $\dfrac{6\sqrt{7}}{7}$

23. **Write** Anton wants to estimate the quotient of $\dfrac{\sqrt{145}}{2\sqrt{9}}$. How should he do this?
(103)

24. Subtract $\dfrac{2r}{r-4} - \dfrac{6}{12-3r}$.
(90)

25. Solve and graph $|x - 16| \leq 12$.
(91)

26. Martha built a new playroom. She determined that the rectangular reading area
(93) is $(9x^2 + 44x - 5)$ square feet. The width is $(x + 5)$ feet. What is the length?

27. (Volleyball) A server's hand is 3 feet above the floor when it hits the volleyball.
(96) After the volleyball is hit, it has an initial velocity of 23 feet per second. What is
its height after 1 second? Use $h = -16t^2 + vt + s$.

28. **Multi-Step** Tickets for the Valley High School production of *Romeo and Juliet* are
(97) $5 for adults and $4 for students. In order to cover expenses, at least $2500 worth
of tickets must be sold.

    a. Write an inequality that describes this situation.

    b. Graph the inequality.

    c. If 200 adult and 400 student tickets are sold, will the expenses be covered?

29. **Generalize** Consider the equation $(x - 5)(x + 8) = 0$. How can you quickly tell
(98) what the roots are?

30. The graph of $f(x) = x^2 + bx + 3$ has an axis of symmetry $x = 4$. What is the value
(Inv 10) of b?

Graphing Absolute-Value Functions

---

1. Vocabulary A _____ is the simplest function of a particular type, or
(Inv 6) family.

Simplify.

2. $3 \cdot 2 + 2|-5|$
(5)

3. $5 \cdot 8 - 4|-6|$
(5)

4. $4|x - 2| = 60$
(74)

5. $-3|x + 4| = 36$
(74)

New Concepts   A function whose rule has one or more absolute-value expressions is called
an **absolute-value function.** The absolute-value parent function is $f(x) = |x|$.

> **Example 1**   **Graphing the Absolute-Value Parent Function**
>
> Graph the absolute-value parent function $f(x) = |x|$.
>
> **SOLUTION**
>
> Use a table to graph the function.

x	y
−2	2
−1	1
0	0
1	1
2	2

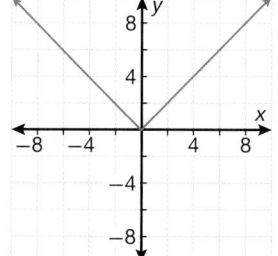

The absolute-value parent function forms the shape of a "V." The equation
of the axis of symmetry of the absolute-value parent function is $x = 0$. The
point on the axis of symmetry of the absolute-value graph, or the "corner"
of the graph, is the **vertex of an absolute-value graph.**

Math Reasoning

Write Why is "axis
of symmetry" an
appropriate name?

The absolute-value function has two slopes. If the graph opens upward, the
slope of the graph on the left of the axis of symmetry is -1. The slope of the
graph on the right side of the axis of symmetry is 1.

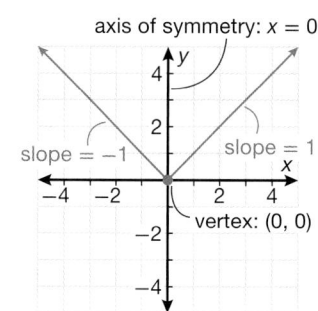

Translations of Absolute-Value Graphs

The absolute-value parent function can be translated by adding or subtracting constants.

Vertical Translation

If a constant k is added outside the absolute-value bars, the graph is translated up or down k units.
For $f(x) = |x| + k$:

- Graph translates up if $k > 0$.
- Graph translates down if $k < 0$.
- Coordinate of vertex is $(0, k)$.

The graph of $f(x) = |x| + k$, where $k = 1$, is shown.

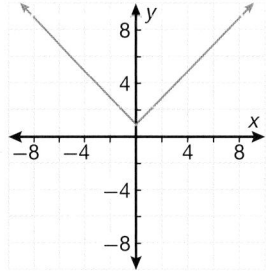

The graph of $f(x) = |x| + k$, where $k = -1$, is shown.

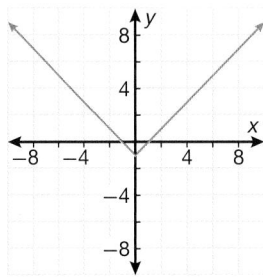

Horizontal Translation

If a constant h is subtracted inside the absolute-value bars, the graph is translated right or left h units.
For $f(x) = |x - h|$:

- Graph translates right if $h > 0$.
- Graph translates left if $h < 0$.
- Coordinate of vertex is $(h, 0)$.

The graph of $f(x) = |x - h|$, where $h = 1$, is shown.

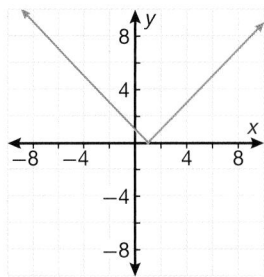

The graph of $f(x) = |x - h|$, where $h = -1$, is shown.

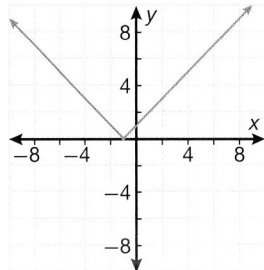

Reading Math

For positive h values, the graph moves right relative to the graph of the parent function and $f(x) = |x - h|$. For negative h values, the graph moves left and $f(x) = |x + h|$.

Online Connection
www.SaxonMathResources.com

Example 2 · Translating Absolute-Value Graphs

Graph the function and give the coordinates of the vertex.

a. $f(x) = |x| - 2$

SOLUTION

Use a table to graph the function.

x	-3	-2	-1	0	1	2	3
y	1	0	-1	-2	-1	0	1

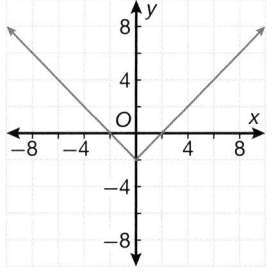

The graph of the parent function is translated down 2 units. The vertex is $(0, -2)$.

b. $f(x) = |x + 3|$

SOLUTION

Use a table to graph the function.

x	-6	-3	0	3	6
y	3	0	3	6	9

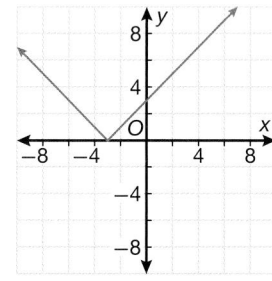

The graph of the parent function is translated left 3 units. The vertex is $(-3, 0)$.

Multiple Translations of Absolute-Value Graphs	
Vertical and Horizontal Translation If a constant h is subtracted inside the absolute-value bars and a constant k is added outside the bars, as in $f(x) = |x - h| + k$. The graph is translated both vertically and horizontally. The vertex is at (h, k).	The graph of $f(x) = |x - h| + k$, where $h = 1$ and $k = 1$, is shown. 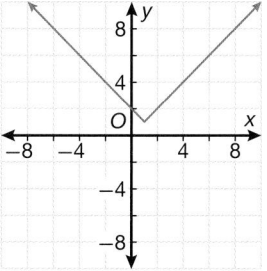

Example 3 · Graphing Multiple Translations

Graph the function and give the coordinates of the vertex.

$f(x) = |x - 4| + 1$

SOLUTION

The graph of the function is determined by translating the parent function. Evaluate how the function is different from the parent function.

The vertex is $(4, 1)$.

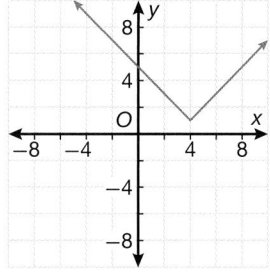

Hint

Knowing how to translate the graph of $y = |x|$ using h and k can replace the use of a table of values to find points on the graph.

Reflections, Stretches, and Compressions of Absolute-Value Graphs
The absolute-value parent function can be reflected, stretched, and compressed by multiplying by a constant a.   If $a < 0$, then the graph is reflected across the x-axis.   If $|a| > 1$, then the graph is stretched vertically, or away from the x-axis.   If $|a| < 1$, then the graph is compressed vertically, or toward the x-axis.

Example 4 **Reflecting, Stretching, and Compressing Absolute-Value Graphs**

Describe the graph of each function.

(a.) $f(x) = 3|x|$

SOLUTION

$a = 3$, so $|a| = 3$.

Since $|a| > 1$, the graph is stretched vertically.

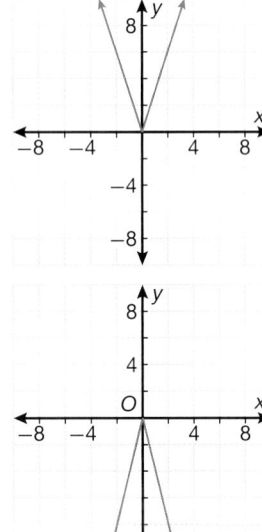

(b.) $f(x) = -4|x|$

SOLUTION

$a = -4$, so $|a| = 4$.

Since $a < 0$, the graph is reflected across the x-axis. Since $|a| > 1$, the graph is stretched vertically.

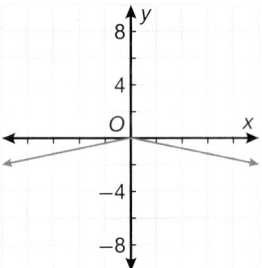

(c.) $f(x) = -0.2|x|$

SOLUTION

$a = -0.2$, so $|a| = 0.2$.

Since $a < 0$, the graph is reflected across the x-axis. Since $|a| < 1$, the graph is compressed vertically.

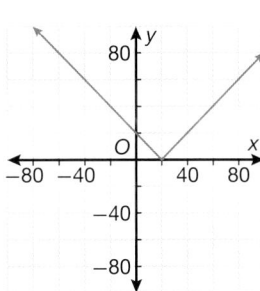

Example 5 **Application: Travel**

A helicopter pilot is flying from town A to town B at 60 miles per hour. To make sure he is on course, he will fly over a landmark that he knows is 20 miles from town A. Write and graph the distance from the landmark as a function of minutes of flight time.

SOLUTION

Let a = rate = 60 mph = 1 mile per minute

Let h = time from landmark = $\frac{20}{1}$ = 20 minutes

Let k = closest distance to landmark = 0 miles

$f(x) = 1|x - 20| + 0$

$f(x) = 1|x - 20|$

Graph each function and give the coordinates of the vertex.

a. $f(x) = |x| + 2$.
(Ex 2)

b. $f(x) = |x + 2|$.
(Ex 2)

c. $f(x) = |x - 1| + 2$
(Ex 3)

Describe the graph of each function.
(Ex 4)

d. $f(x) = 4|x|$

e. $f(x) = -2|x|$

f. $f(x) = -0.5|x|$

g. The distance of a truck to a manhole cover is given by the function
(Ex 5) $f(t) = |t| + 25$. Write the function representing the distance of a truck starting at the same location, but traveling twice as fast.

Practice   Distributed and Integrated

*1. Estimate Without graphing the function, which direction would the function
(107) $f(x) = |x| - 6$ shift the parent function?

2. Solve $\sqrt{2x} = 14$. Check your answer.
(106)

3. Write $5y - 29 = -14x$ in standard form.
(35)

*4. Multiple Choice What absolute-value function is shown by the graph?
(107)

  A $f(x) = 2|x|$ **B** $f(x) = 0.5|x|$

  C $f(x) = -5|x|$ **D** $f(x) = -0.5|x|$

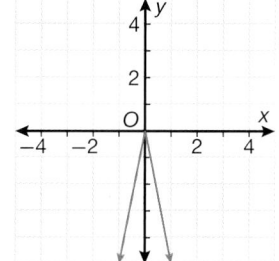

5. Translate the inequality $3b + \frac{2}{5} \geq 1\frac{3}{5}$ into a sentence.
(45)

*6. (**Boating**) The path of a sailboat is represented by the function
(107) $f(x) = \left|\frac{3}{5}x - 30\right| + 30$. At what point does the sailboat tack (turn)?

*7. Write Why does the graph of an absolute-value function not extend past the vertex?
(107)

8. Solve the system of linear equations: $\begin{array}{l} 4y = -3x - 4 \\ 4x + 6 = -5y \end{array}$.
(63)

*9. Geometry The perimeter of the square is 20 centimeters. Solve for x.
(106)

*10. Error Analysis Two students found the solution for a radical equation. Which
(106) student is correct? Explain the error.

Student A	Student B
$\sqrt{x} + 7 = 14$	$\sqrt{x} + 7 = 14$
$\sqrt{x} = 7$	$\sqrt{x} + 49 = 196$
$x = 49$	$\sqrt{x} = 147$
	$x = 21{,}609$

11. Jason built a new deck with an area of $(-20x + 100 + x^2)$ square feet. The width
(93) is $(x - 10)$ feet. What is the length?

*12. Multi-Step A triangular brace is constructed in the shape of a right triangle. The
(106) two legs of the brace are $\sqrt{x + 5}$ and $\sqrt{x}$ units long.

    a. What expression could be used to solve for the length, l, of the third side
of the brace?

    b. Simplify the equation so it does not contain any radicals.

    c. Find the value of x for which the length of the third side of the brace is equal
to 10.

13. Coordinate Geometry Find the coordinates of the point(s) at which the graphs of
(106) $y = x$ and $y = \sqrt{x}$ intersect.

14. Find the next 3 terms of the sequence 125, 25, 5, 1.
(105)

*15. Carbon Dating Scientists can use the ratio of radioactive carbon-14 to carbon-12 to
(105) find the age of organic objects. Carbon-14 has a half-life of about 5730 years, which
means that after 5730 years, half the original amount remains. Carbon dating can date
objects to about 50,000 years ago, or about 9 half-lives. About what percent of the
original amount of carbon-14 remains in objects about 50,000 years old?

*16. Error Analysis Two students find the 5th term in a geometric series that has a common
(105) ratio of $\frac{1}{2}$ and a first term of 6. Which student is correct? Explain the error.

Student A	Student B
$A(n) = ar^{n-1}$	$A(n) = ar^{n-1}$
$= 6 \cdot \left(\frac{1}{2}\right)^4$	$= 6 \cdot \frac{1}{2} \cdot 4$
$= \frac{3}{8}$	$= 12$

17. Solve by graphing on a graphing calculator. Round to the nearest tenth.
(100)
$$-11x^2 + x = -4$$

Solve and graph each inequality.

18. $|x - 4| + 15 \geq 21$ **19.** $|x| + 45 \leq 34$
(101)   (91)

20. (Football) NCAA rules require that the circumference c of a football, measured around
(101) its widest part, 21 inches, to vary by no more than 0.25 inches. Write and solve an
absolute-value inequality that models the acceptable circumferences. What is the least
acceptable circumference?

21. (Area of a Pool) Maria wants to increase the radius of a pool by 3 meters.
(102) The new area of the pool is 200.96 square meters.
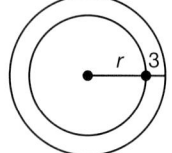

    a. Write a formula to find the original radius of the pool.

    b. Solve the formula.

    c. What will the new diameter of the pool be?

***22.** Graph the function $f(x) = |x| + 3$.
(107)

23. Multiple Choice Solve $-3x^2 + 24x = 36$.
(104)
    A $x = -8$ or 0 **B** $x = -6$ or 2 **C** $x = 2$ or 6 **D** $x = 0$ or 8

24. Analyze Determine what values of c would make the equation $x^2 - 50x = c$ have
(104) no solution.

Simplify.

25. $\dfrac{\dfrac{4x}{2x+12} + \dfrac{x}{3x+18}}{\dfrac{8x^2}{x^2+8x+12}}$
(92)

26. $\sqrt{\dfrac{20}{3}}$
(103)

27. Multi-Step A businessman makes \$50 profit on each item sold. He would like to
(94) make \$950 plus or minus \$100 total each week.

    a. Write an absolute-value equation for the minimum and maximum profit he
    desires.

    b. What is the minimum and maximum number of items he needs to sell each
    week?

28. (School Dance) Tickets for the school dance are \$4 for middle school students and \$6
(97) for high school students. In order to cover expenses, at least \$600 worth of tickets
must be sold. Write an inequality that models this situation and graph it.

29. Multi-Step A painting is 5 inches by 4 inches. The frame around it is x inches wide.
(98)
    a. Write expressions for the length and width of the picture with the frame.

    b. The total area of the picture and frame is 42 square inches. What is the
    width of the frame?

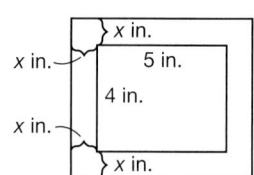

30. Justify Explain how to transform $\dfrac{x}{x-3} = \dfrac{4}{x}$ to $x^2 = 4x - 12$.
(99)

Identifying and Graphing Exponential Functions

Warm Up

1. **Vocabulary** In the expression 3^5, 5 is the _____.
(3)

Simplify.

2. 4^2
(3)

3. 6^{-3}
(3)

4. $2 \cdot 5^{-2}$
(3)

5. $5 \cdot 2^{-1}$
(3)

New Concepts In a geometric sequence, any term, except the first, can be found by multiplying the previous term by the common ratio. In the geometric sequence 2, 6, 18, 54, 162, …, the common ratio is 3.

The sequence can also be written like this: 2, $2(3)^1$, $2(3)^2$, $2(3)^3$, $2(3)^4$, …. Or, with a_1 representing the first term and r representing the common ratio, it can be written as a_1, $a_1(r)^1$, $a_1(r)^2$, $a_1(r)^3$, $a_1(r)^4$, ….

Using n as the term number, observe that the nth term of a geometric sequence can be found by using the rule $a_n = a_1 r^{n-1}$.

Notice that the independent variable n occurs in the exponent of the function rule. Any function for which the independent variable is an exponent is an **exponential function.**

Exponential Function
An exponential function is a function of the form $f(x) = ab^x$, where a and b are nonzero constants and b is a positive number not equal to 1.

Reading Math

The value of b in an exponential function is comparable to r in a geometric sequence.

Example 1 **Evaluating an Exponential Function**

Evaluate each function for the given values.

a. $f(x) = 5^x$ for $x = -3$, 0, and 4.

SOLUTION

Use the order of operations.

$f(-3) = 5^{-3} = \dfrac{1}{5^3} = \dfrac{1}{125}$, $f(0) = 5^0 = 1$, $f(4) = 5^4 = 625$

Hint

$a^{-n} = \dfrac{1}{a^n}$

b. $f(x) = 2(4)^x$ for $x = -1$, 1, and 2.

SOLUTION

Use the order of operations. Evaluate exponents before multiplying.

$f(-1) = 2(4)^{-1} = 2 \cdot \dfrac{1}{4} = \dfrac{2}{4} = \dfrac{1}{2}$

$f(1) = 2(4)^1 = 2(4) = 8$

$f(2) = 2(4)^2 = 2(16) = 32$

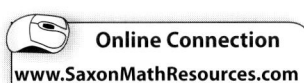
Online Connection
www.SaxonMathResources.com

The common ratio of a geometric sequence is comparable to the base of an exponential function. For any exponential function, as the x-values change by a constant amount, the y-values change by a constant factor. For $f(x) = 4(2)^x$, as each x-value increases by 1, each y-value increases by a factor of 2.

Change: $+1$

x	-1	0	1	2	3
$f(x)$	2	4	8	16	32

Change: $\times 2$

The base 2 of the exponential function $f(x) = 4(2)^x$ is the common ratio of the sequence 2, 4, 8, 16, 32, ….

Example 2 Identifying an Exponential Function

Determine if each set of ordered pairs satisfies an exponential function. Explain your answer.

a. $\left\{ (0, -3), \left(-2, -\frac{1}{3}\right), (1, -9), (-1, -1) \right\}$

SOLUTION

Arrange the ordered pairs so that the x-values are increasing.

$\left\{ \left(-2, -\frac{1}{3}\right), (-1, -1), (0, -3), (1, -9) \right\}$

The x-values increase by the constant amount of 1.

Divide each y-value by the y-value before it.

$-1 \div -\frac{1}{3} = -1 \times -3 = 3$

$-3 \div -1 = 3$

$-9 \div -3 = 3$

Because each ratio is the same, 3, the base $b = 3$. The set of ordered pairs satisfies an exponential function.

b. $\{(6, 150), (4, 100), (8, 200), (2, 50)\}$

SOLUTION

Arrange the ordered pairs so that the x-values are increasing.

$\{(2, 50), (4, 100), (6, 150), (8, 200)\}$

The x-values increase by the constant amount of 2.

Divide each y-value by the y-value before it.

$100 \div 50 = 2$

$150 \div 100 = 1\frac{1}{2}$

$200 \div 150 = 1\frac{1}{3}$

Because the ratios are not the same, the ordered pairs do not satisfy an exponential function.

To graph an exponential function, make a table of ordered pairs and plot the points. The graph will always form a curve that comes close to, but never touches, the x-axis.

Example 3 Graphing $y = ab^x$

Graph each function by making a table of ordered pairs.

a. $y = 5(2)^x$

SOLUTION

Choose both positive and negative x-values.

x	y
-2	1.25
-1	2.5
0	5
1	10
2	20

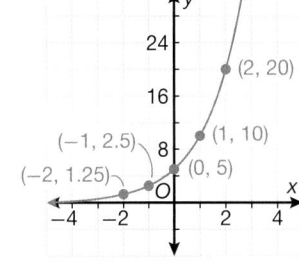

b. $y = -(3)^x$

SOLUTION

x	y
-1	$-\dfrac{1}{3}$
0	-1
1	-3
2	-9
3	-27

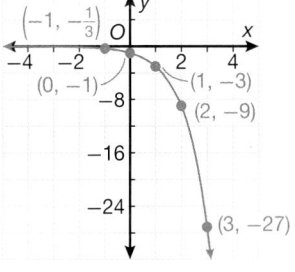

c. $y = 6\left(\dfrac{1}{2}\right)^x$

SOLUTION

x	y
-2	24
-1	12
0	6
1	3
2	1.5

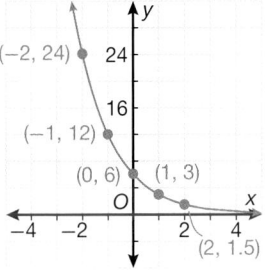

Caution

Due to limitations of scale, graphs of exponential functions often appear to touch the x-axis. The graph will approach but never touch the x-axis. Since $a \neq 0$ and $b \neq 0$, then $y \neq 0$.

Math Reasoning

Generalize Compare the domains and ranges of the functions in Examples 3a and 3b.

A graphing calculator is helpful with comparing graphs of functions and formulating rules based on the values of a and b.

Example 4 Comparing Graphs

Using a graphing calculator, graph each pair of functions on the same screen. Tell how the graphs are alike and how they are different.

(a.) $y = 3(2)^x$ and $y = -3(2)^x$

SOLUTION

Use **Y=** to enter the equations. Use **GRAPH** to graph the equations.

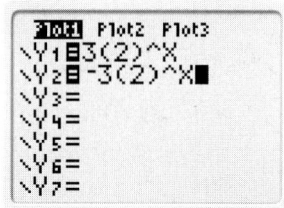 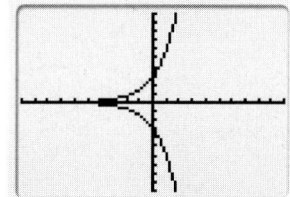

Alike: Both graphs are symmetric about the x-axis. For any x-value, the absolute values of the corresponding y-values are the same.

Different: When $a = 3$, the y-values increase from left to right. When $a = -3$, the y-values decrease from left to right.

(b.) $y = 3(2)^x$ and $y = 3\left(\dfrac{1}{2}\right)^x$

SOLUTION

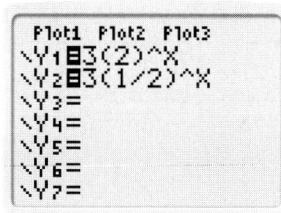 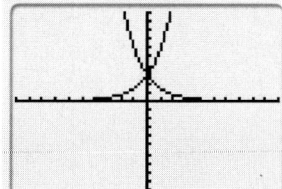

Alike: Both graphs are above the x-axis and symmetric about the y-axis. For any y-value, the absolute values of the corresponding x-values are the same.

Different: When $b = 2$, the y-values increase from left to right. When $b = \frac{1}{2}$, the y-values decrease from left to right.

Example 5 Application: Population

The exponential function $y = 12.28(1.00216)^x$ models the approximate population of Pennsylvania from 2000 to 2006, where x is the number of years after 2000 and y represents millions of people. Use a graphing calculator to find the approximate population of Pennsylvania in 2005. Assuming the model does not change, when will the population reach 13 million?

Caution

The variable y represents millions of people. The table entry $y_1 = 12.413$ means 12.413 million.

SOLUTION Enter the function rule into the Y= editor. Access the Table function by pressing `2nd` `GRAPH` TABLE. Since 2005 is 5 years after 2000, find the y-value for $x = 5$. The population was about 12,413,000. To find when the population will reach 13 million, scroll down until y equals 13 or more. It occurs during the 27th year after 2000, or 2027.

X	Y₁	
0	12.28	
1	12.307	
2	12.333	
3	12.36	
4	12.386	
5	12.413	
6	12.44	

X=5

X	Y₁	
23	12.905	
24	12.933	
25	12.961	
26	12.989	
27	13.017	
28	13.045	
29	13.073	

X=27

Lesson Practice

Evaluate each function for the given values.
(Ex 1)

a. Evaluate $f(x) = 2^x$ for $x = -4, 0$, and 5.

b. Evaluate $f(x) = -3(3)^x$ for $x = -3, 1$, and 3.

Determine whether each set of ordered pairs satisfies an exponential function. Explain your answer.
(Ex 2)

c. $\{(3, -12), (6, -24), (12, -48), (9, -36)\}$

d. $\{(3, 108), (1, 12), (2, 36), (4, 324)\}$

Graph each function by making a table of ordered pairs.
(Ex 3)

e. $y = 2(3)^x$ **f.** $y = -4(2)^x$ **g.** $y = 2\left(\dfrac{1}{4}\right)^x$

Using a graphing calculator, graph each pair of functions on the same screen. Tell how the graphs are alike and how they are different.

h. $y = \left(\dfrac{1}{3}\right)^x$ and $y = -\left(\dfrac{1}{3}\right)^x$
(Ex 4)

i. $y = -2(3)^x$ and $y = -2\left(\dfrac{1}{3}\right)^x$
(Ex 4)

j. The exponential function $y = 8.05(1.01683)^x$ models the approximate population of North Carolina from 2000 to 2006, where x is the number of years after 2000 and y represents millions of people. Use a graphing calculator to find the approximate population of North Carolina in 2006. Assuming the model does not change, when will the population reach 10 million?
(Ex 5)

Practice   Distributed and Integrated

*1. Evaluate the function $f(x) = 2(5)^x$ for $x = -2, 0$, and 2.
(108)

2. Graph the function $f(x) = |x - 2|$.
(107)

*3. Justify Why is $f(x) = 4(1)^x$ not an exponential function?
(108)

*4. Multiple Choice Which could be the function graphed?
(108)

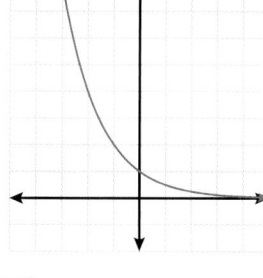

A $y = -\left(\dfrac{1}{2}\right)^x$ **B** $y = \left(\dfrac{1}{2}\right)^x$

C $y = -(2)^x$ **D** $y = 2^x$

*5. (Population) The exponential function $y = 20.85(1.0212)^x$ can model the
(108) approximate population of Texas from 2000 to 2006, where x is the number
of years after 2000 and y represents millions of people. Assuming the model
does not change, what is the difference in expected populations for 2010 and 2020?

*6. Verify Show that the set $\{(3, -4), (2, -1), (5, -64), (4, -16)\}$ is an exponential
(108) function when $b = 4$.

7. Name the corresponding sides and angles if $\triangle RST \sim \triangle NVQ$.
(36)

*8. Multi-Step Graph the parent function $f(x) = |x|$. Translate the function down
(107) by 2. Then reflect the function across the x-axis. What is the new function?

9. Is the graph an absolute-value function? Explain.
(107)

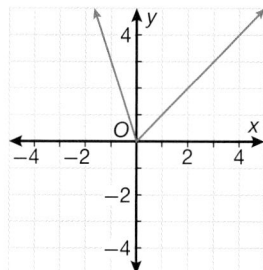

10. Evaluate $\sqrt[3]{x}$ when $x = (-4)^3$.
(46)

*11. Geometry Describe why the function $f(x) = |x|$ is in the shape of a "V".
(107)

12. Error Analysis Two students found the solution to a radical equation. Which student
(106) is correct? Explain the error.

Student A	Student B
$\sqrt{x + 3} = 6$	$\sqrt{x + 3} = 6$
$x + 9 = 36$	$x + 3 = 36$
$x = 27$	$x = 33$

13. Solve $\sqrt{x} - 2 = 8$. Check your answer.
(106)

*14. Write the equation of the function graphed.
(107)

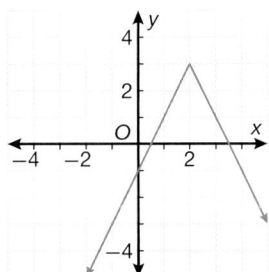

15. Assuming that y varies inversely as x, what is y when $x = 8$, if $y = 55$ when
(64) $x = 11.6$?

16. (Meteorology) In the mountains snow will accumulate quickly in winter. If the
(106) average accumulation can be described using the expression $12\sqrt{x}$, find the
value of x when the accumulation is equal to 108 inches?

17. Solve and graph the inequality $\dfrac{|x|}{8} - 10 < -9$.
(101)

Solve.

18. $x^2 = -9$
(102)

19. $12|x + 9| - 11 = 1$
(94)

20. (Building) Tom's house has two square rooms. He knocks down a wall separating
(102) the rooms. The area of the new room is 338 square feet. What were the dimensions
of the original rooms?

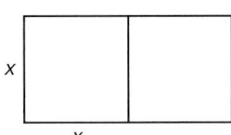

21. Simplify $\dfrac{\dfrac{24a^2b}{7c^2}}{\dfrac{8ab^2}{49c^2}}$.
(92)

22. Find the missing term of the perfect-square trinomial: $x^2 + 7x +$ _____.
(104)

*23. **Multiple Choice** What is the common ratio of the geometric sequence $-\dfrac{5}{8}, -\dfrac{5}{16},$
(105) $-\dfrac{5}{32}, -\dfrac{5}{64}, \ldots$?

   A -2 **B** $-\dfrac{1}{2}$ **C** $\dfrac{1}{2}$ **D** 2

*24. (Landscaping) Li is designing a triangular flower bed in one corner of her
(103) rectangular yard. She plans on making one leg of the triangle $1\frac{11}{12}$ meters long
and the other leg $2\frac{5}{12}$ meters long. She wants to know how much edging material
she needs to buy to place along the hypotenuse of the triangle. Write a rational
expression to show how much material Li needs to buy.

25. **Analyze** Is the sequence $-72, -57.6, 46.08, 36.864, \dots$ geometric? Explain.
(105)

26. Find the quotient of $(36x + 12x^2 + 15) \div (2x + 1)$.
(93)

27. **Multi-Step** Amber drove $\dfrac{7x^2}{x^2 - 49}$ miles on Monday and $\dfrac{x - 1}{4x + 28}$ miles on Tuesday
(95) while delivering pizzas.

    a. What is the total distance she drove?

    b. If her rate was $\dfrac{7}{7x + 49}$ miles per hour, how much time did it take her to deliver
    pizzas on Monday and Tuesday?

28. (Construction) A box needs to be built so that its rectangular top has a length that
(98) is 3 more inches than the width, and so that its area is 88 square inches. Find the
length and the width.

29. **Multi-Step** Sherry can enter all weekly data into the computer in 16 hours. When
(99) she works with Kim, they complete the data entry in 9 hours 36 minutes.

    a. Convert 9 hours 36 minutes to hours.

    b. Write an equation to find how long it would take Kim to enter the same
    data.

    c. How long would it take Kim to enter the data alone?

30. **Analyze** If the y-coordinate of the ordered pair represents the maximum
(100) height of the path of a ball thrown into the air, what does the x-coordinate
represent?

Graphing Systems of Linear Inequalities

Warm Up

1. Vocabulary A(n) _____ (*inequality, equality*) is a mathematical
statement comparing quantities that are not equal.
[45]

2. Graph $y < 2x + 3$.
[97]

3. Is the boundary of the graph of $y \leq 3x + 5$ solid or dashed?
[97]

4. Is the shading above or below the boundary line on the graph
of $y \geq 2x - 6$?
[97]

New Concepts

Recall that a system of linear equations is a set of two or more equations
with the same variables.

The solution of the system below is $(1, 2)$ because the ordered pair $(1, 2)$
makes both equations true.

$y = x + 1$

$y = 2x$

$y = x + 1$	$y = 2x$
$2 = 1 + 1$	$2 = 2(1)$
$2 = 2$	$2 = 2$

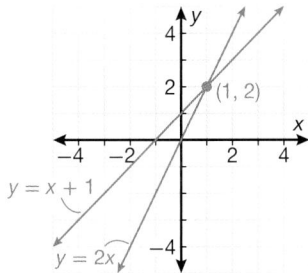

The coordinates also identify the point of
intersection of the two lines.

Likewise, a **system of linear inequalities** is a set of linear inequalities with the
same variables.

Math Reasoning

Verify Show that
$(-4, -4)$ is not a solution
of the system.

In the system shown below, all of the ordered pairs in the overlapping region
satisfy both inequalities. For example, $(3, 2)$ lies in the overlapping region
and makes both inequalities true.

$y \leq x + 1$

$y \leq 2x$

$y \leq x + 1$	$y \leq 2x$
$2 \leq 3 + 1$	$2 \leq 2(3)$
$2 \leq 4$	$2 \leq 6$

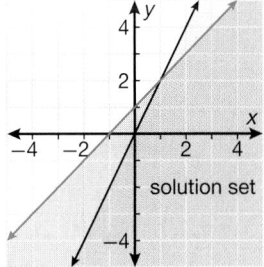

solution set

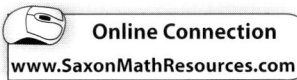
Online Connection
www.SaxonMathResources.com

A **solution of a system of linear inequalities** is an ordered pair or set of
ordered pairs that satisfy all the inequalities in the system. Therefore, all the
ordered pairs in the overlapping region make up the solution of the system.

Example 1 Solving by Graphing

Graph each system.

(a.) $y > \dfrac{1}{4}x - 3$

$y \le 3x + 4.$

SOLUTION

Graph each inequality on the same plane. Every point in the overlapping region is a solution.

Check Substitute a point in the overlapping region to see that it satisfies both inequalities. The point $(0, 0)$ is convenient to substitute.

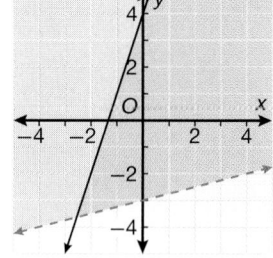

$$y > \dfrac{1}{4}x - 3 \qquad y \le 3x + 4$$

$$0 > \dfrac{1}{4}(0) - 3 \quad 0 \le 3(0) + 4$$

$$0 > -3 \ \checkmark \qquad 0 \le 4 \ \checkmark$$

(b.) $y < 4$

$2y + 2 > -6x.$

SOLUTION

Write the second inequality in slope-intercept form.

$$2y + 2 > -6x$$

$$2y > -6x - 2$$

$$y > -3x - 1$$

Check See if $(0, 0)$ satisfies both inequalities.

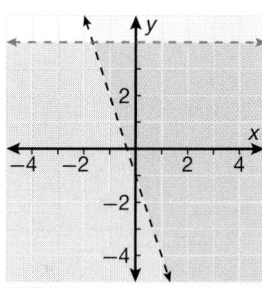

$$y < 4 \qquad\qquad 2y + 2 > -6x$$

$$0 < 4 \ \checkmark \qquad 2(0) + 2 > -6(0)$$

$$2 > 0 \ \checkmark$$

Caution

Do not forget to use a dashed line for the boundary line when the inequality has $<$ or $>$.

Example 2 Solving with a Graphing Calculator

Graph the system on a graphing calculator.

$$y < \dfrac{3}{4}x + 2$$

$$y \ge -\dfrac{1}{5}x + 4$$

SOLUTION Enter both functions. Use the arrow keys to move to the symbol to the left of Y_1 and press enter until the symbol shows the lower half of a plane shaded. For Y_2, select the symbol with the upper half shaded.

Note that for many graphing calculators, the option to choose between a strict and non-strict inequality does not exist.

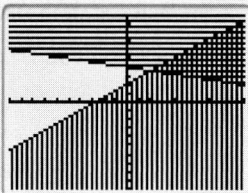

Graphing Calculator Tip

For help with graphing inequalities, refer to the graphing calculator keystrokes in Graphing Calculator Lab 9 on p. 645.

Remember that a system of equations is inconsistent when there are no solutions. This occurs when the slopes of the lines are the same and the y-intercepts are different.

The system has no solutions because the lines are parallel.

$$y = -\frac{2}{3}x - 2$$

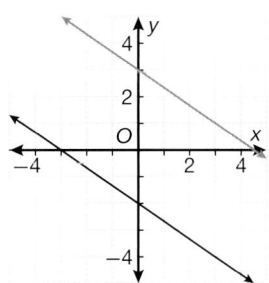

$$y = -\frac{2}{3}x + 3$$

When the equal signs in these equations are replaced with inequality symbols, the system may or may not have a solution set.

Example 3 | **Solving Systems of Inequalities with Parallel Boundary Lines**

Graph each system.

a. $y \leq -\frac{2}{3}x - 2$

$$y \geq -\frac{2}{3}x + 3$$

SOLUTION

The two solution sets do not intersect, so the system has no solution.

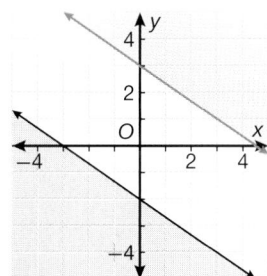

b. $y \geq -\frac{2}{3}x - 2$

$$y \leq -\frac{2}{3}x + 3$$

SOLUTION

The solution set is the region between the parallel lines.

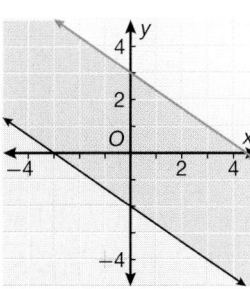

Math Reasoning

Generalize When the boundary lines are parallel, what must be true about the inequality symbols for one graph to be a subset of the other?

c. $y \geq -\frac{2}{3}x - 2$

$$y \geq -\frac{2}{3}x + 3$$

SOLUTION

The solutions of $y \geq -\frac{2}{3}x + 3$ are a subset of the solutions of $y \geq -\frac{2}{3}x - 2$.

The solutions of the system are the same as the solutions of $y \geq -\frac{2}{3}x + 3$.

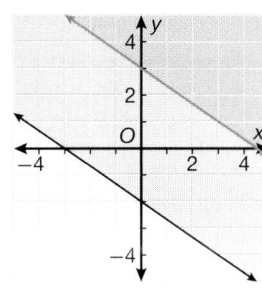

Example **4**   Application: Employment

Lena has to earn at least \$210 per week from two part-time summer jobs. She can work up to 15 hours per week at Job A, which pays \$12 per hour, and can work up to 35 hours per week at Job B, which pays \$10 per hour. She is not allowed to work more than 40 hours per week. Graph the possible combinations of hours Lena can work per week.

SOLUTION

Write a system of inequalities where x is the number of hours worked per week at Job A, and y is the number of hours worked per week at Job B.

$x \leq 15$	no more than 15 hours at Job A
$y \leq 35$	no more than 35 hours at Job B
$12x + 10y \geq 210$	must earn at least \$210 per week
$x + y \leq 40$	cannot work more than 40 hours per week

The region where all four solution sets intersect shows the possible combinations of hours at each job. One possible combination is 9 hours at Job A and 20 hours at Job B.

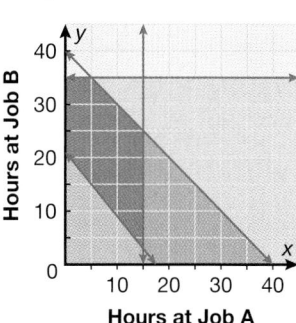

Math Reasoning

Verify Verify that Lena can make at least \$210 working 9 hours at Job A and 20 hours at Job B.

Lesson Practice

Graph each system.
(Ex 1)

a. $y > -2x - 1$

$y \leq \dfrac{1}{5}x + 4$

b. $6y + 6 > -2x$

$y < 2$

c. Graph the system on a graphing calculator.
(Ex 2)

$y \geq x - 6$

$y \leq -x + 3$

Graph each system.
(Ex 3)

d. $y > \dfrac{1}{2}x - 4$

$y > \dfrac{1}{2}x$

e. $y < \dfrac{1}{2}x - 4$

$y > \dfrac{1}{2}x$

f. $y > \dfrac{1}{2}x - 4$

$y < \dfrac{1}{2}x$

g. Brett has \$30 with which to buy dried strawberries and dried pineapple
(Ex 4) for a hiking trip. The dried strawberries cost \$3 per pound and the dried pineapple costs \$2 per pound. Brett needs at least 2 pounds of strawberries and 3.5 pounds of pineapple. Graph the possible combinations of pounds of each dried fruit that Brett can buy.

*1. **Multiple Choice** Which system is represented in the graph?
(109)

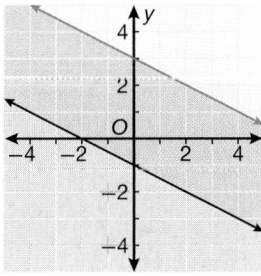

A $\quad y \le -0.5x + 3$
$\quad\quad y \ge -0.5x - 1$

B $\quad y \le -0.5x + 3$
$\quad\quad y \le -0.5x - 1$

C $\quad y \ge -0.5x + 3$
$\quad\quad y \ge -0.5x - 1$

D $\quad y \ge -0.5x + 3$
$\quad\quad y \le -0.5x - 1$

*2. **Sports** The requirements for a major league baseball are shown in
(109) the graph. Write the system of inequalities that matches the graph.

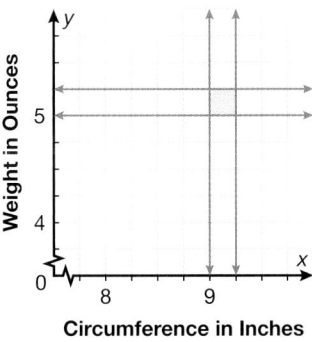

3. Graph the function $f(x) = -3|x|$.
(107)

*4. **Write** Explain how to represent the solution set of $\begin{array}{l} y \le -3x + 4 \\ y < 2x - 1 \end{array}$.
(109)

*5. **Verify** Graph the solution set of $\begin{array}{l} y \ge -x \\ y \le 2x \end{array}$ to verify that $(1, -2)$ is not a
(109) solution of the system.

*6. Evaluate the function $f(x) = 3\left(\frac{1}{3}\right)^x$ for $x = -2, 0,$ and 2.
(108)

7. If the original price was increased 44% to a new price of $900, what was the
(47) original price?

Simplify.

8. $10\sqrt{8x^2y^3} - 5y\sqrt{98x^2y}$
(69)

9. $\sqrt{\dfrac{24y^8}{6x^3}}$
(103)

10. **Error Analysis** Student A said that the following set satisfies an exponential function
(108) because there is a common ratio of 3 among the y-values. Student B said that this
is not so. Which student is correct? Explain the error.

$$\{(3, 1), (5, 3), (6, 9), (7, 27)\}$$

*11. **Multi-Step** Niall has a baseball card whose value, in dollars, x years after he acquired
(108) it, is represented by the function $f(x) = 4.8(1.25)^x$. If Niall bought the card in the
year 2000, how much more is it worth in 2010 than it was in 2005?

*12. **Geometry** Mr. Flores gives the length of a rectangle, in inches, as $f(x) = 16\left(\frac{1}{2}\right)^x$,
(108) where x is the number of times he cuts the length in half. What is the length of the
rectangle after Mr. Flores has cut it in half 4 times? 6 times?
0 times?

*13. **Probability** For the function $f(x) = 7(5)^x$, what is the probability that for a
(108) randomly chosen x-value from the domain of $\{0, 1, 2, 3, 4, 5\}$, $f(x)$ is a number
between 100 and 1000?

14. Is the graph an absolute-value function? Explain.
(107)

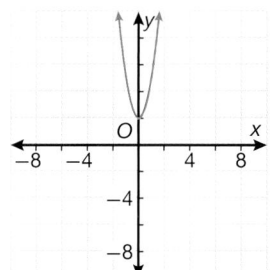

*15. Graph the system $\begin{array}{l} y > \frac{1}{4}x + 3 \\ y > -\frac{1}{4}x + 3 \end{array}$.
(109)

16. **Baseball** An outfielder catches a ball 120 feet from the pitcher's mound and
(107) throws it to home. If $d = |90t - 120|$ represents the ball's distance from the
pitcher's mound, how would the graph change if the outfielder caught the ball 100
feet from the pitcher's mound?

17. **Renovations** Nadia is using 48 square tiles to cover a floor. The tiles come in
(102) 6-inch, 12-inch, and 13-inch sizes. If the total area of the floor is 6912 square inches,
which tile size will fit best?

18. **Projectile Motion** The equation for the time in seconds (t) it takes an object to
(104) strike the ground is $-4.9t^2 - 53.9t = -127.4$. When will the object strike the
ground?

19. Find the next 3 terms of the sequence 5, 4.5, 4.05, 3.645, ….
(105)

*20. **Multiple Choice** Which of the following radical equations has no solution?
(106)
A $\sqrt{x - 3} = x - 9$ **C** $\sqrt{x} + 7 = -2$

B $13\sqrt{x} = 65$ **D** $\sqrt{x + 10} = \sqrt{2x + 8}$

21. **Write** Why is it important to isolate the radical in a radical equation?
(106)

22. Jim's rectangular home gym has an area of $(x^2 - 144)$ square feet. The length
(93) is $(x - 12)$ feet. What is the width?

Solve.

23. $4|x + 2| - 9 = 19$
(94)

24. $x^2 = -49$
(102)

25. $2\left|\dfrac{x}{4} - 6\right| = 8$
(94)

26. Multi-Step A pitcher throws a softball. The height in feet is represented by the
(96) function $h = -16t^2 + 47t + 5$.

    a. How high is the ball after 1 second?

    b. How high is the ball when it is released?

    c. What is the initial velocity of the ball?

27. (Gardening) It takes a boy 2 hours to pull all the weeds in the garden. It takes his sister
(99) 4 hours. How long will it take them if they pull weeds together?

28. Multi-Step Andrew hits a golf ball into the air. Its movement forms a parabola given by
(100) the quadratic equation $h = -16t^2 + 31t + 7$, where h is the height in feet and t is the time
in seconds.

    a. Find the time t when the ball is at its maximum height. Round to the nearest
    hundredth.

    b. Find the time t when the ball hits the ground. Round to the nearest
    hundredth.

    c. Find the maximum height of the arc the ball makes in its flight. Round to the nearest
    hundredth.

29. Write Describe the similarities and differences between solving the inequality
(101) $2|x| + 1 < 7$ and solving the inequality $|2x + 1| < 7$.

30. If the area of a rectangle is represented by the expression $3x^2 + 22x - 45$ and
$(Inv 9)$ the width by the expression $(x + 9)$, what would the length be?

Using the Quadratic Formula

1. Vocabulary A _____ equation can be written in the form
(84)
$ax^2 + bx + c = 0$, where a is not equal to 0.

Find the value of c to complete the square for each expression.

2. $x^2 + 8x + c$ **3.** $x^2 + 9x + c$
(104)   (104)

4. Solve $x^2 + 10x = 24$ by completing the square. Check your answer.
(104)

New Concepts   Different methods are used to solve quadratic equations. One method is applying the **quadratic formula.** The quadratic formula is derived by completing the square of the standard form of the quadratic equation $ax^2 + bx + c = 0$.

Math Language

A **quadratic equation** is an equation whose graph is a parabola.

$$ax^2 + bx + c = 0$$

$$\frac{ax^2}{a} + \frac{bx}{a} + \frac{c}{a} = 0 \qquad \text{Divide by the coefficient of } x^2.$$

$$x^2 + \frac{bx}{a} = -\frac{c}{a} \qquad \text{Subtract the constant } \frac{c}{a} \text{ from both sides.}$$

$$x^2 + \frac{bx}{a} + \left(\frac{b}{2a}\right)^2 = -\frac{c}{a} + \left(\frac{b}{2a}\right)^2 \qquad \text{Add } \left(\frac{b}{2a}\right)^2 \text{ to complete the square.}$$

$$x^2 + \frac{bx}{a} + \frac{b^2}{4a^2} = -\frac{c}{a} + \frac{b^2}{4a^2} \qquad \text{Simplify.}$$

$$\left(x + \frac{b}{2a}\right)^2 = \frac{b^2 - 4ac}{4a^2} \qquad \text{Write the left side as a squared binomial and the other side with the LCD.}$$

$$\sqrt{\left(x + \frac{b}{2a}\right)^2} = \pm\sqrt{\frac{b^2 - 4ac}{4a^2}} \qquad \text{Take the square root.}$$

$$x + \frac{b}{2a} = \pm\frac{\sqrt{b^2 - 4ac}}{2a} \qquad \text{Simplify.}$$

$$x = \frac{-b \pm \sqrt{b^2 - 4ac}}{2a} \qquad \text{Solve.}$$

Quadratic Formula
For the quadratic equation $ax^2 + bx + c = 0$, $$x = \frac{-b \pm \sqrt{b^2 - 4ac}}{2a} \text{ when } a \neq 0.$$

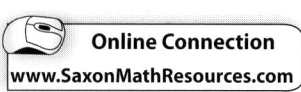

Online Connection
www.SaxonMathResources.com

The quadratic formula can be used to solve any quadratic equation.

Example 1 — Solving a Quadratic Equation in Standard Form

Use the quadratic formula to solve $x^2 - 9x + 20 = 0$ for x.

SOLUTION

$$x = \frac{-b \pm \sqrt{b^2 - 4ac}}{2a}$$
Use the quadratic formula.

$$= \frac{-(-9) \pm \sqrt{(-9)^2 - 4(1)(20)}}{2(1)}$$
Substitute 1 for a, -9 for b, and 20 for c.

$$= \frac{9 \pm \sqrt{81 - 80}}{2}$$

$$= \frac{9 \pm \sqrt{1}}{2} = \frac{9 \pm 1}{2}$$
Simplify.

$$x = 5 \text{ and } 4$$

Check Verify that 5 and 4 make the original equation true.

$$x^2 - 9x + 20 = 0$$
$$(5)^2 - 9(5) + 20 \overset{?}{=} 0$$
$$25 - 45 + 20 \overset{?}{=} 0$$
$$0 = 0 \quad \checkmark$$

$$x^2 - 9x + 20 = 0$$
$$(4)^2 - 9(4) + 20 \overset{?}{=} 0$$
$$16 - 36 + 20 \overset{?}{=} 0$$
$$0 = 0 \quad \checkmark$$

Example 2 — Rearranging Quadratic Equations before Solving

Use the quadratic formula to solve $-18x + x^2 = -32$ for x.

SOLUTION Rearrange the equation into the standard form $ax^2 + bx + c = 0$.

Hint

Rearrange terms and their corresponding signs to match the form $ax^2 + bx + c = 0$.

$$x^2 - 18x + 32 = 0$$
Write the equation in standard form.

$$x = \frac{-b \pm \sqrt{b^2 - 4ac}}{2a}$$
Use the quadratic formula.

$$= \frac{-(-18) \pm \sqrt{(-18)^2 - 4(1)(32)}}{2(1)}$$
Substitute 1 for a, -18 for b, and 32 for c.

$$= \frac{18 \pm \sqrt{324 - 128}}{2}$$

$$= \frac{18 \pm \sqrt{196}}{2} = \frac{18 \pm 14}{2}$$
Simplify.

$$x = 16 \text{ and } 2$$

Check Verify the solutions for x.

$$-18x + x^2 = -32$$
$$-18(16) + (16)^2 \overset{?}{=} -32$$
$$-288 + 256 \overset{?}{=} -32$$
$$-32 = -32 \quad \checkmark$$

$$-18x + x^2 = -32$$
$$-18(2) + (2)^2 \overset{?}{=} -32$$
$$-36 + 4 \overset{?}{=} -32$$
$$-32 = -32 \quad \checkmark$$

Example 3 **Finding Approximate Solutions**

Use the quadratic formula to solve for x. Then use a graphing calculator to find approximate solutions and verify them.

$5x^2 - 3x - 1 = 0$

SOLUTION

$5x^2 - 3x - 1 = 0$

$x = \dfrac{-b \pm \sqrt{b^2 - 4ac}}{2a}$ Use the quadratic formula.

$= \dfrac{-(-3) \pm \sqrt{(-3)^2 - 4(5)(-1)}}{2(5)}$ Substitute the values for a, b, and c.

$x = \dfrac{3 \pm \sqrt{9 + 20}}{10} = \dfrac{3 \pm \sqrt{29}}{10}$

To find the approximate solutions, use a calculator with a square root key. Round the solutions to the nearest ten thousandth.

The solutions are $\dfrac{3 + \sqrt{29}}{10} \approx 0.8385$ and $\dfrac{3 - \sqrt{29}}{10} \approx -0.2385$.

Check

On a graphing calculator, graph the related function $y = 5x^2 - 3x - 1$ to check that the approximate solutions are the zeros of the graph.

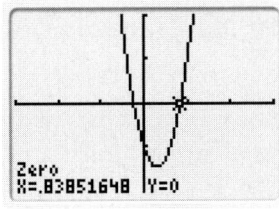
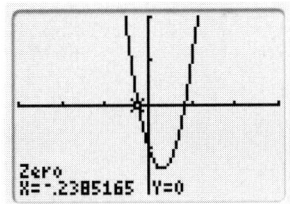

Graphing Calculator Tip

For help with graphing quadratic equations, see the graphing calculator keystrokes in Lab 8 on p. 583.

Example 4 **Recognizing a Quadratic Equation With No Real Solutions**

Use the quadratic formula to solve $2x^2 + 3x + 4 = 0$ for x.

SOLUTION

$x = \dfrac{-b \pm \sqrt{b^2 - 4ac}}{2a}$

$= \dfrac{-(3) \pm \sqrt{(3)^2 - 4(2)(4)}}{2(2)}$ Substitute the values for a, b, and c.

$x = \dfrac{-3 \pm \sqrt{9 - 32}}{4} = \dfrac{-3 \pm \sqrt{-23}}{4}$

The square root of a negative number cannot be taken, so there are no real solutions.

Example 5 Application: Object in Motion

From an initial height s of 70 meters in a stadium, Luis tosses a ball up at an initial velocity v of 5 meters per second. Use the equation $-4.9t^2 + vt + s = 0$ to find the time t when the ball hits the ground.

SOLUTION

Substitute the values into the quadratic formula. Then solve.

$$-4.9t^2 + 5t + 70 = 0$$

$$t = \frac{-b \pm \sqrt{b^2 - 4ac}}{2a}$$

$$= \frac{-(5) \pm \sqrt{(5)^2 - 4(-4.9)(70)}}{2(-4.9)}$$

$$= \frac{-5 \pm \sqrt{25 + 1372}}{-9.8}$$

$$= \frac{-5 \pm \sqrt{1397}}{-9.8}$$

$$\approx \frac{-5 \pm 37.3765}{-9.8}$$

$$t \approx -3.3037 \text{ and } t \approx 4.3241$$

Check

$$-4.9(4.3241)^2 + 5(4.3241) + 70 \approx -91.6194 + 21.6205 + 70 \approx 0 \quad \checkmark$$

The ball will land on the ground in approximately 4.3241 seconds.

Hint

When the solutions deal with time, we only consider positive values for solutions.

Lesson Practice

a. Use the quadratic formula to solve for x.
(Ex 1)
$$x^2 + 3x - 18 = 0$$

b. Use the quadratic formula to solve for x.
(Ex 2)
$$-72 - 14x + x^2 = 0$$

c. Use the quadratic formula to solve for x.
(Ex 2)
$$x^2 + 80 = 21x$$

d. Use the quadratic formula to solve for x. Then use a graphing calculator
(Ex 3) to find approximate solutions and verify them. Round the solutions to the nearest ten thousandth.
$$9x^2 + 6x - 1 = 0$$

e. Use the quadratic formula to solve $4x^2 + 5x + 3 = 0$ for x.
(Ex 4)

f. From an initial height s of 50 meters on a cliff, Janet tosses a ball upward
(Ex 5) at an initial velocity v of 6 meters/second. At what point does the ball fall back to the ground? Round the solution to nearest ten thousandth.

Use the quadratic formula to solve for x. Check the solutions.

*1. $x^2 - 2x - 35 = 0$
(110)

*2. $x^2 - 10x + 25 = 0$
(110)

*3. **Multi-Step** Determine why $16h^2 + 25 = 40h$ has only 1 solution using the quadratic
(110) formula.

    a. Rearrange the equation into the $ax^2 + bx + c = 0$ form.

    b. What is different about $b^2 - 4ac$?

    c. **Generalize** When will the equation $ax^2 + bx + c = 0$ have only 1 solution?

4. Compare: $12,000 \bigcirc 1.2 \times 10^3$.
(37)

5. Find the zeros of the function. $y = x^2 + 12x + 36$
(96)

6. Describe the graph of an indirect variation when the constant of variation
(Inv 7) is positive.

7. Identify the outlier or outliers in the data set.
(48)

    number of cars for sixteen households: 3, 2, 2, 1, 2, 3, 6, 2, 1, 1, 1, 3, 2, 2, 2, 1, 3

*8. **Predict** Use mental math to predict whether the quadratic formula is necessary to
(110) solve $3b^2 + 15b - 20 = 0$. Solve.

*9. (**Soccer**) A 1.5-meter-tall soccer player bounces a soccer ball off his head at a velocity
(110) of 7 meters per second upward. Use the formula $h = -4.9t^2 + v_0t + h_0$ to estimate
how many seconds it will take the ball to hit the ground.

*10. **Error Analysis** For the system of inequalities graphed, Student A said that
(109) $(1, -4)$ is a solution of the system and Student B said that $(4, 2)$ is a solution of
the system. Which student is correct? Explain the error.

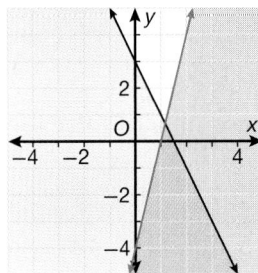

11. Graph the system $\begin{array}{l} y \leq 2 \\ x \geq 2 \end{array}$.
(109)

*12. **Multi-Step** A student group is planning on washing cars in an effort to raise at least
(109) $300. They want to charge $5 for a basic wash, which will take about 10 minutes, and
$15 for a detailed wash, which will take about 30 minutes. They have the car-wash
lot rented for 8 hours. Write and graph a system of linear inequalities to describe this
situation. Explain your findings.

13. **Geometry** Suppose the perimeter of a rectangle must be less than 50 units and
(109) the width must be greater than 5 units. Graph a system of linear inequalities to
describe this situation. Give one set of possible dimensions for the rectangle.

14. Evaluate the function $f(x) = -3(6)^x$ for $x = -2, 0$, and 2.
(108)

15. **Error Analysis** Which student correctly evaluated $f(x) = 2(3)^x$ for $x = 2$? Explain
(108) the error.

Student A	Student B
$f(x) = 2(3)^x$	$f(x) = 2(3)^x$
$= 6^x$	$= 2(3)^2$
$= 6^2 = 36$	$= 2(9) = 18$

*16. **Chemistry** Amaro uses $f(x) = 10\left(\frac{1}{2}\right)^x$ to give the amount remaining from 10 grams
(108) of a radioactive substance after x number of half-lives. Which graph represents
this function?

Graph A   **Graph B**   **Graph C**

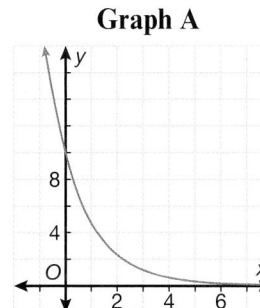   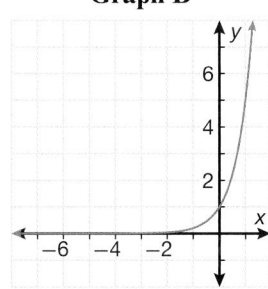   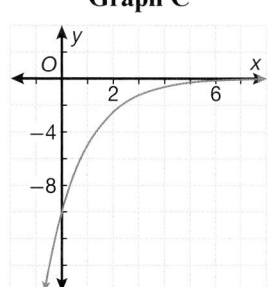

17. Simplify $\dfrac{\sqrt{15xy}}{3\sqrt{10xy^3}}$.
(103)

18. Subtract $\dfrac{5x^2}{10x - 30} - \dfrac{2x - 5}{x^2 - 9}$.
(95)

19. **Astronomy** Astronomers can use the formula $T = \sqrt{d^3}$ to find the time T it takes a
(103) planet to orbit the Sun (in earth years), knowing the distance d of the planet from
the Sun (in astronomical units, AU). If Mars is about $\frac{3}{2}$ AU from the Sun, about
how long does it take Mars to orbit the Sun in earth years? Give your answer as a
rational expression.

20. **Multiple Choice** What is the absolute-value function of the graph?
(107)

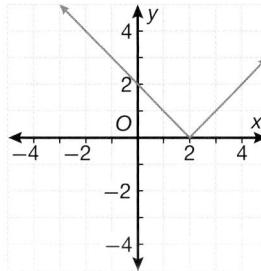

A $f(x) = |x + 2|$ **B** $f(x) = |x - 2|$

C $f(x) = |x| + 2$ **D** $f(x) = |x| - 2$

21. Solve $p^2 + 13p = -50$ by completing the square.
(104)

*22. (**Compound Interest**) The formula for a fund that compounds interest is
$A_n = P\left(1 + \frac{r}{n}\right)^{nt}$, where A is the balance, P is the initial amount deposited, r is the annual interest rate, t is the number of years, and n is the number of times the interest is compounded per year. Gretchen deposits \$1500 into an account that pays 4.5% interest compounded annually. Write the first 4 terms of the sequence representing Gretchen's balance after t years. Round to the nearest cent.
(105)

23. Solve $\sqrt{x + 11} = 16$. Check your answer.
(106)

*24. Analyze Are the graphs for $f(x) = 5|x|$ and $f(x) = |5x|$ the same? Explain.
(107)

25. Solve the equation $9\left|\frac{x}{2} - 6\right| - 27$.   **26.** Factor $x^2 + 42 + 13x$.
(94)   *(72)*

27. Multi-Step Lisa plans to shop for books and magazines and she plans to spend no more than \$32. Each book costs \$14 and each magazine costs \$4.
(97)

   a. Write an inequality that describes this situation.

   b. Graph the inequality.

   c. If Lisa wants to spend exactly \$32, what is a possible number of each she can spend her money on?

28. (**Volleyball**) Diego hits a volleyball into the air. The ball's movement forms a parabola given by the quadratic equation $h = -16t^2 + 3t + 14$ where h is the height in feet and t is the time in seconds. Find the maximum height of the path the volleyball makes and the time when the volleyball hits the ground. Round to the nearest hundredth.
(100)

29. Multi-Step When the temperature (t) of the gas neon is within $1.25°$ of $-247.35°C$ it will be in a liquid form. This can be modeled by the absolute-value inequality $|t - (-247.35)| < 1.25$.
(101)

   a. Solve and graph the inequality $|t - (-247.35)| < 1.25$.

   b. One endpoint of the graph represents the boiling point of neon, the temperature at which neon changes from liquid to gas. The other endpoint represents the melting point, at which neon turns from solid to liquid. The higher temperature is the boiling point and the lower temperature is the melting point. What is the boiling point of neon? What is the melting point?

30. Measurement The following formula represents the area of circle A: $\pi r^2 - 165.05 \text{ m}^2 = 0$. What is the approximate measurement, in meters, of the radius r? Use 3.14 for π.
(102)

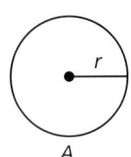

A

Investigating Exponential Growth and Decay

Water Flow Rates

Water flows from a crack in the side of a swimming pool, initially releasing one gallon of water. The crack continues to widen as water continues to flow from the pool. For every second after that, the amount flowing from the pool doubles. The table below shows the relationship between time and the amount of water flowing.

Time (s)	Amount of Water (gal)
0	1
1	2
2	4
3	8

Math Reasoning

Analyze What characteristics of the data and the graph indicate that this data does not model a linear function?

1. Create a graph of the data.

2. **Predict** How many gallons of water flow from the pool in the fourth second?

Near the origin the graph looks similar to a parabola, however it grows much more quickly. The graph models exponential growth. **Exponential growth** is a situation where a quantity always increases by the same percent for a given time period.

Stock Exchange

The annual number of shares S in billions traded on the New York Stock Exchange from 1990 to 2000 can be approximated by the model $S = 39(1.2)^x$, where x is the number of years since 1990.

3. Create a table of values like the one below. Round each share to the nearest billion.

x	S
0	39
2	56
4	
6	
8	
10	

Math Reasoning

Analyze In the exponential growth equation $f(x) = kb^x$ what is the domain? Why?

Online Connection
www.SaxonMathResources.com

4. Plot the coordinates. Connect the points with a smooth curve.

5. Use the graph to estimate the number of shares traded in 1997.

6. **Verify** Use the equation to calculate the exact number of shares traded in 1997 algebraically.

Exponential growth is modeled by the function $f(x) = kb^x$, where $k > 0$. The percent of growth b, expressed as a decimal number, is greater than 1.

Exploration Analyzing Different Values of k in the Exponential Growth Function

Materials

• several sheets of notebook paper

Step 1: Take one sheet of notebook paper. Fold it in half. Unfold the paper and count the number of rectangular regions formed. Record the number of folds and regions in a table like the one below.

Folds	Regions
0	1
1	2
2	
3	
4	

Refold the paper along the initial crease you made and fold it in half again. Continue counting regions and folding in half at least four times.

Step 2: Take three sheets of notebook paper and stack them. Repeat Step 1. Create and complete a table like the one below.

Folds	Regions
0	3
1	6
2	
3	
4	

Step 3: Take five sheets of notebook paper and stack them. Repeat Step 1. Create and complete a table like the one below.

Folds	Regions
0	5
1	
2	
3	
4	

Math Reasoning

Analyze Why are each of the three functions named using function notation?

7. Plot the points on one coordinate plane. Let $x =$ the number of folds. Let $y =$ the number of regions. Connect the point for each set of data with a smooth curve.

The data in the Exploration are included in the graphs of the functions $f(x) = 2^x$, $g(x) = 3(2)^x$, and $h(x) = 5(2)^x$, respectively. All three functions are of the form $y = k(b)^x$.

8. What is the y-intercept of each function? Compare the y-intercept of each equation to $y = kb^x$. Name the y-intercept of $y = kb^x$.

9. Generalize How does changing the value of k affect the graph of the function?

10. Formulate As the number of folds increase, what happens to the number of regions on the folded paper? What is the b-value for each equation? Write an equation in the form $y = k(b)^x$ to model situations in which y doubles as x increases.

11. For any function $y = k(b)^x$, what does k represent in any situation when $x = 0$?

The period of time required for a quantity to double in size or value is called **doubling time**. The equation will be of the form $y = k(2)^x$.

Just as data can grow exponentially, some data can model exponential decay. **Exponential decay** is a situation where a quantity always decreases by the same percent in a given time period.

Carbon-14 dating is used to find the approximate age of animal and plant material after it has decomposed. The half-life of carbon-14 is 5730 years. So, every 5730 years half of the carbon-14 in a substance decomposes. Find the amount remaining from a sample containing 100 milligrams of carbon-14 after four half lives.

12. How many years are there in four half-lives?

13. Create and complete a table like the one below.

Number of Half-Lives	Number of Years	Amount of Carbon-14 Remaining (mg)
0	0	100
1	5730	
2	11,460	
3	17,190	
4	22,920	

14. How much of the sample remains after 22,920 years?

Exponential decay is modeled by the function $f(x) = kb^x$, where $k > 0$ and $0 < b < 1$. Since the value of b is a positive number less than 1, as x increases, the value of $f(x)$ decreases by b.

An exponential decay function can model the amount of a substance in the body over time. Many diabetes patients take insulin. The exponential function $f(x) = 100 \left(\frac{1}{2}\right)^x$ describes the percent of insulin in the body after x half-lives. The **half-life** of a substance is the time it takes for one-half of the substance to decay into another substance.

15. About what percent of insulin would be left in the body after 8 half-lives?

16. Write Describe the effect that the b-value has on the amount of substance remaining as the number of half-lives x increases.

Caution

Do not divide the original amount of a substance by 3 to calculate the amount of a substance left after three half-lives.

Hint

Since x usually represents time in decay equations, $x > 0$.

Math Reasoning

Analyze Why does $f(x)$ decrease as x increases?

17. **Predict** Graph the functions $f(x) = 100\left(\frac{1}{2}\right)^x$ and $g(x) = 50\left(\frac{1}{2}\right)^x$. How does the value of k in each equation compare to the y-intercept? How does the k-value affect the graph of the function?

Match the following exponential growth and decay equations to the graphs shown. Explain your choices.

18. $y = 2(0.5)^x$

19. $y = 2(3)^x$

20. $y = (0.25)^x$

21. $y = 0.25(2)^x$

Graph A

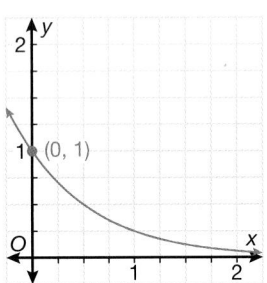

Graph B

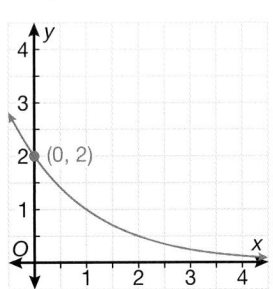

Graph C

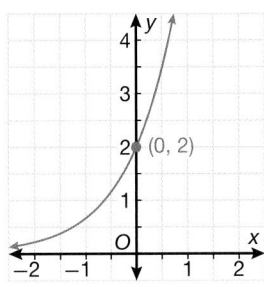

Graph D

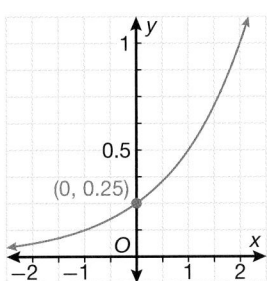

Investigation Practice

a. **Formulate** Alex invested \$500 in an account that will double his balance every 8 years. How many times will the amount in the account double in 32 years? Write an equation to model the account balance y after x doubling times. What will his balance be in 32 years?

b. **Formulate** Radioactive glucose is used in cancer detection. It has a half-life of 100 minutes. How many half-lives are in 24 hours? Write an equation to model the amount y remaining of a 100 milligram sample after x half-lives. How much of a 100 milligram sample remains after 24 hours?

Use the equation $f(x) = \left(\frac{1}{2}\right)^x$ to answer each problem.

c. Does the equation model exponential growth or exponential decay? Explain.

d. How does the graph of $f(x) = \left(\frac{1}{2}\right)^x$ compare to the graph of $g(x) = \left(\frac{1}{3}\right)^x$?

e. How does the graph of $f(x) = \left(\frac{1}{2}\right)^x$ compare to the graph of $h(x) = 2^x$?

Match the following exponential growth and decay equations to the graphs shown. Explain your choices.

f. $y = 3(0.5)^x$

g. $y = 3(2)^x$

h. $y = (4)^x$

i. $y = 2(0.25)^x$

Graph A

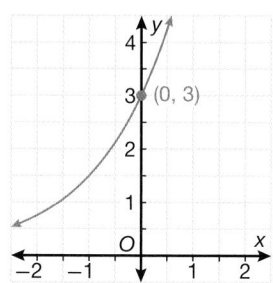

Graph B

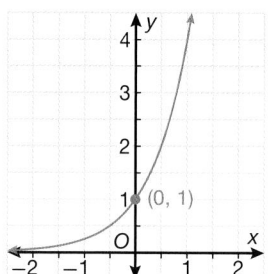

Graph C

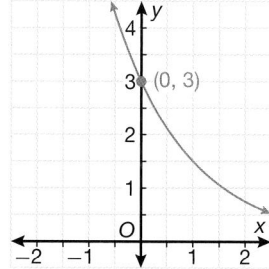

Graph D

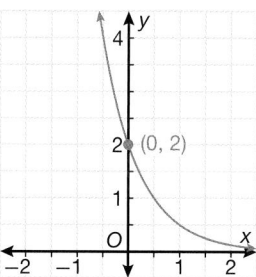

Solving Problems Involving Permutations

Warm Up

1. **Vocabulary** _____ (*Experimental, Theoretical*) probability is found (14) by analyzing a situation and finding the ratio of favorable outcomes to all possible outcomes.

2. What is the probability of rolling a number greater than 3 on a number (14) cube labeled 1–6?

3. What is the probability of rolling a number greater than 7 on a number (14) cube labeled 1–6?

Identify each set of events as independent or dependent.

4. Rolling a 5 on one number cube and a 3 on another. (33)

5. Drawing a blue marble from a bag, keeping it, and then drawing a red (33) marble.

New Concepts
A tree diagram can be used to determine the number of ways 2 pairs of pants and 4 shirts can be arranged to make different outfits. However, the number of possible outcomes can be determined by multiplying the number of ways the first event can occur by the number of ways the second event can occur.

first event		second event		total possible outcomes
2 pairs of pants	×	4 shirts	=	8 outfits

This method is an application of the Fundamental Counting Principle. The Fundamental Counting Principle can be used to determine the number of possible outcomes in situations involving independent events.

Fundamental Counting Principle
If an independent event M can occur in m ways and another independent event N can occur in n ways, then the number of ways that both events can occur is $$m \cdot n.$$ Example: A restaurant offers 4 entrées and 5 vegetable dishes. How many meals with one entrée and one vegetable dish are possible?   20 meals may be ordered since $4 \cdot 5 = 20$.

Math Reasoning

Predict How many different pizzas would be possible if you had 5 choices for toppings and 2 choices for crust?

Example **1** **Using the Fundamental Counting Principle**

A 1-topping pizza can be ordered with a choice of 4 different toppings: pepperoni, sausage, mushrooms, or onion. There is also a choice of different types of crust: thin, thick, or traditional. Find the number of ways that a 1-topping pizza can be ordered using the Fundamental Counting Principle.

SOLUTION

Determine the number of ways each event can occur and then find their product.

4 types of toppings × 3 types of crust = 12 possible pizza combinations

Check Use a tree diagram to verify that there are 12 possible pizza combinations.

Topping	Crust	Outcomes
Pepperoni	Thin	Pepperoni Thin
	Thick	Pepperoni Thick
	Traditional	Pepperoni Traditional
Sausage	Thin	Sausage Thin
	Thick	Sausage Thick
	Traditional	Sausage Traditional
Mushrooms	Thin	Mushroom Thin
	Thick	Mushroom Thick
	Traditional	Mushroom Traditional
Onions	Thin	Onion Thin
	Thick	Onion Thick
	Traditional	Onion Traditional

The tree diagram verifies that there are 12 possible outcomes.

When a group of people or objects are arranged in a certain order, the arrangement is called a **permutation.** The unique ways that 5 different colored blocks can be arranged are examples of permutations.

The factorial operation can be used to find different ways to arrange a set of n different items, where the first item may be selected n different ways, the second item may be selected $n - 1$ ways, and so on.

Factorial
The factorial $n!$ is defined for any natural number n as $n! = n(n - 1)\ldots(2)(1)$.
Zero factorial is defined to be 1. $0! = 1$.
Example: $5! = 5 \cdot 4 \cdot 3 \cdot 2 \cdot 1$

There are $n!$ ways to position n students in a line. For example, the number of ways 6 students can be positioned in a line can be described by 6!. As each position in the line is filled, the number of students that can be chosen to fill each position decreases by 1.

1st	**2nd**	**3rd ...**
6 Students	5 Students	4 Students

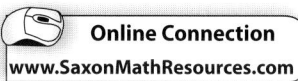

Online Connection
www.SaxonMathResources.com

Notice only 5 students can be chosen for the 2nd position because 1 student has already filled the 1st position. Continuing this pattern shows that 6 students can be arranged in order 6!, or $6 \cdot 5 \cdot 4 \cdot 3 \cdot 2 \cdot 1 = 720$, different ways.

Example 2 **Simplifying Expressions with Factorials**

(a.) Find 7!.

SOLUTION

7!

$= 7 \cdot 6 \cdot 5 \cdot 4 \cdot 3 \cdot 2 \cdot 1 = 5040$ Write the factors of 7! and multiply.

(b.) Find $\frac{9!}{4!}$.

SOLUTION

$\frac{9!}{4!}$

$= \dfrac{9 \cdot 8 \cdot 7 \cdot 6 \cdot 5 \cdot \cancel{4} \cdot \cancel{3} \cdot \cancel{2} \cdot \cancel{1}}{\cancel{4} \cdot \cancel{3} \cdot \cancel{2} \cdot \cancel{1}}$ Write the factors of 9! and 4!.

$= 9 \cdot 8 \cdot 7 \cdot 6 \cdot 5 = 15{,}120$ Multiply.

Exploration **Finding Possibilities When Order is Important**

Materials

• index cards
• 4 different colored ribbons

(a.) On an index card, list all possible ways that the 4 colored ribbons can be arranged.

(b.) On a second index card, list all possible ways that any two of the four colored ribbons can be arranged.

When choosing 3 of 8 contestants as finalists in a competition, order doesn't matter. However, in naming a first, second, and third place from the 8 contestants, the order does matter. Since order is important it is a permutation.

Permutation
The number of permutations of n objects taken r at a time is given by the formula $_nP_r = \frac{n!}{(n-r)!}$.

Example 3 **Finding the Number of Permutations**

(a.) Your school is running a recycling campaign in which 6 classes are competing to see who can collect the most recyclable materials. In how many ways can the classes finish in first through sixth place?

SOLUTION

This is a permutation of 6 things taken 6 at a time.

Caution

Remember that 0! is equal to 1, not 0.

$_nP_r = \dfrac{n!}{(n-r)!}$ Write the formula.

$_6P_6 = \dfrac{6!}{(6-6)!} = \dfrac{6!}{0!}$ Simplify.

$= \dfrac{6 \cdot 5 \cdot 4 \cdot 3 \cdot 2 \cdot 1}{1}$ Write the factors of 6! and 0!.

$= 720$ Multiply.

b. A total of 6 classes are competing to see who can collect the most recyclable materials. In how many different ways can the classes finish in first and second place?

SOLUTION

This is a permutation of 6 things taken 2 at a time.

$$_nP_r = \frac{n!}{(n-r)!} \qquad \text{Write the formula.}$$

$$_6P_2 = \frac{6!}{(6-2)!} = \frac{6!}{4!} \qquad \text{Simplify.}$$

$$= \frac{6 \cdot 5 \cdot \cancel{4} \cdot \cancel{3} \cdot \cancel{2} \cdot \cancel{1}}{\cancel{4} \cdot \cancel{3} \cdot \cancel{2} \cdot \cancel{1}} = 6 \cdot 5 \qquad \text{Write the factors of 6! and 4!. Then simplify.}$$

$$= 30 \qquad \text{Multiply.}$$

Math Reasoning

Generalize Another way to think about permutations of $_nP_r$ is to multiply the first r numbers of $n!$. So $_5P_3$ would be $5 \cdot 4 \cdot 3 = 60$. Explain how to find $_7P_2$ and then find its value.

Example 4 Application: Uniform Numbers

The 15 members of a softball team have uniform numbers 1 through 15. They are introduced randomly at a pep rally. What is the probability that the first 4 players introduced will have uniform numbers 1, 2, 3, and 4 in that order?

SOLUTION

Of the possible permutations only 1, 2, 3, 4 is favorable.

The probability is represented by:

$$\frac{\text{number of ways to choose 1, 2, 3, 4}}{\text{number of ways to choose 4 numbers}} = \frac{1}{_{15}P_4} = \frac{1}{15 \cdot 14 \cdot 13 \cdot 12} = \frac{1}{32{,}760}$$

Lesson Practice

a. While trying to schedule a flight for vacation, you are given two choices for departure and four choices for the return flight. How many ways can you schedule your flights for the trip?
(Ex 1)

b. A video game character has 6 choices each for hair color, face, attitude, and outfit as well as a choice of male or female. How many different characters are possible?
(Ex 1)

c. Find 5!.
(Ex 2)

d. Find $\frac{6!}{3!}$.
(Ex 2)

e. You are selecting your class schedule for the school year. If there are 7 periods and each of the seven classes are taught each period, how many possible ways are there for your schedule to be determined?
(Ex 3)

f. There are 10 people in the Activities Club. In how many different ways can a president, vice-president and treasurer be selected from the club members?
(Ex 3)

g. A popular TV series ran for 10 seasons. You are buying the seasons
(Ex 4) from an online DVD service. If each season arrives at random, what is the probability that the first 5 seasons you receive in the mail are the first 5 seasons that were made, in the correct order?

Practice Distributed and Integrated

*1. Draw a tree diagram to represent the possible outcomes of flipping a coin
(111) three times.

*2. Multiple Choice Evaluate 10!.
(111)

A 3,628,800 **B** 362,880 **C** 55 **D** 9

*3. (Video Rental) For movie night, you want to rent one drama, one comedy, and one
(111) science fiction movie. The video store has 5 new releases for drama, 6 new releases for comedy, and 3 new releases for science fiction. How many possible movie combinations are there?

4. Simplify the rational expression $\frac{3d}{2x^3} - \frac{5d}{2x^3}$ if possible.
(51)

Find the zeros of each function.

5. $y = x^2 - 8x + 16$
(96)

6. $y = 3x^2 + 36x - 39$
(96)

*7. Model Draw a tree diagram to determine the number of possible outcomes of
(111) earning an A, B, or C in history, English, and math classes.

*8. Justify Explain how to find the number of outfits possible if you have 5 shirts and
(111) 4 pairs of pants to choose from.

*9. Use the quadratic formula to solve $c^2 + 16c - 36 = 0$. Check the solutions.
(110)

*10. Estimate Find the best whole number estimate for the solutions to $70 - 52x = -x^2$.
(110)

11. Find and correct the error the student made in graphing $\begin{matrix} y - 2.5 > 0 \\ y - 4 < -2x \end{matrix}$.
(109)

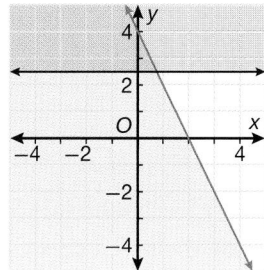

12. Graph the system $\begin{matrix} 4x - 2y < 6 \\ y + 1 \geq 2x \end{matrix}$.
(109)

13. Solve $r^2 - 24r = -144$ by completing the square.
(104)

*14. Error Analysis Two students used the quadratic formula to solve a quadratic
(110) equation. Which student is correct? Explain the error.

Student A	Student B
$8a = -10a^2 + 1$	$8a = -10a^2 + 1$
$8a - 10a^2 + 1 = 0$	$10a^2 + 8a - 1 = 0$
$x = \dfrac{-(-10) \pm \sqrt{-10^2 - 4(8)(1)}}{2(8)}$	$x = \dfrac{-8 \pm \sqrt{8^2 - 4(10)(-1)}}{2(10)}$
$x = \dfrac{10 \pm \sqrt{100 + 32}}{16}$	$x = \dfrac{-8 \pm \sqrt{64 + 40}}{20}$
$x = \dfrac{10 \pm \sqrt{132}}{16}$	$x = \dfrac{-8 \pm \sqrt{104}}{20}$
$x = \dfrac{10 \pm 2\sqrt{33}}{16}$	$x = \dfrac{-8 \pm 2\sqrt{26}}{20}$
$x = \dfrac{5 \pm \sqrt{33}}{8}$	$x = \dfrac{-4 \pm \sqrt{26}}{10}$

*15. (Space Shuttle) The external tank of the space shuttle separates after 8.5 minutes at
(110) a velocity of 28,067 kilometers per hour. Can the formula $-4.9t^2 + v_0 t + y_0 = 0$ be
used to find the distance above earth? Explain.

16. Measurement The length of a piece of wood must measure between 15 and
(109) 17 centimeters and the width must measure between 9 and 11 centimeters. Write
a system of linear inequalities to represent the possible dimensions of the wood
piece, in inches, given that 1 inch is equal to 2.54 centimeters.

17. (Business) The total profit on a particular skateboard is represented as $p^2 - 7p$
(104) where p is the number of units sold in thousands. How many units need to be sold
to have a profit of \$23,750? Round to the nearest hundred.

18. Find the next 3 terms of the sequence $\dfrac{1}{2187}, \dfrac{1}{729}, \dfrac{1}{243}, \dfrac{1}{81}, \ldots$.
(105)

19. (Chemistry) Oxygen evaporation from a body of water increases with the
(106) temperature. This process of oxygen depletion can be modeled by the
expression $\dfrac{\sqrt{x}}{6}$ where x is the temperature in C°. What value of x corresponds to
an evaporation of 9 cubic feet of oxygen?

20. Graph the function $f(x) = 3|x|$.
(107)

21. Multiple Choice Which function is not an exponential function?
(108) **A** $y = 4(3)^x$ **B** $y = -4(3)^x$ **C** $y = 4^3 x$ **D** $y = 4\left(\dfrac{1}{3}\right)^x$

22. Analyze For an exponential function with $a = 5$ and $b = 3$, why is it necessary to put
(108) parentheses around the 3 when writing the function rule?

23. Geometry The diagram shows a right triangle with a hypotenuse that is
(1) an irrational number. What set of numbers would include the
hypotenuse?

24. Evaluate $x^2 - 8x + 15$ and its factors for $x = -2$.
(72)

25. ⎡Oven Temperature⎤ The actual temperature (t) of Jeannine's oven varies by no more
(101) than 9°F from the set temperature. Jeannine sets her oven to 350°F. Write an
absolute-value inequality that models the possible actual temperatures inside the
oven. What is the lowest possible temperature?

26. Multi-Step The length of a picture is 2 inches greater than
(98) its width. A 3-inch-wide border is added to the bottom of
the picture for a scrapbook page.

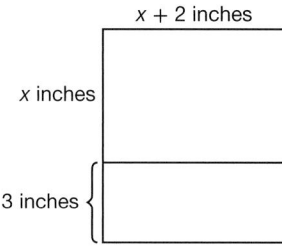

a. Write expressions for the width and length of the
picture with the border.

b. The area of the picture with the border is 110 square
inches. Find the length and width of the original photo.

27. Multi-Step Jasmine wants to plant tulips around the perimeter of her property. The
(102) property is the shape of a square. The area of the yard is 21,000 square feet and
the area of the house is 1500 square feet.

a. Write a formula to find the length of the sides of the property.

b. Solve for x.

c. Jasmine changes her mind and decides to buy enough bulbs to plant them 6
inches apart along just one edge of the property. How many bulbs will she need
if she starts at the first corner and goes to the second corner?

28. Justify Explain how to simplify $\dfrac{6}{\sqrt{5} - 7}$.
(103)

29. Subtract $\dfrac{2x^2}{x^2 - 49} - \dfrac{x - 7}{x^2 - 6x - 7}$.
(95)

*30. If $f(x) = \dfrac{1}{3}^x$ and $g(x) = 3^x$, which function represents exponential growth and
(Inv. 11) which function represents exponential decay?

Graphing and Solving Systems of Linear and Quadratic Equations

Warm Up

1. *(55)* **Vocabulary** A set of linear equations with the same variables is called a _____ of linear equations.

2. *(84)* Write $2x^2 = -x + 8$ in standard form.

3. *(29)* Solve $5x - y = 4 + 9x$ for y.

4. *(9)* Evaluate $50 - 2x^2$ for $x = -5$.

5. *(55)* **Multiple Choice** Which ordered pair is a solution of the system $\begin{array}{l} x - y = 7 \\ 2x + y = -1 \end{array}$?

  A $(2, -5)$ **B** $(6, -1)$ **C** $\left(\dfrac{8}{3}, -\dfrac{13}{3}\right)$ **D** $(3, -4)$

New Concepts

The equations $y = 14 - 4x$ and $y = x + 4$ are a system of linear equations. The solution $(2, 6)$ is a point at which the graphs of the equations intersect.

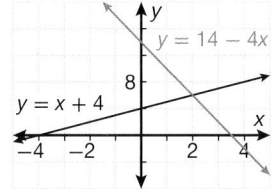

A system of equations can also consist of a linear equation and a quadratic equation. The graphs of three systems each consisting of a quadratic equation, $y = x^2$, and a linear equation are shown.

System A

$y = x^2$

$y = x + 6$

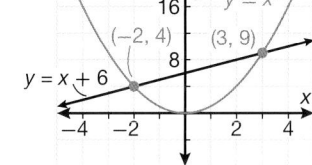

System A has two solutions because the graphs of the system intersect at two points.

System B

$y = x^2$

$y = 2x - 1$

System B has only one solution.

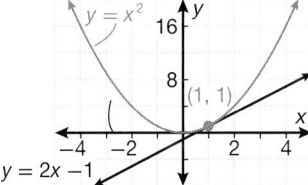

System C

$y = x^2$

$y = 3x - 5$

System C has no solution because the graphs do not intersect.

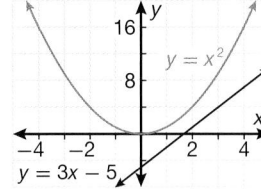

Math Reasoning

Analyze What are the coordinates of the vertex for every equation of the form $y = ax^2$?

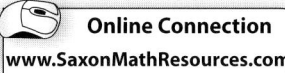
Online Connection
www.SaxonMathResources.com

Example 1 Solving by Graphing

Solve each system of equations by graphing. Then check the solution.

a. $\quad y = x^2$
$\qquad y = 4$

SOLUTION Graph the parabola $y = x^2$ and the horizontal line $y = 4$.

The line intersects the parabola at $(2, 4)$ and $(-2, 4)$. The solution of the system is the ordered pairs $(2, 4)$ and $(-2, 4)$.

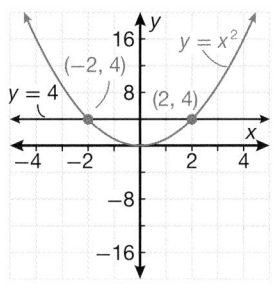

Check

$y = x^2$	$y = x^2$
$4 \overset{?}{=} (2)^2$	$4 \overset{?}{=} (-2)^2$
$4 = 4$ ✓	$4 = 4$ ✓

b. $\quad y = x^2$
$\qquad y = -4x - 4$

SOLUTION Graph the parabola and the line.

The line intersects the parabola at only one point. The solution is $(-2, 4)$.

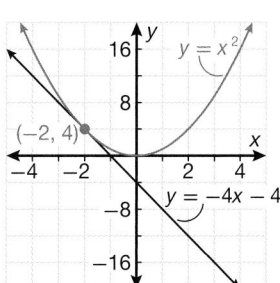

Check

$y = x^2$	$y = -4x - 4$
$4 \overset{?}{=} (-2)^2$	$4 \overset{?}{=} -4(-2) - 4$
$4 = 4$ ✓	$4 = 4$ ✓

c. $\quad y = 2x^2 - 9$
$\qquad y = 4x - 9$

SOLUTION The graphs of $y = 2x^2 - 9$ and $y = 4x - 9$ show two points of intersection. The coordinates of those two points are $(2, -1)$ and $(0, -9)$.

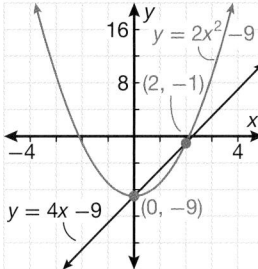

Check Verify that $(2, -1)$ is a solution.

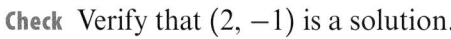

$y = 2x^2 - 9$	$y = 4x - 9$
$-1 \overset{?}{=} 2(2)^2 - 9$	$-1 \overset{?}{=} 4(2) - 9$
$-1 = -1$ ✓	$-1 = -1$ ✓

Verify that $(0, -9)$ is a solution.

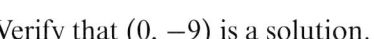

$y = 2x^2 - 9$	$y = 4x - 9$
$-9 \overset{?}{=} 2(0)^2 - 9$	$-9 \overset{?}{=} 4(0) - 9$
$-9 = -9$ ✓	$-9 = -9$ ✓

Caution

Be sure to check all solutions in both of the original equations of the system.

Example 2 Solving with a Graphing Calculator

Solve each system of equations by using a graphing calculator.

a. $y = \frac{x^2}{2} - 3$

$y = x - 3$

SOLUTION

Enter $Y_1 = \frac{x^2}{2} - 3$ and $Y_2 = x - 3$.

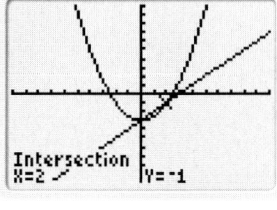

The display shows two graphs: a parabola and a line.

Use TRACE to approximate the solutions first. Then confirm the answers using INTERSECT.

The display shows the coordinates of the two points of intersection.

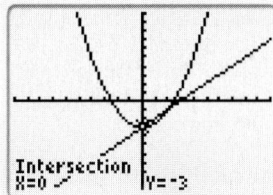

The first point of intersection is $(2, -1)$ and the second point of intersection is $(0, -3)$.

Check

Substitute $(2, -1)$ into both equations.

$$y = \frac{x^2}{2} - 3 \qquad\qquad y = x - 3$$

$$\qquad\qquad\qquad\qquad -1 \overset{?}{=} 2 - 3$$

$$-1 \overset{?}{=} \frac{(2)^2}{2} - 3 \qquad -1 = -1 \ \checkmark$$

$$-1 = -1 \ \checkmark$$

Substitute $(0, 3)$ into both equations.

$$y = \frac{x^2}{2} - 3 \qquad\qquad y = x - 3$$

$$\qquad\qquad\qquad\qquad -3 \overset{?}{=} 0 - 3$$

$$-3 \overset{?}{=} \frac{(0)^2}{2} - 3 \qquad -3 = -3 \ \checkmark$$

$$-3 = -3 \ \checkmark$$

b. $y = x^2$

$y = 2x - 2$

SOLUTION

Enter $Y_1 = x^2$ and $Y_2 = 2x - 2$.

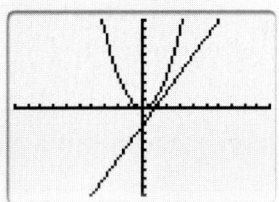

The display shows two graphs: a parabola and a line.

The display shows that the parabola and the line do not intersect, so there are no solutions to this system.

If the calculator is used to find a point of intersection, an error message is displayed.

Example 3 **Solving Using Substitution**

Solve each system of equations by substitution.

a. $y = x^2 + 5x - 1$
$y = 5x + 3$

SOLUTION

$x^2 + 5x - 1 = 5x + 3$ — Substitute the quadratic equation into the linear equation.

$\underline{-5x - 3 \quad -5x - 3}$ — Add the expression $-5x - 3$ to both sides.

$x^2 - 4 = 0$ — Recognize the left side of the equation as a difference of squares.

$(x + 2)(x - 2) = 0$ — Factor.

$x + 2 = 0$ and $x - 2 = 0$ — Solve both equations.

$x = -2 \qquad x = 2$

Determine the corresponding values of y by substituting the values of x into either equation.

$y = 5x + 3$	$y = 5x + 3$
$y = 5(-2) + 3$	$y = 5(2) + 3$
$y = -10 + 3$	$y = 10 + 3$
$y = -7$	$y = 13$

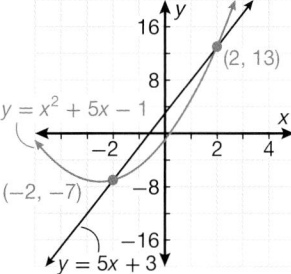

The solutions are the ordered pairs $(-2, -7)$ and $(2, 13)$. The solutions appear at the intersections of the two graphs.

b. $y = x^2 + 7x + 3$
$y = 2x - 3$

SOLUTION

$x^2 + 7x + 3 = 2x - 3$ — Substitute the quadratic equation into the linear equation.

$\underline{-2x + 3 \quad -2x + 3}$ — Add the expression $-2x + 3$ to both sides.

$x^2 + 5x + 6 = 0$ — Recognize the left side of the equation as a trinomial that can be factored.

$(x + 3)(x + 2) = 0$ — Factor.

$x + 3 = 0$ and $x + 2 = 0$ — Solve both equations.

$x = -3$ and $x = -2$

Determine the values of y.

$y = 2x - 3$	$y = 2x - 3$
$y = 2(-3) - 3$	$y = 2(-2) - 3$
$y = -6 - 3$	$y = -4 - 3$
$y = -9$	$y = -7$

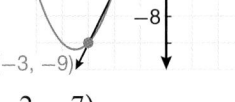

The solutions are the ordered pairs $(-3, -9)$ and $(-2, -7)$.

Math Reasoning

Verify Show that the ordered pairs $(-2, -7)$ and $(2, 13)$ are solutions to Example 3a and that the ordered pairs $(-2, -7)$ and $(-3, -9)$ are the solutions to Example 3b.

Example 4 · Application: Avalanches

A ski patrol fires an explosive arrow to trigger a controlled avalanche. The path of the arrow is modeled by the equation $y = -\frac{x^2}{1600} + 2x$ and the shape of the mountainside is modeled by $y = \frac{3x}{4}$ where x is the horizontal distance and y is the vertical distance. At what altitude will the arrow strike the mountain? (Assume all dimensions are in feet.)

SOLUTION

Understand The path of the arrow is modeled by a parabola. The mountainside is modeled by a straight line.

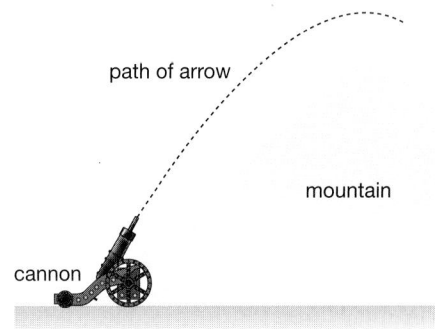

$$y = -\frac{x^2}{1600} + 2x$$

$$y = \frac{3x}{4}$$

Plan The equation of the arrow's path and the equation of the shape of the mountain form a system of equations.

Solving this system will determine the points at which the two graphs intersect.

Solve One way of solving the system is by graphing the two equations. The cannon is located at the base of the mountain, so both graphs pass through $(0, 0)$. The non-origin solution to the system is $(2000, 1500)$. The altitude at which the arrow will strike the side of the mountain is 1500 feet.

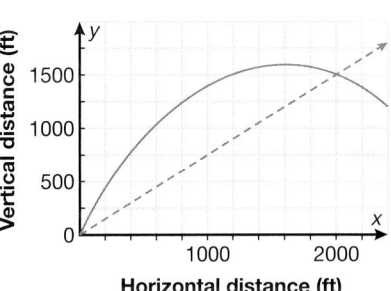

Check

$$y = \frac{3x}{4}$$
$$1500 \overset{?}{=} \frac{3(2000)}{4}$$
$$1500 \overset{?}{=} \frac{6000}{4}$$
$$1500 = 1500 \ \checkmark$$

$$y = -\frac{x^2}{1600} + 2x$$
$$1500 \overset{?}{=} -\frac{2000^2}{1600} + 2(2000)$$
$$1500 \overset{?}{=} -\frac{4,000,000}{1600} + 4000$$
$$1500 \overset{?}{=} -2500 + 4000$$
$$1500 = 1500 \ \checkmark$$

Math Reasoning

Write Describe the meaning of the x-coordinate in the solution $(2000, 1500)$.

Lesson Practice

Solve each system of equations by graphing.
(Ex 1)

a. $y = x^2$
  $y = 16$

b. $y = x^2$
  $y = 6x - 9$

c. $y = x^2$
  $y = -2x + 3$

Solve each system of equations by using a graphing calculator.
(Ex 2)

d. $y = \dfrac{x^2}{2} + 1$

$y = -\dfrac{3x}{2}$

e. $y = -2x^2 - 1$

$y = -x - 2$

Solve each system of equations by substitution.
(Ex 3)

f. $y = x^2 - 3x - 17$

$y = -3x + 8$

g. $y = x^2 + 7x + 5$

$y = 2x - 1$

h. (Physics) A gardener places a sprinkler at the bottom of a gently rising
(Ex 4) hillside described by the equation $y = \dfrac{2x}{5}$. The equation $y = -\dfrac{x^2}{25} + x$
represents the path of the water. If the water splashes onto a rock on the
hillside, what is the rock's altitude? (Assume all dimensions are in feet.)

Practice   Distributed and Integrated

*1. Solve this system by graphing: $\begin{array}{l} y = -x^2 + 12 \\ y = -x + 6 \end{array}$.
(112)

*2. Multiple Choice Which system of equations has no solution?
(112)

A $\begin{array}{l} y = x^2 + 2 \\ y = 3 \end{array}$
   B $\begin{array}{l} y = x^2 - 2 \\ y = 3 \end{array}$
   C $\begin{array}{l} y = -x^2 + 2 \\ y = 3 \end{array}$
   D $\begin{array}{l} y = -x^2 - 2 \\ y = -3 \end{array}$

3. Simplify the rational expression $c^{-2}f^{-5} + \dfrac{6}{c^2 f^5}$, if possible.
(51)

4. Write a compound inequality that represents all real numbers that are greater than
(73) -4 and less than 8.

*5. (Architecture) In a European castle, a room with an arched ceiling is covered by a
(112) slanted roof. The ceiling is modeled by the equation $y = -x^2 + 4$ and the roofline
by the equation $y = -2x + 5$. Assume that the dimensions are in meters. What are
the coordinates for the point of intersection of the roof with the ceiling assuming
that the vertex of the parabola is $(0, 4)$?

*6. Analyze A system of three equations consists of the quadratic equation $y = x^2$ and
(112) two linear equations that do not describe the same line. What is the maximum
number of ordered pairs in the solution set? Explain.

7. A six-sided number cube is rolled three times. How many outcomes are possible?
(111)

*8. Error Analysis Two students are finding the value of $_6P_6$. Which student is correct?
(111) Explain the error.

Student A	Student B
$_6P_6 = \dfrac{6!}{(6-6)!}$	$_6P_6 = \dfrac{6!}{(6-6)!}$
$= \dfrac{6!}{0!}$	$= \dfrac{6!}{0!}$
$=$ undefined	$= \dfrac{720}{1} = 720$

9. **Geometry** A triangle can be classified according to its sides or according to its
(111) angles. There are three side length categories—equilateral, isosceles, and
scalene—and three angle categories—acute, obtuse, and right.

   a. How many possibilities are there for classifying triangles according to both
   sides and angles?

   b. How many of these triangles are not possible? Which ones are they?

10. **Multi-Step** There are 7 runners on the track team. Runners will be selected
(111) randomly for the first, second, third, and final positions on the 4-member
relay team.

   a. How many different relay teams can be formed?

   b. What is the probability that a runner at random is chosen to be on the
   relay team?

11. Use the quadratic formula to solve $x^2 - 60 + 17x = 0$. Check the solutions.
(110)

12. **Multiple Choice** What are the solutions to $2a^2 + 20a - 30 = 0$?
(110)

A $20 \pm 4\sqrt{10}$ $\qquad\qquad$ **B** $-20 \pm \sqrt{10}$

C $-5 \pm 2\sqrt{10}$ $\qquad\qquad$ **D** $-5 \pm \sqrt{10}$

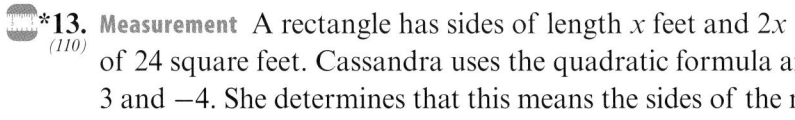***13.** **Measurement** A rectangle has sides of length x feet and $2x + 2$ feet with an area
(110) of 24 square feet. Cassandra uses the quadratic formula and finds that x equals
3 and -4. She determines that this means the sides of the rectangle are -4 by -6
or 3 by 8. Why is she incorrect?

14. (**Construction**) Suzanne would like to place a fence around her rectangular yard, which
(110) has a perimeter of 200 feet. The fencing for the front length of the house will cost $5
per foot and the fencing for the side and back of the yard will cost $3 per foot. Her
total cost is $720. What are the dimensions of her property?

15. Find the next 3 terms of the sequence $-0.032, 0.16, -0.8, 4, \ldots$.
(105)

16. (**Paper Folding**) Solange folds a piece of paper, making two rectangles. When she
(105) folds it again, she makes 4 rectangles. Each fold doubles the number of rectangles.
A sequence describing this process is 2, 4, 8, …. If someone folds a piece of paper is
12 times, how many rectangles did the 12 folds form?

17. Solve the equation $\frac{\sqrt{x}}{6} = 12$. Check your answer.
(106)

18. (**Population**) The exponential function $y = 11.35(1.00183)^x$ can model the
(108) approximate population of Ohio from 2000 to 2006, where x is the number of
years after 2000 and y represents millions of people. What was the population
in 2003?

19. Evaluate the function $f(x) = -2(4)^x$ for $x = -2, 0,$ and 2.
(108)

20. **Multiple Choice** Which system has no solutions?
(109)

A $\begin{array}{l} y < 2 \\ y < 1 \end{array}$ $\quad$ **B** $\begin{array}{l} y > 2 \\ y > 1 \end{array}$ $\quad$ **C** $\begin{array}{l} y < 2 \\ y > 1 \end{array}$ $\quad$ **D** $\begin{array}{l} y > 2 \\ y < 1 \end{array}$

21. Analyze What inequality symbols should go into the boxes so that the solution set
(109) lies between the lines and does not include the boundary points?

$$y \;\boxed{}\; \frac{3}{5}x + 7$$

$$y \;\boxed{}\; \frac{3}{5}x + 1$$

22. Find the zeros of the function $y = x^2 - 6x - 72$.
(96)

23. Graph the inequality $4x - y \le -5$.
(97)

24. Multi-Step A girl takes 4 hours to complete a job. Her mother can complete the
(99) same job in 3 hours. Her little sister takes 6 hours to complete it.

  a. Write an equation representing how long it takes the three of them to complete
  the job working together.

  b. How long will it take to complete the job, in hours, if all three famiy members
  work together?

  c. How many minutes is that?

25. ⬭ Biking ⬭ Dustin and Roberto leave their house at the same
(102) time. Dustin rides his bike 49 feet east. Roberto rides his
bike 81 feet south. Use the formula $(49)^2 + (81)^2 = x^2$ to
find the distance between Dustin and Roberto.

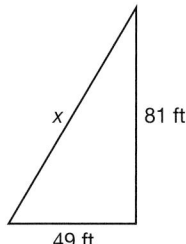

x   81 ft

49 ft

*26. Formulate In the system $\begin{array}{l} y = x^2 - 3 \\ y = a \end{array}$, a is a real number. What is the minimum value
(112) of a so that the system will have two solutions?

27. Multi-Step A race-car driver is driving at a rate of $\sqrt{10,800}$ miles per hour. How
(103) long does it take the driver to go 85 miles? Give the answer as a rational expression
in simplest form. (Hint: distance = rate times time)

  a. Write the equation to find the driver's travel time using the given values.

  b. Find the solution.

28. Write Tell how to remove any coefficients of the x^2-term in a quadratic equation
(104) before completing the square.

*29. Describe the transformation of $f(x) = -x^2 + 2$ from the parent quadratic function.
(Inv 10)

*30. Charlotte invested $1000 in an account that doubles her balance every 7 years.
(Inv 11) Does this situation model exponential growth or decay? Express the function that
represents this situation. After 42 years, how many times will her balance have
doubled? What will that balance be after 42 years?

Interpreting the Discriminant

1. **Vocabulary** The _____ is the number or expression under a radical symbol.
(13)

Evaluate each expression for the given values.

2. $-x^2 - xy - y$ for $x = -5$ and $y = -1$
(9)

3. $b^2 + 3ab - a$ for $a = -7$ and $b = -2$
(9)

4. $ab - 5b^2$ for $a = 3$ and $b = 4$
(9)

5. $7y^2z + 9$ for $y = -3$ and $z = -1$
(9)

New Concepts

The quadratic formula is one method used to solve quadratic equations. Recall the quadratic formula for a quadratic equation of the form $ax^2 + bx + c = 0$ is:

$$x = \frac{-b \pm \sqrt{b^2 - 4ac}}{2a}$$

In the formula, the expression under the radical sign, $b^2 - 4ac$, is called the **discriminant.**

Consider the graphs below and the value of the discriminant for each equation.

$0 = x^2 - 4x + 3$

$b^2 - 4ac \qquad a = 1, b = -4, c = 3$

$= (-4)^2 - 4(1)(3) \qquad$ Substitute.

$= 4$

There are 2 x-intercepts. The discriminant is positive.

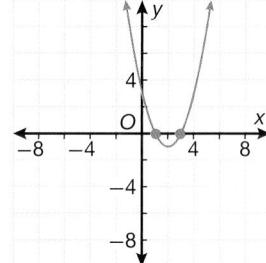

$0 = x^2 - 4x + 4$

$b^2 - 4ac \qquad a = 1, b = -4, c = 4$

$= (-4)^2 - 4(1)(4) \qquad$ Substitute.

$= 0$

There is one x-intercept. The discriminant is zero.

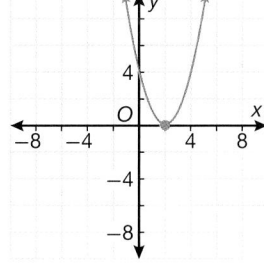

$0 = x^2 - 4x + 5$

$b^2 - 4ac \qquad a = 1, b = -4, c = 5$

$(-4)^2 - 4(1)(5) \qquad$ Substitute.

$= -4$

There are no x-intercepts. The discriminant is negative.

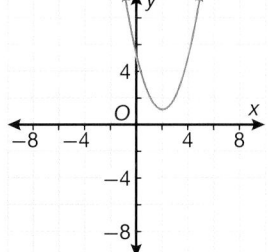

Online Connection
www.SaxonMathResources.com

Math Reasoning

Analyze What does the discriminant tell about the real solutions of a quadratic equation? What does the discriminant not tell about the solutions of a quadratic equation?

The value of the discriminant indicates the number of solutions.

Using the Discriminant
For the quadratic equation $ax^2 + bx + c = 0$ where $a \neq 0$, find the value of the discriminant, $b^2 - 4ac$, to determine the number of real solutions, which represents the number of x-intercepts of the graph of its related function.
If $b^2 - 4ac < 0$, then there are no real solutions and no x-intercepts.
If $b^2 - 4ac = 0$, then there is one real solution and one x-intercept.
If $b^2 - 4ac > 0$, then there are two real solutions and two x-intercepts.

If $b^2 - 4ac = 0$, then there is one real solution, which means there is one x-intercept. The real solution is the x value at the vertex of the parabola, which will be on the x-axis. The solution is called a **double root** of the equation.

Example 1 Finding the Number of Solutions Without Solving

Use the discriminant to find the number of real solutions to the equation. Then state the number of x-intercepts of the graph of the related function.

a. $x^2 - 3x + 9 = 0$

SOLUTION

$b^2 - 4ac$

$= (-3)^2 - 4(1)(9)$ Substitute.

$= 9 - 36$ Simplify.

$= -27$

There are no real solutions, so the graph has no x-intercepts.

b. $2x^2 - 3x - 4 = 0$

SOLUTION

$b^2 - 4ac$

$= (-3)^2 - 4(2)(-4)$ Substitute.

$= 9 + 32$ Simplify.

$= 41$

There are two real solutions, so the graph has two x-intercepts.

c. $x^2 + 8x + 16 = 0$

SOLUTION

$b^2 - 4ac$

$= 8^2 - 4(1)(16)$ Substitute.

$= 64 - 64$ Simplify.

$= 0$

There is one real solution, so the graph has one x-intercept.

Example 2 Application: Baseball

A baseball is thrown in the air with an initial velocity of 20 feet per second from 5 feet off the ground. Use the equation $h = -16t^2 + 20t + 5$ to model the situation. Will the ball reach a height of 30 feet?

SOLUTION

$$h = -16t^2 + 20t + 5$$

$$30 = -16t^2 + 20t + 5 \qquad \text{Substitute 30 for } h.$$

$$0 = -16t^2 + 20t - 25 \qquad \text{Set the equation equal to 0.}$$

Use the discriminant to determine if the ball will reach a height of 30 feet.

$$b^2 - 4ac = 20^2 - 4(-16)(-25)$$
$$= 400 - 1600$$
$$= -1200$$

Since the discriminant of the equation is negative, there are no solutions. The ball will not reach a height of 30 feet.

Math Reasoning

Generalize What are the values of a, b, and c in the quadratic equation $x^2 - 4 = 0$?

Lesson Practice

Use the discriminant to find the number of real solutions to the equation. Then state the number of x-intercepts of the graph of the related function.

a. $x^2 - 2x - 35 = 0$
(Ex 1)

b. $4x^2 + 20x + 25 = 0$
(Ex 1)

c. $2x^2 - 3x + 7 = 0$
(Ex 1)

d. A football is punted from 2 feet off the ground with an initial velocity of 60 feet per second. Use the equation $y = -16t^2 + 60t + 2$ to model the situation. Will the ball reach a height of 45 feet?
(Ex 2)

Practice   Distributed and Integrated

*1. Find the value of the discriminant of the equation $3x^2 - x + 2 = 0$.
(113)

2. The new rectangular basketball court at the high school has a width of $9x^2 + x + 36$ and a length of $4x^2 + 2x + 2$. What is the perimeter of the new court?
(53)

3. Solve $6|z - 3| = 18$.
(74)

4. Find 8!.
(111)

*5. Multiple Choice Which is a possible value for the discriminant of the equation
(113) graphed?

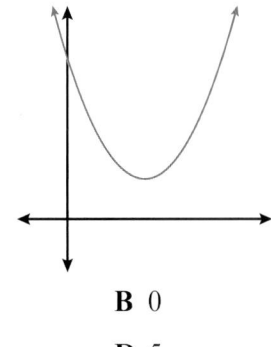

A −5

B 0

C 3

D 5

*6. Model Draw the graph of a quadratic equation that has a discriminant
(113) that is greater than zero.

*7. Generalize Describe the values of the discriminant that indicate two real
(113) solutions.

*8. Solve this system $\begin{aligned} y &= -\frac{x^2}{2} + 8 \\ y &= -2x + 10 \end{aligned}$ by graphing.
(112)

*9. Error Analysis Two students are solving the system of equations $\begin{aligned} y &= x^2 + 3 \\ y &= -3x + 1 \end{aligned}$
(112) by substitution. Which student is correct? Explain the error.

Student A	Student B
$y = x^2 + 3 \qquad y = -3x + 1$ $x^2 + 3 = -3x + 1$ $x^2 + 3 + 3x - 1 = 0$ $x^2 + 3x + 2 = 0$ $(x + 2)(x + 1) = 0$ So, $x = -2$, $x = -1$, and the solutions are $(-2, 7)$ and $(-1, 4)$.	$y = x^2 + 3 \qquad y = -3x + 1$ $x^2 + 3 - 3x + 1 = 0$ $x^2 - 3x + 4 = 0$ no solution

10. Geometry For safety reasons, a guy wire must connect the top of a utility pole to
(112) the ground at a particular angle. The utility pole is located at the base of a hill
described by the equation $y = -\frac{x^2}{25} + 2x$. The equation for the correct angle of
the wire is $y = -x + 14$. At what altitude on the hill should the ground stake be
located? (Assume all dimensions are in feet.)

*11. In designing a necklace, a goldsmith places a gold wire on a workbench so that
(112) the wire takes on the shape of a parabola described by the equation $y = \frac{x^2}{2}$. The
goldsmith then lays a straight wire across the first so that the second follows the
equation $y = \frac{x}{6} + 6$. Use a graphing calculator to determine the coordinates for the
points of intersection. Round answers to the nearest whole number.

*12. Error Analysis Two students are finding the number of ways to choose a president
(111) and a vice president from a list of eight candidates. Which student is correct?
Explain the error.

Student A	Student B
$_8P_2 = \dfrac{8!}{(8-2)!}$ $= \dfrac{8!}{6!}$ $= 56$	$_8P_2 = \dfrac{8!}{2!}$ $= 20{,}160$

13. (**Dining**) A restaurant offers a choice of 3 sandwiches, 3 chips, and 5 soft drinks.
(111) How many different meal combinations are offered?

14. Probability A CD has 9 tracks. The CD player is set to play the songs randomly so
(111) that each song plays only once. What is the probability that the first 3 songs are
the first 3 tracks in order?

15. Solve the equation $\sqrt{x} + 2 = 8$. Check your answer.
(106)

16. (**Architecture**) An architect is designing a structure that merges two different right
(106) triangles along the hypotenuse of each triangle. The hypotenuse of one triangle
is $\sqrt{x + 2}$ units long and the hypotenuse of the second is $\sqrt{2x - 4}$. At what value
of x are the two lengths equal?

17. Graph the function $f(x) = |x + 4|$.
(107)

*18. Multi-Step A plot of land is 143 square feet with dimensions of x and $x + 2$. What
(110) is the perimeter of the plot of land?

a. Use the quadratic formula to find the dimensions of the plot of land.

b. What is the perimeter of the plot of land?

19. Multi-Step Emmanuel throws a football into the air. Its movement forms a parabola
(100) given by the quadratic equation $h = -16t^2 + 14t + 50$, where h is the height in feet
and t is the time in seconds.

a. Find the time t when the ball is at its maximum height. Round to the nearest
hundredth.

b. Find the time t when the ball hits the ground. Round to the nearest hundredth.

c. Find the maximum height of the arc the ball makes in its flight. Round to the
nearest tenth.

20. (**Firefighting**) A forest ranger is stationed at the Delilah Lookout fire tower in the
(103) Sequoia National Forest in California. The distance d (in miles) he can see to
the horizon can be estimated by the formula $d = \sqrt{\dfrac{3h}{2}}$, where h is the height of
the observer's eyes (in feet) above sea level. If Delilah Lookout is located at an
elevation of 5176 feet above sea level, write a radical expression that shows the
distance the ranger can see to the horizon.

21. Graph the system:
$$y \ge -\frac{3}{5}x + 3$$
$$y \ge \frac{3}{4}x + 3$$
(109)

22. **Analyze** Compare $-4.9t^2 + v_0t + y_0 = 0$ and $-4.9t^2 + v_0t = 0$.
(110)

23. Write the inequality that is graphed on the coordinate plane.
(97)

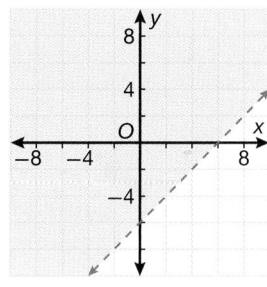

*24. **Projectile Motion** A projectile is shot up in the air from the ground with an initial velocity of 84 feet per second. Using $y = -16t^2 + 84t$, write an equation to model the situation and use the discriminant to determine if the projectile will reach a height of 200 feet.
(113)

25. Find the roots of $36x = 9x^2 + 36$.
(98)

26. **Finance** The amount of money Ricardo has after x years of investing \$100 at his local bank is $f(x) = 100(1.065)^x$. Which graph could represent this function?
(108)

A 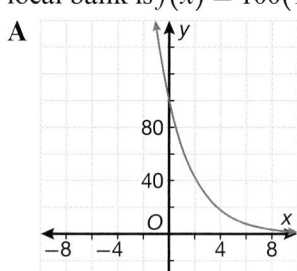 B 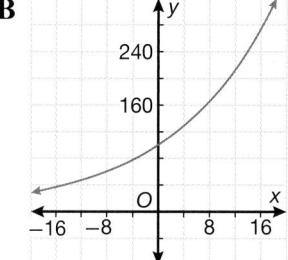 C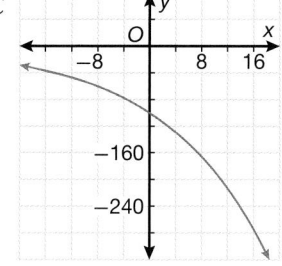

27. **Multi-Step** The time in minutes t it takes for a projectile to strike the ground is described by the equation $-4.9t^2 - 29.4t + 34.3 = 0$.
(104)
   a. Write the quadratic equation in the form $x^2 + bx = c$.

   b. Find the real-number solutions by completing the square.

   c. At what time does the object strike the ground? Explain your answer.

28. **Verify** The fifth term of a geometric sequence is -1. The first is -81. Randy thinks the common ratio is $\frac{1}{3}$. Robin says it could be $-\frac{1}{3}$. Could both be correct? Explain.
(105)

29. If a quadratic function has been vertically compressed, does that mean the parabola is wider or narrower than the parent quadratic function $f(x) = x^2$?
(Inv 10)

30. For all real values of the domain, describe the relationship between the graphs of an exponential growth and an exponential decay function.
(Inv 11)

Graphing Radical Functions

A graphing calculator can be used to graph radical functions and to locate points on the graph.

Graph the function $y = 2\sqrt{x - 1}$.

1. To enter the equation into the **Y=** editor, press the [Y=] key. Then press 2 [2nd] [x^2] [X,T,θ,*n*] [−] 1 [ )].

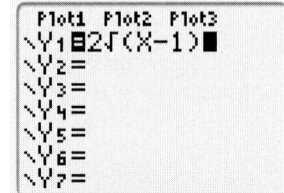

2. Graph the function by pressing [ZOOM] **6:ZStandard.**

3. Press [TRACE] and use the [▶] key to move along the *x*-axis until the cursor locates a point on the graph.

   The first point on the graph appears to be (1.064, 0.505).

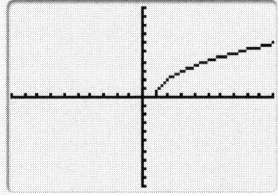

4. Investigate actual points on the graph of $y = 2\sqrt{x - 1}$.

   Press [2nd] [WINDOW](TBLSET) 0 [ENTER] 1. Then press [2nd] [GRAPH](TABLE).

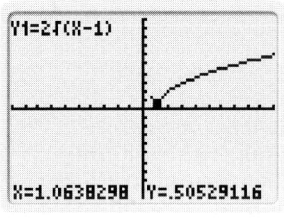

   The first point on the graph is (1, 0). Note that this is different from (1.064, 0.505); the graph does not appear to pass through the point (1, 0). Therefore, it is important to use the Table feature to determine values of the function.

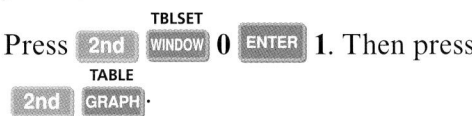

Lab Practice

a. Graph the function $y = 3\sqrt{x + 2}$. At what point does the graph start?

b. Graph the function $y = 2\sqrt{x + 2}$. At what point does the graph start?

Graphing Square-Root Functions

Warm Up

1. Vocabulary Radicals that have the same radicands and roots such as
$2\sqrt{7} + 4\sqrt{7}$ are _____, and radials that have different radicands and/or
roots such as $4\sqrt{7} + 2\sqrt{11}$ are _____.
(69)

Add or subtract.

2. $-6\sqrt{2} + 8\sqrt{2}$
(69)

3. $31\sqrt{5} - 13\sqrt{5}$
(69)

Find each product.

4. $(7 + \sqrt{6})(4 - \sqrt{9})$
(76)

5. $(\sqrt{3} - 12)^2$
(76)

New Concepts

The square root of a number x is the number whose square is x.

$$\sqrt{9} = 3 \qquad 3^2 = 9$$

The square root of x can be a function. For the function $y = \sqrt{x}$ when x is 9,
y is 3 since the square root of 9 is 3. Use the table to make connections with
the graph.

Math Language

A **function** is a
mathematical
relationship that pairs
each value in the domain
with exactly one value in
the range.

x	y
0	0
1	1
4	2
9	3
16	4

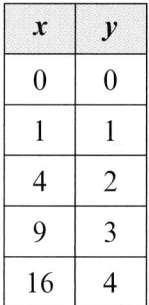

A **square-root function** is a function that contains a square root of a variable.

Example **1** **Graphing a Square-Root Function**

Make a table of $y = 2\sqrt{x} + 1$. Then graph the function.

SOLUTION

Evaluate the function when x is 0, 1, 4, and 9.

Hint

Try choosing x values
that are perfect squares.
This may make it easier
to graph.

$y = 2\sqrt{0} + 1 = 2(0) + 1 = 1$
$y = 2\sqrt{1} + 1 = 2(1) + 1 = 3$
$y = 2\sqrt{4} + 1 = 2(2) + 1 = 5$
$y = 2\sqrt{9} + 1 = 2(3) + 1 = 7$

x	y
0	1
1	3
4	5
9	7

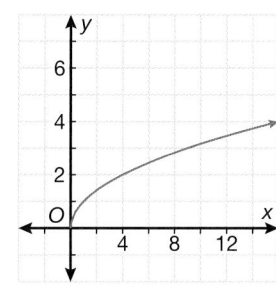

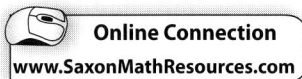

Online Connection
www.SaxonMathResources.com

In order for a square root to be a real number, the radicand cannot be negative.

Example **2** **Determining the Domain of a Square-Root Function**

a. Determine the domain of $y = \sqrt{x - 4}$.

SOLUTION

The domain is the values for x that make the radicand greater than or equal to zero. Solve $x - 4 > 0$.

$x - 4 \geq 0$ Set the radicand greater than or equal to 0.

$\quad x \geq 4$ Solve for x by adding 4 to both sides.

The domain is the set of all real numbers greater than or equal to 4.

b. Determine the domain of $y = 3\sqrt{\dfrac{x}{2} + 4} - 7$.

SOLUTION

$\dfrac{x}{2} + 4 \geq 0$ Set the radicand greater than or equal to 0.

$\dfrac{x}{2} \geq -4$ Subtract 4 from both sides.

$\quad x \geq -8$ Multiply both sides by 2.

The domain is the set of all real numbers greater than or equal to -8.

All square-root functions look similar to the graph of $y = \sqrt{x}$, which is called the parent function. A transformation of a function is an alteration of the parent function that produces a new function.

Compare the parent function $y = \sqrt{x}$ to the function $y = \sqrt{x} + 3$.

x	$y = \sqrt{x}$	$y = \sqrt{x} + 3$
0	0	3
1	1	4
4	2	5
9	3	6
16	4	7

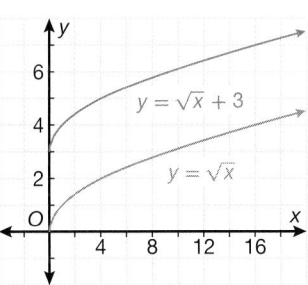

The function $y = \sqrt{x} + 3$ has been shifted 3 units up from the parent function $y = \sqrt{x}$. Transformations that involve vertical and horizontal shifting are called translations.

Transformations of the Graph of $f(x) = \sqrt{x}$
Vertical translation: The graph of $f(x) = \sqrt{x} + c$ is c units up from the parent graph if $c > 0$ and the graph is c units down from the parent graph if $c < 0$.
Horizontal translation: The graph of $f(x) = \sqrt{x - c}$ is c units to the right of the parent graph if $c > 0$ and the graph is c units to the left of the parent graph if $c < 0$.

Example 3 Translating the Square-Root Functions

a. Describe the transformations applied to the parent function to form $y = \sqrt{x} - 3$.

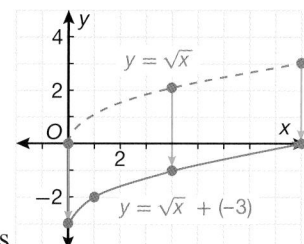

SOLUTION

This function can be written in the form $f(x) = \sqrt{x} + c$ by changing -3 to $+ (-3)$. The function can be written as $y = \sqrt{x} + (-3)$ which is a translation of the parent function that shifts the graph 3 units down.

b. Describe the transformations applied to the parent function to form $y = \sqrt{x + 2}$.

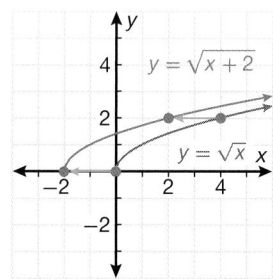

SOLUTION

This function $y = \sqrt{x + 2}$ is written in the form $f(x) = \sqrt{x - c}$, where c is -2, which is a translation of the parent function 2 units left.

Math Reasoning

Analyze What is the domain of $g(x) = \sqrt{-x}$?

Reflections of the Graph of $f(x) = \sqrt{x}$
If $f(x) = \sqrt{x}$, then $g(x) = -\sqrt{x}$ is a reflection of the graph of f across the x-axis.
If $f(x) = \sqrt{x}$, then $g(x) = \sqrt{-x}$ is a reflection of the graph of f across the y-axis.

Example 4 Reflecting a Square-Root Function

a. Describe the transformations applied to the parent function to form $y = -\sqrt{x}$.

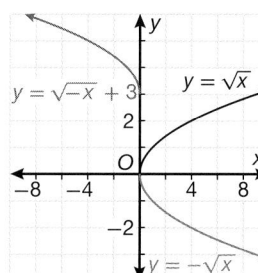

SOLUTION

The graph of $y = -\sqrt{x}$ is a reflection of the parent function over the x-axis.

b. Describe the transformations applied to the parent function to form $y = \sqrt{-x} + 3$.

SOLUTION

The graph of $y = \sqrt{-x} + 3$ is a reflection of the parent function over the y-axis, and then a vertical shift of 3 units up.

Example **5** Application: Horizon

The distance d (in kilometers) that Meliza can see on a clear day to the horizon from a height of h meters is approximately $d = \sqrt{15h}$. Find the distance she can see from a height of 2160 meters.

SOLUTION

Evaluate $d = \sqrt{15h}$ for $h = 2160$ m.

$d = \sqrt{15(2160)}$

$\quad = \sqrt{32400} = 180$

180 km is the distance she can see from a height of 2160 m.

Lesson Practice

a. Graph $y = 3\sqrt{x + 1}$ using a table.
(Ex 1)

Determine the domain of each of the following functions.
(Ex 2)

b. $f(x) = \sqrt{\dfrac{x}{3}}$ ⠀⠀⠀⠀⠀⠀⠀⠀**c.** $f(x) = \sqrt{x - 2}$

Describe the transformations applied to the parent function to form the given function.

d. $f(x) = \sqrt{x} - 2$ ⠀⠀⠀⠀⠀⠀⠀**e.** $f(x) = \sqrt{x - 2}$
(Ex 3) ⠀⠀⠀⠀⠀⠀⠀⠀⠀⠀⠀⠀⠀⠀⠀⠀*(Ex 3)*
f. $f(x) = -\sqrt{x + 3}$ ⠀⠀⠀⠀⠀⠀**g.** $f(x) = \sqrt{-x} - 4$
(Ex 4) ⠀⠀⠀⠀⠀⠀⠀⠀⠀⠀⠀⠀⠀⠀⠀⠀*(Ex 4)*

h. (**Physics**) An acorn fell from a tree limb. The function $t = 0.45\sqrt{x}$
(Ex 5) represents how many seconds it takes something to fall from a height of x meters to the ground. Estimate how long it would take the acorn to fall if the limb were 8 meters above the ground.

Practice **Distributed and Integrated**

Solve.

1. $|z + 5| + 11 = 10$ ⠀⠀⠀⠀⠀⠀⠀⠀⠀**2.** $10x^2 = 70x$
(74) ⠀⠀⠀⠀⠀⠀⠀⠀⠀⠀⠀⠀⠀⠀⠀⠀⠀⠀⠀⠀*(98)*

3. $24x = 32x^2$ ⠀⠀⠀⠀⠀⠀⠀⠀⠀⠀⠀⠀**4.** $\dfrac{5}{x + 1} - \dfrac{2}{x} = \dfrac{5}{10x}$
(98) ⠀⠀⠀⠀⠀⠀⠀⠀⠀⠀⠀⠀⠀⠀⠀⠀⠀⠀⠀⠀*(99)*

*5. Multiple Choice Evaluate the equation $y = \sqrt{x + 6} - 1$ for $x = 2$.
(114)
⠀**A** $\sqrt{2}$ ⠀⠀⠀⠀⠀⠀**B** $\sqrt{7}$ ⠀⠀⠀⠀⠀⠀**C** $2\sqrt{2} - 1$ ⠀⠀⠀⠀⠀**D** no solution

*6. (**Oceanography**) A good approximation of the speed of a wave in deep ocean water
(114) is given by the equation $y = \sqrt{10d}$. In this equation, y is the wave's speed in meters per second and d is the ocean's depth in meters. What is the speed of a wave if the depth is 400 meters? Round to the nearest whole number.

*7. Analyze Given the function $f(x) = \sqrt{\dfrac{4x}{3} - 1}$, for what values of x will $f(x)$ be
(114) greater than 5? Show your work.

*8. Analyze Explain how to graph $f(x) = \sqrt{x - 2} + 3$ in terms of its parent function.
(114)

9. Find the value of the discriminant of the equation $2x^2 - 5x - 4 = 0$.
(113)

*10. **Error Analysis** Two students are using the discriminant to find the number of
(113) real solutions to the equation $5x^2 - 3x = 2$. Which student is correct? Explain
the error.

Student A	Student B
$5x^2 - 3x = 2$ $b^2 - 4ac = (-3)^2 - 4(5)(2)$ $\quad = 9 - 40$ $\quad = -31$ As the discriminant is negative, there are no x-intercepts.	$5x^2 - 3x = 2$ $5x^2 - 3x - 2 = 0$ $b^2 - 4ac = (-3)^2 - 4(5)(-2)$ $\quad = 9 + 40$ $\quad = 49$ As the discriminant is positive, there are two x-intercepts.

*11. **Geometry** The length of a rectangle is $x + 12$ inches and the width is $x + 8$ inches.
(113) Is there a value for x that makes the area of the rectangle 50 square inches?
Explain your reasoning.

*12. **Multi-Step** The equation $288 = (3 + x)(6 - x)$ can be used to determine if the base
(113) of a rectangular box with a length of $(3 + x)$ inches and a width of $(6 - x)$ inches
can have an area of 288 square inches.

a. Write the equation setting it equal to zero.

b. Use the equation to find the values of a, b, and c.

c. Find the value of the discriminant.

d. Can a box with these dimensions be made? Explain.

13. Solve this system by graphing: $\begin{aligned} y &= x^2 + 3 \\ y &= -2x + 3 \end{aligned}$.
(112)

*14. **Error Analysis** Two students are solving the system of equations $\begin{aligned} y &= x^2 + 4x \\ y &= -4 \end{aligned}$ by
(112) substitution. Which student is correct? Explain the error.

Student A	Student B
$y = x^2 + 4x \qquad y = -4$ $x^2 + 4x = -4$ $(x^2 + 4x) - 4 = 0$ $x^2 + 4x - 4 = 0$ no solution	$y = x^2 + 4x \qquad y = -4$ $x^2 + 4x = -4$ $(x^2 + 4x) + 4 = 0$ $x^2 + 4x + 4 = 0$ $(x + 2)(x + 2) = 0$ So, $x = -2$, and the solution is $(-2, -4)$.

*15. (**Physics**) Miguel is standing at the base of a ramp. He tosses a ball into the air. The
(112) path of the ball is described by the equation $y = -x^2 + 7x$. The equation $y = x$
represents the ramp. At what altitude does the ball strike the ramp? Assume that
dimensions are in feet.

16. **Measurement** On what scale would the distance between the x-coordinates in the
(112) solution set of the system $\begin{aligned} y &= \dfrac{x^2}{2} \\ y &= 4x - 6 \end{aligned}$ be 8 centimeters?

17. Graph the function $f(x) = |x| - 2$.
(107)

18. (Temperature) The temperature outside yesterday was 65°. Today the temperature
(107)　changed by $|5°|$. Give the possible temperatures outside today.

19. Determine if the set of ordered pairs $\{(6, 3), (4, 2), (2, 1), (8, 4)\}$ satisfies an
(108)　exponential function.

20. (Engineering) A small bridge has a weight limit of 8000 pounds. A photographer
(109)　wants to photograph at least 5 vehicles on the bridge. The cars weigh about
1800 pounds each and the motorcycles weigh about 600 pounds each. There
must be at least one car and four motorcycles in the photo. Graph a system of
linear equations to describe the situation. Give two combinations of cars and
motorcycles that are solutions.

21. Use the quadratic formula to solve $x^2 = 19x - 60$. Check the solutions.
(110)

22. Multiple Choice There are three numbers in a locker combination: 19, 22, and 28.
(111)　How many different ways can the numbers be arranged?
　　A 3　　　　　　　**B** 6　　　　　　　**C** 12　　　　　　　**D** 24

✎ *23. Write Explain what types of situations apply to permutations.
(111)

24. Multi-Step In a bowling lane, the distance (d) from the foul line to the center of
(101)　the Number 1 pin should be 60 feet and should vary from this length by no more
than $\frac{1}{2}$ inch.
　a. Convert 60 feet to inches.

　b. Write and solve an absolute-value inequality that models the acceptable
　　distances from the foul line to the center of the Number 1 pin.

　c. If the diameter of the base of the Number 1 pin is $4\frac{1}{8}$ inches, what is the shortest
　　possible distance between the foul line and the front of the Number 1 pin?

25. Evaluate $y = \sqrt{2x} + 3$ for $x = 8$.
(114)

26. (Property) Mr. Kinsey's property is in the shape of a right triangle. The legal description
(104)　states that the property has an area of 900 yd^2 and that the base of the property is 30
yards longer than the height. What are the actual dimensions of the property?

27. Multi-Step A company gives its employees a 4% raise at the beginning of every year.
(105)　This year, Jordan earns $32,000.
　a. Write a rule that can be used to find Jordan's salary after n years.

　b. How many years will it take for Jordan to earn $40,000?

　c. What will Jordan's salary be in 12 years? Round to the nearest cent.

28. Analyze Write the radical equation $\sqrt{x + 3} = 2x$ so that the equation has no radical
(106)　and is equal to zero.

29. Has the graph of the parent quadratic function been stretched or compressed to
(Inv 10)　produce the graph $f(x) = 4x^2 + 2$?

30. Describe the similarity and difference between the graphs of $f(x) = 3^x$ and
(Inv 11)　$g(x) = 4 \cdot 3^x$.

Graphing Cubic Functions

Warm Up

1. Vocabulary The polynomial $x - 5x^2 + 3x^3 - 1$ written in _____ form
(53) is $3x^3 - 5x^2 + x - 1$.

Find the degree of each polynomial expression and write the polynomial in descending order.

2. $8 + x^2 + 2x$
(53)

3. $2x^3 - 6x + x^4$
(53)

4. Simplify $(125)^{\frac{1}{3}}$.
(46)

5. Multiple Choice Which value is equivalent to $\sqrt[3]{-343}$?
(46)

    A 7   **B** -7 **C** 114.3   **D** -114.3

New Concepts

A **cubic function** is a polynomial function in which the greatest power of any variable is 3. In other words, a cubic function is a polynomial function of degree 3.

The degree of a polynomial function determines many characteristics of its graph.

Function Type	Graph	Degree	x-Intercepts (Maximum)	End Behavior
Linear		1	1	Ends go in opposite directions.
Quadratic		2	2	Ends go in the same direction.
Cubic		3	3	Ends go in opposite directions.

Reading Math

The equation $y = x^3$ is read, "y is equal to x cubed" or "y is equal to x to the third power."

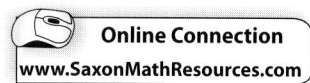

Online Connection
www.SaxonMathResources.com

The parent function for cubic polynomials is $y = x^3$. The graph of $y = -x^3$ is related to the graph of the parent function $y = x^3$.

Example 1 Graphing Cubic Functions

Evaluate the cubic parent function $y = x^3$ and the function $y = -x^3$ for $x = -2, -1, 0, 1,$ and 2. Then graph the functions.

SOLUTION Make tables of values. Then plot points to graph the functions.

x	-2	-1	0	1	2
y	-8	-1	0	1	8

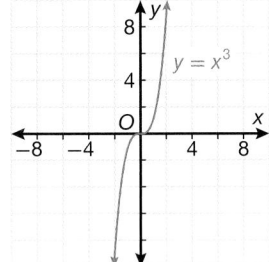

x	-2	-1	0	1	2
y	8	1	0	-1	-8

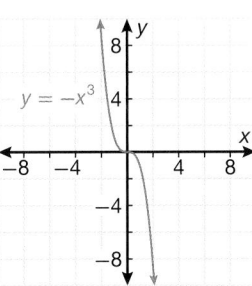

Math Reasoning

Generalize Which transformation changes the graph of $y = x^3$ into the graph of $y = -x^3$?

Example 2 Solving Cubic Equations by Graphing

a. Solve $0 = x^3 - 1$ by graphing.

SOLUTION

To solve $0 = x^3 - 1$, begin by graphing the related function $y = x^3 - 1$.

Then find the x-intercepts of $y = x^3 - 1$ since these are the x-values where $y = 0$.

The only x-intercept is near 1, so the approximate solution to $0 = x^3 - 1$ is $x \approx 1$.

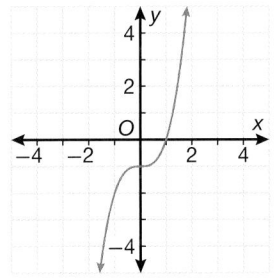

Math Reasoning

Verify In Example 2a, how can you check whether $x = 1$ is the exact solution or not?

b. Solve $2 = -2x^3 - 7$ by graphing.

SOLUTION

Write $2 = -2x^3 - 7$ so that one side is equal to zero. Then graph the related function and find its x-intercepts.

Subtracting 2 from both sides of $2 = -2x^3 - 7$ gives the equation $0 = -2x^3 - 9$. To solve $0 = -2x^3 - 9$, graph the related function $y = -2x^3 - 9$.

The only x-intercept is between -1 and -2, at about -1.7.

The approximate solution to $2 = -2x^3 - 7$ is $x \approx -1.7$.

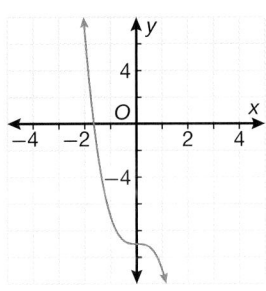

Hint

Another way to solve $2 = -2x^3 - 7$ is to graph $y = -2x^3 - 7$ and $y = 2$, and then to find the x value(s) at their point(s) of intersection.

Example 3 Solving Cubic Equations Using a Graphing Calculator

Solve $-2x^2 = \frac{1}{2}x^3 - 1$ by graphing on a graphing calculator.

SOLUTION

Graphing Calculator Tip

For help with graphing functions, refer to the graphing calculator keystrokes in Lab 3 on p. 305.

Write $-2x^2 = \frac{1}{2}x^3 - 1$ so that one side is equal to zero. Then graph the related function and find its x-intercepts.

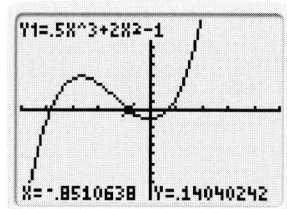

Adding $2x^2$ to both sides of the original equation gives the equation $0 = \frac{1}{2}x^3 + 2x^2 - 1$. Use the graphing calculator to graph the related function $y = \frac{1}{2}x^3 + 2x^2 - 1$.

The graph shows that there are three x-intercepts. Trace to estimate their values.

Math Language

Remember that the **zeros** of a function are its x-intercepts or solutions.

The approximate solutions are $x \approx -3.9$, $x \approx -0.8$, and $x \approx 0.7$.

For better estimates, use the Zero function. To the nearest hundredth, the solutions are $x \approx -3.87$, $x \approx -0.79$, and $x \approx 0.66$.

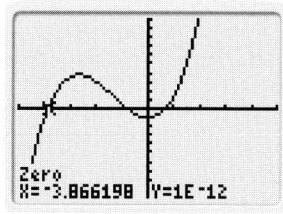

Example 4 Application: Volume of a Cube

A cube of pure gold weighing 100 pounds would have a volume of about 143 cubic inches. Use a graphing calculator to estimate the side length of a 100-pound cube of gold.

SOLUTION

The formula for the volume of a cube is $V = s^3$. To graph this equation on a graphing calculator, let y represent V and x represent s. Then graph $y = x^3$.

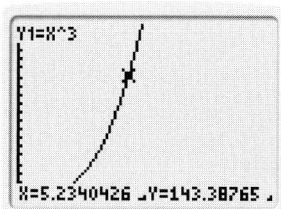

Adjust the window to make sure that 143 is included in the y-values.

Window Settings

$X\text{min} = 0$

$X\text{max} = 12$

$Y\text{min} = 0$

$Y\text{max} = 200$

Trace to estimate the x-value where $y = 143$.

When $y = 143$, $x \approx 5.2$.

The side length of a cube of gold weighing 100 pounds would be about 5.2 inches—about the width of a DVD case.

a. Graph $y = x^3 + 1$.
(Ex 1)

b. Solve $0 = -4x^3$ by graphing.
(Ex 2)

c. Solve $3 = -x^3 + 8$ by graphing.
(Ex 2)

d. Solve $x^2 - \frac{1}{4} = \frac{1}{4}x^3$ by graphing on a graphing calculator.
(Ex 3)

e. The volume of a rectangular prism is represented by the equation $V = x^3 + 4$. Use a graphing calculator to find the volume when $x = 25.5$ units.
(Ex 4)

Practice Distributed and Integrated

Solve and check.

1. $\dfrac{x - 2}{x + 7} = \dfrac{x - 6}{3x + 21}$
(99)

2. $\dfrac{x - 4}{x + 1} = \dfrac{x + 5}{2x + 2}$
(99)

*3. Graph the cubic function $y = \frac{1}{3}x^3$. Use it to solve the equation $0 = \frac{1}{3}x^3$.
(115)

*4. Multiple Choice Which equation represents a cubic function?
(115)

A $y = 3x - 4y$ **B** $y = 6x^2 + 2$

C $y = x^3 - 4x + 1$ **D** $y = 10x^4 + 3x^2 - 5$

*5. (Capacity) The volume of a box is represented by the equation $V = x^3 - 4$. Use a table or graph to find the value of x that corresponds to a volume of 23 cubic units.
(115)

*6. (Games) The volume of a whiffle ball is represented by the equation $V = \frac{4}{3}\pi r^3$. Use a graphing calculator to graph the equation and then use the graph to estimate the volume of air in a ball with a radius of 2 inches.
(115)

*7. Write Describe the characteristics of the graph of a cubic function.
(115)

*8. Formulate Write an example of a cubic function.
(115)

9. Evaluate $y = \sqrt{4x} - 5$ for $x = 3$. Round to the nearest tenth.
(114)

*10. Error Analysis Two students are evaluating the equation $y = \sqrt{2x - 5} + 2$ for $x = 6$. Which student is correct? Explain the error.
(114)

Student A	Student B
$y = \sqrt{2x - 5} + 2$	$y = \sqrt{2x - 5} + 2$
$y = \sqrt{2 \cdot 6 - 5} + 2$	$y = \sqrt{2 \cdot 6 - 5} + 2$
$y = \sqrt{2} + 2$	$y = \sqrt{12 - 5} + 2$
	$y = \sqrt{7} + 2$

11. Multi-Step An apple fell from a tree limb. The function $t = 0.45\sqrt{x}$ represents how long it takes an object to fall from a height of x meters.
(114)

   a. Graph the function. (Hint: Increment the x-axis by 1 and the y-axis by 0.1, and if a graphing calculator is not used, then use the following values for x: 0, 4, 9, and 16.)

   b. Use the graph to estimate how long it took the apple to fall if the limb was 12 meters above the ground.

12. Use the discriminant to find the number of real solutions of the equation $6x^2 + 2x - 1 = 0$.
(113)

*13. Error Analysis Two students are using the discriminant to find the number of real solutions to the equation $2x^2 + 3x - 4 = 0$. Which student is correct? Explain the error.
(113)

Student A	Student B
$2x^2 + 3x - 4 = 0$ $b^2 - 4ac = 3^2 - 4(2)(4)$ $\quad = 9 - 32$ $\quad = -23$ As the discriminant is negative, there are no x-intercepts.	$2x^2 + 3x - 4 = 0$ $b^2 - 4ac = 3^2 - 4(2)(-4)$ $\quad = 9 + 32$ $\quad = 41$ As the discriminant is positive, there are two x-intercepts.

14. (Gardening) The length of a garden is $6 + x$ meters and the width is $10 - x$ meters. Write an equation to model the area of the garden, and use the discriminant to determine if there is a value for x that will allow the area of the garden to be 50 square meters.
(113)

15. Measurement The length of a fence is $15 - x$ feet and the width is $12 + x$ feet. Can the fence enclose an area of 200 square feet? Explain.
(113)

16. Determine if the set of ordered pairs $\left\{\left(-3, \frac{1}{8}\right), \left(-1, \frac{1}{2}\right), \left(-2, \frac{1}{4}\right), \left(-4, \frac{1}{16}\right)\right\}$ satisfies an exponential function.
(108)

17. Graph the system $\begin{array}{l} 21x + 7y \geq -14 \\ \frac{1}{2}y \leq -x + 2 \end{array}$.
(109)

18. Geometry If the area of the triangle is 48 square units, what are the lengths of the base and the height to the nearest whole number?
(110)

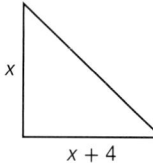

x

$x + 4$

*19. Graph the cubic function $y = 3x^3$. Use it to solve the equation $0 = 3x^3$.
(115)

20. A new 3-digit area code is being created for new telephone numbers. If the first digit must be even but not 0, the second digit is 0 or 1, and the third digit can be any number except 0, how many new area codes are possible?
(111)

21. Multiple Choice Which system of equations has the solution $(-1, 1)$?
(112)

A $y = x^2$
    $y = x + 6$

B $y = x^2$
    $y = 6$

C $y = x^2$
    $y = -2x - 1$

D $y = x^2$
    $y = -x + 6$

*22. Analyze A system of three equations consists of a quadratic, given by
(112) $y = x^2 - 3$, and two linear equations. One linear equation intersects the parabola at two points. If the second linear equation is parallel to the first, how many solutions does the system have? Explain.

23. (Accessories) Candida has plans to shop for hair bows and does not plan on
(97) spending more than \$20. Each big bow costs \$5 and each small bow costs \$2. Write an inequality and graph it to describe the situation.

24. Solve $-x^2 + 2 = -7x$ by using a graphing calculator. Round to the nearest tenth.
(100)

25. Multiple Choice Solve $x^2 + 7 = -42$.
(102)

A 7 **B** ± 7 **C** no solution **D** $\pm 7\sqrt{1}$

26. (Phone Chains) In order to relay information quickly, staff at a school use a phone
(105) chain. The superintendent first notifies 3 people of a snow day. In the second set of calls, these 3 people each call 2 people. Each person called then calls 2 other people. How many sets of calls need to be made to notify 96 people?

27. Multi-Step A square frame is to be made so that its side length is $\sqrt{x + 1}$.
(106)
a. What is the perimeter of the square?

b. For what value of x will the perimeter of the frame be equal to 8 units?

28. Generalize Look at the function $f(x) = -0.5|x|$. How can you find the direction of
(107) the "V" without graphing it?

29. (Football) The distance d from the goal post in feet of a football during a field goal
(107) kick is represented by the function $d = |60t - 90|$ where t is the time in seconds. If the ball were kicked at 80 feet per second how would the graph change?

30. Write, in order, the function that grows the slowest to the one that grows the
(Inv 11) fastest: exponential, linear, quadratic.

Solving Simple and Compound Interest Problems

Warm Up

1. **Vocabulary** Two equivalent ratios form a _____.
(31)

2. Change 24% to a fraction and a decimal.
(SB 7)

3. Change $\frac{1}{40}$ to a decimal and a percent.
(SB 7)

4. Find 25% of 250.
(42)

5. 36 is what percent of 1125?
(42)

New Concepts

Money that is borrowed or invested is called principal. Interest is money paid for the use of that money. If money is borrowed, interest is paid. If money is invested, interest is earned.

Simple interest is interest paid on the principal only. To find simple interest, use the formula $I = Prt$.

<table>
<tr><td colspan="2" align="center">**Simple Interest Formula**
$I = Prt$</td></tr>
<tr><td>I</td><td>the amount of interest</td></tr>
<tr><td>P</td><td>the principal</td></tr>
<tr><td>r</td><td>the annual rate, a percent expressed as a decimal</td></tr>
<tr><td>t</td><td>the time in years</td></tr>
</table>

Math Language

Even though the account value grows as interest is earned, **simple interest** is only paid on the original amount deposited into the account.

Example 1 Finding Simple Interest

a. An account is opened with $4000. The bank pays 5% simple interest annually. How much interest will be earned in 3 years?

SOLUTION

Use the simple interest formula.

The principal P is 4000. The rate r is 5%, or 0.05. The time t is 3.

$I = Prt$	Write the formula, then evaluate.
$= 4000(0.05)(3)$	Substitute the values of the variables.
$= 600$	Simplify.

The account will earn $600 interest in 3 years.

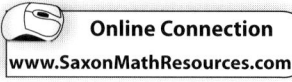
Online Connection
www.SaxonMathResources.com

b. $12,500 is invested for 15 years at 4% simple interest. How much money will be in the account after 15 years?

SOLUTION

Use the simple interest formula.

The principal P is 12,500. The rate r is 4%, or 0.04. The time t is 15.

$I = Prt$	Write the formula, then evaluate.
$= 12{,}500(0.04)(15)$	Substitute the values of the variables.
$= 7500$	Simplify.

The account will earn $7500 interest in 15 years.

Add this interest to the original amount invested to find the total amount in the account.

$$12{,}500 + 7500 = 20{,}000$$

There will be $20,000 in the account after 15 years.

c. $6000 is borrowed at 8.5% simple interest. The total amount of interest paid is $2040. For how many years was the money borrowed?

SOLUTION

Use the simple interest formula and solve for t.

The principal P is 6000. The interest I is 2040. The rate r is 8.5% or 0.085.

$I = Prt$	Write the formula.
$2040 = 6000(0.085)t$	Substitute the values of the variables.
$2040 = 510t$	Simplify.
$4 = t$	Divide both sides by 510.

The money was borrowed for 4 years.

d. After 18 months, $738 had been earned on an $8200 investment. What was the interest rate?

SOLUTION

Use the simple interest formula and solve for r.

The principal P is 8200. The interest I is 738. The time t is $\frac{18}{12} = 1.5$ years.

$I = Prt$	Write the formula.
$738 = 8200 \cdot r \cdot 1.5$	Substitute the values of the variables.
$738 = 12{,}300r$	Simplify.
$0.06 = r$	Divide both sides by 12,300.

Convert 0.06 to a percent. The interest rate was 6%.

Hint

The time in the simple interest formula must be in years. There are 12 months in 1 year. To change the units from months to years, divide by 12.

The amount in an account grows faster with **compound interest.** Compound interest is interest that is paid on both principal and on previously-earned interest. The compound interest formula gives the total amount accumulated after a given number of years.

Compound Interest Formula	
$$A = P\left(1 + \frac{r}{n}\right)^{nt}$$	
A	the total amount after t years
P	the principal
r	the annual rate, a percent expressed as a decimal
t	the time in years
n	the number of times interest is compounded each year

┌ **Example** **2**   **Finding Compound Interest**

(a.) $5000 is invested at 6% compounded annually. Find the value of the investment after 10 years.

SOLUTION

The principal P is 5000. The rate r is 6% or 0.06. The time t is 10 years.

$A = P(1 + r)^t$ 　　　　　Write the formula, then evaluate.

$\quad = 5000 \cdot (1 + 0.06)^{10}$ 　　Substitute the values of the variables.

$\quad = 5000 \cdot (1.06)^{10}$ 　　　Simplify inside the parentheses.

$\quad = 5000 \cdot 1.790847697$ 　Simplify the power, and do not round.

$\quad = 8954.24$ 　　　　　　Multiply, and round to the nearest penny.

The value of the investment will be $8954.24.

(b.) $5000 is invested at 6% compounded quarterly. Find the value of the investment after 10 years.

SOLUTION

The principal P is 5000. The rate r is 6% or 0.06. The time t is 10 years and $n = 4$ because quarterly means four times per year.

$A = P\left(1 + \frac{r}{n}\right)^{nt}$ 　　　　　Write the formula, then evaluate.

$\quad = 5000\left(1 + \frac{0.06}{4}\right)^{4(10)}$ 　Substitute the values of the variables.

$\quad = 5000 \cdot (1.015)^{40}$ 　　Use the order of operations to simplify.

$\quad = 5000 \cdot 1.814018409$ 　Simplify the power and do not round.

$\quad = 9070.09$ 　　　　　　Multiply and round to the nearest penny.

The value of the investment will be $9070.09.

Math Reasoning

Justify Explain why the formula for interest compounded annually is $A = P(1 + r)^t$.

Hint

Use a calculator to evaluate the power and to multiply the result by the principal.

Example 3 Comparing Simple and Compound Interest

a. An account has $1000 and earns 20% simple interest. Make a table to find the total amount in the account after 1, 2, 5, and 10 years.

SOLUTION

Years	$Prt = I$		Total in Account
1	$(1000)(0.20)(1)$	$= 200$	$1000 + $200 = $1200
2	$(1000)(0.20)(2)$	$= 400$	$1000 + $400 = $1400
5	$(1000)(0.20)(5)$	$= 1000$	$1000 + $1000 = $2000
10	$(1000)(0.20)(10)$	$= 2000$	$1000 + $2000 = $3000

b. An account has $1000 and earns 20% interest compounded annually. Make a table to find the total amount in the account after 1, 2, 5, and 10 years.

SOLUTION

Years	$A = P(1 + r)^t$	Total in Account
1	$A = 1000(1 + 0.20)^1$	$1200
2	$A = 1000(1 + 0.20)^2$	$1440
5	$A = 1000(1 + 0.20)^5$	$2488.32
10	$A = 1000(1 + 0.20)^{10}$	$6191.74

c. Use the table in **a** to graph the account earning simple interest and the table in **b** to graph the account earning compound interest on the same coordinate plane. Compare the growth of the two accounts over time.

SOLUTION

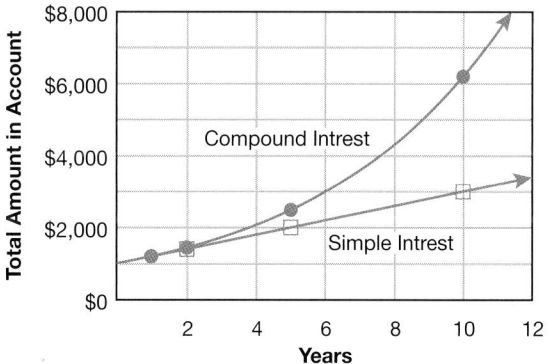

Simple interest grows *linearly* because it adds the same amount each year. Compound interest grows *exponentially* because it pays interest on the previously-earned interest as well as the principal. The account earning compound interest grows more rapidly than the account earning simple interest.

Example 4 **Application: Retirement Investments**

Two people plan to retire at age 65. A 25-year-old woman invests $2000 in a bond that pays 7% per year, compounded annually. A 45-year-old man invests $5000 in a bond that pays 7% per year, also compounded annually. Whose investment will be worth more when they reach retirement age and by how much?

SOLUTION

Use $A = P(1 + r)^t$ to calculate the value of the investment for each person.

For the 25-year-old woman, $P = 2000$, $r = 0.07$, and $t = 40$.

$A = 2000(1 + 0.07)^{40}$	Substitute.
$A = 2000(1.07)^{40}$	Add inside the parentheses.
$A = 29{,}948.92$	Simplify using the order of operations.

The total value of her account will be $29,948.92.

For the 45-year-old man, $P = 5000$, $r = 0.07$, and $t = 20$.

$A = 5000(1 + 0.07)^{20}$	Substitute.
$A = 5000(1.07)^{20}$	Add inside the parentheses.
$A = 19{,}348.42$	Simplify using the order of operations.

The total value of his account will be $19,348.42. The woman's investment will be worth $10,600.50 more.

Math Reasoning

Analyze Why was the man's account value less than the woman's?

Lesson Practice

a. An account is opened with $5600. The bank pays 4% simple interest annually. How much interest will be earned in 10 years?
(Ex 1)

b. $25,000 is invested for 12 years at 6% simple interest. How much will be in the account after 12 years?
(Ex 1)

c. $4500 is borrowed at 2.5% simple interest. The total amount of interest paid is $562.50. For how many years was the money borrowed?
(Ex 1)

d. After 15 months, $130 had been earned on a $2600 investment. What was the interest rate?
(Ex 1)

e. $12,000 is invested at 4% compounded annually. Find the value of the investment after 30 years.
(Ex 2)

f. $12,000 is invested at 4% compounded quarterly. Find the value of the investment after 30 years.
(Ex 2)

g. An account has $2500 and earns 12% simple interest. Complete the table to find the total amount in the account after 1, 2, 5, and 10 years.
(Ex 3)

Years	$Prt = I$	Total Amount in Account
1		
2		
5		
10		

h. A second account has $2500 and earns 12% compounded annually. Complete the table to find the total amount in each account after 1, 2, 5, and 10 years.
(Ex 3)

Principal	Rate	Years	Total Amount in Account
$2500	12%	1	
$2500	12%	2	
$2500	12%	5	
$2500	12%	10	

i. Use the table in problem **g** to graph the account earning simple interest and the table in problem **h** to graph the account earning compound interest on the same coordinate plane. Compare the growth of the two accounts over time.
(Ex 3)

j. [Retirement Investments] Two people plan to retire at age 60. A 30-year-old man invests $4000 in a bond that pays 5% per year, compounded annually. A 40-year-old man invests $6000 in a bond that pays 5% per year, also compounded annually. Whose investment will be worth more when they reach retirement age and by how much?
(Ex 4)

Practice   Distributed and Integrated

*1. $900 is invested at 3% simple interest for 5 years. How much interest is earned?
(116)

*2. Write Explain the difference between simple and compound interest.
(116)

*3. Formulate The graph shows the value of a money market account that pays compound interest. How much principal was originally invested?
(116)

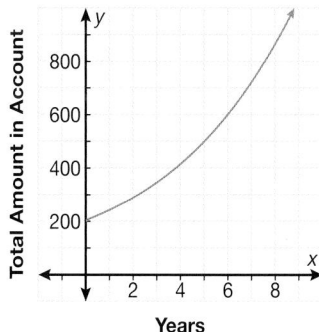

4. [Population] The exponential function $y = 3.45(1.00617)^x$ can model the approximate population of Oklahoma from 2000 to 2006, where x is the number of years after 2000 and y represents millions of people. Assuming the model does not change, predict when the population will reach 4 million?
(108)

*5. **Multiple Choice** $600 is invested at 11% simple interest. What is the value of
(116) the investment after 14 years?

    A $924   **B** $1524   **C** $2586.26   **D** $92,400

*6. (**Mutual Funds**) Over the past 20 years, a mutual fund averages paying
(116) 10% interest compounded annually. If a woman had invested $3000
originally, how much would her account be worth now?

*7. Graph the cubic function $y = -3x^3$. Use the graph to find the roots of the equation.
(115)

8. **Error Analysis** Two students write the equation "y equals x cubed plus
(115) five." Which student is correct? Explain the error.

Student A	Student B
$y = x^3 + 5$	$y = x^2 + 5$

 9. **Geometry** The formula for the volume of a cube is $V = s^3$. Graph the
(115) equation and find the volume of the cube if the side length is 2 units.

*10. **Multi-Step** The volume of a packing container is given by
(115) the function $y = x^3 + 5$.

    a. Make a table of values for the equation.

    b. Graph the equation.

    c. Find the volume when x is 3 feet.

11. Evaluate $y = 3\sqrt{7x + 2} - 7$ for $x = 2$.
(114)

12. (**Physics**) The speed at which an object in free fall drops is modeled by the
(114) equation $y = 8\sqrt{x}$. In this equation, y is the speed in feet per second and
x is the distance fallen in feet. What is the speed of an apple after it falls a
distance of 8 feet? Round to the nearest tenth.

*13. **Error Analysis** Two students are determining the domain and range of the
(114) function $f(x) = \sqrt{x - 5} + 1$. Which student is correct? Explain the error.

Student A	Student B
$f(x) = \sqrt{x - 5} + 1$	$f(x) = \sqrt{x - 5} + 1$
$x - 4 \geq 0$	$x - 5 \geq 0$
$x \geq 4; y \geq 0$	$x \geq 5; y \geq 1$

14. **Measurement** The function $s = \sqrt{A}$ gives the side length of a square with area A.
(114) What is the side length of a square that has an area of 625 square feet?

15. Graph the system $\begin{array}{l} y \geq \frac{2}{5}x - 4 \\ y \leq 0 \end{array}$.
(109)

16. Use the quadratic formula to solve $46 + 16x = -x^2$. Find approximate answers
(110) to four decimal places.

17. (Sports) The American League Central Division in Major League Baseball has
(111) 5 teams. How many different ways are there for the teams to finish first through fifth?

18. Solve this system by graphing: $\begin{aligned} y &= 2x^2 - 6x + 1 \\ y &= -x - 4 \end{aligned}$.
(112)

19. Multiple Choice How many x-intercepts does the equation $y = 4x^2 + 8x - 2$ have?
(113)
    A 0   **B** 1   **C** 2   **D** 3

20. Write Explain what the discriminant tells about the graph of a quadratic
(113) equation.

21. Solve $4x^2 + 8 = -6x$ by using a graphing calculator. Round to the nearest tenth.
(100)

22. Solve and graph the inequality $|4x - 3| + 1 > 10$.
(101)

23. (Structural Engineering) The water pressure p on a dam is a function of the depth
(106) of the water x behind the dam: $p = 4905\sqrt{x}$. For what value of x is the pressure equal to 44,145?

24. Multi-Step Graph the function $f(x) = |x| - 4$, and then translate the function to
(107) the left by 2. What is the vertex of this new function?

*25. \$4500 is borrowed at 3.5% simple interest. The total amount of interest paid is
(116) \$1260. For how many years was the money borrowed?

*26. (Credit Cards) A man uses a credit card to make a \$1200 purchase. The credit card
(116) charges 22% annual interest compounded monthly and requires no payments for the first year. At the end of one year, how much will he owe?

27. Justify Why is $f(x) = 4(-2)^x$ not an exponential function?
(108)

28. Multi-Step Study the numbers in the sequence.
(103)

$$3, \sqrt{3}, 1, \frac{\sqrt{3}}{3}, \frac{1}{3}, \dots$$

    a. Find the pattern.

    b. What is the next term in the sequence?

29. If $f(x) = 3x^2 - 12x + 2$, where is the axis of symmetry located? Give the x- and
(Inv 10) y-coordinates of the vertex.

30. Identify which function is linear, quadratic, exponential growth, and exponential
(Inv 11) decay: $f(x) = \left(\frac{1}{5}\right)^x$, $g(x) = x^2$, $h(x) = 5^x$, and $j(x) = 5x$.

Using Trigonometric Ratios

Warm Up

1. (85) **Vocabulary** A ratio is the comparison of two quantities using _____.

2. (85) If the two legs of a right triangle measure 9 inches and 12 inches, find the length of the hypotenuse.

3. (85) In a right triangle, one leg measures 10 inches and the hypotenuse measures 17 inches. Find the length of the other leg.

Decide if the following are Pythagorean triples or not.

4. (85) 6, 10, 8　　　　　　　　　　　　**5.** (85) 8, 12, 20

New Concepts

Recall that a right triangle has one right angle and two acute angles. In the triangle, $\angle C$ is the right angle and $\angle A$ and $\angle B$ are the acute angles.

Using $\angle A$ in the triangle, the leg across from the angle is called the opposite leg and the leg next to $\angle A$ is called the adjacent leg. The hypotenuse is always opposite the right angle and is always the longest side of the triangle.

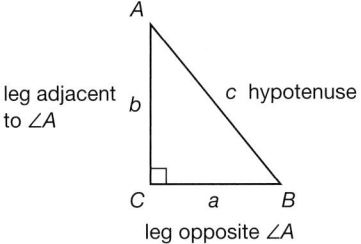

Hint

The three trigonometric ratios of sine, cosine, and tangent can be remembered using the mnemonic device:

SOH-CAH-TOA
(pronounced "sew-ka-toe-a"). **S**ine equals **O**pposite leg over **H**ypotenuse, **C**osine equals **A**djacent leg over **H**ypotenuse, and **T**angent equals **O**pposite leg over **A**djacent leg. This can also be written as $S\frac{o}{h}\ C\frac{a}{h}\ T\frac{o}{a}$.

In any right triangle, there are six **trigonometric ratios** that can be written using two side lengths of the triangle in relation to the angles of the triangle. The three most common trigonometric ratios are sine, cosine, and tangent, abbreviated sin, cos, and tan, respectively.

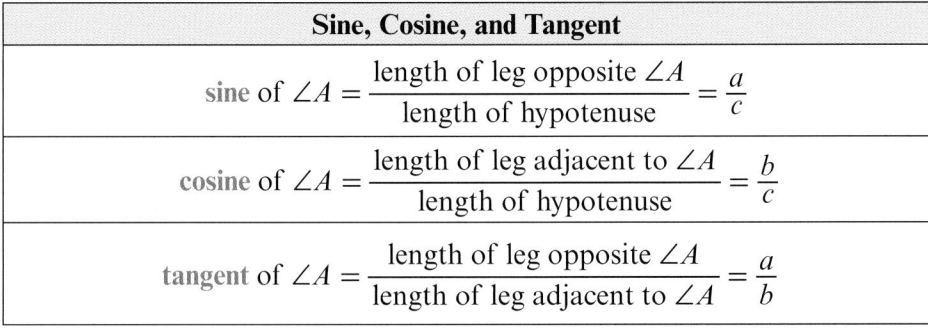

Sine, Cosine, and Tangent
sine of $\angle A = \dfrac{\text{length of leg opposite } \angle A}{\text{length of hypotenuse}} = \dfrac{a}{c}$
cosine of $\angle A = \dfrac{\text{length of leg adjacent to } \angle A}{\text{length of hypotenuse}} = \dfrac{b}{c}$
tangent of $\angle A = \dfrac{\text{length of leg opposite } \angle A}{\text{length of leg adjacent to } \angle A} = \dfrac{a}{b}$

Online Connection
www.SaxonMathResources.com

In addition to the three trigonometric ratios previously discussed, there are three other trigonometric ratios called cosecant, secant, and cotangent, abbreviated csc, sec, and cot, respectively.

Cosecant, Secant, and Cotangent
cosecant of $\angle A = \dfrac{\text{length of hypotenuse}}{\text{length of leg opposite } \angle A} = \dfrac{c}{a}$
secant of $\angle A = \dfrac{\text{length of hypotenuse}}{\text{length of leg adjacent to } \angle A} = \dfrac{c}{b}$
cotangent of $\angle A = \dfrac{\text{length of leg adjacent to } \angle A}{\text{length of leg opposite } \angle A} = \dfrac{b}{a}$

Example 1 **Finding Trigonometric Ratios**

a. Using the right triangle, find sin B, cos B, and tan B.

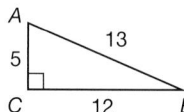

SOLUTION

$$\sin B = \frac{\text{opposite leg}}{\text{hypotenuse}} = \frac{5}{13}$$

$$\cos B = \frac{\text{adjacent leg}}{\text{hypotenuse}} = \frac{12}{13}$$

$$\tan B = \frac{\text{opposite leg}}{\text{adjacent leg}} = \frac{5}{12}$$

b. Using the right triangle, find all six trigonometric ratios for $\angle A$.

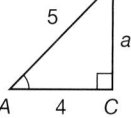

SOLUTION

First find the length of side a using the Pythagorean Theorem.

$$a^2 + b^2 = c^2$$
$$a^2 + 4^2 = 5^2$$
$$a^2 + 16 = 25$$
$$a^2 = 9$$
$$a = 3$$

$$\sin A = \frac{a}{c} = \frac{3}{5} \qquad \cos A = \frac{b}{c} = \frac{4}{5}$$

$$\tan A = \frac{a}{b} = \frac{3}{4} \qquad \csc A = \frac{c}{a} = \frac{5}{3}$$

$$\sec A = \frac{c}{b} = \frac{5}{4} \qquad \cot A = \frac{b}{a} = \frac{4}{3}$$

Example 2 **Using a Calculator with Trigonometric Ratios**

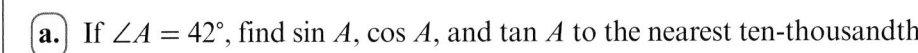

a. If $\angle A = 42°$, find sin A, cos A, and tan A to the nearest ten-thousandth.

SOLUTION

Use a calculator to find the value of the trigonometric ratios.

SIN	42	ENTER		sin $A \approx 0.6691$
COS	42	ENTER		cos $A \approx 0.7431$
TAN	42	ENTER		tan $A \approx 0.9004$

b. If $\angle A = 33°$, find csc A, sec A, and cot A to the nearest ten-thousandth.

SOLUTION

Use a calculator.

| SIN | 33 | ENTER | x^{-1} | ENTER | **OR** | 1 | ÷ | SIN | 33 | ENTER |

csc $A \approx 1.8361$

| COS | 33 | ENTER | x^{-1} | ENTER | **OR** | 1 | ÷ | COS | 33 | ENTER |

sec $A \approx 1.1924$

| TAN | 33 | ENTER | x^{-1} | ENTER | **OR** | 1 | ÷ | TAN | 33 | ENTER |

cot $A \approx 1.5399$

Example 3 **Using Trigonometry to Find Missing Side Lengths**

Use a calculator to find trigonometric ratio values.

a. Find the value of x. Round to the nearest hundredth.

SOLUTION

Since the missing side is opposite the angle and the adjacent side length is given, use the tangent ratio.

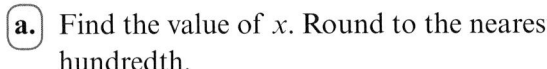

$$\tan 28° = \frac{x}{9}$$

$$9 \cdot \tan 28° = x$$

$$4.79 \approx x$$

b. Find the value of x and y. Round to the nearest hundredth.

SOLUTION

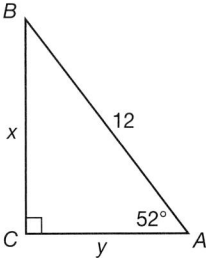

$$\sin A = \frac{\text{opposite leg}}{\text{hypotenuse}} \qquad \cos A = \frac{\text{adjacent leg}}{\text{hypotenuse}}$$

$$\sin 52° = \frac{x}{12} \qquad \cos 52° = \frac{y}{12}$$

$$12 \cdot \sin 52° = x \qquad 12 \cdot \cos 52° = y$$

$$9.46 \approx x \qquad 7.39 \approx y$$

Inverse trigonometric functions can be used to find missing angle measures. On a calculator, these are $\sin^{-1}$, $\cos^{-1}$, and $\tan^{-1}$. Because they are inverse functions, $\sin^{-1}(\sin A) = A$, and the same principle follows for cosine and tangent.

Math Reasoning

Generalize When do you use the sine function and when do you use the inverse sine ($\sin^{-1}$) function?

Example 4 Using Trigonometry to Find Missing Angle Measures

a. Find the measure of $\angle A$. Round to the nearest hundredth of a degree.

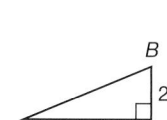

SOLUTION

Use the cosine ratio since you know the adjacent leg and the hypotenuse.

$$\cos A = \frac{6}{11}$$

$$\cos^{-1}(\cos A) = \cos^{-1}\left(\frac{6}{11}\right)$$

$$\angle A \approx 56.94°$$

b. Find the measures of $\angle A$ and $\angle B$. Round to the nearest hundredth of a degree.

SOLUTION

Use the tangent ratio since you know the lengths of the legs.

$$\tan A = \frac{2}{5} \qquad\qquad \tan B = \frac{5}{2}$$

$$\tan^{-1}(\tan A) = \tan^{-1}\left(\frac{2}{5}\right) \qquad \tan^{-1}(\tan B) = \tan^{-1}\left(\frac{5}{2}\right)$$

$$\angle A \approx 21.80° \qquad\qquad \angle B \approx 68.20°$$

Hint

You can also find the measure of the second acute angle of a right triangle by subtracting the first angle from 90°. For example, if m $\angle A = 21.80°$, then m $\angle B = 90° - 21.80° = 68.20°$.

Example 5 Application: Indirect Measurement

If an airplane takes off at a 35° angle with the ground, how far has the plane traveled horizontally when it reaches an altitude of 10,000 feet?

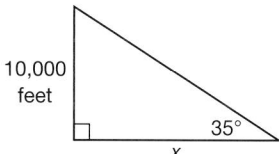

SOLUTION

Use the tangent ratio since the problem involves both legs.

$$\tan 35° = \frac{10,000}{x}$$

$$x \cdot \tan 35° = \frac{10,000}{\cancel{x}} \cdot \cancel{x}$$

$$x \cdot \tan 35° = 10,000$$

$$x = \frac{10,000}{\tan 35°} \approx 14,281$$

The plane has traveled about 14,281 feet horizontally.

a. Using the right triangle, find sin A, cos A,
(Ex 1) and tan A.

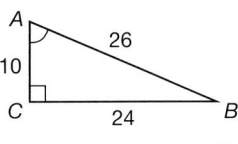

b. Using the right triangle, find all six
(Ex 1) trigonometric ratios for $\angle B$.

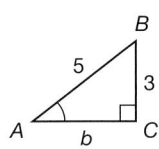

c. If $\angle A = 49°$, find sin A, cos A, and tan A. Round to the nearest ten-
(Ex 2) thousandth.

d. If $\angle A = 67°$, find csc A, sec A, and cot A. Round to the nearest ten-
(Ex 2) thousandth.

e. Find the value of x. Round to the
(Ex 3) nearest hundredth.

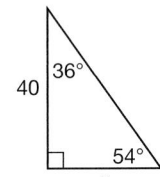

f. Find the value of x and y. Round to the nearest hundredth.
(Ex 3)

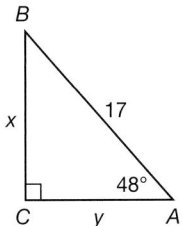

g. Find $\angle A$ and $\angle B$.
(Ex 4)

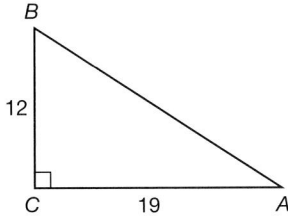

h. A 10-foot ladder is placed on the side of a building 4 feet away from the
(Ex 5) base of the building along the ground. Find the measure of the angle
the ladder makes with the ground.

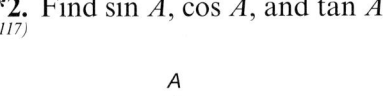

Practice **Distributed and Integrated**

*1. Find sin A, cos A, and tan A.
(117)

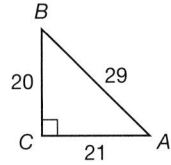

*2. Find sin A, cos A, and tan A.
(117)

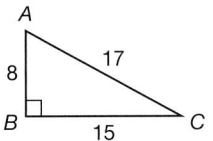

3. Write an equation for a direct variation that includes the point, (24, 3).
(56)

*4. If $\angle A = 77°$, find sin A, cos A, and tan A to the nearest ten-thousandth.
(117)

*5. Error Analysis Two students are finding the measure of $\angle A$. Which student is correct? Explain the error.
(117)

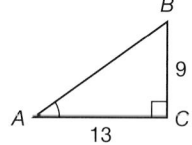

Student A	Student B
$\tan A = \dfrac{9}{13}$	$\tan A = \dfrac{13}{9}$
$\tan^{-1}(\tan A) = \tan^{-1}\left(\dfrac{9}{13}\right)$	$\tan^{-1}(\tan A) = \tan^{-1}\left(\dfrac{13}{9}\right)$
$A \approx 34.7°$	$A \approx 55.3°$

*6. Geometry In a right isosceles triangle, the acute angles are congruent. Find the measures of the acute angles. Then use the sine or cosine ratio to find the length of a leg of a right isosceles triangle to the nearest hundredth if the hypotenuse is 5 centimeters.
(117)

*7. Multi-Step You are standing on the roof of a 70-foot-tall building looking across at another building. Use the picture to answer the questions.
(117)

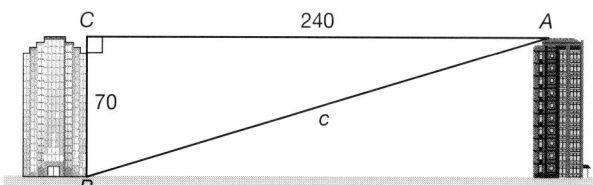

    a. Find the distance from the bottom of the building where you are standing to the top of the other building.

    b. Find the measure of $\angle A$.

*8. (Nature) A tree casts a shadow of 25 feet along the ground. The angle from the ground to the top of the tree is 45°. How tall is the tree?
(117)

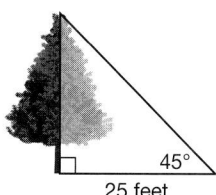

9. If $1100 is borrowed for 2 years at 9% simple interest, how much interest is paid?
(116)

*10. (Navigation) A submarine begins diving from the water's surface at an angle of 7°. How far below the water's surface is the submarine after it has traveled 3.4 miles?
(117)

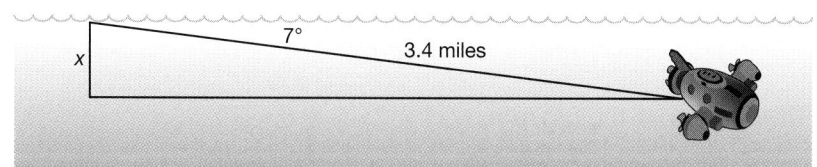

*11. Generalize Explain the meaning of opposite leg and adjacent leg to an acute angle in a right triangle.
(117)

12. **Error Analysis** A \$1500 investment earns 8% simple interest. Two students find the
(116) value of the account after 25 years. Which student is correct? Explain the error.

Student A	Student B
$I = Prt$ $I = 1500 \cdot 0.08 \cdot 25$ $I = 3000$ \$3000	$I = Prt$ $I = 1500(0.08)(25)$ $I = 3000$ $3000 + 1500 = 4500$ \$4500

13. **Multi-Step** A boy plans to invest \$100 in an account that pays 10% interest
(116) compounded annually for 10 years. Another option is an account that earns 20%
interest compounded annually for 5 years. Which will earn him more money, and
how much more?

14. Graph the cubic function $y = x^3 + 3$. Use the graph to evaluate the equation
(115) for $x = 0$.

15. **Error Analysis** Two students draw a graph of the equation $y = 2x^3$. Which student
(115) is correct? Explain the error.

Student A	Student B
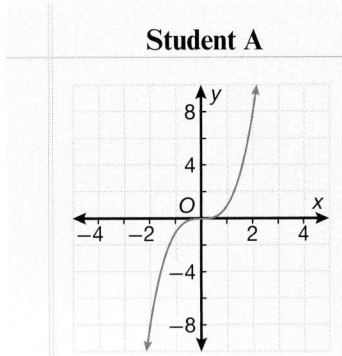	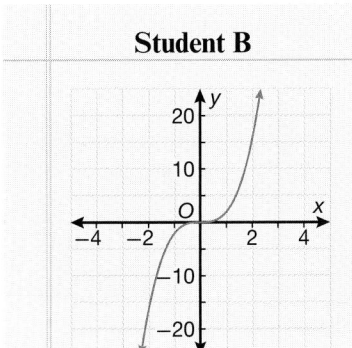

16. **Packaging** A rectangular box has a volume of $V = x^3 + 3$ cubic units. Use a table
(115) or graph to find the value of x that corresponds to a volume of 30 cubic units.

17. Use the quadratic formula to solve $2x^2 + 9 = 9x$. Check the solutions.
(110)

18. Find $_{12}P_3$.
(111)

19. Solve $x^2 + 5 = 9$.
(102)

20. **Astronomy** Near a planet, a satellite follows a trajectory described by the equation
(112) $y = \frac{x^2}{8} + \frac{7}{4}$. The trajectory is intercepted by a radio signal represented by the line
$y = -\frac{9x}{8}$. At what coordinates will the radio signal intersect the trajectory?

21. Use the discriminant to find the number of real solutions of the equation
(113) $x^2 + 2x - 2 = 0$.

22. **Multiple Choice** What is the domain of the function $f(x) = 2\sqrt{x + 6} - 1$?
(114)
   A $x \geq -5$ **B** $x \geq -6$ **C** $x \geq 6$ **D** $x \geq 0$

23. **Write** Describe the graph of $f(x) = \sqrt{x + 4}$ in terms of its parent function.
(114)

24. Solve and graph the inequality $3|8x + 2| < 12$.
(101)

25. **Multi-Step** The sum of the squares of two consecutive odd numbers is 74.
(104)
   a. Write expressions for two consecutive odd numbers.

   b. Write an equation to represent the problem.

   c. What is the possible solution(s)?

*26. If $\angle A = 81°$, find csc A, sec A, and cot A to the nearest ten-thousandth.
(117)

27. **Multi-Step** Anita figures that the value of her car, in thousands of dollars,
(108) can be approximated by $f(x) = 15\left(\frac{4}{5}\right)^x$, where x is the number of years
after the car's manufacture. Evaluate the function for $x = 0$, 1, and 2 and
then sketch the function.

28. **Justify** Explain why $\begin{matrix} y > 4 \\ y < 4 \end{matrix}$ has no solutions but $\begin{matrix} y \geq 4 \\ y \leq 4 \end{matrix}$ does.
(109)

29. What does a half-life mean? If a substance's half-life is 25 hours, how many
(Inv 11) half-lives are there in 150 hours?

30. (Tennis) A tennis instructor has a budget of $2000 to buy new rackets. He will
(78) receive 2 free rackets when he places his order. The number of rackets, y, that he
can get is given by $y = \frac{2000}{x} + 2$, where x is the price per racket.
   a. What is the horizontal asymptote of this rational function?

   b. What is the vertical asymptote?

   c. If the price per racket is $200, how many rackets will he receive?

Solving Problems Involving Combinations

Warm Up

1. Vocabulary A _____ (*permutation, factorial*) is an arrangement of
(111) outcomes in which the order does matter.

Simplify.

2. 7!
(111)

3. $\dfrac{6!}{4!}$
(111)

Simplify.

4. $_7P_3$
(111)

5. $_9P_4$
(111)

New Concepts

In Lesson 111, you learned about permutations, a selection of items where order does matter. In some cases, however, the final group of items is all that matters, not the order in which the items were selected. A **combination** is a grouping of items where order does not matter.

Example 1 **Comparing Combinations to Permutations**

A teacher puts 4 essay questions on a test. They are labeled A, B, C, and D. Students are required to choose 3 questions to answer.

a. How many permutations of the 3 questions are possible?

SOLUTION

First, find the number of permutations.

$$_4P_3 = \frac{4!}{(4-3)!} = \frac{4!}{1!}$$
$$= \frac{4 \cdot 3 \cdot 2 \cdot 1}{1} = 24.$$

There are 24 permutations of the 3 test questions.

Math Reasoning

Analyze Why are there more permutations than combinations?

b. How many combinations of the 3 questions are possible?

SOLUTION

As the order of the questions chosen does not matter, choosing ABC is the same as ACB, CAB, CBA, BCA, and BAC. So, to find the number of combinations, list the 24 permutations and then cross out the duplicate sets.

ABC	ABD	~~ACB~~	ACD	~~ADB~~	~~ADC~~
~~BAC~~	~~BAD~~	~~BCA~~	BCD	~~BDA~~	~~BDC~~
~~CAB~~	~~CAD~~	~~CBA~~	~~CBD~~	~~CDA~~	~~CDB~~
~~DAB~~	~~DAC~~	~~DBA~~	~~DBC~~	~~DCA~~	~~DCB~~

That leaves 4 combinations of the 3 test questions.

In Example 1, there are 6 times as many permutations as combinations. For each set of 3 letters, there are $3 \cdot 2 \cdot 1 = 6$ different ways to order the letters. To find the number of combinations, $_nC_r$, when selecting r out of n items, divide the number of permutations, $_nP_r$, by the number of ways to order r items, $r!$.

That is, $_nC_r = \dfrac{_nP_r}{\text{number of ways to order } r \text{ items}} = \dfrac{\frac{n!}{(n-r)!}}{r!} = \dfrac{n!}{r!(n-r)!}$.

Combination Formula
The number of combinations of n items taken r at a time is $$_nC_r = \dfrac{n!}{r!(n-r)!}.$$

Example 2 Finding the Number of Combinations

a. At a restaurant 2 side dishes may be chosen. There are a total of 6 side dish choices. How many combinations are there?

SOLUTION

$_nC_r = \dfrac{n!}{r!(n-r)!}$ Use the combination formula.

$_6C_2 = \dfrac{6!}{2!(6-2)!}$ Substitute $n = 6$ and $r = 2$.

$= \dfrac{6!}{2!4!}$ Simplify inside parentheses.

$= \dfrac{720}{2 \cdot 24} = 15$ Simplify.

There are 15 ways to choose 2 side dishes.

b. A company delivers fruit to its customers every month. There are 16 different types of fruit. Each customer can choose 12 types of fruit each year. How many combinations can each customer make?

SOLUTION

$_nC_r = \dfrac{n!}{r!(n-r)!}$ Use the combination formula.

$_{16}C_{12} = \dfrac{16!}{12!(16-12)!}$ Substitute 16 for n and 12 for r.

$= \dfrac{16!}{12!4!}$ Simplify inside parentheses.

$= \dfrac{16 \cdot 15 \cdot 14 \cdot 13 \cdot 12!}{12!4!}$ Rewrite 16! as $16 \cdot 15 \cdot 14 \cdot 13 \cdot 12!$.

$= \dfrac{16 \cdot 15 \cdot 14 \cdot 13}{4!}$ Cancel 12!.

$= 1820$ Simplify.

There are 1820 ways to choose 12 fruits.

Example 1   **Matching Function Families and Graphs**

a. Which of the following graphs represents an exponential function?

Graph A   Graph B   Graph C

SOLUTION

Graph B displays the shape of an exponential function.

b. Use the graph to identify the function family.

SOLUTION

This graph has the shape of the quadratic function. It is the graph of $f(x) = -x^2 + 3$.

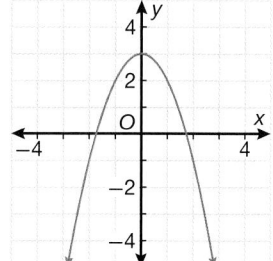

c. Use the graph to identify the function family.

SOLUTION

This graph has the shape of a linear function. It has a slope of 2 and a y-intercept of 1. It is the graph of $f(x) = 2x + 1$.

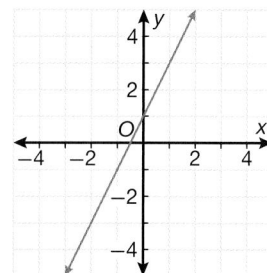

Example 2   **Matching Function Families and Tables**

Use each table of values to identify the function family.

a.

x	-3	-2	-1	0	1	2	3
$f(x)$	$\frac{1}{27}$	$\frac{1}{9}$	$\frac{1}{3}$	1	3	9	27

SOLUTION

Plot the points on a graph and connect them using a smooth curve. From the graph you can tell that the function belongs to the exponential function family. It is a graph of $f(x) = 3^x$. The values for $f(x)$ increase more steeply as x increases, so it shows exponential growth.

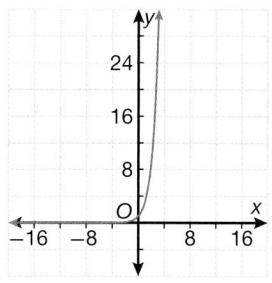

b.

x	-3	-2	-1	0	1	2	3
$f(x)$	8	3	0	-1	0	3	8

SOLUTION

Plot the points on a graph and connect them using a smooth curve.

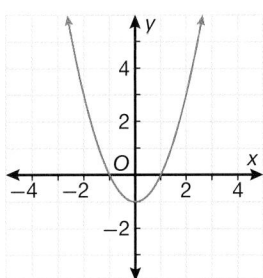

You can see that this function has a graph similar to the graph of $f(x) = x^2$, but it is translated down one unit. This function belongs to the quadratic function family. It is the graph of $f(x) = x^2 - 1$.

c. Identify the table of values that shows a linear function family.

Table 1

x	-3	-2	-1	0	1	2	3
$f(x)$	-9	-4	-1	0	-1	-4	-9

Table 2

x	-3	-2	-1	0	1	2	3
$f(x)$	$\frac{1}{125}$	$\frac{1}{25}$	$\frac{1}{5}$	1	5	25	125

Table 3

x	-3	-2	-1	0	1	2	3
$f(x)$	0	2	4	6	8	10	12

SOLUTION

For a function to be linear, it must have a constant rate of change. Determine which of these tables shows a constant rate of change of $f(x)$ as x increases by 1.

Table 1: In the first row, $f(-3) = -9$ and $f(-2) = -4$, which is a difference of 5. But the difference between $f(-2)$ and $f(-1)$ is only 3. This is not a constant rate of change, so the function is not linear.

Table 2: The difference between $f(1)$ and $f(2)$ is 20, but the difference between $f(2)$ and $f(3)$ is 100, so this function is also not linear.

Table 3: $f(-3) = 0$ and $f(-2) = 2$, which is a difference of 2. Each time x increases by 1, the value of $f(x)$ increases by 2. This is a constant rate of change.

Table 3 shows a linear function.

Caution

A constant rate of change does not have to be a positive number. In the function $f(x) = -3x$, the constant rate of change is -3. Each time x increases by 1, $f(x)$ decreases by 3.

Example 3 Identifying the Function Family from a Description

For each description, state whether the description best fits a linear, quadratic, or exponential function.

a. The rate of change is always the same. The graph is always decreasing.

SOLUTION

Because the rate of change is always the same, the function is linear.

b. The rate of change is not always the same. The graph is always increasing. The graph is a curve that gets steeper as the x-values increase.

SOLUTION

The rate of change is not always the same, so the function family is not linear. The graph is always increasing, so it is not quadratic.

The function is exponential.

c. The rate of change is not always the same. The graph changes direction at a minimum point at which $y = -1$.

SOLUTION

The rate of change is not constant, so the function family is not linear. It has a minimum point at which $y = -1$ where the graph changes direction, so it is quadratic.

d. The graph is always decreasing. The graph is a curve that gets less steep as the x-values increase.

SOLUTION

The graph is always decreasing, so it is not quadratic.

The graph is a curve that gets less steep as x increases, so it is exponential.

Math Reasoning

Justify The graph of a function crosses the x-axis twice. Could the function be linear? Explain.

Linear, quadratic, and exponential functions can be used to model real-world situations.

Linear models apply to situations with a constant rate of change. An example of a function with a positive rate of change is the distance traveled by a train that travels at a constant speed. An example of a function with a negative rate of change is the amount of water left in a bucket with a constant leak.

Quadratic models may apply in situations with a maximum or minimum value because the graph of a quadratic function changes direction at the vertex. For example, if a ball is thrown up in the air, its height at time t is modeled by a quadratic function.

Exponential models can be used for situations where values are always increasing or always decreasing, but not at a constant rate. Examples of exponential situations are population growth and radioactive decay.

Example 4 — Identifying an Appropriate Model

Identify the appropriate model for each of the following situations.

a. the height of a ball thrown upward from an initial height of 5 feet

SOLUTION

When a ball is thrown upward, it goes up for a short time and then changes direction and comes down again. Its height has a maximum value. Therefore, a quadratic function models this situation.

b. the cost of a tank of gas when gas costs $3.25 per gallon

SOLUTION

The cost of gas is a constant rate. For every additional gallon, the price of the tank of gas increases by $3.25. Therefore, a linear function models this situation.

c. the number of bacteria cells in a laboratory dish when each cell divides into two cells every day

SOLUTION

Imagine the first day there was only one cell in the dish. The next day, there would be 2 cells, and the following day, 4 cells. The number of cells doubles every day, so it is not a constant rate of change but an increasing rate of change. Therefore, an exponential function models this situation.

Math Reasoning

Formulate Write a function that could be used to find the cost of gas in Example 4b.

Lesson Practice

Identify the function family represented by each graph.
(Ex 1)

a. 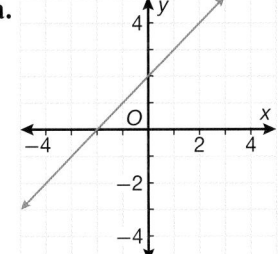   **b.** 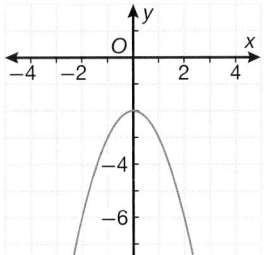   **c.**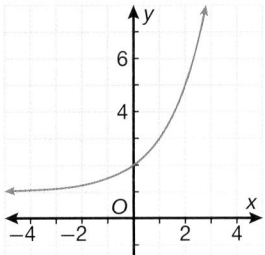

Use the table of values to identify the function family.
(Ex 2)

d.

x	−2	−1	0	1	2
$f(x)$	4	7	10	13	16

e.

x	−2	−1	0	1	2
$f(x)$	4	2	0	2	4

Tell whether the function family is linear, quadratic, or exponential.
(Ex 3)

f. The graph is always increasing with a constant rate.

g. The graph changes direction at a maximum of 3.

h. The graph is always increasing and it gets steeper as x increases.

Identify the appropriate model for each of the following situations.
(Ex 4)

    i. the height of an arrow that is shot upwards from the edge of a cliff

    j. the number of radioactive particles remaining in a sample when, at the end of each hour, the number of radioactive particles is half of what it was at the beginning of the hour

    k. the amount of money you can earn babysitting when you charge $5 per hour of babysitting

Practice   Distributed and Integrated

*1. **Error Analysis** Students were asked to write an equation that has a quadratic
(119) parent function. Which student is correct? Explain the error.

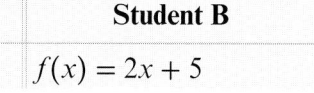

Student A	**Student B**
$f(x) = 2(x - 1)^2 - 4$	$f(x) = 2x + 5$

*2. Identify the function family.
(119)

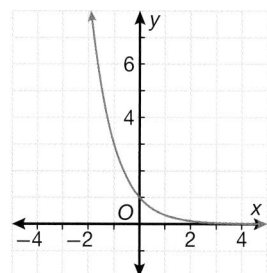

*3. Identify the function family.
(119)

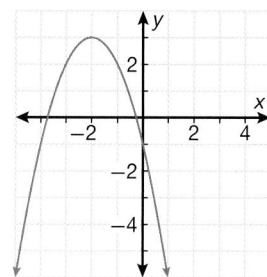

*4. **Write** How can a parent function be used to graph a family of functions?
(119)

*5. (**Interior Decorating**) A type of carpet sells for $12 per square foot. Installation is an
(119) additional $500. A function can be written to determine the price for installing carpet in a square room with floor x feet in length. Identify the function family and the parent function.

6. Error Analysis Two students find $_{18}C_5$. Which student is correct? Explain the error.
(118)

Student A	Student B
$_{18}C_5 = \dfrac{18!}{5!(18-5)!}$ $= 8568$	$_{18}C_5 = \dfrac{18!}{(18-5)!}$ $= 1{,}028{,}160$

*7. Multi-Step A restaurant charges \$16 for a large pizza plus \$1.50 per topping.
(119)
a. Which type of function best describes the cost of a pizza?

b. Write a function that describes the cost of a pizza with x toppings.

8. (Jewelry) A jewelry store sells necklaces for the cost of the chain plus the cost of the
(119) beads. Chains cost \$20 each, and beads cost \$7.50 each. To which function family does the equation that describes the cost of a necklace with x beads belong?

*9. Multiple Choice Which of the following describes the graph of $y = 5^x$?
(119)
A quadratic **B** linear **C** exponential **D** none of these

*10. Geometry A triangle has base b and height $b - 4$. If its area is written as a function,
(119) to which function family does the function belong?

11. Identify the function family to which $y = 2 - 1100x$ belongs.
(119)

*12. Write A fair coin is flipped many times in a row. The probability of all flips
(119) resulting in heads is given by $P(\text{all heads}) = \left(\frac{1}{2}\right)^x$, where x is the number of flips. What type of function is this?

13. Multi-Step A teacher randomly selects 4 helpers from her class of 22.
(118)
a. How many ways can 4 helpers be selected?

b. What is the probability that Shawn, Tonia, Torie, and Reid are all chosen?

*14. If $\angle A = 14°$, find $\sin A$, $\cos A$, and $\tan A$ to the nearest ten-thousandth.
(117)

15. Error Analysis Two students are finding the value of x in the figure. Which student
(117) is correct? Explain the error.

Student A	Student B
$\sin 63° = \dfrac{x}{21}$ $21 \cdot \sin 63° = x$ $18.71 \approx x$	$\cos 63° = \dfrac{x}{21}$ $21 \cdot \cos 63° = x$ $9.53 \approx x$

*16. (Aviation) An airplane begins making its descent at an
(117) angle of 11° with the horizontal. If the plane is at an altitude of 8000 feet and will remain at this angle throughout its descent, how far away is the plane from its landing point?

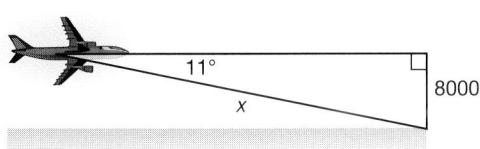

Example 2   Finding Geometric Probability with Circles

A target is made of two concentric circles. The outer circle has a radius of 12 inches. The inner circle has a radius of 4 inches. What is the probability that a dart will land in the inner circle?

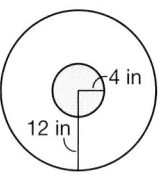

Hint

When finding the ratio of the areas of two circles, leave the areas in terms of π to make simplification easier.

SOLUTION

$$\frac{\text{favorable outcomes}}{\text{total outcomes}} = \frac{\text{shaded area}}{\text{entire area}}$$

$$= \frac{\pi(4)^2}{\pi(12)^2} \qquad \text{Use } A = \pi r^2 \text{ to find the areas.}$$

$$= \frac{16\pi}{144\pi} = \frac{1}{9} \qquad \text{Simplify.}$$

The probability that a dart will land in the inner circle is $\frac{1}{9}$.

Recall that the formula for the complement of an event is:

$$1 - P(A) = P(not\ A)$$

Example 3   Finding the Probability of the Complement

Math Language

The **complement** of an event is all the outcomes in the sample space that are not included in the event.

a. A town is represented by a circle with a diameter of 50 miles. There is a square park with side length 5 miles located within the town. What is the probability that a raindrop would land in the town, but not the park?

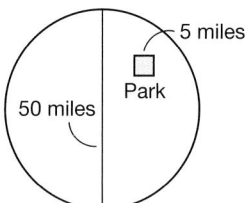

SOLUTION

Find the probability of the complement of the raindrop landing in the park.

$$P(\text{not landing in the park}) = 1 - P(\text{landing in the park})$$

$$= 1 - \frac{\text{area of park}}{\text{area of town}}$$

$$= 1 - \frac{5^2}{\pi(25)^2} \qquad \text{Use the area formulas.}$$

$$= 1 - \frac{25}{625\pi} \qquad \text{Simplify the powers.}$$

$$\approx 0.99 \qquad \text{Subtract.}$$

The probability of a raindrop landing in the town but not the park is 99%.

b. A carnival game has the player release an air-filled balloon towards a square wall. In the middle of the wall is a triangular target. What is the probability that the balloon will not hit the target?

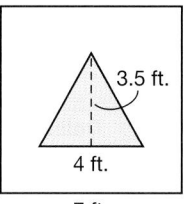

SOLUTION

Find the probability of the complement of the balloon hitting the target.

P(not hitting the target) $= 1 - P$(hitting the target)

$$= 1 - \frac{\text{area of the triangle}}{\text{area of square wall}}$$

$$= 1 - \frac{\frac{1}{2} \cdot 4 \cdot 3.5}{7^2} \qquad \text{Use the area formulas.}$$

$$= 1 - \frac{7}{49} \qquad \text{Multiply and square 7.}$$

$$= 1 - \frac{1}{7} \qquad \text{Simplify the fraction.}$$

$$= \frac{6}{7} \qquad \text{Subtract.}$$

The probability of not hitting the target is $\frac{6}{7}$.

Example **4** **Application: Zoning**

Math Reasoning

Analyze When calculating with the area of circles, why are some answers exact and some approximate?

A new school is being built. All students live within a 4-mile radius of the school, and homes are evenly distributed throughout the area. Planners think that students who live within 0.5 mile of the school would walk to school. Students who live between 0.5 and 2 miles would ride a bike, a city bus, or a private car to school. Students who live between 2 and 4 miles from the school would ride the school bus. What is the probability of a student not walking to school?

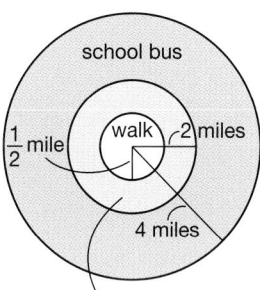

SOLUTION

Find the complement of a student walking to school.

P(not walking to school) $= 1 - P$(walking to school)

$$= 1 - \frac{\text{area of walking circle}}{\text{total area}}$$

$$= 1 - \frac{\pi (0.5)^2}{\pi (4)^2} \qquad \text{Use the area formulas.}$$

$$= 1 - \frac{0.25\pi}{16\pi} \qquad \text{Simplify the powers.}$$

$$= 1 - \frac{1}{64} \qquad \text{Simplify the fraction.}$$

$$= \frac{63}{64} \qquad \text{Subtract.}$$

The probability of not walking to school is $\frac{63}{64}$.

a. A rectangular swimming pool is 15 feet by 30 feet. A raft in the pool is 2 feet by 3 feet. A beach ball is thrown randomly into the pool. What is the probability that the ball hits the raft?
(Ex 1)

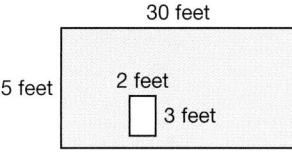

b. A child's crown is made by cutting the 6-inch center out of a 10-inch paper plate. The plate is then decorated by sprinkling it with glitter. What is the probability that a piece of glitter misses the crown?
(Ex 2)

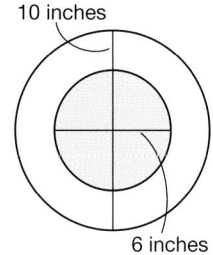

c. A round piece of cardboard with radius 4 inches is used to make a mask. A two-inch square hole is cut for a mouth piece. If a piece of popcorn is tossed at the mask, what is the probability that it will miss the mouth hole?
(Ex 3)

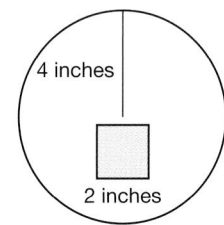

d. A rectangular yard is 10 feet by 15 feet. Tulips are planted in a triangular area that has a 5-foot base and a height of 6 feet. A bird lands in the yard. What is the probability that it does not land in the tulip garden?
(Ex 3)

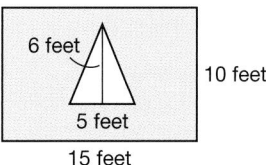

e. (**Puzzles**) A rug in the kindergarten class has various shapes on it. One student steps onto the rug. What is the probability that he is not standing on the square?
(Ex 4)

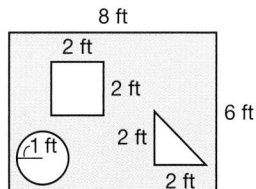

*1. Find the probability of landing in the shaded area.
(120)

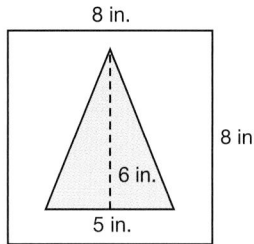

2. Write Explain what geometric probability is.
(120)

3. **Generalize** A system of equations consists of a quadratic and a linear equation. If
(112) the graphs of the two equations do not intersect, what can you conclude about the
solution to the system?

*4. **Verify** Show that the probability of landing in the shaded region is $\frac{1}{2}$.
(120)

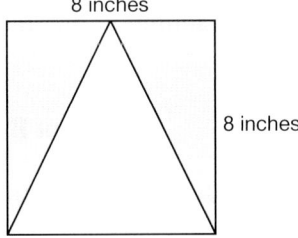

8 inches

8 inches

5. Find $_7C_2$
(118)

6. (**Manufacturing**) A number cube is made with side lengths of 5 centimeters.
(115) Use the function $V = s^3$ to find the volume of plastic that is contained in the
number cube.

*7. **Multiple Choice** A parachutist will land in a rectangular field with a circular landing
(120) area as her target. What is the probability that she will land on target?

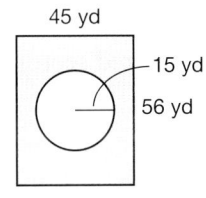

45 yd

15 yd

56 yd

A ≈ 0.09 **B** ≈ 0.28 **C** ≈ 0.72 **D** ≈ 0.92

8. (**Jewelry**) To make a friendship bracelet, 8 beads are used. How many different
(118) combinations of beads could be on the bracelet if there are 20 different beads?

*9. (**Puzzles**) A children's stacking puzzle teaches shapes. A child randomly points to the
(120) puzzle. What is the probability that the child's finger lands on the shaded part of
the square?

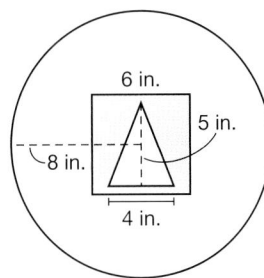

6 in.

5 in.

8 in.

4 in.

10. **Model** Draw right $\triangle ABC$ with right angle C so that $\sin A = \frac{3}{5}$ and $\cos A = \frac{4}{5}$.
(117)

11. What is the domain of $f(x) = 3\sqrt{x} - 5$?
(114)

12. Find the 4th term in the geometric series that has a common ratio of -1.1 and a
(105) first term of 7.

Investigating Matrices

Materials

• graph paper
• graphing calculator

The table shows the price of tickets sold at a local movie theater.

Type	Matinee	Regular
Child	$5	$7
Student	$6	$8
Adult	$9	$11

Use a matrix to organize data, such as the price of movie tickets. A **matrix** is a rectangular array of numbers in horizontal rows and vertical columns. Each number in a matrix is called an element. An **element** is any individual object or member belonging to a set.

Below is a matrix for the ticket prices.

$$\begin{bmatrix} 5 & 7 \\ 6 & 8 \\ 9 & 11 \end{bmatrix}$$

Notice that the entries in the table above correspond to the elements in the matrix.

(**Fundraiser**) The table below shows the number of items sold during the first day of a school fundraiser.

Items Sold on First Day

Item	Medium	Large
T-shirts	10	7
Hats	3	2
Sweatshirts	4	9

1. **Model** Use the data in the table to create a matrix that represents the situation.

2. Explain how to use the matrix to calculate the total number of sweatshirts sold during the first day of the fundraiser. How many sweatshirts were sold?

The dimensions of a matrix with m rows and n columns are $m \times n$. Each element has a specific position in the matrix that is relative to its row and column.

Complete the statements. Refer to the matrix of the number of items sold during the school fundraiser's first day.

3. The matrix has _____ rows and _____ columns.

4. The dimensions of the matrix are _____.

Online Connection
www.SaxonMathResources.com

5. The element in the third row, second column is _____.

6. Describe the dimensions of a matrix representing data about a school fundraiser with five types of items available in four different sizes.

Since matrices are a method of organizing information, sometimes they are added or subtracted to get new information. Matrices that have the same dimensions can be added subtracted.

The table shows the number of items sold during the second day of the fundraiser.

Items Sold on Second Day

Item	Medium	Large
T-shirts	8	3
Hats	1	5
Sweatshirts	4	7

7. **Generalize** Explain how to find the total number of large hats sold during the first two days of the fundraiser.

8. **Formulate** Explain how to use matrices to find the total number of large hats sold during the first two days of the fundraiser.

9. Use matrices to model the sum of the items sold during the first two days. Then add the matrices using a graphing calculator.

10. Find the difference between the two matrices. How many more medium hats were sold on the first day than on the second day?

Matrix addition also has a geometric application.

Exploration **Using Matrix Addition to Transform Geometric Figures**

11. Complete the following table by finding the coordinates of the vertices of $\triangle ABC$.

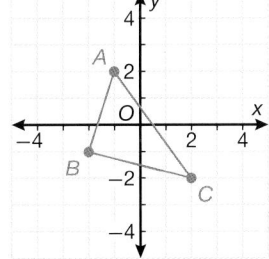

	Point A	Point B	Point C
x-coordinate	−1	−2	
y-coordinate		−1	−2

12. Use the data in the table to create matrix A.

13. Using a graphing calculator find the sum $A + B$, when $B = \begin{bmatrix} 3 & 3 & 3 \\ 2 & 2 & 2 \end{bmatrix}$.

14. Use the elements of $A + B$ as the coordinates of the vertices of $\triangle A'B'C'$. Plot the vertices of $\triangle A'B'C'$ to create a graph of the triangle.

15. **Write** Describe the relationship between $\triangle ABC$ and $\triangle A'B'C'$.

16. What matrix would translate $\triangle ABC$ one unit to the left and three units down?

17. What matrix was used to translate $\triangle ABC$ to $\triangle A'B'C'$ using matrix addition?

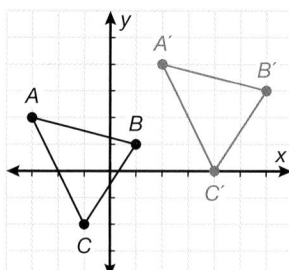

You can also transform a geometric figure through scalar multiplication. **Scalar multiplication** multiplies a matrix A by a scalar c. To find the resulting matrix cA, multiply each element of A by c.

Exploration **Using Scalar Multiplication to Transform Geometric Figures**

18. Predict Use matrix A from the previous Exploration. What would be the effect of multiplying each element in matrix A by 2?

19. Find the matrix $2A$ using a graphing calculator.

20. Use the elements of $2A$ as the coordinates of the vertices of $\triangle A''B''C''$. Plot the vertices of $\triangle A''B''C''$ to create a graph of the triangle.

21. Write Describe the relationship between $\triangle ABC$ and $\triangle A''B''C''$.

22. What matrix would create a triangle one-fourth the size of $\triangle ABC$?

23. Describe the relationship between $\triangle ABC$ and $\triangle A'B'C'$.

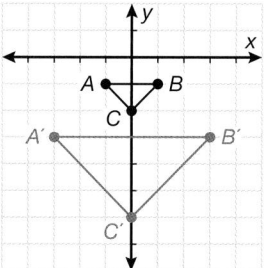

The first table shows how much money Abram and two friends earned doing chores last summer. The second table shows how much money they made this summer.

Money Earned Last Summer

	Mowing Lawns	Washing Cars	Babysitting
Abram	$15	$55	$0
Paul	$75	$10	$30
Leila	$20	$40	$35

Money Earned This Summer

	Mowing Lawns	Washing Cars	Babysitting
Abram	$25	$60	$10
Paul	$85	$20	$35
Leila	$30	$60	$40

a. How can matrices be used to calculate how much more money each person made during the second summer?

b. Use a matrix operation to display the additional money each person made during the second summer. How much more money did Paul make during the second summer than the first?

c. Use scalar multiplication to find the vertices of a quadrilateral whose area is one-fourth of the quadrilateral shown.

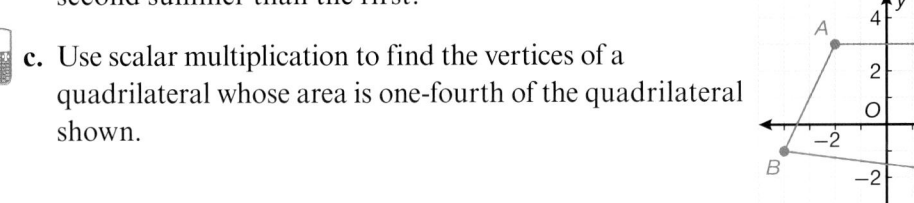

Graphing and Solving Nonlinear Inequalities

New Concepts

A quadratic inequality in two variables can be written in four different forms

$$y < ax^2 + bx + c \qquad y \le ax^2 + bx + c$$
$$y > ax^2 + bx + c \qquad y \ge ax^2 + bx + c$$

Using a procedure similar to graphing linear equalities a quadratic inequality can be graphed.

Example 1 Graphing a Quadratic inequality

a. Graph $y > x^2 + 4x - 5$.

SOLUTION

Step 1: Graph $y = x^2 + 4x - 5$ as a boundary. Use a dashed curve because the inequality symbol is $>$.

Step 2: Shade inside the parabola since the solution consists of y-values greater than the y-values on the parabola for the corresponding x-values.

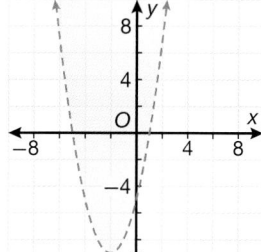

Check Test a point in the solution region. Substitute $(1, 3)$ into the inequality

$$y > x^2 + 4x - 5$$
$$3 \overset{?}{>} (1)^2 + 4(1) - 5$$
$$3 \overset{?}{>} 1 + 4 - 5$$
$$3 > 0 \quad \checkmark$$

b. Graph $y \le x^2 + 2x - 8$.

SOLUTION

Step 1: Graph $y \le x^2 + 2x - 8$ as a boundary. Use a solid curve because the inequality symbol is $\le$.

Step 2: Shade below the parabola since the solution consists of y-values less than the y-values on the parabola for the corresponding x-values.

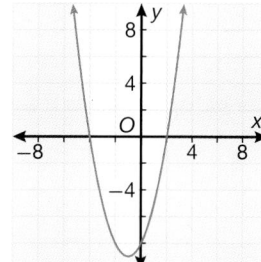

Check To verify the solution region test a point. Substitute $(3, -4)$ into the inequality.

$$y \le x^2 + 2x - 8$$
$$-4 \overset{?}{\le} (3)^2 + 2(3) - 8$$
$$-4 \overset{?}{\le} 9 + 6 - 8$$
$$-4 \le 7 \quad \checkmark$$

A quadratic inequality in one variable can be written in four different forms

$$ax^2 + bx + c < 0 \qquad ax^2 + bx + c \leq 0$$
$$ax^2 + bx + c > 0 \qquad ax^2 + bx + c \geq 0$$

Quadratic inequalities can be solved using tables, graphs, or algebraic methods.

Example 2   Solving with a Table

Solve $x^2 - 2x \leq 3$ using a table.

SOLUTION

Step 1: Write the inequality as $x^2 - 2x - 3 \leq 0$.

Step 2: Make a table of values.

x	-5	-4	-3	-2	-1	0	1	2	3	4	5
$x^2 - 2x - 3$	32	21	12	5	0	-3	-4	-3	0	5	12

The inequality $x^2 - 2x - 3 \leq 0$ is true for values of x between -1 and 3 inclusively. The solution of the inequality is $-1 \leq x \leq 3$.

Example 3   Solving with a Graphing Calculator Table

Solve $x^2 - x - 4 \leq 2$ using a graphing calculator.

SOLUTION

Step 1: Use a graphing calculator to graph each side of the inequality. Set **Y1** equal to $x^2 - x - 4$ and set **Y2** equal to 2.

Step 2: View the table comparing the two equations.

Step 3: Identify the values of x where **Y1** $= x^2 - x - 4$ are less than or equal to the values of **Y2** $= 2$.

The solution set is $-2 \leq x \leq 3$.

Example 4   **Solving with a Graphing Calculator Graph**

Solve $x^2 + 2x - 6 < 2$ using a graphing calculator.

SOLUTION

Step 1: Use a graphing calculator to graph each side of the inequality. Set **Y1** equal to $x^2 + 2x - 6$ and set **Y2** equal to 2.

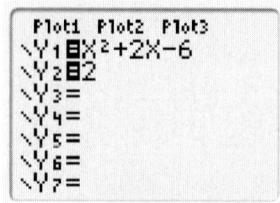

Step 2: Calculate the points of intersection.

Step 3: Identify the values of x where $\mathbf{Y1} \leq \mathbf{Y2}$.

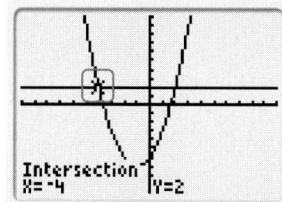 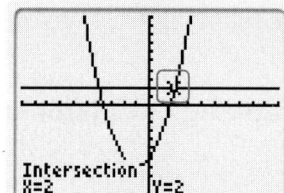

The solution set is $-4 < x < 2$.

Lesson Practice

   a. Graph $y > x^2 - 6x + 8$.
(Ex 1)

   b. Graph $y \leq x^2 - 4x - 5$.
(Ex 1)

   c. Solve $x^2 - 3x \leq 4$ using a table.
(Ex 2)

   d. Solve $x^2 - 5x + 10 \leq 4$ using a graphing calculator.
(Ex 3)

   e. Solve $x^2 - 6x - 5 < 2$ using a graphing calculator.
(Ex 4)

Graphing Piecewise and Step Functions

New Concepts

When a function has a different rule for different pieces of its domain, it is called a **piecewise function.** This kind of function is a combination of two or more functions. It assigns a different value to each domain interval. A piecewise function that is constant for each part of the domain is called a **step function.**

Example 1 Evaluating a Step Function

Evaluate the function for $x = -4$, $x = -2$, and $x = 6$.

$$f(x) = \begin{cases} 10 \text{ if } x \leq -2 \\ 8 \text{ if } x > -2 \end{cases}$$

SOLUTION

When $x = -4$, then $f(-4) = 10$ because $-4 \leq -2$.

When $x = -2$, then $f(-2) = 10$ because $-2 \leq -2$.

When $x = 6$, then $f(6) = 8$ because $6 > -2$.

Example 2 Evaluating a Piecewise Function

Evaluate the function for $x = -4$, $x = -2$, and $x = 6$.

$$f(x) = \begin{cases} 2x - 1 & \text{if } x < 6 \\ 8x^2 & \text{if } x \geq 6 \end{cases}$$

SOLUTION

When $x = -4$, then $x < 6$. Use the piece of the function, $f(x) = 2x - 1$.

$$\begin{aligned} f(-4) &= 2(-4) - 1 && \text{Substitute } -4 \text{ for } x \text{ into } f(x). \\ &= -8 - 1 && \text{Multiply 2 and } -4. \\ &= -9 && \text{Simplify.} \end{aligned}$$

When $x = -2$, then $x < 6$. Use the piece of the function, $f(x) = 2x - 1$.

$$\begin{aligned} f(-2) &= 2(-2) - 1 && \text{Substitute } -2 \text{ for } x \text{ into } f(x). \\ &= -4 - 1 && \text{Multiply 2 and } -2. \\ &= -5 && \text{Simplify.} \end{aligned}$$

When $x = 6$, then $x \geq 6$. Use the piece of the function, $f(x) = 8x^2$.

$$\begin{aligned} f(6) &= 8 \cdot 6^2 && \text{Substitute 6 for } x \text{ into } f(x). \\ &= 8 \cdot 36 && \text{Simplify the exponent.} \\ &= 288 && \text{Multiply.} \end{aligned}$$

Example 3 Graphing a Step Function

Graph the function.

$$f(x) = \begin{cases} -1 & \text{if } x \le 4 \\ 3 & \text{if } x > 4 \end{cases}$$

SOLUTION

Graphing a step function is a lot like graphing inequalities. You will use open circles to indicate > or < and closed circles to show ≤ or ≥.

Begin by considering the function at $x = 4$. This is where the "steps" separate. Because $f(4) = -1$, graph the point $(4, -1)$ with a closed circle. $f(x) = -1$ for $x \le 4$. Draw a ray from the point extending to the left, along the line $y = -1$. This is one horizontal step.

Next consider the other piece, $f(x) = 3$ for $x > 4$.

At $(4, 3)$, draw an open circle because $f(4) \neq 3$. Draw a ray going to the right. This is another horizontal step.

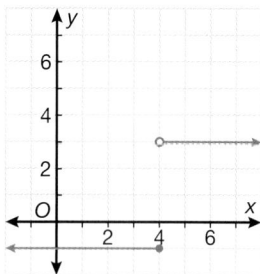

Example 4 Graphing a Piecewise Function

Graph the function.

$$f(x) = \begin{cases} -2x + 3 & \text{if } x \le -1 \\ -5x & \text{if } -1 < x \le 2 \\ x^2 - 10 & \text{if } x > 2 \end{cases}$$

SOLUTION

The function is made of two linear pieces and a quadratic piece with a domain divided at $x = -1$ and $x = 2$. Find the value of the two surrounding functions for these values to see if the graph is continuous.

Use a table to find points and graph each piece. The shaded regions are coordinates that will not be included in the graph of $f(x)$.

x	$f(x) = -2x + 3$	$f(x) = -5x$	$f(x) = x^2 - 10$
-3	9		
-2	7		
-1	5	5	
0		0	
1		-5	
2		-10	-6
3			-1
4			6
5			15

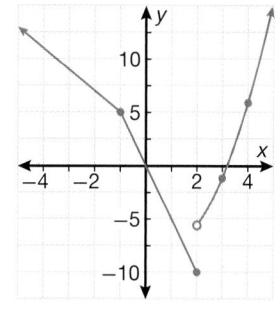

Graph each value. There will be an open circle at $(2, -6)$ and a closed circle at $(2, -10)$ to clearly show the value of the function at $x = 2$. No open circle is needed at $x = -1$ because the function is connected at that point by the two pieces of the function.

Example 5 | Application: Ticket Prices

At an amusement park, children under three years of age are free. Ages 3 to 12 pay \$20. Everyone older than 12 pays \$30. Write the function that represents this information, and graph the function.

SOLUTION

First, identify the intervals for the independent variables. Let x represent age in years.

under three $\qquad x < 3$

ages 3 to 12 $\qquad 3 \leq x \leq 12$

older than 12 $\qquad x > 12$

Then, write the function rule. $f(x)$ is the price of the ticket.

$$f(x) = \begin{cases} 0 & \text{if } x < 3 \\ 20 & \text{if } 3 \leq x \leq 12 \\ 30 & \text{if } x > 12 \end{cases}$$

Graph the function.

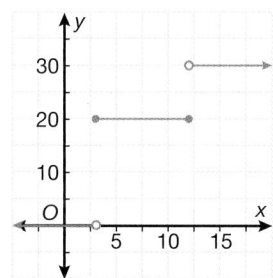

Lesson Practice

Evaluate each step function for the values given.

(Ex 1)

a. $f(x) = \begin{cases} -2 & \text{if } x \leq 1 \\ 4 & \text{if } x > 1 \end{cases}$ for $x = -3$ and $x = 10$.

b. $f(x) = \begin{cases} 6 & \text{if } x < 9 \\ -11 & \text{if } x \geq 9 \end{cases}$ for $x = 8$ and $x = 9$.

Evaluate each piecewise function for the values given.

(Ex 2)

c. $f(x) = \begin{cases} 2x^3 & \text{if } x < 0 \\ 10 - 3x & \text{if } x \geq 0 \end{cases}$ for $x = 4$ and $x = -1$.

d. $f(x) = \begin{cases} 3x & \text{if } x \leq -1 \\ x - 5 & \text{if } x > -1 \end{cases}$ for $x = -5$ and $x = 1$.

Graph each step function.

(Ex 3)

e. $f(x) = \begin{cases} 7 & \text{if } x < 5 \\ 2 & \text{if } x \geq 5 \end{cases}$

f. $f(x) = \begin{cases} 3 & \text{if } x < -3 \\ 0 & \text{if } -3 \leq x < 3 \\ -3 & \text{if } x \geq 3 \end{cases}$

Graph each piecewise function.

(Ex 4)

g. $f(x) = \begin{cases} 4x & \text{if } x < -2 \\ 2x + 2 & \text{if } x \geq -2 \end{cases}$

h. $f(x) = \begin{cases} 3x & \text{if } x \leq 1 \\ 6x - 3 & \text{if } 1 < x < 2 \\ -x^2 & \text{if } x \geq 2 \end{cases}$

i. (Ex 5) (Allowance) A child less than 5 years old does not get an allowance. Starting at 5 years old, he gets 3 times his age per month. At 10 years, the rate increases to 4 times his age per month. Write the function that represents this information, and graph the function.

j. (Ex 5) (Rides) At an amusement park, there are 15 rides that have no height requirement. If a person is at least 4 feet tall, there are a total of 20 available rides. To be granted access to all 24 rides in the park, a person must be at least 4.5 feet tall. Write a function that represents the number of available rides based on a person's height. Sketch a graph of that function.

Understanding Vectors

New Concepts

To say that you biked 3 miles tells how far you went, but to say that you biked 3 miles north tells how far you went and in what direction. A **vector** is a quantity with both magnitude (size) and direction. "3 miles north" can be represented by a vector.

A vector is represented by a line segment with a half-arrow that indicates direction, not a continuation of the segment infinitely as in a ray. This vector can be named $\overrightarrow{MN}$ or $\vec{v}$.

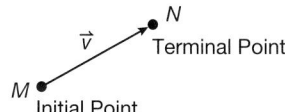

N
Terminal Point
$\vec{v}$
M
Initial Point

Component form is also used to name a vector. It identifies the horizontal change (x) and vertical change (y) from the initial point to the terminal point in the form, $\langle x, y \rangle$. The horizontal change is positive to the right and negative to the left. The vertical change is positive up and negative down.

Example 1 Writing Vectors in Component Form

Write each vector in component form.

a. $\overrightarrow{AB}$

SOLUTION

The horizontal change from A to B is 5.

The vertical change from A to B is -2.

The component form of $\overrightarrow{AB}$ is $\langle 5, -2 \rangle$.

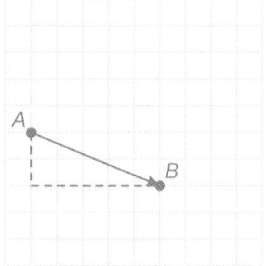

b. $\overrightarrow{RS}$ with $R(-1, 4)$ and $S(6, 3)$.

SOLUTION

$\overrightarrow{RS} = \langle x_2 - x_1, y_2 - y_1 \rangle$ Horizontal change is $x_2 - x_1$ and vertical change is $y_2 - y_1$.

$\overrightarrow{RS} = \langle 6 - (-1), 3 - 4 \rangle$ Substitute the coordinates of the given points. Subtract the initial point's coordinates from the terminal point's coordinates.

$\overrightarrow{RS} = \langle 7, -1 \rangle$ Simplify.

The length of the vector is called its magnitude. It is written $\left| \overrightarrow{EF} \right|$ or $|\vec{v}|$. Derived from the distance formula, the formula for the length of a vector is

$$\left| \langle a, b \rangle \right| = \sqrt{a^2 + b^2}.$$

Finding the Magnitude of a Vector

Find the magnitude of the vector to the nearest tenth.

$\langle -3, 5 \rangle$

SOLUTION

$$\left| \langle a, b \rangle \right| = \sqrt{a^2 + b^2}$$

$$\left| \langle -3, 5 \rangle \right| = \sqrt{(-3)^2 + 5^2}$$

$$= \sqrt{9 + 25}$$

$$= \sqrt{34}$$

$$\approx 5.8$$

The direction of a vector is the angle formed by it and a horizontal line. Begin at the positive x-axis and measure counterclockwise to the vector. Then, use inverse trigonometric functions to find the angle.

Example **3** **Finding the Direction of a Vector**

Find the direction of the vector to the nearest degree.

A boat's velocity is given by the vector $\langle 4, 8 \rangle$.

SOLUTION

First, draw the vector on a coordinate plane. Use the origin as the initial point.

The horizontal change and the vertical change make right triangle FGH. $\angle G$ is the angle formed by the vector and the x-axis.

$\tan G = \dfrac{8}{4}$.

So $m\angle G = \tan^{-1}\left(\dfrac{8}{4}\right) \approx 63°$.

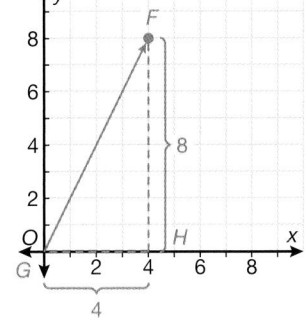

Equal vectors are two vectors that have the same magnitude and direction. They do not have to have the same initial and terminal points.

Parallel vectors may have different magnitudes, but have the same or opposite direction. Equal vectors are always parallel vectors.

Example **4** **Identifying Equal and Parallel Vectors**

a. Identify equal vectors.

SOLUTION

Equal vectors have the same magnitude and direction.

$\overrightarrow{AB} = \overrightarrow{GH}$

b. Identify parallel vectors.

SOLUTION

Parallel vectors have the same or opposite directions.

$AB \| GH$ and $CD \| EF$

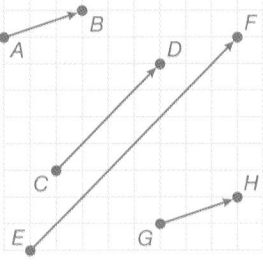

Write each vector in component form.
(Ex 1)

a. Write the vector in component form.

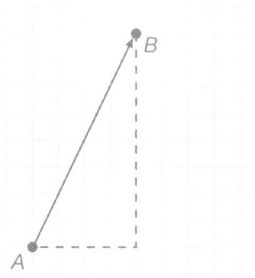

b. Write the vector in component form.

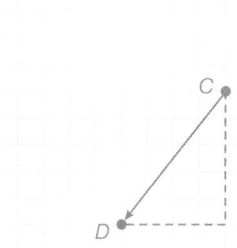

Write each vector in component form.
(Ex 1)

c. $\overrightarrow{PQ}$ with $P(2, -6)$ and $Q(1, -1)$.

d. $\overrightarrow{JK}$ with $J(3, 7)$ and $K(8, -2)$.

Find the magnitude of each vector to the nearest tenth.

e. $\langle 2, -9 \rangle$ f. $\langle 6, 12 \rangle$

g. $\boxed{\textbf{Water Current}}$ The river's current is given by the vector $\langle 3, 1 \rangle$. Find the
(Ex 3) direction of the vector to the nearest degree.

i. Identify the equal vectors.   j. Identify the parallel vectors.
(Ex 4)   *(Ex 4)*

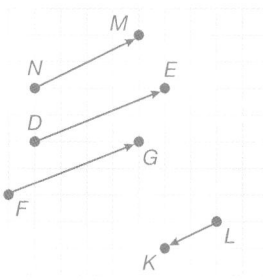

Using Variation and Standard Deviation to Analyze Data

New Concepts

$$\{1, 2, 3, 4, 5, 6, 7, 8, 9\}$$

The mean of the data set is 5. **Standard deviation** measures how the data is spread from the mean. It is a measure of variation.

The **variance,** represented by the symbol σ^2, is the average of the squared differences from the mean. To calculate the variance.

- Find the mean of the data.
- Subtract each value from the mean and square the result.
- Find the average of the squared results.

The standard deviation, represented by the symbol σ, is the square root of the variance.

Example 1 Finding the Standard Deviation

Ten students are asked how many CDs they own. Their responses are recorded in the data set.

$$\{10, 15, 13, 20, 8, 11, 10, 9, 14, 16\}$$

Find the standard deviation of the data.

SOLUTION

First, find the mean of the data by adding the data and dividing by 10.

$$\frac{10 + 15 + 13 + 20 + 8 + 11 + 10 + 9 + 14 + 16}{10} = \frac{126}{10} = 12.6$$

Next, subtract each value in the data set from the mean and square the result.

Value (x)	10	15	13	20	8	11	10	9	14	16
Difference ($12.6 - x$)	2.6	−2.4	−0.4	−7.4	4.6	1.6	2.6	3.6	−1.4	−3.4
Difference Squared $(12.6 - x)^2$	6.76	5.76	0.16	54.76	21.16	2.56	6.76	12.96	1.96	11.56

Now, find the average of the differences squared.

$$\frac{6.76 + 5.76 + 0.16 + 54.76 + 21.16 + 2.56 + 6.76 + 12.96 + 1.96 + 11.56}{10}$$

$$= \frac{124.4}{10} = 12.44.$$

Finally, take the square root to get the standard deviation. $\sqrt{12.44} \approx 3.53$

The standard deviation describes the spread of the data. When the standard deviation is low, the data tends to be close to the measure of central tendency, or mean. When the standard deviation is high, the data is more spread out.

An outlier is a number that is much greater or much less than the other values in the data set. Outliers have a great impact on the mean and standard deviation and can cause them to misrepresent the data set. One way to determine whether a value is an outlier is to see if it is more than 3 standard deviations from the mean.

Example 2 **Examining Outliers**

The population of southern states is shown. Find the mean and standard deviation of the data. Identify any outliers, and if one is found, explain how it affects the mean.

State	TX	OK	AK	LA	MS	AL	FL	GA	NC	SC	VA	WV	MD	DE	KY	TN
Population in millions	22.9	3.5	2.8	4.5	2.9	4.6	17.8	9.1	8.7	4.2	7.6	1.8	5.6	0.8	4.1	6.0

SOLUTION

First, find the mean of the state populations.

$$\frac{22.9 + 3.5 + 2.8 + 4.5 + 2.9 + 4.6 + 17.8 + 9.1 + 8.7 + 4.2 + 7.6 + 1.8 + 5.6 + 0.8 + 4.1 + 6.0}{16}$$

$$\approx 6.7$$

Next, subtract each value in the data set from the mean and square the result.

Now, find the average of the difference squared, $\frac{518.89}{16} \approx 32.43$, and take the square root to get the standard deviation.

$$\sqrt{32.43} \approx 5.69$$

An outlier would be outside the 3 standard deviations from the mean, $6.7 \pm 3(5.69)$.

Negative population would not make sense, so check to see if any state has a greater population than $6.7 + 3(5.69) = 23.77$ million.

There are no outliers in this data because there are no populations larger than 23.77 million. All data is within 3 standard deviations of the mean.

Population x	Difference $(6.7 - x)$	Difference Squared $(6.7 - x)^2$
22.9	−16.2	262.44
3.5	3.2	10.24
2.8	3.9	15.21
4.5	2.2	4.84
2.9	3.8	14.44
4.6	2.1	4.41
17.8	−11.1	123.21
9.1	−2.4	5.76
8.7	−2	4
4.2	2.5	6.25
7.6	−0.9	0.81
1.8	4.9	24.01
5.6	1.1	1.21
0.8	5.9	34.81
4.1	2.6	6.76
6.0	0.7	0.49

Some data is said to be normally distributed. The shape of the data looks like a bell, so it is often called a "bell-shaped curve." The mean is at the center.

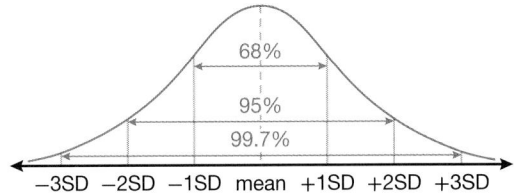

As the graph indicates, 68% of the data falls within one standard deviation of the mean. 95% of the data falls within two standard deviations of the mean, and 99.7% of the data falls within three standard deviations of the mean.

Example 3   Using the Normal Distribution

The ages of people at a park are normally distributed. The mean is 18 years and the standard deviation is 6 years. Between what two ages do 95% of the ages fall?

SOULTION

Because it is a normal distribution, 95% of the data falls within 2 standard deviations of the mean.

$$18 \pm 2(6) = 18 \pm 12$$

95% of the ages fall between 6 and 30.

Lesson Practice

Find the standard deviation of the data.

a. *(Ex 1)* An ATM machine records the values of the withdrawals made in one day.
$$\{20, 100, 20, 200, 20, 20, 100, 20, 80, 20, 20, 40, 100, 40, 100\}$$

b. A group of students is asked how many movies they watched in the last month. Their responses are recorded in the data set.
$$\{4, 10, 6, 8, 4, 5, 30, 4, 2, 3, 1\}$$

Find the mean and standard deviation of the data. Identify any outliers, and if one is found, explain how it affects the mean.

c. *(Ex 2)* Twelve students are asked how many books they read last year. Their responses are recorded in the data set.
$$\{12, 15, 30, 14, 13, 9, 10, 10, 11, 12, 14, 8\}$$

d. *(Ex 1)* A teacher records the scores on a test.
$$\{90, 95, 90, 85, 80, 80, 90, 40, 95, 90, 85, 90, 95, 80, 100\}$$

e. *(Ex 3)* (Test Results) The results on a test are normally distributed with a mean of 85 and a standard deviation of 5. Between what two scores are 68% of the scores?

f. *(Ex 3)* (Salaries) The salaries of educators are normally distributed with a mean of $35,000 and a standard deviation of $10,000. Between what two scores are 99.7% of the salaries?

Evaluating Expressions with Technology

New Concepts

A graphing calculator can help you evaluate expressions for several values of the variable.

Example 1 **Using a Graphing Calculator to Evaluate Expressions**

(a.) Use a graphing calculator to evaluate $3x^2 + 2x - 1$ for $x = 50, 150, 250, 350$ and 450.

SOLUTION

Press [Y=].

Enter $3x^2 + 2x - 1$ for Y_1.

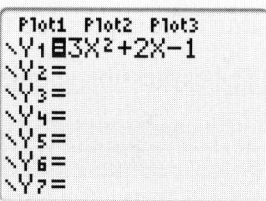

Press [2nd] [WINDOW] (TBLSET) to set the table values.

Enter the first value of x, 50, for **TblStart.**

For Δ**Tbl**, enter the difference in the x-values, 100.

Press [2nd] [GRAPH] (TABLE).

In the first column, you will see the values of x.

The second column shows the value of the expression for each value of x.

(b.) Use the table to find the value of the expression when $x = 550$.

SOLUTION

Find 550 in the first column, and look across from it. The value is 908,599.

(c.) Use the table to find the value of x if the expression is equal to 368,199.

SOLUTION

Find 368,199 in the second column. It is next to $x = 350$.

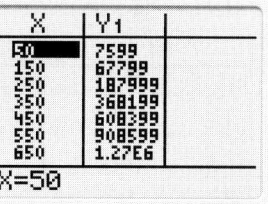

Fraction Operations

Skills Bank Lesson 3

To add or subtract fractions with unlike denominators, first find a common denominator.

Example 1 Adding and Subtracting Fractions

a. Add $\frac{5}{6}$ and $\frac{3}{8}$.

SOLUTION

Method 1: Multiply to find a common denominator.

$6 \cdot 8 = 48$

$\frac{5}{6}\left(\frac{8}{8}\right) + \frac{3}{8}\left(\frac{6}{6}\right)$ Multiply by fractions equal to 1.

$= \frac{40}{48} + \frac{18}{48}$ Add.

$= \frac{58}{48}$ Simplify.

$= \frac{29}{24}$ or $1\frac{5}{24}$

Method 2: Find the lowest common denominator (LCD).

Multiples of 6: 6, 12, 18, 24, …

Multiples of 8: 8, 16, 24, …

The LCD is 24.

$\frac{5}{6}\left(\frac{4}{4}\right) + \frac{3}{8}\left(\frac{3}{3}\right)$ Multiply by fractions equal to 1.

$= \frac{20}{24} + \frac{9}{24}$ Add.

$= \frac{29}{24}$ or $1\frac{5}{24}$

b. Subtract $\frac{1}{2}$ from $\frac{7}{8}$.

SOLUTION

$\frac{7}{8} - \frac{1}{2}\left(\frac{4}{4}\right)$ Write equivalent fractions using a denominator of 8.

$= \frac{7}{8} - \frac{4}{8} = \frac{3}{8}$

Example 2 Multiplying and Dividing Fractions

a. Multiply $\frac{2}{3} \cdot \frac{5}{6}$.

SOLUTION

Multiply the numerators and denominators. Then simplify if possible.

$\frac{2}{3} \cdot \frac{5}{6} = \frac{10}{18}$

$= \frac{5}{9}$

b. Divide $\frac{5}{4} \div \frac{3}{5}$.

SOLUTION

Write the reciprocal of $\frac{3}{5}$ and then multiply.

$\frac{5}{4} \cdot \frac{5}{3} = \frac{25}{12}$ Multiply by $\frac{5}{3}$.

$= \frac{25}{12}$ or $2\frac{1}{12}$

Skills Bank Practice

Add, subtract, multiply, or divide. Simplify if possible.

a. $\frac{7}{12} + \frac{3}{8}$ **b.** $\frac{9}{10} - \frac{4}{5}$ **c.** $\frac{5}{9} \cdot \frac{3}{4}$ **d.** $\frac{2}{16} \div \frac{9}{8}$ **e.** $\frac{5}{8} - \frac{5}{16}$ **f.** $\frac{7}{10} + \frac{8}{15}$

Divisibility

Skills Bank Lesson 4

A number is **divisible** by another number if the quotient is a whole number without a remainder.

Divisibility Rules
A number is divisible by …
2 if its last digit is even (0, 2, 4, 6, or 8).
3 if the sum of its digits is divisible by 3.
4 if its last two digits are divisible by 4.
5 if its last digit is 0 or 5.
6 if it is divisible by both 2 and 3.
9 if the sum of its digits is divisible by 9.
10 if its last digit is 0.

Example 1 Determining the Divisibility of Numbers

a. Determine whether 24 is divisible by 2, 3, 4, 5, and 6.

SOLUTION

2	The last digit is even.	24	divisible
3	The sum of the digits is divisible by 3.	$2 + 4 = 6$	divisible
4	The last two digits are divisible by 4.	24	divisible
5	The last digit is not 0 or 5.	24	not divisible
6	The number is divisible by both 2 and 3.		divisible

24 is divisible by 2, 3, 4, and 6.

b. Determine whether both the numerator and denominator in the fraction $\frac{16}{60}$ are divisible by 2, 3, 4, and 5.

SOLUTION

2	The last digit is even.	16	60	both divisible
3	The sum of the digits in 16 is not divisible by 3.	$1 + 6 = 7$	$6 + 0 = 6$	not both divisible
4	The last two digits are divisible by 4.	16	60	both divisible
5	The last digit in 16 is not 0 or 5.	16	60	not both divisible

Both the numerator and denominator in $\frac{16}{60}$ are divisible by 2 and 4.

Skills Bank Practice

Determine whether each number is divisible by 2, 3, 4, 5, 6, 9, and 10.

a. 90   **b.** 830   **c.** 1024

d. Determine whether both the numerator and denominator in the fraction $\frac{12}{54}$ are divisible by 2, 3, 4, 5, and 6.

Equivalent Decimals, Fractions, and Percents

Skills Bank Lesson 5

Numbers can be written as decimals, fractions, and percents. The table shows common fractions and their equivalent decimals and percents.

Fraction	Decimal	Percent
$\frac{1}{4}$	0.25	25%
$\frac{1}{2}$	0.5	50%
$\frac{3}{4}$	0.75	75%
$\frac{1}{5}$	0.2	20%
$\frac{1}{8}$	0.125	12.5%

Example 1 — Writing Fractions As Decimals and Percents

Find the equivalent decimal and percent for each fraction.

a. $\frac{7}{10}$

SOLUTION

$$10)\overline{7.0} = 0.7$$

Find the equivalent decimal. Divide the numerator by the denominator.

$0.70 = 70\%$

Find the equivalent percent. Move the decimal two places to the right.

$\frac{7}{10}$ is equivalent to 0.7 and 70%.

b. $\frac{2}{9}$

SOLUTION

$2 \div 9 = 0.\overline{2}$

Divide the numerator by the denominator.

$0.\overline{2} = 22.\overline{2}\%$

Move the decimal two places to the right.

$\frac{2}{9}$ is equivalent to $0.\overline{2}$ and $22.\overline{2}\%$.

Skills Bank Practice

Write the equivalent decimal and percent for each fraction.

a. $\frac{3}{5}$

b. $\frac{4}{10}$

c. $\frac{3}{8}$

d. $\frac{5}{11}$

e. $\frac{7}{9}$

f. $\frac{3}{4}$

Repeating Decimals and Equivalent Fractions

A **terminating decimal,** such as 0.75, has a finite number of decimal places.

A **repeating decimal,** such as 0.333… and 0.353535…, has one or more digits after the decimal point repeating indefinitely. A repeating decimal can be written with three dots or a bar over the digit or digits that repeat, such as $0.\overline{3}$ and $0.\overline{35}$.

Example 1 Writing an Equivalent Fraction for a Terminating Decimal

Write each decimal as a fraction in simplest form.

a. 0.35

SOLUTION

$0.35 = \dfrac{35}{100}$ The decimal is in the hundredths place, so use 100 as the denominator.

$\dfrac{35}{100} = \dfrac{7}{20}$ Simplify.

b. 1.9

SOLUTION

$1.9 = 1\dfrac{9}{10}$ The decimal is in the tenths place, so use 10 as the denominator.

Example 2 Writing an Equivalent Fraction for a Repeating Decimal

Write 0.272727… as a fraction.

SOLUTION

To eliminate the repeating decimal, subtract the same repeating decimal.

$n = 0.272727…$ Let n represent the fraction equivalent to 0.272727…

$100n = 27.272727…$ Since 2 digits repeat, multiply both sides of the equation by 10^2 or 100.

$$\begin{aligned} 100n &= 27.272727… \\ -n &= -0.272727… \end{aligned}$$ Subtract the original equation.

$99n = 27$ Combine like terms.

$n = \dfrac{27}{99} = \dfrac{3}{11}$ Divide both sides by 99 and simplify.

0.272727… is equivalent to $\dfrac{3}{11}$.

Skills Bank Practice

Write an equivalent fraction in simplest form for each decimal.

a. 0.85 **b.** 1.75 **c.** 0.575757… **d.** $0.\overline{81}$

e. 0.48 **f.** 1.25 **g.** 0.363636… **h.** $0.44\overline{4}$

Equivalent Fractions

Skills Bank Lesson 7

Fractions that represent the same amount or part are called **equivalent fractions.**

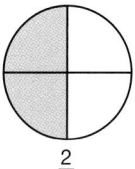
$\frac{2}{4}$

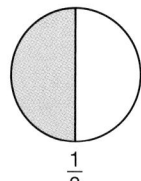
$\frac{1}{2}$

Example 1 Finding Equivalent Fractions

For each fraction, write two equivalent fractions.

a. $\frac{3}{4}$

b. $\frac{36}{40}$

SOLUTION

Choose any whole number. Multiply the numerator and the denominator by that number.

$$\frac{3}{4} = \frac{3 \cdot 3}{4 \cdot 3} = \frac{9}{12}$$

$$\frac{3}{4} = \frac{3 \cdot 5}{4 \cdot 5} = \frac{15}{20}$$

$\frac{3}{4}$ is equivalent to $\frac{9}{12}$ and $\frac{15}{20}$.

SOLUTION

Find a number that is a factor of the numerator and the denominator. Divide both by that number.

$$\frac{36}{40} = \frac{36 \div 4}{40 \div 4} = \frac{9}{10}$$

$$\frac{36}{40} = \frac{36 \div 2}{40 \div 2} = \frac{18}{20}$$

$\frac{36}{40}$ is equivalent to $\frac{9}{10}$ and $\frac{18}{20}$.

Example 2 Writing Fractions in Simplest Form Using the GCF

Simplify.

$$\frac{24}{48}$$

SOLUTION

Find the greatest common factor (GCF) of 24 and 48. The GCF is 24.

$$\frac{24}{48} = \frac{24 \div 24}{48 \div 24} = \frac{1}{2} \qquad \text{Divide the numerator and denominator by 24.}$$

Skills Bank Practice

For each fraction, write two equivalent fractions.

a. $\frac{3}{7}$ **b.** $\frac{1}{5}$ **c.** $\frac{54}{72}$ **d.** $\frac{120}{360}$

Simplify.

e. $\frac{14}{24}$ **f.** $\frac{30}{36}$ **g.** $\frac{75}{100}$

h. $\frac{48}{60}$ **i.** $\frac{90}{360}$

Estimation Strategies

Skills Bank Lesson 8

To estimate is to find an approximate answer. Rounding numbers is one way to estimate.

Rounding Rules	
If the digit to the right of the rounding digit is > 5, round up.	Round 35,679 to the nearest thousand. 35,679 rounds up to 36,000.
If the digit to the right of the rounding digit is < 5, round down.	Round 35,479 to the nearest thousand. 35,479 rounds down to 35,000.
If the digit to the right of the rounding digit = 5, then round up.	Round 35,579 to the nearest thousand. 35,579 rounds up to 36,000.

Compatible numbers are numbers that are close in value to the actual numbers and are easy to add, subtract, multiply, or divide. Compatible numbers can be used to estimate. An overestimation is an estimate greater than the exact answer. An underestimation is an estimate less than the exact answer.

Example 1 Estimate by Rounding

a. Sally has $23 to buy two shirts. One shirt is $9.75, and the other shirt is $10.95. Explain whether Sally should overestimate or underestimate the total cost. Then estimate the total cost and tell whether Sally has enough money to buy both shirts.

SOLUTION Sally should overestimate. If her estimate is more than the actual cost, then she has enough money to buy both shirts.

$9.75 + $10.95   To overestimate, round each number up.

$10.00 + $11.00 = $21.00

The actual cost will be less than $23.00, so Sally has enough money.

b. Alan plans to drive 575 miles to his aunt's house. He can drive 65 mi/hr. About how long will the trip take?

SOLUTION Alan should underestimate his speed.

Round 575 up to 600. Round 65 mi/hr down to 60.

$600 \div 60 = 10$ Distance divided by rate is equal to time.

It will take Alan about 10 hours to drive to his aunt's house.

Skills Bank Practice

a. Rico has $30 to buy school supplies. He wants to buy 2 packages of pens for $2.75 each, a backpack for $12.50, and 4 notebooks for $1.99 each. Tell whether Rico should overestimate or underestimate the total cost. Then estimate the total and tell whether Rico has enough money.

b. Jordan drives 120 miles. If his car gets 32 miles per gallon of gas, about how much gas will he use?

Greatest Common Factor (GCF)

Skills Bank Lesson 9

The **greatest common factor,** or **GCF,** is the largest factor two or more given numbers have in common. For example, 2 and 5 are common factors of 10 and 20, but 5 is the greatest common factor.

One way to find the GCF is to make a list of factors and choose the greatest factor that appears in each list. Another way is to divide by prime factors.

Example 1 Finding the GCF

a. Find the GCF of 24 and 60.

SOLUTION

24: 1, **2, 3, 4, 6,** 8, **12,** 24   List the factors of each number.

60: 1, **2, 3, 4,** 5, **6,** 10, **12,** 15, 20, 30, 60   Find the greatest common factor.

2, 3, 4, 6, and 12 are common factors.

The GCF of 24 and 60 is 12.

b. Find the GCF of 54 and 72.

SOLUTION

2	54	72	Divide both numbers by the same prime factor.
3	27	36	Keep dividing until there is no prime factor that
3	9	12	divides into both numbers without a remainder.
	3	4	

$2 \cdot 3 \cdot 3$ or $2 \cdot 3^2 = 18$

The GCF of 54 and 72 is 18.

Example 2 Using the GCF to Simplify Fractions

a. Write $\frac{21}{28}$ in simplest form.

SOLUTION Divide 21 and 28 by the GCF, 7.

$$\frac{21}{28} = \frac{21 \div 7}{28 \div 7} = \frac{3}{4}$$

b. Write $1\frac{9}{12}$ in simplest form.

SOLUTION Divide 9 and 12 by the GCF, 3.

$$\frac{9}{12} = \frac{9 \div 3}{12 \div 3} = \frac{3}{4}$$

$$1\frac{9}{12} = 1\frac{3}{4}$$

Skills Bank Practice

Find the GCF.

a. 72 and 60   **b.** 54 and 89   **c.** 21 and 56   **d.** 120 and 960

e. 3, 6, and 12   **f.** 7, 21, and 49   **g.** 4, 22, and 40   **h.** 20, 45, and 80

Write each fraction in simplest form.

i. $\frac{8}{12}$ **j.** $\frac{15}{25}$ **k.** $\frac{16}{64}$ **l.** $\frac{110}{150}$ **m.** $\frac{52}{65}$

Least Common Multiple (LCM) and Least Common Denominator (LCD)

Skills Bank Lesson 10

The **least common multiple,** or **LCM,** is the smallest whole number, other than zero, that is a multiple of two or more given numbers.

Example 1 Finding the LCM

a. Find the LCM of 6 and 10.

SOLUTION

List the multiples of each number.

Multiples of 6: 6, 12, 18, 24, **30,** 36, 42, 48, 54, **60,** …

Multiples of 10: 10, 20, **30,** 40, 50, **60,** …

30 and 60 are common multiples.   Find the common multiples that are in both lists.

The LCM of 6 and 10 is 30.   Find the least common multiple.

b. Find the LCM of 12 and 18.

SOLUTION

$$
\begin{array}{c|cc}
2 & 12 & 18 \\
3 & 6 & 9 \\
  & 2 & 3
\end{array}
$$

Divide both numbers by the same prime factor.

Keep dividing until there is no prime factor that divides into both numbers without a remainder.

$2 \cdot 3 \cdot 2 \cdot 3$ or $2^2 \cdot 3^2 = 36$. The LCM of 12 and 18 is 36.

The **least common denominator,** or **LCD,** is the least common multiple of two or more denominators.

Example 2 Finding the LCD and Writing Equivalent Fractions

Find the LCD of $\frac{3}{8}$ and $\frac{5}{12}$. Use the LCD to write equivalent fractions.

SOLUTION The LCM of 8 and 12 is 24, so 24 is the LCD.

$$\frac{3}{8} = \frac{3 \cdot 3}{8 \cdot 3} = \frac{9}{24}$$ Write an equivalent fraction using a denominator of 24.

$$\frac{5}{12} = \frac{5 \cdot 2}{12 \cdot 2} = \frac{10}{24}$$ Write an equivalent fraction using a denominator of 24.

$\frac{3}{8}$ and $\frac{5}{12}$ are equivalent to $\frac{9}{24}$ and $\frac{10}{24}$.

Skills Bank Practice

Find the LCM.

a. 9 and 15   **b.** 20 and 25   **c.** 24 and 48   **d.** 14 and 21

e. 25, 50, and 100   **f.** 8, 16, and 48   **g.** 2, 3, and 20

h. Use the LCD to write equivalent fractions for $\frac{1}{2}$ and $\frac{7}{15}$.

Mental Math

Skills Bank Lesson 11

Mental math means to find an exact answer quickly in your head. Mental math strategies use number properties.

Example 1   Using Properties to Add or Multiply Whole Numbers

a. Find the sum of $32 + 3 + 48 + 57$.

SOLUTION

$32 + 3 + 48 + 57$	Look for sums that are multiples of 10.
$= 3 + 57 + 32 + 48$	Use the Commutative Property.
$= (3 + 57) + (32 + 48)$	Use the Associative Property.
$= 60 + 80$	Add.
$= 140$	

b. Find the product of $2 \cdot 44 \cdot 5$.

SOLUTION

$2 \cdot 44 \cdot 5$	Look for products that are multiples of 10.
$= 2 \cdot 5 \cdot 44$	Use the Commutative Property.
$= (2 \cdot 5) \cdot 44$	Use the Associative Property.
$= 10 \cdot 44$	Multiply.
$= 440$	

c. Find the product of $8 \cdot 47$.

SOLUTION

$8 \cdot 47$	
$8 \cdot 47 = 8 \cdot (40 + 7)$	"Break apart" 47 into $40 + 7$.
$= (8 \cdot 40) + (8 \cdot 7)$	Use the Distributive Property.
$= 320 + 56$	Multiply.
$= 376$	Add.

Skills Bank Practice

Find each sum or product.

a. $24 + 15 + 16 + 15$ **b.** $6 \cdot 12 \cdot 5$

c. $58 \cdot 4$ **d.** $6 + 31 + 34 + 9$

e. $34 \cdot 7$ **f.** $4 \cdot 62 \cdot 25$

g. $8 + 67 + 12 + 3$ **h.** $33 \cdot 9$

Prime and Composite Numbers and Prime Factorization

A **prime number** is a number that has exactly two factors, 1 and itself. For example, 5 is a prime number because its only factors are 1 and 5.

A **composite number** has more than two factors. For example, 8 is a composite number because its factors are 1, 2, 4, and 8.

The number 1 is neither prime nor composite.

Example 1 Determining Whether a Number is Prime or Composite

Determine whether each number is prime or composite.

a. 18

b. 13

SOLUTION

1, 2, 3, 6, 9, 18   List the factors.

18 is a composite number.

SOLUTION

1, 13   List the factors.

13 is a prime number.

Every composite number can be written as the product of two or more prime numbers. This product is called the **prime factorization** of a number.

Example 2 Using a Factor Tree to Find the Prime Factorization

36

SOLUTION

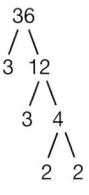

Choose any two factors of 36. Continue to factor until each branch ends in a prime number.

The prime factorization of 36 is $2 \cdot 2 \cdot 3 \cdot 3$ or $2^2 \cdot 3^2$.

Skills Bank Practice

Determine whether each number is prime or composite.

  a. 17   **b.** 15   **c.** 32   **d.** 29

Find the prime factorization of each number.

  e. 72   **f.** 28   **g.** 34   **h.** 24

  i. 76   **j.** 32   **k.** 45   **l.** 52

Classify Angles and Triangles

Skills Bank Lesson 13

You can classify an angle by its measure.

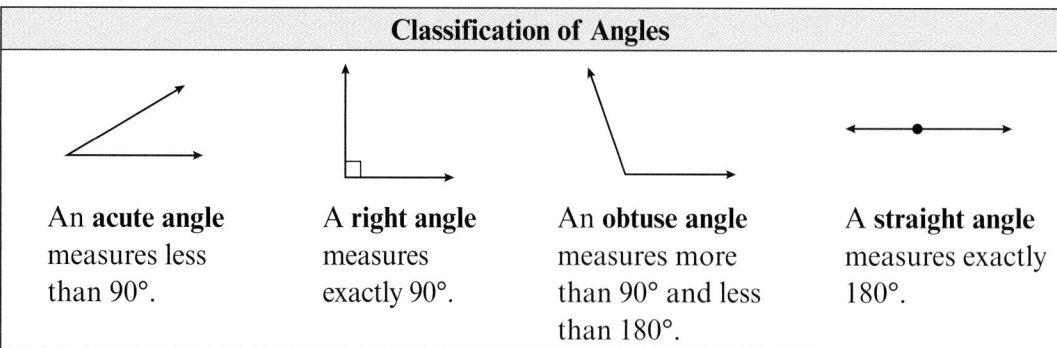

Classification of Angles

An **acute angle** measures less than 90°.

A **right angle** measures exactly 90°.

An **obtuse angle** measures more than 90° and less than 180°.

A **straight angle** measures exactly 180°.

You can classify a triangle by its angle measures.

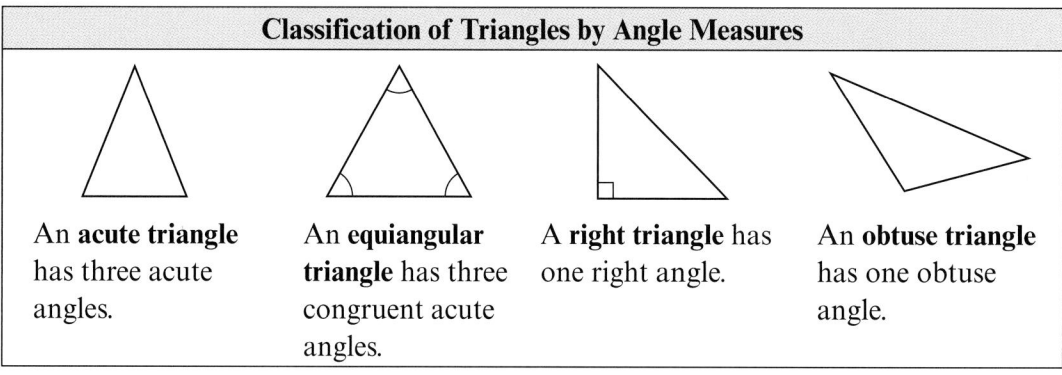

Classification of Triangles by Angle Measures

An **acute triangle** has three acute angles.

An **equiangular triangle** has three congruent acute angles.

A **right triangle** has one right angle.

An **obtuse triangle** has one obtuse angle.

You can also classify a triangle by its side lengths.

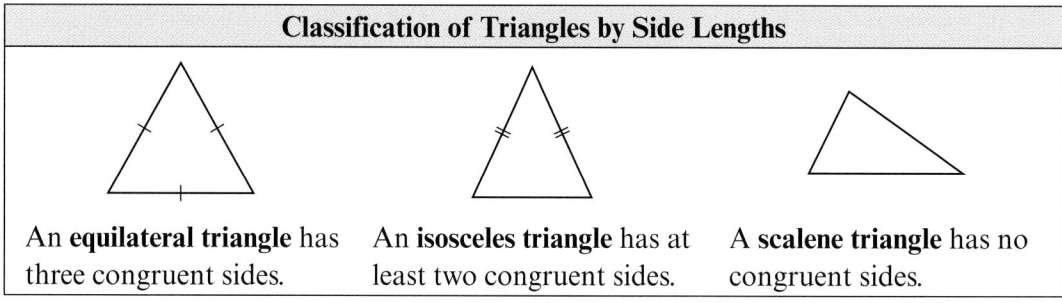

Classification of Triangles by Side Lengths

An **equilateral triangle** has three congruent sides.

An **isosceles triangle** has at least two congruent sides.

A **scalene triangle** has no congruent sides.

Example 1 — Classifying Angles

Classify each angle according to its measure.

a.

SOLUTION

This is a straight angle, because the figure is a line and the angle measures 180°.

b.

SOLUTION

This is an obtuse angle, because the angle measure is greater than 90° but less than 180°.

c.

SOLUTION

This is an acute angle because the angle measure is less than 90°.

d.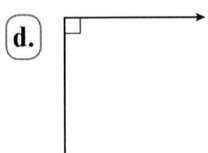

SOLUTION

This is a right angle because the angle measure is equal to 90°.

Example 2 — Classifying Triangles

Classify each triangle according to its angle measures and side lengths.

a.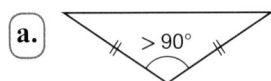

SOLUTION

The figure has one obtuse angle and at least 2 congruent sides. So, this is an obtuse isosceles triangle.

b.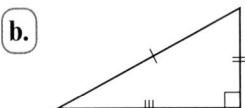

SOLUTION

The figure has one right angle and no congruent sides. So, this is a right scalene triangle.

Skills Bank Practice

Classify each angle according to its measure.

a.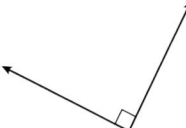

b.

c.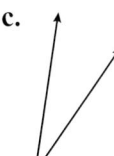

Classify each triangle according to its angle measures and side lengths.

d.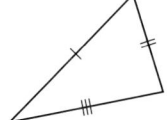

e.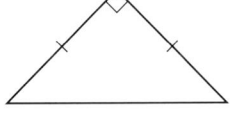

f.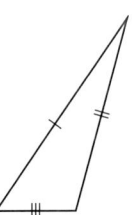

Congruence

Skills Bank Lesson 16

Congruent segments are segments that have the same length.

Congruent angles are angles that have the same measure.

Figures are congruent if all of their corresponding angles and sides are congruent.

Hint

The symbol for congruent is ≅.

Congruent Triangles		
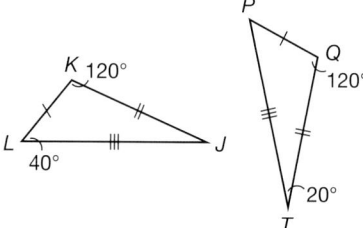	**Corresponding Angles**	**Corresponding Sides**
Statement: $\triangle ABC \cong \triangle DEF$	$\angle A \cong \angle D$ $\angle B \cong \angle E$ $\angle C \cong \angle F$	$\overline{AB} \cong \overline{DE}$ $\overline{BC} \cong \overline{EF}$ $\overline{AC} \cong \overline{DF}$ $\dfrac{AB}{DE} = \dfrac{BC}{EF} = \dfrac{AC}{DF}$

In a congruence statement, the order of the letters shows which angles and sides are congruent.

Example 1 **Identifying the Corresponding Angles and Sides**

Find the congruent angles and sides. Then write a congruence statement.

SOLUTION

$\angle D \cong \angle I$ $\angle D$ corresponds to $\angle I$.

$\angle E \cong \angle H$ $\angle E$ corresponds to $\angle H$.

$\angle F \cong \angle G$ $\angle F$ corresponds to $\angle G$.

$\overline{DE} \cong \overline{IH}$ $\overline{DE}$ corresponds to $\overline{IH}$.

$\overline{EF} \cong \overline{HG}$ $\overline{EF}$ corresponds to $\overline{HG}$.

$\overline{DF} \cong \overline{IG}$ $\overline{DF}$ corresponds to $\overline{IG}$.

$\triangle DEF \cong \triangle IHG$

Skills Bank Practice

Write a congruence statement for each pair of figures.

a.

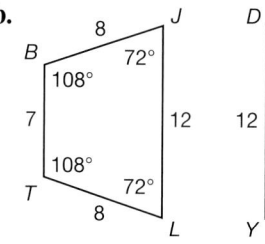

b.

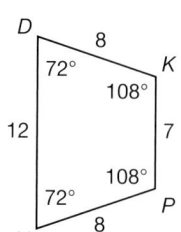

Estimate the Perimeter and Area of Figures

Perimeter is the distance around a figure. The perimeter of a polygon is the sum of its side lengths. The **area** of a figure is the amount of surface it covers.

Perimeter and Circumference Formulas	Area Formulas
Rectangle $P = 2l + 2w$ or $P = 2(l + w)$ **Circle** $C = 2\pi r$ or $C = \pi d$	**Rectangle** $A = lw$ **Circle** $A = \pi r^2$

Example 1 Estimating Perimeter

a. Estimate the perimeter of the figure.

8 feet

8 feet

SOLUTION

Estimate the length of the top, sides, and bottom of the figure.

right and left: ≈ 8 feet

bottom: 8 feet

top: ≈ 8 feet

$$P \approx 4(8)$$

The perimeter is about 32 feet.

b. Estimate the perimeter of the trapezoid.

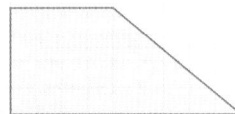

SOLUTION

Find the length of the top, side, and bottom of the trapezoid.

top: 4 units

left: 4 units

bottom: 9 units

Estimate the length of the diagonal line.

diagonal line: ≈ 5 units

$$P \approx 4 + 4 + 9 + 5 \approx 22$$

The perimeter is about 22 units.

Example 2 Estimating Area

Estimate the area of the circle.

SOLUTION

Estimate the area by counting the squares.

12 full squares   4 almost full squares

8 quarter full squares: ≈ 2 8 corners: ≈ 1

The area of the circle is about 19 units^2.

Skills Bank Practice

a. Estimate the perimeter of the figure.
b. Estimate the area of the figure.

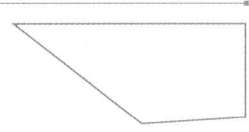

SKILLS BANK

Venn Diagrams

Skills Bank Lesson 30

A **Venn diagram** shows the relationship between sets.

Example 1 Making a Venn Diagram

167 people taste tested two new brands of cereal. 7 people did not like either brand, 100 people liked Brand A, and 110 people liked Brand B. How many people only liked Brand A? Make a Venn diagram to represent the data.

SOLUTION

Draw and label two intersecting circles to show the set of people that liked Brand A and Brand B.

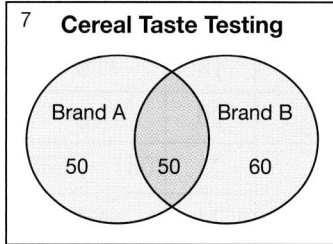

There must be people that liked both brands of cereal, because $100 + 110 + 7 = 217$, and only 167 people taste tested the cereal.

The overlap is $217 - 167 = 50$.

This means 50 people were counted twice because 50 people liked both Brand A and Brand B.

Out of 100 people who liked Brand A, 50 of them also liked Brand B. So, 50 people liked only Brand A.

Skills Bank Practice

Out of a group of 133 people, 55 people carpool to work, 67 take the bus to work, and 30 do not carpool or take the bus to work. Make a Venn diagram. Then use the Venn diagram to find how many people use both a carpool and a bus.

Problem-Solving Strategies

Skills Bank Lesson 31

Sometimes it helps to **draw a diagram** when solving problems.

Example 1 Drawing a Diagram to Solve a Problem

A landscaper is designing a garden. It will have a rectangular flower border around a rectangular fountain. The flower border will be a 3-foot wide border. The water fountain is 7 feet long and 5 feet wide. What is the area of the border?

Understand

You need to find the area of the flower border surrounding the water fountain.

• The flower border and the fountain are both rectangles.

• Fountain: 7 ft × 5 ft

• Border: 3 ft wide

Plan

Draw and label a diagram of the water fountain with the surrounding border. Subtract the area of the fountain from the entire area of the garden.

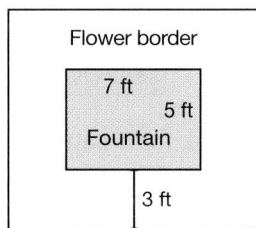

Solve

Find the length and width of the garden.
length: 3 ft + 7 ft + 3 ft = 13 ft
width: 3 ft + 5 ft + 3 ft = 11 ft

Find the area of the garden.   Find the area of the fountain.
$A = lw$ $13 \cdot 11 = 143 \text{ ft}^2$ $A = lw$ $7 \cdot 5 = 35 \text{ ft}^2$

The area of the garden is 143 ft^2.   The area of the fountain is 35 ft^2.

Find the area of the flower border.

Subtract area of fountain from the area of the garden.

$$143 \text{ ft}^2 - 35 \text{ ft}^2 = 108 \text{ ft}^2$$

Check

The area of the fountain and the border is equal to the area of the entire garden.

$$108 \text{ ft}^2 + 35 \text{ ft}^2 = 143 \text{ ft}^2$$

Skills Bank Practice

a. Sajio is building a new rectangular deck around his rectangular pool. The pool is 40 feet long and 30 feet wide. The deck is 6 feet wide. What is the area of the deck?

You can **make a table** to solve problems. A table can help you recognize patterns or relationships.

Example 4 **Making a Table to Solve a Problem**

Sam opened a bank account with $450. At the end of each year, the account earns 5% interest on the balance. If Sam does not deposit or withdraw any money, how much money will he have at the end of 10 years?

Understand

Find the total amount of money Sam will have at the end of 10 years.

- The starting balance is $450.

- Add 5% interest to the balance at the end of every year.

Plan

Make a table with the starting balance and the total amount of interest added at the end of the 1st year. Continue building the table until you have the balance at the end of the 10th year.

Solve

Sam will have $733.02 at the end of 10 years.

Check

The interest each year is increasing. The balance each year is increasing.

Suppose the balance was constant over 10 years.

$22.50 \cdot 10 = $225.

$450 + $225 = $675.

Sam's balance of $733.02 is close to $675, so the answer is reasonable.

End of Year	Add 5% of the balance	Balance
1	$450 + $22.50	$472.50
2	$472.50 + $23.63	$496.13
3	$496.13 + $24.81	$520.94
4	$520.94 + $26.05	$546.99
5	$546.99 + $27.35	$574.34
6	$574.34 + $28.72	$603.06
7	$603.06 + $30.15	$633.21
8	$633.21 + $31.66	$664.87
9	$664.87 + $33.24	$698.11
10	$698.11 + $34.91	$733.02

Skills Bank Practice

Make a table to solve the problem.

a. Gas from an 8550 ft^3 gas tank is used at a rate of 475 ft^3 per day. Gas from a 7200 ft^3 gas tank is used at a rate of 250 ft^3 per day. If no gas is replaced, how much gas will be in each tank when the two tanks hold equal amounts of gas?

Sometimes there are so many numbers in a problem that it can be confusing to solve. To solve **a simpler problem,** rewrite the numbers so they are easier to compute.

Example 5 **Writing a Simpler Problem to Solve a Problem**

In a cycling race, Elio cycled 128 blocks. One block is 1.9 kilometers. If Elio finished in 5.9 hours, what was his average speed?

Understand

Find Elio's average speed.

- Distance: 128 blocks each 1.9 km long

- Time: 5.9 hours

Plan

Find Elio's average speed by using simpler numbers to compute.

Solve

$(128)(1.9)$	Find the total distance of the race.
$= (128)(2 - 0.1)$	Write 1.9 as $2 - 0.1$.
$= 128(2) - 128(0.1)$	Use the Distributive Property.
$= 256 - 12.8$	
$= 243.2$ km	

$d = rt$	Use the distance formula.
$243.2 = r(5.9)$	Solve for r.
$\dfrac{243.2}{5.9} \approx 41.2$ km/hr	

Elio's average speed was about 41.2 km/hr.

Check

Each block is close to 2 miles and 128 is close to 130.

The total distance rounds to 260 kilometers.

Round the time to 6 hours and divide into the distance.

$260 \div 6 \approx 43.3$ km/hr. This is close to 41.2 km/hr.

Skills Bank Practice

a. Frank walked 9 laps around the track. One lap is 1312 feet. Frank walked at a rate of 4 mi/hr. How many minutes did it take him to walk 9 laps?

Subtraction Property of Inequality
(66)

For every real number a, b, and c, if $a < b$, then $a - c < b - c$.

Also holds true for $>$, $\leq$, $\geq$, and $\neq$.

Zero Exponent Property
(32)

For every nonzero number x, $x^0 = 1$.

Zero Product Property
(98)

For every real number a and b, if $ab = 0$, then $a = 0$ and/or $b = 0$.

Formulas

Perimeter

Rectangle	$P = 2l + 2w$ or $P = 2(l + w)$
Square	$P = 4s$

Circumference

Circle	$C = \pi d$ or $C = 2\pi r$

Area

Rectangle	$A = lw$
Triangle	$A = \frac{1}{2}bh$
Trapezoid	$A = \frac{1}{2}(b_1 + b_2)h$
Circle	$A = \pi r^2$

Surface Area

Cube	$S = 6s^2$
Cylinder	$S = 2\pi r^2 + 2\pi rh$
Cone	$S = \pi r^2 + \pi rl$

Volume

Where B is the area of the base of a solid figure,

Prism or cylinder	$V = Bh$
Pyramid or cone	$V = \frac{1}{3}Bh$

Linear Equations

Slope formula	$m = \frac{y_2 - y_1}{x_2 - x_1}$
Slope-intercept form	$y = mx + b$
Point-slope form	$y - y_1 = m(x - x_1)$
Standard form	$Ax + By = C$

Quadratic Equations

Standard form	$ax^2 + bx + c = 0$
Axis of symmetry	$x = -\frac{b}{2a}$
Discriminant	$b^2 - 4ac$
Quadratic formula	$x = \frac{-b \pm \sqrt{b^2 - 4ac}}{2a}$

Sequences

nth term of an arithmetic sequence

$$a_n = a_1 + (n - 1)d$$

nth term of an geometric sequence

$$a_n = a_1 \cdot r^{n-1}$$

Trigonometric Ratios

$$\text{sine of } \angle A = \frac{\text{length of leg opposite } \angle A}{\text{length of hypotenuse}}$$

$$\text{cosine of } \angle A = \frac{\text{length of leg adjacent to } \angle A}{\text{length of hypotenuse}}$$

$$\text{tan of } \angle A = \frac{\text{length of leg opposite } \angle A}{\text{length of leg adjacent to } \angle A}$$

Percents

$$\text{Percent of change} = \frac{\text{amount of change}}{\text{original amount}}$$

Permutations and Combinations

$P(n, r)$ — permutation of n things taken r at a time

$$_nP_r = \frac{n!}{(n - r)!}$$

$C(n, r)$ — combination of n things taken r at a time

$$_nC_r = \frac{n!}{r!(n - r)!}$$

$n!$ — $n! = n \cdot (n - 1) \cdot (n - 2) \cdot \ldots \cdot 3 \cdot 2 \cdot 1$

Probability

$$P(\text{event}) = \frac{\text{number of favorable outcomes}}{\text{total number of outcomes}}$$

$P(A)$ — probability of event A

Probability of complement

$$P(\text{not event}) = 1 - P(\text{event})$$

Probability of independent events

$$P(A \text{ and } B) = P(A) \cdot P(B)$$

Probability of dependent events

$$P(A \text{ then } B) = P(A) \cdot P(B \text{ after } A)$$

Probability of mutually exclusive events

$$P(A \text{ or } B) = P(A) + P(B)$$

Probability of inclusive events

$$P(A \text{ or } B) = P(A) + P(B) - P(A \text{ and } B)$$

Additional Formulas

Direct variation $\quad y = kx$

Inverse variation $\quad y = \frac{k}{x}; x \neq 0$

Distance formula $\quad d = \sqrt{(x_2 - x_1)^2 + (y_2 - y_1)^2}$

Distance traveled $\quad d = rt$

Exponential decay $\quad y = kb^x; k > 0, 0 < b < 1$

Exponential growth $\quad y = kb^x; k > 0, b > 1$

Midpoint of a segment $\quad M = \left(\frac{x_1 + x_2}{2}, \frac{y_1 + y_2}{2}\right)$

Symbols

Comparison Symbols

$<$	less than
$>$	greater than
$\leq$	less than or equal to
$\geq$	greater than or equal to
$\neq$	not equal to
$\approx$	approximately equal to

Geometry

$\cong$	is congruent to
$\sim$	is similar to
$^\circ$	degree(s)
$\angle ABC$	angle ABC
$m\angle ABC$	the measure of angle ABC
$\triangle ABC$	triangle ABC
$\overleftrightarrow{AB}$	line AB
$\overline{AB}$	segment AB
$\overrightarrow{AB}$	ray AB
AB	length of $\overline{AB}$
⌐	right angle
$\perp$	is perpendicular to
$\parallel$	is parallel to

Real Numbers

$\mathbb{R}$	the set of real numbers
$\mathbb{Q}$	the set of rational numbers
$\mathbb{Z}$	the set of integers
$\mathbb{W}$	the set of whole numbers
$\mathbb{N}$	the set of natural numbers

English	Example	Spanish

D

direct variation
(56)

A relationship between two variables, x and y, that can be written in the form $y = kx$, where k is a nonzero constant, called the constant of variation.

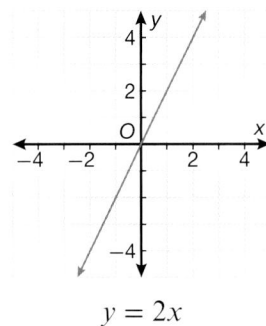

$$y = 2x$$

variación directa
(56)

Relación entre dos variables, x e y, que puede expresarse en la forma $y = kx$, donde k es una constante distinta de cero, denominada la constante de variación.

---

discontinuous function
(78)

A function whose graph has one or more jumps, breaks, or holes.

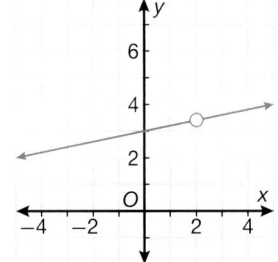

función discontinua
(78)

Función cuya gráfica tiene uno o más saltos, interrupciones u hoyos.

---

discrete data
(Inv 2)

Data that cannot take on any real-value measurement within an interval.

datos discretos
(Inv 2)

Datos que no admiten cualquier medida de valores reales dentro de un intervalo.

---

discrete event
(80)

An event that has a finite number of outcomes.

suceso discreto
(80)

Un suceso que tiene un número finito de resultados posibles.

---

discrete graph
(Inv 2)

A graph made up of unconnected points.

Water Park Attendance

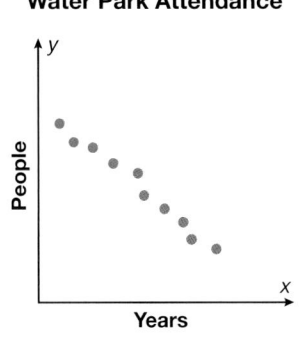

gráfica discreta
(Inv 2)

Gráfica compuesta de puntos no conectados.

---

discriminant
(113)

The discriminant of the quadratic equation $ax^2 + bx + c = 0$ is $b^2 - 4ac$.

The discriminant of $3x^2 - 2x - 5$ is $(-2)^2 - 4(3)(-5)$ or 64

discriminante
(113)

El discriminante de la ecuación cuadrática $ax^2 + bx + c = 0$ es $b^2 - 4ac$.

---

disjunction
(73)

A compound statement that uses the word *or*.

$x < -1$ OR $x \geq 2$

disyunción
(73)

Enunciado compuesto que contiene la palabra *o*.

English	Example	Spanish

D

---

domain
(25)

The set of input values of a function or relation.

The domain of $y = \sqrt{x}$ is $x \geq 0$.

dominio
(25)

Conjunto de valores de entrada de una función o relación.

---

double root
(113)

Two equal roots in a quadratic equation are sometimes called a double root.

$$x^2 - 4x + 4 = 0$$
$$x = 2, 2$$

raíz doble
(113)

Dos raíces iguales en una ecuación cuadrática a veces son llamadas una raíz doble.

---

double-bar graph
(22)

A graph that shows two bar graphs together and compares two related sets of data.

gráfica de doble barra
(22)

Una gráfica que muestra dos gráficas de barras juntas y compara los conjuntos de datos relacionados.

---

double-line graph
(22)

A graph with two line graphs together that compare two related sets of data.

gráfica de línea doble
(22)

Una gráfica con dos gráficas lineales juntas que comparan dos conjuntos de datos relacionados.

---

doubling time
(Inv 11)

The period of time required for a quantity to double in size or value.

tiempo de duplicación
(Inv 11)

El período de tiempo requerido para que una cantidad duplique su tamaño o valor.

E

---

element of a set
(Inv 12)

An item in a set.

elemento de un conjunto
(Inv 12)

Componente de un conjunto.

English	Example	Spanish

E

empty set (1) A set with no elements.	The solution set of $|x| < -1$ is the empty set, $\{\ \}$, or $\varnothing$.	**conjunto vacío** (1) Conjunto sin elementos.
equation (19) A mathematical sentence that shows that two expressions are equivalent.	$x + 5 = 7$ $4 + 3 = 8 - 1$ $(x - 2)^2 + (y - 3)^2 = 4$	**ecuación** (19) Enunciado matemático que indica que dos expresiones son equivalentes.
equivalent equations (19) Equations that have the same solution set.	$x + 2 = 4; x = 2$ $2x + 4 = 8; x = 2$	**ecuaciones equivalentes** (19) Ecuaciones que tienen el mismo conjunto solución.
equivalent inequalities (50) Inequalities that have the same solution set.	$x + 3 < 5; x < 2$ $2x + 6 < 10; x < 2$	**desigualdades equivalentes** (50) Desigualdades que tienen el mismo conjunto solución.
event (Inv 1) An outcome or set of outcomes in a probability experiment.	In the experiment of rolling a number cube, the event of "an even number" consists of 2, 4, and 6.	**suceso** (Inv 1) Resultado o conjunto de resultados en un experimento de probabilidades.
excluded values (78) Values of x for which a function or expression is not defined.	The excluded values of $f(x) = \dfrac{(x + 3)}{(x + 1)(x - 4)}$ are $x = -1$ and $x = 4$, which would make the denominator equal to 0.	**valores excluidos** (78) Valores de x para los cuales no está definida una función o expresión.
experimental probability (Inv 1) The ratio of the number of times an event occurs to the number of trials, or times, that an activity is performed.		**probabilidad experimental** (Inv 1) Razón entre la cantidad de veces que ocurre un suceso y la cantidad de pruebas, o veces, que se realiza una actividad.
exponent (3) The number that indicates how many times the base in a power is used as a factor. $3^4 \longleftarrow$ exponent	$2^4 = 2 \cdot 2 \cdot 2 \cdot 2 = 16$ 4 is the exponent	**exponente** (3) Número que indica la cantidad de veces que la base de una potencia se utiliza como factor. $3^4 \longleftarrow$ exponente

English	Example	Spanish

E

exponential decay
(Inv 11)

An exponential function of the form $f(x) = ab^x$ in which $0 < b < 1$. If r is the rate of decay, then the function can be written $y = a(1 - r)^t$, where a is the initial amount and t is the time.

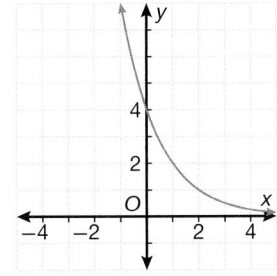

decremento exponencial
(Inv 11)

Función exponencial del tipo $f(x) = ab^x$ en la cual $0 < b < 1$. Si r es la tasa decremental, entonces la función se puede expresar como $y = a(1 - r)^t$, donde a es la cantidad inicial y t es el tiempo.

---

exponential function
(108)

A function of the form $f(x) = ab^x$, where a and b are real numbers with $a \neq 0$, $b > 0$, and $b \neq 1$.

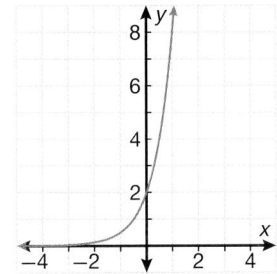

función exponencial
(108)

Función del tipo $f(x) = ab^x$, donde a y b son números reales con $a \neq 0$, $b > 0$ y $b \neq 1$.

---

exponential growth
(Inv 11)

An exponential function of the form $f(x) = ab^x$ in which $b > 1$. If r is the rate of growth, then the function can be written $y = a(1 + r)^t$, where a is the initial amount and t is the time.

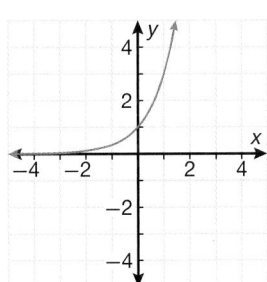

crecimiento exponencial
(Inv 11)

Función exponencial del tipo $f(x) = ab^x$ en la que $b > 1$. Si r es la tasa de crecimiento, entonces la función se puede expresar como $y = a(1 + r)^t$, donde a es la cantidad inicial y t es el tiempo.

---

extraneous solution
(99)

A solution of a derived equation that is not a solution of the original equation.

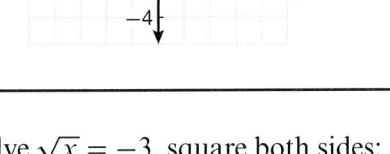

To solve $\sqrt{x} = -3$, square both sides; $x = 9$
Check: $\sqrt{9} = 3$ is false; so 3 is an extraneous solution.

solución extraña
(99)

Solución de una ecuación derivada que no es una solución de la ecuación original.

F

factor
(2)

A number or expression that is multiplied by another number or expression to get a product.

$10 = 2 \cdot 5$
2 and 5 are factors of 10
$x^2 - 4 = (x + 2)(x - 2)$
$(x + 2)$ and $(x - 2)$ are factors of $x^2 - 4$

factor
(2)

Número o expresión que se multiplica por otro número o expresión para obtener un producto.

English	Example	Spanish

F

factorial
(111)

If n is a positive integer, then n factorial, written $n!$, is $n \cdot (n - 1) \cdot (n - 2) \cdot ... \cdot 2 \cdot 1$. The factorial of 0 is defined to be 1.

$$6! = 6 \cdot 5 \cdot 4 \cdot 3 \cdot 2 \cdot 1 = 720$$

factorial
(111)

Si n es un entero positivo, entonces el factorial de n, expresado como n!, es $n \cdot (n - 1) \cdot (n - 2) \cdot ... \cdot 2 \cdot 1$. Por definición, el factorial de 0 es 1.

---

family of functions
(Inv 6)

A set of functions whose graphs have basic characteristics in common.

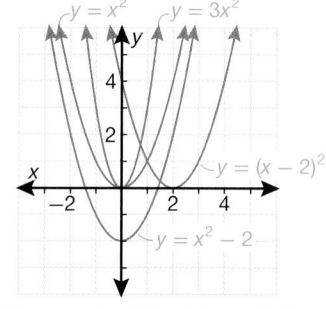

familia de funciones
(Inv 6)

Un conjunto de funciones cuyas gráficas tienen las características básicas en común.

---

finite set
(1)

A set with a fixed number of elements.

$$\{1, 2, 3, 4\}$$

conjunto finito
(1)

Un conjunto con un número fijo de elementos.

---

frequency distribution
(80)

A table or graph that shows the number of observations falling into several ranges of data values.

Grade Range	Frequency (Number of Students)
0 to 40	3
41 to 60	18
61 to 80	27
81 to 100	2

distribución de frecuencias
(80)

Una tabla o gráfica que muestra el número de observaciones que se encuentran dentro de varios rangos de valores de datos.

---

function
(25)

A type of relation that pairs each element in the domain with exactly one element in the range.

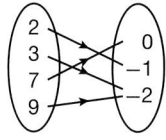

función
(25)

Tipo de relación que hace corresponder a cada elemento del dominio exactamente un elemento del rango.

---

function notation
(25)

If x is the independent variable and y is the dependent variable, then the function notation for y is $f(x)$, read "f of x," where f names the function.

equation: $y = 3x$

function notation: $f(x) = 3x$

notación de función
(25)

Si x es la variable independiente e y es la variable dependiente, entonces la notación de función para y es $f(x)$, que se lee "f de x", donde f nombra la función.

English	Example	Spanish

G

geometric sequence
(105)

A sequence in which the ratio of successive terms is a constant r, called the common ratio, where $r \neq 0$ and $r \neq 1$.

3, 6, 12, 24, …
The ratio is 2.

sucesión geométrica
(105)

Sucesión en la que la razón de los términos sucesivos es una constante r, denominada razón común, donde $r \neq 0$ y $r \neq 1$.

greatest common factor (GCF) of an expression
(38)

The product of the greatest integer and the greatest power of each variable that divides evenly into each term of the expression.

máximo común divisor (MCD) de una expresión
(38)

Producto del entero mayor y la potencia mayor de cada variable que divide exactamente cada término de la expresión.

H

half-life
(Inv 11)

The half-life of a substance is the time it takes for one-half of the substance to decay into another substance.

vida media
(Inv 11)

La vida media de una sustancia es el tiempo que tarda la mitad de la sustancia en desintegrarse y transformarse en otra sustancia.

histogram
(62)

A bar graph used to display data grouped in class intervals. The width of each bar is proportional to the class interval, and the area of each bar is proportional to the frequency.

Age of Visitors

(bar graph: Frequency vs. Ages, with bars for 5–9, 10–4, 15–19, 20–24, 25–29, 30–34)

histograma
(62)

Gráfica de barras utilizada para mostrar datos agrupados en intervalos de clases. El ancho de cada barra es proporcional al intervalo de clase y el área de cada barra es proporcional a la frecuencia.

hypothesis
(Inv 4)

The part of a conditional statement following the word *if*.

hipótesis
(Inv 4)

La parte de un enunciado condicional que sigue a la palabra *si*.

I

identity
(28)

An equation that is true for all values of the variables.

$$2x + 6 = 2(x + 3)$$

identidad
(28)

Ecuación verdadera para todos los valores de las variables.

English	Example	Spanish
I		
inclusive events (68) Events that have one or more outcomes in common.	In the experiment of rolling a number cube, rolling an odd number and rolling a number less than 3 are inclusive events because both contain the outcome 1.	**sucesos inclusivos** (68) Sucesos que tienen uno o más resultados en común.
inconsistent system (67) A system of equations or inequalities that has no solution.	$$x + y = 2$$ $$x + y = 1$$	**sistema inconsistente** (67) Sistema de ecuaciones o desigualdades que no tiene solución.
independent events (33) Events for which the occurrence or non-occurrence of one event does not affect the probability of the other event.	From a bag containing 4 green marbles and 2 red marbles, drawing a green marble, replacing it, and then drawing a red marble.	**sucesos independientes** (33) Dos sucesos son independientes si el hecho de que ocurra o no uno de ellos no afecta la probabilidad del otro suceso.
independent system (67) A system of equations that has exactly one solution.	$$x + y = 6$$ $$x - y = 2$$ Solution: (4, 2)	**sistema independiente** (67) Sistema de ecuaciones que tiene sólo una solución.
independent variable (20) The input of a function; a variable whose value determines the value of the output, or dependent variable.	For $y = 3x + 2$, x is the independent variable.	**variable independiente** (20) Entrada de una función; variable cuyo valor determina el valor de la salida, o variable dependiente.
inductive reasoning (Inv 4) The process of reasoning that a rule or statement is true because specific cases are true.		**razonamiento inductivo** (Inv 4) Proceso de razonamiento por el que se determina si una regla o enunciado es verdadero porque ciertos casos específicos son verdaderos.
inequality (45) A statement that compares two expressions by using one of the following signs $<$, $>$, $\leq$, $\geq$, or $\neq$.	$x \geq 3$ —2 0 2 4	**desigualdad** (45) Enunciado que compara dos expresiones utilizando uno de los siguientes signos: $<$, $>$, $\leq$, $\geq$, o $\neq$.
infinite set (1) A set with an unlimited, or infinite, number of elements.	Set of Integers $\{..., -3, -2, -1, 0, 1, 2, 3, ...\}$	**conjunto infinito** (1) Conjunto con un número de elementos ilimitado o infinito.

English	Example	Spanish
integer *(1)* A member of the set of whole numbers and their opposites.	$\dots, -3, -2, -1, 0, 1, 2, 3, \dots$	**entero** *(1)* Miembro del conjunto de números cabales y sus opuestos.
intersection of sets *(1)* The intersection of two sets is the set of all elements that are common to both sets, denoted by $\cap$.	$A = \{1, 2, 3\}$ $B = \{2, 3, 4, 5\}$ $A \cap B = \{2, 3\}$	**intersección de conjuntos** *(1)* La intersección de dos conjuntos es el conjunto de todos los elementos que son comunes a ambos conjuntos, expresado por $\cap$.
inverse *(Inv 5)* A conditional statement formed by negating both the hypothesis and the conclusion.	Statement: If a figure has three sides, then it is a triangle. Inverse: If a figure does not have three sides, then it is not a triangle.	**inverso** *(Inv 5)* Un enunciado condicional formado al negar tanto la hipótesis como la conclusión.
inverse operations *(19)* Operations that undo each other.	Addition and subtraction are inverse operations: $4 + 3 = 7,\ 7 - 4 = 3$ Multiplication and division are inverse operations: $2 \cdot 4 = 8,\ 8 \div 2 = 4$	**operaciones inversas** *(19)* Operaciones que se anulan entre sí.
inverse variation *(64)* A relationship between two variables, x and y, that can be written in the form $y = \frac{k}{x}$, where k is a nonzero constant and $x \neq 0$.	$y = \dfrac{6}{x}$ 	**variación inversa** *(64)* Relación entre dos variables, x e y, que puede expresarse en la forma $y = \frac{k}{x}$, donde k es una constante distinta de cero y $x \neq 0$.
irrational number *(1)* A real number that cannot be written as a ratio of integers.	$\sqrt{3},\ \pi$	**número irracional** *(1)* Número real que no se puede expresar como una razón de enteros.

English	Example	Spanish

J

joint variation
(Inv 8)

A relationship among three variables that can be written in the form $y = kxz$, where k is a nonzero constant.

variación conjunta
(Inv 8)

Relación entre tres variables que se puede expresar en la forma $y = kxz$, donde k es una constante distinta de cero.

L

leading coefficient
(53)

The coefficient of the first term of a polynomial in standard form.

$$4x^2 + 2x + 5$$
4 is the leading coefficient

coeficiente principal
(53)

Coeficiente del primer término de un polinomio en forma estándar.

like radicals
(69)

Radical terms having the same radicand and index.

$$5\sqrt{3x} \text{ and } \sqrt{3x}$$

radicales semejantes
(69)

Términos radicales que tienen el mismo radicando e índice.

like terms
(18)

Terms with the same variables raised to the same powers.

$$2x^2y^3 \text{ and } 5x^2y^3$$

términos semejantes
(18)

Términos con las mismas variables elevadas a los mismos exponentes.

line graph
(22)

A graph that uses line segments to show how data changes.

Car Acceleration

gráfica lineal
(22)

Gráfica que utiliza segmentos de líneas para mostrar cambios en los datos.

line of best fit
(71)

The line that comes closest to all of the points in a data set.

línea de mejor ajuste
(71)

Línea que más se acerca a todos los puntos de un conjunto de datos.

linear equation
(30)

An equation whose graph is a line.

ecuación lineal
(30)

Un enunciado cuya gráfica es una línea.

English	Example	Spanish

L

linear function
(30)

A function that can be written in the form $y = mx + b$, where x is the independent variable and m and b are real numbers. Its graph is a line.

función lineal
(30)

Función que puede expresarse en la forma $y = mx + b$, donde x es la variable independiente y m y b son números reales. Su gráfica es una línea.

linear inequality in one variable
(50)

An inequality that can be written in one of the following forms: $ax < b$, $ax > b$, $ax \le b$, $ax \ge b$, or $ax \ne b$, where a and b are constants and $a \ne 0$.

$$2x + 4 \le 3(x + 5)$$

desigualdad lineal en una variable
(50)

Una desigualdad que puede expresarse de una de las siguientes formas: $x < b$, $ax > b$, $ax \le b$, $ax \ge b$ o $ax \ne b$, donde a y b son constantes y $a \ne 0$.

linear inequality in two variables
(97)

An equation that can be written in one of the following forms: $y < mx + b$, $y > mx + b$, $y \le mx + b$, $y \ge mx + b$, or $y \ne mx + b$, where m and b are real numbers.

$$4x + 2y > 7$$

desigualdad lineal en dos variables
(97)

Ecuación que puede expresarse de una de las siguientes formas: $y < mx + b$, $y > mx + b$, $y \le mx + b$, $y \ge mx + b$ o $y \ne mx + b$, donde m y b son números reales.

literal equation
(29)

An equation that contains two or more variables.

$$d = rt$$
$$A = \frac{1}{2}bh$$

ecuación literal
(29)

Ecuación que contiene dos o más variables.

M

matrix
(Inv 12)

A rectangular array of numbers enclosed in brackets.

$$\begin{bmatrix} 1 & 0 & 3 \\ -2 & 4 & 5 \\ 0 & 7 & -3 \end{bmatrix}$$

matriz
(Inv 12)

Arreglo rectangular de números encerrados entre corchetes.

maximum of a function
(89)

The y-value of the highest point on the graph of the function.

máximo de una función
(89)

Valor de y del punto más alto en la gráfica de la función.

English	Example	Spanish

M

mean
(48)

The sum of all the values in a data set divided by the number of data values. Also called the average.

Data set: 4, 5, 6, 7

Mean: $\dfrac{4 + 5 + 6 + 7}{2} = 11$

media
(48)

Suma de todos los valores de un conjunto de datos dividido por el número de valores de datos. También llamada promedio.

---

measure of central tendency
(48)

A measure that describes the center of a data set.

mean, median, or mode

medida de tendencia central
(48)

Medida que describe el centro de un conjunto de datos.

---

median
(48)

If there are an odd number of data values, the median is the middle value. If there are an even number of values, the median is the average of the two middle values.

Data set: 7, 8, ⑩, 12, 14

Median: 10

Data set: 4, 6, ⑦, 10, 11, 12

Median: $\dfrac{7 + 10}{2} = 8.5$

mediana
(48)

Dado un número impar de valores de datos, la mediana es el valor del medio. Dado un número par de valores, la mediana es el promedio de los dos valores del medio.

---

midpoint
(86)

The point that divides a segment into two congruent segments.

x • x
Midpoint

punto medio
(86)

Punto que divide un segmento en dos segmentos congruentes.

---

minimum of a function
(89)

The y-value of the lowest point on the graph of the function.

(0, −3)

mínimo de una función
(89)

Valor de y del punto más bajo en la gráfica de la función.

---

mode
(48)

The value or values that occur most frequently in a data set. If all values occur with the same frequency, the data set is said to have no mode.

Data set: 3, 5, 7, 7, 10 Mode: 7

Data set: 2, 4, 4, 6, 6, Modes: 4 and 6

Data set: 2, 4, 5, 8, 9 No mode

moda
(48)

El valor o los valores que se presentan con mayor frecuencia en un conjunto de datos. Si todos los valores se presentan con la misma frecuencia, se dice que el conjunto de datos no tiene moda.

English	Example	Spanish

M

monomial
(53)

A number or a product of numbers and variables with whole-number exponents, or a polynomial with one term.

$5x^3y^2$

monomio
(53)

Número o producto de números y variables con exponentes de números cabales, o polinomio con un término.

---

multiplicative inverse of a number
(11)

The reciprocal of the number.

The multiplicative inverse of 6 is $\frac{1}{6}$.

inverso multiplicativo de un número
(11)

Recíproco de un número.

---

mutually exclusive events
(68)

Two events are mutually exclusive if they cannot both occur in the same trial of an experiment.

In the experiment of rolling a number cube, rolling a 2 and rolling an odd number are mutually exclusive events.

sucesos mutuamente excluyentes
(68)

Dos sucesos son mutuamente excluyentes si ambos no pueden ocurrir en la misma prueba de un experimento.

N

natural number
(1)

A counting number.

1, 2, 3, 4, 5, …

número natural
(1)

Número que se utiliza para contar.

---

negative correlation
(71)

Two data sets have a negative correlation if one set of data values increases as the other set decreases.

correlación negativa
(71)

Dos conjuntos de datos tienen una correlación negativa si un conjunto de valores de datos aumenta a medida que el otro conjunto disminuye.

---

numeric expression
(9)

An expression that contains only numbers and operations.

$2 \cdot 5 + (6 - 8)$

expresión numérica
(9)

Expresión que contiene únicamente números y operaciones.

	English	Example	Spanish

O

odds
(33)

A comparison of favorable and unfavorable outcomes.

The odds in favor of an event are the ratio of the number of favorable outcomes to the number of unfavorable outcomes. The odds against an event are the ratio of the number of unfavorable outcomes to the number of favorable outcomes.

The odds in favor of rolling a 4 on a number cube are 1:5.

posibilidades
(33)

Comparación de los resultados favorables y desfavorables.

Las posibilidades a favor de un suceso son la razón entre la cantidad de resultados favorables y la cantidad de resultados desfavorables. Las posibilidades en contra de un suceso son la razón entre la cantidad de resultados desfavorables y la cantidad de resultados favorables.

---

opposite
(6)

The opposite of a number a, denoted $-a$, is the number that is the same distance from zero as a, on the opposite side of the number line. The sum of opposites is 0.

opuesto
(6)

El opuesto de un número a, expresado $-a$, es el número que se encuentra a la misma distancia de cero que a, del lado opuesto de la recta numérica. La suma de los opuestos es 0.

---

order of magnitude
(3)

The order of magnitude of a quantity is the power of 10 nearest the quantity.

orden de magnitud
(3)

El orden de magnitud de una cantidad es la potencia de diez más cercana a la cantidad.

---

order of operations
(4)

A rule for evaluating expressions: First, perform operations in parentheses or other grouping symbols. Second, evaluate powers and roots. Third, perform all multiplication and division from left to right. Fourth, perform all addition and subtraction from left to right.

orden de las operaciones
(4)

Regla para evaluar las expresiones: Primero, realizar las operaciones entre paréntesis u otros símbolos de agrupación. Segundo, evaluar las potencias y las raíces. Tercero, realizar todas las multiplicaciones y divisiones de izquierda a derecha. Cuarto, realizar todas las sumas y restas de izquierda a derecha.

English	Example	Spanish

O

ordered pair
(20)

A pair of numbers that can be used to locate a point on a coordinate plane. The first number indicates the distance to the left or right of the origin, and the second number indicates the distance above or below the origin.

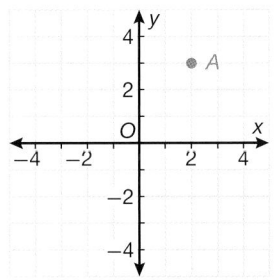

The coordinates of *A* are (2, 3).

par ordenado
(20)

Par de números que se pueden utilizar para ubicar un punto en un plano coordenado. El primer número indica la distancia a la izquierda o derecha del origen y el segundo número indica la distancia hacia arriba o hacia abajo del origen.

---

origin
(20)

The intersection of the *x*- and *y*-axes in a coordinate plane. The coordinates of the origin are (0, 0).

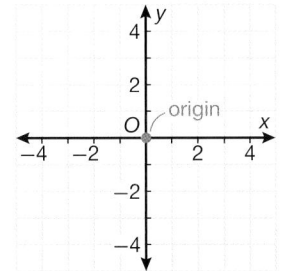

origen
(20)

Intersección de los ejes *x* e *y* en un plano coordenado. Las coordenadas de origen son (0, 0).

---

outcome
(Inv 1)

A possible result of a probability experiment.

The outcomes are 1, 2, 3, 4, 5, 6 in the experiment of rolling a number cube.

resultado
(Inv 1)

Resultado posible de un experimento de probabilidades.

---

outlier
(48)

A data value that is far removed from the rest of the data. A value less than $Q_1 - 1.5(\text{IQR})$ or greater than $Q_3 + 1.5(\text{IQR})$ is considered to be an outlier.

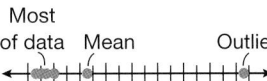

valor extremo
(48)

Valor de datos que está muy alejado del resto de los datos. Un valor menor que $Q_1 - 1.5(\text{IQR})$ o mayor que $Q_3 + 1.5(\text{IQR})$ se considera un valor extremo.

P

parabola
(84)

The shape of the graph of a quadratic function. Also, the set of points equidistant from a point *F*, called the *focus*, and a line *d*, called the *directrix*.

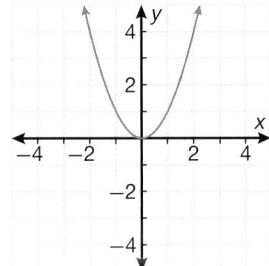

parábola
(84)

Forma de la gráfica de una función cuadrática. También, conjunto de puntos equidistantes de un punto *F*, denominado *foco*, y una línea *d*, denominada *directriz*.

---

parallel lines
(65)

Lines in the same plane that do not intersect.

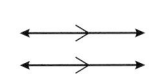

líneas paralelas
(65)

Líneas rectas en el mismo plano que no se cruzan.

English	Example	Spanish
P		

parent function
(Inv 6)

The most basic function of a family of functions, or the original function before a transformation is applied.

$f(x) = x^2$ is the parent function for $h(x) = x^2 + 5$.

función madre
(Inv 6)

La función más básica de una familia de funciones o la función original antes de aplicar una transformación.

---

percent
(42)

A ratio that compares a number to 100.

$$\frac{16}{100} = 16\%$$

porcentaje
(42)

Razón que compara un número con 100.

---

percent of change
(47)

An increase or decrease given as a percent of the original amount. Percent increase describes an amount that has grown. Percent decrease describes an amount that has been reduced.

porcentaje de cambio
(47)

Incremento o disminución dada como un porcentaje de la cantidad original. El porcentaje de incremento describe una cantidad que ha aumentado. El porcentaje de disminución describe una cantidad que se ha reducido.

---

perfect square
(13)

A number whose positive square root is a whole number.

49 is a perfect square because $\sqrt{49} = 7$.

cuadrado perfecto
(13)

Número cuya raíz cuadrada positiva es un número cabal.

---

perfect-square trinomial
(60)

A trinomial whose factored form is the square of a binomial. A perfect-square trinomial has the form $a^2 - 2ab + b^2 = (a - b)^2$ or $a^2 + 2ab + b^2 = (a + b)^2$.

$x^2 + 10x + 25$ is a perfect-square trinomial, because $x^2 + 10x + 25 = (x + 5)^2$.

trinomio cuadrado perfecto
(60)

Trinomio cuya forma factorizada es el cuadrado de un binomio. Un trinomio cuadrado perfecto tiene la forma $a^2 - 2ab + b^2 = (a - b)^2$ o $a^2 + 2ab + b^2 = (a + b)^2$.

---

permutation
(111)

An arrangement of a group of objects in which order is important.

For objects P, Q, R, S, there are 12 different permuations of 2 objects. PQ, PR, PS, QR, QS, RS, QP, RP, SP, RQ, SQ, SR

permutación
(111)

Arreglo de un grupo de objetos en el cual el orden es importante.

---

perpendicular lines
(65)

Lines that intersect at 90° angles.

líneas perpendiculares
(65)

Líneas que se cruzan en ángulos de 90°.

English	Example	Spanish

P

---

point-slope form
(52)

$y - y_1 = m(x - x_1)$ where m is the slope and (x_1, y_1) is a point on the line.

$y - 4 = 2(x - 5)$

forma de punto y pendiente
(52)

$y - y_1 = m(x - x_1)$, donde m es la pendiente y (x_1, y_1) es un punto en la línea.

---

polynomial
(53)

A monomial or a sum or difference of monomials.

$3x^2 + 4xy - 8y^2$

polinomio
(53)

Monomio o suma o diferencia de monomios.

---

positive correlation
(71)

Two data sets have a positive correlation if both sets of data values increase.

correlación positiva
(71)

Dos conjuntos de datos tienen correlación positiva si los valores de ambos conjuntos de datos aumentan.

---

principal square root
(46)

The positive square root of a number, indicated by the radical sign.

$\sqrt{64} = 8$

raíz cuadrada principal
(46)

Raíz cuadrada positiva de un número, expresada por el signo de radical.

---

probability
(Inv 1)

A number from 0 to 1 (or 0% to 100%) that describes how likely an event is to occur.

A bag contains 4 green marbles and 5 purple marbles. The probability of randomly choosing a purple marble is $\frac{5}{9}$.

probabilidad
(Inv 1)

Número entre 0 y 1 (o entre 0% y 100%) que describe cuán probable es que ocurra un suceso.

---

proportion
(31)

An equation that states that two ratios are equal.

$\frac{3}{4} = \frac{9}{12}$

proporción
(31)

Ecuación que establece que dos razones son iguales.

Pythagorean triple
(85)

A set of three nonzero whole numbers a, b, and c such that $a^2 + b^2 = c^2$.

The numbers 3, 4, and 5 are a Pythagorean triple because $3^2 + 4^2 = 5^2$.

Tripleta de Pitágoras
(85)

Conjunto de tres números cabales distintos de cero a, b y c tal que $a^2 + b^2 = c^2$.

English	Example	Spanish

Q

quadrant
(20)

One of the four regions into which the x- and y-axes divide the coordinate plane.

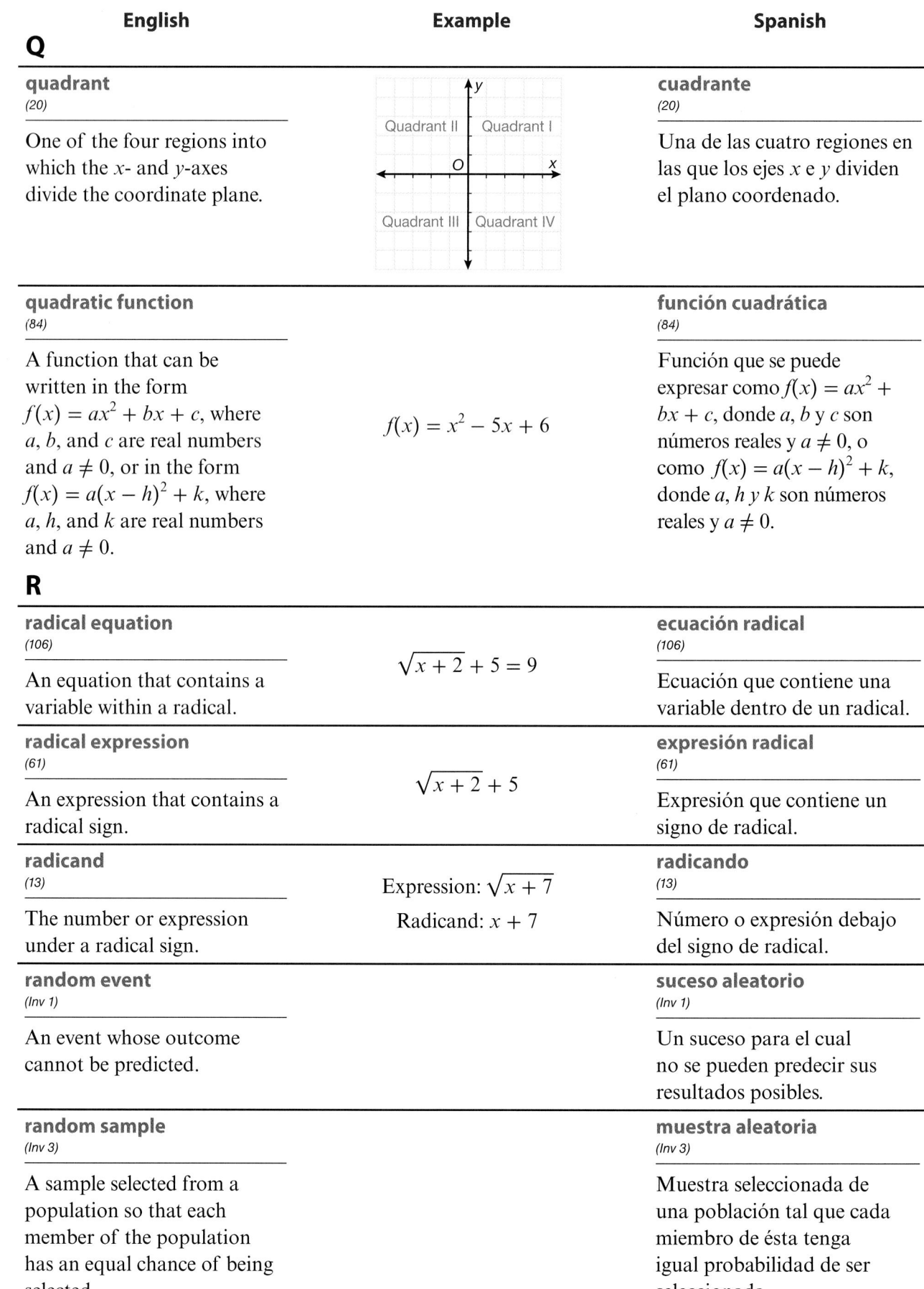

cuadrante
(20)

Una de las cuatro regiones en las que los ejes x e y dividen el plano coordenado.

---

quadratic function
(84)

A function that can be written in the form $f(x) = ax^2 + bx + c$, where a, b, and c are real numbers and $a \neq 0$, or in the form $f(x) = a(x - h)^2 + k$, where a, h, and k are real numbers and $a \neq 0$.

$$f(x) = x^2 - 5x + 6$$

función cuadrática
(84)

Función que se puede expresar como $f(x) = ax^2 + bx + c$, donde a, b y c son números reales y $a \neq 0$, o como $f(x) = a(x - h)^2 + k$, donde a, h y k son números reales y $a \neq 0$.

R

---

radical equation
(106)

An equation that contains a variable within a radical.

$$\sqrt{x + 2} + 5 = 9$$

ecuación radical
(106)

Ecuación que contiene una variable dentro de un radical.

---

radical expression
(61)

An expression that contains a radical sign.

$$\sqrt{x + 2} + 5$$

expresión radical
(61)

Expresión que contiene un signo de radical.

---

radicand
(13)

The number or expression under a radical sign.

Expression: $\sqrt{x + 7}$
Radicand: $x + 7$

radicando
(13)

Número o expresión debajo del signo de radical.

---

random event
(Inv 1)

An event whose outcome cannot be predicted.

suceso aleatorio
(Inv 1)

Un suceso para el cual no se pueden predecir sus resultados posibles.

---

random sample
(Inv 3)

A sample selected from a population so that each member of the population has an equal chance of being selected.

muestra aleatoria
(Inv 3)

Muestra seleccionada de una población tal que cada miembro de ésta tenga igual probabilidad de ser seleccionada.

English	Example	Spanish
R		

English	Example	Spanish
range (25) The set of output values of a function or relation.		**rango** (25) Conjunto de los valores de salida de una función o relación.
range of a function (25) The set of all possible output values of a function.	The range of $y = 2x^2$ is $y \geq 0$.	**rango de una función** (25) Conjunto de todos los valores de salida posibles de una función o relación.
range of a set of data (48) The difference between the greatest and least values in the data set.	The data set $\{2, 4, 6, 8, 10\}$ has a range of $10 - 2 = 8$.	**rango de un conjunto de datos** (48) La diferencia entre los valores mayor y menor en un conjunto de datos.
rate (31) A ratio that compares two quantities measured in different units.	$\dfrac{65 \text{ miles}}{1 \text{ hour}} = 65 \text{ mi/hr}$	**tasa** (31) Razón que compara dos cantidades medidas en diferentes unidades.
rate of change (41, 44) A ratio that compares the amount of change in the dependent variable to the amount of change in the independent variable.		**tasa de cambio** (41) Razón que compara la cantidad de cambio de la variable dependiente con la cantidad de cambio de la variable independiente.
ratio (31) A comparison of two numbers by division.	$\dfrac{1}{3}$ or 1:3	**razón** (31) Comparación de dos números mediante una división.
rational equation (99) An equation that contains one or more rational expressions.	$\dfrac{x + 3}{x^2 - 2x - 3} = 2$	**ecuación racional** (99) Ecuación que contiene una o más expresiones racionales.
rational expression (39) An algebraic expression whose numerator and denominator are polynomials and whose denominator has a degree ≥ 1.	$\dfrac{x + 3}{x^2 - 2x - 3}$	**expresión racional** (39) Expresión algebraica cuyo numerador y denominador son polinomios y cuyo denominador tiene un grado ≥ 1.

English	Example	Spanish

R

rational function
(78)

A function whose rule can be written as a rational expression.

$$f(x) = \frac{x + 3}{x^2 - 2x - 3}$$

función racional
(78)

Función cuya regla se puede expresar como una expresión racional.

---

rational number
(1)

A number that can be written in the form $\frac{a}{b}$, where a and b are integers and $b \neq 0$.

$$4, 2.75, 0.\overline{4}, -\frac{4}{5}, 0$$

número racional
(1)

Número que se puede expresar como $\frac{a}{b}$, donde a y b son números enteros y $b \neq 0$.

---

rationalizing the denominator
(103)

A method of rewriting a fraction by multiplying by another fraction that is equivalent to 1 in order to remove radical terms from the denominator.

$$\frac{1}{\sqrt{3}} \cdot \frac{\sqrt{3}}{\sqrt{3}} = \frac{\sqrt{3}}{3}$$

racionalizar el denominador
(103)

Método que consiste en escribir nuevamente una fracción multiplicándola por otra fracción equivalente a 1 a fin de eliminar los términos radicales del denominador.

---

real number
(1)

A rational or irrational number. Every point on the number line represents a real number.

número real
(1)

Número racional o irracional. Cada punto de la recta numérica representa un número real.

---

reciprocal
(11)

For a real number $a \neq 0$, the reciprocal of a is $\frac{1}{a}$. The product of reciprocals is 1.

The reciprocal of 2 is $\frac{1}{2}$.

recíproco
(11)

Dado el número real $a \neq 0$, el recíproco de a es $\frac{1}{a}$. El producto de los recíprocos es 1.

---

reflection
(Inv 6)

A transformation across a line, called the line of reflection. The line of reflection is the perpendicular bisector of each segment joining a point and its image.

reflexión
(Inv 6)

Transformación sobre una línea, denominada la línea de reflexión. La línea de reflexión es la mediatriz de cada segmento que une un punto con su imagen.

---

relation
(25)

A set of ordered pairs.

$$\{(2, 3), (3, 4), (4, 5), (6, 7)\}$$

relación
(25)

Conjunto de pares ordenados.

English	Example	Spanish

R

relative frequency
(62)

In an experiment, the number of times an event happens divided by the total number of trials.

frecuencia relativa
(62)

En un experimento, el número de veces de ocurrencia de un suceso dividido entre el número total de intentos.

root of an equation
(98)

Any value of the variable that makes the equation true.

4 is a root of $2x + 3 = 11$.

raíz de una ecuación
(98)

Cualquier valor de la variable que transforme la ecuación en verdadera.

S

sample space
(14)

The set of all possible outcomes of a probability experiment.

The sample space in the experiment of rolling a number cube is $\{1, 2, 3, 4, 5, 6\}$.

espacio muestral
(14)

Conjunto de todos los resultados posibles de un experimento de probabilidades.

scale
(36)

The ratio of any length in a drawing to the corresponding actual length.

1 cm : 6 mi

escala
(36)

Razón entre una longitud cualquiera en un dibujo y la longitud real correspondiente.

scale drawing
(36)

A drawing that uses a scale to represent an object as smaller or larger than the original object.

Scale: 1 in.: 5 ft

dibujo a escala
(36)

Dibujo que utiliza una escala para representar un objeto como más pequeño o más grande que el objeto original.

scale factor
(36)

The ratio of a side length of a figure to the corresponding side length of a similar figure.

Original 6 in., 2 in. Enlarged 9 in., 3 in.

Scale Factor: $\dfrac{9}{6} = 1.5$

factor de escala
(36)

La razón de la longitud de un lado de una figura a la longitud del lado correspondiente de una figura similar.

English	Example	Spanish

S

---

scatter plot
(71)

A graph with points plotted to show a possible relationship between two sets of data.

diagrama de dispersión
(71)

Gráfica con puntos dispersos para demostrar una relación posible entre dos conjuntos de datos.

---

scientific notation
(37)

A method of writing very large or very small numbers, by using powers of 10, in the form $m \times 10^n$, where $1 \leq m < 10$ and n is an integer.

$$1{,}420{,}000{,}000 = 1.42 \times 10^9$$

notación científica
(37)

Método que consiste en escribir números muy grandes o muy pequeños utilizando potencias de 10 del tipo $m \times 10^n$, donde $1 \leq m < 10$ y n es un número entero.

---

secant of an angle
(117)

The reciprocal of the cosine function. In a right triangle, the secant of angle A is the ratio of the length of the hypotenuse to the length of the leg adjacent to the angle.

$$\sec A = \frac{\text{hypotenuse}}{\text{adjacent}}$$

secante de un ángulo
(117)

Inversa de la función coseno. En un triángulo rectángulo, la secante del ángulo A es la razón de la longitud de la hipotenusa a la longitud del cateto adyacente al ángulo.

---

sequence
(34)

A list of numbers that often form a pattern.

$$1, 2, 4, 8, 16, \ldots$$

sucesión
(34)

Lista de números que generalmente forman un patrón.

---

set
(1)

A collection of items called elements.

conjunto
(1)

Grupo de componentes denominados elementos.

---

similar
(36)

Two figures that have the same shape, but not necessarily the same size.

semejantes
(36)

Dos figuras con la misma forma pero no necesariamente del mismo tamaño.

---

simple event
(14)

An event resulting in a single outcome.

The event of rolling a die and it landing on 4 is a simple event.

suceso simple
(14)

Suceso que tiene sólo un resultado.

English	Example	Spanish
S		

simple interest
(116)

A fixed percent of the principal. For principal P, interest rate r, and time t in years, the simple interest is $I = Prt$.

interés simple
(116)

Porcentaje fijo del capital. Dado el capital P, la tasa de interés r y el tiempo t expresado en años, el interés simple es $I = Prt$.

---

simplify
(4)

To perform all indicated operations.

$$12 - 10 + 8$$
$$2 + 8$$
$$10$$

simplificar
(4)

Realizar todas las operaciones indicadas.

---

simulation
(Inv 1)

A model of an experiment, often one that would be too difficult or time-consuming to actually perform.

simulación
(Inv 1)

Modelo de un experimento; generalmente se recurre a la simulación cuando realizar dicho experimento sería demasiado difícil o llevaría mucho tiempo.

---

sine
(117)

In a right triangle, the sine of angle A is the ratio of the length of the leg opposite the angle to the length of the hypotenuse.

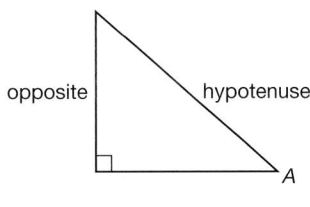

$$\sin A = \frac{\text{opposite}}{\text{hypotenuse}}$$

seno
(117)

En un triángulo rectángulo, el seno del ángulo A es la razón entre la longitud del cateto opuesto al ángulo y la longitud de la hipotenusa.

---

slope
(41, 44)

A measure of the steepness of a line. If (x_1, y_1) and (x_2, y_2) are any two points on the line, the slope of the line, known as m, is represented by the equation $m = \frac{y_2 - y_1}{x_2 - x_1}$.

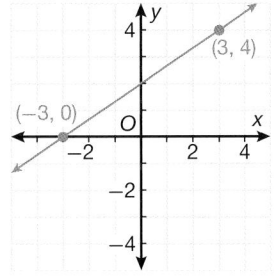

$$m = \frac{y_2 - y_1}{x_2 - x_1} = \frac{0 - 4}{-3 - 3} = \frac{-4}{-6} = \frac{2}{3}$$

pendiente
(41, 44)

Medida de la inclinación de una línea. Dados dos puntos (x_1, y_1) y (x_2, y_2) en una línea, la pendiente de la línea, denominada m, se representa por la ecuación $m = \frac{y_2 - y_1}{x_2 - x_1}$.

---

slope-intercept form
(49)

A line with slope m and y-intercept b can be written in the form $y = mx + b$.

$$y = -3x + 5$$

The slope is -3.

The y-intercept is 5.

forma de pendiente-intersección
(49)

Una línea con pendiente m e intersección con el eje y en b se puede expresar como $y = mx + b$.

English	Example	Spanish

S

English	Example	Spanish
solution of a linear equation in two variables *(35)* An ordered pair or set of ordered pairs that satisfies the equation.	$(2, 3)$ is a solution of the equation $3x + 4y = 18$.	**solución de una ecuación lineal de dos variables** *(35)* Un par ordenado o conjunto de pares ordenados que satisfacen la ecuación.
solution of a linear inequality in two variables *(97)* An ordered pair or set of ordered pairs that satisfies the inequality.	$(1, 4)$ is a solution of the inequality $3x + 4y > 18$.	**solución de una desigualdad lineal de dos variables** *(35)* Un par ordenado o conjunto de pares ordenados que satisfacen la desigualdad.
solution of a system of linear equations *(55)* An ordered pair or set of ordered pairs that satisfies all the equations in the system.	$(7, 1)$ is a solution of $\begin{matrix} x - y = 6 \\ x + y = 8 \end{matrix}$.	**solución de un sistema de ecuaciones lineales** *(55)* Un par ordenado o conjunto de pares ordenados que satisfacen todas las ecuaciones en el sistema.
solution of a system of linear inequalities *(109)* An ordered pair or set of ordered pairs that satisfies all the inequalities in the system.	$(2, 1)$ is a solution of $\begin{matrix} x - y < 6 \\ x + y < 8 \end{matrix}$.	**solución de un sistema de desigualdades lineales** *(109)* Un par ordenado o conjunto de pares ordenados que satisfacen todas las desigualdades en el sistema.
solution of an equation in one variable *(19)* A value of the variable that makes the equation true.	6 is a solution of $2x + 3 = 15$.	**solución con una variable de una ecuación** *(19)* Un valor de la variable que satisface la ecuación.
solution of an equation in two variables *(49)* An ordered pair or set of ordered pairs that satisfies the equation.	$(2, 3)$ is a solution to the equation $x + y^2 = 11$.	**solución de una ecuación con dos variables** *(19)* Un par ordenado o conjunto de pares ordenados que satisface la ecuación.
solution of an inequality in one variable *(50)* A value or set of values that satisfies the inequality.	4 is a solution of $x + 3 < 10$.	**solución con una variable de una desigualdad** *(50)* Un valor de la variable que satisface la desigualdad.

English	Example	Spanish
S		

solution of an inequality in two variables *(97)*	$(2, 3)$ is a solution of $x + y > 2$.	**solución de una desigualdad de dos variables** *(97)*
An ordered pair or set of ordered pairs that satisfies the inequality.		Un par ordenado o conjunto de pares ordenados que satisface la desigualdad.
square root *(13)*	$\sqrt{25}$ is 5 because $5^2 = 5 \cdot 5 = 25$.	**raíz cuadrada** *(13)*
A number that is multiplied by itself to form a product is called a square root of that product.		El número que se multiplica por sí mismo para formar un producto se denomina la raíz cuadrada de ese producto.
square-root function *(114)*	$y = \sqrt{5x} - 6$	**función de raíz cuadrada** *(114)*
A function whose rule contains a variable under a square-root sign.		Función cuya regla contiene una variable bajo un signo de raíz cuadrada.
standard form of a linear equation *(35)*	$3x + 5y = 6$	**forma estándar de una ecuación lineal** *(35)*
$Ax + By = C$, where A, B, and C are real numbers.		$Ax + By = C$, donde A, B y C son números reales.
standard form of a polynomial *(53)*	$3x^4 - 2x^3 - 6x^2 + 2x - 1$	**forma estándar de un polinomio** *(53)*
A polynomial in one variable is written in standard form when the terms are in order from greatest degree to least degree.		Un polinomio de una variable se expresa en forma estándar cuando los términos se ordenan de mayor a menor grado.
standard form of a quadratic equation *(96)*	$3x^2 + 4x - 1 = 0$	**forma estándar de una ecuación cuadrática** *(96)*
$ax^2 + bx + c = 0$, where a, b, and c are real numbers and $a \neq 0$.		$ax^2 + bx + c = $, donde a, b y c son números reales y $a \neq 0$.
standard form of a quadratic function *(84)*	$f(x) = 2x^2 - 3x + 5$	**forma estándar de una función cuadrática** *(84)*
$f(x) = ax^2 + bx + c$, where a does not equal 0.		$f(x) = ax^2 + bx + c$, donde a no es igual a 0.

GLOSSARY/ GLOSARIO

English	Example	Spanish

S

---

stem-and-leaf plot
(22)

A graph used to organize and display data by dividing each data value into two parts, a stem and a leaf.

Stem	Leaves
2	2, 4, 5, 6
3	1, 2, 4
4	4, 7, 9

Key: 3|1 means 3.1

diagrama de tallo y hojas
(22)

Gráfica utilizada para organizar y mostrar datos dividiendo cada valor de datos en dos partes, un tallo y una hoja.

---

system of linear equations
(55)

A system of equations in which all of the equations are linear.

$$2x + 4y = 2$$
$$x - 2y = 5$$

sistema de ecuaciones lineales
(55)

Sistema de ecuaciones en el que todas las ecuaciones son lineales.

---

system of linear inequalities
(109)

A system of inequalities in two or more variables in which all of the inequalities are linear.

$$y \leq x + 1$$
$$y < -x + 3$$

sistema de desigualdades lineales
(109)

Sistema de desigualdades en dos o más variables en el que todas las desigualdades son lineales.

T

---

tangent of an angle
(117)

In a right triangle, the tangent of angle A is the ratio of the length of the leg opposite the angle to the length of the leg adjacent to the angle.

$$\tan A = \frac{\text{opposite}}{\text{adjacent}}$$

tangente de un ángulo
(117)

En un triángulo rectángulo, la tangente del ángulo A es la razón entre la longitud del cateto opuesto al ángulo y la longitud del cateto adyacente al ángulo.

---

term of an expression
(2)

A part of an expression to be added or subtracted

$$4x^2 + 3x$$

$4x^2$ and $3x$ are terms.

término de una expresión
(2)

Parte de una expresión que debe sumarse o restarse.

---

term of a sequence
(34)

An element or number in the sequence.

6 is the third term in the sequence
2, 4, 6, 8, …

término de una sucesión
(34)

Elemento o número de una sucesión.

English	Example	Spanish

T

theoretical probability
(14)

The ratio of the number of equally likely outcomes in an event to the total number of possible outcomes.

In the experiment of rolling a number cube, the theoretical probability of rolling an even number is $\frac{3}{6} = \frac{1}{2}$.

probabilidad teórica
(14)

Razón entre el número de resultados igualmente probables de un suceso y el número total de resultados posibles.

---

translation
(Inv 6)

A transformation in which all the points of a figure move the same distance in the same direction; the figure is moved along a vector so that all of the segments joining a point and its image are congruent and parallel.

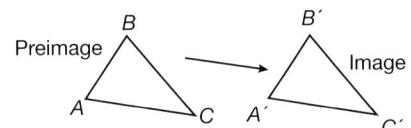

traslación
(Inv 6)

Transformación en la que todos los puntos de una figura se mueven la misma distancia en la misma dirección; la figura se mueve a lo largo de un vector de forma tal que todos los segmentos que unen un punto a su imagen son congruentes y paralelos.

---

trend line
(71)

A line on a scatter plot that helps show the correlation between data sets more clearly. *See also* line of best fit.

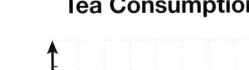
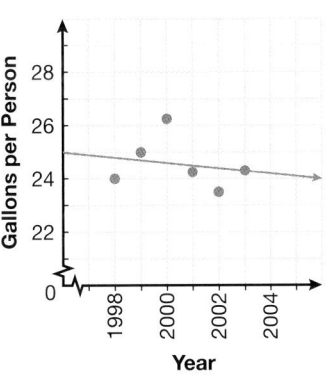

línea de tendencia
(71)

Línea en un diagrama de dispersión que sirve para mostrar la correlación entre conjuntos de datos más claramente. *Ver también* línea de mejor ajuste.

---

trigonometric ratio
(117)

A ratio of two sides of a right triangle.

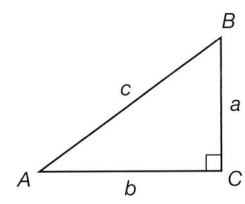

$$\sin A = \frac{a}{c},\ \cos A = \frac{b}{c},\ \tan A = \frac{a}{b}$$

razón trigonométrica
(117)

Razón entre dos lados de un triángulo rectángulo.

---

trinomial
(53)

A polynomial with three terms.

$$4x^2 + 2xy - 7y^2$$

trinomio
(53)

Polinomio con tres términos.

English	Example	Spanish

U

union
(1)

The union of two sets is the set of all elements that are in either set, denoted by $\cup$.

$$A = \{1, 2, 3\}$$
$$B = \{2, 3, 4, 5\}$$
$$A \cup B = \{1, 2, 3, 4, 5\}$$

unión
(1)

La unión de dos conjuntos es el conjunto de todos los elementos que se encuentran en ambos conjuntos, expresado por $\cup$.

---

unit rate
(31)

A rate in which the second quantity in the comparison is one unit.

$$\frac{60 \text{ mi}}{1 \text{ h}} = 60 \text{ mi/h}$$

tasa unitaria
(31)

Tasa en la que la segunda cantidad de la comparación es una unidad.

---

unlike radicals
(69)

Radicals with a different quantity under the radical.

$3\sqrt{5}$ and $2\sqrt{6}$

radicales distintos
(69)

Radicales con cantidades diferentes debajo del signo del radical.

---

unlike terms
(18)

Terms with different variables or the same variables raised to different powers.

$3xy^2$ and $4x^2y$

términos distintos
(18)

Términos con variables diferentes o las mismas variables elevadas a potencias diferentes.

V

variable
(2)

A symbol used to represent a quantity that can change.

In the expression $x + 5$, x is the variable.

variable
(2)

Símbolo utilizado para representar una cantidad que puede cambiar.

---

vertex of a parabola
(89)

The highest or lowest point on a parabola

vértice de una parábola
(89)

Punto más alto o más bajo de una parábola.

---

vertex of an absolute-value graph
(107)

The point on the axis of symmetry of the graph.

vértice de una gráfica de valor absoluto
(107)

Punto en el eje de simetría de la gráfica.

English	Example	Spanish

V

vertical-line test
(25)

A test used to determine whether a relation is a function. If any vertical line crosses the graph of a relation more than once, the relation is not a function.

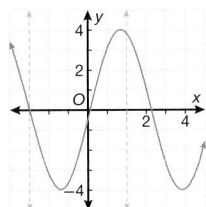 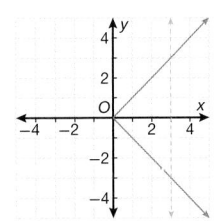

prueba de la línea vertical
(25)

Prueba utilizada para determinar si una relación es una función. Si una línea vertical corta la gráfica de una relación más de una vez, la relación no es una función.

W

whole number
(1)

A member of the set of natural numbers and zero.

$$0, 1, 2, 3, \ldots$$

número cabal
(1)

Conjunto de los números naturales y cero.

X

x-axis
(20)

The horizontal axis in a coordinate plane.

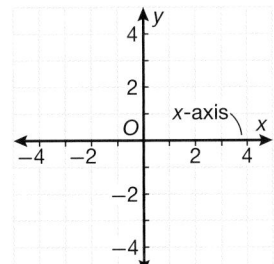

eje x
(20)

Eje horizontal en un plano coordenado.

x-coordinate
(20)

The first number in an ordered pair, which indicates the horizontal distance of a point from the origin on the coordinate plane.

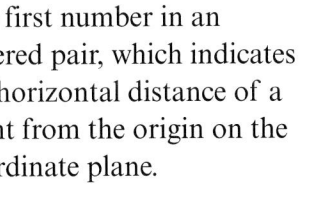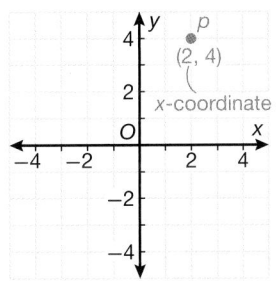

coordenada x
(20)

Primer número de un par ordenado, que indica la distancia horizontal de un punto desde el origen en un plano coordenado.

x-intercept
(35)

The x-coordinate(s) of the point(s) where a graph intersects the x-axis.

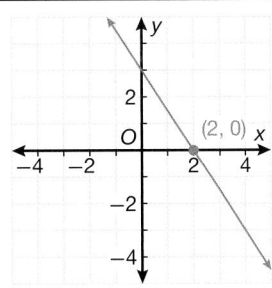

The x-intercept is 2.

intersección con el eje x
(35)

Coordenada/s x de uno o más puntos donde una gráfica corta el eje x.

English	Example	Spanish

Y

y-axis
(20)

The vertical axis in a coordinate plane.

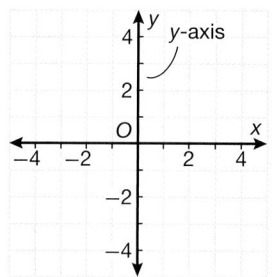

eje y
(20)

Eje vertical en un plano coordenado.

y-coordinate
(20)

The second number in an ordered pair, which indicates the vertical distance of a point from the origin on the coordinate plane.

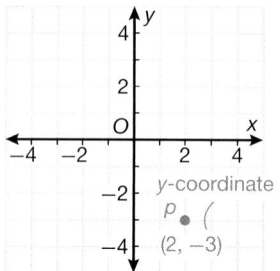

coordenada y
(20)

Segundo número de un par ordenado, que indica la distancia vertical de un punto desde el origen en un plano coordenado.

y-intercept
(35)

The y-coordinate(s) of the point(s) where a graph intersects the y-axis.

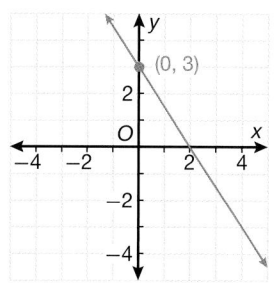

The y-intercept is 3.

intersección con el eje y
(35)

Coordenada/s y de uno o más puntos donde una gráfica corta el eje y.

Z

zero of a function
(89)

For the function f, any number x such that $f(x) = 0$.

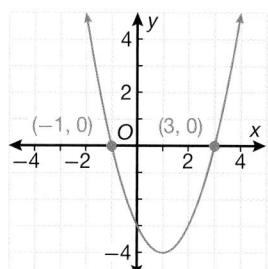

cero de una función
(89)

Dada la función f, todo número x tal que $f(x) = 0$.

Index

B

Bar graphs, 127–128, 159

Binomials, 336
mental math, 392
multiplication of, 390
multiplication with trinomial, 378
polynomial division by, 617–618
product of sum and difference of, 391
special products of, 390
square of, 391

Binomial squares, 697

Box-and-whisker plot
analyzing, 346
comparing data with, 347
data including outliers, 346
defined, 345
displaying data in, 345–346

Boxplot. *See* **box-and-whisker plot**

Braces, 31

Brackets
simplifying expressions with, 32
as symbols of inclusion, 31

C

Calculator. *See* **Graphing Calculator**

Central tendency
measures of, 299
outliers effect on, 300

Chance, 76

Circle graphs, 130
misleading, 160

Circumference, 226

Closed sets, 4
under addition, 24
under subtraction, 28

Closure, 4

Coefficients, 7

Combinations
compared to permutations, 804
defined, 804
finding number of, 805
formula for, 805
probability, 806

Combining like terms, 153
with and without exponents, 98–99

Common denominators, 631

Common difference, 211

Common factors, 271

Common ratio, 705

Commutative property
of addition, 63
of multiplication, 63

Comparison
of algebraic expressions, 44
of algebraic expressions with exponents, 44
of rational expressions, 48

Completing the square process, 697–700

Complex fractions
defined, 609
factoring to simplify, 610
simplification by dividing, 609–610
simplification by using the reciprocal of the denominator, 610
simplification of, 609–611

Compound events, 523

Compound inequalities
defined, 481
multi-step, 678
writing from a graph, 483

Compound interest, 790
vs. simple interest, 791

Compression, 723

Conclusions, 254

Conditional statements, 254
contrapositive of, 320
converse of, 320
inverse of, 320

Congruent angles, 223

Conjugates
of irrational numbers, 693
used to rationalize denominators, 693

Conjunction
defined, 481
solving, 482
writing, 481–482

Connections. *See* **Math to Math Connections**

Consistent systems, 437

Constant of variation, 462
defined, 362

Constants, 7

Continuous data, 118

Continuous graph, 118

Contrapositive, 320

Convenience sampling method, 187

Converse, 320

Conversion factor, 36

Coordinate, 110

Coordinate plane
defined, 110
graphing on, 110–111

Correlation
defined, 467
identification of, 468
lack of, 467
positive and negative, 467

Cosecant, 797

Cosine, 796

Cotangent, 797

Counterexample, 4

Cross products, 191

Cross products property, 191

Cubic functions
defined, 782
graphing, 783–784
solving by graphing, 783
solving with graphing calculator, 784

Currency, 39

D

Data
comparing, 300
misleading, 159–160
range of set of, 300

Decimal equations
solving, 140
two-step, 141

Decimal parts, 141

Deductive reasoning, 254

Degree of monomials, 335

Degree of polynomials, 336

Denominators
conjugate used to rationalize, 693
rationalization of, 691–692
simplifying before rationalization of, 692
simplifying with opposite, 594

Dependent equations, 436

Dependent events
calculating probability of, 206
defined, 204
probability of, 204–205
situations involving, 205

Dependent systems of equations
defined, 436
solving for, 437

Dependent variables
defined, 111
determination of, 112
identification of, 111

Difference of two squares, 545

Direction
of a parabola, 552

Direct variation
defined, 362, 462
vs. inverse variation, 462–463
from ordered pairs, 363

Direct variation equation
graphing, 364
writing and solving, 364

Discontinuous functions, 511

Discounts, 295

Discrete data, 118

Discrete events, 523

Discrete graphs, 118

Discriminant
determination of, 769
use of, 770

Disjunction
defined, 482
solving, 483
writing, 482–483

Distance
calculating with Pythagorean
theorem, 563–564
between two points, 564

Distributing over addition, 243

**Distributing over multiple
operations,** 245

Distributing over subtraction, 244

Distributive property
polynomials and, 375
radical expressions, 501
simplifying expressions with,
80–81
to simplify rational expressions,
243
used in substitution, 383
using, 154

Division
in algebraic expressions, 93
distributing over, 245
of inequalities by a negative
number, 458
of inequalities by a positive
number, 457
of numbers in scientific
notation, 232
one-step equations solved by,
120–122
of polynomials, 617–618
of polynomials with a zero
coefficient, 619
of positive and negative
fractions, 58
of radical expressions, 691–692
of rational expressions, 578
of signed numbers, 58
simplification of complex
fractions by, 609–610
solving equations by, 122

Division properties
of equality, 120
of an inequality, 457

Domain, 146, 181

Double-bar graphs, 128

Double-line graphs, 128–129

Double root, 770

E _____

Elements, 2, 826

Ellipsis, 211

Equation of a line
given two points, 330
from a graph, 309
in point slope form, 330
in slope-intercept form, 307
in standard form, 217

Equations
absolute-value, 487–488
addition of, 412
classifying systems of, 438
defined, 103
equivalent, 103
evaluation and solution of, 134
of line of best fit, 464–465, 467
matching to graphs, 180–181
multiplication of one, 413
multiplication of two, 414
of parallel lines, 424–425
of perpendicular lines, 426
roots of, 655

in slope-intercept form, 307
solution of, in one variable, 103
solved by addition, 105
solved by division, 122
solved by multiplication, 121
solved by subtraction, 105
subtraction of, 413
of two variables, 308
with variables on both
sides, 164–165
writing, given a point, 363

Equivalent equations, 103

Equivalent fractions
to add with unlike
denominators, 632, 633
to subtract with unlike
denominators, 632, 633, 664

Equivalent inequalities, 315

Estimate. *See* **Math Reasoning**

Error Analysis, 5, 11, 15, 20, 25, 30,
35, 41, 42, 45, 46, 50, 51, 60, 61,
67, 68, 73, 78, 79, 83, 84, 85, 91,
92, 96, 97, 101, 102, 107, 108, 115,
126, 131, 137, 143, 151, 156, 157,
167, 168, 175, 185, 196, 201, 209,
216, 221, 228, 234, 247, 248, 252,
261, 268, 273, 281, 287, 293, 297,
298, 304, 312, 313, 318, 328, 333,
334, 341, 350, 359, 367, 374, 380,
387, 394, 401, 410, 417, 423, 427,
429, 435, 440, 442, 447, 448, 453,
454, 461, 471, 472, 478, 479, 485,
491, 498, 503, 508, 509, 515, 521,
527, 536, 537, 541, 542, 549, 555,
562, 568, 575, 581, 591, 597, 607,
612, 613, 614, 621, 622, 628, 629,
635, 636, 643, 653, 660, 661, 667,
668, 675, 681, 682, 683, 688, 689,
694, 695, 703, 709, 710, 711, 718,
725, 732, 740, 746, 747, 759, 766,
772, 773, 780, 785, 786, 794, 801,
802, 807, 814, 815, 822, 823

Estimation of square roots, 70

Evaluate, 43

Excluded values, 322
determining, 510

Experimental probability, 53–54, 524

Exploration, 23, 37, 53, 74, 121, 127,
164, 225, 230, 249, 256, 337, 361,
376, 390, 399, 418, 474, 523, 648,
698, 756

Exponential decay, 751
defined, 751

continuous, 118
double-bar, 128–129
double-line, 128–129
finding zeros from, 586–587
of functions, 179–180
identification of, as a function, 148
identification of, as a relation, 148
identifying domain and range, 181
identifying range, 181
line, 128–129
line, misleading, 159
matching equations to, 180
matching to tables, 179–180
of relationships, 117
representing data with, 525
statistical, 127–128
stem and leaf plots, 128

Greatest common factor (GCF)
of algebraic expressions, 238
factoring trinomials using, 517
factoring with, 571
of monomials, 237
simplifying expressions with, 239

Grouping polynomials, 570–571

H

Half-life, 751

Higher-Order Thinking Skills. *See also* **Math Reasoning**

Histograms
creating, 408
defined, 408
drawing lab, 404–405

Horizontal lines, 258

Horizontal translations, 777

Hypothesis, 254

I

Identification
of dependent variables, 111
of independent variables, 111
of ordered pairs, as a function, 147
of ordered pairs, as a relation, 147
of properties, 64
of quadratic equations, 550–551

Identity, defined, 165

Identity property
of addition, 63
of multiplication, 56, 63

Inclusive events, defined, 444

Inconsistent equations, 436

Independent events
defined, 204
probability of, 204–205
situations involving, 204

Independent system, 437

Independent variables, 146
defined, 111
identification of, 111

Indirect measurement, 224

Inductive reasoning, defined, 254

Inequalities
addition property of, 430
compound, 481–482
defined, 282
division of, by negative numbers, 458
division of, by positive numbers, 457
equivalent, 315
graphing, 314–315
linear, of one variable, 314
multiplication property of, 455
multi-step absolute-value, 678
multi-step compound, 538
with operations inside absolute-value symbols, 679–680
simplifying before solving, 533
solving by addition, 430
solving by multiplication, 455
solving by subtraction, 432
special cases, 533
subtraction property of, 432
translating sentences into, 282
translating words into, 283
with variables on both sides, 532–533
and words, 282
writing from a graph, 316

Infinite set, defined, 2

Input variables. *See* **independent variables**

Integer exponents, 324

Integers, defined, 2

Intercepts, 217

Interest, 788–792

Interquartile range (IQR), 346

Intersection of sets, 4

Inverse of conditional statements, 321

Inverse operations, 104, 165, 712–713
defined, 120
use of, 121

Inverse property of multiplication, 56

Inverse variation
defined, 418, 462
vs. direct variation, 462–463
graphing, 420
identifying, 419
modeling, 418
product rule for, 419

Investigations
analyzing bias in sampling, surveys, and bar graphs, 187–189
choosing a factoring method, 598–601
comparing direct and inverse variations, 462–463
using deductive and inductive reasoning, 254–256
determining probability of event, 53–54
on experimental probability, 54
identifying and writing joint variation, 529–531
investigating exponential growth and decay, 749–753
investigating matrices, 826–829
using logical reasoning, 320–321
transforming linear functions, 396–399
transforming quadratic functions, 676–677

Irrational numbers
conjugate of, defined, 693
defined, 2

J

Joint variations, 529–531

Justify. *See* **Math Reasoning**

L

Labs
calculating intersection of two lines, 352–353
characteristics of parabolas, 583–584
creating a table, 177–178

Multiple variable expressions, 86–87

Multiplication

in algebraic expressions, 93

associative property of, 63

of binomial and a trinomial, 378

of binomials, 390

of binomials with radical expressions, 501

commutative property of, 63

identity property of, 56, 63

of inequalities by a negative number, 456

of inequalities by a positive number, 455

inverse property of, 56

of numbers in scientific notation, 231

of one equation, 413

one-step equations solved by, 120–121

of polynomials, 375

by powers of ten, 140

of rational expressions, 576–577

scalar, 828

of signed numbers, 57

solving equations by, 121

of two equations, 414

Multiplication properties of equality, 120

Multiplication property of inequalities, 455–456

Multiplication Property of −1, 56

Multiplication property of zero, 56

Multi-step, 6, 10, 16, 21, 26, 30, 35, 41, 42, 46, 50, 51, 61, 67, 72, 83, 84, 90, 91, 92, 96, 101, 102, 108, 109, 115, 116, 125, 126, 133, 138, 139, 144, 145, 151, 157, 158, 162, 163, 168, 175, 184, 185, 186, 194, 195, 196, 202, 203, 210, 216, 222, 228, 229, 235, 241, 242, 247, 261, 262, 267, 269, 273, 274, 280, 281, 286, 287, 291, 292, 297, 298, 302, 303, 311, 312, 313, 318, 327, 328, 333, 340, 348, 351, 358, 366, 367, 372, 373, 374, 380, 381, 388, 389, 394, 395, 402, 403, 411, 416, 421, 422, 423, 427, 428, 429, 433, 434, 440, 441, 442, 447, 448, 452, 454, 460, 461, 473, 479, 480, 484, 485, 486, 491, 492, 498, 499, 503, 504, 508, 509, 515, 516, 521, 522, 527, 528, 535, 537, 540, 541, 548, 549, 554, 555, 561, 562, 567, 569, 574, 575, 580, 582, 590, 591, 596, 597, 607, 608, 613, 614, 615, 621, 623, 629, 630, 635, 636, 637, 644, 653, 654, 660, 661, 667, 668, 674, 675, 683, 688, 689, 690, 694, 696, 702, 704, 709, 711, 718, 719, 725, 726, 732, 734, 740, 741, 746, 748, 760, 767, 768, 773, 774, 780, 781, 786, 787, 794, 795, 801, 802, 803, 807, 808, 815, 816, 822, 823

Multi-step absolute-value inequalities, 678

Multi-step compound inequalities, 538–539

defined, 538

Multi-step equations, 153–154

Multi-step inequalities, 506

Multi-step proportions, 192

Mutually exclusive events

defined, 443

probability of, 443

N

Natural numbers, defined, 2

Negative coefficients, 135

Negative correlation, 467–468

Negative exponents

evaluation of expressions with, 198

property of, 197

simplifying, 198

simplifying with, 244

Numbers

decimal parts of, 141

rules for adding with different signs, 23

rules for adding with same sign, 23

Numeric coefficients, 7

Numeric expressions vs. algebraic expressions, 43–44

O

Odds

calculating, 207

defined, 206

One-step equations

algebra tiles to solve, 104

solved by addition or subtraction, 103

solved by multiplication or division, 120–121

Opposites, 27

factoring with, 571

Ordered pairs

defined, 110, 217

direct variation from, 363

identification of, as a function, 147

Order of magnitude, defined, 13

Order of operations rules, 17

Origin, defined, 110

Outliers, 300, 346

box-and-whisker plot with, 346

effects of, 300

Output variables. *See* **dependent variables**

P

Parabola, 551

direction of, 552

vertex of, 585

Parallel lines

defined, 424

determining, 424

equations of, 424–425

Parent functions, 396, 809

Parentheses

simplifying expressions with, 17

as symbols of inclusion, 31

Parentheses and absolute value symbols, 31

Percent, defined, 263

Percentage

defined, 263

using an equation to find, 263

Percent of change

defined, 294

increase or decrease, 294

Percent problems, 263

Perfect squares

defined, 69

simplifying with, 398

Perfect square trinomials, 543, 697

factored form of, 543

factoring, 544

Perimeter
defined, 226
similar figures ratio of, 226

Permutations, 754–756
combinations compared to, 804
defined, 756

Perpendicular lines
described, 110
determining, 425
equations of, 425–426
slope (of a line) of, 425

Pie graphs/charts. *See* **circle graphs**

Point-slope form, 330

Polygons, classification of, 564–565

Polynomials
addition and subtraction of, 338
addition of, 338
defined, 336
degree of, 336
distributive property and, 376
division of, 617–619
division of, by binomials, 617–618
division of, by long division, 618–619
division of, by monomials, 616
factoring by grouping, 570–572
factoring of, 238
four-term, 570
least common multiple (LCM) of, 370
multiplication by a monomial, 375
multiplication of, 375
multiplication of rational expressions containing, 577
products of, 376
rearranging before grouping, 570–571
standard form of, 336
subtraction of, 338
with a zero coefficient, division of, 619

Population, 187

Positive and negative fractions,
division of, 58

Positive coefficients, two-step equations with, 135

Positive correlation, 467–468

Possibilities, 756

Power, 12

Power property of exponents, 13

Powers
raising numbers to, 57
simplifying expressions with, 251

Powers of ten
multiplication by, 140
simplifying with, 400

Power of a power, 249–250

Power of a product, 250

Power of a quotient, 251

Predict. *See* **Math Reasoning**

Prime factorization, 236–237

Prime numbers, 236

Principal, 788

Principal square roots, 288

Probability
combinations, 804–806
dependent events calculation, 205
of independent and dependent events, 204–205
multi-step problems involving, 207
of mutually exclusive events, 443
of inclusive events, 444

Probability of event, 53–54

Product property of exponents, 198

Product rule, 197
of exponents, 13
for inverse variation, 419

Product property of radicals, 500

Properties
of addition and multiplication, 63
of equality, 104, 120
identification of, 64
use of, 64

Properties of equality
division, 120
multiplication, 120

Proportions
cross products solution to, 191
defined, 191
to find a percentage, 264
multi-step, 192
writing and solving, 223

Pythagorean theorem, 556–557
calculating distance with, 563–564
converse of, 558
justification of, 556
missing side lengths calculation, 557

Pythagorean triple, 558

Quadrants, defined, 110

Quadratic equations
approximating solutions, 686
completing the square to solve, 697–700
graphing linear equations and, 761
identification of, 550–551
missing terms, 657
solutions by graphing, 669–671
solutions by graphing calculator, 671–672
solving by factoring, 655, 656
solving using square roots, 684–685

Quadratic formula
approximate solutions to, 744
defined, 742
rearranging before solving, 743–744
recognizing, with no real solutions, 744
standard form, 743

Quadratic functions
defined, 550
finding zeros of, 640–641
graphing, 638–639
graphing using a table, 551
identifying characteristics of, 585–586
standard form of, 550, 638

Quotient property for exponents, 199

Radical equations, 712–715
solving by isolating square roots, 714
solving with square roots on both sides, 715

Radical expressions, 500–501
addition of, 449
distributive property, 501
division of, 691–692
multiplication of binomials with, 501
simplifying, 398–399, 500

Radical functions, 775

Radicand, 69

Random number generator, 52

Random sampling method, 187

Range, 146
    of functions, identifying in graphs, 181

Range of set of data, 300

Rates
    converting, 190
    defined, 190

Rates of change
    defined, 256
    determination from a graph, 256
    determination from a table, 257

Rational equations
    defined, 662
    solving for, using LCD, 663

Rational expressions
    addition and subtraction of, 592–593
    common denominators for, 631
    common factors, 271
    comparison of, 48
    defined, 243
    distributive property to simplify, 243
    division of, 578
    with like denominators, 322
    multiplication and division of, 576–577
    simplifying, 270, 323
    with unlike denominators, 632–633

Rational functions
    defined, 510
    graphing, 511–512

Rationalization
    defined, 691
    of denominator, 691–692

Rational numbers
    defined, 2
    multiplication of, 57
    ordering, 48
    simplifying expressions with, 32

Rational proportions, 662–663

Ratios, defined, 190

Reading Math, 2, 22, 59, 75, 81, 99, 106, 111, 122, 148, 223, 224, 282, 283, 430, 431, 476, 481, 482, 505, 510, 519, 525, 602, 701, 706, 721, 727, 728, 755, 782

Real-number addends, 23

Real numbers
    addition and subtraction of, 47–48
    classification of, 2–3

    defined, 2
    division of, 58
    multiplication of, 56
    properties of, used to simplify expressions, 63
    rules for adding, 23
    sets of, closed under addition, 24
    subsets of, 2–3
    subtraction of, 27

Real World Connections. *See* **Applications**

Reasoning. *See* **Math Reasoning**

Reciprocals, 136, 797

Rectangles, 701

Recursive formulas, 212

Reflections, 397
    of absolute-value graphs, 723
    of square-root functions, 778

Relation
    defined, 146
    determining domain and range of, 146
    ordered pairs of, 147

Relationships, 117

Relations vs. functions, 146

Relative frequency, 407

Roots. *See also* **square roots**
    of equations, 655
    higher-order, 289
    simplifying, 289

S

Sample, 187

Sample spaces, 74–75

Sampling, 187

Scalar multiplication, 828

Scale drawing, 225

Scale factor, 223

Scatter plots
    defined, 466
    graphing, 466
    making and analyzing, 466–467
    matching situations to, 468

Scientific notation
    comparing expressions with, 232
    division of numbers in, 232
    multiplying numbers in, 231
    vs. standard form, 230
    writing numbers in, 231

Secant, 797

Segment of a line, 563–564

Sequences
    arithmetic, 211
    defined, 211
    term of, 211

Sets
    defined, 2
    intersection of, 4
    union of, 4

Signed numbers
    division of, 58
    multiplication of, 57

Similar figures, 223
    finding measures in, 224
    ratio of perimeter, area and volume in, 226

"Similar to" symbol, 223

Simple event, 74

Simple interest, 788–789
    vs. compound interest, 791

Simple random sampling method, 187

Simplify/simplification

Sine, 796

Slope (of a line)
    defined, 257, 329
    determination from a graph, 257
    from a graph, 276
    of parallel lines, 424
    of perpendicular lines, 425
    using slope formula, 275
    from a table, 276
    from two points, 275

Slope formula, 275

Slope-intercept form
    defined, 307
    equation of a line in, 308
    equations in, 307

Special products, 543–544

Square-root functions
    defined, 776
    determining domain of, 777
    graphing, 776
    reflections of, 778
    translations of, 778

Square roots, 288
    calculating and comparing, 69–70
    comparing expressions involving, 70

estimation of, 70

finding products of, 399

of perfect squares, 69

positive and negative values of, 288

principal, 288

solving by isolating, 714

Standard form

of linear equations, 217

of polynomials, 336

of quadratic functions, 550

vs. scientific notation, 231

used to graph, 218

Stem-and-leaf plots, 128

analyzing, 407

creating, 406

Stratified random sampling method, 187

Stretches of absolute-value graphs, 723

Subsets, 2

Substitution

distributive property used in, 383

linear and quadratic equations system solved by, 764

linear equations solved by, 382

rearranging before, 384

steps for solving by, 382

Subtraction

closed sets under, 28

distributing over, 244

of equations, 413

equations solved by, 105

fraction equations solved by, 106

inequalities solved by, 432

of polynomials, 338

of rational expressions with like denominators, 592

of rational expressions with unlike denominators, 594, 633, 664

of real numbers, 27

Subtraction property

of equality, 104

of inequalities, 432

Symbols of inclusion

comparing expressions with, 32

simplifying and comparing expressions with, 31

Symmetry, 587

Systematic random sampling method, 187

Systems of linear equations, 437

solving by elimination, 412–414

solving by graphing, 355–356

solving by substitution, 382–386

solving special systems, 436–439

T

Tables

to graph functions, 179–180

representing data with, 525

slope (of a line) from, 276

Tangent, 796

Technology

See also **Graphing Calculator.**

See also **Labs.**

spreadsheets, 843–845

Term of a sequence, defined, 211

Terms of an expression, 8

Theoretical probability

calculating, 75

finding, 74

Transformations, 777

Translations, 396, 777

of absolute-value functions, 721–722

of square-root functions, 778

Tree diagrams, 205

Trend lines, 466

Trigonometric ratios, 796–797

Trigonometry

finding missing angle measures, 798–799

finding missing side lengths, 798

Trinomial, 336

Trinomials

evaluating, 477

factoring, 474–477, 493–496, 517–518, 572

multiplication with binomial, 378

with tiles, 474–475

Two points

equation of a line given, 330

writing an equation using, 330

Two-step decimal equations, 141

Two-step equations

with fractions, 136

with negative coefficients, 135

with positive coefficients, 135

solutions to, 134

Two-step inequalties, 505

Two variables, equations of, 308

U

Undefined expressions, 270

Union of sets, 4

Unit analysis, 36–39

Unit rate, defined, 190

Unlike denominators

adding and subtracting with, 633–665

using equivalent fractions to subtract, 664

Unlike radicals, defined, 449

V

Variable expressions

multiple, simplification and evaluation of, 86–88

Variables, 7

on both sides, solving for, 172

simplifying with, 400

solved a formula for, 172

solving for, 171

Variation graphs, 463

Vertex

identifying, 585–586

of absolute-value function, 720

of parabola, 585

Vertical lines, 258

Vertical line test, 147

Vertical translations, 777

Volume

converting units of, 38

similar figures ratio of, 226

Voluntary sampling method, 187

W

Whole numbers, defined, 2

Word problems

translating between algebraic expressions and, 94

words and phrases to algebraic expressions, 93

Words

and inequalities, 282

translating into algebraic expressions, 93

Write. *See* **Math Reasoning**

X

x-axis, 110

x-coordinate, 110

x-intercept
finding, 217
graphing, 218
locating on graph, 218

Y

y-axis, 110

y-coordinate, 110

y-intercept
finding, 217
graphing, 218
locating on graph, 218
and slope of a line, 307

Z

Zero exponents, 197–198

Zero of the function, 583

Zero product property, 655

Zeros
finding, from axis of symmetry,
587–588
finding from graphs, 586–587
multiplication property of, 56